English Translation of
the Meanings of

AL-QUR'AN

The Guidance for Mankind

O Rabb! Open for me my heart

By
Muhammad Farooq-i-Azam Malik

© *Copyright 1997*
The Institute of Islamic Knowledge
Houston, Texas U.S.A.

© All Rights of Publication Reserved

Translator: *Muhammad Farooq-i-Azam Malik*

Fifth
Edition: English Only   25,000   October, 2002

Library of
Congress Cat. #   97-070435

ISBN #   0-911119-77-9

Printer: **RR Donnelley & Sons Company**
1009 Sloan Street
Crawfordsville, IN 47933 - USA

Publisher: **The Institute of Islamic Knowledge**
P. O. Box 8307
Houston, Texas 77288-8307, USA

Tel: (281) 448-4080   Fax: (713) 526-9090

Web Site: To read Al-Qur'an online, get more copies or to
sponsor its distribution, visit our website:

al-quraan.org -or- jihad-bil-quraan.com

E-Mail: information@al-quraan.org
webmaster@al-quraan.org
suggestions@al-quraan.org

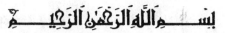

In the name of Allah, the Compassionate, the Merciful

Dedicated
To
Mankind

Attention Please:

The Holy Qur'an is revealed in Arabic so the Qur'an is only the Arabic Text, not its translation in any other language.

Whoever finds any mistake in this translation of the meaning of Al-Qur'an, the Guidance for Mankind, we request him to write us, indicating the mistake and its place along with the correct translation. We thank all those who will point out these mistakes to improve this translation for seeking the pleasure of Allah. Allah is the Guardian over what we say.

Please note that the requirement of reading this Book is to touch it with clean hands.

Biography of: *Muhammad Farooq-i-Azam Malik*

Mr. Malik, Chairman of the Board of Trustees and Dean of the Institute of Islamic Knowledge (IIK), was born in the year 1943 in a village called Machhiwal near Lalamusa, District Gujrat in the Province of Panjab, Pakistan.

He completed the Arabic reading of the Qur'an at the age of 7 and completed the meaning of The Qur'an in 8 years at the age of 16. He completed his B.A. Honors in Islamic Studies and Arabic Language winning the Panjab University Scholarship. Then he joined Government Law College at Lahore where he completed his LL.B. Major in Islamic Law *(Shari'ah)* in 1965. During his internship as a junior lawyer, he completed his M.A. Economics in 1966. He worked as an attorney for 5 years, then migrated to the United States as a permanent resident to work as a foreign attorney in 1970. The company which offered him the job went out of business during the oil embargo. He then left the profession and completed his MBA with a major in Accounting from Long Island University at New York in 1975. After completing his MBA he moved to Houston and joined the Internal Audit Division of Foley's, a leading retailer, where he worked for 18 years.

During high school studies, Mr. Malik started an organization called Anjuman-e-Islâh-e-Mu'âshra *(Social Welfare Society)* to reform 'Aqeedah and fight against social evils and un-Islamic local customs. This organization worked in all the surrounding villages and was successful in achieving most of its objectives. During his college life he started Tarjuma-tul-Qur'an *(Translation of the Holy Qur'an)* sessions at various Masâjid.

In the United States he started Dars-e-Qur'an *(Qur'anic Study Sessions)* at Bronx and Manhattan in New York City. Most of his Dars-e-Qur'an participants are the founding members of different Islamic Centers. He is among the pioneers of Islamic Circle of North America (ICNA). After moving to Houston in 1975 he was elected three times as the Treasurer of ISGH. As treasurer, he organized Accounting and Check-o-Matic systems. He was then elected twice as the Director of Religious Affairs and one time as the Director of Education. In these positions he organized the Zonal system of ISGH for children's Islamic Education and Qur'anic Tajweed. Then he was elected as the President of ISGH. In that position he lead the community in buying the Zonal facilities at the North, Southwest, Southeast, Northwest and Bear Creek areas and putting these facilities in Owqâf (Trust) with North American Islamic Trust (NAIT). He also accomplished the amendments to the ISGH Constitution and Bylaws for the future unlimited growth of the Muslim Community in Greater Houston area. He also served as Chairman of the Planning and Administration Committee and developed short term and long term plans for the ISGH. At the national level, he was Vice Chairman of ISNA's Islamic Coordinating Committee, a member of NAIT's Board of Advisers and is now a member of NAIT's Board of Trustees.

Mr. Malik completed this magnificent project in 5 1/2 years. He is also the author of well known manuals of Al-Zakah (the Islamic financial responsibility), Al-Wasiyyah (the Islamic Will - a mandatory Commandment for the residents of North America) and a Da'wah booklet called: "What is Islam and Who are the Muslims?"

4

AT A GLANCE

ACKNOWLEDGMENTS

I would like to express my sincere appreciation and deep thanks to IIK Trustees and all those who were associated with development of the manuscript of this translation of Al-Qur'an during the last ten years.

I started this project in March 1992 with the grace of Allah and sent typed copies of the completed parts for review to a number of scholars of the Qur'an in the USA., Canada, Saudi Arabia, Egypt and Pakistan. I received critical and useful suggestions for its improvement. The draft was then sent to the major Islamic Institutions including Jâme-Al-Azhar in Egypt, Ummal Qura University at Makkah-tul Mukarramah, Islamic University at Madinah-tul Munawwarah and Muslim World League in Saudi Arabia, and International Islamic University Islamabad in Pakistan for their reviews and input.

My thanks are to my parents, especially my mother *(may Allah bless her soul and award her Paradise)* who taught me to read the Qur'an and persuaded me to learn its translation and tafseer, and to my wife Mamoona who extended her full support during this project. My thanks are also due, to all those Muslims and non-Muslims who participated in the project; especially those who critically evaluated the usage of various English words during the translation process and discussed in detail those words which could be interpreted in meanings other than what I meant in the translation. The entire translation was fully discussed during our daily Dars-e-Qur'an and was completed in three years and seven months. My thanks are also due to Dr. Haroon Rashid, Dr. Aziz Siddiqi, Dr. Naila, Amir Ja'fri, Noveed, Zaheer, Amy Lipke, Hassan Igram, Sayyid Syeed, Batul Bowman, G. A. Khan, Azra Khan, Shabbir Dadabhoy, Javed Rashid and Dr. Farooq Ahmad for their help in the development of this manuscript and checking the typographical and linguistic errors .

I am indebted to the translators, authors and their publishers whose work I have frequently consulted during the translation process. I would like to express my gratitude to Sheikh Dr. Mahmood Ahmad Ghazi, Vice President, of Islamic University at Islamabad and Hafiz Nazar Ahmad of the Muslim Academy Lahore, Pakistan. I am also obliged to Fadeelat Sheikh Abdul Aziz Bin Abdullah Bin Muhammad Âle Al-Sheikh, Grand Mufti, Kingdom of Saudi Arabia, Sheikh Dr. Sâleh Bin Abdullah Al-'Ubûd of Islamic University at Madinah-tul-Munawwarah, Sheikh Dr. Ali Bin Muhammad Nasir Faqeehi and Dr. V. Abdur Rahim of King Fahd Qur'an Printing Complex at Madinah-tul-Munawwarah for their help in getting in-depth reviews and editing done through Dr. Abdul Majeed Al-'Ubaidi, Abdul Razzaq Abdul Majeed and Muhammad Luqmân As-Salfi from the Department of Education, Ifta, Da'wah and Irshâd, Kingdom of Saudi Arabia.

In conclusion, I must say that all the merit of conveying the message of Allah in this manuscript is entirely due to the bounty of Allah and if there are faults and mistakes, in it, they are entirely mine and I seek Allah's forgiveness for any such inadvertent error. Readers are requested that if they find any error or have any suggestion, please do not hesitate to write us. May Allah help us all to work together for His pleasure. *Â'meen!*

Muhammad Farooq-i-Azam Malik

The Institute of Islamic Knowledge
Houston, Texas, USA

Sûrahs (Chapters) Index

Juz (Parts) Index

To embrace Islam one is required only to
make the following statement (*Kalimah)*, and then follow
the Qur'an and traditions of the Prophet Muhammad, peace be upon him.

Lâ Ilâha Illallahu Muhammadur Rasoolullah

There is none worthy of worship except Allah (the One and Only God) and
Muhammad is the Rasool (Messenger / Prophet) of Allah

FOREWORD

Praise be to Allah Almighty (God), who is the Cherisher and Sustainer of the Universe. May the peace and blessings of Allah Almighty be upon Muhammad, the Seal of the Prophets, who said:

"The best among you is he who learns and teaches the Qur'an."

The Qur'an is the Message from Allah Almighty for the whole of mankind. Since the language of The Qur'an is Arabic, there is a language barrier for those who do not understand Arabic. This translation, in contemporary English, is an effort to facilitate the understanding of the Qur'an. This is also the fulfillment of an obligation on us to convey the Message of Allah in the language of those people to whom the Message is being presented. As Allah has said in Sûrah Ibrâheem, the Divine Message should be presented in the addressee's own language:

"We have not sent any Rasool (messenger) except that he spoke the language of his own people so that he could explain to them clearly." (Sûrah 14, verse 4)

It may be asked: Is there any need for a fresh English Translation? To those who ask this question, I would like to request that they take any particular passage and compare it with any other translation they choose. If they find that I have helped them even the least bit further in understanding its meaning or appreciating its beauty or catching something of the grandeur of the original, I would claim that my humble attempt is justified. I started this project with Duâ *(prayer)* which was made by the Prophet Musa (pbuh):

"O my Rabb! Open my heart, ease my task and remove the impediment from my speech so that people may understand what I say."
(Sûrah 20, verses 25-28)

If you see the cover page of publications by the Institute of Islamic Knowledge you will notice the start of this prayer *"Rabbish Rahli Sadri"* is the logo of the Institute. The objective of the Institute is to present the Message of Allah in a language which the people of North America can easily understand.

It is the duty of every Muslim, male or female, to read The Qur'an and understand it according to one's own capacity. If any one of us attains some knowledge or understanding of the Qur'an by study or contemplation, both outward and inward, it is one's duty, according to one's capacity to instruct others, and share with them the joy and peace which resulted from contact with the spiritual world. The Qur'an is to be read, not only with the tongue, voice and eyes, but with the best light that our intellect can provide, and even more, with the truest and purest light which our heart and conscience can give us. It is in this spirit that I would like the readers to approach the Qur'an.

The reader should know that given the depth and sublimity of the Qur'anic text, a literal translation into another language is virtually impossible. The reader would agree that any translation of the Qur'an can never be equal to or be the replacement of the original, therefore, no translations including this, however accurate they may be, can be designated as the Qur'an. But translation is one of the avenues available to us to share this priceless gift of Almighty Allah. There are, however, some significant differences between the two languages, English and Arabic. For example, English is very deficient when it comes to 2nd person pronouns, of which now a days only these are used: "you," "your," and "yours." The old "ye," "thou," and "thee" as well as their possessive persons are obsolete. English is also restricted in meanings for "Man" as opposed to "Woman;" similarly "Mankind" and "People" are inadequate expressions. Bearing in mind the limitations of the English language and its correlating words to translate expression, we have tried to make the Message of the Qur'an simple and as close to the original Arabic meaning, used at the time of the Prophet, as possible. The English as compared to the Arabic has changed with the passage of time. The English spoken in England is not the same as that spoken in United States of America, and even in United States, the English spoken in New York is not the same as that spoken in Texas. The task of translation will never cease. As people grow and change, so does their language. This humble effort is merely to facilitate the present generation in understanding the Eternal Message of the Qur'an. There are some Arabic words which cannot be translated into English; for example: Allah, Rabb, Rasool and Shirk. These are written in transliteration and their meanings are explained in the Glossary of Qur'anic Words and Terms on pages 95 through 102.

The method of translation followed here is based on the theme and subject matter discussed in the verses of the Qur'an rather than the literal translation. Literal translation into English cannot create the same continuity in English as in the Arabic text, the reader may not enjoy the force of the Arabic language and the effects of Allah's speech. It may appear to be a group of lifeless sentences without any correlation to each other. It does not affect the soul, arouse the sentiments or bring tears into one's eyes as does the Qur'anic Arabic text. When reading the literal English translation, one sometimes wonders whether it is the same Qur'an which challenged the world to produce one chapter or even one verse like it. The reason for this is, that in literal translation the focus is on the words rather than the message of the Qur'an. Actual Qur'anic language is so powerful that it will even melt stones, as the Qur'an itself states:

> *"If we would had sent down this Qur'an on a mountain, you would have seen it humble itself and split asunder from the fear of Allah..."*
> *(Sûrah 59, verse 21)*

The force of the Qur'anic address was admitted by the opponents of the Prophet, who were afraid and used to say to pagan Arabs: "Don't listen to the Qur'an, its language affects like magic and anyone who listens cannot resist." Those effects cannot be recreated in a translation.

There is another reason why literal translation does not serve the purpose of understanding the Divine Message. The text of the Qur'an is a speech and an address, and was not given to the Prophet Muhammad (peace be upon him) in the form of a book. The addressees were aware of their environment and their problems, therefore, solutions presented in the Qur'an were enough for their understanding. Unless we are aware of the environment, circumstances and problems faced by the community at the time of the Prophet Muhammad (pbuh), to which Qur'anic guidelines and solutions were provided, we will not be able to understand its message. For this reason, the biography of the Prophet Muhammad (pbuh) is being presented. Historical background, time of the revelation, and the problems faced by the community are stated prior to the translation of each Sûrah (chapter). The reader is advised to frequently refer to these backgrounds while reading the actual text of the Qur'anic translation for better understanding.

It is very difficult to understand the Qur'anic teachings without knowing the condition of the world at the time when the Qur'an was revealed to the Prophet Muhammad (peace be upon him). At that time Judaism, Christianity and other religions were unable to address and solve the real issues faced by humanity in social, economic, moral and political aspects of life. Allah Almighty bestowed His favors upon mankind by selecting Muhammad (peace be upon him), an illiterate person from the most backward region of the world, for His Message. In that region tribes were at war most of the time. A tribal war based on the petty issue of drinking water from a well lasted 500 years, killing thousands of human beings on both sides. People used to kill their daughters by burying them alive. Allah's message, the Qur'an, not only united those tribes, solved their social, economic and political problems, but made them the torchbearers of Islam. Islam, through its insistence on consciousness and knowledge, created in its followers a spirit of intellectual curiosity and independent inquiry, resulting in a splendid era of learning and scientific research. Qur'anic teachings penetrated in countless ways and byways into the minds of medieval Europe and gave rise to the revival of Western culture which we call, the Renaissance. In the course of time, these teachings became largely responsible for the birth of what is described as the "Age of Science:" the age in which we are now living.

The reader should know that Muhammad (peace be upon him) did not receive any education and could not read or write even his own name. Thus, he was not exposed to any Jewish or Christian literature or books. He was 40 years old when he was chosen by Allah Almighty for delivering His message. His whole life was known to his people. He was a successful businessman and had earned the titles of Al-Ameen (the Trustworthy) and Al-Siddeeq (the Truthful) for his behavior and interaction with the community. He never made any speech worth mentioning prior to his commission as a Rasool (Messenger and Model for people) of Allah. Then came the revelation of the Qur'an, a masterpiece of the Arabic language, which challenged the Arabs (who used to call the non-Arabs as 'Ajamees, which means those who do not know how to speak) to produce "even one verse" like the verses of the Qur'an. The challenge was not to a single person or even to the Arabs only, it was and still is to all mankind, allowing them to use the help of their gods or idols, and no one has ever been able to, and never will, meet this challenge. The reader should also ask himself, "Can a book of this size and volume, which does not have any contradictions or grammatical errors, even though revealed in a 23 - year time span, be attributed to an unlettered man?"

It is noteworthy that Arabs were proud of their language and Arabic was at its peak. There was no other art form than the art of language which could occupy the interest of the people. This challenge was repeated many times in the Qur'an, both at Makkah and Madinah. It is meant to convince the opponents of Islam that the Qur'an, which is matchless in its literary excellence and subject matter, could not be produced by any human being. It must, therefore, have been revealed only by Allah.

Unlike the Bible, as it exists today, where the name of Isa (Jesus) and his disciples is mentioned numerous times, the name of the Prophet "Muhammad" (peace be upon him) is mentioned only four times in the Qur'an. Each time it is mentioned for a specific purpose:

1. *"Muhammad is no more than a Rasool of Allah, like the Rasools that passed away before him ..."*   *(Sûrah 3, verse 144)*

   This verse prohibits the followers of the Prophet Muhammad (pbuh) from elevating his status to Godhead or to attribute him as a son of God, similar to what the Christians did to Jesus (pbuh).

2. *"Muhammad is not the father of any your men (he is not going to leave any male heir), but he is the Rasool of Allah and the Seal of the Prophets."*
                                  (Sûrah 33, verse 40)

   This verse indicates that the dynasty of the Prophet Muhammad (pbuh) ended with him, so that no one could claim superiority over others by being his descendant and no one could claim to be the prophet of Allah after him, since he is the Seal (last) of the Prophets.

3. *"As for those who believe and do good deeds and believe in what is revealed to Muhammad - and that is the Truth from their Rabb - He will remove from them their sins and improve their condition."*   *(Sûrah 47, verse 2)*

This verse reaffirms that the Qur'an is the true revelation from Allah and only those who will believe in it and act accordingly (since no way of life other than Islam is acceptable to Allah), will have good life in this world and qualify for salvation in the Hereafter (life after death).

4. *"Muhammad, the Rasool of Allah, and those with him are strong against the unbelievers and kind to each other..."*   *(Sûrah 48, verse 29)*

This verse indicates the characteristics of the followers of the Prophet Muhammad (pbuh); that they should stand firm against transgression and cooperate with each other in promoting good deeds.

I am fully aware that my renderings can not "do justice" to the depth of the meaning of the Qur'an. However, this translation is the result of not only my efforts, but also the efforts, input, advice and suggestions by dozens of Ulema, and hundreds of American new-Muslims and non-Muslims. Furthermore , in depth reviews were done with the help of Fadeelat Sheikh Abdul Aziz Bin Abdullah Bin Muhammad Âle Al-Sheikh, Grand Mufti of the Kingdom of Saudi Arabia, Sheikh Sâleh Bin Abdullah Al-'Ubûd, Chancellor of Islamic University at Madinah-tul-Munawwarah, Sheikh Dr. Ali Bin Muhammad Nasir Faqeehi and Dr. V. Abdur Rahim of King Fahd Qur'an Printing Complex at Madinah-tul-Munawwarah through Dr. Abdul Majeed Al-'Ubaidi, Abdul Razzaq Abdul Majeed and Muhammad Luqmân As-Salfi from the Department of Education, Ifta, Da'wah and Irshâd, Kingdom of Saudi Arabia.

In conclusion, I would like to request the reader and those whom Allah has blessed with knowledge to inform us if they find any error or have a suggestion for improvement to get reward from Allah Almighty. *Insha Allah,* next edition will be improved accordingly. Please pray for me, my family, my friends who encouraged me to take on this heavy task, the reviewers and the editors who helped in fine-tuning this work. I also pray for you and all mankind; may Allah bless everyone with His mercy and provide the reader His true guidance. May Allah help us all to strive hard for His cause and His pleasure.   *Â'meen!*

Your Well Wisher

Muhammad Farooq-i-Azam Malik
27th Day of Rajab, 1423

THE PROPHET MUHAMMAD
(May Allah's blessings and peace be upon him)

HIS MISSION

Historical Background

Prior to the advent of the Prophet Muhammad (peace be upon him) the entire world had plunged into darkness. The light of civilization had faded away from Egypt to China and from Persia to Rome. The Roman and Persian empires, the two world powers, were in the worst state of tyranny and terrorism. Emperors were considered gods or representatives of gods. With the clergy and army being at their disposal, they had strangled the common man through heavy taxes, bribes and forced labor. Devastating wars, frequent changes in ruling dynasties, and large territories frequently passing from one empire to another caused newer forms of oppression. Churches and temples, on changing hands, became places of worship of each conqueror in turn. All over the world, the common man was deprived of the basic necessities of life and could not even raise his voice in protest. Freedom was unknown and no religion or philosophy could guide him. Religion had become a profitable trade in the hands of religious orders in alliance with the ruling class. Greek philosophy had lost its force, the teachings of Confucius and Mani were forgotten. Buddhist, Vedantic, and Christian teachings had become ineffective. When humanity despaired and found no way of escape, the crisis reached its peak. It was at this critical stage that Allah Almighty (God) selected a redeemer of humanity from a tribal area of the Arabian peninsula, which neither the Roman empire nor the Persian empire wanted to annex due to its barbarism, lack of yielding to any discipline, and utter moral degradation.

In midst of this degradation, the Prophet Muhammad (pbuh) was assigned a mission to redeem humanity from the slavery of men (kings, emperors, clergymen, etc.) towards the service of One Almighty God. He stood up single-handed to change the entire world, while those who hated evil, like him, and were unable to reform their surroundings, had retired to forests and mountain caves and became monks. The Prophet Muhammad (pbuh) on the other hand, boldly faced the situation, challenged the Roman Empire, the Persian Empires and the rest of the world alike, and crushed them to restore freedom for all.

The Mission of the Prophet MUHAMMAD (peace be upon him):

The mission of Muhammad (pbuh) was to redeem humanity from the clutches of slavery, to transform the whole life of man from within and without, his individual as well as his community life. This all-embracing program was not taken up haphazardly but was the result of firm conviction, deep meditation and contemplation. For years, the deep questions of life, its meaning and purpose, engaged the Prophet's mind. Every year for one month, in the cave of Hira, he examined his own capacities and thought over the world's condition, devoted his mind to the basic problems which afflicted the human society, but did not take any practical step until he received guidance through Divine Revelations. The greatest truth was that Allah is the Master of the universe and man is His servant. It was from this seed that the tree of wholesome civilization grew.

The revolutionary proclamation of the Prophet: "Lâ Ilâha Illallah" (there is no god but Allah), although brief, has tremendous significance. It was a declaration that there is no divine being except "Allah," the only God, Who should be obeyed, loved, worshipped, praised and remembered. From Him one should expect all good and His displeasure one should fear. He will reward the good and punish the wicked. He is regarded as the master, ruler and lawgiver. His injunctions must be obeyed, and His prohibitions avoided. Lives must be molded according to His will. Everything must be sacrificed on His command and His pleasure should be made the ideal of life. It was this comprehensive meaning of divinity that was condensed into the single phrase "Lâ Ilâha Illallah" (there is no god but Allah).

Human society was suffering because these attributes of divinity were appropriated by different people and innumerable divinities were ruling over society, such as social rites, tribal traditions, ruler and clergy dominance under which man was powerless. Lâ Ilâha Illallah struck at the root of all this. One who believed in this proclamation, declared that he did not recognize any other greatness except that of God, did not submit to any other rule, did not recognize any other law or code of conduct and would not bow before any other power, nor seek anyone else's pleasure. This proclamation was in fact the declaration of man's freedom.

The second part of this proclamation, "Muhammad-ur-Rasool-Allah" (Muhammad is the Messenger of Allah), declared that the only means of uplift and social reform was the Prophethood established by Allah (Almighty God). That real knowledge is provided through Revelation, which guides the thinking of mankind. That the Prophet Muhammad (pbuh) has completed the chain of Prophethood and that he was the last Rasool (Messenger) of Allah. That life's purpose can be secured from this source alone and it is only through Divine guidance that humanity can successfully advance towards its true goal of achieving the pleasure of Allah and inheriting Paradise. It was this interpretation of the proclamation that was made the first pillar of Islam. To embrace Islam, one has only to say and believe in this slogan. When this belief entered men's hearts, it changed the entire outlook of man and gave birth to a new humanity on the march towards progress and rectitude.

The Prophet's Mission and the Modern World

Non-Muslims study the teachings of Plato, Socrates, Marx, Einstein etc., without any prejudice, but there are innumerable prejudices in the way of seeking guidance from the mission of the Prophet Muhammad (pbuh). There is a notion that Muhammad (pbuh) is the Prophet of the Muslims only, therefore, non-Muslims have nothing to learn from him. This is incorrect. Muhammad (pbuh) was assigned for the guidance of Mankind as is ordained in the Qur'an: "Say; O mankind, I am the Rasool of Allah towards all of you." This includes all human beings: Muslims, Jews, Christians, Buddhists, Hindus, people of other religions and atheists as well.

The life of the Prophet is often not studied as a whole, but in fragments. An unbiased study of his biography clearly indicates that the personality which shines in the background of the European renaissance and whose hand could be traced behind democracy, international movements and religious reforms is none else but Muhammad (pbuh). Studying a mission and the sponsor of the mission can never lead to a true appraisal if there is an overdose of biased and hostile literature on the subject, which can prejudice the minds of even those who are not absolutely averse to the Truth.

The Qur'an's message is for all of humanity, for the whole world of the East and the West, for black and white, for the classes and the masses, for employees and their employers, for men and women of all walks of life, for all religions and political persuasions, for the rulers and the ruled, for the learned and the ignorant and for every man in every field of activity. The Qur'an deals with "Man" (which is used in the Qur'an to mean men as well as women) and not with his civilization, ethnicity, language or color. Man's birth, growth, senses of good and bad, hot and cold, laughter and crying, happiness and sorrow, are all the same. Time has changed, civilizations have changed, but 'Man' is the same as it was at the time of the creation of Adam and will remain the same until the Last Day. That's why Allah's message is for all times: it is applicable to us today as it was applicable at the time of the Prophet Muhammad (pbuh) fourteen hundred years ago.

Prophet's Ranking and Status in Human History

I would like to quote only non-Muslim scholars to present unbiased opinions about this topic. Michael H. Hart in his book *'The 100, A Ranking of the Most Influential Persons in History'* published in 1989 by Carol Publishing Group, New York, ranked Muhammad (pbuh) as #1 in the history of mankind in both religious and secular influence. He writes:

"My choice of Muhammad to lead the list of the world's most influential persons may surprise some readers and may be questioned by others, but he was the only man in history who was supremely successful on both the religious and secular levels...... Of a humble origin, Muhammad founded and promulgated one of the world's great religions, and became an immensely effective political leader. Today, thirteen centuries after his death, his influence is still powerful and pervasive...... Furthermore, Muhammad (unlike Jesus) was a secular as well as a religious leader. In fact, as a driving force behind the Arab conquests, he may well rank as the most influential political leader of all times....... It is the unparalleled combination of secular and religious influence which I feel entitles Muhammad to be considered the most influential single figure in human history."

A famous French scholar, Lamartine says:

"If greatness of purpose, smallness of means, and astounding results are the three criteria of human genius, who could dare to compare any great man in modern history with Muhammad. The most famous men created arms, laws and empires only. They founded, if anything at all, no more than material powers which often crumbled away before their eyes. This man moved not only armies, legislations, empires, people and dynasties but millions of men in one-third of the then inhabited world; and more than that, he moved the altars, the gods, the religions, the ideas, the beliefs and souls. On the basis of a Book, every letter of which has become law, he created a spiritual nationality, which blended together people of every tongue and of every race. He has left for us as the indelible characteristic of this Muslim nationality, the hatred of false gods and the passion for the one and immaterial God. Philosopher, Orator, apostle, legislator, warrior, conqueror of ideas, restorer of rational dogmas, of a cult without images, the founder of twenty terrestrial empires and of one spiritual empire, that is Muhammad. As regards all standards by which human greatness may be measured we may well ask, is there any man greater than he is? (Historledela Turquie, Paris, Vol.1, pp.276-277 by Lamartine)."

A famous British scholar, George Bernard Shaw says:

"I have always held the religion of Muhammad in high estimation because of its wonderful vitality. It is the only religion, which appears to possess that assimilating capability to the changing phases of existence which can make itself appeal to every age. I have prophesied about the faith of Muhammad that it would be acceptable tomorrow as it is beginning to be acceptable to the Europe of today. Medieval ecclesiastics, either through ignorance or bigotry, painted Muhammadanism in the darkest colors. They were, in fact, trained to hate both the man Muhammad and his religion. To them Muhammad was anti-Christ. I have studied him, the wonderful man, and in my opinion far from being an anti-Christ he must be called the savior of Humanity. I believe that if a man like him were to assume the dictatorship of the modern world he would succeed in solving the problems in a way that would bring it the much-needed peace and happiness. Europe is beginning to be enamored of the creed of Muhammad. In the next century it may go still further in recognizing the utility of that creed in solving its problems, and it is in this sense that you must understand my prediction." ('A collection of Writings of some of the Eminent Scholars' p.77, by the Woking Muslim Mission, 1933 edition).

With this brief historical background, the Prophet's mission, relevancy of his mission to the modern world and his ranking and status in human history, let us look at the highlights of his life and the Divine Message revealed to him.

THE PROPHET MUHAMMAD

(May Allah's blessings and peace be upon him)

The Rasool (Messenger) of Allah for Mankind

HIS LIFE

At Makkah :

Muhammad (peace be upon him) son of Abdullah, son of Abdul Muttalib, of the tribe of Quraish, was born at Makkah on the 12th of Rabi-al-Awwal (22nd April, 571 A.D.) fifty-three years before the Hijrah. His father died before he was born, and he was brought up first by his grandfather, Abdul Muttalib, and, after his grandfather's death, by his uncle, Abu Tâlib. As a young boy he travelled with his uncle in the merchants' caravan to Syria. Despite the prevalence of corruption, debauchery, gambling, drinking and other vices, he kept himself isolated, chaste, and pure. He never bowed before the idols as was the prevailing practice of his family and tribe. He joined a body of like-minded youth who formed an association to help the poor and the oppressed people against their oppressors, which was called "Hilful Fudhool." His wisdom enabled him to diffuse an ugly situation caused by tension among the various tribes (at the time of rebuilding the Ka'bah) claiming the right to adjust the 'black stone'. He suggested that the stone be put on a sheet of cloth and leader of each tribe hold the sheet, raise the stone and put it in its place.

Birth of the Prophet

His youth

When he became old enough to choose a profession, he chose the honorable profession of trade. He earned such a reputation that the most prominent capitalists of Makkah wished to invest their money in business through him. In this profession he made another journey to Syria in the service of a wealthy widow named Khadijah. So faithfully did he transact the widow's business, and so excellent was his behavior reported by her old servant who had accompanied him, that soon afterwards, she married her young agent. The marriage proved a very happy one, though she was fifteen years older than him. Throughout the twenty-six years of their life together, he remained devoted to her. After her death, when he took other wives, he always mentioned her with the greatest love and reverence. This marriage gave him rank among the notables of Makkah, while his conduct earned for him the surnames of Al-Ameen (the Trustworthy) and Al-Siddeeq (the Truthful).

His profession

His marriage

The Makkans claimed descent from Prophet Abraham through Isma'il (Ishmael), and tradition stated that their temple, the Ka'bah, had been built by Abraham for the worship of One God. It was still called the House of Allah, but the chief objects of worship there were a number of idols which were called

The Hunafa

intercessors and daughters of Allah. The few who felt disgust at this idolatry which had prevailed for centuries, longed for the religion of Abraham and tried to find out what had been its teaching. Such seekers of the truth were known as Hunafa (singular- Hanif), a word originally meaning "those who turn away' (from the existing idol-worship), but later signifying "upright" or "by nature upright" because such persons held the way of truth and right conduct. These Hunafa did not form a community. They were the agnostics of their day, each seeking truth by the light of his own inner consciousness. Muhammad (peace be upon him) became one of them. It was his practice to retire from his family for one month each year to a cave in the desert for meditation. His place of retreat was Hira, a cave in a desert hill not far from Makkah, and his chosen month was Ramadhân.

The first revelation

It was there one night toward the end of a quiet month that the first revelation came to him. He was forty years old at that time. He was meditating when he heard a voice say: "Read!" He said: "I cannot read." The voice again said: "Read" He said: "I cannot read". A third time the voice repeated: "Read!" He said: "What may I read"? The voice said:

> *"Read: In the name of your Rabb (Lord) Who created.*
> *Created man from a leechlike mass. Read! Your Lord is the*
> *Most Gracious, Who taught by the pen, taught man what he*
> *knew not."* (Sûrah 96 Âyat 1-5)

The vision at the Cave of Hira

The words remained "as if inscribed upon his heart." He went out of the cave on to the hillside and heard the same awe-inspiring voice say: "O Muhammad! You are Allah's messenger, and I am Gabriel." Then he raised his eyes and saw the angel, in the likeness of a man, standing in the sky above the horizon. And again the voice said: "O Muhammad! You are Allah's messenger, and I am Gabriel." Muhammad (peace be upon him) stood quite still, turning away his face from the brightness of the vision, but wherever he turned his face, the angel was there confronting him. He remained there a long time till at length the angel vanished. He returned in great distress of mind to his wife Khadijah. He was shivering. He asked his wife to cover him with a heavy blanket. He related his vision to Khadijah. She did her best to reassure him, saying that his conduct had been such that Allah would not let a harmful spirit come to him. Later she took him to her cousin Waraqa bin Naufal, a very old man, "who knew the Scriptures of the Jews and Christians." He declared his belief that the heavenly messenger Gabriel who came to Prophet Musa of old had come to Muhammad, and that he was chosen as the Prophet of his people. He further said, "People will not believe him, they will persecute him, expel him and wage war against him. I wish I could live long enough to support him."

To understand the reason for the Prophet's diffidence and his extreme distress of mind after the vision at the cave of Hira, it must be remembered that the Hunafa sought true religion in nature and regarded with distrust the intercourse with spirits of which men "avid of the Unseen," sorcerers and soothsayers and even poets, boasted in those days. Moreover, he was a man of humble and devout nature, a lover of quiet and solitude. The very thought of being chosen to face mankind alone, with such a Message, scared him at first. Recognition of the Divine nature of the call he had received involved a change in his whole mental outlook sufficient to disturb a sensitive and honest mind, which also involved the forsaking of his quiet way of life. With the continuance of the revelations and the conviction that they brought, at length he accepted the tremendous task imposed on him, becoming filled with an enthusiasm of obedience which justifies his proudest title: "The Slave of Allah."

His distress of mind

The words which were conveyed to him when in a state of trance by Gabriel from Allah are held sacred by the Muslims and are never confounded with those which the Prophet spoke when no physical change was apparent in him. The former are the Sacred Book , called The Qur'an , which means, "The Reading," the Reading of the man who knew not how to read. The Prophet's own words of preaching or sayings are called Al-Hadith.

Basic Difference in The Qur'an and Hadith

For the first three years of his Mission, the Prophet preached only to his family and his close friends, while the people of Makkah in general regarded him as one who had lost his mind. The first, who responded to his call and embraced Islam, was his wife Khadijah. The second, his first cousin Ali (whom he had adopted). The third, his servant Zaid (a former slave). His old friend Abu Bakr also with some of his slaves and dependents were among those early converts.

First converts

At the end of the third year, the Prophet received the command to "rise and warn," whereupon he began to preach in public. He pointed out the wretched folly of idolatry and that the tremendous laws of day and night, life and death, growth and decay, are in the power of Allah and attest to His Sovereignty. When he began to speak against their gods, the Quraish became actively hostile, persecuting his poor disciples, mocking and insulting him. The one consideration which prevented them from killing him was fear of the blood-vengeance of the clan to which his family belonged. Strong in his inspiration, the Prophet went on warning and pleading, while the Quraish did all they could to ridicule his teaching, and reject his followers.

Beginning of persecution

The converts of the first four years were mostly humble folk, who were unable to defend themselves against oppression. So cruel was the persecution that the Prophet advised all who could to emigrate to Abyssinia, a Christian country. In spite of persecution and emigration, the small community of Muslims grew in

The pilgrimage of some new Muslims to Abyssinia

number. The Quraish were seriously alarmed. The idol worship at the Ka'bah, the holy place to which all Arabia made pilgrimage, was first among their vested interests. During the season of the pilgrimage they posted men on all the roads to warn the tribes against the madman who was preaching in their midst. They tried to compromise with the Prophet by offering to accept his religion if he would so modify it as to make room for their gods as intercessors with Allah, they offered to make him their king if he would give up attacking idolatry. When their efforts at negotiation failed, they went to his uncle Abu Tâlib, offering to give him the best of their young men in place of Muhammad, to give him all that he desired, if only he would let them kill Muhammad and be done with him. Abu Tâlib

refused. The exasperation of the idolaters was increased by the conversion of Umar, one of their stalwarts. They grew more and more hostile, till things came to the point that they decided to ostracize the Prophet's whole clan, idolaters who protected him as well as Muslims who believed in him. Their chief men drew up

a document forbidding themselves to hold any interaction with the Prophet's clan. They all signed it, and it was deposited in the Ka'bah. Then for three years, the Prophet was isolated from his kinfolk in their stronghold which was situated in one of the gorges that run down to Makkah. Only at the time of pilgrimage could he go out and preach, or did any of his kinfolk dare to go into the city.

At length, some kind hearts among Quraish grew weary of the boycott of old friends and neighbors. They managed to have the document which had been

placed in the Ka'bah brought out for reconsideration. It was found that all the writing had been destroyed by termite, except the words Bismil-Lah, Allahumma ("In Your name, O Allah"). When the elders saw that marvel, the ban was removed, and the Prophet was again free to go about the city. But meanwhile the opposition to his preaching had grown stronger. He had little success among the Makkans, and the attempt which he made to preach in the city of Ta'if was unsuccessful. His Mission appeared to be a failure, judged by worldly standards.

At the season of yearly pilgrimage, he came upon a little group of men who heard him gladly. They had come from Yathrib, a city more than two hundred

miles away, which has since become world-famous Al-Madinah, "the City" par excellence. At Yathrib, there were Jewish tribes with learned rabbis, who had often spoken to the pagans of a Prophet soon to come among the Arabs. With his help, the Jews would destroy the pagans as the nations of 'Ad and Thamûd had been destroyed in the past for their idolatry. When the men from Yathrib saw Muhammad, they recognized him as the Prophet whom the Jewish rabbis had described to them. On their return to Yathrib, they told what they had seen and

heard, with the result that at the next season of pilgrimage, a deputation came from Yathrib purposely to meet the Prophet. They swore allegiance to him, which is called, the first pact of Al-'Aqabah. They then returned to Yathrib with a Muslim teacher in their company, and soon "there was not a house in Yathrib wherein there was not mention of the messenger of Allah."

In the following year, at the time of pilgrimage, seventy-three Muslims from Yathrib came to Makkah to vow allegiance to the Prophet and invite him to their city, which is called the second pact of Al-'Aqabah. They swore to defend him as they would defend their own wives and children. It was then that the Hijrah, the migration to Yathrib, became possible and he only waited for "Allah's permission to migrate."

Second pact of Al -'Aqabah

Soon after this pact, the Muslims who were in a position to migrate, began to sell their property and to leave Makkah for Yathrib. The Quraish came to know what was going on. They hated Muhammad for that, but were afraid of what he might become, if he escaped from them. It would be better, they concluded, to kill him. The death of Abu Tâlib had removed his chief protector; but still they had to reckon with the vengeance of his clan upon the murderer. They cast lots and chose a slayer out of every clan. All those were to attack the Prophet simultaneously and strike together, as one man. Thus his blood would be on all Quraish.

Plot to murder the Prophet

The last of the able Muslims to remain in Makkah were Abu Bakr, Ali and the Prophet himself. Abu Bakr, a man of wealth, had bought two riding-camels and retained a guide in readiness for the migration. The Prophet waited only for Allah's command. It came at length. It was the night marked for his murder. The conspirators surrounded his house. He gave his cloak to Ali, asked him to lie down in bed so that anyone looking in may think, Muhammad is laying there. They were to strike him as he came out of the house, in the night or early morning. He knew they would not hurt Ali. He threw dust towards them, and it is said that a blindness fell upon the would-be murderers, and he was able to pass them without being noticed. He went to Abu Bakr's house and both of them went together to a cave called "Thore" in the desert hills and hid there for three days until the futile chase was over. Abu Bakr's son and daughter and his herdsman brought food and news after nightfall. Once a search party came quite near them in their hiding place. Abu Bakr was fearful, but the Prophet said; "Fear not! Allah is with us." When the coast was clear, Abu Bakr had riding camels and a guide brought to the cave at night and they set out to Yathrib.

The migration to Yathrib - called "Al-Hijrah" (June 20, 622 AD)

Cave of Thore

After travelling for many days by unfrequented paths, the escapees reached a suburb of Yathrib, where, for weeks, the people of the city had been waiting and watching for the Prophet till heat drove them to shelter. The travelers arrived in the heat of the day, after the watchers had retired. It was a Jew who called out to the Muslims in derisive tones that he whom they were waiting for had arrived at last.

Prophet's arrival at Yathrib

Hijrah made a
clear division
in Prophet's
mission

Such was the Hijrah, the migration from Makkah to Yathrib (called Madinah), which is the beginning of the Muslim era. Thirteen years of humiliation, persecution and seeming failure of prophccy were over. Ten years of success, the fullest that has ever crowned one man's endeavor, had begun. The Hijrah makes a clear division in the Prophet's Mission. Till then he had been a preacher only. Henceforth he was the ruler of a State, at first a very small one, which grew in ten years to be the empire of Arabia.

Hijrah was the
start of a new
calendar for
the Islamic
State

This Hijrah was a turning point in the mission of the Prophet and start of the new calendar for the Islamic State. The kind of guidance which he and his people needed after the Hijrah was not the same as that which they had before. The Madani Sûrahs differ, therefore, from the Makkan Sûrahs. The Makkan Sûrahs give guidance to the individual soul and to the Prophet as a Warner; the Madani Sûrahs give guidance to a growing social and political community and to the Prophet as exemplar, lawgiver and reformer.

At Madinah :

The Jews

The hypocrites

In the first year of Hijrah to Yathrib, the Prophet made a solemn treaty with the Jewish tribes, which secured them equal rights of citizenship and full religious liberty in return for their support of the new State. But their idea of a Prophet was one who would give them dominion, not one who made the Jews as brothers of every Arab who might happen to believe as they did. When they found that they could not use the Prophet for their own ends, they tried to shake his faith and his Mission through seducing some professing Muslims who had reason to resent the Prophet's coming (the hypocrites), since it took away their local influence. In the Madani Sûrahs, there is frequent mention of these Jews and Hypocrites.

The Qiblah

Till then the Qiblah (the place toward which the Muslims turn their faces in prayer) had been Jerusalem. The Jews imagined that the choice implied a leaning toward Judaism and that the Prophet stood in need of their instruction. He received command to change the Qiblah from Jerusalem to the Ka'bah at Makkah. The first section of Part II of Al-Qur'an relates to this Jewish controversy.

The
expeditions

The Prophet's first concern at Yathrib was to establish public congregational prayers and lay down the constitution of the State; but he did not forget that the Arabs had sworn to make an end to his religion. After he had been in Yathrib for twelve months several small expeditions went out, led either by the Prophet himself or other immigrants from Makkah. These are generally represented as warlike but, considering their weakness and the fact that this did not result in fighting, they couldl hardly have been war like, though it is certain that they were prepared to resist attack. It is noteworthy that in those expeditions only immigrants from Makkah took part; not the natives of Yathrib; the reason being that the Yathrib men who had sworn their oath of allegiance at Al-'Aqabah, foresaw fighting in defense, and not fighting in the field. Blood was shed and booty taken in only one of those early expeditions, and even then it was against the Prophet's orders. One purpose of those expeditions may have been to familiarize the immigrant Muslims to the surroundings of Yathrib (Madinah) in the warlike situations, because for thirteen years they had been strict pacifists, and it is clear from several passages of the Qur'an that many of them hated the idea of fighting even in self-defence.

In the second year of the Hijrah, the Makkan merchants' caravan was returning from Syria as usual by a road which passed not far from Yathrib. Makkans had pledged to use the profit of this business trip in war against the newly formed Islamic State. The Prophet had the option to capture the caravan or wait and fight the war planned by the Quraish. As its leader, Abu Sufyân, approached the territory of Yathrib, he learned the Prophet's design to capture the caravan. he, immediately, sent a camel-rider on to Makkah, who arrived in a worn-out state and shouted frantically from the valley to hasten to the rescue, otherwise they would lose both wealth and honor. A force comprised of over 1,000 warriors was sent on its way to Yathrib; less, it would seem, with the hope of saving the caravan than with the idea of punishing the raiders, since the Prophet might have taken the caravan before the relief force started from Makkah.

The Battle of Badr

The army of Quraish had advanced more than half the way to Yathrib before the Prophet set out. The two parties--the army of Quraish and the Prophet with his 313 companions -- were heading for the water of Badr. Abu Sufyân, the leader of the caravan, turned to the coast-plain and safely passed Yathrib. The Muslims met the army of Quraish by the water of Badr. Before the battle, the Prophet was prepared still further to increase the odds against him. He gave leave to all the Ansâr (natives of Yathrib) to return to their homes unreproached, since their oath did not include the duty of fighting in the field; but the Ansâr were only hurt by the suggestion that they could possibly desert him in a time of danger. The battle went at first against the Muslims, but ended in a signal victory for them.

The victory of Badr gave the Prophet new prestige among the Arab tribes; but this war created a feud of blood between the Quraish and the Islamic State, in addition to the old religious hatred. Those passages of the Qur'an which refer to the battle of Badr give warning of much greater struggles yet to come.

The Battle of Uhud

In fact, in the following year, an army of 3,000, under the leadership of Abu Sufyân, came from Makkah to destroy Yathrib. The Prophet's first idea was merely to defend the city, a plan of which Abdullah bin Ubeyy, the leader of

"Hypocrites" (or lukewarm Muslims), strongly approved. But the men who had fought at Badr and believed that God would help them against any odds thought, it would be a shame to wait behind the walls. The Prophet, approving of their faith and zeal, gave way to them, and set out with an army of 1,000 men toward Mt. Uhud, to face the enemy. Abdullah bin Ubeyy was much offended by the change of plan so he withdrew with his men, about a fourth of the army.

Despite the heavy odds, the battle on Mt. Uhud would have been an even greater victory than that at Badr for the Muslims but for the disobedience of a band of fifty archers whom the Prophet had set to guard a pass against the enemy cavalry. Seeing their companions victorious, these men left their post, fearing to lose their share of the spoils. The cavalry of the Quraish rode through the gap and fell on the exultant Muslims. The Prophet himself was wounded and the cry arose that he was slain, till someone recognized him and shouted that he was still alive, a shout to which the Muslims rallied, gathering around the Prophet. This battle cost the Muslims seventy lives, including Hamza, an uncle of the Prophet.

On the following day, the Prophet again rallied forth with what remained of his army, that the Quraish should know that he was still in the field, possibly deterring them from attacking the city. The stratagem succeeded, thanks to the behavior of a friendly Beduin who met the Muslims and conversed with them and afterwards met the army of Quraish. Questioned by Abu Sufyân, he said that Muhammad was in the field, stronger than ever, and thirsting for revenge for yesterday's affair. On that information, Abu Sufyân decided to return to Makkah.

The loss which they suffered on Mt. Uhud lowered the prestige of the Muslims with the Arab tribes and also with the Jews of Yathrib. Tribes which had inclined toward the Muslims now inclined toward Quraish. The Prophet's followers were attacked and killed whenever they went abroad in little companies. Khubaib, one of his envoys, was captured by a desert tribe and sold to the Quraish, who tortured him to death in Makkah publicly. And the Jews, despite their treaty, now hardly concealed their hostility. They even went so far in flattery of Quraish as to declare the religion of the pagan Arabs superior to Al-Islam. The Prophet was obliged to take punitive action against some of them. The tribe of Bani Nadheer were besieged in their strong towers, subdued and forced to emigrate. The Hypocrites sympathized with the Jews and secretly edged them on.

In the fifth year of the Hijrah, the idolaters made a great effort to destroy Al-Islam in the War of the Clans or War of the Trench, as it is variously called. The Quraish with all their clans and the tribe of Ghatfân with all their clans, an army of 10,000 men, rode against Yathrib. The Prophet, by the advise of Salmân, the Persian, caused a deep trench to be dug before the city, and himself led the work

Expulsion of Bani Nadheer

The Battle of Trench

of digging it. The army of the clans was stopped by the trench, a novelty in Arab warfare. It seemed impossible for cavalry, which formed their strength to overcome this tactic. They camped in sight of it and showered their arrows daily on its defenders. While the Muslims were awaiting the assault, news came that Bani Quraizah, a Jewish tribe of Yathrib which had till then been loyal, had gone over to the enemy. The case seemed desperate. But the delay caused by the trench had damped the ardor of the clans, and one Muslim, whose conversion to Islam was not yet known to the unbelievers, managed to sow distrust between the Quraish and their Jewish allies, as a result both hesitated to act. Then came a bitter wind from the sea, which blew for three days and nights so terribly that not a tent could be kept standing, not a fire could be lighted, not a pot boiled. The tribesmen were in utter misery. At length, one night the leader of the Quraish decided that the torment could be borne no longer and gave the order to retire. When Ghatfân awoke next morning they found the Quraish had gone with their bags and baggage.

On the day of the return from the trench the Prophet ordered an attack on the treacherous Bani Quraizah, who, conscious of their guilt, had already taken to their towers of refuge. After a siege of nearly a month they had to surrender unconditionally. They begged that they might be judged by a member of the Arab tribe of which they were adherents. The Prophet granted their request. But the judge, upon whose favor they had counted, condemned their men to death, their women and children to slavery.

Punishment of Bani Quraizah

Early in the sixth year of the Hijrah, the Prophet led a campaign against Bani Al-Mustaliq, a tribe who was preparing to attack the Muslims. It was during the return from that campaign that 'Aisha, his young wife, was left behind and brought back to camp by a soldier, an incident which gave rise to the scandal denounced in Sûrah An-Nûr. It was this campaign, when Abdullah bin Ubeyy, the Chief of Hypocrites, said: "As soon as we return to the city, the mightier will expel the weaker" at sight of a quarrel between Muhâjireen (immigrants from Makkah) and Ansâr (natives of Yathrib).

The slander against the Prophet's wife, 'Aisha

In the same year the Prophet had a vision in which he found himself entering the holy place at Makkah unopposed; therefore, he decided to attempt the pilgrimage. Besides a number of Muslims from Yathrib (which we shall henceforth call Al-Madinah) he called upon the friendly Arabs, whose numbers had increased since the miraculous defeat of the clans, to accompany him, but most of them did not respond. Attired as pilgrims, and taking with them the customary offerings, a company of fourteen hundred journeyed to Makkah. As they drew near the holy valley they were met by a friend from the city, who warned the Prophet that Quraish had put on their leopard-skins (the badge of valor) and

Attempt of pilgrimage to Makkah

had sworn to prevent his entering the sanctuary; their cavalry was on the road before him. On that, the Prophet ordered a detour through mountain gorges and came down at last into the valley of Makkah and encamped at a spot called Al-Hudaibiyah. From there he tried to open negotiations with Quraish, explaining that he came only as a pilgrim. The first envoy he sent towards the city was maltreated and his camel hamstrung. He returned without delivering his message. The Quraish on the other side sent an envoy who was threatening in tone, and very arrogant. Another of their envoys was too familiar and had to be reminded sternly of the respect due to the Prophet. It was he who, on his return to the city, said: "I have seen Caesar and Khosroes in their pomp, but never have I seen a man honored as Muhammad is honored by his companions."

The Prophet sought some envoy who would inspire respect from the Quraish. Uthmân bin Affân was finally chosen because of his kinship with the powerful Umayyad family. While the Muslims were awaiting his return the news came that he had been killed. It was then that the Prophet sitting under a tree at Al-Hudaibiyah, took an oath from all his companions that they would stand or fall together (Bai't-e-Ridwan). After a while, however, it became known that Uthmân was alive. Some people, who came out from the city to hurt the Muslims in their camp, were captured before they could do any harm and brought before the Prophet, who forgave them on their promise to renounce hostility. Then proper envoys came from the Quraish. After some negotiation, truce of Al-Hudaibiyah was signed. For ten years there were to be no hostilities between the parties. The Prophet was to return to Al-Madinah without visiting the Ka'bah, but in the following year he could perform the pilgrimage with his companions. Quraish promised to evacuate Makkah for three days to allow him to do so. Deserters from Quraish to the Muslims during the period of the truce were to be returned; but it was not so for the deserters from the Muslims to Quraish. Any tribe or clan who wished to be a part of the treaty as allies of the Prophet might do so, and any tribe or clan who wished to be part of the treaty as allies of Quraish might do so.

There was dismay among the Muslims at these terms. It was during the return journey from Al-Hudaibiyah towards Madinah when the Sûrah #48, entitled "Al-Fat-h" was revealed. Allah declared that truce to be a clear-cut victory for the Muslims, and in fact, it proved to be the greatest victory that the Muslims had till then achieved. War had been a barrier between them and the idolaters, but now both parties met and talked together, and the new religion spread more rapidly. In the two years which elapsed between the signing of the truce and the fall of Makkah, the number of converts was greater than the total number of all previous converts. The Prophet had travelled to Al-Hudaibiyah with 1,400 men. Two years later, when the Makkans broke the truce, he marched against them with an army of 10,000.

In the seventh year of the Hijrah, the Prophet led a campaign against Khaiber, the stronghold of the Jewish tribes in North Arabia, which had become a hornet's nest of his enemies. The forts of Khaiber were reduced one by one, and the Jews of Khaiber became thenceforth tenants of the Muslims until the expulsion of the Jews from Arabia in the Caliphate of Umar. On the day when the last fort surrendered, Ja'far, son of Abu Tâlib, the Prophet's first cousin, arrived with all who remained of the Muslims who had fled to Abyssinia to escape from persecution in the early days. They had been absent from Arabia for fifteen years. It was at Khaiber that a Jewess prepared for the Prophet poisoned meat, of which he only tasted a morsel without swallowing it, then warned his companions that it was poisoned. One Muslim, who had already swallowed a mouthful, died immediately. The woman who cooked the meat was brought before the Prophet. When she said that she had done it on account of humiliation of her people, the Prophet let her go.

In the same year the Prophet's vision was fulfilled: he visited the holy place at Makkah unopposed. In accordance with the terms of the truce idolaters evacuated the city, and from the surrounding heights watched the procedure of the Muslims. At the end of the stipulated three days the chiefs of Quraish sent word to remind the Prophet that the time was up. He then withdrew, and the idolaters reoccupied the city.

In the eighth year of the Hijrah, hearing that the Byzantine (Roman) emperor was gathering a force in Syria for the destruction of Al-Islam, the Prophet sent 3,000 men to Syria under the command of his freedman Zaid. The campaign was unsuccessful but it did impress the Syrians with a notion of the reckless valor of the Muslims. The 3,000 did not hesitate to fight against the Roman army of 100,000 troops. When all the three leaders appointed by the Prophet had been killed, the survivors obeyed Khâlid Ibn Al-Waleed, who by his strategy and courage, managed to preserve a remnant and return with them to Al-Madinah.

In the same year, the Quraish broke the truce by attacking a tribe that was in alliance with the Prophet and massacring them even in the sanctuary at Makkah. Afterwards they were afraid because of what they had done. They sent Abu Sufyân to Al-Madinah to ask for the existing treaty to be reaffirmed. They hoped that he would arrive before the tidings of the massacre. But a messenger from the injured tribe had been before him, and his embassy was fruitless.

Then the Prophet summoned all the Muslims capable of bearing arms and marched to Makkah. Quraish were overawed. Their cavalry put up a show of defense before the town, but were routed without bloodshed; and the Prophet entered his native city as the conqueror. The inhabitants expected vengeance for their past misdeeds but the Prophet proclaimed a general amnesty. Only a few known criminals were arrested, and most of them were in the end forgiven. In their relief and surprise, the whole population of Makkah hastened to swear allegiance. The Prophet caused all the idols which were in the sanctuary to be destroyed, saying: "Truth has come and darkness has vanished," then the Islamic call for prayer was heard in Makkah.

The Battle of Hunain

In the same year, there was an angry gathering of pagan tribes eager to regain the Ka'bah. The Prophet led 12,000 men against them. At Hunain, in a deep ravine, his troops were ambushed by the enemy and almost put to flight. It was with difficulty that they were rallied to the Prophet and his bodyguard of faithful companions who alone stood firm. But the victory, when it came, was complete and the booty enormous, for many of the hostile tribes had brought out with them everything that they possessed.

The conquest of Ta'if

The tribe of Thaqeef was among the enemy at Hunain. After that victory their city of Ta'if was besieged by the Muslims, and finally reduced. Then the Prophet appointed a governor at Makkah, and himself returned to Al-Madinah to the enormous joy of the Ansâr, who had feared that now that Prophet had regained his native city, he might forsake them and make Makkah the capital.

The Tabûk expedition

In the ninth year of the Hijrah, hearing that Roman army was again being mustered in Syria, the Prophet called on all the Muslims to support him in a great campaign. The far distance, the hot season, the fact that it was harvest time and the prestige of the enemy caused many hypocrites to excuse themselves, and many more to stay behind without excuse. Those defaulters are denounced in the Qur'an, but the campaign ended peacefully. The army advanced to Tabûk, on the confines of Syria, and there learned that the enemy had retreated.

Declaration of immunity

Although Makkah had been conquered and its people were now Muslims and the official order of the pilgrimage had been changed; the pagan Arabs were allowed to perform it in their manner and the Muslims in their manner. It was only after the pilgrims' caravan had left Al-Madinah in the ninth year of the Hijrah, when Al-Islam was dominant in North Arabia, that the Declaration of Immunity, as it is called, was revealed. The Prophet sent a copy of it by a messenger to Abu Bakr, leader of the pilgrimage, with the instruction that Ali was to read it to the multitudes at Makkah. Its purpose was that, after that year, Muslims only were to make the pilgrimage, exception being made for such of the idolaters as had a treaty with the Muslims and had never broken their treaty nor supported anyone against them. Such were to enjoy the privileges of their treaty for the term thereof, but when their treaty expired they would be as other idolaters. That proclamation marks the end of idol-worship in Arabia.

The ninth year of the Hijrah is called the Year of Deputations, because from all parts of Arabia deputations came to Al-Madinah to swear allegiance to the Prophet and to hear the Qur'an. The Prophet had become, in fact, the emperor of Arabia, but his way of life remained as simple as before.

The number of the campaigns which he led in person during the last years of his life is 27, in nine of which there was hard fighting, the number of the expeditions which he planned and sent out under other leaders is 38. He personally controlled every detail of organization, judged every case and was accessible to every suppliant. In those ten years he destroyed idolatry in Arabia; raised woman from the status of a chattel to complete legal equality with man; effectually stopped the drunkenness and immorality which had till then disgraced the Arabs; made men to live with faith, sincerity and honest dealing; transformed tribes who had been for centuries content with ignorance into a people with the greatest thirst for knowledge; and for the first time in history made universal human brotherhood a fact and principle of common law. His support and guide in all that work, was The Qur'an.

In the tenth year of the Hijrah, he went to Makkah as a pilgrim for the last time - his "pilgrimage of farewell," it is called - when from Mount 'Arafât he addressed to an enormous throng of pilgrims. He reminded them of all the duties Islam enjoined upon them and that they would one day have to meet their Lord, Who would judge each one of them according to his work. An extract of the address is as follows:

"...I declare this truth that there is no god except Allah and I declare this truth that Muhammad is His servant and His messenger.

O servants of Allah, I advise you to worship Him and I persuade you to do so.

O people! Listen to me carefully as I speak clearly, for I do not think I will have the opportunity to meet you here after this year.

O people! Your blood and your property have been sanctified to one another ...., just as this month, this year, this day in this city are sanctified.

Beware that I have conveyed the word to you. O Allah! Be my Witness!

So whosoever has anything in trust should return it to its owner.

Amounts of usury of the days of ignorance are remitted and first of all I remit the claims of usury of my uncle 'Abbâs bin Abdul Muttalib....

Beware that I have conveyed the word. O Allah! Be my Witness!

O People! Your women have been given some right in respect of you and you have been given some rights in respect of them. It is incumbent on them to let no one enter into their sleeping chambers except you and do not let any one enter into your house whose entry is not liked by you. And they should not commit any adultery.......

After me, do not go back to the ways of idolatry and do not slay each other.

I am leaving with you two things, as long as you follow them, you will never go astray, and those are the Book of Allah (The Qur'an) and my Sunnah (What I said and what I did).

Beware that I have conveyed the word. O Allah! Be my Witness!

O people! Your God is one, and your ancestor is also one. You are all the progeny of Adam who was created from dust. The most respected before Allah amongst you is one who is most Godfearing. No Arab has preference over a non-Arab or a non-Arab over an Arab. Preference if any is on the basis of 'who fear Allah the most'....

Those who are present here should convey these words to those who are absent. Possibly those who are absent may remember and observe these things more carefully than those present.

O people! Allah has assigned a specific share of inheritance to each heir. To will more than one-third of one's property is not permitted.

The child belongs to one on whose bed (marriage) it is born, and the adulterer shall be stoned."

At the end of the discourse, he asked: "Have I not conveyed the message?" And from that great multitude of men, who a few months or years before had all been conscienceless idolaters, the shout went up: "O' Allah! Yes!" The Prophet said: "O' Allah! You are my witness! O Allah! You are my Witness! O Allah! You are my Witness!"

It was during that last pilgrimage when the following verse of the Qur'an was revealed, declaring Al-Islam to be Allah's chosen religion:

"This day I have perfected your religion for you, completed My Favors upon you and approved Al-Islam as the Deen (The Way of Life) for you." (Sûrah 5, Ayâh 3)

The Prophet considered this verse as an announcement of his approaching death. Soon after his return to Al-Madinah he fell ill. The tidings of his illness caused dismay throughout Arabia and anguish to the folk of Al-Madinah, Makkah and Ta'if, the hometowns. At early dawn on the last day of his earthly life he came out from his home beside his mosque (Masjid Al-Nabawi) at Al-Madinah and joined the congregation prayer, which Abu Bakr had been leading since his illness. And there was great relief among the people who supposed him well again. When, later in the day, on the 12th of Rabi-al-Awwal, 11 A.H., the rumor grew that he was dead, Umar threatened those who spread the rumor with dire punishment, declaring it a crime to think that the messenger of God could die. He was storming at the people in this strain when Abu Bakr came into the mosque and overheard him. Abu Bakr went to the chamber of his daughter 'Aisha, where the Prophet lay. Having ascertained the fact, and kissed the dead man's forehead, he went back into the mosque. The people were still listening to Umar, who was saying that the rumor was a wicked lie, that the Prophet who was all in all to them could not be dead. Abu Bakr went up to Umar and tried to stop him by a whispered word. Then, finding he would pay no heed, Abu Bakr called to the people, who, recognizing his voice, left Umar and came crowding around him. He first gave praise to Allah, and then said: "O people! Lo! As for him who used to worship Muhammad (peace be upon him), Muhammad is dead. But as for him who used to worship Allah, Allah is Alive and dies not." He then recited the verse of the Qur'an:

"And Muhammad is no more than a Rasool of Allah, like the Rasools that passed away before him. If he dies or is killed, will you turn back on your heels (become unbelievers)? He who turns back on his heels will do no harm to Allah; soon Allah will reward the thankful." (Sûrah 3, Ayâh 144)

"And," says the narrator, an eye-witness, "it was as if the people had not known that such a verse had been revealed till Abu Bakr recited it." And another witness tells how Umar used to say: "Directly I heard Abu Bakr recite that verse as if my feet were cut from beneath me and I fell to the ground. May Allah be pleased with him!"

THE COMPILATION
OF
AL-QUR'AN

The Qur'an was put in writing at the direction of the Prophet himself

All the Sûrahs of the Qur'an had been recorded in writing at the direction of the Prophet before his death, and many Muslims had committed the whole Qur'an to memory. But the written Sûrahs were dispersed among the people; and when, in a battle which took place during the Caliphate of Abu-Bakr - that is to say, within two years of the Prophet's death - a large number of those who knew the whole Qur'an by heart were martyred, a collection of the whole Qur'an was made and put in writing. In the Caliphate of Uthmân, all existing copies of Sûrahs were called in, and an authoritative version, based on Abu-Bakr's collection and the testimony of those who had memorized the whole Qur'an, was compiled exactly in the present form and order, the arrangement of which was ordered by the Prophet himself, the Caliph Uthmân and his helpers being Companions of the Prophet and the most devout students of the revelation (for details about the recording and preservation of the Qur'an, please refer to page # 783-785). The Qur'an has thus been very carefully preserved by Allah Almighty Himself as He stated in the Qur'an:

"Surely, We have revealed this reminder (the Qur'an); and We will surely preserve it Ourself." (Sûrah 15, Âyah 9)

Arrangement of the verses of The Qur'an

The arrangement of the verses of the Qur'an is not easy to understand. Revelations of various dates and on different subjects are to be found together in Sûrahs; some of the Madinah Sûrahs, though of late revelation, are placed first and the very early Makkan Sûrahs at the end. But the arrangement is not haphazard, as some have hastily supposed. A closer study will reveal a sequence and significance -- as, for instance, with regard to the placing of the very early Makkan Sûrahs at the end and Madani Sûrah (Al-Baqarah) in the beginning.

Peculiarity of Arabic text and its English translation

There is another peculiarity which is disconcerting in translation though it proceeds from one of the beauties of the original, and is unavoidable without abolishing the verse-division of great importance for reference. In Arabic, the verses are divided according to the rhythm of the sentences. Verses end naturally when there are strong pauses, although the sentence may go on in the next verse or in several subsequent verses. That is of the spirit of the Arabic language; but attempts to reproduce such rhythm in English have the opposite effect to that produced by the Arabic. A detailed discussion about the translation and how to study the Qur'an is provided in "Guidelines to study the Qur'an" on page # 103.

SYNOPSIS OF SÛRAHS (CHAPTERS)

JUZ (PART) - 1

AL-FÂTIHA: 1

    Supplication to Allah for guidance taught by Allah Himself.   1:[1-7]   111

AL-BAQARAH: 2

    Claim of the Qur'an that it contains no doubtful statement.

        The Qur'an is a guide for those who are God-conscious.   2:[1-5]   115

    Warning is of no use for those who reject faith.   2:[6-7]

    Hypocrites and the consequences of hypocrisy.   2:[8-16]

        Examples of hypocrite's deeds.   2:[17-20]   116

    Allah's demand to worship Him.   2:[21-22]

    Claim of the Qur'an to be the Book of Allah.   2:[23-24]

    Reward for the believers.   2:[25]

    Parable of gnat may confound many and enlighten many.   2:[26-27]   117

    How can you deny Allah?   2:[28-29]

    The story of Adam's creation: 2:[30]

        Victory of knowledge.   2:[31-33]

        Angels show respect to Adam.   2:[34-35]

        Shaitân caused Adam to lose paradise.   2:[36]

        Adam's repentance and his forgiveness.   2:[37]   118

    Need of Allah's revelations for guidance.   2:[38-39]

    Allah's covenants with the Children of Israel.   2:[40-43]

    Do you advise others and forget yourselves?   2:[44]

    Allah's help comes with patience and Salah (Prayers).   2:[45-46]

    Criminals will find no way out on the Day of Judgment.   2:[47-48]

    Israelites' deliverance from Pharaoh's persecution: 2:[49-50]   119

        Their sin of worshipping the Calf.   2:[51-52]

        Their repentance through slaying the culprits.   2:[53-54]

        Those who wanted to see Allah face to face were put

        to death, then Allah gave them life again and provided

        them with heavenly food.   2:[55-57]

        Their discontent and disbelief.   2:[58-59]

    Miracle of providing water in the desert from a rock.   2:[60]

    Israelites rejected the heavenly food and

        Their disobedience and transgression.   2:[61]   120

    Real believers have nothing to fear or to regret.   2:[62]

    Israelites covenant with Allah: 2:[63-64]

        Punishment for the violation of Sabbath.   2:[65-66]

        Their attitude in sacrificing a cow on Allah's command.   2:[67-71]   121

        Miracle of bringing the dead body back to life and

JUZ (PART) - 3

JUZ (PART) - 5

Al-Fâtiha is also called: "Seven verses worthy of
oft-recitation."

Proclaim the commandments of Allah publicly and turn away
from the Mushrikeen. 15:[87-99] 321

NAHL: 16

Allah has sent down His revelations to warn that there is no
god but Him.
He has created cattle for the benefit of human beings. 16:[1-9] 323
It is He Who sends down water from the sky for drinking and
agriculture.
He set mountains to stabilize the earth.
Allah has bestowed so many favors, you cannot even
count them. 16:[10-21] 324
The unbelievers are arrogant and they will be held responsible
for that attitude. 16:[22-25]
On the Day of Judgment, Allah will humiliate the arrogant and
cast them into hell while the righteous will be awarded
paradise. 16:[26-34] 325
Allah has sent the Rasools to warn against the unbelievers'
excuse: "If Allah wanted, we would have not worshipped
anyone else." 16:[35-40]
Allah has promised a good abode for those who migrate for
His sake. 16:[41-44] 326
Do the unbelievers feel secure against the wrath of Allah. 16:[45-50]
Whenever unbelievers are in distress they call upon Allah
Alone; no sooner does He relieve them that they start
committing shirk. 16:[51-60]
If Allah were to punish mankind for wrong doings, He would
not leave even an animal around the wrongdoers.
As water gives life to dead land so does the Qur'an to the
human soul. 16:[61-65] 327
There is a lesson for mankind in the lives of animals i.e.,
milk-producing animals and the honeybee. 16:[66-70]
There is a lesson in the process of your own creation: Why,
then, believe in deities who have no power to create
anything and disbelieve in Allah, the Creator? 16:[71-76] 328
There are also signs of Allah in the lives of the birds and the
animals. 16:[77-83]
On the Day of Judgment a witness will be called from each
nation and the unbelievers will face the reality of their
invented false gods. 16:[84-89] 329
Allah commands to do justice, do good to others, and give to

JUZ (PART) : 17

AL-ANBIYÂ': 21

AL-MU'MINÛN: 23

AN-NÛR: 24

Salah *(Prayer)* keeps one away from shameful deeds and
    Do not argue with the People of the Book except in
    good taste.   29:[45-51]   446
Those who believe in falsehood and disbelieve Allah shall be
    the losers.
    How many creatures are there who do not carry their
    provisions with them ? Allah provides them as He
    provides you.   29:[52-63]   447
The life of this world is nothing but pastime, the real life is
    the life Hereafter.
    Those who strive in Our cause, We do guide them to
    Our Way.   29:[64-69]

AR-RUM: 30

The Romans' *(Christians)* defeat at the hands of Persia *(Pagans)*
    was taken as a sign of the Muslims' defeat at the hands of
    Arab unbelievers, so Allah gave good tidings for the Roman
    victory as well as the Muslim victory in a few years.   30:[1-10]   452
It is Allah Who originates creation and then repeats it and
    to Him everyone will be brought for final Judgment.   30:[11-19]
The creation of Man, his consort, heavens, earth, language,
    colors, sleep, quest for work, lightening, rain and
    growth of vegetation - all are the signs from Allah.   30:[20-27]   453
The wrongdoers are led by their own appetites without real
    knowledge.
    True faith and the nature of sects.   30:[28-32]
When an affliction befalls people, they call upon Allah, but
    when He relieves them, lo! They start committing shirk.   30:[33-37]   454
Commandment to give one's relatives their due and likewise to
    the poor and the travellers in need.   30:[38-40]
Mischief in the land is the result of Man's own misdeeds, that
    is how Allah lets them taste the fruit of their deeds.   30:[41-45]
Allah sent His Rasools for the guidance of people; some
    believed while others rejected. Allah subjected the guilty
    to His retribution and helped the Believers. Allah said:
    "O Prophet, you cannot make the dead to hear you."   30:[46-53]   455
It is Allah Who has created you and shall bring you to justice
    on the Day of Judgment.   30:[54-60]

LUQMÂN: 31

The Qur'an is the Book of Wisdom, a Guide and a Blessing

No intercession before Allah can avail any one except for
whom He permits it.

The Prophet Muhammad (pbuh) is for the entire mankind. 34:[22-30] 481

Those who disbelieve in the Qur'an and prior scriptures, will
have yokes placed around their necks before being tossed
into hell.

Wealth and children are not the indications of Allah's
pleasure.   34:[31-36]

It is belief that brings you close to Allah not the wealth or
children.

Whatever you spend in charity, Allah will pay you back.

Unbeliever's statements about the Prophet and the Qur'an. 34:[37-45] 482

The unbelievers are asked to ponder upon their wrong
statements - the Truth has come, falsehood neither
originates nor restores anything.   34:[46-50]

On the Day of Judgment the unbelievers will want to believe
but it will be of no avail to them.   34:[51-54] 483

FÂTIR: 35

None can withhold or award blessings besides Allah.

Shaitân is your enemy: so consider him as such.   35:[1-7]   486

That person who considers his evil deeds to be good, cannot be
guided to the Right Path.   35:[8-9]

Let all those who are seeking honor know that real honor is in
the obedience of Allah.   35:[10-11]

Allah has created water, day, night, the sun and the moon, all
for man's benefit.

Deities besides Allah can neither hear, nor response.

They do not own even equal to a thread of a date-stone. 35:[12-14] 487

Mankind is in need of Allah, while He is not in need of any one. 35:[15-18]

The living and the dead are not alike. You cannot make those
who are buried in the grave hear you.   35:[19-26]

Those who recite the Qur'an, establish Salah *(prayer)* and give
charity may hope for Allah's blessings and rewards.

Those who disbelieve, shall have a painful punishment
in the hellfire forever.   35:[27-37] 488

Allah has not sent any Book which has a provision of Shirk
(worshipping any one else besides Allah).   35:[38-41] 489

Plotting evil recoils none but the author of it.

If Allah was to punish people for their wrong doings,
He would have not left even an animal around.   35:[42-45]

Jinns having blood relations with Allah are utterly false. 37:[149-166] 501
Allah has promised to help His Rasools and His devotees. 37:[167-182]

SÂD: 38

The Qur'an is full of admonition. Unbelievers are in sheer
    arrogance for calling the Prophets, liars. 38:[1-14] 504
The story of the Prophet Daûd with whom mountains and
    birds used to sing the rhymes of Allah. 38:[15-26] 505
    The story of the two litigants who came to Daûd
    for a decision. 38:[15-26]
Allah has not created the heavens and the earth in vain. 38:[27-29]
The story of Sulaimân's inspection of steeds to be used in Jihâd.
    The Prophet Sulaimân's prayer of granting him a kingdom,
    similar of which may not be granted to any one else. 38:[30-40]
The story of Ayûb *(Job)*, his sickness and relief. 38:[41-48] 506
The Qur'an is but a reminder about the reward of Paradise and
    punishment of the hellfire. 38:[49-64]
The mission of a Rasool is to warn people and declare that
    there is no divinity except Allah. 38:[65-70] 507
Story of the creation of Adam and disobedience of Iblees
    (Shaitân). 38:[71-88]

AZ-ZUMAR: 39

The mushrikeen try to justify their worship of saints saying that
    it may bring them closer to Allah. 39:[1-6] 509
On the Day of Judgment, no bearer of burden shall bear
    the burden of another. 39:[7-9]
Believers who cannot practice their faith *(Islam)* should migrate
    to other places where they can do so.
    The real losers are those who shall lose their souls and
    their families on the Day of Judgment. 39:[10-18] 510
No one can rescue the one against whom the sentence of
    punishment has been decreed. 39:[19-21]
The Qur'an is consistent in its verses though it repeats its
    teachings in different ways.
    Allah has cited every kind of parable in the Qur'an so
    that people may learn a lesson. 39:[22-31] 511

JUZ (PART): 24

Who can be more wicked than the one who invents a lie against
    Allah?
    If Allah intends to harm you, no one can save you and if
    He intends to bestow His blessings, no one can withhold it. 39:[32-41] 512

It is Allah Who recalls the souls of people upon their death
  and of the living people during their sleep. 39:[42-46] 512
If the wrong doers possess all the treasures of the earth and
  much more besides it, they will gladly offer it as a ransom
  to redeem themselves on the Day of Judgment. 39:[47-52] 513
Those who have transgressed against their souls should not
  despair of Allah's mercy, they should repent while they
  can. 39:[53-63]
Worship Allah and be among His thankful servants and
  On the Day of Judgment, the Book of Deeds will be
  laid open and justice will be done with all fairness. 39:[64-70] 514
After Judgment, unbelievers will be driven to Hell and the
  righteous will be led to Paradise. 39:[71-75]

GHÂFIR / AL-M'UMIN: 40

No one disputes the revelations of Allah except the kuffâr
  (unbelievers).
  The angels who bear the Throne of Allah pray for those
  who repent and follow the Right Way. 40:[1-9] 516
A scene from the Day of Judgment.
  Furtive looks and the secret thoughts. 40:[10-20] 517
Those who denied the Prophets and Allah's revelations were
  all destroyed. 40:[21-22]
The Prophet Musa was sent to Fir'aun, Hamân and Qarûn.
  Fir'aun intended to kill the Prophet Musa. 40:[23-27]
An excellent speech of one of the relatives of Fir'aun in favor
  of the Prophet Musa. 40:[28-37] 518
Allah saved that believer from the plots of Fir'aun and destroyed
  the people of Fir'aun; now they are presented before the fire
  of Hell morning and evening *(punishment of the graves).* 40:[38-50] 519
Allah does help His Rasools and the believers in this world's
  life and will help them in the life Hereafter.
  Your Rabb says: "Call on Me, I will answer your prayers" 40:[51-60]
No one has the right to be worshipped except Allah, the
  Creator and the Rabb of the worlds. 40:[62-68] 520
Those who argue about the revelations of Allah, will soon
  find out the Truth.
  Allah has sent many Rasools before Muhammad (pbuh);
  some are mentioned in the Qur'an and some are not. 40:[69-78] 521
Cattle are the signs of Allah for the people of understanding.
  Belief after seeing the scourge of Allah is of no avail
  to the disbelievers. 40:[79-85]

FUSSILÂT / HA-M'EEM AS-SAJDAH: 41

The Qur'an is a giver of good news and an admonition. Woe to those who deny the Hereafter and do not pay Zakah.	41:[1-8]	524
The story of the creation of the earth, mountains, seasons, skies and heavens.	41:[9-12]	
Warning to the disbelievers and the example of Allah's scourge upon the nations of 'Ad and Thamûd.	41:[13-18]	525
On the Day of Judgment, people's own ears, eyes and skins will bear witness against them relating to their misdeeds.	41:[19-25]	
Those who do not listen to the Qur'an shall be sternly punished and those who say our God is Allah and then stay firm on it, angels are assigned for their protection.	41:[26-32]	526
The best in speech is the one who calls people towards Allah, does good deeds and says: "I am a Muslim." Example of Allah's signs. Nothing is said to Muhammad (pbuh) which was not said to the prior Prophets. The Qur'an is a guide and healing for the believers.	41:[33-44]	527
The Book given to the Prophet Musa was similar to the Qur'an.	41:[45-46]	

JUZ (PART) - 25

On the Day of Judgment all other gods to whom people worship besides Allah shall vanish.	41:[47-51]	528
Have you ever considered that if the Qur'an is really from Allah and you deny it, what will happen to you.	41:[52-54]	

ASH-SHU'ARÂ: 42

The heavens might have broken apart from above those who elevate Allah's creatures to His rank, if the angels were not begging forgiveness for the residents of earth.	42:[1-9]	532
Islam is the same Deen *(way of life)* which was enjoined on Nûh *(Noah)*, Ibrâheem *(Abraham)*, Musa *(Moses)* and Isa *(Jesus)*. They were all ordered to establish Deen-al-Islam and do not create division *(sects)* in it.	42:[10-19]	533
He who desires the harvest in the Hereafter shall be given manifolds, but he who desires in this life shall be given a portion here but shall have no share in the Hereafter.	42:[20-29]	534
Whatever afflictions befall upon people are the result of their own misdeeds. True believers are those who establish Salah, give charity and defend themselves when oppressed.	42:[30-43]	

Admonish the unbelievers and bear with them in patience and
Admonish with the Qur'an.   50:[36-45]   577

AZ-ZÂRIYÂT: 51

Surely the Day of Judgment shall come to pass, only the
perverse persons turn away from this truth.   51:[1-23]   580
The story of the Prophet Ibrâheem, when he was given the
good news of having a son.   51:[24-30]

JUZ (PART) - 27

The same angels who gave good news to Ibrâheem annihilated
the nation of homosexuals.   51:[31-37]   581
There is a lesson in the stories of Fir'aun, 'Ad, Thamûd and
people of Nûh.   51:[38-46]
Allah, Who built the heavens and spread out the earth, has
assigned the Prophet Muhammad (pbuh) to be a Warner
for mankind   51:[47-60]   582

AT-TÛR: 52

Deniers of truth will be put in the fire of hell.
The reward for the righteous will be paradise in which
they will show gratitude for Allah's graciousness.   52:[1-28]   585
The mission of the Prophet and the response to the
disbelievers' arguments.   52:[29-49]   586

AN-NAJM: 53

Scene of the first revelation, brought by angel Gabriel to
the Prophet Muhammad (peace be upon him).
Allah gave him a tour of the heavens, the paradise and
other great signs.   53:[1-18]   589
Lât, Uzza and Manât *(goddesses of Arabs)* are nothing but
names invented by the pagan Arabs.   53:[19-25]
The angels have no share in divinity, nor can they intercede
without permission.
Do not claim piety for yourselves, Allah knows who is
Godfearing and pious.   53:[26-32]
No soul shall bear the burden of another; there shall be
nothing for a person except what he strived for.   53:[33-62]   590

AL-QAMAR: 54

The Day of Judgment is drawing near, yet the unbelievers are
not paying heed to the signs of Allah.   54:[1-8]   592

We have made the Qur'an easy to understand the admonition,
    so is there any who would take the admonition? 54:[9-22]   592
Story of Thamûd and Lût who called their Prophets liars, to
    show how terrible was Allah's scourge and how clear
    was His warning? 54:[23-40]   593
People of Fir'aun were seized for disbelieving Allah's warning.
    The same warning has come to you, will you not take
    admonition? 54:[41-44]

AR-RAHMÂN: 55

It is Allah Who created man, taught the Qur'an and taught him
    how to convey his feelings and thoughts. 55:[1-16]   596
Allah is the Rabb of the easts and the wests and He puts the
    laws to regulate oceans, its products and ships. 55:[17-25]
All that exists will perish except Allah, Who is busy in mighty
    tasks all the time. 55:[26-32]
No one can run away from the jurisdiction of Allah.
    Sinners will be punished in hell. 55:[33-45]   597
Righteous will be rewarded in paradise with lush gardens,
    springs, fruits, bashful virgins and much more. 55:[46-78]   598

AL-WÂQI'A: 56

Scene of Doomsday when mankind will be divided into
    three groups:
    A. Reward for the foremost group. 56:[1-26]   600
    B. Reward for the right-hand group. 56:[27-38]
    C. Punishment for the left-hand group. 56:[39-56]   601
Admonition to the disbelievers with the examples of creation. 56:[57-74]
Testimony of Allah about the Qur'an. 56:[75-96]   602

AL-HADEED: 57

All that is in the heavens and earth glorifies Allah, Who created
    the heavens and earth in six periods and has the knowledge
    of everything.
    Those who spend in charity will be richly rewarded. 57:[1-10]   605
On that day, the true believers will have their light shining
    before them while the hypocrites will have their fate no
    different than the disbelievers.
    Those who spend in charity will be repaid manifold
    and also be given liberal reward besides it. 57:[11-19]   606
Life of this world is but play, amusement and illusion.
    Do not grieve for the things that you miss, nor overjoy
    at what you gain. 57:[20-25]   607

Prophets Nûh *(Noah)*, Ibrâheem *(Abraham)* and Isa *(Jesus)*
were sent for guidance to the Right Way. As for the
monasticism, people instituted it themselves.   57:[26-29]   607

adhere to His laws.   65:[8-12]   647

AT-TAHREEM: 66

Do not make something unlawful which Allah has made lawful
and wives of the Prophet are admonished on their
behavior with him.   66:[1-7]   651

O believers! Turn to Allah in sincere repentance if you want to
be forgiven.

Example of the wives of Nûh and Lût who will go to hell and
example of Fir'aun's wife and Maryam who will go to
paradise.   66:[8-12]   652

JUZ (PART) - 29

AL-MULK: 67

Kingdom of the universe belongs to Allah.

     The lower heaven is decorated with the lamps *(stars)*.

     Conversation between the dwellers of hell and her guards.   67:[1-14]   655

No one can help you against Allah.

     No one can provide you sustenance besides Allah.

     No one can save you from the punishment of Allah.   67:[15-30]   656

AL-QALAM: 68

Allah has declared Muhammad (pbuh) to be of the highest
moral character.

     Do not yield to any disbelieving oath-monger, slanderer
or wicked person.   68:[1-16]   658

What happened to the arrogant stingy owners of a garden who
did not want to pay charity?   68:[17-33]

Allah is not going to treat the Muslims as He will treat the
guilty. Why don't the disbelievers understand this?   68:[34-43]   659

Those who do not believe in Allah's revelations are led step
by step towards destruction.   68:[44-52]

AL-HÂQQAH: 69

Description of the Day of Resurrection and of the Day of Judgment   69:[1-18]   661

Righteous people and their reward and

     Sinful people and their punishment.   69:[19-37]

The Qur'an is the word of Allah and not of the Prophet, and is
a reminder for those who fear Allah *(God)*.   69:[38-52]   662

AL-MA'ÂRIJ: 70

The Day of Judgment will be equal to fifty thousand years and
the disbelievers will wish to save themselves from the

punishment at the expense of their children, wives, brothers and relatives, but it will not happen. 70:[1-35] 664
Paradise is not for the disbelievers.
The disbelievers will have downcast eyes and countenances distorted with shame. 70:[36-44] 665

NÛH: 71
The Prophet Nûh's preaching and submission to Allah after exhausting all his efforts. 71:[1-20] 667
The Prophet Nûh's prayer not to leave any unbeliever on the surface of the earth and Allah granted his wish. 71:[21-28]

AL-JINN: 72
A beautiful speech of the jinns who embraced Islam after hearing the Qur'an.
Jinns also have different religions and sects, among jinns there are some Muslims and some deviators from the Truth. 72:[1-15] 673
Mosques are built for the worship of Allah, so invoke no one else besides Him. 72:[16-19]
The Rasools do not have the power to harm or benefit anyone, their mission is just to convey Allah's message.
Only Allah knows the unseen, He reveals it to whom He chooses from the Rasools. 72:[20-28] 674

AL-MUZZAMMIL: 73
Allah ordered the Prophet not to stand in prayer the whole night.
Those who oppose the Prophet will be treated with heavy fetters and blazing fire.
The Qur'an is a reminder for those who seek to find the Right Way. 73:[1-19] 577
Read from the Qur'an as much as you easily can.
Whatever you spend in the way of Allah, you will find it in the Hereafter. 73:[20] 678

AL-MUDDATHTHIR: 74
Instructions to the Prophet for cleanliness and patience. 74:[1-7] 681
The Day of Judgment will be very difficult, especially for those who deny Allah's revelations and oppose His cause. 74:[8-31]
Actions which lead to hellfire are: Not offering Salah, not feeding the poor, wasting time in vain talk and denying the Day of Judgment. 74:[32-56] 682

AL-QIYÂMAH: 75

Be aware of the Day of Resurrection and Judgment, from
    which there is no escape.75:[1-15]   684
Allah Himself took the responsibility of the Qur'an.
    The last moments of disbeliever's death.   75:[16-30]
The disbelievers do not believe because they never took
    Al-Islam seriously.   75:[31-40]

AD-DAHR: 76

The universe was there before mankind existed, then Allah
    created man, provided him with guidance and gave him
    free will; either to believe or to disbelieve.   76:[1-12]   688
An exemplary life in paradise for those who choose to believe.   76:[13-22]
Allah sent this Qur'an gradually according to the issues faced
    by mankind.
    This is an admonition for those who want to adopt the
    way to their Rabb *(God)*.   76:[23-31]   689

AL-MURSALÂT: 77

Allah swears in the name of life-giving winds, rain and angels
    that the Day of Judgment will be established.
    Woe on that day to the disbelievers!   77:[1-28]   692
On that day; the disbelievers will be asked to walk towards
    the hell which they used to deny.   77:[29-40]
The righteous will be given all that they desire.   77:[41-45]   693
A warning to the disbelievers.   77:[46-50]

JUZ (PART) - 30

AN-NABÂ': 78

The creation of the heavens , earth, mountains and vegetation
    clearly points towards the Day of Judgment.
    Resurrection and man's accountability in the court of
    Allah.   78:[1-30]   696
The righteous will be well pleased and disbelievers will wish
    that they could remain merely dust.   78:[31-40]

AN-NAZI'ÂT: 79

Death, Day of Resurrection and Life after death.   79:[1-14]   699
The story of Musa when he called Fir'aun to his Rabb, he
    denied Allah and was seized for punishment.   79:[15-26]
The creation of man is not harder than the creation of the
    heavens, earth and its contents.   79:[27-33]
Punishment and reward on the Day of Judgment.   79:[34-46]

AL-A'LÂ: 87

Glorify Allah; Allah has taken the responsibility of the Prophet's
    memory about The Qur'an. It is a reminder and those who
    heed its reminders will be successful in the Hereafter.   87:[1-19]   716

AL-GHÂSHIYAH: 88

Condition of the disbelievers and the believers on
    the Day of Judgment.   88:[1-16]   718
Wonders of nature, admonition and accountability.   88:[17-26]

AL-FAJR: 89

Admonition for social welfare through the examples of prior
    nations.   89:[1-14]   720
What should be avoided to do real social welfare.   89:[15-20]
Day of Judgment will be too late to heed the admonition.
    Allah's address to the believers.   89:[21-30]

AL-BALAD: 90

Admonition to the disbelievers of Makkah.
    Allah has given you one tongue and two lips to control it.
    Qualities of a righteous person.   90:[1-20]   722

ASH-SHAMS: 91

Success depends on keeping the soul pure and failure depends
    on corrupting it.   91:[1-10]   724
The corrupted people of Thamûd were leveled to the ground.   91:[11-15]

AL-LAIL: 92

For good people, Allah will facilitate the easy way and for the
    wicked, the hard way.
    What benefit will he get from wealth, if he himself is
    doomed.   92:[1-21]   726

AD-DHUHÂ: 93

Good news to Muhammad *(pbuh)* that the later period will be
    better for him than the earlier.   93:[1-11]   728

AL-INSHIRÂH: 94

Allah expanded the chest of the Prophet, lightened his burden
    and exalted his fame.   94:[1-8]   730

AT-TEEN: 95

Man is made the best creatures of all, except the disbelievers.   95:[1-8]   732

AL-'ALAQ: 96

Read in the name of Allah, Who created man and taught him
by the pen.
Those who forbid from the worship of Allah will be
dragged to hell by their forelock.

AL-QADR: 97

The night of Qadr is better than one thousand months.

AL-BAIYYINAH: 98

The people of the Book did not get divided into sects until
after receiving guidance.
They were also commanded to establish Salah and
pay Zakah.

AZ-ZALZALAH: 99

The earth will report whatever happened on her and men shall
be shown their Books of Deeds

AL-'ADIYÂT: 100

An example of horses who are more grateful to their owners
than men to their Rabb.

AL-QÂRI'AH: 101

A scene explaining the Day of Judgment.

AT-TAKÂTHUR: 102

The cause of man's destruction is mutual rivalry for worldly
gains.
Real success is in working for the life Hereafter.

AL-'ASR: 103

Formula for the way to salvation.

AL-HUMAZAH: 104

The slanderer, defamer and stingy shall be thrown into the
blazing fire.

AL-FEEL: 105

Allah has the power to defeat an army with elephants
through the flock of birds.

THE ARTICLES OF FAITH

"To believe in Allah, His angels, His books, His Rasools, the Last Day, and to believe in the Divine Decree (Al-Qadar), both, the Good and the Evil thereof." *(Reported by Bukhari and Muslim)*

I. Allah: Belief and conviction in the existence of Allah and His Oneness (Tawheed). Tawheed is divided into three categories to facilitate its understanding:

a) **Tawheed Al-Rububiyah** (The Unity of His Lordship): To believe that Allah Alone is the Rabb of this universe. He is the Creator, the Owner, the Nourisher, the Maintainer, the Sustainer, and the Executor of all of its affairs. All creation has been created by Him and Him Alone.

b) **Tawheed Al-Uluhiyah** (The Unity of His Worship): To believe that Allah is the only Ilâh (God, object of adoration and worship), and that all acts of worship (such as prayer, prostration, fasting, animal sacrifice, and invocations) must be directed towards Allah and Allah Alone. These acts of worship, internal and external, must be done in a manner that is prescribed by Allah and that is pleasing to Him, which means total obedience of His laws and commandments. This is the reason for which the Rasools were sent and the Books revealed.

c) **Tawheed Al-Asma wa As-Sifât** (The Unity of His Names and Attributes): To believe in all the names and attributes of Allah in their absolute forms without any imperfections as described by Allah for Himself or by His Rasool, peace be upon him; without giving them meanings other than their obvious meanings, without giving Him new names and attributes or taking away any of them, and without making any similarities of them with His creation.

II. His Angels: To believe in the existence of the angels, their names, attributes, characteristics, and duties as described in the Qur'an and authentic Sunnah of the Prophet (peace be upon him). They are a creation from amongst the creations of Allah. He has created them from light and they are in total obedience to Him Alone. They are assigned many duties, from amongst them is Jibrâ'el, who has brought down all the revelations to the various Rasools, Isrâfeel, who is in-charge of blowing the trumpet that will cause all to be destroyed and which will resurrect the bodies on the Day of Judgment, and Mikâ'eel, who is responsible for the rain and vegetation.

III. His Books: To believe in all the Books or Revelations sent by Allah to His various Rasools as a mercy and guidance for mankind. From amongst them are the Taurât (Torah) revealed to Musa (Moses), the Injeel (Gospel) revealed to 'Isa (Jesus), the Zuboor (Psalm) revealed to Daûd (David) and the Qur'an revealed to Muhammad, peace be upon them all. To believe that the Qur'an is the final, complete, and unchanged revelation of Allah towards all of mankind and will stay as such until the Day of Judgment, and that all previous revelations have been abrogated by this final revelation.

IV. His Rasools (Messengers): To believe in all the Rasools as mentioned in the Qur'an and that Allah had sent a Messenger to every nation. To believe that the Rasools communicated Allah's Message completely, properly and promptly, and that they have no divine status or attributes. They all proclaimed the same fundamental beliefs and teachings. From amongst them are Nûh (Noah), Ibrâheem (Abraham), Musa (Moses), 'Isa (Jesus) and the last of them and seal of the Prophets is Muhammad, peace be upon him, who came as a Rasool for the whole of mankind.

V. The Last Day (the Hereafter): To believe in everything that the Qur'an or the Prophet, peace be upon him, has mentioned about the final hour. It includes all that will occur before the trumpet will be blown and after the Resurrection, the events pertaining to the Day of Judgment in which everyone will be held accountable for his/her deeds and will be rewarded with paradise or punished in Hell.

VI. The Belief in the Divine Decree (Al-Qadar), both, the Good and the Evil thereof: To believe that Allah had the knowledge of everything before their existence. This would, therefore, include all the affairs of His creation in respect to obedience, disobedience, life spans, and sustenance. That all things were recorded in the Preserved Tablet *(Al-Lauh Al-Mahfoodh)* before He created the heavens and the earth. That all things came into existence by Divine Decree and Allah Alone created them. Nothing has come to existence by any other means and nothing happens, good or evil, without His permission. The evil, which is mentioned, refers to the evil that happens as a result of mans disobedience of Allah.

GLOSSARY
Of Qur'anic Words and Terms

Allah   AL - Ilâh (The God); it is the proper name of the only Supreme Being Who exists necessarily by Himself. This word comprises all the attributes of perfection. This word is neither feminine nor plural and has never been applied to any other being. This word has no corresponding word in English or in any other language of the world.

A.b.p.h.   (Abph) = Allah be pleased with her, or, Allah be pleased with him.

A'râf   Literally it means an elevated place or an elevated portion of earth or ground. This term is used for the walls (heights) that divide Paradise from Hell.

Ansâr   Helper, defender, protector. This name was given as an honorary distinction to those of the inhabitants of Madinah who were the first to extend assistance to the Prophet Muhammad (pbuh) and who gave a hearty welcome to the emigrants, fraternized with them and defended the Prophet with their wealth and lives.

'Asr   An unlimited extent of time during which people pass away and become extinct. 'Asr is also a name used for one of the five prescribed prayers, offered in the late afternoon.

Dar-ul-Islam   Home of Peace.. A State or Country ruled by Islamic Law (Qur'an and Sunnah), where Muslims and Non-Muslims are at peace to practice their respective beliefs.

Deen   Religion, judgement, way of life. Islam is called 'Al-Deen,' the way of life, as it is not a religion of rituals but a complete way of life including spiritual, social, economical and political systems providing guidance for private, public, national and international issues.

Fir'aun   Pharaoh. This was the title used for the kings of Egypt.

Furqân   Any thing that makes a separation or distinction between truth and falsehood. It also means proof, evidence, or demonstration. The Divine Book revealed to the Prophet Moses and The Qur'an are also called 'Furqân' as distinguishing between truth and falsehood.

Hajj	To perform the religious rites and ceremonies of the pilgrimage. This term is used for the obligatory pilgrimage to Makkah in Saudi Arabia during the lunar month of Zul-Hajj. It is obligatory on every Muslim once in a life time who can afford the necessary expenses to and back.
Harâm	Sanctuary, sacred, sanctified. This term is used for the territory of Makkah and its inviolable suburbs.
Hijrah	Name of the Islamic Calendar based on the day of the Prophet's migration from Makkah to Madinah.
Iddat	Literally it means counting or to count. This term is used relating to the waiting period for a woman, after the divorce or death of her husband, before she is allowed to remarry in order to make sure that no pregnancy exists from the prior marriage.
Ihrâm	To enter upon performance of those acts of Hajj (pilgrimage) or of Umrah whereby certain things become forbidden that were lawful before that state. This term is also used for the special garment worn by pilgrims during Hajj or Umrah.
I'tikâf	To remain constantly in one place. This term is used for devoting one's self for the worship of Allah in a Mosque for the last ten days of the month of Ramadhân (Fasting).
Ilâh	God, an entity worthy of worship
Imân	Belief, true faith, heartfelt belief.
Jihad	Striving to implement Allah's Commandments and the Prophet's Sunnah (way of life) and to struggle in the path of Allah (God) including fight for His cause. Jihâd is one of the three elements of Imân (Faith) in Islam.
Jinn	A definite order of conscious being, intelligent, corporeal and normally invisible, created out of smokeless flame, as men are created

from clay. They were created before Adam. They eat, drink and propagate their species, and are subject to death, the same way as human beings, though as a rule they are invisible to the human eye. They can manifest themselves to human beings at will, mostly in the animal form.

Jizya — Compensation. This term is used for a tax that is taken from the non-Muslim subjects of an Islamic State or Government whereby the Islamic Government assures their protection.

Juz — One of the thirty parts of the Qur'an.

Ka'bah — The square or cubic, a swelled one or one that becomes prominent. This term is specifically used for the cube shaped building in the center of the Sacred Mosque in Makkah. It is the first house of worship built on earth by Adam. It was destroyed during Noah's flood and was re-erected by Ibrâheem (Abraham) and Isma'il (Ishmael). It is a massive stone building oblong in shape, 55 feet in length, 45 feet in width, and with height, a little more than its length, standing in the middle of open parallelogram of about 500 feet by 530 feet known as the sacred Mosque and having a door 7 feet above the ground.

Mujâhid — The one who strives or struggles in the way of Allah (God), and if required goes forth to fight in the cause of Islam.

Al-Masjid-al-Harâm — The Sacred Mosque in Makkah which has the Ka'bah in its center.

Mahram — That relationship which is declared sacred or which is forbidden or unlawful for marriage. The examples are immediate family members, real aunts, real uncles, real nephews and real nieces.

Muhâjireen — Immigrants. This term is more specifically used for those Muslims who migrated from Makkah to Madinah for the cause of Islam. They joined the Prophet leaving all their belongings behind.

Mushrik — Infidel, associator, idol worshipper, worshipper of any one else besides Allah (God) or the one who associates someone as partner of Allah (God) or the one who commits shirk. For details see 'shirk.'

P.b.u.h.	(pbuh) = Peace be upon him.
P.b.u.t.	(pbut) = Peace be upon them.
Prophet	A Messenger of Allah, selected by Him to pass on His message which was given through the Book of Revelations and Shari'ah (Islamic Laws) to a Rasool. For example: the Prophet Yahya (John) was a prophet during the time Isa (Jesus) who was a Rasool. Therefore, he (John) was required to follow the Book and Shari'ah given to Isa (Jesus) - peace be upon them both.
Qiblah	It is the direction of Ka'bah in Makkah towards which Muslims turn their faces during prayers from anywhere in the world.
Rabb	Translated in most English translations as 'Lord.' Stands for: Master, Owner, Sustainer, Provider, Guardian, Sovereign, Ruler, Administrator, Organizer. Allah is the Lord of the Universe in all these senses.

Of the Attributes of the Divine Being, the one that occupies the first place in the Qur'an is Rabb. It is this attribute which, after Allah, is mentioned most frequently, occurring 967 times in the Qur'an; and, lastly, it is the name by which God is most often addressed in prayers. Its significance, according to Imam Râghib, is the fostering of a thing in such a manner as to make it attain one condition after another until it reaches its goal of perfection. Hence Rabb is the Lord Who not only gives to the whole creation its means of sustenance, but has also preordained for each kind a sphere of capacity and, within that sphere, provided the means by which it continues gradually to attain its goal of perfection.

It may be noted here that the Qur'an adopts the word Rabb instead of the word "ab" (meaning father) which is frequently used by the Christians in addressing God. The significance carried by the word "ab" is very limited in comparison with the word Rabb. Another peculiarity regarding this Attribute may be noted here. It is never used absolutely but always as "my Rabb" or "our Rabb" or "your Rabb" or "thy Rabb" or "Rabb of the worlds".

The reason is plain. The Nourisher or Sustainer can be spoken of only in relation to something which He nourishes or sustains. He is spoken of repeatedly as the Rabb (or Sustainer) of believers as well as of unbelievers, of the Muslims as well as their opponents, which is a clear evidence of the broadness of the conception of God in Islam.

Rasool   A Prophet who is given the Book of Revelations and Shari'ah (Islamic Law), and is selected by Allah (God) to pass on His message and be a Model for a particular nation like Ibrâheem (Abraham), Lût (Lot), Musa (Moses), Isa (Jesus) or for the whole mankind like Muhammad - peace be upon them all. All Rasools were also Prophets but all Prophets were not necessarily Rasools.

Rahmân   Kind, beneficent, compassionate, mercy giving.
Raheem   Merciful.

These two attributes not only occupy the highest place after Rabb with regard to the frequency of their occurrence, but their importance is also indicated by bringing them immediately after the attribute of Rabb in the opening chapter, and further by heading with every Sûrah of the Qur'an in the well-known formula Bismillah-ir-Rahmân-ir-Raheem. The closely related Names Rahmân and Raheem, translated as Compassionate and Merciful respectively. They occur 400 times in the Qur'an, while these attributes in verb form showing of mercy occurs about 170 times bringing the total to about 570. No other attribute, with the exception of Rabb, is so frequently repeated. Both these words are active participle nouns of different forms from the same root rahmah, which signifies tenderness requiring the exercise of beneficence, and thus comprises the idea of love and mercy.

The two words are applicable to two different states of the exercise of Allah's mercy; the first for that state, when man has not done anything to deserve it and Allah exercises His unbounded mercy in bestowing His gifts on him, and the second to that state, when man does something to deserve His mercy, and His mercy is, therefore, repeatedly exercised for him.

Thus, it is Rahmân, Who creates for man all those things which make his life possible on this earth, and it is Raheem, Who gives him the fruits of his labor; or, again, it is Rahmân Who, by His revelation, shows man the right way to develop his faculties, and it is Raheem Who rewards the faithful for the good they do.

It is not only the frequent occurrence of the two names, Rahmân and Raheem and the importance attached to them by placing them at the heading of each chapter, which shows that the attribute of mercy is the most predominant of all the attributes of Allah. The Qur'an has gone further and laid the greatest stress in explicit words on the immeasurable vastness of His Divine Mercy.

Risâlat   Message. This term is used for the institution of delivering the Divine Messages. An individual who is chosen by Allah (God) for this purpose is called a Rasool. For details see 'Rasool.'

Rûh   The Soul of man. It is the command of Allah. A man is a component of body and soul. When the soul leaves the body the person is dead. This earthly life is the world of body in which the soul is the guest and the world hereafter will be the world of soul where body will be the guest. Since the soul never dies, therefore, the life hereafter will be an eternal life.

Sadaqât   Alms, charity. This term is used for whatever is given for the pleasure of Allah (God) to the needy or that which is sanctified to God's service.

Sakeenah   Tranquillity or peace of mind.

Salah   An obligatory prayer in the prescribed form which must be offered five times a day at prescribed times. The prescribed timings are Fajr (before sunrise), Dhuhr (afternoon), 'Asr (late afternoon), Maghrib (after sunset) and 'Isha (nightfall).

Shirk   It has no equivalent in English. It is a combination of idolatry, atheism, heathenism, polytheism, paganism, egoism, etc. One may be guilty of shirk even if one is not an idol worshipper and even if one professes to believe in Allah. Shirk is to ascribe any of the exclusive attributes or characteristics or powers or rights of Allah to any one or to associate any one with Him in any form, shape or way whatsoever.

Shorakâ'	Partners, imaginary partners or associates ascribed to Allah by mushrikeen. This term is used for all those to whom the Mushrikeen rendered a share of Divine honors, such as angels, jinns, devils, idols, saints or their statutes.
Sunnah	Dispensation, tradition, way of doing things. This term is specifically used for dealings of Allah (God) with His creatures and also the traditions and the actions of the Prophet Muhammad (pbuh) which are in accordance with the commandments of Allah.
Sûrah	A chapter of the Qur'an.
Tâghût	One who rebels against Allah and claims himself to be the master and sovereign of Allah's servants and forces them to become his own servants. The Arabic word Tâghût literally applies to everyone who transgresses the limits; such entity may be Shaitân or a priest or a religious or political leader or a king or a state.
Tawheed	The opposite of Shirk. It is the doctrine that Allah is One Being, He is Unique in His Person, in His Attributes, in His Powers and in His Rights. He has no offspring, no partner and no associate in any way or capacity whatsoever. He Alone is the Creator, the Cherisher, the Sustainer, the Sovereign, the Ruler and the only Deity worthy of worship.
Tawâf	To circumambulate. This term is used to circumambulate the Ka'bah counter clock wise seven times starting from the corner of the Black Stone and ending the circle at the same place.
Tayammûm	It is a process of ablution when water is not available or some medical condition prevents someone to use water. It is done with clean dust or sand, by clapping the palms of the hands on it and passing them over the hands up to elbows, repeating the same process and passing the hands over the face as if they were being washed with water.
Taurât	Torah. It is the name of the Holy Book containing the Divine Message given to the Prophet Musa *(Moses)* for the guidance of Fir'aun *(Pharaoh)*, his chiefs and the Children of Israel.

Umrah	A voluntary pilgrimage to the Ka'bah at any time other than the Hajj days.
Wali	To be very near to any one, protector, friend, patron, benefactor, helper. This term is used for the friendship of Allah (God) or friendship of Shaitân (Satan). It is also used for the guardianship of a child.
Yaume	A Day, a Stage or a Time Period. It may be equivalent to one thousand years as mentioned in Sûrah #32 (*As-Sajdah*) Verse #5, or fifty thousand years as mentioned in Sûrah #70 (*Al-Ma'arij*) Verse #4.
Zakah	Literally means - growth and increase as well as purification. The payment of Zakah purifies and cleans the remaining wealth because it is blessed by Allah for compliance with His commandment. Zakah is considered an act of worship relating to one's wealth. The giving of Zakah leads to increase of wealth in this world, develops the religious merits in the next and purifies the giver from sins. The divine verse: "Take from their property Sadaqât (Charity) in order to purify them from their sins" illustrates the spirit of Zakah. The Zakah is an obligatory charity enjoined on the members of the Muslim community, so as to take a portion of the surplus money from the comparatively wealthy members of the society and be given it to the destitute, needy and the welfare projects. It is also used for spreading the message of Al-Islam.
Zaboor	Name of the Holy Book containing the Divine message given to the Prophet Dawôôd (David). It is also called Psalms.

GUIDELINES FOR STUDYING THE QUR'AN

The reader should understand the real nature of the Qur'an. Whether one believes it to be a revealed book or not, one should consider, as a starting point, the claim that the Qur'an has put forward by itself and its bearer, the Prophet Muhammad (peace be upon him), that this is a Divine Guidance.

Before a reader begins to study the Qur'an, he should realize that unlike all other writings, this is a unique book with the Supreme Author, an Eternal Message and Universal Relevance. Its contents are not confined to a particular theme or style, but contain the foundation of an entire system of life, covering a whole spectrum of issues, which range from articles of faith to moral teachings; rights and obligations; crime and punishment; personal and public laws; social, economic and political regulations; local and international treaties; guidelines for war and peace; and a host of private and community concerns. These issues are discussed in a variety of ways, such as direct stipulations, reminders of Allah's favors on His creation, admonition, and glad tidings. Stories of past communities are narrated, followed by the lessons to be learned from actions and their consequences.

Unlike conventional books, the Qur'an does not contain information, ideas and arguments about specific themes arranged in a literary order. That's why a stranger to the Qur'an, on his first approach to it, is baffled when he does not find the enunciation of its theme or its division into chapters and sections or separate instructions for different aspects of life arranged in a serial order. On the contrary, what he finds is something with which he has not been familiar before and which does not conform to his concept of a book. He finds that it deals with creeds, gives moral instructions, lays down laws, invites people to Islam, admonishes the unbelievers, draws lessons from historical events, administers warnings, and gives glad tidings, and all these are blended together. The same subject is repeated in different ways and one topic follows the other without any apparent connection. Sometimes, a new topic crops up in the middle of another without any apparent reason; the speaker, the addressees, and the direction of the address changes without any notice. Historical events are presented, but not as in history books. The problems of philosophy and metaphysics are treated in a manner different from that of the textbooks on those subjects. Man and the universe are mentioned in a language different from that of the natural sciences. Likewise, it follows its own method of solving cultural, political, social, and economic problems and deals with the principles and injunctions of law in a manner quite different from that of the sociologists, lawyers and jurists. Morality is taught in a way that has no parallel in the whole literature on the subject.

In order to understand the Qur'an thoroughly, it is essential to know the nature of this Book, its central idea and its aim and object. The reader should also be well acquainted with its style, the terms it uses and the method it adopts to explain things. He or she should also keep in view the background and circumstances under which a certain passage was revealed.

* **THE SUBJECT** it deals with is MANKIND: it discusses those aspects of his life that lead either to his real success or to his failure.

* **THE TOPICS** of the Qur'an are Three:

    Tawheed   that there is only one God (Allah). To realize and maintain His Oneness in all actions which directly or indirectly relate to Him. To believe that: Allah is One without any partner in His dominion and His actions *(Raboobiyyah)*, Allah is One without similitude in His essence and attributes *(Asmâ wa Sifât)* and Allah is one without any rival in His divinity and in His worship *(Uloohiyyah wa 'Ibâdah)*. These three aspects of Tawheed over lap and are inseparable. The omission of any of these aspects is called *"Shirk,"* the association of partners with Allah, which in fact is idolatry.

    Risâlah   that Allah has assigned Rasools (Prophets) to deliver His message, provide knowledge about those unseen facts, such as angels, hell and paradise about which human beings have no means to know, and to provide a model of living in accordance with His commandments.

    Âkhirah   that mankind is in test here in this life and will be held accountable for all good or bad deeds on the Day of Judgement. Then righteous people will be rewarded for their good deeds in Paradise while the bad people will be punished for their bad deeds in Hellfire.

* **THE CENTRAL THEME** that runs throughout the Qur'an is the exposition of Reality and the invitation to the Right Way based on it. It declares that Reality is the same one that was revealed by Allah Himself to Adam at the time of his appointment as vicegerent, and to all the Prophets after him. The Right Way is the same one that was taught by all the Prophets. It also points out that all theories contradictory to this Reality, invented by people about God and the rest of His creation are false, and the ways of life based on them are erroneous and lead to disastrous consequences.

* **THE AIM and OBJECT** of the revelations is to invite mankind to the Right Way and to present clearly the Guidance which he has lost because of his immature and underdeveloped art of preserving the Divine Guidance through writing it down, prior to the advent of the Prophet Muhammad (pbuh).

* **THE QUR'AN IS ONE INTEGRAL WHOLE** in which every verse and sentence has an intimate bearing on other verses and sentences, all of them clarifying and amplifying one another. Its real meaning can only be grasped when we correlate every one of its statement with what has been stated elsewhere in its pages through a cross-reference, always subordinating the particular to general and incidental to intrinsic, realizing that the "Qur'an is its own best commentary." The Qur'an's cross-references are like check digits to

verify its own contents in Allah's scheme of protecting this Eternal Message. As Allah has stated in Al-Qur'an:

"We have revealed this Reminder and We are going to preserve it." (15:9)

If the reader keeps these four basic things in mind, he or she will find that in this Book there is no incongruity in the style, no gap in the continuity of the subject, and no lack of interconnection between its various topics. As a matter of fact, this Book contains no irrelevancy anywhere with regard to its Subject, its Central Theme and its Aim. From its very beginning to its end, the different topics it deals with are so intimately connected with its Central Theme that they are like the beautiful gems of the same necklace, despite their different colors and sizes. The Qur'an keeps the same object in view, whether it is relating to the story of the creation of the earth or the heavens or man, or is referring to the manifestations in the universe or stating events from human history. As the aim of the Qur'an is to guide man and not to teach nature, history, philosophy, science or art, it does not concern itself with these subjects. The only thing which the Qur'an is concerned with, is, to expound the Reality, to remove misunderstandings and misconceptions about it, to impress the Truth upon the mind, to warn of the consequences of wrong attitudes and to invite humanity to the Right Way. The same is true relating to the criticism of various creeds, moral system, and the problems of metaphysics. That's why it states, discusses or cites an example only to the extent relevant to its Central Theme and to its invitation around which every other topic revolves. When the Qur'an is studied in this light, no doubt is left that there is a continuity of subject throughout the Book.

Another thing that causes mental confusion is the assertion that the Qur'an is a complete code of life. But when one reads it, one does not find detailed rules and regulations regarding social, cultural, political, and economic problems. One is, therefore, baffled to see that it does not contain any detailed regulations even about Salah (prayers) and Zakah (charity), which are such important obligatory duties that the Qur'an itself lays great emphasis on them over and over again. That's why the casual reader cannot understand how this Book can be called a complete code. This confusion is caused because the reader loses sight of the fact that Allah did not only send down the Book but also appointed His Rasool to demonstrate its teachings by putting them into actual practice. To illustrate this, we may take the case of the construction of a building. If only a plan of the proposed building is laid down and no engineer is appointed to supervise and direct its construction, then every detail must be supplied. But if an engineer is also appointed along with the plan to construct the building on the spot, obviously there is no need for a detailed plan. In that case, only a sketch with its essential features will suffice. It would, therefore, be wrong to find fault with such a plan as being incomplete. As Allah appointed the Prophet Muhammad (pbuh) along with His Message (the Qur'an), only general principles and absolutely essential instructions were needed, and not their details.

The one and only prerequisite for understanding the Qur'an is to study it with an open and detached mind. Whether one believes it to be a revealed book or not, one should, as much as possible, free one's mind of bias in favor of or against it and get rid of all preconceived opinions, and then approach it with the sole desire of understanding it. Those people who study it with preconceived notions of their own, read only their own ideas between its lines and cannot, therefore, grasp what the Qur'an wants to convey.

If one wishes to have deep knowledge of it, one will have to go through it several times and each time from a different point of view. Those who desire to make a thorough study of the Qur'an should read it at least twice for the sole purpose of understanding the overall system of life it presents. It is a Book that has been sent down to invite people to start a movement and to lead its followers and direct their activities towards the achievement of its mission. One has, therefore, to go to the battlefield of life to understand its real meaning. That's why a quiet and amiable person like the Prophet Muhammad (pbuh) had to come out of his seclusion, start the Islamic Movement and fight against the rebellious world. It was the Qur'an that urged him to declare war against every kind of falsehood and engage in conflict with the leaders of disbelief without any consideration of the consequences.

It is obvious that one cannot possibly grasp the truth contained in the Qur'an by merely reciting its words. Some verses and some chapters of the Qur'an themselves tell that they were revealed at such and such time and brought such and such instructions to guide the Islamic Movement. For others, one must find out the time of revelation in the life of the Prophet to understand the problems the people were facing and the guidance accordingly provided. The same formula applies to its Commandments, its moral teachings, its instructions about economics and culture and its laws regarding different aspects of human life. These things can never be understood unless they are put into practice. It is thus obvious that those individuals and communities who discard it from practical life cannot understand its meaning and gain guidance by mere lip-service to it.

Last but not least, one should also keep in mind that the names of the Sûrahs (Chapters) have not been used to indicate the subject of the Sûrahs. It would, therefore, be wrong to translate the names of Sûrahs; such as Al-Baqarah into "The Cow" or "The Heifer" because this would imply that the Sûrah is dealing with the subject of "The Cow". Just like it would be wrong to translate any English name like Rice, Wolf, Bill, Bush or Baker into its equivalent in Arabic, Urdu or other languages. As mentioned in the Foreword, some Arabic words which cannot be translated into English are written in transliteration, such as Allah, Rabb, Rasool, and so on. Please refer to the Glossary of Qur'anic Words and Terms, to understand their meanings in detail.

The true knowledge is with Allah, May Allah guide me and the reader towards the Right Way.

Â'meen.

English Translation of
the Meanings of

AL-QUR'AN

The Guidance for Mankind

By
Muhammad Farooq-i-Azam Malik

The Institute of Islamic Knowledge
Houston, Texas U.S.A.

IMPORTANT INFORMATION

In the name of Allah, the Compassionate, the Merciful.

**Before you start reading the translation of the meaning of
the Qur'anic Text, you should know the following:**

1. After this page all *Italic* typewriting is the explanation and information relating to the Sûrah's (chapter's) period of revelation, major issues, Divine laws and Guidance provided in that Sûrah, and a brief historical background for the reader to understand the Divine Message in context.

2. In the Translation, an effort is made to use regular type for translating the meanings of Arabic Text, and *Italic* type to clarify the meaning of the verse - the way it is meant by Allah (swt) in the context of the Divine Guidance according to the authentic traditions of the Prophet Muhammad (peace be upon him). Please note that it is not a word for word translation *(Tarjumah)* but a translation of the meanings of Al-Qur'an *(Tarjumâni)*.

3. [ ] indicates the completion of one verse of the Arabic Qur'anic Text and the number of this verse is written in this superscript parenthesis.

4. For better understanding we have spelled out the names of those who are meant in verses where "he," "she," or "they" are mentioned. The word "he" does not mean male gender, it also means female unless specifically used in comparison to a female.

5. The English text is grouped into paragraphs. Paragraphs are the combination of those verses which contain the same theme, incident, law, example or guidance about a particular issue. For an easy reference there is a numerical identification of the Sûrât (Chapter) and the Ayât (verses).

6. We have not translated the Qur'anic words which can not be translated or if translated could have limited or confusing meaning, such as Allah, Rabb, Rasool, Tawheed, Shirk, Salah and Zakah.

7. Parenthesis ( ) is used to explain the immediately preceding term, name or word. Arabic names or terms used in the text which are not translated in ( ) are explained in the "Glossary of Words and Qur'anic Terms" on pages 95 through 102.

**May Allah Almighty bless you with the Guidance
you are looking for!**

Â'meen!

JUZ (PART): 1

1: AL-FÂTIHA

Period of Revelation:

It is one of the very early Revelations. In fact, we learn from authentic Traditions that it was the first complete Sûrah (Chapters) revealed to the Prophet (pbuh). Before this, only a few miscellaneous verses were revealed which form parts of Sûrah 'Alaq, Muzzammil and Muddaththir.

Prayer and Divine Guidance:

* This Sûrah (Chapter) is known as Sab'a Mathani (Seven Oft-Repeated Verses).
* It is also called Umm-al-Kitâb (Mother of the Book), foundation and essence of the Qur'an.
* Its recitation is mandatory in each Islamic Prayer (Salah). It is recited at least seventeen times daily in the five obligatory prayers.
* This Prayer is taught by Allah (Almighty God) Himself to mankind, as a favor, to let them know the format of a Prayer which is acceptable to Him.

This Prayer is for all those who want to study His Message. It is placed at the very beginning to teach the reader that if he sincerely wants to benefit from Al-Qur'an, he should offer this prayer to the Rabb (Lord) of the Universe. Al-Fâtiha teaches that the best thing for a man is to pray for "guidance towards the Right Way" and to study Al-Qur'an with the mental attitude of a seeker of truth, and to recognize that the Rabb (Lord) of the Universe is the source of all knowledge. One should, therefore, begin the study of Al-Qur'an with a prayer to Allah (Almighty God) for seeking His guidance.

It is important to know that the real relation between Al-Fâtiha and Al-Qur'an is not that of an introduction to a book but that of a prayer and its answer. Al-Fâtiha is the prayer from the devotee, and the rest of Al-Qur'an is the answer from Allah. The devotee prays to Allah to show him the "Right Way" and Allah places the whole of Al-Qur'an before him in answer to his prayer, as if to say:

"This is the Guidance that you have asked for"

Appendix I

Al - Qur'an

PARTS AND CHAPTERS

The Qur'an has been divided into 30 parts (Juz) in equal size for the convenience of reciting the Qur'an in the night prayers, called Tarâweeh, during the month of Ramadân, the 9th month in the Lunar Calendar designated for fasting. Reading of the Qur'an on a daily basis is also considered a pious duty by every Muslim and is actually performed in practice by every literate man, woman, and child. The Juz is further divided into Rakûh which is like a section in English. These Rakûhs are also of various lengths. One of the thirty parts of the Qur'an is called a 'Juz' in Arabic and Sipârah or simply Pârah in Persian and Urdu languages. If you read a 'Juz' every day, you complete the whole reading of the Qur'an in a month of thirty days. Usually the arithmetical quarters of a 'Juz' (one-fourth, one-half, three-quarters) are also marked in the Arabic text as al-ruba: al-nisf, and al-thalathah.

The whole of the Qur'an is arranged in 114 Sûrahs of various lengths. Each Sûrah consists of a number of Âyât (verses). A Sûrah is usually spoken of as a chapter in English, but that translation is hardly satisfactory. The word Sûrah has been left un-translated as a technical term in Islamic literature. The Âyah or verse's division is usually determined by the rhythm and cadence in the Arabic text. Sometimes an Âyah (verse) contains many sentences. Sometimes a sentence is divided by a break in an Âyah. But usually, there is a pause in meaning at the end of an Âyah.

For easy identification and convenience, the Sûrahs are numbered and the consecutive number is shown just before the title of the Sûrah in English. In Arabic, the number of the 'Juz' and the title of the Sûrah are given at the head of every page in the Sûrah. Sûrah numbers and Âyah numbers are also written at the end of each paragraph in each Sûrah. The most convenient form of quotation is to write the name of the Sûrah and then the Âyah: thus 2:120 means the 120th Âyah of the second Sûrah.

JUZ (PART): 1

1: AL-FÂTIHA

This Sûrah, revealed at Makkah, has 1 section and 7 verses.

In the name of Allah, the Compassionate, the Merciful. [1]

All praise is for Allah, the Rabb of the Worlds.[2]

The Compassionate, the Merciful. [3]

Master of the Day of Judgment. [4]

You Alone we worship and You Alone we call on for help. [5]

Guide us to The Right Way. [6]

The Way of those whom You have favored; not of those who have earned Your wrath, or of those who have lost The Way. [7]

[Â'meen]   1:[1-7]

Supplication to Allah taught by Allah Himself

Al-Fâtiha:	*Means opening or entrance of the Holy Qur'an.*
Rabb:	*Translated in most English translations as "Lord". Stands for: Master, Owner, Sustainer, Provider, Guardian, Sovereign, Ruler, Organizer, Administrator. Allah is the Lord of the Universe in all these senses. Rabb, as compared to 'Ab' (used by Christians for God, which means father), is a very comprehensive attribute. It implies that He not only gives to the whole creation its means of sustenance but also preordains for each a sphere of capacity, and within that sphere, provides the means by which it continues gradually to attain its goal of perfection.*

Appendix II

THE ABBREVIATED LETTERS (Al-Muqattaât)

Certain Sûrahs have certain initials prefixed to them, which are called the Muqattaât (abbreviated letters). A number of conjectures have been made as to their meaning. Opinions are divided as to the exact meaning of each particular letter or combination of letters, and it is agreed that only Allah knows their exact meaning.

Their presence is not inconsistent with the character of the Qur'an as a "plain book:" The book of nature is also a plain book, but how few can fully understand it. Everyone can get out of the Qur'an plain guidance for his life according to his capacity for spiritual understanding. As his capacity grows, so will his understanding grow. The whole Book is a record for all time. It must necessarily contain truths that only gradually unfold themselves to humanity.

This is not a mystery of the same class as "mysteries" by which we are asked to believe against the dictates of reason. If we are asked to believe that one is three and three is one, we can give no intelligible meaning to the words. If we are asked to believe that certain initials have a meaning which will be understood in the fullness of time or of spiritual development, we are asked to draw upon faith but we are not asked to do any injustice to our reason.

There are 29 letters in the Arabic alphabet (counting hamzah and alif as two letters), and there are 29 Sûrahs which have abbreviated letters prefixed to them. One of these Sûrahs (# 42) has two sets of abbreviated letters, but we need not count this Sûrah twice. If we take the half of the alphabet, omitting the fraction, we get 14, and this is the number of letters which actually occur in the Muqattaât. The 14 letters, which occur in various combinations, are:

1.	Alif	8.	Qâf
2.	Hâ	9.	Kâf
3.	Râ	10.	Lâm
4.	Sin	11.	M'eem
5.	Sâd	12.	Nûn
6.	Tâ	13.	Hâ
7.	Ain	14.	Yâ

The science of phonetics tells us that our vocal sounds arise from the expulsion of air from the lungs, and the sounds are determined by the way in which the breath passes through the various organs of speech, e.g., the throat (guttural), or the various positions of the tongue to the middle or front of the palate or to the teeth, or the play of the lips. It is amazing that everyone of these kinds of sounds is represented in these abbreviated letters.

2: AL-BAQARAH

Period of Revelation:

Though it is a Madani Sûrah (revealed at Madinah), it follows naturally a Makki Sûrah (revealed at Makkah) Al-Fâtiha, which ended with the prayer: "Guide us to the Right Way." This Sûrah begins with the answer to that prayer, "This is the guidance that you have asked for." The greater part of Al-Baqarah was revealed during the first two years of the Prophet's residence at Madinah.

Major Issues, Divine Laws and Guidance:

*   Claim of the Qur'an: "This is the Book which contains no doubt."
*   Creation of Adam, man's nature, and his destiny.
*   The Children of Israel and the People of the Book (Jews and Christians).
*   Israelites' sin of worshipping the statue of a calf.
*   Punishment of Israelites for violation of Sabbath.
*   Nature of Jews' belief.
*   Allah orders not to prevent the people from coming to Masâjid.
*   Ibrâheem and his sons were neither Jews nor Christians but were Muslims.
*   Abraham (Ibrâheem), Ishmael (Isma`il), and their building of the Ka'bah.
*   Change of Qiblah (direction in prayers) towards the Ka'bah in Makkah.
*   Allah orders not to profess any faith blindly.
*   The moon is created to determine the time periods i.e. months and years.
*   Hypocrisy vs. True faith.
*   Ayat-ul-Kursi (Verse of the Throne of Allah).
*   Allah orders the believers to enter into Islam completely.
*   Punishment of a murtad (a Muslim who becomes a Non-Muslim).
*   It is unlawful to marry a mushrik (who worship someone else besides Allah).
*   Victory is not by numbers but by Allah's help.
*   Confrontation of Ibrâheem and Namrûd (the king of his time).
*   What makes charity worthless.
*   Taking usury is like declaring war against Allah and his Rasool.
*   All business dealings relating to deferred payments must be in writing.
*   Retaliation against oppression.
*   Non compulsion in religion.
*   Divine Laws are promulgated relating to the following categories:

Food	Retribution	Wills
Fasting	Bribery	Jihâd
Self-defense	Evidence	Pilgrimage
Charity	Drinking	Bloodwit

Gambling	*Marriage*	*Orphans*
Menstruation	*Oaths*	*Divorce*
Alimony	*Nursing*	*Widows*
Usury	*Buying on Credit*	*Debts*
Loans	*Pledge/Mortgage*	

*   *Believers supplication to Allah.*

      Guidance is also provided concerning social, cultural, economic, political and legal issues through addressing the Jews who were acquainted with the Unity of Allah, Prophethood, Revelation, the Hereafter and Angels. The Jews professed to believe in the law which was revealed by Allah to their Prophet Moses (pbuh). In principle, their religion was the same (Islam) that was being taught by the Prophet Muhammad (pbuh). Although they were originally Muslims, they had swerved from the real Islam and made innovations and alterations to their religion. As a result, they had fallen victims to hair splitting and sectarianism, so much so that they had even given up their original name "Muslim" and adopted the name "Jew" instead, and made religion a monopoly of the children of Israel. This was Jews religious condition when the Prophet went to Madinah and invited them to the True Religion. More than one third of this Sûrah (Chapter) addresses the Children of Israel. A critical review of their history, moral degeneration and religious perversions has been made, to draw clear lines of demarcation between the essentials and nonessentials of the True Religion. The Jews are warned not to mix up the Truth with Falsehood.

      During this period, a new type of Muslims called "Munâfiqûn" (hypocrites), had emerged. There were some who had entered the fold of Islam merely to harm it from within. There were others who were surrounded by Muslims, and become "Muslims" to safeguard their worldly interests. They, therefore, continued to have relations with the unbelievers so that if they became successful, their interests would remain secure. Allah has, therefore, briefly pointed out the characteristics of the hypocrites in this Sûrah. Later on when their mischievous deeds became manifest, detailed instructions were given in Sûrah At-Tauba.

      In brief, this Sûrah is an invitation towards the Divine Guidance. All stories, examples and incidents mentioned in this Sûrah revolve around this central theme. This Sûrah particularly addresses the Jews and cites many incidents from their history to admonish and advise them that accepting the Guidance revealed to the Prophet Muhammad (pbuh) is in their best interest. They should, therefore, be the first to accept it, because this Message is basically the same as was revealed to the Prophet Musa (Moses), peace be upon him.

2: AL-BAQARAH

This Sûrah, revealed at Madinah, has 40 sections and 286 verses.

In the Name of Allah, The Compassionate, The Merciful.

SECTION: 1

Alif L'âm M'eem.[1]   This is the Book *(the Qur'an)* in which there is no doubt. *(Since its author, Allah, the Creator of the universe, possesses complete and perfect knowledge, there is no room for doubt about its contents.)* It is a guidance for the God conscious,[2] who believe in the Unseen, establish Salah *(five regular daily prayers)* and spend in charity out of what We have provided for their sustenance;[3] who believe in this Revelation *(the Qur'an)* which is sent to you *(O Muhammad)* and *the Revelations* which were sent before you *(Torah, Psalms, Gospel...)* and firmly believe in the Hereafter.[4] They are on true Guidance from their Rabb and they are the ones who will attain salvation.[5]   2:[1-5]

Surely, those who reject Faith; it is the same, whether you warn them or you do not, they will not believe.[6]   Allah has sealed their hearts and their hearing; on their eyes there is a veil, and there is a grievous punishment for them.[7]   2:[6-7]

SECTION: 2

There are some people who say: "We believe in Allah and the Last Day;" yet, they are not *true* believers.[8]   They *try to* deceive Allah and the believers. However, they deceive none except themselves; yet, they do not realize it.[9]   In their hearts is a disease *(of doubt and hypocrisy, and because of their misbehavior)* Allah has increased their disease and they shall have a painful punishment for the lies they have told.[10]   When it is said to them: "Do not make mischief on earth," they say: "We make peace."[11] Beware! They are the ones who make mischief but they do not realize it.[12]   When they are told: "Believe as the others believe," they *sarcastically* ask: "Should we believe like fools?" Be aware! They themselves are the fools, if only they could understand.[13] When they meet the believers they say: "We are believers," but when they are alone with their shaitâns, they say: "We are really with you; we were only mocking *the believers.*"[14]   Allah will throw back their mockery on them and leave them alone in their trespasses; so they wander to and fro like the blind.[15]   These are the people who barter guidance for error: but their bargain is profitless and they are not going to be guided.[16]   2:[8-16]

Al-Qur'an is free from all doubts

It is a guide for the God-conscious

Warning is of no avail for those who reject faith

Hypocrites and consequences of hypocrisy

Examples of their deeds

Their example is that of a man who kindled a fire; when it illuminated all around him Allah took away their light *(their eyesight)* and left them in utter darkness: they could see nothing.[17] Deaf, dumb, and blind, they will never return *to the Right Way.*[18] Or *another example is that* of a dark storm-cloud in the sky charged with thunder and lightning. They press their fingers to their ears at the sound of each stunning thunderclap for fear of death: Allah is encircling the unbelievers from all sides.[19] The lightning *terrifies them* as if it was going to snatch away their eyesight; whenever it flashes they walk on; when it becomes dark, they stand still. And if Allah wanted He could have taken away their hearing and their sight; for Allah has power over everything.[20]   2:[17-20]

SECTION: 3

Allah's demand to worship Him Alone

O mankind! Worship your Rabb Who created you and created those who came before you; *by doing this* you may become pious.[21] It is He Who has made the earth a resting place for you and the sky a canopy; and it *is He Who* sends down rain from the sky for the growth of fruits for your sustenance. Therefore, do not knowingly set up rivals to Allah.[22]   2:[21-22]

The claim of The Qur'an to be the Book of Allah

If you are in doubt concerning that which We have sent to Our servant *(Muhammad),* then produce one Sûrah like this; and call your witnesses *(gods that you call upon)* besides Allah *to assist you,* if you are right *in your claim.*[23] But if you are unable to do so, and you can never do so, then fear the Hell fire, whose fuel is men and stones which is prepared for the unbelievers.[24]

     2:[23-24]

Reward for the believers

Give glad tidings to those who believe and do good deeds, for them there will be Gardens beneath which rivers flow. Whenever they will be given fruits to eat they will say: "This is similar to the one we used to eat before," for they will be provided *fruits* which will resemble *the fruits on the earth*; and for them there will be chaste virgin spouses, and they shall live therein for ever.[25]

     2:[25]

Parable of gnat may confound many and enlighten many

Allah does not hesitate to use the similitude of a gnat or an even more insignificant *creature.* Those who believe, know that it is the truth from their Rabb; as for the unbelievers, they will say: "What does Allah mean by such a similitude?" By such *a similitude,* Allah confounds many and enlightens many. He confounds none except the transgressors:[26] those who break Allah's

Covenant after affirming it, and who cut aside what Allah has ordered to be united and cause mischief on earth. It is they, who are the losers.[27]   2:[26-27]

How can you deny Allah? You were lifeless and He gave you life. He will cause you to die, then again will bring you to life; and then you will ultimately return to Him ?[28]   It is He, Who has created for you all that there is in the earth; and directed Himself towards the sky and fashioned it into seven heavens. He has perfect knowledge of everything.[29]   2:[28-29]

How can you deny Allah?

SECTION: 4

Note that occasion, when your Rabb said to the angels: I am going to place a vicegerent on earth. They said: "Will You place there one who will make mischief and shed blood while we glorify Your praises and sanctify Your name?" *Allah* said: "I know what you know not."[30]   2:[30]

Story of Adam's creation

He taught Adam the names of all things; then He presented those things to the angels and said: "Tell Me the names of these, if what you say is true?" (*This was to show Adam's superior qualities).*[31]   "Glory to You," they replied, "we have no knowledge except what You have taught us: in fact You are the One who is perfect in knowledge and wisdom."[32]   *Allah* said: "O Adam! Tell them their names." When Adam told them their names, *Allah* said: "Did I not tell you that I know the secrets of the heavens and the earth, and I know what you reveal and what you conceal?"[33]   2:[31-33]

Victory of knowledge

When We ordered the angels: "Prostrate before Adam *in respect,*" they all prostrated except Iblees *(name of Shaitân)* who refused in his arrogance and became a disbeliever.[34] *To Adam* We said: "Dwell with your wife in Paradise and eat anything you want from its bountiful food from wherever you wish, but do not approach this tree, or you shall both become transgressors."[35]   2:[34-35]

Angels show respect to Adam

But Shaitân *tempted them with the tree to disobey Allah's commandment* and caused them to slip therefrom (paradise), and get them expelled from where they were. We said: "Get down from here, some of you being enemies to others, and there is for you in the earth an abode and provisions for a specified period."[36]   2:[36]

Shaitân caused Adam to lose paradise

Then Adam received appropriate words from his Rabb *and*

repented, and Allah accepted his repentance. Surely, He is the Acceptor of Repentance, the Merciful.[37]   2:[37]

Adam's repentance and his forgiveness

"Get down from here all of you," We said *at the time of Adam's departure from Paradise.* "Henceforth there shall come to you guidance from Me, those who *accept and* follow that guidance shall have nothing to fear or to grieve.[38]   But those who reject and defy Our revelations will be inmates of Hellfire, wherein they shall live forever."[39]   2:[38-39]

Need of Allah's revelations for guidance

SECTION: 5

O children of Israel! Remember My favors which I bestowed upon you; fulfill your covenant *(firm commitment)* with Me and I will fulfill My covenant with you, and fear none but Me.[40] Believe in My revelations, which are confirming your scriptures; do not be the first one to deny My revelations, and do not sell them for a petty price, fear Me and Me Alone.[41]   Do not mix the Truth with falsehood, or knowingly conceal the truth.[42]   Establish Salah *(prayers)*; give Zakah *(charity)*; and bow down with those who bow down *in worship.*[43]   2:[40-43]

Allah's covenants with the Children of Israel

Would you ask others to be righteous and forget to practice it yourselves? Even though you read your *Holy* Book? Have you no sense?[44]   2:[44]

Do you advise others and forget yourselves?

Seek Allah's help with patience and Salah; it is indeed hard *to be punctual in offering Salah* except for those who fear Allah,[45] who are certain in their mind that they are going to meet their Rabb and that they are going to return to Him *for final judgment.*[46]   2:[45-46]

Allah's help comes with patience and Salah

SECTION: 6

O' Children of Israel! Remember My favors which I bestowed upon You; that I preferred you to all other nations *of your time for My message.*[47] Guard yourselves against the Day on which one soul shall not avail another - no intercession shall be accepted, no ransom shall be taken and no help shall be given.[48]

2:[47-48]

Criminals will find no way out on the Day of Judgment

Remember, when We delivered you from the people of Fir'aun *(Pharaoh):* they had subjected you to severe torment, killing your sons and sparing your daughters; you were facing a tremendous trial from your Rabb.[49]   And when We parted the Sea for you,

Israelites deliverance from Pharaoh's persecution

taking you to safety, and drowned Fir'aun's people before your very eyes.[50]   2:[49-50]

Remember, when We made an appointment of forty nights with Musa *(Moses), in his absence* you took the calf *for worship,* thus committing a wicked transgression.[51]   Even then We forgave you, so that you might become grateful.[52]   2:[51-52]

Israelites sin of worshipping the calf

Remember, when We gave Musa *(Moses)* the Holy Book *(Torah)* and the criterion of right and wrong so that you might be rightly guided.[53] *Remember,* when Musa *returned with the Divine Book, he* said to his people: "O my people! You have indeed grievously wronged yourselves by taking the calf for worship; so turn in repentance to your Creator and slay the culprits among you; that will be best for you in His sight." He accepted your repentance; surely, He is the Forgiving, the Merciful.[54]   2:[53-54]

Their repentance through slaying the culprits

Remember, when you said: "O Musa *(Moses)*! We shall never believe you until we see Allah with our own eyes," a thunderbolt struck you while you were looking on *and you fell dead.*[55] Then We raised you up after your death; so that you might be grateful.[56]   We even provided you the shade of clouds and sent down to you al-manna *(sweet dish)* and al-salwâ *(quail's meat)* saying: "Eat of the good things, We have provided for you;" *inspite of these favors your forefathers violated our commandments.* However, *by violating our commandments,* they did not harm Us, but they harmed their own souls.[57]   2:[55-57]

Israelites who wanted to see Allah directly were put to death, then Allah gave them life again and provided them with heavenly food

Remember, when We said: "Enter this town and eat whatever you wish to your hearts' content; make your way through the gates, with humility saying; 'we repent.' We shall forgive you your sins and We shall increase the provisions for the righteous among you.[58]   But the wrongdoers changed Our Words from that which they were asked to say, so We sent down a scourge from heaven as a punishment for their transgression.[59]   2:[58-59]

Israelites discontent and disbelief

SECTION: 7

Remember, when Musa *(Moses)* prayed for water for his people; We said: "Strike the rock with your staff." Thereupon, twelve springs came out of it. Each tribe was assigned its own drinking-place. *Then they were commanded*: "Eat and drink of what Allah has provided and do not create mischief in the land."[60]

2:[60]

The miracle of providing water from a rock

Remember, when you said: "O Musa *(Moses)*! We cannot endure one kind of food; call on your Rabb to give us *a variety of food* which the earth produces, *such as* green-herbs, cucumbers, garlic, lentils, and onions." 'What?' He asked. 'Would you exchange the better for the worse? *If that's what you want,* get down to a city; there you will find what you have asked for. *Gradually, they became so degraded that* shame and misery were brought upon them and they drew upon themselves the wrath of Allah; this was because they went on rejecting the commandments of Allah and killed His prophets unjustly, *furthermore*, it was the consequence of their disobedience and transgression.[61]   2:[61]

Israelites rejected the heavenly food

Israelites disobedience and transgression

SECTION: 8

Surely, those who believed and those who were Jews, Christians or Sabians *(before the advent of Prophet Muhammad)* - those *among them* who believed in Allah and the Last Day and performed good deeds - will be rewarded by their Rabb; they will have nothing to fear or to grieve.[62]   2:[62]

Real believers have nothing to fear or to regret

Remember, O Children of Israel when We took a covenant from you and when We lifted the Mount *(Toor)* over your heads saying: "Hold firmly to what We have given you *(Torah)* and follow the commandments therein, so that you may become pious."[63]   But even after that you backed out; if there would not have been the Grace and Mercy of Allah upon you, you surely would have been among the losers.[64]   2:[63-64]

Israelites covenant with Allah

You very well know the story of those of you who transgressed in the matter of the Sabbath; We ordered them: "Be detested apes".[65]   Thus, We made them an example to their own people and to succeeding generations, and a lesson to those who are God-conscious.[66]   2:[65-66]

Punishment for the violation of Sabbath

Remember, when Musa *(Moses)* said to his people: "Allah commands you to sacrifice a cow," they replied, "do you ridicule us?" Musa answered, "I seek the protection of Allah from being one of the ignorant."[67]   "Request your Rabb," they said, "to give us some details of that *cow*." Musa replied: "Allah says, the *cow* should neither be too old nor too young but of middle age;" do, therefore, what you are commanded![68]   "Request your Rabb again" they said, "to clarify for us her color." Musa replied: "Allah says, the said *cow* should be of a rich and deep yellow color pleasing

Israelites attitude in sacrificing a cow on Allah's command

to the eyes."[69]   Again they said: "Request your Rabb to clarify for us the exact type of *cow* she should be, because to us all cows look alike; if Allah wills, we shall be rightly guided."[70]   Musa replied: "Allah says, the said *cow* should have neither been used to till the soil nor water the fields; a healthy one, free from blemish with no spot on her." "Now you have brought us the accurate description," they said. Then they slaughtered her, after they had almost declined.[71]   2:[67-71]

SECTION: 9

And remember the incident, when you killed a man and started disputing *as to who killed him,* Allah made it known what you concealed.[72]   So, We said: "Strike the dead body with a piece of the *slaughtered cow.*" Thus Allah brought the dead to life and showed you His Signs so that you may understand *His power to restore life.*[73]   But, *even after seeing that* your hearts became hard like a rock or even harder, for there are some rocks from which rivers gush out, and there are some which break asunder and water comes out of them, and there are some which fall down with the fear of Allah. Allah is not unaware of what you do.[74]   2:[72-74]

Miracle of bringing the dead body back to life

The Israelites reaction to the miracle

Do you, *O Believers,* still hope that they *(people of the Book)* will believe in what you say, when some of them have already heard the word of Allah and perverted it, knowingly, after they understood it?[75]   When they meet the believers *(Muslims),* they say: "We too are believers," but when they *(people of the Book)* meet each other in private, they say: "Would you disclose to the believers *(Muslims)* what Allah has revealed to you? So that they *(Muslims)* may use it as an argument against you in *the court* of your Rabb? Have you no sense?"[76]   Do they not really know that Allah knows what they conceal and what they reveal?[77]   2:[75-77]

People of the Book are hopeless victims of hypocrisy

Among them, there are some illiterates who do not know their *Holy* Book; except that they follow their own desires and do nothing but conjecture.[78]   Woe to those, who write the Book with their own hands and then say: "This is from Allah," so that, they may sell it for a petty price! Woe to them, for what their hands have written and woe to them, for what they have earned.[79]

2:[78-79]

Among them there are some who attribute their own writings to Allah

The Jews say: "The fire shall not touch us except for a few days." Ask them: "Have you obtained such a promise from Allah which Allah would not break ? Or do you assert against Allah what

Jews' false claim and its punishment

you do not know?"[80]   Yea! Those who commit evil and become encircled in sins are the inmates of Hellfire; they shall live therein for ever.[81]   *As for* those who believe and do good deeds, they will be the residents of Paradise and live therein forever.[82]

2:[80-82]

SECTION: 10

Israelites made a covenant and broke it

Remember, when We took a covenant *(firm commitment)* from the children of Israel: "You shall worship none but Allah; be good to your parents, relatives, orphans and destitute, speak fair to the people, establish 'Salah', and pay 'Zakah.'" But you broke the covenant, except a few of you, and you paid no heed.[83]

2:[83]

Their behavior with their own people

Also remember another covenant which We took from you: That you shall not shed blood among yourselves and you shall not expel your own people from your homes; you confirmed it and you are witness to it.[84]   Yet, there you are, killing your own people, expelling a group amongst you from their homes, backing each other with sin and aggression; and if they come to you as captives, you trade them for ransoms whereas their expulsion was unlawful for you to begin with. Do you believe in a part of your *Holy Book* and reject the rest? So, what other punishment do such people among you, who behave like this, deserve, than disgrace in this world and to be driven to grievous punishment on the Day of Judgment? Allah is not unaware of what you do.[85]   Such are the people who trade in the life of Hereafter for the life of this world; so neither their punishment shall be lightened nor shall they be helped.[86]

Their punishment for breaking the covenant

2:[84-86]

SECTION: 11

Advent of the Prophet Isa *(Jesus)*

Indeed, to Musa *(Moses)* We gave the Book *(Torah)* and sent after him other Rasools in succession; then We gave Isa *(Jesus)*, the son of Maryam *(Mary)*, clear Signs and strengthened him with the Holy Spirit *(Gabriel)*. Why is it that whenever there came to you a Rasool *with a message* which did not suit your desires, you became so arrogant that to some of them you called impostors and others you killed![87]   They say: "Our hearts are in secure wrappers;" but the fact of the matter is that Allah has cursed them for their disbelief, so little is that which they believe.[88]

2:[87-88]

Jews rejected the truth knowingly

Now when there has come to them a Book from Allah confirming *the Holy Books of Torah and Gospel* which they already have - even though before this they used to pray *for the coming of the Prophet Muhammad* to gain victory against the unbelievers - when there came to them that which they *very well* recognize, they *knowingly* rejected it; Allah's curse is on such disbelievers.[89] What a bad is that for which they have sold away their souls! They deny Allah's revelation merely because of their grudge, that Allah should send His grace *(only on an Israelite rather than)* on whom He pleases from His servants *(Muhammad)*! They have drawn on themselves wrath upon wrath, and for such disbelievers there is a disgraceful punishment.[90]   2:[89-90]

When they are asked to believe in what Allah has revealed, they reply: "We only believe in what Allah has sent to us *(Torah)*, and we reject what is beside that," while it is the truth confirming their own scriptures! Well, ask them, "If you sincerely believe in what was sent to you, why did you kill the Prophets of Allah *who were sent to you from amongst yourselves* before?"[91]   Indeed, Musa *(Moses)* came to you with clear Signs, no sooner was he away from you, than you committed evil by *worshipping* the calf.[92]   2:[91-92]

Nature of the Jews' belief

Remember, when We took a Covenant from you and We lifted the Mount of Toor over your heads *saying:* "Take what We have given you firmly and listen to Our Commandments," you replied: "we have heard but we will not obey." So much was the love of that calf in their hearts due to their unbelief. Tell them: "If you are real believers, then why does your faith prompt you to do such evil things?"[93]   2:[93]

Their love for the calf was more than their love for Allah

Say *O Muhammad*: "If the Home of the Hereafter is exclusively for you and not for the rest of mankind, then wish for death if you are true in your claim!"[94]   But they will never wish for death, because *they are fully aware of the consequences* of what they have sent before them for the Hereafter. Allah knows the wrongdoers.[95]   You will find them the greediest of men for life, even greedier than the mushrikeen; each one of them wishes to be given a life of a thousand years; but the grant of such a life will not save them from the punishment, for Allah is watching whatever they do.[96]   2:[94-96]

Jews' claim of exclusive right to inherit paradise is put to test

SECTION: 12

Say *O Muhammad*: "Whoever is the enemy of Jibrâ'el *(Gabriel)* should know that he revealed this *Qur'an* to your heart by Allah's command, which confirms previous scriptures, and is a

Their animosity for Jibrâ'el and other angels

guidance and good news for the believers."[97]   *Let them know that* whoever is an enemy of Allah, His angels, His Rasools, Jibrâ'el *(Gabriel)* and Mika'el *(Michael)*;   Allah is an enemy to such unbelievers.[98]   2:[97-98]

We have sent down to you clear revelations: no one can deny them except the transgressors.[99]   Has it not been *the case* that every time they made a covenant a group of them threw it aside? But *the fact is that* most of them do not believe.[100]

2:[99-100]

Israelites faithless-ness

Their accusation against the Prophet Solomon (Sulaimân)

When there came to them a Rasool from Allah confirming their own *Holy* Book, a group from those to whom the *Holy* book was given cast off the Book of Allah behind their backs as if they knew nothing about it,[101]   and accepted what the shaitâns falsely attributed to the kingdom of Sulaimân; not that Sulaimân was an unbeliever, it were the shaitâns who were unbelievers; they taught witchcraft to the people and that which was revealed to the two angels, Hâroot and Mâroot in *the city of* Bâbil (Babylon). Yet, these two *angels* never taught magic to anyone without saying: "We have been sent to tempt you; do not renounce your faith." *In spite of this warning,* those people kept on learning from both of them, the magic of which could cause discord between husband and wife; although they could harm none with it except with Allah's permission. They learned, indeed, what harmed them and did not profit them; even though they knew fully well that the buyers of *magic* would have no share in *the happiness of* the Hereafter. Surely, they sold their souls for a bad price, if they could understand it![102]   If they would have believed *(accepted Islam)* and kept themselves away from evil, there would have been a better reward from Allah, if they could understand it![103]   2:[101-103]

Their learning of witchcraft

SECTION: 13

Etiquettes of addressing the Prophet of Allah

O Believers, do not say *to our Rasool*: Râ'inâ (an *ambiguous word for: "Listen, may you become deaf" or "Our shepherd" or in Judeo-Arabic language conveys the sense, "our evil one.")* But say: 'Unzurnâ *("look upon" us "or pay attention" to us)* and listen *to him* carefully; and *remember that* there is a painful punishment for the unbelievers.[104]   The unbelievers among the People of the Book, and the mushrikeen, would never wish that any good be sent down to you, *O Muhammad,* from your Rabb, but Allah chooses for His special Mercy whom He pleases, and Allah is the most Gracious.[105]   2:[104-105]

We do not abrogate any of Our verses *of the Qur'an* or cause it to be forgotten except that We substitute it with something better or similar; don you not know that Allah has full power over everything?[106]   Do you not know that to Allah belongs the dominion of the heavens and the earth, and that besides Allah, you have no protector or helper![107]   2:[106-107]

Abrogation and/ or substitution of the verses of the Qur'an

Do you intend to ask your Rasool *(Muhammad)* questions as Musa *(Moses)* was asked before? But whoever barters belief for unbelief, has indeed lost the direction of the Right Way.[108]

2:[108]

Questioning the Prophet

Many among the people of the Book *(Jews and Christians)* wish they could somehow turn you back from belief to unbelief, due to their selfish envy, after the truth has become quite clear to them. Forgive them and bear with them until Allah brings about His decision; rest assured that Allah has power over everything.[109]

2:[109]

Envy of Jews and Christians

Establish Salah *(Prayers)* and pay Zakah *(obligatory charity)*, and whatever good you send ahead of you *to the Hereafter* for yourselves, you shall find it with Allah; surely, Allah is watching all your actions.[110]   2:[110]

Open-ended credit account for the Hereafter

They say: "None shall enter paradise except the one who is a Jew or a Christian." These are their vain desires. Say *O Muhammad*: "Let us have your proof if you are right in your claim."[111]   Yea! Whoever submits himself entirely to Allah and is a doer of good deeds, will be rewarded by his Rabb; and will have nothing to fear or to grieve.[112]   2:[111-112]

The Jews' and Christians' false claim to inherit paradise

SECTION: 14

The Jews say: "The Christians are not on the right track," and the Christians say: "It is the Jews who are not on the right track," yet, both read their *Holy* Books *(Torah or Gospel)*. And those who have no knowledge *(the pagan Arabs)* say like to what both of them say; so Allah will judge between them in their dispute on the Day of Judgment.[113]   2:[113]

Religious prejudice of the Jews and the Christians

Who is more unjust than the one who prevents people from the Masâjid *(mosques)* of Allah, and to mention His name therein, and strives to ruin them? It is not proper for such people to enter them except with fear. For them there is disgrace in this world and grievous punishment in the Hereafter.[114]   2:[114]

Order not to prevent people from coming to the Masâjid

All directions belong to Allah

To Allah belong the East and the West; whichever direction you turn your face, you will face Allah. Surely, Allah is All-Embracing and All-Knowing.[115]　　　2:[115]

The accusation against Allah of having a son

They say: "Allah has taken to Himself a son;" Allah is above such things! Rather, to Him belongs all that is in the heavens and in the earth; all are obedient to Him.[116] He is the Originator of the heavens and the earth ! When He decrees a thing, He needs only to say, "Be," and there it becomes.[117]　　　2:[116-117]

The Qur'an is the knowledge of truth

Those who have no knowledge ask: "Why does Allah not speak to us *face to face* or send us a sign ?" The same demand was made by those before them: they all have the same mentality. We have already shown clear signs to those whose faith is firm.[118] *What clearer sign could there be than this Book?* We have sent you *(O Muhammad)* with the Truth *(Al-Islam)* and made you the bearer of good news and warning; now, you will not be called upon to answer about the actions of the companions of the blazing fire.[119]
2:[118-119]

Jews and Christians will never be pleased with you

The Jews and the Christians will never be pleased with you, until you follow their faith. *O Muhammad,* tell them *:* "Allah's guidance is the only guidance;" and if after all the knowledge you have received, you yield to their desires, there shall be none to protect you or help you from the wrath of Allah.[120]　　　Those to whom We have given the book and who read it as it ought to be read, they are the ones who believe in it; as for those who reject it, they are for sure the losers.[121]　　　2:[120-121]

SECTION: 15

Accountability on the Day of Judgment

O Children of Israel! Remember the special favor which I bestowed upon you; that I exalted you above all other nations.[122] Guard yourselves against the Day when one soul shall not avail another, no ransom shall be taken, no intercession shall profit anyone, and no help shall be given.[123]　　　2:[122-123]

Ibrâheem was made the Leader of mankind

Remember, when Ibrâheem *(Abraham)* was tested by his Rabb with certain commands, he fulfilled them. *Allah* said: "Surely, I will make you the leader of mankind." "What about my offspring?" Asked Ibrâheem. "My pledge," said *Allah*, "will not apply to the evil doers."[124]　　　2:[124]

Remember, when We made the House *(the Ka'bah)* a center and sanctuary for mankind *saying:* "Take the station of

Ibrâheem as a place of prayer." We entrusted Ibrâheem and Isma'il to cleanse Our House for those who walk around it, who meditate in it, and who kneel and prostrate in prayers.[125] Remember when Ibrâheem said: "My Rabb, make this *(Makkah)* a secure town and provide its people with plenty of food from fruits, those of them who believe in Allah and the Last Day." He answered, "As for those who do not, I shall also provide for them in this life, though in the Hereafter I shall drag them to the torture of Hellfire and it is an evil destination indeed!"[126]   2:[125-126]

Importance of the Ka'bah

Prayer of Ibrâheem for the city of Makkah

Remember, when Ibrâheem *(Abraham)* and Isma'il *(Ishmael)* raised the foundations of the House *and prayed*: "Accept this from us, O our Rabb, You are the one who hears all and knows all.[127] O our Rabb, make us both Muslims *(submissive to You)*; and make our descendants, a nation that will be Muslims *(submissive to You)*. Show us our rites of worship and accept our repentance; surely, You are the Acceptor of repentance, the Merciful.[128] O our Rabb, appoint from among them a Rasool who shall recite to them Your Revelations and teach them the Book and the Wisdom, and purify them; surely, You are the All-Mighty, the Wise."[129]   2:[127-129]

Ibrâheem and Isma'il pray for the appointment of a Prophet from the City of Makkah

SECTION: 16

Who but a foolish man would renounce the faith of Ibrâheem? We chose him in this worldly life, and in the Hereafter, he will be among the righteous.[130] When his Rabb asked him: "Be a Muslim," he answered: "I have become a Muslim to the Rabb of the worlds."[131] This was the legacy that Ibrâheem left to his sons and so did Ya'qoob *(Jacob)*, when he said: "O my sons! Allah has chosen for you this Deen *(way of life)*, therefore, die not unless you are Muslims."[132]   2:[130-132]

Islam: the religion of Ibrâheem

Ibrâheem's advice to his sons

Were you present when death approached Ya'qoob *(Jacob)*? He asked his sons: "Who will you worship after me?" They replied: "We will worship *the same One God* Who is your Rabb and the Rabb of your forefathers Ibrâheem, Isma`il and Ishâq *(Isaac)*, and to Him we all submit as Muslims."[133]   2:[133]

Ya'qoob's advice to his sons

They were a people that have passed away. They shall reap *the fruits* of what they did, and you shall for what you do. You shall not be questioned about what they did.[134] *Jews and Christians* say: "Be Jews or Christians, you shall then be rightly guided." *O Muhammad,* say: "By no means! We follow the faith of Ibrâheem,

Jews & Christians vs. Faith of Ibrâheem

the upright one; and he was not one of the mushrikeen *(those who worship others beside Allah)*."[135]   2:[134-135]

The order of Allah to believe in all the Prophets without discrimination

Say: "We believe in Allah and that which is revealed to us; and what was revealed to Ibrâheem *(Abraham)*, Isma`il *(Ishmael)*, Ishâq *(Isaac)*, Ya'qoob *(Jacob)* and their descendants, and that which was given to Musa *(Moses)*, Isa *(Jesus)* and other Prophets from their Rabb. We do not discriminate between any of them, and to Him *(Allah)* we have surrendered ourselves *(in Islam)*."[136] So, if they believe *(accept Islam)* like you have believed, they shall be rightly guided; if they reject it, they will surely fall into dissension *(divide into differing factions)*; Allah will be your sufficient defender against them, and He hears and knows everything.[137]

2:[136-137]

Baptism is from Allah

Baptism is the baptism of Allah; and who is better than Allah in baptizing? Him do we worship.[138]   2:[138]

Say, *O Muhammad*: "Would you dispute with us concerning Allah, who is our Rabb and your Rabb as well? We shall be accountable *to Him* for our deeds and you for yours; to Him Alone we are devoted.[139]

Ibrâheem and his sons were neither Jews nor Christians

Do you claim that Ibrâheem *(Abraham)*, Isma`il *(Ishmael)*, Ishâq *(Isaac)*, Ya'qoob *(Jacob)* and their descendants were all Jews or Christians? Say: Are you more knowledgeable than Allah?" Who is more unjust than the one who hides the testimony received from Allah? Allah is not unaware of what you do.[140] That was a nation which has already passed away. They are responsible for what they did and you are responsible for what you do, you shall not be questioned about their deeds.[141]

2:[139-141]

JUZ (PART): 2

SECTION: 17

The foolish will ask: "Why did they turn away from the Qiblah *(the direction in prayer)* towards which they used to face?" *O Muhammad*, say: "East and West belong to Allah; He guides whomever He wishes to the Right Way."[142]   2:[142]

Q i b l a h (direction in prayers)

We have made you a moderate Ummah *(nation)* so that you may testify against mankind and that your own Rasool may testify against you. We decreed your former Qiblah only to distinguish those who are the real followers of the Rasool from those who would turn away *from the faith.* It was indeed a hard test except for those whom Allah has guided. Allah does not want to make your faith fruitless. Allah is Compassionate and Merciful to mankind.[143]   2:[143]

The order of Allah to change Qiblah

O Muhammad, many a time, We have noticed you turning your face towards heaven; now, We shall make you turn towards a Qiblah that will please you. Turn your face *(during Salah)* towards the Al-Masjid Al-Harâm *(Ka'bah)*; wherever you are, turn your face in that direction. Surely, those were given the Book know that it is the truth from their Rabb. Allah is not unaware of what they do.[144]   Even if you give every proof to the people of the Book, they will not accept your Qiblah, nor will you accept theirs. Neither of them *(the Jews and Christians)* are the followers of each other's Qiblah. If, after all the knowledge you have been given, you yield to their desires then surely, you will be among the wrongdoers.[145]   Those, to whom We have given the Book *(Jews and Christians)* recognize this fact as they recognize their own sons. Nevertheless, a group of them deliberately conceal the truth.[146] The truth is from your Rabb; therefore, you should never be among those who doubt.[147]   2:[144-147]

The Ka'bah in Makkah was made the new Qiblah

SECTION: 18

Everyone has a direction towards which one turns, therefore, emulate *one another* in good deeds. Wherever you are, Allah will bring all of you together; Allah has power over all things.[148] From where ever you come forth, turn your face *during Salah* towards the Al-Masjid-al-Harâm; this is indeed the Truth from your Rabb. Allah is not unaware of what you do.[149]   Again, from where ever you come forth, turn your face *during Salah* towards the Al-Masjid-al-Harâm; and wherever you are, face towards it, so that

The order to face towards Ka'bah as Qiblah during Salah (prayers)

people will not have any argument against you, except those among them, who are wrongdoers. Do not fear them; fear Me, so that I may perfect My favors to you and that you may be rightly guided,[150] just as *We bestowed Our favor upon you when* We sent among you a Rasool of your own, who recites to you Our revelations, sanctifies you, teaches you the Book and wisdom, and teaches you that which you did not know.[151]   Therefore, remember Me, and, I will remember you, be grateful to Me and never deny Me.[152]

2:[148-152]

SECTION: 19

Prescription to seek Allah's help

O' You who believe! Seek My help with patience and prayer: surely, Allah is with those who are patient.[153]   2:[153]

Martyrs are not dead

Do not say about those who are slain in the cause of Allah *(martyrs)*, that they are dead. Nay, they are alive, but you do not perceive it.[154]   2:[154]

Allah will test the Believer's belief

We shall surely test *your steadfastness* with fear and famine, with loss of property, life and produce. Give good news to those who endure with patience;[155]   who, when afflicted with calamity, say: "We belong to Allah and to Him we shall return."[156] Such are the people on whom there are blessings and Mercy from Allah; and they are the ones that are rightly guided.[157]

2:[155-157]

Safâ and Marwâ are the symbols of Allah

Behold! Safâ and Marwâ *(two hills in the Al-Masjid Al-Harâm)* are among the symbols of Allah. So anyone who performs Hajj *(obligatory pilgrimage to Makkah)* or Umrah *(optional visit to Makkah)* to the House, there is no blame if one goes around *(perform s'ayy)* between them; and anyone who does good voluntarily *should know that* surely, Allah is Appreciative, All-Knowerl.[158]   2:[158]

The curse of Allah, the angels and all mankind is on those who conceal the truth

Those who conceal the clear proofs and the guidance, after We have made it clear in the Book for mankind, will have Allah's curse and that of those who are entitled to curse;[159]   except those who repent, reform and let the truth be known; I will accept their repentance, for I am the Receiver of Repentance, the Merciful.[160] Surely, those who are unbelievers and die while they are unbelievers, they are the ones on whom is the curse of Allah, the angels and all mankind,[161]   they will live in it for ever; neither their punishment shall be lightened nor shall they be given respite.[162] Your God is one God; there is no one worthy of worship except Him, the Compassionate, the Merciful.[163]   2:[159-163]

SECTION: 20

Surely, in the creation of the heavens and the earth, in the alternation of the night and the day, in the sailing of the ships through the ocean for the profit of mankind, in the rain which Allah sends down from the skies, with which He revives the earth after its death and spreads in it all kinds of animals, in the change of the winds and the clouds between the sky and the earth that are made subservient, there are signs for rational people.[164]   2:[164]

Signs from nature to recognize Allah

There are some who take *for worship* other deities besides Allah *(mushrikeen)*, they love them as they should love Allah, whereas the believers are strong in love for Allah. If those who are unjust could visualize *(the Day of Judgement)* when they will see the chastisement, *they would come to know* for sure, that all powers belong to Allah and that Allah is stern in retribution.[165]   On that Day, those leaders who were being followed, when faced with their punishment, will renounce those who followed them and the bonds which united them will break asunder.[166]   The followers will say: "If it could be possible for us to live again, we would renounce them as they have renounced us today." Thus, Allah will show them the fruits of their deeds. They will sigh with regret, and shall not be able to come out of the Hell fire.[167]   2:[165-167]

The mushrikeen will have severe punishment

The followers of misguided leaders will regret on the Day of Judgement

SECTION: 21

O Mankind! Eat of what is lawful and clean on the earth and do not follow the footsteps of Shaitân, surely, he is your open enemy.[168]   He enjoins you to commit evil and indecency, and to say certain things against Allah about which you have no knowledge.[169]   2:[168-169]

Do not follow the footsteps of Shaitân

When it is said to them: "Follow what Allah has revealed." They reply: "Nay! We will follow what our forefathers practiced." Well! Even if their forefathers had no sense at all and lacked guidance?[170]   The parable of those who reject faith is like cattle which, *call out to them as one may*, hear nothing but a shout and a cry *since they are unable to understand*; they are deaf, dumb, blind, and understand nothing.[171]   2:[170-171]

Do not profess the faith blindly

O believers! Eat the clean things which We have provided you and give thanks to Allah, if you worship only Him.[172]   He has forbidden you to eat dead meat, blood, the flesh of swine, and that on which any name other than Allah has been invoked; but, if

Prohibited *(Harâm)* food

someone is compelled by absolute necessity, intending neither to sin nor to transgress, they shall incur no sin. Surely, Allah is Forgiving, Merciful.[173]   2:[172-173]

Those who hide the truth for worldly gains swallow nothing but fire

Surely, those who conceal any part of the Book which Allah has revealed and sell His revelations for a petty price *(material gain)*, swallow nothing but fire into their bellies. On the Day of Resurrection, Allah will neither speak to them nor purify them and they shall have painful punishment.[174]   These are the kind of people who barter guidance for error and forgiveness for punishment. How patient are they, to reach hell fire![175]   Their doom is because Allah has revealed the Book with the truth; surely, those who argue about the Book *(the Qur'an)* are in extreme schism *(divergence)*.[176]   2:[174-176]

SECTION: 22

Islamic definition of righteousness

Righteousness is not whether you turn your face towards East or West; but righteousness is to believe in Allah, the Last Day, the Angels, the Books and the Prophets, to spend wealth, inspite of love for it, on relatives, orphans, helpless, needy travellers, those who ask for and on the redemption of captives; to establish Salah *(prayers)*, to pay Zakah *(charity)*, to fulfill promises when made, to be steadfast in poverty, hardship and at the time of war. Those are the ones who are truthful and those are the ones who are the pious.[177]   2:[177]

Islamic laws of retribution

O believers! Retaliation is prescribed for you in the cases of murder: a free man for a free man, a slave for a slave, and a female for a female. But, if the killer is pardoned by the brother of the slain *(sparing the killer's life by accepting the blood-money)*, then blood-money should be demanded with fairness and payment should be made with gratitude. This is a concession and a mercy from your Rabb. Now, whoever exceeds the limits after this, shall have a painful punishment.[178]   O men of understanding! There is *security of* life for you in the law of retaliation, so that you may become pious.[179]   2:[178-179]

Commandment of Allah to execute a "will"

The will is made obligatory before the death of anyone of you who is leaving some property behind, to bequest it equitably to his parents and relatives. This is a duty incumbent on the righteous.[180]   If anyone changes *the bequest* after hearing it, the sin of it then is on those who make the change. Allah hears and knows everything.[181]   But there is no blame on the one who suspects an error or an injustice on the part of the testator and brings about a settlement among the parties. Allah is Forgiving, Merciful.[182]   2:[180-182]

SECTION: 23

O believers! Fasting is prescribed for you as it was prescribed for those before you, so that you may become pious.[183] *Fast the* prescribed number of days; except if any of you is ill or on a journey, then *fast a* similar number of days later. For those who can not endure it *for medical reasons,* there is a ransom: the feeding of one poor person *for each missed day.* Whoever does more good *than this* voluntarily, it is better for him. However, if you truly understand *the rationale of fasting,* it is better for you to fast.[184]
2:[183-184]

The obligation of fasting

It is the month of Ramadân in which the Qur'an was revealed, a guidance for mankind with clear teachings showing the Right Way and a criterion *of truth and falsehood.* Therefore, anyone of you who witnesses that month should fast therein, and whoever is ill or on a journey shall fast a similar number of days later on. Allah intends your well-being and does not want to put you to hardship. He wants you to complete the prescribed period so that you should glorify His Greatness and render thanks to Him for giving you guidance.[185]   2:[185]

The revelation of the Qur'an and fasting in the month of Ramadân

When my servants question you about Me, tell them that I am very close *to them.* I answer the prayer of every suppliant when he calls Me; therefore, they should respond to Me and believe in Me, so that they may be rightly guided.[186]   2:[186]

Allah is very close to His devotees

It is made lawful for you to approach your wives during the nights of the fasts; they are an apparel for you and you for them. Allah knows that you were committing dishonesty to your souls. So He has relented towards you and pardoned you. Now, you may approach *your wives* and seek what Allah has ordained for you. Eat and drink until the white thread of dawn appears to you distinct from the black thread of night, then complete your fast till nightfall. Do not approach your wives during I'tikâf *(retreat in the mosques for certain period with intention to worship Allah).* These are the limits set by Allah: do not ever violate them. Thus Allah makes His revelations clear to mankind so that they may become pious.[187]
2:[187]

Husband-wife relationship is permitted during the nights of the Fasting month

Timings of fasting

Bribing is a sin

Do not misappropriate one another's property unjustly, nor bribe the judges, in order to misappropriate a part of other people's property, sinfully and knowingly.[188]   2:[188]

SECTION: 24

The moon is to determine time periods

They question you about the new moons. Tell them: they are to determine the periods of time for the *benefit of* mankind and for the Hajj *(pilgrimage)*. It is not righteous to enter your houses from the back doors *during Hajj times*. Righteousness is to fear Allah. Enter your houses through the proper doors and fear Allah so that you may prosper.[189]   2:[189]

Order to fight for a just cause

Fight in the cause of Allah those who fight against you, but do not exceed the limits. Allah does not like transgressors.[190] Kill them wherever they confront you *in combat* and drive them out of the places from which they have driven you. *Though killing is bad*, creating mischief is worse than killing. Do not fight them within the precincts of the Al-Masjid-al-Harâm unless they attack you there; but if they attack you, put them to the sword; that is the punishment for such unbelievers.[191] If they cease hostility, then surely, Allah is Forgiving, Merciful.[192] Fight against them until there is no more disorder and Allah's supremacy is established. If they desist, let there be no hostility except against the oppressors.[193]   2:[190-193]

Retaliation is made lawful even in the sacred months

The Sacred month, *in which fighting is prohibited*, is to be respected if the same is respected by the enemy: sacred things too are subject to retaliation. Therefore, if anyone *transgresses a prohibition and* attacks you, retaliate with the same force. Fear Allah, and bear in mind that Allah is with the righteous.[194]   2:[194]

Commandment to give charity

Give generously for the cause of Allah and do not cast yourselves into destruction by your own hands. Be charitable: Allah loves those who are charitable.[195]   2:[195]

Hajj and Umrah (pilgrimage to Makkah)

Complete the Hajj *(obligatory pilgrimage to Makkah)* and the Umrah *(optional visit to Makkah)* for the sake of Allah. If you are prevented *from proceeding*, then send such offering for sacrifice as you can afford and do not shave your head until the offerings have reached their destination. But, if any of you is ill or has an ailment in his scalp, *which necessitates shaving*, he must pay ransom either by fasting or feeding the poor or offering a sacrifice. If, in peacetime, anyone wants to take the advantage of performing

Umrah and Hajj together, he should make an offering which he can afford; but if he cannot afford it, he should fast three days during the Hajj and seven days on his return making ten days in all. This order is for the one whose household is not in the precincts of Al-Masjid Al-Harâm. Fear Allah and know that Allah is strict in retribution.[196]   2:[196]

SECTION: 25

Hajj is in the well known months. One who undertakes to perform it, must abstain from husband-wife relationship, obscene language, and wrangling during Hajj. Whatever good you do, Allah knows it. Take necessary provisions with you *for the journey*, but piety is the best of all provisions. Fear Me, O People endowed with understanding.[197]   There is no blame on you, if you seek the bounty of your Rabb *during this journey*. When you return from Arafât, *(stop at Muzdalifah and)* praise Allah at Al-Mash'ar Al-Harâm. Praise Him as He has guided you, for before this you were of the people who had lost the Right Way.[198]   Then return from where the people return and seek Allah's forgiveness; surely, Allah is Forgiving, Merciful.[199]   When you have fulfilled your sacred duties, praise Allah as you used to praise your forefathers or with deeper reverence. There are some who say: "Our Rabb! Give us abundance in this world." Such people will not have any share in the hereafter.[200] But there are others who say: "Our Rabb! Give us the good life, both in this world and in the Hereafter and save us from the torment of the fire."[201]   Such people shall have their due share *in both worlds* according to what they have earned, Allah is swift in settling the accounts.[202]   Celebrate the praises of Allah during the appointed days *(11th, 12th and 13th of Dhul-Hijjah)*. There is no sin if anyone hastens to leave *Mina* after two days and there is no sin to stays there a day longer, provided he spends *these days* in piety. Fear Allah and remember that you will surely be gathered before Him.[203]

2:[197-203]

Among the people, there is one whose speech fascinates you in this worldly life; he may even call upon Allah to witness what is in his heart, yet, he is your staunch opponent.[204]   And when he leaves you, he directs his efforts towards causing mischief in the land, destroying crops and cattle. Allah, *Whom he makes his witness,* does not like mischief.[205]   When it is said to him "Fear Allah," arrogance carries him off to sin. Hell will be the proper place for such a person, which is indeed an evil refuge.[206]   And among people there is one who would give away his life to seek the

Restrictions during Hajj

Performance of Hajj (pilgrimage)

Hypocrisy
vs.
True belief

pleasure of Allah. Allah is affectionate to His devotees.[207]

2:[204-207]

Commandment of entering into Islam completely

O believers! Enter into Islam completely and do not follow the footsteps of Shaitân, surely, he is your open enemy.[208] If you falter after clear signs have come to you, then keep in mind that Allah is Mighty, Wise.[209] Are they waiting for anything other than Allah to come down to them in the covers of clouds and the angels and make His decision known? Ultimately, all matters will be presented to Allah *for decision*.[210] 2:[208-210]

SECTION: 26

Believers will rank above the disbelievers on the Day of Judgement

Ask the Children of Israel, how many clear signs We have given them. Anyone who substitutes the favor of Allah *(changes the revelations of Allah)* after it has come to him, *should know that* Allah is strict in retribution.[211] The life of this world is charming to those who are unbelievers and they mock at those who believe, but *they forget that* those who fear Allah will rank above them on the Day of Resurrection; Allah gives sustenance without measure to whom He wants.[212] 2:[211-212]

Mankind was one nation having one religion

Mankind was one nation *having one religion. Later, when people invented other religions, Allah* appointed Prophets as bearers of good news and warnings; and revealed to them the Book with the True Guidance to settle the matters of dispute between people. But, the very people to whom it was given, started disputes after the clear proofs had come to them, because of rivalry between one another. Allah has guided the believers by His will to the truth in those matters in which they had differences. Allah guides whom He pleases towards the Right Way.[213] 2:[213]

The way to paradise passes through trials

Do you think that you will enter paradise *without any trials* while you have known the examples of those who passed away before you? They were afflicted with suffering and adversity and were so violently shaken up that even the Rasool and the believers with him cried out: "When will Allah's help come?" Be aware! Allah's help is ever close.[214] 2:[214]

Charity and fighting (for just cause) is made obligatory

They ask you what they should spend in charity. Say: "Whatever you spend with a good *heart, give it* to parents, relatives, orphans, the helpless, and travellers in need. Whatever good you do, Allah is aware of it.[215] Fighting has been made obligatory for you, much to your dislike. It is quite possible that something which you do not like is good for you and that something which you love is bad for you. Allah knows, and you do not know.[216]

2:[215-216]

SECTION: 27

They ask you about war in the Sacred Month. Tell them: "Fighting in this month is a big *offence*; but to prevent from the path of Allah, to deny Him, to prevent an access to, and expel His worshippers from Al-Masjid-al-Harâm are more severe *crimes* in the sight of Allah, and mischief is worse than killing. *As for unbelievers*: they will not cease fighting until they succeed in turning you back from your religion, if they can; if any of you turns back from his religion and dies as an unbeliever, his deeds will become void in this life and in the hereafter. He will be the inmate of the hellfire, to live in there forever.[217]   Surely, those who believed, migrated and struggled in the path of Allah, they are the ones who can hope for the mercy of Allah; Allah is Forgiving, Merciful."[218]   2:[217-218]

> Fighting during the Sacred Months is a heinous sin

> Punishment for 'mûrtad' (the one who turns back from Islam)

They ask you about drinking and gambling. Tell them: "There is great sin in both, *although they may* have some benefit for men; but their sin is greater than their benefit." They ask you what they should spend; tell them: "What is beyond your needs." Thus, Allah makes His revelations clear to you, so that you may reflect upon[219]   this world and the hereafter. They ask you about orphans. Tell them: "It is best to look for their welfare; and if you mix your affairs with theirs *(become copartners)*, then they are your brothers; Allah knows who means harm and who means their welfare. If Allah wanted, He could be hard on you in this matter, surely, Allah is Mighty, Wise."[220]   2:[219-220]

> Drinking and gambling are sinful (First Order of prohibition)

> The commandment to deal with orphans justly

Do not marry mushrik women until they become believers; a believing slave woman is better than a free mushrik woman even though she may be more attractive to you. *Likewise,* do not marry mushrik men until they become believers: a believing slave is better than a free mushrik even though he may be more pleasing to you. These *mushrikeen* invite you to the hellfire while Allah invites you towards paradise and forgiveness by His grace. He makes His revelations clear to mankind so that they may take heed.[221]

2:[221]

> It is unlawful to marry a mushrik male or female

SECTION: 28

They ask you about menstruation. Tell them: "This is a discomfort; therefore, keep away from women *(do not have*

Prohibition of husband wife relationship during menstruation

sexual intercourse) during their menstrual periods and do not approach them until they are clean again. When they have cleansed themselves then you may approach them in the manner Allah has enjoined for you. Surely, Allah loves those who turn to Him in repentance and love those who keep themselves clean.[222] Your wives are your tilth; so go to your tilth when you like. Take care of your future and refrain from the displeasure of Allah. Bear in mind that you shall meet Him *in the Hereafter,* and give good news to the believers.[223]   2:[222-223]

Do not misuse oaths taken in the name of Allah

Do not make Allah's *name* as an excuse in your oaths against your dealing justly, behaving piously and making peace between people; Allah hears and knows everything.[224] Allah will not hold you accountable for what is inadvertent in your oaths, but He will hold you accountable for what you intended in your hearts; Allah is Forgiving, Forbearing.[225]   2:[224-225]

A limitation on renouncing husband wife relationship

Those who renounce *conjugal relationship with* their wives on oath, have a limitation of four months. If they reconcile *and restore their relationship,* surely, Allah is Forgiving, Merciful.[226] But, if they decide to divorce them, *they may do so,* surely, Allah hears and knows everything.[227]   2:[226-227]

Waiting period for remarriage is three menstruation periods after divorce

Divorced women must keep themselves waiting for three menstrual periods, it is not lawful for them to hide what Allah has created in their wombs, if they believe in Allah and the Last Day. In such cases, their husbands have a right to take them back in that period, if they desire reconciliation. Women have rights, similar to those exercised against them in an equitable manner, although men have a status *(degree of responsibility)* above them. Allah is Mighty, Wise.[228]   2:[228]

SECTION: 29

Laws relating to divorce

The pronouncement of *revocable* divorce is only allowed twice: then, she should be allowed to stay with honor or let go with kindness. It is not lawful for you to take anything back which you have given them except when both parties fear that they may not be able to follow the limits set by Allah; then, if you fear that they both will not be able to keep the limits of Allah, there is no blame, if, by mutual agreement the wife compensates the husband to obtain divorce. These are the limits set by Allah; do not transgress them, and those who transgress the limits of Allah are the wrongdoers.[229] So, if a husband divorces his wife *three times*, it is not lawful for him to remarry her until after she has married another man. In case he divorces her, there is no blame on either of them if they reunite in marriage, provided they feel that they can keep the limits of Allah. These are the limits of Allah which He makes clear to the people of understanding.[230]　　　　　2:[229-230]

When you divorce women and they have reached the end of their waiting period ('Iddat) either allow them to stay with honor or let them go with kindness; but you should not retain them to harm them or to take undue advantage; if anyone does that, he wrongs his own soul. Do not take Allah's revelations as a joke. Remember the favors of Allah upon you and the fact that He sent down the Book and Wisdom for your guidance. Fear Allah and know that Allah has knowledge of everything.[231]　　　　　2:[231]

Commandment of honorable and kind treatment to divorced women

SECTION: 30

When you have divorced women and they have reached the end of their waiting period, do not prevent them from marrying their prospective husbands if they have come to an honorable agreement. This is enjoined on everyone amongst you who believes in Allah and the Last Day. This is more virtuous and chaste for you; Allah knows what you do not know.[232]　　　　　2:[232]

There is no restriction on divorcees for remarriage

The mothers shall breast-feed their offspring for two whole years if *the father* wishes the breast-feeding to be completed. The reasonable cost of their maintenance and clothing will be the responsibility of the child's father. No one should be charged with more than they can afford. Neither a mother should be made to suffer on account of her child nor a father on account of his child. The *father's* heirs are under the same obligation. But, if with mutual agreement, they both decide to wean the child, there is no blame on them. If you decide to have a foster-mother for your offspring, there is no blame on you, provided you pay what you have promised to pay in an honorable manner. Fear Allah and beware that Allah observes your actions.[233]　　As for those of you who die and leave widows behind, let the widows abstain *from marriage* for four months and ten days: when they have reached the end of this period, there is no blame on you for what they do for themselves in a decent manner. Allah is aware of what you do.[234]　　　　　2:[233-234]

Commandment of breast feeding the babies

Widows are commanded to wait four months and ten days before remarriage

There is no blame on you, if you make a hint of marriage proposal *during their waiting period* openly or keep it in your hearts. Allah knows that you will naturally cherish them in your

There is no restriction on the remarriage of widows

hearts; however, be careful not to make any secret agreement except that you speak to them in an honorable manner. Do not confirm the marriage tie until the prescribed waiting period expires. You should know that Allah is aware of what is in your hearts, so fear Him. Bear in mind that Allah is Forgiving, Forbearing.[235]

2:[235]

SECTION: 31

Commandments relating to dowry in the case of a divorce

There is no blame on you, if you divorce women before the marriage is consummated or the dowry is settled. Pay them something anyhow, the rich man according to his means and the poor according to his, a reasonable amount in all fairness. This is an obligation on the righteous people.[236]   And if you divorce them before the marriage is consummated but after the fixation of a dowry, give them half of their dowry unless the woman wants to waive it or the man, in whose hand is the marriage tie, agrees to forego *(and pay the dowry in full)*. To forego *and give full dowry* is closer to piety. Do not forget to show kindness to each other. Surely, Allah observes your actions.[237]   2:[236-237]

Commandment for guarding the Salah (Prayers)

Guard your Salahs *(obligatory prayers)* especially the middle Salah and stand up with true devotion to Allah.[238]   If you are in danger, pray on foot or while riding; and when you are safe, remember Allah in the manner that He has taught you which you did not know before.[239]   2:[238-239]

Executing a "Last Will and Testament" is made obligatory

Those of you who die and leave widows, should bequeath for them a year's maintenance without causing them to leave their homes; but if they leave *the residence* on their own, there is no blame on you for what they chose for themselves in a fair way. Allah is Mighty, Wise.[240]   Reasonable provisions must also be made for divorced women. That is an obligation upon those who fear Allah.[241]   That's how Allah makes His Revelations clear to you so that you may understand.[242]   2:[240-242]

SECTION: 32

Fight in the path of Allah without the fear of death since there is no escape from death

Have you reflected on the case of thousands of people *(Israelites)* who fled their homes for fear of death? Allah said to them: "Die" *(gave them death)*. Then He gave them life again. Surely, Allah is bountiful to mankind, but most of the people do not pay thanks.[243]   O believers, fight in the path of Allah *without fear of death* and bear in mind that Allah hears and knows everything.[244]   2:[243-244]

Who will loan to Allah a beautiful loan which Allah will increase manifold? Allah alone can decrease and increase wealth, and to Him you all shall return.[245]   Have you not reflected on what the leaders of the children of Israel *demanded from one of their Prophets* after the death of Musa *(Moses)*? "Appoint for us a king," they said, "and we will fight in the cause of Allah." The Prophet replied: "What if you refuse to fight when you are ordered to do so?" They replied, "How could we refuse to fight in the cause of Allah, while we have been driven out from our homes and from our children?" But when, *on their demand,* they were ordered to fight, all refused except a few of them. Allah knows the wrongdoers.[246]   2:[245-246]

Israelites asked for a king to fight in the way of Allah

Their Prophet told them: "Allah has appointed Talût *(Saul)* to be your king." They replied: "How can he be our king when some of us are more deserving than he? Besides, he is not rich." The Prophet said: "Allah has chosen him to rule over you and blessed him with more knowledge and a bigger stature. Allah grants kingship to whom He pleases and Allah is All-Sufficient for His creatures' needs and All-Knowing."[247]   *Furthermore,* their Prophet told them: "The sign of his appointment as a king is that there will come to you the chest in which there is tranquillity from your Rabb, the residue of relics which the family of Musa *(Moses)* and the family of Haroon *(Aaron)* left behind, and that *chest* will be carried by the angels. Surely, therein is a sign for you if you are true believers."[248]   2:[247-248]

Allah appointed Talût to be their king

SECTION: 33

When Talût marched forth with his army, he said: "Allah will test you at a certain river; anyone who will drink from its water, shall cease to be my soldier, and those who will not drink to quench their thirst with its water except a sip or so from the hollow of their hands, shall *fight* on my side." They all drank from it, *inspite of this warning,* except a few of them. When he and those who believed with him crossed the river, they said: "We have no power *left* this day against Jalût *(Goliath)* and his warriors." But the believers, who knew they would meet Allah, replied: "It has often happened that a small group, by the grace of Allah, has vanquished a mighty army. Allah is with those who endure with patience."[249]

2:[249]

Majority of Israelites' failed in the test of their belief

Victory is not dependent on numbers

When they advanced to face Jalût *(Goliath)* and his war-

Believer's prayer
for a victory

Allah reaffirmed
the Prophethood of
M u h a m m a d
(pbuh)

riors, they prayed: "Our Rabb! Fill our hearts with steadfastness, make our steps firm, and help us *(give us victory)* against the unbelievers."[250]   They put the *unbelievers* to flight by the leave of Allah, and Daûd *(David)* killed Jalût. Allah gave Daûd the kingdom and wisdom, and taught him what else He pleased. If Allah had not been repelling one set of people by the might of others, there would indeed be disorder on earth, but Allah is Gracious to all the worlds.[251]   These are the revelations of Allah; We recite them to you in truth. Surely, you *O Muhammad,* are one of Our Rasools.[252]   2:[250-252]

JUZ (PART): 3

These are the Rasools *(which We have sent for the guidance of mankind)*. We have exalted some above others. To some Allah spoke directly; others He raised high in ranks; to Isa *(Jesus)*, the son of Maryam *(Mary)*, We gave clear Signs and supported him with the Holy Spirit. If Allah had so willed, succeeding generations would not have fought against each other after they had received clear signs; but they disputed, as a result, there were some who believed, while others rejected. Yet, If Allah wanted, they would not have fought each other; but Allah does, what He intends.[253]

2:[253]

Ranks of Rasools

SECTION: 34

O believers! Spend out of the sustenance which We have provided for you before the arrival of that Day when there will be no bargaining, friendship or intercession. It is the unbelievers who are wrongdoers.[254]   2:[254]

Spending in charity

Allah! There is no god but He: the Ever-Living, the Sustainer of all existence. He neither slumbers nor sleeps. To Him belongs all that is in the heavens and the earth. Who can intercede with Him without His permission? He knows what is before them and what is behind them. They cannot gain access to any thing out of His knowledge except what He pleases. His kursiyy *(chair)* is more vast than the heavens and the earth, and guarding of these both does not fatigue Him. He is the Exalted, the Supreme.[255]

2:[255]

Allah's Attributes " A y a t - u l - Kursiyy"

There is no compulsion in religion. True guidance has been made clearly distinct from error. Therefore, whoever renounces 'Tâghoot' *(false deities - Shaitân)* and believes in Allah has grasped the firm hand-hold that will never break. Allah, *Whose hand-hold you have grasped,* hears all and knows all.[256]   Allah is the Waliyy *(Protector)* of those who believe, He brings them out of the depth of darkness and leads them into the light. As for the unbelievers, their waliyy *(protector)* is Tâghoot *(false deities - Shaitân)*, they takes them out of the light and leads them into the depths of darkness. *As a result,* they will become the companions of the Hell fire and shall live therein forever.[257]   2:[256-257]

There is no compulsion in religion

Waliyy of Allah vs. Waliyy of Shaitân

SECTION: 35

Have you ever reflected upon the one *(Namrud)*, who,

Confrontation of Ibrâheem and Namrud

because Allah had given a kingdom, argued with Ibrâheem *(Abraham)* about his Rabb. When Ibrâheem said: "My Rabb is He Who has power to give life and to cause death." He replied: "I too have the power to give life and to cause death." Ibrâheem said: "Well, Allah causes the sun to rise from the east; just make it rise from the west." Thus, the unbeliever was confounded; Allah does not guide the wrongdoers.[258]   2:[258]

Example of bringing dead to life

Or take another example of the one *(Ezra)* who passed by a town which had fallen down upon its roofs. He exclaimed: "How can Allah bring this dead township back to life?" Thereupon, Allah caused him to die, and after one hundred years brought him back to life. *Allah* asked: "How long did you remain here?" *Ezra* replied: "*Perhaps* a day or part of a day." *Allah* said: "Nay! You have remained here for one hundred years: now just have a look at your food and drink; they are not rotten; and then look at your donkey *and see that his very bones have decayed*. We have done this to make you a Sign for mankind. Look at the bones of your donkey, how We bring them together then clothe them with flesh *and bring it back to life*! When this all was shown clearly to him, he said: "Now I know that Allah has power over everything."[259]
2:[259]

Ibrâheem's question of life after death

Yet, another example is when Ibrâheem said: "My Rabb! Show me how you give life to the dead." He replied: "Have you no faith in this?" *Ibrâheem* humbly submitted: "Yes! But I ask this to reassure my heart." *Allah* said: "Take four birds; cause them to incline towards you *(train them to follow your direction)*, *cut them into pieces and* scatter those pieces on hilltops, then call them back; *Allah will bring them back to life and* they will come to you right away. Then know that Allah is All-Mighty, All-Wise."[260]
2:[260]

SECTION: 36

The parable of spending in Charity

The parable of those who spend their wealth in the way of Allah, is that of a grain that sprouts into seven ears, each bearing one hundred grains. Allah gives manifold increase to whom He wishes. Allah is All-Sufficient for His creatures' needs and All-Knowing.[261]   Those who spend their wealth in the cause of Allah and do not follow their charity with reminders of their generosity or injure the feeling of the recipient, shall get their reward from their Rabb; they shall have nothing to fear or to grieve.[262]   Kind words and forgiveness are better than charity followed by injury.

Allah is Self-sufficient, Forbearing.[263]   2:[261-263]

O believers! Do not make your charity worthless by reminders of your generosity or by injury to the recipients feelings, like him who spend his wealth to be seen by people and believe neither in Allah nor in the Last Day. His parable is like a hard barren rock covered with a thin layer of soil; a heavy rain falls, leaving it just a bare stone. Such people will not gain any reward that they thought they had earned. Allah does not guide the unbelievers.[264]   2:[264]

What makes charity worthless

The example of those who spend their wealth to seek the pleasure of Allah and assuring *reward for* themselves is like a garden on a high and fertile ground: when heavy rain falls on it, it yields up twice its normal produce; and if no rain falls, even a light moisture is sufficient. Whatever you do, is in the sight of Allah.[265] Would any one of you like that his garden, which is full of palm trees, grape vines, and all kinds of fruits and watered by running streams, be blasted and consumed by a fiery whirlwind at the time when he has become too old and his children are too feeble *to earn anything*? Thus Allah makes His revelations clear to you so that you may ponder over them.[266]   2:[265-266]

Charity vs. Showing off

SECTION: 37

O believers, spend in Allah's Way the best portion of the wealth you have lawfully earned and that which We have produced for you from the earth, and do not pick out for charity those worthless things that you yourselves would not accept but with closed eyes. Bear in mind that Allah is Self-Sufficient, Praiseworthy.[267]   Shaitân threatens you with poverty and prompts you to commit what is indecent, while Allah promises you His forgiveness and bounties, and Allah is All-Sufficient for His creatures' needs and All-Knowing.[268]   He grants wisdom to whom He pleases; and whoever is granted wisdom is indeed given a great wealth, yet, none except people of understanding learn a lesson from it.[269]   2:[267-269]

Spend the best portion of your wealth

Allah's promise vs. Shaitân's promise

Whatever you spend in charity or whatever vow you make, surely, Allah knows it. The wrongdoers shall have no helpers.[270] To give charity in public is good, but to give to the poor in private is better and will remove from you some of your sins. Allah is aware of your actions.[271]   *O Prophet,* you are not responsible for their guidance, it is Allah Who guides whom He pleases. Whatever wealth you spend in charity, it is to your own advantage; provided

Giving charity in public is good but giving in private is better

Who is eligible for receiving charity

you give to seek the pleasure of Allah. Whatever wealth you spend for the sake of Allah, will be paid back to you in full, and you will not be wronged.[272]   Charity is for those needy people who are engaged so much in the cause of Allah that they cannot move about in the land *to earn their livelihood:* the ignorant think that they are wealthy on account of their modest behavior. You can recognize them by their look because they do not make insistent demands on people. Whatever you spend on them, surely, Allah knows it.[273]

2:[270-273]

SECTION: 38

Reward for giving charity

Those who spend their wealth in charity by night and day, secretly and openly, they will have their reward from their Rabb. They shall have nothing to fear or to grieve.[274]   2:[274]

Prohibition of usury

Those who live on usury will not rise up before Allah except like those who are driven to madness by the touch of Shaitân. That is because they say: "Trading is no different than usury, but Allah has made trading lawful and usury unlawful. He who has received the admonition from his Rabb and has mended his way may keep his previous *gains*; Allah will be his judge. Those who turn back *(repeat this crime)*, they shall be the inmates of hellfire wherein they will live forever.[275]   Allah decreases usury and increases charity. Allah does not like any sinning disbeliever.[276]

2:[275-276]

Taking usury is like declaring war against Allah and His Rasool

Those who believe and do good deeds, establish Salah (prayers), and give Zakah (charity), will have their reward with their Rabb. They will have nothing to fear or to grieve.[277]   O you who have believed! Fear Allah and waive what is still due to you from usury if you are indeed believers. [278]   If you fail to do so, war shall be declared against you by Allah and His Rasool. If you repent, you may retain your principal, causing no loss to debtor and suffering no loss.[279]   If the debtor is in a difficulty, grant him time till it is easy for him to repay; but if you waive *the sum* by way of charity, it will be better for you, if you understand it.[280]   Fear the Day when you shall all return to Allah; when every one shall be paid in full what they have earned and none shall be dealt with un-justly.[281]   2:[277-281]

SECTION: 39

O believers! When you deal with each other in lending for a fixed period of time, put it in writing. Let a scribe write it down with justice between the parties. The scribe, who is given the gift of literacy by Allah, should not refuse to write; he is under obligation to write. Let him who incurs the liability *(debtor)* dictate, fearing Allah his Rabb and not diminishing anything from the settlement. If the borrower is mentally unsound or weak or is unable to dictate himself, let the guardian of his interests dictate for him with justice. Let two witnesses from among you bear witness to all such documents, if two men cannot be found, then one man and two women of your choice should bear witness, so that if one of the women forgets anything the other may remind her. The witnesses must not refuse when they are called upon to do so. You must not be averse to writing *(your contract)* for a future period, whether it is a small matter or big. This action is more just for you in the sight of Allah, because it establishes stronger evidence and is the best way to remove all doubts; but if it is a common commercial transaction concluded on the spot among yourselves, there is no blame on you if you do not put it in writing. You should have witnesses when you make commercial transactions. Let no harm be done to the scribe or witnesses; and if you do so, you shall be guilty of transgression. Fear Allah; it is Allah that teaches you and Allah has knowledge of everything.[282]   2:[282]

> *Commandment of writing down all business dealings - loans, debts and buying on credit*

> *Witnesses are required in all major business transactions*

If you are on a journey and cannot find a scribe *to write down the transaction,* then transact your business by taking possession of a pledge. If one of you entrust another *with a pledge*, let the trustee discharge his trust faithfully and let him fear Allah, his Rabb. Do not conceal testimony, and whoever conceals it, his heart is surely sinful. Allah is aware of all your actions.[283]   2:[283]

SECTION: 40

> *If writing is not possible, take a security deposit - pledge / mortgage*

To Allah belongs all that is in the heavens and in the earth. Whether you reveal what is in your minds or conceal it, Allah will call you to account for it. He, *however, has full authority to* pardon or punish anyone He pleases. Allah has complete power over everything.[284]   2:[284]

> *Allah will call all actions to account*

The Rasool has believed in the Guidance which has been revealed to him from his Rabb and so do the believers. They all believe in Allah, His angels, His books and His Rasools. *They say:* "We do not discriminate against anyone of His Rasools" - and they say: "We hear and we obey. Grant us Your forgiveness, O our Rabb; to You we shall all return."[285]   Allah does not burden any human being with more than he can bear. Everyone will enjoy *the credit*

> *True belief of Prophets and Muslims*

Believer's suppli-
cation to Allah

of his deeds and suffer *the debits* of his wrongdoings. *The believers say:* "Our Rabb! Do not punish us if we forget or make a mistake. Our Rabb! Do not place on us a burden as You placed on those before us. Our Rabb! Lay not on us the kind of burden that we have no strength to bear. Pardon us, Forgive us, Have mercy on us. You are our Protector, help us against the unbelievers."[286]

2:[285-286]

3: Â'L-E-'IMRÂN

Period of Revelation:

This Sûrah (Chapter), revealed at Madinah, consists of three discourses. The first discourse (vv. 1-32 and vv. 64-120) appears to have been revealed soon after the Battle of Badr. The second discourse (vv. 33-63) was revealed in 9 A.H. when the deputation from the Christians of Najrân visited the Prophet. The third discourse (vv. 121-200) was revealed after the Battle of Uhud.

Major Issues, Divine Laws and Guidance

* Allah's testimony about Himself.
* Decisive vs. Allegorical verses of the Qur'an.
* The True religion in the sight of Allah is only Islam.
* The only religion acceptable to Allah is Islam.
* Live Islam and die as a Muslim in order to get salvation.
* Followers of Isa (Jesus) were Muslims.
* Birth of Maryam (Mary), Yahya (John) and Isa (Jesus) peace be upon them.
* 'Mubahla' (calling for Allah's decision if the birth of Jesus is disputed). He was born without a father, as Adam (first man) was born without parents and Eve (first woman) was born without a mother.
* Life and death is from Allah.
* There is no escape from death.
* Those who are killed in the path of Allah are not dead, but are alive.
* Muhammad (pbuh) is no more than a Rasool/Prophet of Allah.
* Prohibition to take the unbelievers as protectors.
* Critical review and lessons taught during the Battle of Uhud.
* The first House of Allah ever built on earth is that of Ka'bah at Makkah.

As in Sûrah Al-Baqarah, the Jews were invited to accept the guidance. Similarly, in this Sûrah, the Christians are admonished to give up their erroneous beliefs and accept the guidance of the Qur'an. At the same time, the Muslims are instructed to nourish the virtues that may enable them to carry out their obligation of spreading the Divine guidance.

The believers had met with all sorts of trials and hardships about which they were forewarned in Sûrah Al-Baqarah. Even though they had come out victorious in the Battle of Badr, they were not out of danger yet. Their victory had aroused the enmity of all those powers in Arabia which were opposed to the Islamic movement. Threatening events had begun to appear on all sides and the Muslims were in a perpetual state of fear and anxiety. This state of emergency was also adversely affecting its economy which had already been badly disturbed by the influx of Muslim refugees from other places.

The Jewish clans, who lived in the suburbs of Madinah, started discarding the treaties of alliance which they had made with the Prophet at his arrival from Makkah. They had discarded the treaties to the extent that during the Battle of Badr, these "People of the Book" sided with the pagan Quraish, in spite of the fact that their fundamental Articles of Faith - such as Oneness of Allah, Prophethood and life after death - were the same as those of the Muslims. After the Battle of Badr, they openly began to approach various Arab clans against the Muslims. The magnitude of the peril may be judged from the fact that even the life of the Prophet himself was always in danger. His Companions used to sleep in their armor and keep watch at night to guard against any sudden attack. Whenever the Prophet happened to be out of sight, even for a short while, they would at once set out in search of him.

Jews even approached the Quraish and challenged their ego to avenge the defeat that they had suffered at Badr and promised to help them from within. As a result, the Quraish marched against Madinah with an army of three thousand warriors and a battle took place at the foot of mount Uhud. The Prophet marched out of Madinah with one thousand men to fight the enemy. On their way to the battlefield, three hundred hypocrites deserted the army and returned to Madinah to discourage the believers. A small band of hypocrites, however, remained among the seven hundred who accompanied the Prophet. They played their part and did their best to create mischief and chaos in the ranks of the believers during the battle. This was the first clear indication of the fact that within the fold of Muslim community there was quite a large number of saboteurs who were always ready to conspire with the external enemies to harm their own brethren.

These devices of the hypocrites, played a major role in the setback at Uhud, even though the weaknesses of the Muslims also contributed to it. The Muslims were a new community, formed on a new ideology and had not as yet gotten thorough moral training. Naturally, in this second hard test of their physical and moral strength, some weaknesses came to the surface. That is why a detailed critical review of the Battle of Uhud is made in this Sûrah which was needed to warn the Muslims of their shortcomings and to issue instructions for their reform.

3: Â'L-E-'IMRÂN

This Sûrah, revealed at Madinah, has 20 sections and 200 verses.

In the name of Allah, The Compassionate, The Merciful

SECTION: 1

Alif L'âm M'eem[1]

Allah! There is no god but He; the Living, the Eternal.[2] He has revealed to you this Book with the Truth, confirming the scripture which preceded it, as He revealed the Tawrât *(Torah)* and Injeel *(Gospel),*[3] before this, as a guidance for mankind and also revealed this Al-Furqân *(criterion for judgment between right and wrong).* Surely, those who reject Allah's revelations will be sternly punished; Allah is Mighty, capable of retribution.[4] Surely, nothing in the earth or in the heaven is hidden from Allah.[5] It is He Who shapes you in the wombs of your mothers as He pleases. There is no god but He; the Mighty, the Wise.[6]   3:[1-6]

It is Allah Who has revealed Torah, Gospel and Qur'an

He is the One Who has revealed to you the Book. Some of its verses are decisive - they are the foundation of the Book - while others are unspecific. Those, in whose hearts is perversity, follow the unspecific part, seeking discord through giving it their own interpretation, but no one knows its true interpretation except Allah. Those who are well grounded in knowledge say: "We believe in it; it is all from our Rabb." None will take heed except the people of understanding.[7] *They say:* "Our Rabb, do not let our hearts deviate *from the truth* after you have guided us, and grant us Your own mercy; You are the Grantor of bounties without measure.[8] Our Rabb, You will surely gather all mankind before You on the Day about which there is no doubt; surely, Allah does not break His promise."[9]   3:[7-9]

Qur'an's decisive vs. allegorical verses

Supplication of the believers to remain steadfast upon belief

SECTION: 2

Surely, neither their wealth nor their children will save the unbelievers from the wrath of Allah: they are the ones who will become the fuel for hellfire.[10] Their end will be the same as that of the people of Fir'aun *(Pharaoh)* and their predecessors who denied Our revelations, so Allah called them to account for their sins. Allah is strict in retribution.[11] *O Muhammad,* say to the unbelievers: "Soon you will be overpowered and driven together to Hell - which is a horrible refuge.[12] Indeed there was a sign

Wealth or children will not be a defense against disbelief

(lesson) for you in the two armies which met on the battlefield *(of Badr)*: one was fighting for the cause of Allah and the other had rejected *Allah*; the believers saw with their own eyes that the unbelievers were twice their number. But *the result of the battle proved that* Allah strengthens with His own aid whom He pleases. Surely, there is a lesson in this for those who have sight.[13]

3:[10-13]

Battle of Badr was a sign of Allah's favors

The life of men is tempted by *love and* desire for women, children, the hoarding of treasures of gold and silver, branded horses, *wealth of* cattle and plantations. These are the comforts for the *transitory* life of this world; the excellent abode, however, is with Allah.[14]　Say : "Shall I tell you of better things than these, with which the righteous will be rewarded by their Rabb? There will be gardens beneath which rivers flow, where they will live forever with spouses of perfect chastity and the good pleasure of Allah. Allah is watching His servants *very closely*."[15]　*The righteous people are* those who pray: "Our Rabb! We sincerely believe in You: please forgive our sins and save us from *the agony of* the hellfire;"[16]　who are steadfast, sincere, obedient, and charitable, and who seek forgiveness *from Allah* in the last hours of the night.[17]　　　　　　　3:[14-17]

Comforts of this life vs. The life in the hereafter

Allah Himself has testified to the fact that there is no god but He and so do the angels and those of knowledge - standing firm on justice.　There is no god but He, the Mighty, the Wise.[18] Surely, the only Deen *(true religion and the Right Way of life)* in the sight of Allah is Islam. Those to whom the Book was given did not differ except out of envy among themselves, and after true knowledge had come to them. *They should know that* Allah is swift in calling to account those who deny His revelations.[19]　So if they argue with you *(O Muhammad),* tell them: "I have submitted myself entirely to Allah and so have those who follow me." Then ask those who are given the Book and those who are illiterate *(Arab pagans)*: "Will you also submit yourselves *to Allah*?" If they become Muslims they shall be rightly guided but if they turn back, *you need not worry,* because your sole responsibility is to convey the Message. Allah is watching all His servants *very closely*.[20]

3:[18-20]

Testimony of Allah about Himself.

True religion in the sight of Allah is only Al-Islam

SECTION: 3

Give a warning to those who deny Allah's revelations, who slay the Prophets without any justification, and who kill those from among the people who enjoin justice, that there is a painful punishment for them.[21]   They are the ones whose deeds will become void in this world and in the Hereafter, and they will have no helpers.[22]   Have you not seen the behavior of those *(Jews)* who have been given a portion of the Book? When they are invited to settle their disputes according to the Book of Allah, some of them turn back and decline.[23]   This is because they say: "The fire of Hell shall not touch us except for a few days." In their religion they are deceived by their own self-invented   beliefs.[24] What will they do when We will gather them together on the Day which is sure to come, when every soul will be given what it has earned and there shall be no injustice?[25]   3:[21-25]

Warning of a painful punishment for disbelief

Jews and Christians are being deceived by their own self-invented beliefs

Say: "O Allah! Owner of the Kingdom, You give the kingdom to whom You please and take away the kingdom from whomsoever You please; You give honor to whom You please and disgrace whom You please; all the good is in Your hand; surely, You have power over everything.[26]   You cause the night to pass into the day and You cause the day to pass into the night; You draw the living from the dead and You draw the dead from the living; and You provide sustenance for anyone You wish   without measure."[27]   3:[26-27]

It is Allah Who gives or takes away the kingdom and honor

Let not the believers make unbelievers their protectors instead of the believers; anyone who does so will have nothing to hope for from Allah - except if you do so as a precaution *to guard yourselves* against their tyranny. *Anyhow,* Allah warns you to fear Him: because with Allah is your final refuge.[28]   Say: "Whether you conceal what is in your heart or reveal it, it is known to Allah. He knows whatever is in the heavens and whatever is in the earth. Allah has full power over everything.[29] On the Day *of Judgment,* when every soul will be confronted with whatever good it has done - and those who have done bad deeds will wish that their evil deeds were a long way off. Allah cautions you to beware of Him. Allah is full of kindness towards His devotees.[30]   3:[28-30]

Prohibition of taking disbelievers as protectors

SECTION: 4

Say *to the people, O Muhammad:* "If you sincerely love Allah, then follow me; Allah will also love you and forgive you your sins. Allah is Forgiving, Merciful."[31]   *Also* tell them, "Obey Allah and His Rasool." *Inspite of this,* if they turn back, *then warn them, that* Allah does not love the disbelievers.[32]   3:[31-32]

Commandment to obey and follow the Prophet

Adam, Noah, the families of Ibrâheem and 'Imrân were exalted

Indeed Allah exalted Adam, Nûh *(Noah)*, the family of Ibrâheem *(Abraham)* and the family of'Imrân above all the worlds.[33] They were the offsprings of one another. Allah hears all and knows all.[34]   3:[33-34]

Birth and growth of Maryam (Mary - the mother of Jesus)

Allah heard when the wife of 'Imrân said, "O my Rabb! I dedicate to Your service what is in my womb. Please accept it from me. You Alone hear all and know all."[35]   When she gave birth *to a girl instead of a boy*, she said: "My Rabb! I have given birth to a girl," - Allah knew very well what she had delivered - and that the male is not like the female. I have named her Maryam *(Mary)* and I seek Your protection for her and her children from *the mischief of Shaitân, the accursed.*"[36]   Her Rabb graciously accepted her. He made her grow up as a good person and entrusted her to the care of Zakariyya. Whenever Zakariyya entered the sanctuary to see her, he found with her food. He asked, "O Maryam! From where did you get it?" She replied, "It came from Allah. In fact, Allah gives to whom He wants without measure."[37]   3:[35-37]

Supplication of Zakariyya for granting him a son and Allah granted his wish and gave him a son called Yahya *(John)*

Thereupon, Zakariyya prayed to his Rabb saying: "O my Rabb! Grant me a righteous child as Your special favor; surely, You hear all prayers."[38]   As he stood praying in the Mihrâb *(a prayer place in the sanctuary),* the angels called out to him saying: "Allah gives you good news of a son to be named Yahya *(John)*, he will confirm the word of Allah, he will be a great leader, chaste and a Prophet from among the righteous."[39]   He said: "O my Rabb! How can I have a son now that I have reached an old age and my wife is barren?" "Such is the will of Allah," was the answer, " *Allah* does what He wants."[40]   *Zakariyya* said: "My Rabb! Grant me a sign." It was said: "Your sign is that you will not be able to speak to people for three days except through gestures. *During this time you should* remember your Rabb very much and glorify Him in the evening and in the morning."[41]   3:[38-41]

SECTION: 5

Allah chose Maryam (Mary) for His service and exalted her over all the women of the world

There came the time when angels said: "O Maryam! Surely, Allah has exalted you, purified you, and preferred you for His service over all the women of the worlds.[42]   O Maryam! Be obedient to your Rabb, prostrate and bow down in worship with other worshippers."[43]   *O Muhammad*, this is the news from the Unseen which We are revealing to you. You were not present with them when *priests of the temple* cast their pens to decide which of them should be the guardian of Maryam; nor were you with them when they argued about it.[44]　　　　　　　　　3:[42-44]

When the angels said "O Maryam!　Allah gives you the good news with a Word from Him *that you will be given a son*: his name will be Al-Maseeh (Messiah), Isa *(Jesus Christ),* the son of Maryam. He will be noble in this world and the Hereafter; and he will be from those who are very close *to Allah.* [45]　　He will speak to the people in the cradle and in his maturity and he will be among the righteous."[46]　　　　　　　　　3:[45-46]

Hearing this, Maryam said, "O my Rabb! How can I have a son when no man has ever touched me?" He replied, "Even so, Allah creates however He wants; whenever He decides to do anything, He only says to it, 'Be,' and it is![47]　　*Allah* will teach *your son* the Book, the Wisdom, the Tawrât *(Torah)*, and the Injeel *(Gospel)*[48]　　and send him forth as a Rasool to the Children of Israel *with this message*: 'I have brought you signs *of my appoint-ment* from your Rabb. I shall make for you the likeness of a bird from clay; I shall breathe into it and, with Allah's leave, it will become a living bird. I shall heal him who was born blind and the leper, and raise the dead to life, by Allah's leave. *Furthermore,* I will tell you what you have eaten and what you have stored in your houses. Surely, these are the signs *to convince* you, if you are believers.[49]　　*I am appointed to* confirm that which is before me from the Tawrât *(Torah)* and to make lawful to you some of the things forbidden to you. I have brought you the signs from your Rabb, therefore, fear Allah and obey me.[50]　　In fact, Allah is my Rabb as well as your Rabb, therefore, worship Him; this is the Right Way.'"[51]　　　　　　　　　3:[47-51]

When Isa *(Jesus)* found out that they *(most of the children of Israel)* had no faith, he asked: "Who will help me in the cause of Allah?" The Disciples replied: "We will help you in the cause of Allah. We believe in Allah. Be our witness that we are Muslims."[52] *Then they invoked Allah and said: "Our* Rabb! We believe in what you have revealed and we follow Your Rasool. Please count us with those who bear witness."[53]　　　　　　　　　3:[52-53]

The *unbelievers* plotted *to kill Isa* and Allah also devised a plan *to raise him up,* and Allah is the best in planning.[54]　　3:[54]

SECTION: 6

Remember, when Allah said: "O Isa *(Jesus)*! I am going to

Allah gave Mary a noble son called Isa *(Jesus)*

Birth of Isa *(Jesus)* son of Maryam

Miracles given to Isa *(Jesus)*

Followers of Isa *(Jesus)* were also called Muslims

Plot to kill Isa *(Jesus)*

Allah's promise to clean Isa (Jesus) of those who rejected him

recall you *(from your mission)* and raise you up to Myself. I will clean you of those who rejected you and exalt your followers above the unbelievers until the Day of Resurrection; then to Me shall be your return and I shall judge those matters in which you have been disputing.[55] Those who are unbelievers will be punished with severe punishment in this world and the Hereafter; they shall have no helpers.[56] As for those who believe and do good deeds, Allah will pay them their full reward. Allah does not love the wrongdoers."[57]

3:[55-57]

The birth of Isa (Jesus) without father is like the creation of Adam without parents

This revelation which We recite to you is full of signs and is a wise reminder.[58] In fact, the example of *the birth of* Isa *(Jesus)* in the sight of Allah is like the example of Adam *who had no father or mother*, whom He created out of dust, then said to him: "Be" and he was.[59] *This is* the Truth from your Rabb, therefore, do not be of those who doubt it.[60] If anyone disputes with you concerning this matter *(the birth of Jesus)* after full knowledge has come to you, say: "Come! Let us gather our sons and your sons, our women and your women, ourselves and yourselves: then let us earnestly pray and invoke the curse of Allah on the liars."[61] Verily, this is the absolute true explanation. *The fact of the matter is that* there is no god but Allah; and for sure Allah is the Mighty, the Wise.[62] But, if they turn away *from accepting this challenge, it will be clear proof of their mischief* and Allah has full knowledge of mischief-mongers.[63]

"Mubahla:"
[Calling for Allah's decision if Isa's (Jesus) birth is disputed]

3:[58-63]

SECTION: 7

The commandment of calling the Jews and Christians to get together on what is common between them and Muslims

Say: "O people of the Book! Let us get together on what is common between us and you: that we shall worship none but Allah; that we shall not associate any partners with Him; that we shall not take from among ourselves any lords beside Allah." If they reject your invitation then tell them: "Bear witness that we are Muslims *(who have surrendered to Allah)*."[64] O people of the Book! Why do you argue with us about Ibrâheem, *as to whether he was a Jew or a Christian? You know that* the Tawrât *(Torah)* and the Injeel *(Gospel)* were revealed long after him? Have you no sense at all?[65] So far, you have been arguing about things of which you had some knowledge! Must you now argue about that of which you know nothing at all? Allah knows while you do not.[66] Ibrâheem was neither a Jew nor a Christian but he was a Muslim, true in faith. He was not one of the Mushrikeen *(who set up partners with Allah)*.[67] Surely, the people nearest to Ibrâheem are those who follow him, this Prophet *(Muhammad)* and those who believed *in his message*, Allah is the Protector of the believers.[68] Some of the People of the Book want to mislead you; but they mislead none except themselves, but they do not realize it.[69] O People of the Book! Why do you deny the revelations of Allah when you know *that they are true*?[70] O People of the Book! Why do you confound the truth with falsehood and knowingly conceal the truth?[71]   3:[64-71]

The religion of Ibrâheem was Islam and the Muslims are his followers

SECTION: 8

Some of the People of the Book say *to one another:* "Believe in what is revealed to the believers *(Muslims)* in the morning and deny it in the evening; so that they *(the Muslims)* may follow suit *and abandon their faith.*[72] Do not believe anyone except the one who follows your own religion." *O Muhammad,* tell them: "The only true guidance is the guidance of Allah." *These people of the Book do not believe* that revelation could be sent to anyone *besides themselves,* like that which has been sent to you; or that they will ever argue with you in the presence of your Rabb. Tell them: "Surely, grace is in the hands of Allah: He bestows it on whom He pleases; Allah is All-Sufficient for His creatures needs and is All-Knowing."[73] He chooses for His mercy whom He pleases, Allah is the Owner of mighty grace.[74]   3:[72-74]

Hypocrites among Jews and Christians

Among the People of the Book there are some, who, if you trust them with a heap of gold, will readily return it back; and there are others, who, if you trust them with a single dinar *(silver coin),* will not return it back unless you constantly keep on demanding; because they say, "We are not going to be called to account for our behavior with the illiterates *(non Jews).*" Thus they deliberately ascribe a lie to Allah - *knowing well that He never permitted such wrongdoing.*[75] Yes! Those who keep their promise and guard themselves against evil *are His beloved*, for Allah loves only those who guard themselves against evils.[76] In fact, those who sell the covenants of Allah and their own oaths for a petty price, shall have no portion in the hereafter. Allah will neither speak to them nor even look at them nor cleanse them *from their sins* on the Day of Judgment. They shall have painful punishment.[77] There are some among them who twist their tongues pretending a quote from their *Holy* Book; so that you may think that what they read is a part of the Book, whereas, in fact, it is not a part of the Book. They also assert, "It is from Allah" whereas, in fact, it is not from Allah. Thus they deliberately ascribe a lie to Allah.[78]   3:[75-78]

Among the Jews and Christians there are some good people and some bad

There are some Jews and Christians who cheat in quoting their Holy Books

Isa *(Jesus)* never asked to worship him instead of Allah

It is not possible for a man whom Allah has given the Book, the authority and the Prophethood, that he would say to the people: "Worship me instead of Allah." On the contrary he would say: "Be pious scholars of the Rabb in accordance with the *Holy* Book you have been teaching and reading."[79] He would never ask you to take angels and prophets as your lords. Would he ask you to disbelieve after you have become Muslims *(believers)*?[80]

3:[79-80]

SECTION: 9

The covenant of Allah with all the Prophets concerning the Last Prophet (Muhammad)

Remember, when Allah took the covenant of the Prophets, saying: "Now that you have been given the Book and Wisdom; there will come to you a Rasool who will confirm that which is with you, you will have to believe in him and help him *in his mission*." *Then* He said "Do you affirm this covenant and agree to take this heavy responsibility?" They replied, "Yes, we do affirm." *Allah* said, "Very well, bear witness to this and I too bear witness with you."[81] So, if anyone turns back after this, he will become the transgressor.[82] 3:[81-82]

No religion is acceptable to Allah other than Al-Islam

Are they looking for a religion other than the Deen *(religion and Way of Life)* of Allah *knowing well* that everything in the heavens and in the earth, willingly or unwillingly, has submitted to Him? And to Him, they shall all return.[83] *O Prophet,* say: "We believe in Allah and what is revealed to us and what was revealed to Ibrâheem *(Abraham)*, Isma'il *(Ishmael)*, Ishâq *(Isaac)*, Ya'qoob *(Jacob)* and the Descendants *(the Prophets who were the offspring of Jacob)*; and in that which was given to Musa *(Moses)*, Isa *(Jesus)* and other Prophets from their Rabb; we do not discriminate between any one of them, and to Allah do we submit ourselves *as Muslims*."[84] If anyone is looking for a religion other than Islam, *then let it be known that* it will not be accepted from him; and in the Hereafter, he will be among the losers.[85] 3:[83-85]

The reward for the disbelievers is the curse of Allah, the Angels and all mankind

How can it be that Allah would guide those people who commit Kufr *(reject faith)* after their Imân *(acceptance of faith)*, bearing witness that the Rasool is true, and clear proofs have come to them? Allah does not guide such wrongdoers.[86] The reward of such people is that upon them is the curse of Allah, the angels and all mankind.[87] They shall remain under it forever; neither will their punishment be lightened nor will they be given respite,[88] except those who repent after this and mend their ways, verily Allah is Forgiving, Merciful.[89] Surely, those who disbelieve after their belief *(acceptance of Islam)* then go on adding to their disbelief, their repentance will never be accepted; because they *intentionally* chose to go astray.[90] Surely, those who are unbelievers and died while they were unbelievers, if they were to fill the whole earth with gold and offer it as a ransom for each one of them, that would not be accepted. These are the ones who shall have painful punishment, and shall have no helpers.[91]   3:[86-91]

Disbelievers who die as disbelievers will have an everlasting painful punishment

JUZ (PART): 4

SECTION: 10

Criteria of righteousness

You can never attain righteousness unless you spend *in the cause of Allah* that which you dearly cherish; and whatever you spend, surely, it is known to Allah.[92]   3:[92]

Lawful and unlawful food for the Children of Israel

All food, *that is lawful in Islamic Law,* was also halâl *(lawful)* for the children of Israel except what Israel *(Ya'qoob)* made harâm *(unlawful)* for himself before the Tawrât *(Torah)* was revealed *to Musa.* Ask them: "Bring the Tawrât *(Torah)* and read *a passage* from it *in support of your objection,* if what you say is true."[93]   Then, whoever fabricates a lie against Allah after this, will indeed be unjust.[94]   Say: "Allah has declared the truth. *If you are sincere,* then follow the faith of Ibrâheem; who was upright and not a mushrik."[95]   3:[93-95]

The first House of Allah on Earth

Indeed, the first House *for the worship of Allah* ever built for mankind is the one at Bakkah *(Makkah)*, a blessed site and a guidance for all the worlds.[96]   In it are clear signs; the Station of Ibrâheem *(Abraham)*. Whoever enters it, is safe. Performance of Hajj *(pilgrimage)* to this House is a duty to Allah for all who can afford the journey to it; and the one who disobeys *this commandment should know* that Allah is Self-sufficient, beyond the need of any from the worlds.[97]   3:[96-97]

Disbelief of the Jews and Christians

Say: "O people of the Book! Why do you deny the revelations of Allah? Allah Himself is a witness to your actions."[98] Say: "O people of the Book! Why do you obstruct the believers from the path of Allah and desire that they follow the crooked way while you yourselves are witnesses *to the Truth*? Allah is not unmindful of what you do."[99] O believers! If you were to obey a group of those who were given the Book, they would turn you back from belief to unbelief.[100]

Do not obey the Jews or Christians

Just think, how can you turn away from belief *on their statements,* when Allah's revelations are being recited to you and Allah's Rasool is among you? Whoever holds fast to Allah, will indeed be guided towards the Right Way.[101]   3:[98-101]

SECTION: 11

O believers! Fear Allah as He should be feared and die not but as true Muslims.[102]   All together hold fast to the rope of Allah *(Faith of Islam)* and be not divided among yourselves. Remember

Allah's favors upon you when you were enemies; He united your hearts, so by His favor you became brethren; you were at the brink of the fiery pit and He saved you from it. Thus Allah makes His revelations clear to you, so that you may be rightly guided.[103]

3:[102-103]

Let there arise from among you a band of people who should invite to righteousness, enjoin good and forbid evil; such are the ones, who shall be successful.[104]   Be not like those, who became divided into sects and who started to argue against each other after clear revelations had come to them. Those *responsible for division and arguments* will be sternly punished[105]   on the Day when some faces will be brightened *with joy* and others darkened *with gloom*. To the dark-faced sinner *it will be said*: "Did you adopt the way of disbelief after embracing the True Faith? Then taste the punishment for having adopted the way of disbelief."[106]   As for the bright-faced ones, they will be in Allah's Mercy and abide therein forever.[107]   These are the Revelations of Allah, We recite them to you in truth; Allah intends no injustice to the worlds.[108]   All that is in the heavens and in the earth belongs to Allah and all matters return to Allah *for decision*.[109]

3:[104-109]

SECTION: 12

You are the best nation which has ever been raised for the *guidance of* mankind. You enjoin good, forbid evil, and believe in Allah. Had the People of the Book *(Jews and Christians)* believed, it would surely have been better for them; among them some are believers but most of them are transgressors.[110]   *Anyhow,* they can do no harm to you except a trifling annoyance; if they do fight against you, they will turn their backs and run away, getting no help from anywhere.[111]   Disgrace will be branded on them wherever they are found except when they are under a covenant *of protection* from Allah and from other people; they have incurred the wrath of Allah. They have been branded with misery because they disbelieved Allah's revelations and slew His prophets unjustly. This is because they disobeyed and transgressed the limits.[112]   Yet, they are not all alike: there are some among the People of the Book who are upright, who recite the revelations of Allah all night long and then prostrate before Him.[113]   They believe in Allah and the Last Day, they enjoin good and forbid evil and rush in emulating each other in good deeds. These are the righteous people.[114]   Whatever good they do, its reward will not be denied to them; Allah knows

---

Live Islam, die as a Muslim, and be not divided among yourselves

Punishment for those who divide Muslims into sects

Muslims are the best nation evolved to enjoin good and forbid evil

Some righteous People of the Book

the pious.[115]   3:[110-115]

Surely, for those who are unbelievers, neither their wealth nor their children shall in the least *protect them* from *the wrath of Allah;* they will be the inmates of the Hellfire and live therein forever.[116]   Example of what they spend in this life is that of a freezing wind which strikes and destroys the tillage of people who have wronged themselves *(it is the lack of faith which makes their reward null and void)*; Allah is not unjust to them; it is they who have done injustice to their own souls.[117]   O believers! Do not make intimate friendships with any but your own people. *The unbelievers* will not miss any opportunity to corrupt you. They desire nothing but your destruction: their malice has become evident from what they say; and what they conceal in their hearts is far worse. We have made Our revelations plain to you, if you want to comprehend.[118]   Whereas you love them, they do not love you even though you believe in their *Holy* Books *(the Psalms, the Torah, and the Gospels)*. When they meet you, they say "We also believe *in your prophet and your Qur'an;"* but when they are alone, they bite their fingertips in rage against you. Say to them: "May you perish in your rage;" surely, Allah knows all the secrets of the heart.[119]   When you are blessed with good fortune, they grieve; but if some misfortune overtakes you, they rejoice. If you are patient and guard yourselves against evil, their schemes will not harm you in any way. Surely, Allah encompasses all their actions.[120]   3:[116-120]

SECTION: 13

O Muhammad, remember that morning when you left your household at an early hour to assign the believers to their battle-posts *(in the Battle of Uhud)*: Allah hears and knows everything.[121] *Remember*, when two parties from among you became fainthearted and Allah protected them *through strengthening their hearts*. In Allah should the believers put their trust.[122]   Allah helped you at *the Battle of* Badr when you were helpless. Therefore, have fear of Allah; perhaps you may become thankful.[123]   *Remember,* when you said to the believers, "Is it not enough that Allah should send down three thousand angels to help you?"[124]   Of course! If you remain patient and pious, Allah will send to your aid *not three thousand but,* five thousand specially marked angels in case of a sudden attack from the enemy.[125]   Allah has told you this as good news and that your hearts may be at ease thereby; victory comes

---

Hypocritical charity

Intimate friendship should be only with the believers

Lessons from the Battle of Uhud

Allah's help to the believers

only from Allah, the Mighty, the Wise.[126]   *(Allah sent the aid of Angels for the believers to offset the aid of shaitâns to the unbelievers)* so that He might cut off a flank of the unbelievers or put them to flight, making them withdraw with utter disappointment.[127]   *O Prophet,* you have no authority to decide the affair; it is up to Allah whether to pardon or punish them since they are wrongdoers.[128] To Allah belongs all that is in the Heavens and in the earth. He pardons whom He pleases and punishes whom He pleases. Allah is Forgiving, Merciful.[129]   3:[121-129]

Prophet does not have the authority to pardon the sinners

SECTION: 14

O believers! Do not consume usury which is compounded over and over again. Have fear of Allah so that you may prosper.[130] Guard yourself against the Fire which is prepared for the unbelievers.[131]   Obey Allah and His Rasool so that you may be shown mercy.[132]   Rush towards the forgiveness from your Rabb to a paradise as vast as the heavens and the earth which is prepared for the righteous people;[133]   those who spend generously in the Way of Allah, whether they are in prosperity or in adversity, who control their anger and forgive other people, Allah loves such charitable people,[134]   who, if they commit an indecency or wrong their own souls, earnestly remember Allah and seek forgiveness for their sins; for no one can forgive sins except Allah, and those who do not knowingly persist *in something wrong* which they have done.[135] Such people will be rewarded with forgiveness from their Rabb beside gardens beneath which rivers flow, to live therein forever. How excellent is the reward for such laborers![136]   3:[130-136]

Prohibition of usury

Allah loves charitable people

As for those, who rejected the Divine Revelations, there have been many examples before you. Travel through the earth and see what was the end of those who rejected *the truth.*[137]   This *(the Qur'an)* is a clear declaration to mankind, a guidance and an admonition to those who are God-conscious![138]   Do not grieve and get disheartened: for you will have the upper hand if you are believers.[139]   If you have suffered a wound, so did the enemy. We alternate these days of varying fortunes among mankind so that Allah may know the true believers and take witnesses *to the truth (grant martyrdom)* from among you, for Allah does not love the unjust people,[140]   and that Allah may purge the believers and destroy the unbelievers.[141]   3:[137-141]

Believers are promised to have upper hand

Do you think that you will enter paradise *without going through the trial*? Allah has not yet tested you to see who among you strive hard for His cause and show patience for His sake.[142] You certainly used to wish for death before you confronted it; now you have seen with your own eyes what it is like.[143]

3:[142-143]

SECTION: 15

Muhammad (pbuh) is no more than a Rasool of Allah

Muhammad is no more than a Rasool of Allah, like the Rasools that passed away before him. If he dies or is killed, will you turn back on your heels *(become unbelievers)*? He who turns back on his heels will do no harm to Allah; soon Allah will reward the thankful.[144]   No one dies without the permission of Allah. The term of every life is fixed. He who desires the reward in this world shall be given it here, and he who desires the reward in the hereafter shall be given it there. Soon We will reward the thankful.[145]

3:[144-145]

Prophets and their followers

Supplication of the believers

In the past, many Prophets have fought, *in the Way of Allah,* with a large number of godly people. They did not lose heart during the adversities that befell them in the path of Allah; they neither showed weakness nor submitted *to falsehood.* Allah loves the steadfast.[146]   Their only words were, "Our Rabb! Forgive our sins and our excesses; establish our feet firmly and give us victory over the unbelievers."[147]   Therefore, Allah gave them the reward in this world and also an excellent reward *awaits them* in the Hereafter. Allah loves such righteous who are good to others.[148]

3:[146-148]

SECTION: 16

Do not follow the unbelievers

O believers! If you yield to the unbelievers, they will drag you back *to unbelief* and you will become the losers.[149]   The fact is that Allah is your Protector and He is the best of all helpers.[150] Soon We shall cast terror into the hearts of the unbelievers for they commit shirk with Allah, for which He has revealed no authority. The hellfire shall be their home; and evil is the home of the wrongdoers.[151]   3:[149-151]

The result of disobeying the Rasool

Allah did indeed fulfill His promise to you, when, with His leave, you defeated them until you flinched and fell into dispute about the order and disobeyed *the Prophet*, after Allah had brought within your sight that which you love. Among you there were some who desired the gain of this world and some who desired the gain of the Hereafter. He allowed you to be defeated in order to test you, but now He has forgiven you, for Allah is gracious to the believers.[152]   *Remember,* how you fled in panic and did not even look back at one another while the Rasool, at your rear, was calling out to you! Consequently, *Allah* inflicted upon you one sorrow after another *to teach you a lesson*; so that you may not grieve for what you lose, nor at any misfortune you may encounter. Allah is well aware of all that you do.[153]   3:[152-153]

Then, after this grief, He bestowed peace on some of you - a slumber, which overcame them - while the others were in anxiety as how to save themselves, holding unjust and wrong suspicions about Allah, the suspicions of ignorance. Now they ask: "Have we any say in the matter?" Tell them: "All matters are in the hands of Allah." They hide in their minds what they dare not reveal to you, saying: "If we had any say in the matter, none of us would have been killed here." Say to them: "Even if you had remained in your homes, those of you who were destined to be killed would nevertheless have been killed; but it was Allah's will to test your faith and purge what was in your hearts. Allah has knowledge of the secrets of your hearts."[154] In fact those of you who turned their backs on the day when the two armies met, they failed in their duty because they were seduced by Shaitân on account of some of their shortcomings. But now Allah has pardoned them; for Allah is Forgiving, Forbearing.[155]

      3:[154-155]

After grief, Allah bestowed peace

There is no escape from death

SECTION: 17

O believers! Do not be like the unbelievers who speak of those brethren of theirs who die during their travels on the earth or while engaged in fighting: "Had they but stayed with us they would not have died or been killed." Allah makes such thinking a cause of regret and anguish in their hearts. It is Allah who gives life and death. Allah is observant of all your actions.[156] If you should die or get killed in the cause of Allah, His forgiveness and mercy will be far better than all the riches you could gather.[157] Whether you die or get killed, all of you will be brought before Allah.[158]

      3:[156-158]

Life and death is from Allah

O Muhammad, it is a great Mercy of Allah that you are very gentle with them; had you been rough or hard-hearted, they would have deserted you. Therefore, pardon them and ask Allah's forgiveness for them. Consult them in the conduct of affairs; and when you make a decision *to do something,* then put your trust in Allah *(hold fast to your decision).* Allah loves those who put their trust in Him.[159]   3:[159]

Consult before making a decision, once decision is made then be firm

Put your trust in Allah

If Allah helps you, then there is none who can overcome you. If He forsakes you, then who else is there other than Him who can help you? *Therefore,* in Allah let the believers put their trust.[160] It is not conceivable that any Prophet would hold back *from the spoils of war*; for anyone who holds back shall bring along whatever he has been withholding on the Day of Resurrection; then every soul shall be paid back in full what it has earned and they shall not be dealt with unjustly.[161]   3:[160-161]

Dignity of the Rasool

Can it be *conceivable* that a person who is seeking the good pleasure of Allah will be like the one who has incurred the wrath of Allah and is ultimately doomed to hell, which is an evil refuge?[162] These *two kinds of people* have quite different levels in the sight of Allah; Allah is observant of all their actions.[163] Allah has done a great favor to the believers that He raised among them a Rasool from among themselves, reciting to them the Revelations of Allah, sanctifying them, and teaching them the Book and Wisdom, although before this, they were in manifest error.[164]   3:[162-164]

Lessons to be learned from the Battle of Uhud

How is it that when you are afflicted with a loss, after you yourselves had inflicted losses twice as heavy *upon your enemy in the Battle of Badr*, you exclaimed: "Whose *fault* was that?" Say *to them*: "It was your own *fault*," Surely, Allah has power over everything.[165] The *misfortune* which befell you when the two armies met *in the Battle of Uhud* was with the leave of Allah so that He might know the true believers[166] and knows the hypocrites. When it was said to them: "Come fight for the cause of Allah or at least defend yourselves," they replied: "Had we known how to fight, we would certainly come with you." On that day, they were nearer to unbelief than to belief; for they uttered with their mouths what was not in their hearts. Allah is quite aware of what they were concealing.[167] Such are the ones who, as they sat *at home*, said of their brothers: "Had they listened to us, they would not have been killed." Ask them: "Avert death from your own selves, *when it comes to you,* if you speak the truth."[168] Never think of those who are

Those who are slain in the cause of Allah are not dead

slain in the cause of Allah are dead. Nay, they are alive, and are being well provided for by their Rabb.[169] They are pleased with what Allah has given them with His grace, and they are also happy to think that there is nothing to fear or to grieve for those believers whom they have left behind and who have not yet joined them *in their bliss*.[170] They feel happy to have received Allah's grace and bounty and *have come to know* that most surely, Allah does not waste the reward of the believers.[171]　　　　　　　　　3:[165-171]

SECTION: 18

As for those, who, even after their injuries *during the Battle of Uhud*, responded to the call of Allah and His Rasool *to follow the Quraish army which was gathering to attack again*, there will be a great reward for such of those who do righteous deeds and refrain from evil,[172]　　who, when the people told them: "Your enemies have mustered a great force against you: fear them," grew more firm in their faith, and replied: "Allah's help is all-sufficient for us. He is the best Disposer of affairs."[173]　　As a result, they returned *home* with blessings and grace from Allah and suffered no harm at all. *Besides this*, they had *the honor of* following what pleased Allah, and Allah is the Owner of mighty grace.[174]　　*Now you must have realized that* it was the Shaitân who was trying to prompt you to fear his followers. But have no fear of them. Fear Me, if you are true believers.[175]　　　　　　　3:[172-175]

O Muhammad, let not those who rush headlong into unbelief, grieve you; surely, they can do absolutely no harm to Allah. Allah intends to give them no share in the Hereafter. They shall have a grievous punishment.[176]　　Those who barter away faith for unbelief will in no way harm Allah. They shall have a painful punishment.[177]　　Let not the unbelievers think that Our granting of respite is good for their souls. We grant them respite so that they may add more to their sins. They shall have a disgraceful punishment.[178]　　　　　　　3:[176-178]

Allah will not leave the believers in their present condition; *you are in this condition only* until He separates the Evil from the Good. Allah will not do this by disclosing to you the secrets of the unseen. *As for disclosing the unseen,* Allah chooses those of his Rasools whom He pleases. Therefore, believe in Allah and His Rasools. If you believe and guard yourselves against evil, you shall have a great reward.[179]　　　　　　　3:[179]

Let not those who are stingy in giving for charity from what Allah has blessed them with, think that it is good for them: nay it is very bad for them. All the wealth they hoarded *with stingy behavior* will be hung around their necks like a collar on the Day of Resurrection. It is Allah who will inherit the heavens and the earth. Allah is well aware of all your actions.[180]　　　　3:[180]

Character of the believers at Uhud

Punishment for bartering belief for unbelief

Adverse conditions are a test from Allah

Punishment for the stingy

SECTION: 19

The Jews insulted Allah and uttered a lie against Him

Allah has heard the statement of those who said: " Allah is poor and we are rich!" Their words are recorded and so is their unjust killings of the Prophets. *On the Day of Judgment,* We shall say: "Taste now the torment of burning!"[181]   Here is the reward of your deeds. Allah is not unjust to His servants." [182]   They also say: "Allah has commanded us to believe in no Rasool unless he shows us a sacrifice consumed by a fire from the Heaven." Ask them: "Other prophets before me have come to you with clear arguments and showed this *miracle* you are asking for. Why did you kill them if what you say is true?"[183]   *O Muhammad* if they reject you *by calling you an impostor,* so did they reject other Rasools before you, although they brought them clear signs, Divine Scriptures, and the enlightening Book.[184]   3:[181-184]

Everyone has to die

Every soul shall taste death. You shall receive your full reward *for everything which you have striven for* on the Day of Resurrection. Whoever is spared from the fire and is admitted into paradise will indeed be successful; for the life of this world is nothing but an illusory enjoyment.[185]   3:[185]

Test of the believers

You shall certainly be tested through your wealth and your persons; and you will certainly hear much that is hurtful from those who were given the Book before you, and from the Mushrikeen. But if you endure with patience and have fear of Allah, this will surely be a proof of your firm determination.[186]   3:[186]

Punishment for claiming credit for something you have not done

When Allah made the covenant with those who were given the Book, they were asked to spread the teachings of the Book to mankind and not to conceal them; but they cast it behind their backs and sold them for a petty price. What a bad bargain they made![187] Those who rejoice in their misdeeds and love to be praised for what they have not actually done, should never think that they will escape the punishment; in fact, they shall have a painful punishment;[188]   for all the dominions of the Heavens and the earth belong to Allah Who has power over everything.[189]

3:[187-189]

SECTION: 20

Signs from nature

Surely, in the creation of the heavens and the earth and the alternation of the night and the day, there are signs for men of understanding.[190]   Those who remember Allah while standing, sitting, and lying on their sides, and meditate on the creation of the heavens and the earth, *then say:* " Our Rabb! You have not created this in vain. Glory to You! Save us from the punishment of Fire.[191] Our Rabb! Those whom You cast into the Fire will be in eternal shame: and there shall be no helper for such wrongdoers.[192] Our Rabb! We have heard someone calling to the faith saying; 'Believe in your Rabb,' so we have believed. Our Rabb! Forgive us our sins, remove from us our evil deeds and make us die with the righteous.[193] Our Rabb! Grant us what You have promised through Your Rasools and save us from the shame on the Day of Resurrection; Surely, You never break Your promise."[194]   3:[190-194]

Supplication of the believers

So their Rabb answers their prayers, *saying:* " I will not let the good deed of any worker among you, whether a male or a female, be wasted. You are *the offspring* of one another. Those who had to leave their homes or were expelled therefrom, and those who suffered persecution for My sake and fought and were killed: I will forgive them their sins and admit them into gardens beneath which the rivers flow; a prize from Allah, and Allah holds the finest prize!"[195]   3:[195]

Acceptance of supplication by Allah

Do not be deceived by the free movement of the unbelievers in this land.[196] Their enjoyment is brief. Their ultimate home shall be hell, an evil resort.[197] As for those who fear their Rabb, there shall be gardens beneath which rivers flow, they will live therein forever, this will be their welcome from Allah; and what Allah possesses is the best for righteous people.[198] There are some among the people of the Book who truly believe in Allah and what has been revealed to you, *O Muhammad,* and what has been revealed to them *before you*. They humble themselves before Allah and do not sell the revelations of Allah for a petty price. For them, there will be a reward from their Rabb. Surely, Allah is very swift in settling the accounts.[199] O believers! Be patient, excel in patience *during confrontation*, hold yourselves ready *for battle* and have fear of Allah so that you may be successful.[200]   3:[196-200]

Do not be deceived by the unbelievers

Be patient and excel in patience

4: AN-NISÂ'

Period of Revelation:

This Sûrah is comprised of several discourses that were revealed on different occasions. Instructions about the division of inheritance and safeguarding the rights of the orphans were revealed after the Battle of Uhud in which 70 Muslims were martyred (vv. 1-28). By the end of 3rd. year After Hijrah (A.H. - Islamic Calendar), a last warning to the Jews (v. 47) was given before the Jewish tribe of Banu Nadheer was expelled from Al-Madinah in A.H. 4. Permission about Tayammûm (ablution with clean earth when water is not available) was given during the expedition of Bani-al-Mustaliq in early A. H. 5.

Major Issues, Divine Laws and Guidance:

* Restriction on number of wives.
* Marriage and the rights of women.
* Laws of inheritance, women are awarded the rights to inherit.
* Acceptable and unacceptable repentance.
* Mahram relations - relatives that are prohibited for marriage.
* Commandment about 'arbitration' in family disputes.
* Second commandment relating to the prohibition of drinking, (first commandment was in Sûrah Al-Baqarah 2:219).
* The one who disputes the decision of the Prophet is not a believer.
* Divine Law, that obedience of the Rasool is in fact the obedience of Allah.
* Allah's command to respond greetings with better greetings.
* Laws about manslaughter , murder and bloodwit.
* Salat-ul-Qasr: permission for short prayer in travelling.
* Salat-ul-Khauf: performing prayer in a state of emergency (war).
* Salah: (prayers) are made obligatory on prescribed timings.
* Prohibition of 'secret counsels' and its exceptions.
* Decree of Allah that He will never forgive a mushrik.
* Allah's commandment to be firm for justice and bear true witness.
* Allah's commandment to boycott un-Islamic meetings.
* The fact that hypocrites will be in the lowest depth of hellfire.
* Isa (Jesus) was neither killed nor crucified.
* Isa (Jesus) was a Prophet of Allah (Almighty God) and His worshipper.
* Stop saying "Trinity" - Allah is the One and Only God.
* The Qur'an carries the same Message that was sent to Nûh (Noah), Ibrâheem (Abraham), Musa (Moses) and Isa (Jesus).
* Allah's commandments relating to family life and community life.

The main theme of this Sûrah is the building of a strong Islamic community. Guidelines are provided to the Muslims for uniting their ranks to be firm and strong. Instructions are given to stabilize the family structure, which is the nucleus of a strong community. Muslims are urged to prepare themselves for defense and to be the torchbearers of Islam. The importance of having a high moral character in building a strong community is emphasized.

Guidelines for the smooth running of family life are provided and methods to settle family disputes are taught. Rules for marriage are prescribed and rights of wife and husband are assigned fairly and equitably. The status of women in the society is determined and the declaration about the rights of orphans is made. Laws and regulations are laid down for the distribution of inheritance. Instructions are given to reform the economic system. The foundation of criminal laws is laid down. Drinking is prohibited. Instructions are given for cleanliness and purification. The Muslims are taught what kind of relations they should have with their Rabb (Lord) and with their fellow human beings. Instructions are given for the maintenance of discipline in the Muslim community.

The moral and religious condition of the People of the Book is reviewed to guide the Muslims, and a warning is given to refrain from following their footsteps. The distinctive features of hypocrisy and true faith are clearly marked for easy identification between the two. The setback in the Battle of Uhud had enabled the pagan Arab tribes, the neighboring Jews, and the hypocrites in Madinah to threaten the Muslims from all sides. At this critical stage, Allah's grace filled the Muslims with courage and gave them the necessary instructions. In order to counteract the rumors that were being spread by the hypocrites, Muslims were asked to make a thorough inquiry about their accuracy and then inform the appropriate leadership. Muslims were experiencing difficulties in offering their Salah during the expeditions when water was not available to perform ablution. In such circumstances Allah granted permission to make Tayammûm (purification with clean earth), and to shorten the Salah (Prayer) or to offer the "Salat-ul-Khauf," when they were faced with danger. Instructions were also given to those Muslims who were living in the enemy camps that they should migrate to Madinah, the Islamic State.

Clear instructions are also given regarding the hypocrites and nonbelligerent tribes. On one hand, the superiority of Islamic morality and culture is established over that of the Jews, Christians and Pagans; on the other hand, their incorrect religious concepts, immorality, and evil actions are criticized to prepare the ground for inviting them to the Right Way.

4: AN-NISÂ'

This Sûrah, revealed at Madinah, has 24 Sections and 176 verses.

In the name of Allah, the Compassionate, the Merciful

SECTION: 1

Creation of mankind

  O mankind! Have fear of your Rabb, the One who created you from a single soul, from that soul He created its mate, and through them He spread countless men and women. Fear Allah, the One in whose name you demand your rights *from one another* and the ties of relationship; surely, Allah is watching you very closely.[1]
         4:[1]

Property of the orphans

  Give orphans the property which belongs to them *when they are able to handle it themselves* and do not substitute *your* worthless things for *their* valuable ones; and do not cheat them of their possession through mixing it up with your own. For this would indeed be a great sin.[2]   4:[2]

Restrictions on number of wives

  If you fear that you shall not be able to treat the orphans with fairness, then marry other women of your choice: two, three or four. But if you fear that you will not be able to maintain justice *between your wives*, then *marry* only one or any slave girl you may own. That will be more suitable , so that you may not deviate *from the Right Way*.[3]   4:[3]

Obligation of dowry

  Give the women *(whom you marry)* their dowries willingly *as an obligation*; but if they, by their own free will, give up to you a portion of it then you may enjoy it with pleasure.[4]
         4:[4]

Do not entrust property to feebleminded people

  Do not entrust your property which Allah has made a means of support for you, to feebleminded people, however, provide such people with food and clothing, speak to them nicely and give them good advice.[5]   4:[5]

Train the orphans to manage their properties

  Observe the orphans *through testing their abilities* until they reach the age of marriage, then if you find them capable of sound judgment, hand over to them their property; and do not consume it wastefully in haste lest they grow up *to demand it*. If *the guardian* is well-off, he should not take compensation *from the orphan's property, bu*t if he is poor let him take a just and reasonable remuneration. When you hand over their property to them, call in some witnesses; *even though* Allah is sufficient in taking the accountability.[6]
         4:[6]

Men will have a share in what their parents and their near relatives leave; and women will have a share in what their parents and their near relatives leave: whether it be a small or large, they shall be *legally* entitled to their shares.[7]   If the relatives, orphans or needy are present at the time of the division of an inheritance, give them something out of it, and speak to them kind words.[8]   Let those *(executors and guardians)* have the same fear in their minds as they would have for their own if they were to leave helpless children behind: they should, therefore, fear Allah and speak for justice.[9]   In fact, those who misappropriate the property of orphans unjustly, swallow but fire into their bellies; they will soon be cast into the blazing fire![10]   4:[7-10]

Laws of inheritance

SECTION: 2

In regard to inheritance, Allah commands you concerning your children: that the share of a boy shall be twice that of a girl. In the case where there are more than two girls, their share will be two thirds of the estate; but if there is only one girl, her share will be one half of the estate. If the deceased left children behind, each of the parents shall get one sixth of the estate, but if the deceased left no children and the parents are the only heirs, the mother shall get one third of the estate, but if the deceased left brothers or *sisters,* then the mother will get one sixth of it. *The distribution in all cases shall be* after fulfilling the terms of any bequest and the payment of debts. With regards to your parents and your children, you do not know who is more beneficial to you, therefore, Allah has issued this ordinance. Surely, Allah is the Knowledgeable, Wise.[11]
                                                    4:[11]

Prescribed shares in inheritance

You shall inherit one half of your wives' estate if they leave no child, but if they leave behind a child then you will get one fourth of their estate, after fulfilling the terms of their *last* will and the payment of debts. Your wives shall inherit one fourth if you leave no child behind you; but if you leave a child, then they shall get one-eighth of your estate; after fulfilling the terms of your *last* will and the payment of debts. If a man or a woman leaves neither ascendant nor descendants but has left a brother or a sister, they shall each inherit one sixth, but if they are more than two, they shall share one third of the estate; after fulfilling the terms of the *last* will and the payment of debts, so that no loss is caused *to anyone.* Thus is the commandment of Allah. Allah is Knowledgeable, Forbearing.[12]   4:[12]

Inheritance of spouse's property

These are the limits set by Allah: those who obey Allah and His Rasool will be admitted to paradise, beneath which rivers flow, to live therein forever, and that will be a Great Achievement.[13] But the ones who disobey Allah and His Rasool, and transgress His limits, they will be cast to Hellfire to live therein forever. They shall have a humiliating punishment.[14]   4:[13-14]

Commandment to abide by the limit of Allah

SECTION: 3

If any of your women are guilty of fornication, ask for four *reliable* witnesses from among yourselves against them; and if they testify *and their guilt is proved*, confine them to their houses until they die or Allah opens some other way out for them *(Allah did open an other way. He abrogating these two verses through the verses of Sûrah An-Noor (24:2-10).*[15]   And the two, *whether married or unmarried,* who are guilty of this offense, punish them both. If they repent and mend their ways, leave them alone. Surely, Allah is the Acceptor of Repentance, Merciful.[16]   4:[15-16]

Initial order relating to the punishment for women guilty of fornication

Repentance with Allah *(right to be forgiven by Allah)* is only for those who do something evil in ignorance and repent as soon as they realize it; Allah will pardon them. Allah is the Knowledgeable, Wise.[17]   There is no repentance for those who persist in their evil deeds until death approaches anyone of them and he says: "surely, now I repent." Similarly, there is no repentance for those who die while they were still unbelievers; for them We have prepared a painful punishment.[18]   4:[17-18]

Acceptable vs. unacceptable repentance

O believers! It is not lawful for you to consider women as a part of your inheritance and retain them against their will in order that you may force them to give up a part of the dowry you have given them, unless they are guilty of proven fornication. Treat them with kindness even if you dislike them; it is quite possible that you dislike something in which Allah has placed much good.[19]

4:[19]

Women should not be treated as a part of estate

If you wish to marry another woman in place of the one you already have, do not take back anything of what you have given her even if it be a heap of gold. Would you take it back through slander and open sin *(accusing her unjustly)*?[20]   And how could you take it back when you have enjoyed conjugal happiness and she had taken from you a firm pledge *of marriage*?[21]   4:[20-21]

Do not take dowry back from women

Do not marry those women whom your fathers had married, - except what happened prior to this commandment. - Surely, it was shameful, disgusting, and an evil practice.[22]   4:[22]

Prohibition from marrying the wife of one's father

SECTION: 4

Forbidden to you *for marriage* are: your mothers, your daughters, your sisters, your paternal aunts, your maternal aunts, daughters of your brothers, daughters of your sisters, your foster-mothers, your foster-sisters, the mothers of your wives, your stepdaughters under your guardianship from those wives with whom you have consummated your marriage, but there is no blame on you *in marrying your stepdaughters* if you have not consummated your marriage *with their mothers, whom you have divorced*, and *also forbidden are* the wives of your own real sons; and to take two sisters in wedlock at the same time, except what happened prior to this commandment; surely, Allah is Forgiving, Merciful.[23]

4:[23]

Women that are prohibited for marriage - "Mahram" relations

JUZ (PART): 5

Prohibited and permitted marriages continued

Also *forbidden for you are* married women, except those who have fallen in your hands *as prisoners of war*. This is the order of Allah *relating to marriage prohibitions*. All women, other than these, are lawful provided you seek *them in marriage* with gifts from your property *(dowry),* desiring chastity and not lust. Give them their dowry as an obligation for the benefit you have received from your marriage relationship. However, there is no blame on you if you change the agreement of dowry with mutual consent. Surely, Allah is the Knowledgeable, Wise.[24]   4:[24]

Permission for marriage with slave girls

If any of you cannot afford to marry a free believing woman, let him marry a slave girls who is a believer; Allah knows how good you are in your faith. You are from one another. Marry them with the permission of their family and give them their fair dowry so that they may live a decent life in wedlock and not live as prostitutes or look for secret illicit relationships. Then, if after marriage they commit adultery, they shall be given half the punishment prescribed for a free *adulteress*. The concession of such a marriage is for those of you who fear that they might commit a sin *if they do not get married*, but it is better for you to practice self-restraint. Allah is Forgiving, Merciful.[25]   4:[25]

SECTION: 5

Allah wishes to guide and forgive

Allah desires to clarify, and guides you to the ways which were followed by the righteous people before you, and turns to you in mercy. Allah is the Knowledgeable, Wise.[26]   Allah wishes to forgive you, but those who follow their lusts wish to see you deviate far away from the Right Way.[27]   Allah wishes to lighten your burdens because humans have been created weak by nature.[28]
4:[26-28]

Respect the ownership of one another's properties

O believers! Do not consume one another's wealth through unlawful means; instead, do business with mutual consent; do not kill yourselves *by adopting unlawful means*. Indeed Allah is Merciful to you.[29]   Anyone who commits such acts of aggression and injustice will soon be thrown into Hellfire, and this is very easy for Allah to do.[30]   4:[29-30]

Avoid heinous sins and do not be jealous

If you avoid the heinous sins which you have been forbidden, We will do away with your small sins and cause you to enter a place of great honor *(paradise)*.[31]   Do not wish for that which Allah has given some of you more than the others. Men will be rewarded according to their deeds and women will be rewarded according to theirs. Ask Allah for His grace. Surely, Allah has perfect knowledge of everything.[32]   4:[31-32]

For every parent and relative, We have appointed the rightful heirs to inherit what they leave. As for those with whom you have made firm agreements, give them their share. Surely, Allah is a Witness to everything.[33]   4:[33]

Laws of inherit-ance are fixed

SECTION: 6

Men are overseers over women because Allah has made the one of them to excel the other, and because men *are required to* spend their wealth *for the maintenance of women.* Righteous women are, therefore, devoutly obedient and guard in *the husband's* absence what Allah requires them to guard *(their husband's property and their own honor).* As to those women from whom you fear disobedience, *first* admonish them, *then* refuse to share your bed with them, *and then, if necessary,* beat them. Then if they obey you, take no further actions against them *and do not make excuses to punish them.* Allah is Supremely Great *and is aware of your actions.*[34]   If you fear a breach of marriage between a man and his wife, appoint one arbiter from his family and another from hers; if they wish to reconcile, Allah will create a way of reconciliation between them. Allah is the Knowledgeable, Aware.[35]

4:[34-35]

Men are overseers over women

Corrective measures for disobedient women

Arbitration in family disputes

Serve Allah and do not commit shirk *(associate any partner with Him),* and be good to your parents, relatives, orphans, the helpless, near and far neighbors who keep company with you, the travellers in need, and the slaves you own. Allah does not love those who are arrogant and boastful,[36]   who are themselves stingy and enjoin others to be stingy, who hide the bounties which Allah has bestowed on them. For such unbelievers We have prepared a disgraceful punishment.[37]   *Similar punishment has been prepared for* those who spend their wealth to show off to the people, believing neither in Allah nor in the Last Day. In fact, the one who chooses Shaitân as his companion has chosen a very evil companion![38]   4:[36-38]

Huqûq-ul-Ibâd (rights of other human beings)

What *harm* would they have suffered if they had believed in Allah and the Last Day and spent *in charity* out of what Allah had given them? Allah Knows them all.[39]   Rest assured, Allah

Witnesses of the Rasools on the Day of Judgment	does not wrong anyone even by an atom's weight. If someone does a good deed He increases it manifold and also gives an extra great reward on His own.[40] *Just imagine,* how they will feel, when We shall bring a witness from every nation and call upon you, *O Muhammad,* to testify against them?[41] On that Day *(the Day of Judgment)* those who rejected faith and disobeyed the Rasool will wish that they were levelled with earth; for they will not be able to hide a single word from Allah![42] 4:[39-42]

SECTION: 7

Prohibition of drinking liquor - (second order)

Tayammum | O believers! Do not offer Salah (prayer) when you are drunk until you are able to understand what you are saying; nor after seminal emission, except when you are travelling, unless you wash your whole body. If you are sick, or on a journey, or one of you has used the toilet, or has had contact with women *(sexual relation with wives)* and can find no water, then make tayammum: take some clean earth and rub your faces and hands with it. Allah is Oft-Pardoning, Oft-Forgiving.[43]   4:[43] |

Behavior of the People of the Book	Have you not considered the case of those to whom a portion of the Book was given? They purchased error for themselves and wish to see you lose the Right Way.[44] Allah knows your enemies very well. Sufficient is Allah to protect you, and Sufficient is Allah to help you.[45] Among the Jews there are some who take the words out of their context and utter them with a twist of their tongues to slander the true Deen *(faith)* and say: "We hear and we disobey;" and "Hear, may you *(O Muhammad)* hear nothing!" And Râ'inâ *(an ambiguous word meaning: "listen, may you become deaf," or "our shepherd," or "in judeo-Arabic language conveying the sense of "our evil one").* If only they had said: "We hear and we obey;" and "Hear us;" and Unzurnâ *("look upon us," or "pay attention to us"):* it would have been better for them and more proper. Due to all this Allah has cursed them for their unbelief. In fact, with the exception of a few, they have no faith.[46] 4:[44-46]

Invitation of Imân to the People of the Book	O people of the Book *(Jews and Christians)*! Believe in what We have revealed *(The Qur'an)*, confirming your own scriptures, before We obliterate your faces and turn them backward, or lay Our curse on you as We laid Our curse on the Sabbath-breakers: and remember that Allah's command is always executed.[47] Surely, Allah does not forgive shirk *(associating any partner with Him)*; and may forgive *sins* other than that if He so pleases. *This is*

because one who commits shirk with Allah, does indeed invent a great sinful lie.[48] Have you not seen those who speak very highly of their own purity *even though they are committing shirk.* In fact, Allah purifies whom He wishes, and they will not be dealt with injustice, even equal to the thread in the cleft of a date-stone.[49] See how they invent a lie against Allah, and this in itself is enough to show their manifest sin.[50]   4:[47-50]

Mushrikeen will not be forgiven

SECTION: 8

Have you not seen those who were given a portion of the Book? They believe in superstition and Tâghoot *(forces of Shaitân)* and say about the unbelievers that they are better guided to the Right Way than the believers![51] Those are the ones whom Allah has cursed, and the one who is cursed by Allah can find no helper.[52] Do they have a share in the kingdom? If they had any *share* they would have not given other people equal to a speck on a date-stone.[53] Or do they envy other people because Allah has given them from His grace? *If so, let them know that* We did give the Book and Wisdom to the descendants of Ibrâheem *(Abraham)*, and blessed them with a great kingdom.[54] But some of them believed in it and some turned away. Sufficient is hell to burn those who turned away.[55]   4:[51-55]

People of the Book tend to take side of Shaitân

Those who rejected Our revelations will soon be thrown into the Fire. No sooner will their skins be burnt off than We shall replace their skins, so that they may taste the real torment. Surely, Allah is Mighty, Wise.[56] As for those who believe and do righteous deeds, We shall admit them to gardens beneath which rivers flow wherein they will live for ever. Therein, they will have chaste spouses, and We shall provide them with cool thick shade.[57] Allah commands you to give back the trusts to their rightful owners, and when you judge between people, judge with fairness. Surely, excellent is the counsel which Allah gives you. Indeed, Allah is ever All-Hearer, All-Seer.[58] O believers! Obey Allah, obey the Rasool and those charged with authority among you. Should you have a dispute in anything, refer it to Allah and His Rasool, if you truly believe in Allah and the Last Day. This *course of action* will be better and more suitable.[59]   4:[56-59]

Fate of the unbelievers and the believers

Who should the believers obey?

SECTION: 9

Have you not seen those who claim that they believe in what has been revealed to you and other prophets before you? Yet, they desire that the judgment *(in their disputes)* be made by

Hypocrites' attitude towards the decision of the Prophet

Tâghoot *(Kâfir laws - Shaitân)* though they were commanded to reject them, and Shaitân's wish is to lead them far astray into deep error.[60]   When it is said to them: "Come to be judged by the Rasool in accordance with what Allah has revealed, " you see that the hypocrites show their utmost hesitation in coming to you.[61] But see how they behave when they get into trouble as a consequence of their own doings? They come to you swearing by Allah that they desired nothing but to promote good and bring about a reconciliation.[62]   Allah knows what really is in their hearts; therefore, leave them alone, admonish them, and speak to them effectual words which may go deep into their hearts.[63]   4:[60-63]

One who disputes the decision of the Prophet is not a believer

We did not send any Rasool but to be obeyed by Allah's leave. If they would have come to you when they had wronged themselves to seek Allah's forgiveness and if the Rasool had also asked Allah's forgiveness for them, they would have found Allah Forgiving, Merciful.[64]   Nay! *O Muhammad* - by your Rabb - they will never be true believers until they accept you as a judge in their disputes, then they do not find any resentment in their hearts against your verdicts and accept them with complete submission.[65] If We had commanded them to sacrifice their lives or to leave their homes, very few of them would have done it. Yet, if they would have done what they were commanded to do, it would have been better for them; not only would their faith have been strengthened,[66]   but We would have given them an extra great reward on Our own[67]   and also guided them to the Right Way.[68]

4:[64-68]

Believers will be in excellent company in the hereafter

Whosoever obeys Allah and the Rasool will be in the company of those whom Allah has blessed - the Prophets, the sincere and steadfast affirmers of truth, the martyrs, and the righteous: What excellent companions they will be![69]   This is the real grace from Allah and sufficient is Allah's infinite knowledge.[70]   4:[69-70]

SECTION: 10

Be prepared for armed conflict (Jihad)

O believers! Prepare yourselves for   encounter, then advance in detachments or all together *as the occasion may require.*[71]   There will be someone among you who will surely lag behind, so that if you face any calamity, he will say: "Allah has been gracious to me that I did not accompany them."[72]   But if you are blessed with grace from Allah, he will say, as if there was no friendship between you and him: "I wish I had been with them; I could have attained a mighty good fortune!"[73] *Let it be known that* only those people should fight in the cause of Allah who are willing to exchange the life of this world for the Hereafter; and whoever fights for the cause of Allah, whether he dies or is victorious, will soon be granted a mighty reward.[74]   4:[71-74]

And what reason do you have not to fight in the cause of Allah, *to rescue* the helpless oppressed men, women, and children who are crying: "Our Rabb! Deliver us from this town whose people are oppressors; raise for us a protector from You and send for us a helper from You." [75]   Those who are believers, fight in the cause of Allah and those who are unbelievers fight in the cause of Tâghoot *(false deities -Shaitân)*: so fight against the helpers of Shaitân; surely, Shaitân's crafty schemes are very weak.[76]   4:[75-76]

Make Jihad to help the oppressed

SECTION: 11

Have you not seen those who were told to restrain their hands *from fighting*, establish Salah *(prayers)* and pay Zakah *(obligatory charity)*. Now, when *at length,* they are commanded to fight, lo! A group of them fear people as they should have feared Allah, or even more than that, and say: "Our Rabb! Why have You ordered us to fight? Could you delay its implementation for a while?" Tell them: "The enjoyment of this worldly life is short, *life of* the hereafter is much better for those who fear Allah, and *rest assured that* you will not be wronged equal to the fiber of a date-stone.[77]   *As for death*, no matter where you may be, death is going to reach you even if you are in fortified towers. When such people are blessed with some benefit, they say: "This is from Allah;" but if they suffer a loss, they say: "this is because of you." *O Muhammad* tell them: "Everything is from Allah." What is the matter with these people that they do not understand a word?[78]   Whatever benefit comes to you *O people*, it is by Allah's grace; and whatever loss you suffer, it is the result of your own doings. We have sent you, *O Muhammad,* as a Rasool to mankind. Allah is your All-Sufficient Witness.[79]   4:[77-79]

Fear Allah and not the people

There is no escape from death

Anyone who obeys the Rasool, in fact, obeys Allah. As for those who pay no heed, *they should know that* We have not sent you as a taskmaster over them.[80]   They will say: "We are at your service!" Yet, when they leave you, some of them *meet together secretly at night to* plot against what you have said. Allah notes down all their plots. Therefore, leave them alone and put your trust in Allah. Allah is your all sufficient trustee.[81]   4:[80-81]

Obedience of the Rasool is in fact the obedience of Allah

Proof that the Qur'an is Divine revelation

Report the important news to responsible persons

Why don't they research the Qur'an? *Don't they realize that* if it was from someone other than Allah, they would find many discrepancies in it.[82]   Whenever they hear news of peace or of danger, they spread it quickly; but if they would report it to the Rasool and to the responsible people among them, it would come to the knowledge of those who could draw the right conclusions. If it had not been for Allah's grace and mercy, all of you with the exception of a few, would have followed Shaitân.[83]   Therefore, *O Muhammad,* fight in the path of Allah, you are accountable for no one except for yourself. Urge the believers *to fight*, it may be that Allah will overthrow the might of the unbelievers, for Allah is the strongest in might and severe in punishment.[84]   4:[82-84]

Respond to greetings with better greetings

Anyone who intercedes for a good cause shall have a share in it, and anyone who intercedes for an evil cause shall also get a share in its burden. Allah has control over everything.[85]   When anyone greets you in a courteous manner, let your greetings be better than his - or at least return the same. Allah keeps account of everything.[86]   Allah! There is no god but He. He will certainly gather you all together on the Day of Resurrection; there is no doubt in it, and who can be more truthful in his words than Allah?[87]

4:[85-87]

SECTION: 12

Fight against hypocrisy and hypocrites

What is the matter with you, *why are you divided into* two groups concerning the hypocrites, while Allah has cast them back *to disbelief* on account of their misdeeds? Do you wish to guide those, whom Allah has left to stray? Whomever Allah has left astray, you cannot find a way for them to be guided.[88]   Their real wish is to see that you become a disbeliever, as they themselves have disbelieved, so that you may become equal to them. So, you should not take friends from their ranks unless they immigrate in the way of Allah; and if they do not, seize them and kill them wherever you find them, and do not take any of them as protectors or helpers.[89]   The exception to this is for those who take refuge with your allies or come over to you because their hearts restrain them both from fighting against you and from fighting against their own people. If Allah had wanted, He would have given them power over you and they might easily have fought against you; therefore, if they withdraw from you and cease their hostility and offer you peace, in that case Allah has not granted you permission *to fight* against them.[90] You will find other *hypocrites* who wish to be safe from you as well as from their own people; but who would plunge into mischief whenever they get an opportunity. Therefore, if they do not keep distance from you and neither offer you peace, nor cease their hostilities against you, seize them and kill them wherever you find them. In their case, We give you clear authority.[91]

4:[88-91]

SECTION: 13

It is not befitting for a believer to kill a believer except by accident, and whoever accidently kills a believer, *he is commanded* to free a believing slave and pay bloodwit to the family of the victim, unless they forgo it as a charity. If the victim, who is a believer, is from a hostile nation, then the freeing of a believing slave *is enough*, but if he belonged to a nation with whom you have a treaty, then bloodwit must be paid to his family along with the freeing of a believing slave. Those who do not have the means *(bloodwit and / or a slave)* must fast two consecutive months: a method of repentance provided by Allah. Allah is the Knowledgeable, Wise.[92] Whoever kills a believer intentionally, his punishment is hell to live therein forever. He shall incur the wrath of Allah, Who will lay His curse on him and prepare for him a woeful punishment.[93]

4:[92-93]

The punishment for killing a believer and laws of bloodwit

O believers! When you struggle in the way of Allah, investigate carefully, and do not say to anyone who offers you a salutation: "You are not a believer" in order to seek worldly gain by this. Allah has abundant spoils for you. Remember that you yourselves were in the same condition before. Allah has conferred His favors on you. Therefore, make a thorough investigation *before considering someone an unbeliever*. Allah is well aware of all your actions.[94]

4:[94]

Investigate properly before jumping to conclusion

Those believers who stay at home - having no physical disability or other reasonable cause - are not equal to those who make Jihad *(struggle)* in the cause of Allah with their wealth and their persons. Allah has granted a higher rank to those who make Jihad with their wealth and their persons than to those who stay at home. Though Allah has promised a good reward for all, Allah has prepared a much richer reward for those who make Jihad for Him than for those who stay at home[95] - they have special higher ranks, forgiveness and mercy. Allah is Forgiving, Merciful.[96]

4:[95-96]

Ranks of the Mujâhideen over the Non-Mujâhideen

SECTION: 14

Oppressed should migrate if possible

When the angels of death cause those people to die who have wronged their souls, they ask: "What was your condition?" They reply: "We were oppressed in the earth." *The angels* say: "Was not the earth of Allah spacious enough for you to emigrate and go somewhere else?" Hell will be their abode and it is a very evil refuge![97] However, those helpless men, women and children who have neither the means to migrate nor strength to escape,[98] They are the ones whom Allah may pardon. Allah is the Pardoning, Forgiving.[99]

Reward for migration in the cause of Allah

He who emigrates in the path of Allah shall find numerous places of refuge in the earth and abundant resources. He who leaves his home to migrate for Allah and His Rasool and dies on the way, his reward becomes due and sure with Allah. Allah is Forgiving, Merciful.[100]   4:[97-100]

SECTION: 15

Salat-ul-Qasr: Shortening of Salah during travel and Salah in the state of war

When you travel in the earth, there is no blame on you if you shorten your prayers, especially when you fear that the unbelievers may attack you, since the unbelievers are your open enemies.[101] When you, *O Muhammad,* are with them, leading their Salah *(prayer in the state of war)*, let one party of them stand up to pray with you, armed with their weapons. After they finish their prostrations, let them withdraw to the rear and let the other party who have not yet prayed come forward to pray with you; and let them also be on their guard, armed with their weapons. The unbelievers wish to see you neglect your arms and your baggage, so that they could suddenly attack to overpower you all in one stroke. However, there is no blame on you if you lay aside your arms because of heavy rain or because you are sick, but you should still be on your guard. Allah has prepared a humiliating punishment for the unbelievers.[102]

When you finish your Salah *(prayers)* remember Allah whether you are standing, sitting or reclining; then as soon as you are safe *(out of danger)* establish regular Salah in full. Surely, Salahs *(prayers)* are made obligatory for the

Salah is obligatory at its prescribed times

believers at their prescribed times.[103] Do not show weakness in following up the enemy; if you are suffering hardships they too are suffering similar hardships; moreover, you have hope to receive reward from Allah while they have none. Allah is the Knowledgeable, Wise.[104]   4:[101-104]

SECTION: 16

We have revealed to you the Book with the Truth so that you may judge between people in accordance with *the Right Way* which Allah has shown you, so be not an advocate for those who betray trust;[105]   seek Allah's forgiveness, surely, Allah is Forgiving, Merciful.[106]   Do not plead on behalf of those who betray their own souls; Allah does not love the treacherous, sinful.[107]   They may hide *their crimes* from people, but they cannot hide them from Allah. He is with them even when they plot *by night* in words that He cannot approve. Allah encompasses all their actions.[108]   You may plead for them in this world's life, but who will plead for them with Allah on the Day of Resurrection? Or who will be their defender?[109]   If anyone does evil or wrongs his own soul and then seeks Allah's forgiveness, he will find Allah Forgiving, Merciful.[110]   Whoever commits a sin, he commits it against his own soul. Allah is knowledgeable, Wise.[111]   But if anyone commits a crime and charges an innocent person with it *(a Muslim from the tribe of Banu Dhafar committed theft and put the blame on a Jew who was innocent)*, he indeed shall bear the guilt of slander and a flagrant sin.[112]   4:[105-112]

Establish justice based on Divine guidance

Warning against Slander and against falsely charging innocents

SECTION: 17

If Allah's grace and mercy were not with you *to save you from their mischief,* a group of them *(tribe of Banu Dhafar)* was determined to lead you astray. They led astray none but themselves, and they cannot do you any harm. Allah has revealed to you the Book and wisdom and taught you what you did not know; great indeed is the grace of Allah upon you.[113]   There is no virtue in most of the secret counsels of the people; it is, however, good if one secretly enjoins charity, kindness, and reconciliation among people; the one who does this to please Allah, will soon be given a mighty reward.[114]   Anyone who is hostile to the Rasool after guidance has been plainly conveyed to him and follows a path other than that of the believers, We shall leave him in the path he has chosen and cast him into hell, which is an evil refuge.[115]   4:[113-115]

Allah's special favors to the Prophet

Prohibition of secret counsel and its limited exception

SECTION: 18

Surely, Allah will never forgive the one who commits shirk *(worship anyone other than Him)* and may forgive anyone else, if He so pleases. One who commits shirk has indeed gone far away

Shirk is an unforgivable sin

from the Right Way.[116]   *The pagans* call upon female deities beside Him; by doing so they call nothing but the rebellious Shaitân[117] on whom Allah has laid His curse; and who has said: "I will take a good portion of Your servants and mislead them.[118] I will create in them false desires and order them to slit the ears of cattle. I will order them to tamper with Allah's creation." Therefore, whoever takes Shaitân as a guardian instead of Allah, has indeed become a clear-cut loser.[119] *Shaitân* makes promises to stir up in them false desires; but Shaitân's promises are nothing but deception.[120]   The home of such people *who follow him* will be hell, from where they will find no way to escape.[121]

Promise of Shai-tân to create false desires

4:[116-121]

As for those who have faith and do righteous deeds, We shall soon admit them to gardens beneath which rivers flow to live therein forever. The promise of Allah is true indeed, and who can be truer in his words than Allah?[122]   The final *result* will neither be in accordance with your desires nor in accordance with the desires of the People of the Book. He who does evil will be requited with evil: he will find no protector or helper besides Allah.[123]   But the one who does righteous deeds, whether a male or a female - provided he or she is a believer - shall enter paradise and no injustice will be done to them, even to the size of a speck.[124]

Promise of Allah to grant paradise to righteous - who can be truer than Allah in promise?

4:[122-124]

Who has a better Deen *(way of life or religion)* than the one who is a Muslim *(submits himself entirely)* to Allah, is a doer of good and follows the faith of Ibrâheem *(Abraham),* the upright one, whom Allah chose to be His friend?[125]   To Allah belongs all that is in the heavens and in the earth. Allah encompasses every-thing.[126]

No one is better than a Muslim

4:[125-126]

SECTION: 19

They ask your decision concerning the women. Tell them: Allah makes His decision concerning them and along with it reminds you about those commandments, recited to you in the Book *(the Qur'an)*, relating to orphan girls to whom you do not give their lawful rights and yet whom you desire to marry. *He also reminds you regarding* the helpless children, and that you stand firm for justice to orphans. Whatever good you do, Allah surely knows it.[127]   If a woman fears cruelty or desertion from her husband, there is no blame if both of them agree to reconcile by means of a compromise, after all compromise is better. Human

Establish justice for women, or-phan girls and helpless children

souls are prone to stinginess and greed, but if you show generosity and fear *Allah in your dealings,* surely, Allah is well aware of your actions.[128]　It is not possible for you to do perfect justice between your wives even if you wish to do so; therefore, *in order to comply with Divine Law,* do not lean towards one wife to the extent that you leave the other hanging in the air *(neither married nor divorced).* If you work out a friendly understanding and fear *Allah,* Allah is Forgiving, Merciful.[129]　If the spouses do separate, Allah will make each one independent of the other out of His own limitless resources, Allah is Ample-giving, Wise.[130]　　　4:[127-130]

　　　To Allah belongs all that is in the heavens and in the earth. We directed the People of the Book before you and now direct you also, to fear Allah and keep your duty to Him. But if you disobey *(you will do so at your own risk)* for to Allah belongs all that is in the heavens and in the earth and Allah is Self-sufficient, Praiseworthy.[131]　*Yes!* To Allah belongs all that is in the heavens and in the earth and Allah is sufficient as a Protector.[132]　If He wanted, He could destroy you all, O mankind, and bring others. Allah has the power to do so.[133]　Anyone who desires the reward of this world *should know that* Allah possesses the rewards of both, this world and the hereafter. Allah hears all and sees all.[134]

4:[131-134]

SECTION: 20

　　　O believers! Stand firm for justice and bear true witness for the sake of Allah, even though it be against yourselves, your parents or your relatives. *It does not matter* whether the party is rich or poor - Allah is the well wisher of both. So let not your selfish desires swerve you from justice. If you distort your testimony or decline to give it, *then you should remember* that Allah is fully aware of your actions.[135]　　　　　　　　　　　　　4:[135]

　　　O believers! Believe in Allah, His Rasool, the Book which He has revealed to His Rasool, and every Book which He previously revealed. He who denies Allah, His angels, His Books, His Rasools and the Last Day has gone far astray.[136]　As for those who accept the faith then renounce it, who again embrace it and again deny it, and go on increasing in unbelief, Allah will neither forgive them nor guide them to the Right Way.[137]　Announce the painful punishment to those hypocrites[138]　who choose the unbelievers to be their protectors rather than believers. Are they seeking honor

Have fear of Allah in your dealings

Commandment to stand firm for justice

The believers are required to believe wholeheartedly

in being with them? Whereas all honor belongs to Allah Alone.[139] He has already revealed for you in the Book that when you hear Allah's revelations being denied or ridiculed by people, you must not sit with them unless they change the topic of their talk, otherwise you shall be considered *guilty* like them. Rest assured that Allah is going to gather the hypocrites and the unbelievers all together in hell.[140]   *These hypocrites are such that* they wait and watch to see *how the wind blows.* If Allah grants you a victory, they say: "Were we not with you?" And if the unbelievers gain success, they will say to them: "Were we not strong enough to fight against you? Yet, we protected you from the believers *(Muslims).*" Allah will judge between you *and them* on the Day of Resurrection. Allah will not leave the way for the unbelievers *to triumph* over the believers.[141]   4:[136-141]

SECTION: 21

Surely, the hypocrites *try to* deceive Allah, whereas, in fact, He has reverted their deception to them; when they stand up for Salah *(prayer)*, they stand reluctantly, merely to be seen by people and do not remember Allah but a little[142] - wavering between *belief and disbelief,* belonging neither to this nor to that. Whom Allah leaves astray, you cannot find a Way for him.[143]   O believers! Do not choose unbelievers to be your protecting friends instead of believers. Would you like to furnish Allah a clear proof against yourselves?[144]   Surely, the hypocrites will be in the lowest depth of Hellfire; and you will not find any helper for them.[145] However, those who repent and mend their ways, hold fast to Allah, and become sincere in their devotion to Allah - they are considered to be with the believers. Allah will soon grant the believers a mighty reward.[146]   Why should Allah punish you if you are grateful and a true believer? Allah is All-Appreciative, All-Knowing.[147]

4:[142-147]

Boycott the un-Islamic gatherings

The hypocrites have double standards

Characteristics of hypocrites and the acts of hypocrisy

The hypocrites will be in the lowest depths of hellfire

JUZ (PART): 6

Allah does not like evil words to be uttered except by someone who is *truly* wronged. Allah hears all and knows all.[148] If you do good deeds openly or in private or forgive an evil, then surely, Allah is Pardoning, Powerful.[149] Those who deny Allah and his Rasool and *those who* intend to draw a line between Allah and His Rasools saying: "We believe in some, and reject the rest" - desiring to take a middle way between *belief and unbelief*[150] - these are the real unbelievers. We have prepared for such unbelievers a humiliating punishment.[151] As for those who believe in Allah and His Rasools and do not discriminate between any of them, We shall soon give them their due rewards. Allah is Forgiving, Merciful.[152]   4:[148-152]

SECTION: 22

The People of the Book ask you to bring down for them a book from Heaven. From Musa *(Moses)* they demanded an even harder *miracle* than that. They asked him: "Make us see Allah with our own eyes." As a result of their wickedness, the thunderbolt overtook them. Then they took the calf for worship after receiving clear revelations. *After all that,* We still pardoned them and gave Musa clear authority.[153] We lifted the mount of Toor over them and took the covenant from them *that they will obey Our commandments. On another occasion,* We commanded them to enter the gates prostrating *in humility. Yet, on another occasion,* We commanded them not to transgress in the matter of the Sabbath and took a solemn commitment from them. [154] *After all this*, they still broke their covenant, rejected the Revelation of Allah, killed the Prophets unjustly. Yet, they say: "Our hearts are in secure wrappings *which have preserved Allah's Word; we need no more."* Nay! Allah has sealed their hearts on account of their disbelief. They have no faith except a little.[155] They went in their unbelief *to such an extent* that they uttered terrible slander against Maryam *(Mary)*.[156] They say: "We have killed the Messiah, Isa *(Jesus), son of* Maryam, the Rasool of Allah." Whereas in fact, neither did they kill him nor did they crucify him but they thought they did *because the matter was made dubious for them*. Those who differ therein are in doubt. They have no real knowledge, they follow nothing but merely a conjecture, certainly, they did not kill him *(Jesus)*.[157] Nay! *The fact is that* Allah took him up to Himself. Allah is Mighty, Wise.[158] There is none of the People of the Book but will believe in this fact

Margin notes

Do not utter evil words

Do not draw a line between Allah and His Rasools in obedience

Most Jews are habitual sinners and violators of Allah's commandments

Jesus was neither killed nor crucified

before his death; and on the Day of Resurrection *Isa (Jesus)* will bear witness against them.[159]   4:[153-159]

Punishing the Jews for their iniquities

Because of the iniquity of those who call themselves Jews, their hindering of many people from the way of Allah,[160] taking of usury in spite of its prohibition, and cheating others of their properties - We made many wholesome things unlawful which were formerly lawful for them. We have prepared a painful punishment for those among them who reject faith.[161] However, those among them who are well-grounded in knowledge and those who truly believe in what has been revealed to you, *O Muhammad,* and what was revealed to other Prophets before you, establish Salah *(prayer)*, pay Zakah *(obligatory charity)*, and believe in Allah and the Last Day, those are the ones who will soon be given a mighty reward.[162]   4:[160-162]

Their only salvation is to become Muslims

SECTION: 23

This Qur'an carries the same message as was sent to Noah, Abraham, Moses and Jesus

O Muhammad, We have sent revelations to you just as We sent to Nûh *(Noah)* and the Prophets who came after him; We also sent revelations to Ibrâheem *(Abraham)*, Isma'il *(Ishmael)*, Ishâq *(Isaac)*, Ya'qoob *(Jacob)*, his descendants, Isa *(Jesus)*, Ayyûb *(Job)*, Yûnus *(Jonah),* Haroon *(Aaron)* and Sulaimân *(Solomon)*, and to Daûd *(David)* We gave the Psalms.[163] *Revelations were also sent to those* Rasools whom We have already mentioned to you and to those Rasools *whose names* We have not mentioned; to Musa *(Moses)* Allah spoke directly.[164] All these Rasools conveyed good news to mankind and admonished them, so that after conveying the message through the Rasools, people should have no excuse to plead against Allah. Allah is Mighty, Wise.[165] *People may or may not believe it,* but Allah bears witness that what He has sent to you, *O Muhammad,* He has sent with His own Knowledge and so do the angels; though Allah's testimony alone is sufficient.[166]   4:[163-166]

Al-Qur'an's authenticity is verified by Allah Himself

Believe in this authentic revelation if you want to attain felicity

Those who reject faith and hinder others from the Way of Allah, have indeed strayed far away from the Path.[167] Surely, Allah will neither forgive those who reject faith and act unjustly; nor guide them to any path[168] other than the path of hell, wherein they will live forever and this is easy for Allah.[169] O mankind! The Rasool has brought you the Truth from your Rabb, so believe in it, it is better for you. If you disbelieve, then you should know that to Allah belongs all that is in the heavens and in the earth. Allah is the Knowledgeable, Wise.[170] O People of the Book! Do not transgress the limits of your religion. Speak nothing but the Truth about Allah. The Messiah, Isa *(Jesus)*, the son of Maryam *(Mary)* was no more than a Rasool of Allah and His Word *"Be"* which He bestowed on Maryam and a Spirit from Him. So believe in Allah and His Rasools and do not say: Trinity (three)." Stop saying that, it is better for you. Allah is only One Deity. He is far above the need of having a son! To Him belongs all that is in the heavens and in the earth. Allah is All-Sufficient as a Disposer of affairs.[171]

4:[167-171]

Stop saying "Trinity" Allah is the One and Only Deity.

SECTION: 24

The Messiah *(Jesus)* never disdained to be the worshipper of Allah nor do the angels who are nearest *to Allah*. Whosoever disdains His worship and is arrogant, will be brought before Him all together.[172]   As for those who have faith and do righteous deeds, He will pay them their due compensation and give them more on His own from His grace, but He will inflict painful punishment on those who are disdainful and arrogant, and they will find none *(of those on whom they rely)* to protect or help them besides Allah.[173]   4:[172-173]

Jesus was a Prophet and worshipper of Allah

O mankind! There has come to you convincing proof *of Truth* from your Rabb. We have sent to you a glorious light *(Al-Qur'an) that shows you the Right Way clearly*.[174]   Now those who believe in Allah and hold fast to Him, *Allah* will soon enter them with His mercy and grace and will show them the Right Way to Himself.[175]   4:[174-175]

Mankind is asked to believe in the message of Al-Qur'an

They ask you for a legal decision *about Al-Kalâlah*. Say: Allah gives you His decision about Al-Kalâlah *(those who leave no ascendants or descendants as heirs)*. If it is a man that dies leaving behind a sister, but no child, she shall inherit one-half of his estate *(rest will go to the spouse and other relatives)*. If it is a woman that dies leaving no child, her brother will inherit all of her estate. If there are two sisters, they both shall inherit two-thirds of the estate *(rest will go to the spouse and other relatives)*; but if there are brothers and sisters, the share of each male shall be equal to that of two females. Thus Allah makes His commandments clear to you lest you go astray. Allah has perfect knowledge of everything.[176]

4:[176]

Legal decision relating to the inheritance of childless persons

5: AL-MÂ'IDAH

Period of Revelation

This Sûrah appears to have been revealed after the treaty of Hudaibiyah at the end of 6 A. H. or the beginning of 7 A. H. It deals with problems that arose from this treaty. The continuity of the subject indicates that most probably the whole Sûrah was revealed as a single discourse at one and the same time.

Major Issues, Divine Laws and Guidance

* Halâl (Lawful) and Harâm (unlawful) in the matters of food.
* Permission to eat the food of Ahl-al-Kitâb (Jews and Christians).
* Permission to marry women of Ahl-al-Kitâb (Jews and Christians).
* Regulations about bath, wudhu and Tayammûm.
* Salah (Prayer) and Zakah (Obligatory Charity) were also obligatory for Jews and Christians.
* Invitation to Jews and Christians to become Muslims.
* Those who do not judge by the Laws which Allah has revealed are declared to be unbelievers, wrong doers and transgressors.
* Warning to guard against corruption of power.
* Punishment for rebellion, disturbing the peace and theft.
* Absolute prohibition of drinking and gambling. (First commandment was in Sûrah Al-Baqarah 2:219 and Second in Sûrah An-Nisâ' 4:43)
* Additional rules for the laws of evidence.
* Miracles of Isa (Jesus) - and the fact that he did not claim divinity.
* Testimony of Isa (Jesus) which he shall give on the Day of Judgement.

Al-Mâ'idah was revealed at the time when the last effort of the Quraish to suppress Islam had been defeated in the Battle of the Ditch, and it had become quite obvious to the Arabs that no power could suppress the Islamic movement. Now Islam was not merely a creed which ruled over the minds and hearts of the people, but had also become a State which was regulating the lives of its people. Therefore, there was a need to formulate Islamic civil and criminal laws in detail and enforce them through Islamic courts. New and reformed ways of trade and commerce were needed to replace the old. Likewise, Islamic laws of marriage and divorce, segregation of the sexes and punishment for adultery, were needed to mold the social life of Muslims. This Sûrah provided the guidelines to the believers in some of these aspects of their lives so that their social behavior, conversation, dress, way of life and culture could take a definite shape of its own.

The treaty of Hudaibiyah was also signed in the same year which gave the Muslims not only peace in their own territory but also respite to spread the Message of Islam in the surrounding territories. The Prophet wrote letters to the rulers of Iran, Egypt, Rome and to the Chiefs of Arab tribes, inviting them to Islam. At the same time the missionaries of Islam spread among the clans and tribes and invited them to accept the Divine Message of Al-Islam.

Now that the Muslims had become a ruling body, there was a danger that power might corrupt them. At this stage of great trial, Allah admonished them over and over again to stick to justice and to guard against the wrong behavior of their predecessors - Jews and Christians. Believers are enjoined to remain steadfast to the Covenant of Obedience to Allah and His Rasool. They should follow Allah's commands and prohibitions in order to save themselves from the evil consequences which were faced by the Jews and the Christians who had violated them. They are instructed to avoid hypocrisy. In continuation of the instructions given in Sûrah An-Nisâ' about the consolidation of the Islamic Community, the Muslims were directed to observe and fulfill all of their obligations. The Jews and the Christians are also admonished to give up their wrong attitudes towards the Right Way and accept the guidance which is being presented by the Prophet Muhammad (peace be upon him).

5: AL-MÂ'IDAH

This Sûrah, revealed at Madinah, has 16 sections and 120 verses.

In the name of Allah, the Compassionate, the Merciful.

SECTION: 1

Fulfill your obligations

O believers! Fulfil your obligations. All four-legged animals from livestock are lawful to you other than those which are hereby announced. However do not violate the prohibition of hunting while you are in Ihrâm *(Hajj dress).* Surely, Allah orders whatever He pleases.[1]   O believers! Do not violate the sanctity of the Symbols of Allah: the Sacred Month , the animals brought for sacrifice, the garlands that mark such animals, and people visiting the Sacred House *(Ka'bah)* to seek the grace and good pleasure of their Rabb. When you put off your Ihrâm *(pilgrim garments)* then you are allowed to hunt. Let not the hatred of some people - who once hindered you from Al-Masjid-al-Harâm - incite you to commit transgression. Cooperate with one another in righteousness and piety, and do not cooperate in sin and transgression. Have fear of Allah. Allah is stern in punishment.[2]   5:[1-2]

Cooperate in piety and not in transgression

Harâm - (Forbidden) meat

You are forbidden to eat *the meat of any animal* that dies by itself *(dead body)*, blood, the flesh of swine *(pig meat)* and that on which any name other than Allah's has been invoked; also that which is strangled to death , killed by a violent blow, killed by a headlong fall and of those beaten or gored to death; and that which has been partly eaten by a wild animal unless you are able to slaughter it *before its death;* and that which is sacrificed on altars; and *forbidden also is* to seek luck or decision by raffling of arrows. All these are sinful acts. Today, the unbelievers have given up all their hope of vanquishing your religion. Have no fear of them, fear Me. Today I have perfected your religion for you, completed my favor upon you and approved Al-Islam as a Deen *(way of life for you).* Anyone who is compelled by hunger to eat *what is forbidden*, not intending to commit sin, will find Allah Forgiving, Merciful.[3]   5:[3]

Al-Islam is declared to be the complete and perfect Deen (way of life)

All good and clean things are lawful

They ask you what food is lawful for them, say: All good and clean things are lawful for you, as well as what you have taught your hunting birds and beasts to catch, trained by you with the knowledge given to you by Allah. Eat what they catch and hold for you, however, pronounce the name of Allah over it. Have fear of

Allah. Allah is swift in settling the accounts.[4]   Today all good clean things have been made lawful for you; and the food of the People of the Book is also made lawful for you and your food is made lawful for them. *Likewise,* marriage with chaste free believing women and also chaste women among the People who were given the Book before you is made lawful for you, provided that you give them their dowries and desire chastity, neither committing fornication nor taking them as mistresses. Anyone who commits Kufr with Imân (*rejects faith*), all his good deeds will become void *(zero)* and in the hereafter, he will be among the losers.[5]

5:[4-5]

The food of the People of the Book is made lawful and marriage with their women is permitted

SECTION: 2

O believers! When you rise up for Salah (*prayer*), wash your faces and your hands as far as the elbows, wipe your heads *with wet hands* and *wash* your feet to the ankles. If you had an emission of semen, then take a full bath. However, if you are sick or on a journey or you have used the toilet or you had intercourse with your women (*your wives*) and you do not find any water then resort to Tayammum - find clean soil and rub your faces and hands with it. Allah does not wish to burden you; He only wishes to purify you and to perfect His favor upon you, so that you may be thankful.[6]

5:[6]

Order for making wudhu (ablution)

Permission of Tayammum

Remember Allah's favor to you and the covenant which He ratified with you when you said: "We hear and we obey." Have fear of Allah; surely, Allah knows the secrets of your hearts.[7]   O believers! Be steadfast for the sake of Allah and bear true witness and let not the enmity of a people incite you to do injustice; do justice; that is nearer to piety. Fear Allah, surely, Allah is fully aware of all your actions.[8]   Allah has promised those who believe and do good deeds that for them there is forgiveness and mighty reward.[9] As for those who reject faith and deny Our revelations, they will be the companions of hellfire.[10]   O believers! Also remember Allah's favor which He *recently* bestowed upon you when He restrained the hands of those who sought to harm you (*Jewish plan to kill the Prophet and eminent companions through an invitation to a dinner which Allah informed him not to attend*). Have fear of Allah; and in Allah let the believers put their trust.[11]

5:[7-11]

Stand as a true witness and establish justice

The plot of the Jews to kill the Prophet and his eminent companions

SECTION: 3

Allah did in fact make a covenant with the Children of Israel and appointed twelve chieftains from among them and said: "I am

Salah and Zakah were obligatory for

the Jews also

with you; if you establish Salah (*prayers*), pay Zakah, believe in My Rasools, support them and give a generous loan to Allah (*spend in charity*), I will certainly forgive you your sins and admit you to gardens beneath which rivers flow. However, if any one of you violates *this covenant,* after this, he will indeed go astray from the Right Way."[12]   Even after that, they broke their covenant; as a result, We laid on them Our curse and hardened their hearts. They tampered with words out of their context and neglected a part of what they were enjoined. You will always find most of them deceitful except for a few of them. Yet, forgive them and overlook *their misdeeds.* Allah loves those who are kind to others.[13]   5:[12-13]

The Jews' habit of being deceitful

Christians too have neglected most of their Book

Likewise, We also made a covenant with those who call themselves Christians, but they too have neglected a part of what they were enjoined. *As a result,* We stirred among them enmity and hatred, which will last till the Day of Resurrection and soon Allah will inform them of what they used to do.[14]   O people of the Book (*Jews and Christians*)! Now Our Rasool has come to you to reveal much of what you have concealed from the Holy Book and to pass over much *which is no longer necessary.* There has come to you from Allah a *new* Light and a clear Book,[15]   with which Allah will guide to the ways of peace all those who seek His good pleasure and bring them out of the depth of darkness into the light by His leave and guide them to the Right Way.[16]   5:[14-16]

Jews and Christians are commanded to embrace Islam

Jesus, son of Mary, is not God or son of God

Indeed, those have committed Kufr (*rejected faith*) who said, "God is the Messiah, son of Maryam." *O Muhammad*, ask them, "Who has the power to prevent Allah if He chose to destroy the Messiah, the son of Maryam, his mother and all that is in the earth? To Allah belongs the heavens and the earth and all that is between them. He creates what He pleases and has power over everything."[17]   5:[17]

False claim of Jews and Christians of being the children of God

The Jews and the Christians say: "We are the children of Allah and His beloved ones." Ask them, "Why then does He punish you for your sins? Nay! In fact, you are human beings like others whom He has created. He forgives whom He pleases and He punishes whom He wills. To Allah belongs the sovereignty of the heavens and the earth and all that is between them, and to Him is the final refuge."[18]   O people of the Book! Indeed Our Rasool has now come to you making clear to you *the teaching of the Right Way*, after a long break in the series of the Rasools, so that you may not

An invitation to Jews and Christians to become Muslims

be able to say, "No one has come to give us good news or to warn us." Now someone has come to give you good news and warn you *so listen to him*. Allah has power over everything.[19]   5:[18-19]

SECTION: 4

Ponder upon the incident when Musa *(Moses)* said to his people: "O my people! Remember the favors which Allah has bestowed upon you. He has raised Prophets from among you, made you kings and gave you that which had not been given to anyone in the worlds."[20] "O my people! Enter the holy land which Allah has assigned for you. Do not turn back, because if you do, you will become losers."[21] They said: "O Musa! A nation of giants live in there, we will not set our foot in it until they leave. As soon as they leave, we will be ready to enter."[22] Thereupon two Allah-fearing men upon whom Allah had bestowed His Grace said: "Attack directly at the city gate, once you enter it, you will surely be victorious. Put your trust in Allah if you are really believers."[23] They replied, "O Musa! We will never enter it so long as they remain therein. Therefore, both you and your Rabb should go and fight, we will stay here."[24] *Hearing this Musa* prayed, "O my Rabb! I have no control over anyone except myself and my brother. Please, set us apart from these disobedient people."[25] *Allah* responded, "Very well, they are forbidden this land for forty years, *during this time* they will wander homeless on the earth, so do not grieve for these disobedient people."[26]   5:[20-26]

Behavior of the Jews with their own Prophet Musa (Moses)

Curse of Allah on the Jews for 40 years

SECTION: 5

Recite to them in all truth the story of Adam's two sons: How each offered a sacrifice, and how the offering of one was accepted while that of the other was not. *The latter* said: "I will kill you." *The former* replied: "Allah only accepts the sacrifice from the righteous.[27] Even if you stretch your hand to kill me, I shall not stretch my hand to slay you, for I fear Allah, the Rabb of the worlds.[28] I intend to let you bear the burden of my sins as well as yours and thus become an inmate of the Fire which is the reward for wrongdoers."[29] The latter's soul prompted him to kill his brother; he killed him and thus became one of the losers.[30] (*He carried around the dead body of his brother and did not know what to do with it*.) Then Allah sent a raven, which dug the ground to show him how to bury the dead body of his brother. "Alas!" He cried, "I failed even to be like this raven *to find some way* to dispose

Story of Adam's sons, one of whom committed the sin of murder

of the dead body of my brother!" So he became full of regrets.[31]

5:[27-31]

Decree of Allah regarding the killing of a human being

On account of that incident, We ordained for the Children of Israel that whoever kills a person, except as a punishment for murder or mischief in the land, it will be *written in his book of deeds* as if he had killed all the human beings and whoever will save a life shall be regarded as if he gave life to all the human beings. Yet, even though Our Rasools came to them *one after the other* with clear revelations, it was not long before, many of them committed excesses in the land.[32]

5:[32]

Punishment of waging war against Allah and His Rasool

The punishment for those who wage war against Allah and His Rasool and strive to create mischief in the land, is death or crucifixion or the cutting off of their hands and feet from opposite sides or exile from the land *based on the gravity of their offense.* This will be their humiliation in this world and in the hereafter they will have grievous punishment,[33] except those who repent before you apprehend them, *in such a case*, you should know that Allah is Forgiving, Merciful.[34]

5:[33-34]

SECTION: 6

Jihad is the way to success

No ransom will save the unbelievers from the punishment

O believers! Fear Allah and seek the means to be closer to Him and make Jihad *(struggle)* in His Way so that you may be successful.[35] As for those who are unbelievers, if they have everything that the earth contains or twice as much to offer as a ransom to redeem themselves from the punishment of the Day of Resurrection, it will not be accepted from them and they shall have a painful punishment.[36] They will desire to get out of the fire but will not be able to do so and they shall have an everlasting punishment.[37]

5:[35-37]

Punishment for the crime of theft

Male or female, whoever is guilty of theft, cut off the hand *(that was used in theft)* of either of them as a punishment for their crime. This is, *exemplary punishment,* ordained by Allah. Allah is Mighty, Wise.[38] But whoever repents after committing the crime and reforms his conduct, Allah will surely turn to him with forgiveness. Allah is Forgiving, Merciful.[39] Do you not know that Allah has sovereignty over the heavens and the earth? He may punish whom He pleases and forgive whom He pleases. Allah has power over everything.[40]

5:[38-40]

Do not provide lip-service;

O Rasool! Do not grieve for those who plunge headlong into unbelief; those who say with their tongues: We believe, but have no faith in their hearts; and *do not grieve for* those Jews, who listen to lies and spy for other people who had never come to you. They tamper with the words *of Allah* and take them out of their context and say: "If you are given such and such *commandment,* accept it; but if it is other than this, reject it." If Allah intends to put anyone to trial, you have no authority in the least to save him from Allah. Such people are those whose hearts Allah does not desire to purify; they will have humiliation in this world and a grievous punishment in the hereafter.[41]   *That is because* they listen to falsehood and eat what is forbidden. Therefore, if they come to you *with their cases,* you may judge between them or refuse to do so. Even if you refuse, they will not be able to harm you the least, but if you do act as a judge, judge between them with fairness, for Allah loves those who judge with fairness.[42]   But why do they come to you for Judgment when they have the Tawrât which contains Allah's commandments? Yet, they turn back after that. In fact, they are not true believers.[43]   5:[41-43]

SECTION: 7

Indeed, We revealed the Tawrât *to Moses*, in which there is guidance and light: By its laws, all the Prophets, who were Muslims, judged those *who call themselves* Jews and so did the rabbis and jurists of law. They were entrusted the protection of Allah's Book and they themselves were witnesses. Have no fear of people; fear Me, and do not sell My revelations for a petty price: those who do not judge by the law which Allah has revealed, are indeed kafirs (*unbelievers*).[44]   We ordained *in Tawrât* for them: "A life for a life, an eye for an eye, a nose for a nose, an ear for an ear, a tooth for a tooth and for a wound an equal retaliation." But if anyone remits the retaliation by way of charity, it will be an act of atonement for him; those who do not judge by the law which Allah has revealed, are indeed the wrongdoers.[45]   5:[44-45]

Then in the footsteps of those Prophets, We sent Isa (*Jesus*), the son of Maryam *(Mary),* confirming whatever remained intact from the Tawrât in his time, and gave him the Injeel *(Gospel)* wherein was guidance and light, corroborating what was revealed in the Tawrât; a guidance and an admonition to those who fear Allah.[46]   Therefore, let the people who follow the Injeel *(Gospel),* judge by the Law which Allah has revealed therein; those who do not judge by the Law which Allah has revealed, are indeed the transgressors.[47]   5:[47-47]

Side notes:

be True believers

If Allah intends to punish, the Rasool cannot save

Laws of Tawrât (Torah)

Those who do not judge by the laws of Allah :

a) They are unbelievers

b) They are wrongdoers

c) They are transgressors

To you, *O Muhammad*, We have revealed this Book with the truth. It confirms whatever has remained intact from the Book which came before it and also to safeguard it. Therefore, judge between them according to Allah's revelations and do not yield to their vain desires, diverging from the truth which has come to you. We have ordained a law and a Way of life for each of you. If Allah wanted, He could have made all of you a single nation. But He willed otherwise in order to test you in what He has given you; therefore, try to excel one another in good deeds. *Ultimately* you all shall return to Allah; then He will tell you the truth of those matters in which you dispute.[48] So, *O Muhammad*, pronounce Judgment among them according to the law which Allah has revealed and do not follow their vain desires, and beware of them lest they tempt you away from a part of that which Allah has revealed to you. If they reject *your Judgment*, then know that it is Allah's wish to scourge them for some of their sins. In fact, most of the people are transgressors.[49] *By rejecting the Divine Law,* do they wish to be judged by the laws of ignorance? Who is a better Judge than Allah for those who believe in Him?[50]   5:[48-50]

SECTION: 8

O believers! Take neither Jews nor Christians as your protecting friends: they are only protecting friends of one another. Whoever of you disobeys this *commandment* will be counted as one of them. Surely, Allah does not guide such wrongdoers.[51] You see that those who have the disease *of hypocrisy* in their hearts move around in their camp saying: "We fear lest a turn of fortune strike us." But soon when Allah gives you victory or a decision according to His will, they will regret for what they are hiding in their hearts.[52] At that time the believers will say: "Are these the same people who solemnly swore by Allah that they would stand beside you?" *As a result* all their deeds will be voided and they will become losers.[53]   5:[51-53]

O believers! Whoever among you renounce his Deen *(Islam), let them do so*; soon Allah will replace them with others whom He will love and they will love Him, who will be humble towards the believers, mighty against the unbelievers, striving hard in the way of Allah, and will have no fear of reproach from any critic. This is the grace of Allah which He bestows on whom He pleases. Allah is All-Sufficient for His creatures' needs and All-Knowing.[54] Your real protecting friends are Allah, His Rasool,

---

Sidebar notes:

Diversity of human race

Establish justice based on Allah's revelations

Do not take Jews or Christians as your protectors

Your protecting friends are: Allah, His Rasool, and your fellow believers

and the fellow believers - the ones who establish Salah *(prayer)*, pay Zakah *(obligatory charity)* and bow down humbly *before Allah*.[55]   Whoever makes Allah, His Rasool and the fellow believers his protecting friends, must know that Allah's party will surely be victorious.[56]   5:[54-56]

SECTION: 9

     O believers! Do not make your protecting friends, those from among the people who were given the Book before you and the unbelievers, who have made your religion a mockery and pastime, fear Allah if you are true believers.[57]   When you call for Salah *(prayers),* they make it as an object of mockery and pastime; this is because they are a people devoid of understanding.[58]   Tell them: "O people of the Book! What makes you against us other than that we believe in Allah and in what has been revealed to us and what was revealed before? The fact is that most of you are rebellious transgressors."[59]   Say: "Should I tell you of those who will have even worse than this in retribution from Allah? They are those whom Allah has cursed; who have incurred His wrath; some of whom were turned into apes and pigs; who worshipped Tâghoot *(false deities - Shaitân)*; are worse in rank and far more astray from the Right Way."[60]
          5:[57-60]

Do not befriend those people who make a mockery of your religion

     When they come to you, they say: "We believe". But in fact, unbelievers they came and unbelievers they departed. Allah knows fully well what they hide in their hearts.[61]   You will see many of them try to beat each other in sin and rancor, and eating what is unlawful. Evil indeed is what they do.[62]   Why do not their Rabbis and the Jurists of laws forbid them from uttering sinful words and eating unlawful things? Evil indeed are their deeds.[63] The Jews say: Allah's hand is tied up! - Nay! Their own hands will be tied up and they will be cursed for what they utter. Both of His hands are free; However, He spends as He pleases. The fact is that the revelations that have come to you from Allah will surely make many of them increase in their wickedness and unbelief. We have stirred among them enmity and hatred till the Day of Resurrection. Every time they kindle the fire of war, Allah extinguishes it. *Now* they are striving to spread mischief in the land. Allah does not love those who do mischief.[64]   If *instead of this rebellious attitude* the people of the Book had believed and become Godfearing, We would certainly have removed their iniquities and admitted them to the gardens of bliss *(paradise)*.[65]   If they would have observed the Laws of Tawrât and the Injeel *(Gospel)* and other Revelations

Jews' deceiving behavior

Jews' slandering Allah

If only the people of the Book had believed, they could have had best of both worlds

which were sent to them from their Rabb, they would have certainly enjoyed abundance from above and from beneath. Though there are some among them on the moderate course; yet, most of them do nothing but evil.[66]   5:[61-66]

SECTION: 10

The Rasool's mission is to deliver Allah's Message

O Rasool! Deliver the Message which has been revealed to you from your Rabb, and if you do not, you have not *fulfilled your duty of* conveying the Message. Allah will protect you from *the mischief of* the people. Surely, Allah does not guide the unbelievers.[67]   Tell them: O people of the Book! You have no ground to stand on unless you observe the Tawrât *(Torah)*, Injeel *(Gospel)* and other revelations that have come to you from your Rabb. This revelation *(the Qur'an)* which has come to you from your Rabb will surely increase the rebellion and disbelief of many of them but you should not grieve for the disbelievers.[68]   Surely, the believers *(Muslims)*, the Jews, the Sabians and the Christians - whoever believes in Allah and the Last Day and does righteous deeds - will have nothing to fear or to grieve.[69]   5:[67-69]

Attitude of the Jews towards the Rasools

Certainly, We took a covenant from the Children of Israel and sent them Rasools. Whenever there came to them a Rasool with *a message* that did not suit their fancies, either they called him an impostor or they put him to death.[70]   They thought no affliction would follow; so they acted blind and deaf. Yet, Allah, *in extreme mercy*, accepted their repentance, but again many acted blind and deaf *towards the message of Allah*. Allah is observant of their actions.[71]   5:[70-71]

Those who say Jesus is God are disbelievers

Certainly, they have disbelieved, who say: "Allah is Al-Maseeh *(the Messiah, Jesus), the son of Maryam (Mary)*." While Messiah himself said: "O children of Israel! Worship Allah, my Rabb and your Rabb." Whoever commits shirk *(joins partners with Allah)*, Allah will deny him the paradise, and the hellfire will be his home. There will be no helper for such wrongdoers.[72]   Certainly they are unbelievers who say: "Allah is one of three in a Trinity." There is none worthy of worship except One God *(Allah)*. If they do not stop saying what they say, a painful punishment will befall the disbelievers among them.[73]   Will they not then turn to Allah and seek His forgiveness? Allah is Forgiving, Merciful.[74]

5:[72-74]

Al-Maseeh *(the Messiah, Jesus)*, the son of Maryam, was no more than a Rasool; many Rasools had already passed away before him. His mother was a sincere steadfast for the truth; they both ate food *like other human beings.* See how the Revelations are made clear to them *to know the reality;* yet, see how they ignore the truth![75]   Say: "Would you worship besides Allah someone who can neither harm nor benefit you? While Allah is He who hears all and knows all."[76]   Tell them: "O people of the Book! Do not transgress the bounds of truth in your religion unjustly, and do not yield to the fancies of those people who went astray before you. They misled many others and have themselves strayed away from the Right Way.[77]   5:[75-77]

Who was Jesus, son of Mary?

SECTION: 11

Those who disbelieved from among the Children of Israel were cursed at the tongue of Daûd *(David)* and Isa *(Jesus),* the son of Maryam *(Mary)*: because they disobeyed and committed excesses.[78]   They would not forbid one another from committing iniquities; evil indeed were their deeds.[79]   As you can see, many of them are taking the side of the unbelievers. Evil is that, which their souls have sent forth for them *for the hereafter.* Because they have incurred the wrath of Allah, so in punishment, they are going to live forever.[80]   Had they believed in Allah, in the Prophet, and in what was revealed to him, they would have never taken *unbelievers* as their protecting friends *instead of believers,* but most of them are rebellious transgressors.[81]   You will find that the most violent in enmity to the believers are the Jews and the mushrikeen *(pagans)*; and nearest in affection to the believers are those who say: "We are Christians." That is because among them, there are men that are priests and monks, and do not behave arrogantly.[82]   5:[78-82]

Disbelievers among the Children of Israel were cursed by the tongues of David and Jesus

Christians are closer to the Muslims than the Jews and Pagans

JUZ (PART): 7

Good Christians recognize the truth and accept Islam

When they *(monks and priests)* listen to that which is revealed to the Rasool, you can see their eyes filled with tears, because they recognize the truth. They say: "Our Rabb! We believe, therefore, write us down among the witnesses of truth.[83] Why should we not believe in Allah and the truth which has come to us and hope that our Rabb will admit us to the company of the righteous?"[84] So Allah has rewarded them with gardens beneath which rivers flow to live therein forever. Such is the recompense of the doers of good.[85] As for those who reject and deny Our revelations, they shall become the inmates of hellfire.[86]

5: [83-86]

SECTION: 12

Do not make halâl things harâm on your own

O believers! Do not make unlawful those wholesome things which Allah has made lawful for you and not transgress; surely, Allah does not love the transgressors.[87] Eat of the lawful and wholesome things which Allah has provided for you. Fear Allah, in Whom you believe.[88] Allah will not call you to account for what is inadvertent in your oaths. But He will hold you accountable for that which you solemnly swear. The penalty for a *broken oath* is to feed ten indigent persons with such food as you normally provide to your own family, or to clothe *ten* needy people, or to free one slave. The one who cannot afford any of these must fast three days. This is the expiation for breaking your oaths. Therefore, be mindful of your oaths. Thus Allah makes clear to you His revelations that you may be thankful.[89]   5:[87-89]

Kaffarah (penalty) for breaking the oath

The prohibition of intoxicants (liquor and drugs) and gambling

O believers! Intoxicants and gambling *(games of chance)*, dedication to stones *(paying tribute to idols)* and using arrows *(for seeking luck or decision)* are the filthy works of Shaitân. Get away from them, so that you may prosper.[90] Shaitân desires to stir up enmity and hatred between you with intoxicants and gambling, to prevent you from the remembrance of Allah and from Salah *(prayers)*. Will you not abstain?[91] Obey Allah and obey the Rasool and abstain *from these things*. If you do not, then you should know that Our Rasool's duty is only to convey My message clearly.[92] There is no blame on those who believe and do good deeds for what they ate in the past, provided they abstain *from those things which have been made unlawful*, then remain steadfast in their belief and do righteous deeds, then abstain themselves *from*

Rasool's duty is only to pass on the Message of Allah

whatever they are forbidden and believe *in Divine Law,* then fear Allah and do good deeds. For Allah loves those who do good deeds.[93]　　　　　　　　　　　　　　5: [90-93]

SECTION: 13

O believers! Allah will put you to trial by making game *(that which is to be hunted)* well within the reach of your hands and your spears in order to see who fears Him, though unseen. There shall, therefore, be a painful punishment for those who transgress after this warning.[94]　O believers! Do not kill game while you are in Ihrâm *(pilgrim garb)*. If anyone kills game intentionally, he will have to pay a penalty through an offering brought to the Ka'bah of a domestic animal equivalent to the one which was killed as determined by two just men among you; or as an expiation, either feed a few indigent or fast their equivalent days, so that he may taste the evil consequences of what he did. Allah has forgiven what happened in the past; but if anyone repeats it now, Allah will inflict retribution on him. Allah is Mighty, Capable of Retribution.[95] Game of the sea and its use as food is lawful for you and the seafarers, but the game of the land is forbidden as long as you are in Ihrâm *(pilgrim garb)*. Have fear of Allah to whom you shall all be assembled.[96]　　　　　　　　　　　5: [94-96]

Prohibition of hunting during Hajj Ihrâm (wearing pilgrim garb)

Kaffarah (penalty) for hunting during Hajj Ihrâm

Allah has made the Ka'bah of the Sacred House an eternal value for mankind, so are the Sacred Months, the animal offerings, and *the animals* which are collared as a mark of dedication; so you must know that Allah has knowledge of what is in the heavens and in the earth and that Allah is well aware of everything.[97]　You should also know that Allah is stern in Retribution, and that Allah is Forgiving, Merciful.[98]　The only duty of the Rasool is to convey *My Message.* Allah knows all what you reveal and what you conceal.[99]　Tell them, "Bad and good are not equal, even though the abundance of the bad may dazzle you; so fear Allah, O people of understanding, that you may prosper!" [100]　　　　5:[97-100]

Allah has made Ka'bah in Makkah, an eternal value for mankind

SECTION: 14

O believers! Do not ask *questions* about things that if revealed to you, may cause you trouble. But if you ask a question about something when the Qur'an is being revealed, it will be made known to you. Allah has pardoned that *what you did in the past*, Allah is Forgiving, Forbearing.[101]　Some people before you did ask such questions and later lost their faith because of those very

Do not ask questions like the nation of Musa (Moses)

Superstitions are prohibited in Islam

things.[102] Allah did not institute *superstitions like those of* a slit-ear she-camel or a she-camel let loose for free pasture or idol sacrifices for twin-births in animals or stallion-camels freed from work; this lie is invented by the unbelievers against Allah, and most of them lack understanding.[103]   When it is said to them: "Come to what Allah has revealed and come to the Rasool." They reply: "Sufficient for us are the ways on which we found our forefathers." What! Even though their forefathers knew nothing and were not rightly guided?[104]   5:[101-104]

Last will and testament, and the required testimony of witnesses

O believers! You are accountable for none but yourselves; anyone who has gone astray cannot harm you if you are on the Right Way. To Allah you shall all return and He will let you know *the truth* of all that you did.[105]   O believers! When death approaches any one of you, let two just men from among yourselves act as witnesses at the time of making your last will; or from others *(non-Muslims)* if you are travelling through the land and the calamity of death overtakes you. If you doubt their honesty, detain them after prayer and let them both swear by Allah: "We will not sell our testimony for any price, even to a relative, and we will not hide the testimony which we will be giving for the sake of Allah; for we shall be sinners if we do so."[106]   If it becomes known that those two were guilty of the sin *of perjury*, then let two other better qualified witnesses from among those who were deprived of their right come forward and testify upon oath, "By Allah, our testimony is truer than theirs. We have not transgressed in our testimony; for we should be wrongdoers if we did so."[107]   By this procedure, it is more likely that they will bear true witness or at least fear that their oaths could be contradicted by subsequent oaths. Have fear of Allah and listen; Allah does not guide those who are disobedient transgressors. [108]   5: [105-108]

SECTION: 15

Favors of Allah upon Jesus and the miracles he was given

On the Day *of Resurrection* when Allah will gather the Rasools and ask: "What response were you given *from your addressees*?" They will say: "We have no knowledge, only You have all the knowledge of the unseen."[109]   Then Allah will ask: "O Isa *(Jesus)* son of Maryam *(Mary)*! Recall my favor upon you and your mother: how I strengthened you with the Holy Spirit *(the angel Gabriel)*, so you could speak to the people in the cradle and in maturity; how I taught you the Book, Wisdom, the Tawrât *(Torah)* and the Injeel *(Gospel)*; how you were able to make the figure of a bird out of a clay, by My permission; how you breathed into it and changed it into a *living* bird, by My permission; how you could heal the born-blind and the lepers, by My permission; how you could bring the dead body back to life, by My permission; how I protected you from *the violence of* the Children of Israel when you came to them with clear signs and the unbelievers among them said: "This is nothing but clear sorcery."[110]   Remember, when I inspired the disciples to have faith in Me and in My Rasool, and they said: 'We believe and bear witness that we have become Muslims."[111] Remember when the disciples asked: "O Isa, son of Maryam! Can your Rabb send down to us from heaven a table spread with food?" And he said: "Have fear of Allah if you are true believers."[112] They said: "We only wish to eat thereof to satisfy our hearts and to know that you have indeed told us the truth, and that we bear witness to it."[113]   Isa, son of Maryam said: "O Allah, our Rabb! Send us from heaven, a table spread with food that it may mark a feast, one of a kind, for us for those before and after us, as a sign from You; and provide us our sustenance, You are the best Sustainer."[114]   Allah responded: "I shall send it down to you, but if any of you disbelieve after that, I shall punish him with a torment which I have never inflicted on anyone in the worlds."[115]

The disciples of Jesus asked for a Table Spread of food as a miracle

5:[109-115]

SECTION: 16

After reminding him of these favors, Allah will say: "O Isa *(Jesus),* son of Maryam *(Mary),* Did you ever say to the people, "worship me and my mother as gods beside Allah?" He will answer: "Glory to You! How could I say what I had no right to say? If I had ever said so, you would have certainly known it. You know what is in my heart, but I know not what is in Yours; for You have full knowledge of all the unseen.[116]   I never said anything other than what You commanded me to say, that is to worship Allah, Who is my Rabb and your Rabb. I was a witness over them as long as I remained among them; but when You called me off, You were the Watcher over them and You are a Witness to everything.[117]   If You punish them, they surely are Your servants; and if You forgive them, You are Mighty, Wise."[118]   Allah will say: "This is the day on which the truthful will profit from their truth; they shall have gardens beneath which rivers flow to live therein forever. Allah is well-pleased with them and they are pleased with Him. This is the mighty achievement."[119]   To Allah belongs the sovereignty of the heavens and the earth and all that is therein; He has power over everything.[120]   5:[116-120]

Testimony of Jesus on the Day of Judgment about Christians

6: AL-AN'ÂM

Period of Revelation

The whole of the Sûrah was revealed at one time during the last year of the Prophet's stay at Makkah. The traditions indicate that it was dictated by the Prophet the same evening that it was revealed.

Major Issues, Divine Laws and Guidance:

* Refutation of shirk (worshipping other deities besides Allah) and guidance towards Tawheed (Oneness of God).
* Reality of the life after death and the Day of Judgement.
* Clarification of self-imposed prohibitions by the Jews that were falsely attributed to Allah.
* Allah's commandments are not irrational taboos, but form the fundamental moral principles of the Islamic society.
* Answers to objections raised against the person and the mission of the Prophet Muhammad, peace be upon him.
* Comfort and encouragement is provided to the Prophet and his followers who were at that time in a state of anxiety and despondency.
* Admonition, warnings and threats are given to the disbelievers to give up their apathy and haughtiness.
* Prohibition of dividing the religion into sects.
* Allah requires the Believer to declare: My Salah (Prayer), my devotion, my life and my death are all for Allah."

It is important to know that the above issues have not been discussed under separate heading; rather the discourse goes on as a continuous whole and these topics are discussed over and over from different angles. The discussion revolves around the major articles of faith: Tawheed, Prophethood and life after death, and their practical application in human life. Side by side with this, it refutes the erroneous beliefs of the Mushrikeen and provides answers to their objections. It also comforts the Prophet and his followers who were then suffering from persecution by the disbelievers.

6: AL-AN'ÂM

This Sûrah, revealed at Makkah, has 20 sections and 165 verses.

In the name of Allah, the Compassionate, the Merciful

SECTION: 1

All praise be to Allah, the One Who has created the heavens and the earth and made the darkness and the light; yet, the unbelievers set up equal partners with their Rabb.[1]   He is the One Who has created you from clay, then decreed a fixed term of life and a specified time *(for your resurrection)* known to Him; yet, you go on doubting![2]   He is the same One Allah in both the heavens and the earth. He knows what you conceal, what you reveal and what you do.[3]   *Yet, the reaction of the people has been that* whenever a revelation came to them from their Rabb, they ignored it.[4]   Now that the truth has come to them, they have denied it. Soon they will come to know the reality which they are ridiculing.[5] Have they not seen how many generations We have destroyed before them? We had made those nations more powerful in the land than yourselves. We sent down for them abundant rain from the sky and made the rivers flow beneath their feet: yet, for their sins We destroyed them all and raised up other generations in their places.[6]

6:[1-6]

O Prophet, if We had sent you a Book written on paper and they touched it with their own hands, the unbelievers would still have said: "This is nothing but plain sorcery!"[7]   They ask: "Why has no angel been sent down to us?" Well, if We had sent down an angel, the matter would have been settled at once and no respite would have been granted after that;[8]   and even if We had sent an angel, We would have certainly sent him in a human form and thus involved them in the same confusion as they are in at this time.[9]   *O Muhammad!* Many Rasools before you were also ridiculed, but in the long run those who ridiculed were hemmed in by the very thing they were ridiculing.[10]   6:[7-10]

SECTION: 2

O Muhammad, say: "Travel through the earth and see what was the end of those who denied the truth."[11]   Ask them: "To whom belongs all that is in the heavens and in the earth?" *If they don't respond,* tell them: "To Allah!" He has decreed mercy for Himself, *that is why He does not punish you for your misdeeds right away.* He will certainly gather you all together on the Day of

---

Allah is the same One God, All-mighty in both the heavens and the earth

If Allah had sent a written Book and an angel with it, the unbelievers still would not have believed

Allah has decreed mercy for Himself that is why He does not punish in this world

Resurrection; there is no doubt about it. Yet, those who have lost their souls will not believe.[12]   To Him belongs all that takes rest in the night and in the day. He is the Hearer, the Knower.[13]   Say: "Should I take as my protector anyone other than Allah, who is the Creator of the heavens and the earth. Who feeds all and is fed by none?" Say: "Nay! I am commanded to be the first of those who submit to Allah *in Islam,* and do not ever be of the mushrikeen."[14] Say: " I fear the torment of a Mighty Day if I disobey my Rabb."[15] He who is delivered *from the torment of* that Day, has indeed received Allah's Mercy; and this is a glorious achievement.[16]   If Allah afflicts you with any harm, none can relieve you other than Him; and if He blesses you with happiness, *you should know that* He has power over everything.[17]   He is the Supreme Authority over His servants; and He is the Wise, the Aware.[18]

What punishment will be on the Day of Judgment?

6: [11-18]

Ask them: " Whose testimony is the most reliable? " *When they say Allah, then* tell them: "Let Allah be Witness between me and you *(that I am the Rasool of Allah);* this Qur'an has been revealed to me by Him so that I may warn you thereby and all those whom it may reach. Can you really testify that there are other gods besides Allah?" Tell them: *"As far as I am concerned,* I will never testify to this!" Say: "Indeed, worthy of worship is One and Only God, and indeed, I am free of the shirk you commit.[19]   Those to whom We have given the Book recognize this fact as they recognize their own sons. *In fact,* those who have lost their souls will not believe.[20]

The Qur'an is revealed to admonish and to declare that there is Only One God: Allah

6: [19-20]

SECTION: 3

Who can be more wicked than a person who forges a lie against Allah or denies His revelations? Surely, the wrongdoers shall never get salvation.[21]   On the Day of Judgment when We gather them all together, We shall ask the mushrikeen: "Where are those deities whom you ascribed *to be My partners*?"[22]   They will have no argument but to say: "By Allah, our Rabb, we were not at all mushrikeen."[23]   See how they will lie against their own souls, and how the deities of their own inventions will leave them in the lurch.[24]   Of them there are some who pretend that they listen to you; but *their prejudices have dulled their faculties and* We have cast veils over their hearts and deafness in their ears so they are unable to understand. Even if they see every one of Our Signs, they will not believe. So much so, that when they come to you, they argue with you. The unbelievers say: "These are nothing but tales

Prejudice has made the people worship deities other than Allah of the old times."[25]   They themselves have turned away from the truth and also forbid other people to believe in it. *With such a behavior* they harm none but their own souls but they do not perceive it.[26]   6:[21-26]

If you could witness *the scene*, when they are made to stand before the hellfire, they will say: "We wish we could return *to earthly life again*; then we would not deny the revelations of our Rabb, and we would join the believers!"[27]   In fact, they will say this because they had come to know the reality which they were concealing before. *As a matter of fact,* even if they be sent back, thcy would certainly repeat the same things which they had been forbidden to do. Indeed they are liars.[28]   *Today* they say: "There is no other life except the life of this world and we shall never be raised to life again."[29]   If you could witness the scene when they are brought before their Rabb; He will ask, "Is this not the reality?" They will say: "Yes, our Rabb, *this is the reality*." He will order: "Well, then taste the punishment for denying this reality."[30]

6: [27-30]

> For sure there is a life after death?

SECTION: 4

Those people are indeed lost who deny that they will ever meet Allah. When the hour *of Doomsday* overtakes them all of a sudden, they will exclaim: "Alas! How negligent we have been about this *Hour*." They will be carrying the burden of their sins on their backs; and evil indeed are the burdens that they carry![31]   The life of this world is nothing but play and amusement, but the life of the hereafter will be better for those who are pious. Will you not use your common sense?[32]   *O Muhammad* We know it well that what they say grieves you: it is not you that they deny, these wrongdoers actually deny the revelations of Allah.[33]   Many Rasools before you were denied but patiently bore with their denial and persecution until Our help came down to them; for none can change the decrees of Allah. You have already received the news of what happened to those Rasools.[34]   If you find their aversion hard to bear, then see if you can make a tunnel in the ground or put a ladder to *ascend* in the skies by which you can bring them a sign. *O Prophet, you know well that* if Allah wanted, He would have given guidance to all. So do not be like the ignorant.[35]   6:[31-35]

> Those who deny the Prophet Muhammad , in fact, deny Allah's revelations

Surely, those who listen *to Our revelations with an open mind will* accept the Truth. As for the dead *(those with closed minds)*, Allah will bring them back to life, *on the Day of Judgment,*

> Those who listen, will accept the Truth

Use your common sense to learn from the signs of nature

Do you not call Allah Alone in real distress?

then to Him they will be returned *for their recompense.* [36] They ask: "Why has a sign not been sent down to him from his Rabb?" Tell them: "Allah is surely able to send down a Sign *if He wants*; but most of them do not understand *the wisdom behind it.*"[37] *If you really want to see the signs of Allah,* just look at any animal that walks upon the earth and any bird that flies in the air; they too are communities like you. We have not left out anything from the Book. They all shall be gathered before their Rabb.[38] Those who deny Our Revelations are deaf and dumb, living in many layers of darkness. Allah leaves astray whom He will, and guides to the Right Way whom He please.[39] Ask them *to think carefully and answer*: "When the punishment of Allah smites you or the last Hour approaches you, do you call for help anyone other than Allah? *Answer me* if you are truthful!"[40] No, on Him Alone you will call, and forget those whom you have set up as His partners; then if He pleases, He relieves you from the affliction about which you have prayed to Him.[41]   6: [36-41]

SECTION: 5

Prosperity in this world is not a reward, but a respite

We did send Rasools before you to other nations and afflicted them with suffering and adversities so that they might call *Allah* in humility.[42] Then why did they not call *Allah* in humility when the sufferings overtook them? But their hearts hardened and shaitân made their sinful acts seem fair to them.[43] When they neglected the warning they had received, then, *instead of punishment,* We opened the gates of every kind of prosperity for them; but just as they were rejoicing in what they were given, We took them by surprise, and lo! They were plunged into despair![44] Thus We cut off the roots of the wrongdoers. All praises are due to Allah, the Rabb of the worlds.[45]   6: [42-45]

Who can restore your hearing and sight if Allah takes them away?

Rasools never claimed that they know the unseen or that they are angels

Ask them: "Just think, if Allah takes away your hearing and your sight and seals up your hearts, is there any deity other than Allah who could restore them to you?" See how We present Our revelations over and over again and yet they turn away.[46] Say: "Just think if the punishment of Allah comes to you whether suddenly or openly, would any be destroyed other than the wrongdoers?"[47] We have sent the Rasools only to give good news and to warn: so those who believe and mend their ways shall have nothing to fear or to grieve.[48] But those who deny Our Revelations shall be punished for their transgression.[49] Say: "I do not claim that I possess the treasures of Allah, or that I know the unseen, nor do I claim that I am an angel. *What I say is that* I follow only that which is revealed to me." Ask them: "Are the blind and the seeing alike? Can you not think?"[50]   6: [46-50]

SECTION: 6

O *Muhammad,* admonish with this *(the Qur'an),* those who have the fear of being assembled before their Rabb in such a condition that there will be no one to protect them or intercede on their behalf other than Him. It may be that, *by this admonition,* they may become righteous.[51]   Do not drive away those *(poor people like Bilal, Ammâr and Sûhaib)* who call on their Rabb morning and evening, seeking only to gain His favor. You are in no way accountable for their deeds nor they are in any way accountable for yours. So, if you drive them away, you shall be counted among the wrongdoers.[52]   That's how We have made some of them *(poor and slaves who accepted Islam)* a means for testing the others *(the chiefs of Quraish),* so that they should say: "Are these the people whom Allah favors among us *(the poor, indigent and low class)*?" Well, does Allah not know best those who are grateful?[53]   When those who believe in Our revelations come to you, say: "Peace be upon you. Your Rabb has decreed mercy upon Himself. If anyone among you commits evil because of ignorance and thereafter repents and mends his ways, you will find Allah Forgiving, Merciful."[54]   Thus, We spell out Our revelations, so that the way of the culprits may become evident.[55]   6:[51-55]

SECTION: 7

O *Muhammad,* tell them: "I am forbidden to worship those whom you call upon besides Allah." Say: "I am not going to follow your wishes; if I do, I would be lost and cease to be from the rightly guided."[56]   Say: "I am on a clear proof from my Rabb which you have denied, but *the scourge of Allah,* which you are in such a rush to see, is not in my power. No one has the authority of passing Judgment except Allah: He declares the truth and He is the best of Judges."[57]   Say: "If what you rush to see were in my power, the matter between you and me would have been settled long ago; but Allah knows best who are the wrongdoers."[58]   He Alone has the keys of the unseen; no one knows them except Him. He knows whatever is in the land and in the sea; there is not a single leaf that falls without His knowledge; there is neither a grain in the darkness of the earth nor anything fresh or dry which has not been recorded in a Clear Book.[59]   He is the One Who takes your souls at night

---

Admonish the unbelievers with this Qur'an

Real belief is a favor of Allah and is irrespective of worldly status

Allah Alone has the authority of passing Judgment and He Alone knows the unseen

(makes you go to sleep) and knows what you do during the day, then the next day raises you up again to complete your allotted span of life. To Him you shall all return, then He will notify you of all that you have done."[60]   6: [56-60]

SECTION: 8

Allah has appointed guardian angels over you

He is the Irresistible *(supreme)* over his servants and sends guardian *angels* over you. At length, when death approaches anyone of you, Our messengers *(angels)* take his soul and they are not negligent in performing their duty.[61]   Then those *souls* are brought back to Allah, their real Master. Beware! He is the Judge and He is the swiftest in settling accounts.[62]   6: [61-62]

Allah is the One Who delivers you from calamities

Ask them: "Who delivers you from *calamities* in the darkness of the land and of the sea, when you call upon Him in open *humility* and silent *terror*: If You deliver us from this *affliction*, we shall become truly grateful."[63]   Say: "Allah delivers you from these and all other calamities; yet, you commit shirk *(worship false deities)*!"[64]   Say: "He has the power to send calamities on you from above and from below or to split you into discordant factions to make you taste the violence of one another. See how We present Our revelations over and over again so that they may understand *the reality*.[65] But your people are rejecting this *(the Qur'an)*, although it is the very truth." Tell them: "I am not appointed as your caretaker.[66]   For every prophecy there is an appointed time, and soon you will come to know."[67]   6: [63-67]

Do not sit with those who argue about Allah's revelations

When you see those who are engaged in arguments about Our revelations, turn away from them until they change their topic of discussion. If Shaitân ever makes you forget this *commandment*, then as soon as you realize, withdraw from the company of wrongdoers.[68]   The righteous people will not be held responsible for the wrongdoers' actions; it is only an admonition - perhaps they may fear *Allah*.[69]   6: [68-69]

Do not associate with those who take their religion as a matter of amusement

Leave alone those people who take their religion as mere play and amusement and are deceived by the life of this world. However, keep on admonishing them with this *(the Qur'an)*, lest their souls be damned by their own *sinful* deeds. They will not have any protector or intercessor to rescue them from Allah, and if they seek to offer every imaginable ransom, it shall not be accepted from them. Such are those who are damned by their own *sinful* deeds. They will get boiling water to drink and painful punishment for their rejection of the Truth.[70]   6: [70]

SECTION: 9

Ask the *mushrikeen*: "Should we call, besides Allah, on others who can neither benefit us nor harm us, and turn upon our heels after Allah has guided us to the Right Way, like the one whom shaitâns has misled and is wandering around in the land, while his friends are calling him to the right way, shouting: "Come this way?" Tell them: "Allah's guidance is the only guidance. We are commanded to surrender *(become Muslims)* to the Rabb of the worlds.[71]   So, establish Salah *(prayer)* and fear Him, before Whom you shall all be assembled *on the Day of Judgment*.[72]   He is the One Who has created the heavens and the earth in all Truth. On the Day when He says: "Be," and it is *(the Day of Resurrection)*. His Word is the truth. He shall be the sole Sovereign on the Day when the trumpet will be blown. He has the full knowledge of the invisible and the visible. He is the Wise, the All-Knowing.[73]

6: [71-73]

Believers are commanded to become Muslims, to establish Salah and to fear Him

Tell them about Ibrâheem *(Abraham)*, who said to Âzar, his father: "Are you taking idols for gods? Surely, I see you and your people in manifest error."[74]   Thus, We showed Ibrâheem the kingdom of the heavens and the earth, so he became one of the firm believers.[75]   When the night drew its shadow over him, he saw a star and said, "this is my Rabb." But when it set, he said: "I do not love *to worship such a god* that fades away."[76]   Afterwards he saw the moon shining, he said; "This is my Rabb." But when it also set, he said: "If my Rabb does not guide me, I shall certainly become one of those who go astray."[77]   Then when he saw the sun with its brighter shine, he said: "This must be my Rabb; it is larger *than the other two*." But when it also set, he exclaimed: "O my people! I am free of your shirk *(associating partners with Allah)*.[78] *As far as I am concerned,* I have turn my face, sincerely, to Him Who has created the heavens and the earth, and I am not one of the mushrikeen."[79]   6: [74-79]

Ibrâheem learned faith through the study of nature with his common sense

When his people started arguing with him, he told them: "Will you argue with me about Allah, whereas He Himself has guided me? I do not fear those whom you take for gods besides Him, *none can harm me* unless my Rabb so wills. The knowledge of my Rabb encompasses everything; why don't you get admonition?[80]   Why should I fear your idols, when you are not afraid of

Arguments of the mushrikeen with Prophet Ibrâheem about Allah

your actions of making them partners with Allah, for which He has not given you any sanction? Which one from the two parties of us deserves to feel secure? *Tell me,* if you know *the truth.*[81] *As a matter of fact* those who believe and do not taint their faith with injustice *(shirk)* will have security and are rightly guided."[82]

6: [80-82]

SECTION: 10

Descendants of the Prophet Ibrâheem including Musa, Isa and Muhammad: none of them were mushrikeen

This was the argument which We gave Ibrâheem *(Abraham)* against his people. We exalt in ranks whom We please; surely, your Rabb is Wise, All-Knowing.[83] We gave him Ishâq *(Isaac)* and Ya'qoob *(Jacob)* and guided them all as We guided Nûh (Noah) before them, and among his descendants were Daûd *(David)*, Sulaimân *(Solomon)*, Ayyûb *(Job)*, Yûsuf *(Joseph)*, Musa *(Moses)* and Haroon *(Aaron)*; thus do We reward the doers of good.[84] *Other descendants include* Zakariyya, Yahya *(John)*, Isa *(Jesus)*, and Ilyâs *(Elias)*; all of them were righteous;[85] and Isma'il *(Ishmael)*, Al-Yas'â *(Elisha)*, Yûnus *(Jonah)* and Lût *(Lot)*. We exalted every one of them over the worlds[86] as *We exalted* some of their forefathers, their children and their brothers. We chose them *for Our service* and guided them to the Right Way.[87] This is the guidance from Allah; He bestows it upon whom He pleases of His devotees. If they had committed shirk *(worshiped anyone else besides Allah)* all their deeds would have become void.[88] Such were the people to whom We gave the Book, authority and Prophethood. Now if these people deny this *guidance, it does not matter*; We would bestow this *guidance* upon other people who would not disbelieve.[89] *O Muhammad,* those were the people who were rightly guided by Allah; therefore, follow their guidance and tell these people: "I am not asking you any payment for this work *of delivering the Message to you,* this *message* is nothing but a reminder to all the worlds."[90]

6: [83-90]

SECTION: 11

Allah is He Who has revealed the Tawrât and the Qur'an

Those people have not appraise Allah with true appraisal, when they said: "Allah has never revealed anything to a human being." Ask them: "Who then sent down the Book *(Torah)* which Musa brought, a light and guidance for mankind? You have transcribed it on separate sheets, showing some and suppressing much, although you have been taught that which neither you nor your forefathers knew before." *If they do not answer,* then just say: "Allah *sent it down,"* and leave them to amuse themselves with their useless chatter.[91]   6: [91]

This is the blessed Book which We have revealed, con-firming what came before it, that you, *O Muhammad,* may warn *the people living in* the Mother City (*Makkah*) and those who live around it. Those who believe in the hereafter, do believe in this *(Book)* and are maintaining their Salah *(prescribed prayers).*[92] Who can be more wicked than the one who invents a lie against Allah, or says: "This was revealed to me," while nothing was revealed to him? Or the one who says: "I can reveal the like of what Allah has revealed?" If you could only see these wrongdoers when they are in the agonies of death and the angels stretch forth their hands saying, "Deliver your souls! Today you will be rewarded with a disgraceful punishment for saying *falsehood* against Allah which you had no right to say and for showing arrogance against His revelations!"[93] *Allah adds to what the angels said,* "So you have come back to Us Alone as We created you at the first time, leaving behind all that which We gave you in that world and We do not see with you your intercessors, whom you claimed to be *Allah's* partners in your affairs; all *your ties* have been cut off and what you presumed has failed you."[94]   6:[92-94]

Those who invent a lie against Allah will face a disgraceful punishment

SECTION: 12

Surely, it is Allah Who causes the seed and the fruit-stone to split *and sprout.* He brings forth the living from the dead and the dead from the living. It is Allah, *Who does all this*; then why are you being misled?[95]   He causes the daybreak *from the dark.* He makes the night for rest and makes *the rising and setting of* the sun and the moon for you to determine times *(days, weeks, months and years);* these are the arrangements of the Almighty, the All-Knowing.[96] He is the One Who has made the stars for you, so that you might find your way thereby in the darkness *whether you are* on the land or the sea. We have spelled out Our revelations very clearly for people of common sense.[97]   He is the One Who has created you from a single soul and granted you dwelling *on Earth* and a resting place *in the hereafter.* We have spelled out Our revelations very clearly for people of understanding.[98]   It is He Who sends down rainwater from the sky and therewith produces vegetation of all kinds: He brings forth green *crops* producing grain piled up *in the ear*, palm-trees laden with clusters of dates hanging within reach, gardens of grapes, olives, and pomegranates; though their fruit resembles in kind yet is different in variety. Look at their

Examples from Allah's creation are clearly spelled out for the understanding of mankind

fruits as they yield and ripen. Behold! In these things there are signs for true believers.[99]   Yet, they make the Jinns *(Genies: a creature created out of fire)* partners with Allah, whereas He is their Creator; and also ascribe to Him sons and daughters without having any knowledge. Glory to Him! *He is* highly exalted far above what they ascribe.[100]   6:[95-100]

SECTION: 13

How could Allah have a son without a spouse?

He is the Originator of the heavens and the earth. How could He have a son when He has no consort? He has created everything and is aware of everything.[101]   That is Allah your Rabb! There is none worthy of worship but He, the Creator of everything. Therefore, worship Him, He is the Guardian *(Disposer of affairs)* over all things.[102]   No vision can grasp Him while He grasps all visions. He is the Subtle, the Aware.[103]   Now, there have

Clear proofs have come to you, if only you could open your eyes to understand

come to you clear proofs from your Rabb to open your eyes. Therefore, anyone who will open his eyes, it is *good* for his own soul and anyone who will play blind, it is to his own *harm*, I am *a Rasool and has* not *been assigned as* a keeper over you.[104]   Thus do We explain Our revelations over and over again so that *the unbelievers* may say: "You have learned *from someone, but not from Allah*" and that it may become clear to the people of understanding.[105]   Follow what is revealed to you from your Rabb; there is none worthy of worship but He, and turn away from the mushrikeen.[106]   If Allah wanted they would have not committed shirk. We have neither appointed you their keeper nor made you their guardian.[107]   6: [101-107]

Do not insult the deities to whom the mushrikeen offer their worship

O believers, do not insult those, whom these *mushrikeen* call upon besides Allah, lest in retaliation they call bad names to Allah out of their ignorance. Thus We have made the deeds of every group of people seem fair to them. In the end they will all return to their Rabb and then, He will inform them of the reality of all that they have done.[108]   These *mushrikeen* solemnly swear by Allah that if a Sign came to them they would most certainly believe *in your Prophethood.* Say: "All signs are vouchsafed by Allah." What should make you understand that if a sign comes to them they will

Guidance depends on the attitude of individuals

still not believe?[109]   We will turn away their hearts and their eyes *from the Truth because of their attitude* which prompted them to disbelieve in the first place, and We will leave them to wander in their rebellious wrongdoing.[110]   6:[108-110]

JUZ (PART): 8

SECTION: 14

Even if We had sent to them the angels, made the dead speak to them, and presented all the different things of the world before them as proof, they would have not believed, unless Allah wanted otherwise *(and forcing someone to believe is not what He wants)*: Yet, most of them act out of ignorance.[111]   Likewise, We made for each Prophet enemies - shaitâns from among the human beings and Jinns - some of them inspire the others with seductive discourses by way of deception. If your Rabb wanted, they would not have done so. Therefore, leave them and that which they invent,[112]   so that the hearts of those who do not believe in the hereafter may be inclined to what they say, and be pleased with it; so that they can earn what they wish to earn.[113]   *Say:* "Should I seek a judge other than Allah, when He is the One Who has revealed this Book *(The Qur'an)* with full details?" Those whom We gave the Book, *before you,* know very well that it is revealed to you from your Rabb with the Truth; therefore, you should not be of those who have doubts.[114]   The Words of your Rabb have been completed with credibility and justice; there is no way to change His Words. He is the All-Hearing, the All-Knowing.[115]

6:[111-115]

All Rasools of Allah had opposition from Shaitân and his followers

If you obey *(other than Allah and His Rasool, then you should know that)* most of the people on earth, will lead you away from the Way of Allah, for they follow nothing but guesswork and preach nothing but falsehood.[116]   In fact, your Rabb knows best those people who have strayed from His Way and He knows best those who are Rightly Guided.[117]   So eat of that *meat* on which Allah's name has been pronounced if you truly believe in His revelations.[118]   Why should you not eat that on which Allah's name has been pronounced, when He has clearly spelled out for you in detail what is forbidden - except in case you are compelled? In fact, many do mislead *people* by their low desires without knowledge. Your Rabb knows best those who transgress.[119]   Eschew all sin whether open or secret: surely, those who earn sin will soon get due punishment for their wrongdoing.[120]   Do not eat of that *meat* on which Allah's name has not been pronounced, since that is most surely a transgression. In fact, shaitâns inspire their friends that they should argue with you, and if you obey them, most surely, you will become mushrikeen.[121]

6:[116-121]

Eat only that meat on which Allah's name has been pronounced

SECTION: 15

When good and bad are treated alike, criminals are appointed as their ringleaders

Can a person who was dead *(ignorant),* and whom We raised to life and gave the Light to walk with among people, be like the one who is in the depths of darkness from which he can never come out? *Since they treat both of them alike,* the actions of the unbelievers seem pleasing to them,[122]　and thus, in every town, We have placed the criminals as their ring leaders to plot therein; they plot against none but their own souls, though they do not perceive it.[123]　Whenever there comes to them a sign *(from Allah)* they say: "We shall not believe until we are given directly that which is given to the Rasools of Allah." Allah knows best with whom to entrust His Message. Soon these criminals will be overtaken by humiliation and by a severe punishment from Allah for their evil plots.[124]　　　　6:[122-124]

Whomever Allah wants to guide, He opens up his chest to Islam

Whomever Allah wills to guide, He opens his chest to Islam and whomever He intends to send astray *(as a result of their arrogance and persistence in sin)*, He makes his chest narrow and constricted that, *at the very idea of Islam,* he feels as if *his soul* were climbing into the sky. That is how Allah places abomination on those who do not believe.[125]　This *(Al-Islam)* is the Way of your Rabb, the straight way: We have spelled out Our revelations for the people who reflect *(use their common sense).*[126]　For them, there will be a home of peace with their Rabb. He will be their protector because of their good deeds.[127]　　　　6:[125-127]

Jinns, and human beings who are misled by them, will all be cast into hell

On the Day when He will assemble them all together, *(Allah will address the Jinns)*: "O assembly of Jinns! You seduced mankind in great numbers." And their votaries from among mankind will say: "Our Rabb, we have both enjoyed each other's fellowship but *alas!* Now we have reached the end of our term which You had decreed for us." Then *Allah* will say: "Now hellfire is your dwelling-place; you will live therein forever unless Allah ordains otherwise." Surely, your Rabb is All-Wise, All-Knowing.[128]　Thus We make wrongdoers the comrades of one another on account of what they used to earn.[129]　　　　6:[128-129]

SECTION: 16

At that time Allah will also ask: "O Assembly of Jinns and mankind! Did not there come to you Rasools from amongst you who proclaimed to you My revelations and warned you about the meeting of this Day?" They will reply: "*Yes they did,* We bear witness against our own souls." Today, this worldly life has deceived them, but on that Day they will testify against their own souls that they were indeed unbelievers.[130]   That is because your Rabb would not destroy towns without just cause while their residents were unaware.[131]   All will be awarded ranks according to their deeds, and your Rabb is not unaware of what they do.[132] Your Rabb is Self-Sufficient, Lord of Mercy. If He wants, He can destroy you all and replace you with others as He pleases, just as He raised you from the offspring of other people.[133]   Surely, what you are being threatened with, must come to pass and you can do nothing to frustrate it.[134]   *O Muhammad,* tell them: "O my people! *If you don't listen to me,* do whatever you want and I'll do whatever I deem right; you will soon find out who is to gain the reward of the hereafter; rest assured that the wrongdoers will not get salvation." [135]

6:[130-135]

On the Day of Judgment unbelievers will confess that they were indeed unbelievers

   They set aside a share from that which Allah has created of their produce and of their cattle, saying: "This is for Allah" - so they pretend - "and this is for our shorakâ' *(deities that they assigned as partners of Allah)*." Their shorakâ's share does not reach Allah, but the share of Allah is given to shorakâ'. Evil is their judgement![136] Their shorakâ' have induced many mushrikeen to kill their own children in order to ruin them and confuse them in their religion. If Allah wanted, they would not have done so. Therefore, leave them and what they invent.[137]   These *mushrikeen* say that such and such cattle and crops are reserved, *in the name of such and such temple,* and no one should eat except those whom we permit - in fact, *these restrictions* they themselves have imposed. Then there are some animals which they have prohibited from riding or carrying loads, and there are still other animals over which they do not pronounce the name of Allah. They have falsely attributed *all these things* to Him. Soon He will punish them for what they have been inventing.[138]   They also say: "What is in the wombs of these cattle is specially reserved for our males and forbidden to our females but if it is stillborn then all can share." He will punish them for their attribution *of such superstitions to Allah.* Surely, He is All-Wise, All-Knowing.[139]   Actual losers are those who kill their own children foolishly without knowledge and forbid food which Allah has provided them, falsely ascribing prohibitions to Allah. Certainly they have gone astray and are not at all rightly guided.[140]

6:[136-140]

Mushrikeen give their deities preference over Allah

Mushrikeen falsely attribute their self-imposed prohibitions to Allah

SECTION: 17

Give Zakah of agriculture on the harvest day

It is He who has created all kinds of plants, trellised and untrellised, palm trees, field crops with produce of different kinds, olive trees and pomegranates, similar in kind yet, different in verity. Eat of their fruit they ripen and give away its due *(the rights of poor and needy - Zakah)* on the day of its harvest. Do not be extravagant, surely, He does not love the extravagant.[141] Of the animals you have, some are for transportation and some are small *(for consumption)*. Eat of that which Allah has provided for you and do not follow the footsteps of Shaitân; surely, he is your open enemy.[142]   6:[141-142]

Falsely attributed prohibition of livestock are clarified

Take eight *heads of cattle*, in pair (male and female): a pair of sheep and a pair of goats, *for example, and* ask them, "Of these, has He forbidden you the males, females or what is contained in the wombs of the females? Answer me based on knowledge, *not superstition,* if what you say is true."[143] *Likewise ask them* about a pair of camels and a pair of cows, "Of these, has He forbidden you the males, females or what is contained in the wombs of the females?" *If they answer, then ask them:* "Were you present when Allah gave you these commandments?" *If not, then* Who can be more unjust than the one who forges a lie against Allah, so that he may mislead mankind without having any knowledge? Surely, Allah does not guide the unjust people.[144]   6:[143-144]

SECTION: 18

Correct prohibitions of livestock are spelled out

O Muhammad tell them: "I did not find in what has been revealed to me anything forbidden to be eaten by one who wishes to eat it, except the meat of an already dead animal, or running blood or the flesh of swine *(pig meat)* - for these are unclean - or profane meat on which a name other than Allah has been invoked." Even so, if anyone is forced by extreme necessity, intending neither disobedience nor transgression, you will find your Rabb Forgiving, Merciful.[145] For those who are Jews, We forbade every animal with undivided hoofs and the fat of oxen and sheep except what is

Explanation of the Jewish prohibitions of live stock

attached to their backs or their intestines or is mixed with their bones. That was the punishment which was awarded for their wilful disobedience. Indeed, what We said is true.[146] Now if they disbelieve you, say: "Your Rabb is the owner of boundless Mercy; but His scourge cannot be averted from criminal people.[147]
     6:[145-147]

In response to this, the mushrikeen will promptly say: "If Allah wanted, neither we nor our forefathers would have committed shirk, or could have made anything unlawful." That is how their ancestors rejected the truth *in the past* until they tasted Our punishment. *If they say so, then* ask them: "Do you have any evidence that you can put before us? *The fact of the matter is,* you believe in nothing but conjecture and follow nothing but falsehood."[148]   Say: *"In contrast to your position,* Allah's argument is conclusive; if it had been His will He could indeed have guided you all."[149]   Say: "Bring your witnesses to prove that Allah did forbid so and so." Even if they so testify, do not testify with them, nor yield to the wishes of those who deny Our revelations, disbelieve in the hereafter and set up others as equals with their Rabb.[150]

6:[148-150]

> The mushrikeen's excuse for being mushrikeen

SECTION: 19

O Muhammad, say: "Come, I will recite what your Rabb has forbidden to you: not to commit shirk with Him, be kind to your parents, not to kill your children making the excuse of the inability to support them - We provide sustenance for you and for them - not to commit shameful deeds whether open or secret, and not to kill any soul forbidden by Allah except for *the requirements of* justice. These are the things which He enjoined you so that you may use reason.[151]   *Furthermore, your Rabb has forbidden you* not to go near the property of an orphan except to improve it, until he attains maturity; *and has commanded you* to give full measure and just weight - We never charge a soul with more than it can bear; and whenever you speak, be just, even if it affects your own relatives, and fulfill your covenant with Allah. These are the things which He has enjoined on you so that you may be mindful.[152]   *He has also said:* Verily, this is My way, the Right Way; therefore follow it and do not follow other ways, for they will lead you away from His way. This is what He enjoined on you so that you may become righteous.[153]   Moreover, *He said,* We gave Musa *(Moses)* the Book to complete Our favor on those who would do good; it contained details of all things, and was a guidance and a mercy, so that they should believe in the *ultimate* meeting with their Rabb."[154]

6:[151-154]

> In Islam, forbidden things are based on fundamental moral principles

SECTION: 20

We have revealed this Book, *similar to the Book given to Musa,* as a blessing; therefore, follow it and adopt a Godfearing attitude so that you may receive mercy.[155]   Lest you say: "The

> The Book of Allah has come to you for guidance so

that there may be no excuse about the true Word of Allah

Those who divide religion into sects are not Muslims

Declare: "My Salah, my devotion, my life and my death are all for Allah."

Book was revealed to two parties before us and we were unaware of what they read,"[156]   or lest you say: "If the Book had been revealed to us, we could have followed its guidance better than them;" a veritable sign has now come to you from your Rabb as guidance and mercy. Who then is more unjust than the one who denies the revelations of Allah and turns away from them? Very soon those who turn away from Our revelations will face dreadful punishment for their aversion.[157]   Are they waiting for anything other than that the angels or your Rabb should come to them or are they waiting to be given a certain sign of your Rabb! On the Day when that certain sign of your Rabb appears, the belief will not profit that soul which did not believe before nor earned any good deeds through its faith. Say to them: "Wait if you will; we too are waiting."[158]   6:[155-158]

Surely, those who divide their religion and break up into sects *(and identify themselves as a sect)*, *O Muhammad,* you have nothing to do with them. Their case will be called to account by Allah Himself; He will inform them as to what they did.[159] Whoever does one good deed will be given credit for ten similar good deeds, and whoever does one bad deed will be punished for only one; and no one will be treated unjustly.[160]   6:[159-160]

O Muhammad, tell them: "As for me, surely, my Rabb has guided me to the Right Way, the ever true Deen, the faith of Ibrâheem *(Abraham),* the upright, who was not of the mushrikeen."[161]   Also say: "Surely, my Salah, my sacrifices, my life, and my death are all for Allah, the Rabb of the Worlds.[162]   He has no partner; thus I am commanded, and I am the first of the Muslims."[163]   Say: "Should I seek another Rabb besides Allah when He is the Rabb of everything?" Every soul will reap the fruits of its own deeds; no bearer of burdens shall bear the burden of another. Ultimately you will return to your Rabb, and He will resolve for you your disputes.[164]   He is the One Who has made you the inheritors of the earth and raised some of you in ranks over others so that He may test you in what He has given you. Surely, your Rabb is swift in retribution; yet, He is also very Forgiving, Merciful."[165]

6:[161-165]

7: AL-A'RÂF

Period of Revelation

The period of its revelation is about the same as that of Al-An'âm, the last year of the Prophet's residence at Makkah, but it cannot be asserted with certainty which of these two was revealed earlier.

Major Issues, Divine Laws and Guidance

* An invitation to the People of the Book (Jews and Christians) to become Muslims.
* A warning is given to the unbelievers about the consequences of their denial through citing the example of punishments which were inflicted upon former people for their wrong attitude towards their Rasools.
* The Jews are warned about the consequences of their hypocritical conduct towards the Prophets.
* Commandment to propagate the message of Islam with wisdom.
* The Rasools as well as the people to whom they are sent will be questioned on the Day of Judgement.
* Commandment to the Believers that they should wear decent and proper dress, and eat pure and good food.
* Dialogue between the residents of paradise, the inmates of hell and the people of A'râf (heights between Paradise and Hell).
* Affluence and adversity are reminders from Allah.
* Muhammad (peace be upon him) is the Rasool for the whole of mankind.
* The fact that the advent of Muhammad (peace be upon him) was described in Torah and the Gospel (Bible).
* The fact that the Jews have fabricated a wrong belief about Allah's forgiveness.
* Mankind's testimony about Allah at the time of Adam's creation.
* Allah created all of mankind from a single soul.
* Allah's commandment to show forgiveness, speak for justice and avoid the ignorant.
* Allah's commandment about listening to the recitation of the Qur'an with complete silence.

The principal subject of this Sûrah is an invitation to the Divine Message sent down to Muhammad (peace be upon him). The Messenger had spent thirteen long years admonishing the people of Makkah without any tangible results, because they had turned a deaf ear to his message and had become so antagonistic that Allah was about to command the Prophet to leave them alone, migrate and turn to other people. That is why they are being admonished to accept the message and a warning is given about the consequences of their wrong attitude. Now that the Prophet was about to receive Allah's commandment to migrate from Makkah, the concluding portion of the address has been directed towards the People of the Book with whom he was going to come into contact at Madinah. During the course of the address to the Jews, the consequence of their hypocritical attitude towards the Prophets is also pointed out clearly, for they professed to believe in Prophet Musa (Moses) but their practices were opposed to his teachings. They were not only disobeying him but were in fact worshipping falsehood.

At the end of the Sûrah, instructions are given to the Prophet and his followers to show patience and exercise restraint in answer to the provocations of their opponents. Since the believers were under pressure and stress, they are advised to be very careful and not to take any step that might harm their cause.

7: AL-A'RÂF

This Sûrah, revealed at Makkah, has 24 sections and 206 verses.

In the name of Allah, the Compassionate, the Merciful

SECTION: 1

Alif L'âm M'eem Sâd.[1] This Book is revealed to you; let there be no discomfort in your heart about it, so that you may thereby warn *the unbelievers* and remind the believers.[2] *Say: "O people,* follow what has been brought down to you from your Rabb and do not follow other patrons besides Him." *Yet,* little do you take admonition.[3]   How many towns have We destroyed *for their sins?* Our scourge took them all of a sudden at night or while they were taking their afternoon rest;[4] and when our scourge fell upon them, their only cry was: "We have indeed been wrongdoers."[5] *On the Day of Judgment,* We shall question those to whom Rasools were sent and We shall also question the Rasools *about Our message and its response.*[6] Then We shall tell their whole story as an eye witness, for We were never absent *at any time or from any place.*[7]   On that Day, the scale of justice shall be established. Those whose scale of good deeds will be heavy, they are the ones who will attain felicity,[8] and those whose scale is light, they shall find themselves in loss, for they had done injustice to Our revelations.[9]   We are the One Who established you on earth, and provided you means of your sustenance therein: *yet,* little it is that you pay thanks.[10]   7:[1-10]

The Rasools as well as the people to whom they were sent shall be questioned on the Day of Judgment

The scale of justice shall be established

SECTION: 2

Indeed, We created you, then We fashioned you, then We asked the angels: "Prostrate yourselves before Adam." They all prostrated accordingly except Iblees *(name of Satan - Shaitân)* who did not join those who prostrated.[11] *Allah* said: "What prevented you from prostrating when I commanded you?" He replied: "I am better than he; you created me from fire and him from clay."[12] *Allah* said: "Get down from here. You have no right to brag here of your superiority. Get out, henceforth you are of the petty ones."[13] *Shaitân* requested: "Give me respite till the Day of Resurrection."[14]   *Allah* said: "The respite *you requested* is hereby granted."[15]   *Shaitân* said: "Since You let me deviate, now I will lie in ambush for mankind on Your Right Way.[16] I Will come upon them from their front, from their rear, from their right, and from their left, and You will not find most of them grateful *to*

The story of Adam and Iblees (Shaitân)

Shaitân vowed to mislead Adam and his descendants

You."[17]   *Allah* said: "Get out from here, despicable and outcast; I will certainly fill hell with you and all of them who follow you."[18]

7:[11-18]

Allah said: "O Adam! Dwell with your wife in paradise and eat any fruit you please; but never approach this tree or you shall both become wrongdoers."[19]   But Shaitân tempted them so that he might reveal to them the private parts of their bodies which they had never seen before. He told them: "Your Rabb has forbidden you to approach this tree only to prevent you from becoming angels or immortals."[20]   And he swore to them both: "I am your sincere adviser."[21]   Thus he cunningly seduced them, and when they ate from the tree, their shame became visible to them and they began to cover themselves with the leaves of the garden. Then their Rabb called out to them: "Did I not forbid you to approach that tree, and did I not warn you that Shaitân was your open enemy?"[22]   They both replied: "Our Rabb! We have wronged our souls. If You do not forgive us and have mercy on us, we shall certainly be of the losers."[23]   *Allah* said: "Go down, some of you are the enemy of others. The Earth will be your dwelling-place and your means of livelihood for a fixed term."[24]   He further said: "Therein you shall live, therein you shall die, and therefrom you shall be raised to life *on the Day of Resurrection*."[25]   7:[19-25]

SECTION: 3

O children of Adam! We have sent down to you clothing to cover your nakedness and as an adornment, however, the best clothing is the clothing of piety. This is one of Allah's revelations so that the people may learn a lesson.[26]   O children of Adam! Let not Shaitân seduce you in the same manner as *he seduced* your parents out of paradise through stripping them of their clothing in order to expose their nakedness. He and his tribe can see you from where you cannot see them. We have made the shaitâns allies to those who do not believe.[27]   Whenever they commit a shameful deed, they say: "We found our forefathers doing this and Allah Himself has commanded us to do so." Tell them: "Nay! Allah never commands what is shameful. Do you attribute to Allah something about which you have no knowledge?"[28]   *O Muhammad,* say to them: "My Rabb has commanded justice and that you set your faces in the right direction at the time of every prayer and call on Him with true devotion. You shall return to Him as He created you in the beginning."[29]   One group He has guided while the other group deserved to be left in error *due to their own choice*; for they took

Shaitân cunningly seduced Adam and Eve to disobey Allah

Their repentance and Allah's conditional acceptance

Children of Adam are warned not to fall into the trap of Shaitân like Adam

Allah never commands what is shameful

the shaitâns for their protectors instead of Allah; yet, they think that they are rightly guided.[30]   O Children of Adam! Put on your adornment *(proper and decent dress)* when you attend your Masjid *at the time of every prayer*. Eat and drink, but do not be extravagant; surely, He does not love the extravagant.[31]   7:[26-31]

SECTION: 4

O Muhammad, ask them: "Who has forbidden you to wear decent clothes or to eat the good food which Allah has provided for His devotees?" Say: "All these things are for the enjoyment of the believers in the life of this world *though shared by others*; but these shall be exclusively theirs on the Day of Resurrection. Thus do We make Our revelations clear for those who have knowledge."[32] Say: "My Rabb has forbidden all indecencies whether open or secret, sin and rebellion against justice, committing shirk with Allah for which He has granted no sanction, and saying things about Allah of which you have no knowledge.[33]   For every nation there is a fixed term; when their term expires, it can neither be delayed for a moment nor can it be made to come early."[34]
7:[32-34]

Command of Allah to wear proper and decent dress and eat good food

O children of Adam! Whenever there come to you Rasools from among you and recite to you My revelations, those who will become righteous and mend their ways will have nothing to fear or to grieve;[35]   but those who deny Our revelations and treat them with arrogance, shall be the inmates of hellfire to live therein forever.[36]   Who can be more unjust than the one who invents a lie against Allah or rejects His revelations? Such people will have their destined portion from the Book (*what was written for them to receive during their life on earth*); until when Our messengers *(angels)* arrive to take away their souls, they will ask: "Where are those gods whom you used to invoke besides Allah?" They will reply: "They have forsaken us" and they will bear witness against themselves *(admit)* that they were indeed kuffâr *(unbelievers)*.[37] *Allah* will say: "Enter the fire and join the nations of Jinns and men who have gone before you." As each nation will enter hell, it will curse its preceding sister till all are gathered there, the last of them will say about the first one: "Our Rabb! These have led us astray; therefore, give them double punishment of the fire." He will answer: "There will be double for all, although you may not know *because of being predecessor or successor in sin and aggression.*"[38]   Then the first will say to the last: "*If we were to blame,*

Children of Adam are directed to follow the Guidance of Allah provided to them through His Rasools

you too, were no better than us; now taste the punishment of your misdeeds."[39]   7:[35-39]

The gates of heaven shall not be opened for the disbelievers

Surely, the gates of Heaven will not be opened for those who deny Our revelations and treat them with arrogance; their admission into paradise will be as impossible as the passing of a camel through the eye of a needle. That is how We shall reward the criminals.[40]   Hell shall be their bed and flames shall be their covering. That is how We shall reward the wrongdoers.[41]

7:[40-41]

Only believers shall enter paradise

As for those who believe and do good deeds - We never burden a soul with more than it can bear - they are worthy of Paradise, wherein they will live forever.[42]   We shall remove whatever ill-feeling they may have in their hearts against one another. Rivers will be flowing beneath them; and they will say: "Praise be to Allah Who guided us this way; we would have never found the Right Way if Allah had not guided us. The Rasools of our Rabb have surely preached us the truth." *At that time* they will hear the announcement: "This is paradise, which you have inherited because of your good deeds."[43]   7:[42-43]

Dialogue between the residents of paradise and the inmates of hell

The residents of paradise will call out to the inmates of the hellfire: "We have indeed found out the promises of our Rabb to be true; have you, also, found the promise of your Rabb to be true?" "Yes," they will answer, and a herald in-between them will proclaim, "the curse of Allah be upon those wrongdoers[44]   who hindered other people from the Way of Allah and sought to make it crooked, and who did not believe in the hereafter."[45]   Between the two, there shall be a veil, and on the A'râf *(heights)* there will be people who will recognize them by their features. They will call out to the residents of Paradise: "Peace be upon you!" They will not have yet entered it, though they will have the hope."[46]   When their eyes will be turned towards the inmates of the hellfire, they will say: "Our Rabb! Do not cast us among these wrongdoers."[47]

7:[44-47]

Dialogue between the people of A'râf and the inmates of hell

The people of the A'râf *(heights)* will call to certain men *(famous personalities from among the inmates of Hell)* whom they will recognize by their features and say: "*Have you found out that* neither your riches nor your arrogant pride have availed you?[48]

Are these *residents of paradise* not the same people about whom you swore that Allah will never bestow His mercy on them?" *Today the same people are being welcomed with the words*, "Enter paradise, you have nothing to fear or to grieve."[49]   Then the inmates of the fire will cry out to the residents of paradise: "Give us some water or some of the food which Allah has provided you." They will reply: "Allah has prohibited both of these things to the unbelievers,[50] who took their religion to be mere amusement and play, and were deceived by their earthly life." *Allah* will say: "Today We will forget them as they forgot the meeting of this Day and rejected Our revelations."[51]   For We have certainly brought them a Book which We have detailed with knowledge, a guidance and blessing for the true believers.[52]   Now are they waiting for its fulfillment *(Day of Judgment)*? On the Day when it is fulfilled, those who have disregarded it, will say: "Indeed the Rasools of our Rabb had come with the truth. Are there any intercessors now, who could intercede on our behalf? Or could we be sent back so that we would not do as we have done before." In fact, they would have lost their souls and the things they had invented will leave them in the lurch.[53]   7:[48-53]

> Inmates of hell shall beg for water and food from the residents of paradise

SECTION: 7

Surely, your Rabb is Allah Who created the heavens and the earth in six Yaums *(days, time periods or stages)* and then established *Himself* on the Throne *in a manner that suits His Majesty*. He makes the night cover the day and the day follow the night in rapid succession. *He created* the sun, the moon and the stars, and made them subservient to His will. *Take a note*: His is the creation, and His is the command. Blessed be Allah, the Rabb of the worlds![54]   Call on your Rabb with humility and in private; for He does not love the transgressors.[55]   Do not create mischief in the land after it has been set in order. Pray to Him in humility and privacy. Surely, the mercy of Allah is always close to the doers of good.[56]   He is the One Who sends the winds bearing good news of His blessings, so when they lift up heavy clouds, We drive them along to a dead land and make the rain fall upon it and bring forth all kinds of fruits *from the same dead land*. Likewise We will raise the dead to life; *this example is given* so that you may learn a lesson *from this observation*.[57]   The good soil yields rich produce by the permission of Allah and barren soil yields nothing but poor produce. Thus do We explain Our revelations over and over again for those who pay thanks.[58]   7:[54-58]

> Allah is the One Who created this universe

> Pray to Allah with fear and hope

SECTION: 8

Indeed, We sent Nûh to his people, and he said: "O my people! Worship Allah, you have no god but He. *If you do not listen to what I say,* I fear for you the punishment of a Mighty Day."[59] The chiefs of his people said: "Surely, we see that you are in evident error."[60]   He replied: "O my people! I am not in error; on the contrary, I am a Rasool from the Rabb of the worlds.[61]   I am appointed to deliver the message of my Rabb and give you friendly advice, for I know from Allah something that you do not know.[62] Do you wonder that there has come to you a message from your Rabb through a man from among yourselves to warn you, so that you may fear Allah in order to receive His mercy?"[63]   But they denied him; as a result, We saved him and all who were with him in the ark, and drowned those who denied Our revelations. Surely, they were a blind people.[64]   7:[59-64]

SECTION: 9

To the people of 'Âd, *We sent* their brother Hûd, who said: "O my people! Worship Allah! You have no god but He. Will you not fear Him?"[65] The chiefs of his people who denied his message said: "We can see that you are foolish and we think that you are lying."[66]   He replied: "O my people! I am not foolish; on the contrary, I am a Rasool from the Rabb of the worlds.[67]   I am conveying the message of my Rabb to you, and I am an honest adviser to you.[68]   Do you wonder that a reminder from your Rabb has come to you through one of your own men to warn you? Remember that He made you successors after the people of Nûh and gave you a tall and strong stature as compared to other people. Therefore, remember the favors that you have received from Allah, so that you may prosper."[69] They replied: "Have you come to us *with the demand* that we should worship Allah Alone and give up those whom our forefathers used to worship? Well, bring us what you are threatening us with if what you say is true!"[70]   *Hûd* said: "You have already incurred the blight and wrath of your Rabb. Would you dispute with me about mere names which you and your forefathers have invented, and for which Allah has revealed no sanction? If so then wait *for the decision of Allah*, I too will wait with you."[71]   We saved him and his companions by Our mercy and We cut off the roots of those who denied Our revelations and did not become believers.[72]   7:[65-72]

SECTION: 10

To the people of Thamûd, *We sent* their brother Sâleh, who said: "O my people! Worship Allah; you have no other god but He. Now a clear proof has come to you from your Rabb; here is Allah's she-camel as a sign for you; therefore, leave her alone to pasture on Allah's land and do not touch her with bad intentions, lest you incur a painful punishment.[73]   Remember how you were made the heirs of 'Ad and settled in the land, capable of building mansions in the valleys and carving out homes in the mountains. Therefore, remember the favors of Allah and do not spread mischief in the land."[74]   The arrogant leaders from his people asked the oppressed among them who had believed: "Do you really believe that Sâleh is a Rasool from his Rabb?" They replied: "We do indeed believe in the revelation with which he has been sent."[75] The arrogant, *who considered themselves superior,* said: "We deny all that you believe in."[76]   Then they hamstrung the she-camel, defied the commandment of their Rabb and *challenged* Sâleh saying: "Bring down the scourge you have threatened us with, if you truly are one of the Rasools."[77]   Thereupon, an earthquake overtook them and they became lifeless bodies in their homes with their faces down.[78]   *Sâleh* left them saying: "O my people! I did indeed convey to you the message of my Rabb and gave you sincere advice but you did not love sincere advisers."[79]

7:[73-79]

We also sent Lût, who said to his people: "Will you do such indecent acts as no one else in the world has committed before you?[80]   You satisfy your lust with men *(homosexuality)* instead of women. Indeed you are a people who have transgressed beyond bounds."[81]   His people had no answer but to say: "Drive them out of your town; these people want to keep themselves pure!"[82]   So We saved him and his family except his wife, who was of those who lagged behind.[83]   We rained upon them a rain of stones *and every one was killed*; see what was the outcome for such criminals.[84]

7:[80-84]

SECTION: 11

To Madyan, *We sent* their brother Shu'aib, who said: "O my people! Worship Allah, you have no god but He. A clear guidance has come to you from your Rabb. Give just measure and weight, do not undersell others in their goods, and do not create mischief in the land after it has been set in order; this is better for

---

The Prophet Sâleh's address to his people, their disbelief and their fate

The Prophet Lût's address to his people, their disbelief and their fate

The Prophet Shu'aib's address to his people, their disbelief and their fate

you if you are *true* believers.[85] Do not sit in ambush on every road to threaten people and hinder from the Way of Allah those who believe in Him, seeking to make His Way crooked. Remember how He multiplied you when you were few in number and see what was the end of the mischief-makers *of prior nations*.[86] If there are some among you who believe in the message with which I have been sent and others who disbelieve it, then be patient until Allah judges between us, for He is the best of all judges."[87]

7:[85-87]

JUZ (PART): 9

The arrogant proud leaders of his people said: "O Shu'aib! We shall certainly drive you and your fellow believers out of our town or you will have to return back to our religion." He replied: "What! *Even it be* against our will?[88]   We would indeed forged a lie against Allah if we return to your religion after Allah has rescued us therefrom. It is not possible for us to return to it unless Allah, our Rabb, wants us to. Our Rabb has vast knowledge of everything. We put our trust in Allah." *Then they prayed:* "Our Rabb! Decide between us and our people with justice, for you are the best of judges."[89]   The leaders who disbelieved from among his people said: "If you follow *Shu'aib,* you shall indeed be losers!"[90]   Thereupon an earthquake overtook them and they became lifeless bodies in their homes with their faces down.[91] Those who called Shu'aib a liar were as though they never lived therein; those who called Shu`aib a liar were the actual losers.[92] Shu'aib left them saying: "O my people! I did indeed convey to you the messages of my Rabb and I did give you good advice; how shall I then be sorry for the people who refused to believe?"[93]

7:[88-93]

SECTION: 12

Whenever We sent a Prophet to a town We afflicted its people with poverty and hardship so that they might humble themselves *to Allah.*[94]   Then We changed their bad condition into good fortune till they became very affluent and said: "Our forefathers also had their hardship and affluence." So! We took them by surprise while they were unaware.[95]   Had the residents of the towns believed and feared *Allah,* We would have showered upon them riches from the heavens and the earth, but they disbelieved; so We seized them for their misdeeds.[96]   Do the people of these towns now feel secure against Our punishment coming to them by night while they might be fast asleep?[97]   Or do the people of these towns feel secure against Our punishment coming to them in the forenoon while they are playing around?[98]   Do these people feel secure against the plan of Allah? In fact, no people feel secure against the plan of Allah except those who are doomed to loss.[99]

7:[94-99]

SECTION: 13

Is it not a guiding lesson to those who inherit the earth after its former occupants, that if We please, We can punish them for

---

Behavior of the unbelievers with Prophet Shu'aib

Adversity and affluence are reminders from Allah

Stories of prior nations are narrated to teach a lesson

their sins and seal their hearts so they would not hear?[100]   Those towns whose stories We related to you, *can serve as examples.* Certainly their Rasools came to them with clear signs, but they *persisted in their unbelief and* would not believe what they had denied before. Thus Allah seal the hearts of the unbelievers.[101] We did not find most of them true to their commitments, rather We found that most of them were transgressors.[102]

7:[100-102]

The Prophet Moses was sent for the guidance of Pharaoh and his chiefs

Then after them, We sent Musa *(Moses) with* Our revelations to Fir'aun *(Pharaoh)* and his chiefs but they too treated *Our revelations* unjustly, so see what was the end of those mischief-makers.[103]   Musa said: "O Fir'aun! I am a Rasool from the Rabb of the worlds.[104]   It is not befitting for me to say anything about Allah except the Truth. I have come to you from your Rabb with clear signs; therefore, send the children of Israel with me."[105] *Fir'aun* asked: "If you have come with a sign then produce it, if what you say is true."[106]   So *Musa* threw down his staff and all of a sudden it became a real serpent.[107]   Then he drew out his hand *from his pocket* and it became shining white to all the beholders.[108]

7:[103-108]

SECTION: 14

Moses' confrontation with the magicians of Pharaoh

The chiefs of Fir'aun's people said: "He indeed is a skilled sorcerer[109] who intends to drive you out from your land." *Fir'aun asked:* "So what do you advise?"[110]   They said: "Put him and his brother off for a while; and send heralds to all the cities[111] to summon every skillful sorcerer to you."[112]   The sorcerers came to Fir'aun and said: "We must certainly have some suitable reward if we prevail!"[113]   "Yes," he answered. *"Not only reward but more:* you shall certainly become my favored courtiers."[114]   Then they asked Musa: "Will you throw, or should we be the first ones to throw?"[115]   *Musa* said: "You throw." So when they threw, they bewitched the eyes of the people and terrified them by a display of a mighty sorcery.[116]   We inspired Musa to throw his staff. No sooner did he throw it than *it became a serpent* and began to swallow up the creation of their sorcery![117]   Thus the truth prevailed and all that they did was of no effect.[118]   *Fir'aun and his people* were defeated and put to humiliation,[119]   and the sorcerers, *since they were professionals and knew that it was not sorcery,* fell down in prostration,[120]   saying: "we believe in the Rabb of the worlds,[121]   the Rabb of Musa and Haroon."[122]

Fir'aun said: "How dare you believe in Him without my permission? In fact, this was a plot which you all had planned to drive the people out of their city, but soon you will know *its consequences*.[123] I will have your hands and your feet cut off on opposite sides and then crucify you all."[124]   They answered: "We will surely return to our Rabb.[125]   *Look at your verdict,* you would take revenge on us simply because we believed in the signs of our Rabb when they were shown to us! O our Rabb! Pour upon us patience and make us die as Muslims."[126]   7:[109-126]

SECTION: 15

The chiefs of Fir'aun's *(Pharaoh's)* people asked him: "Will you leave Musa *(Moses)* and his people free to commit mischief in the land and to forsake you and your gods?" He said: "We will put their sons to death and spare their females; we have irresistible power over them."[127]   Musa said to his people: "Seek help from Allah and be patient. The land belongs to Allah. He gives it as a heritage to those of His servants whom He pleases. *You should know that* final success is for the righteous."[128]   They said: "We were oppressed before you came to us and since you have come to us." He replied: "It is quite possible that your Rabb may destroy your enemy and grant you succession in the land; then He will see how you act."[129]   7:[127-129]

Pharaoh's revenge against the people of Moses

SECTION: 16

We afflicted Fir'aun's people with several years of famine and shortages of fruit so that they might come to their senses.[130] But whenever they had good times they said "It is our due," and whenever evil befell them, they ascribed that bad luck to Musa and those with him. Behold! In fact, their misfortune was in the hands of Allah; yet, most of them do not know.[131]   They said *to Musa*: "No matter what sign you may bring us to put your magic spell on us, we are not going to believe in you."[132]   So We plagued them with flood, locusts, lice, frogs and blood: clear-cut signs; yet, they persisted in their arrogance, for they were a criminal people.[133] Every time the plague befell them, they said: "O Musa! Pray for us to your Rabb as He has made the promise with you, if you help remove the plague from us, we shall truly believe in you and send the Children of Israel with you."[134]   But every time We removed the plague from them to a fixed term which they had to reach, lo! They broke their promise.[135]   Therefore, We inflicted retribution

Scourge of Allah against Pharaoh and his chiefs, and their final destruction on them and drowned them in the sea; for they denied Our signs and became heedless of them.[136]   Thus, We made the people who were oppressed, the inheritors of the eastern and western regions of the lands, which We had blessed. Thus the fair promise of your Rabb was fulfilled for the Children of Israel because they had endured with patience; and We levelled to the ground the great works and fine buildings which Fir'aun and his people had erected *with such pride*.[137]   7:[130-137]

Allah rescued the Children of Israel but they still disbelieved in One God

We made the Children of Israel cross the *(Red)* sea. On their way they came across people who were worshipping their idols. They said: "O Musa *(Moses)* fashion for us a god like the gods of these people." He replied: "You are indeed very ignorant people.[138]   What these people are following is doomed to destruction and their deeds are in vain."[139]   He further said: "Should I seek for you a god for worship other than Allah: when it is He who has exalted you above all the worlds.[140]   Remember that We rescued you from the people of Fir'aun *(Pharaoh)*, who subjected you to cruel torment, putting your sons to death and sparing your women and in that *condition of slavery,* there was a great trial from your Rabb.[141]   7:[138-141]

SECTION: 17

Prophet Musa's communication with Allah

We summoned Musa *to the mount of Tûr* for thirty nights and added ten more to complete the term of forty nights for communion with his Rabb. *(Before leaving)* Musa said to his brother Haroon *(Aaron)*: "You will be in my place among my people; set a good example and do not follow the way of mischief-makers."[142]   When Musa came to Our appointed place and his Rabb spoke to him, he asked: "O my Rabb! Show me *Yourself*, that I may look at You." He answered: "You cannot see Me. Look at the mountain; if it remains firm in its place then you will see Me." When his Rabb manifested to the mountain, He crushed it into fine dust and Musa fell down unconscious. When *Musa* recovered, he said: "Glory be to You! I turn to You in repentance and I am the first of the believers."[143]   *Allah* said: "O Musa! I have chosen you from among mankind to deliver My message and to have conversation with Me: so take what I give you and be thankful."[144]

7:[142-144]

We inscribed for him upon tablets all kind of instructions and details of every thing, *concerning all branches of life, and said*:

"Observe these with firmness and enjoin your people to follow them according to the best of their abilities. Soon I shall show you the homes of the transgressors.[145]   I will turn away from My signs those who are unjustly arrogant in the land, so that even if they see each and every sign they will not believe in it. If they see the Right Way before them, they will not follow it; but if they see a crooked way, they will follow it; this is because they denied Our revelations and were heedless of them.[146]   Those who deny Our signs and the meeting of the Hereafter, their deeds are null. Should they be rewarded but for what they have done?"[147]   7:[145-147]

SECTION: 18

        In his absence, the people of Musa *(Moses) made* an image of a calf *for worship* from their jewelry which produced a mooing sound. Did they not see that it could neither speak to them nor give them guidance? Yet, they took it *for worship* and became wrongdoers.[148]   When they felt ashamed about what they had done and realized that they had gone astray, they said: "If our Rabb does not have mercy on us and pardon us, we shall become losers."[149] When Musa came back to his people, he was extremely angry and sorrowful, and he said: "What an evil thing you have done in my absence! Have you tried to hasten the matter of your Rabb?" He put down the *Holy* Tablets and seized his brother by *the hair of* his head and dragged him closer. *Haroon (Aaron)* cried: "O son of my mother! The people overpowered me and almost killed me; do not make my enemies happy over me and do not count me among the wrongdoers."[150]   *At this Musa* said: "O Rabb! Forgive me and my brother! And admit us to Your mercy, for You are the Most Merciful of all."[151]   7:[148-151]

SECTION: 19

        Those who worshipped the calf did indeed incur the wrath of their Rabb and disgrace in this life; thus do We recompense those who invent falsehoods.[152]   As for those who do evil deeds, then repent and become true believers thereafter, your Rabb is most surely, the Forgiving, Merciful.[153]   When Musa's anger calmed down, he took up the *Holy* Tablets in whose writing there was guidance and mercy for those that fear their Rabb.[154]   Musa chose seventy men from his people *to accompany him* to Our place of meeting. On their way when they were seized by a violent earthquake, he said: "O my Rabb! Had it been Your will, You could have

Musa was given the written tablets of Tawrât (Torah)

Arrogant people cannot get guidance

Israelites started worshipping the calf after witnessing their miraculous deliverance

Worshippers of the calf incurred the wrath of Allah

destroyed them and me long ago. Would You destroy us for the offense committed by some fools among us? That trial was or-dained by You, to let go astray whom You willed and to guide whom You pleased. You are our Guardian, therefore, forgive us and have mercy on us; for You are the best of all forgivers![155]   *O Allah* ordain for us what is good in this life and in the Hereafter, surely, we have turned to You." He replied: "I will inflict My punishment upon whom I please; yet, My mercy encompasses everything. I will ordain *special mercy* for those who are righteous, who pay Zakah *(obligatory charity)* and who believe in Our revelations." [156]   7:[152-156]

The advent of the Prophet Muhammad was described in Torah and Gospel

Those who follow the Rasool, the unlettered Prophet *(Muhammad)* - whom they shall find described in the Tawrât *(Torah)* and the Injeel *(Gospel)*. Who enjoins them what is good and forbids what is evil; who makes pure things halâl *(lawful)* for them and impure things harâm *(unlawful)*; who relieves them from their heavy burdens and from the yokes that were around their necks. Therefore, those who believe in him, honor him, help him, and follow the Light which is sent down with him, will be the ones who will be successful."[157]   7:[157]

SECTION: 20

Muhammad is the Prophet for all of mankind

O Muhammad, say: "O mankind! I am the Rasool of Allah towards all of you, *from the One* to whom belongs the kingdom of the heavens and the earth. There is no deity but Him. He brings to life and causes to die. Therefore, believe in Allah and His Rasool, the unlettered Prophet *(Muhammad)* who believes in Allah and His Word. Follow him so that you may be rightly guided."[158]

7:[158]

Allah provided food and water in the desert to the people of Musa

From among the people of Musa *(Moses)* there were some who guided others with the truth and thereby established justice.[159] We divided them into twelve tribes, as nations; and when his *thirsty* people asked him for water, We revealed to Musa: "Strike the rock with your staff." Thereupon, twelve springs gushed out from the rock, each tribe was specified its drinking place. We caused the clouds to cast shadow over them and sent down to them mannâ *(sweet dish)* and salwâ *(quail's meat)* for their food, *saying*: "Eat of the pure things We have provided for you," *but they rebelled and by doing so* they did Us no harm but they harmed their own souls.[160]   When it was said to them: "Reside in this town and eat therein wherever you wish and say 'Hittatun' *(forgive us)* and enter the gate in a posture of humility; We will forgive you your sins and increase all the more the reward for such righteous people."[161] But the wicked among them changed that word which was said to them. As a result, We sent down a scourge upon them from heaven for their wrong doings.[162]   7:[159-162]

SECTION: 21

Ask them, about the town which was situated on the sea shore, *what happened* when they transgressed in the matter of Sabbath. On the day of their Sabbath the fish appeared before them on the surface of the water but on the days other than their Sabbath they never came near them; thus did We test them because they transgressed.[163]   *Also remind them about the conversation among some of them,* when some of them asked: "Why do you admonish people whom Allah will destroy or sternly punish?" They replied: "To be able to offer an excuse before our Rabb *that we did discharge our duty,* and also in the hope that they may refrain from His disobedience."[164]   However, when they disregarded the reminder, We delivered those who forbade evil and We overtook those who were wrongdoers with stern punishment because of their transgression.[165]   But when after that they exceeded the limits of what they were prohibited, We said to them: "Be detested apes."[166] *Also remind them* when your Rabb declared that He would raise against them others who would afflict them with grievous torment till the Day of Resurrection. Swift is the retribution of your Rabb, yet, He is also the Oft-Forgiving, Most Merciful.[167]   We *broke their unity as a nation and* dispersed them into different communities all over the earth - some of them are righteous and others are the opposite - We tested them with both blessings and misfortunes so that they might turn *to the Right Way.*[168]   7:[163-168]

Jews' test on the day of Sabbath

Jews' violation of Sabbath and Allah's scourge

Then they were succeeded by an evil generation who inherited the Book; they indulged in the vanities of this nether life, saying: "We expect to be forgiven" *assuming that they are favorites of Allah and somehow He will spare them.* Yet, if similar vanities come their way they would again seize them. Was not a covenant taken from them in the Book that they would not speak anything about Allah except the truth? And they have studied what is in *the Book.* Best for the righteous is the home of the hereafter, don't you understand?[169]   As for those who strictly observe the Book and establish Salah *(prayer)*, surely, We never let the reward

Jews' wrong belief about Allah's forgiveness

of such reformers go waste.[170]   Remember when We suspended the mountain over them as though it was an umbrella and they feared it was going to fall on them *and We said*: "Hold firmly to *the Book* that We have given you and be mindful of what is in it, so that you might fear *Allah and obey Him*."[170]   7:[169-171]

SECTION: 22

Mankind's testimony at the time of Adam's creation that Allah is their Rabb

O Prophet, remind mankind about the incident when your Rabb brought into existence the offspring from the loins of Adam and his descendants *(virtually each single individual of mankind)* and made them testify about themselves. *Allah asked them*: "Am I not your Rabb?" They all replied: "Yes! We bear witness that You are." *This We did,* lest you *mankind* should say on the Day of Resurrection: "We were not aware of this fact *that You are our Rabb and that there will be a Day of Judgment*.[172]   or lest you should say: "Our forefathers started the practice of shirk and we just followed, being their descendants. Will you then destroy us on account *of following the sin* committed by those wrongdoers?"[173] Thus do We spell out Our revelations so that they might return *to the Right Way*.[174]   7:[172-174]

Example of those who deny Allah's revelations

Tell them the story of that person to whom We sent our revelations but he turned away from them, As a result, Shaitân persuaded him until he became one of the misguided.[175]   Had it been Our will, We would have exalted him through those *revelations*; but he clung to this earthly life and followed his own desires. His similitude is that of a dog: if you chase it, it lolls out his tongue and if you leave it alone, it still lolls out his tongue. Such are those who deny Our revelations. Tell them these parables, so that they might think over *their behavior to Our revelations*.[176]   Very bad is the example of those people who deny Our revelations and wrong their own souls.[177]   Only he whom Allah guides is rightly guided; and whom He lets go astray, will be the loser.[178]   7:[175-178]

Misguided people are like animals, even worse

Certainly, We have destined many Jinns and human beings for hell; *those are the ones* who have hearts with which they do not understand, they have eyes with which they do not see, they have ears with which they do not hear. They are like animals - or even worse: they are those who are heedless.[179]   Allah has the most beautiful names *(over ninety-nine attributes)*; call on Him by them; and shun those people who use profanity in His Names, such people shall be requited for their misdeeds.[180]　　Among those whom We have created, there are some people who guide others with the truth and establish justice therewith.[181]　　　　　　7:[179-181]

SECTION: 23

　　Those who deny Our revelations, We shall draw them step by step *closer to destruction* in ways that they do not realize,[182] *and even though* I shall grant them respite; My plan is surely strong.[183]　Has it never occurred to them that their companion is not a madman; he is merely a plain Warner.[184]　Have they not pondered over the kingdom of the heavens and the earth　　and whatever Allah has created, and that maybe their hour of death has come closer? In what message after this would they then believe?[185]　None can guide those whom Allah lets go astray and leaves them blundering about in their rebellious transgression.[186] They ask you about the Hour *of Doom* and when it will take place. Say: "Knowledge about it rests only with my Rabb: No one can disclose its proper time except Him. Heavy is its weight in the heavens and the earth. It will not come *gradually* but all of a sudden. They ask you as if you yourself were in search of it. Tell them: "The knowledge about it rests only with Allah though most people do not understand."[187]　*Further,* tell them: "I have no power over any benefit or harm to myself, except what Allah wills. Had I possessed the knowledge of the unseen, I would have acquired many benefits to myself; and no harm would have touched me. I am but a Warner and bearer of good news for the believers."[188]　　7:[182-188]

SECTION: 24

　　He is the one who created you from a single person and from him He created his mate, so that he might find comfort with her. When he covers her, she conceives a light burden and walks around with it. When it grows heavy, they both pray to Allah their Rabb *saying*: "If You will grant us a goodly child, we will be truly thankful."[189]　But when He gives them a goodly child, they both begin to associate partners with Him in what He has given them; but Allah is exalted far above the shirk they commit *of associating other deities with Him as His partners*.[190]　Do they associate with Him those deities who can create nothing but are themselves created![191]　They have neither the ability to help them, nor can they help themselves![192]　If you invite them to guidance they will not follow you. It will be all the same for you whether you call them

Those who deny Allah's revelations are, step by step, drawing closer to destruction

The Prophet himself has no power to benefit anyone or to avert any harm

Allah created all of mankind from a single soul

Reality of those gods whom people worship beside Allah

or hold your peace.[193]   In fact, those whom you call besides Allah are bondmen, like yourselves. Well call them, and let them answer you, if what you say is true![194]   Have they feet to walk with? Have they hands to hold with? Have they eyes to see with? Have they ears to hear with? *O Muhammad,* say: "Call on your shorakâ' *(partners you have set up besides Allah)* and collectively plot against me and give me no respite![195]   My protector is Allah Who has revealed this Book and He is the protecting friend of the righteous.[196]   But those whom you call besides Him have neither the ability to help you, nor can they help themselves.[197]   If you call them to guidance, they cannot even hear *what you say*, and it appears as if they are looking at you, but they do not see.[198]   7:[189-198]

Allah is the Protecting Friend of the righteous

Show forgiveness, enjoin good and avoid the ignorant.[199] If Shaitân tempts you, seek refuge with Allah; for He is the one Who is All-Hearing, All-Knowing.[200]   Those who fear Allah, when they are tempted by Shaitân, they have but to remember Allah and they shall see the light *(right course of action)*![201]   As for their *evil* brothers, they drag them deeper into error and never relax their efforts.[202]   When you, *O Muhammad,* do not bring them a revelation, they say: "Have you not yet invented one?" Tell them: "I follow only what is revealed to me from my Rabb. This Book contains veritable insight from your Rabb, a guidance and a blessing for the true believers."[203]   When the Qur'an is recited, listen to it with full attention so that you may be shown mercy.[204]   Bring your Rabb to remembrance deep in your soul with humility and in reverence without raising your voice, both in the mornings and in the evenings; and be not of those who are heedless.[205]   Surely, those who are near your Rabb *(the angels)* are never too proud to worship Him; they declare His glory and prostrate themselves before Him.[206]   7:[199-206]

Show forgiveness, speak for justice and avoid the ignorant

When the Qur'an is being recited, listen to it with complete silence

8: AL-ANFÂL

Period of Revelation

This Sûrah was revealed in 2 A. H. after the battle of Badr, the first battle between Islam and Kufr. Since it contains a detailed and comprehensive review of the battle, it appears that the whole Sûrah was revealed at the same time.

Major Issues, Divine Laws and Guidance:

* Battle of truth and falsehood.
* Truth should not fear to be cowed down by odds against it.
* Fighting should not be for spoils or gains but for a just cause.
* Laws relating to peace and war.
* Relation of an Islamic state with Muslims living in non-Muslim countries.

The battle of Badr took place in the 2nd year of Hijrah, therefore, rules and regulations relating to peace and a critical review of war have been made in this Sûrah. But this review is quite different from the reviews that are usually made by worldly commanders after a great victory. Instead of gloating over the victory, the moral weaknesses that had come to the surface in that expedition have been pointed out as follows:

1. That the victory was due to the help of Allah rather than to their own valor and bravery has been stressed so that the Muslims should learn to rely on Him and obey Allah and His Rasool.

2. The moral lesson to be learned from the conflict between the truth and falsehood have been explained.

3. The mushrikeen, the hypocrites, the Jews, and the prisoners of war are addressed in a very impressive manner advising them to learn a lesson.

4. Instructions are given in regard to the spoils of war. The Muslims have been told not to regard these as their right but as a bounty from Allah. Therefore, they should accept with gratitude the share that is granted to them out of it and willingly accede to the share which Allah sets aside for His cause, for His Rasool, and for the help of the needy.

5. It gives instructions concerning the laws of peace and war, for these were urgently needed at the stage, in which the Islamic movement had entered. It enjoined the Muslims to refrain from the ways of ignorance whether they are in peace or at war, and thus establish their moral superiority in the world.

6. *This Sûrah also states some articles of the Islamic Constitution which differentiate the status of Muslims living within the limits of Dar-al-Islam (the Abode of Islam) from that of the Muslims living beyond its limits.*

In order to understand the circumstances and conditions which were being faced by the Muslim community and the Islamic State, in relation to which Divine guidance and laws were enacted, it is important to know how the battle of Badr took place.

Battle of Badr

The message of Islam had proved its firmness and stability. However, the Muslims had not yet had an opportunity to demonstrate practically the blessings of the system of life based on Islam. There was neither any Islamic culture, nor any social, economic or political system; nor were there any established principles of war and peace. Therefore, the Muslims had no opportunity for demonstrating those moral principles on which they intended to build their entire system of life; nor had it been proved on the touchstone of trial that the Muslims as a community were sincere in their proclamation of the message. Allah created opportunities for making up these deficiencies at Madinah.

The people of Makkah had realized that Muhammad (peace be upon him), who had a great personality and possessed extraordinary talents, was going to gain a strong footing in Madinah. This would help integrate his followers - whose constancy, determination, and unwavering fidelity to Al-Islam had been tried - into a disciplined community under his wise leadership and guidance. They knew that this would spell death for their old ways of life. They also realized the strategic importance of Madinah to their trade, which was their main source of livelihood. The Muslims could strike at the caravans travelling on the trade route between Yemen and Syria, and thus strike at the root of their economy. The value of the trade done by the people of Makkah on this route amounted to about two hundred thousand dinârs annually.

In Sh'abân, 2 A. H. (February or March, 623 A. D.) a large trade caravan of the Quraish, on its way back from Syria carrying goods worth over 50,000 dinârs with a guard of thirty to forty men, reached the territory from where it could be easily attacked from Madinah. As soon as the caravan entered the dangerous territory, Abu Sufyân, the caravan's leader, despatched a camel rider to Makkah with a frantic appeal for help. This caused great excitement and anger at Makkah. An army of approximately 1000 warriors with great pomp and show marched towards Madinah. They intended not only to rescue the caravan but also to put an end to the rising power of the Muslims and overawe the clans surrounding the route so as to make it absolutely secure for future trade.

The Prophet, who always kept himself well informed, felt that the hour had come to take a bold step; otherwise the Islamic Movement would become lifeless with no chance to rise again. The condition of the Muslim community was still very shaky because the Muslim immigrants from Makkah (Muhâjireen) had not been able to stabilize their economy; their helpers (the Ansâr) from the natives of Madinah, who became Muslims after the Prophet and his followers migrated there from Makkah, had not yet been tested; and the neighboring Jewish clans could not be trusted. Above all, the surrounding clans lived in awe of the Quraish and had all their religious sympathies with them. Therefore, the consequences of the coming attack could not be favorable to the Muslims. A careful study of the situation indicated to the Prophet that he should take a decisive step and go into the battle with whatever strength he could muster and demonstrate whether the Muslim community had the ability to survive or was doomed to perish.

The Prophet's analysis of the situation was supported by Divine inspiration, therefore, he called the Muhâjireen and the Ansâr to a meeting and placed the whole situation before them, without any reservation, saying: "Allah has promised that you will confront one of the two, the trade caravan coming from the north or the army of the Quraish marching from the south. Now, tell me which of the two you would like to confront!" The majority of the people replied that they should go for the caravan. When the Prophet repeated the same question, Miqdâd bin 'Amr, a Muhâjir, stood up and said: "O Rasool of Allah! Please march in the direction which Allah commands you; we will accompany you wherever you go. We will not say like the Israelites: 'You and your Rabb go and fight, we will wait.' In contrast to them we say: 'Let you and your Rabb decide; we will fight by your side to our last breath.'" Even then, he did not announce any decision, but waited for a reply from the Ansâr who had not yet taken part in any confrontation for Islam. As this was the first opportunity for them to prove that they were ready to fulfill their promise of fighting for the cause of Islam, he repeated the question without directly addressing them. At this, Sa'ad bin Mu'az, an Ansâr, stood up and said: "O Rasool of Allah, it appears that you are addressing this question to us." When the Prophet said, "Yes," he replied, "We have believed in you and confirmed that what you have brought is the truth, and have made a solemn pledge with you that we will listen to you and obey you. Therefore, O Rasool of Allah, do whatever you intend to do. We swear by Allah Who has sent you with the truth that we are ready to accompany you to the seashore and if you enter it, we will plunge into it. We assure you that not a single one of us will remain behind or forsake you, for we will not hesitate at all to go to fight, even if you should lead us to the battlefield tomorrow. We will, Insha Allah (Allah willing), remain steadfast in the battle and sacrifice our lives for Islam. We do hope that by the grace of Allah our behavior will gladden your heart. So, trusting in Allah's blessing, take us to the battlefield." After this it was decided that they would march towards the army of the Quraish and not towards the trade caravan.

The number of people who came forward to go to the battlefield was only a little more than three hundred (86 Muhâjireen, 62 from Aus, and 170 from Khazraj). Over and above that, this little army was ill-armed and hardly equipped for battle. Only a couple of them had horses to ride and the others had to take their turn in threes or fours on a camel back. They had a total of 70 camels. They did not even have enough weapons for the battle; only 60 of them had armor. They marched straight to the southwest, wherefrom the army of the Quraish was coming. This is also an indication that, from the very beginning, they had gone out to fight with the army and not to plunder the caravan. If they had aimed at plundering the caravan they would have taken the north-westernly direction rather than the southwest. The two parties met in combat at Badr on the seventeenth day of Ramadân. When the two armies confronted each other and the Prophet noticed that the Quraish army outnumbered the Muslims by three to one and was much better equipped, he raised his hands up in supplication and made this earnest prayer with great humility: "O Allah! Here are the Quraish, proud of their war material. They have come to prove that Your Rasool is false. O Allah! Now send the help that You have promised me. O Allah! If this little army of Your devotees is destroyed, then there will be no one left in the land to worship You."

In this combat the emigrants from Makkah were put to the hardest test because they had to fight against their own relatives, putting to the sword their fathers, sons, brothers, and uncles. It is obvious that only such people could do this who had accepted the truth sincerely and cut off all relations with falsehood. Similarly, the test to which the Ansâr were put was not less hard. So far the Ansâr had only alienated the powerful Quraish and their allies by giving shelter to the Muslims against their wishes, but now, for the first time, they were going to give them a fight and sow the seeds of a long and bitter war with them. This meant that a small town of a few thousand inhabitants was going to wage a war with the whole of Arabia. It is obvious that only such people could take a stand who believed in the Truth of Islam so firmly that they were ready to sacrifice every personal interest for its sake. Allah accepted these sacrifices of the Muhâjireen and the Ansâr because of their true faith, and rewarded them with His help through angels.

The proud, well-armed Quraish were defeated by these ill-equipped devotees of Islam. Seventy men of the Quraish army were killed and seventy captured as prisoners of war. Their arms and equipment came into the hands of the Muslims as spoils of war. All their big chiefs, who were their best soldiers and who had led the opposition to Islam, were killed in this battle. This decisive victory made Islam a power to be reckoned with.

8: AL-'ANFÂL

This Sûrah, revealed at Madinah, has 10 sections and 75 verses.

In the Name of Allah, the Compassionate, the Merciful

SECTION: 1

They ask you about booty *(spoils of war)*. Tell them: "The Booty belongs to Allah and His Rasool: so fear Allah, *end your disputes,* and correct the relations among yourselves: obey Allah and His Rasool if you are true believers."[1] The true believers are those whose hearts tremble with fear, when the name of Allah is mentioned, and whose faith grows stronger as they listen to His revelations and they put their trust in their Rabb,[2] They are those who establish Salah *(prayers)* and spend in charity out of the sustenance which We have given them.[3] Those are the ones who are the true believers; they will have exalted ranks with their Rabb, forgiveness for their sins, and honorable sustenance.[4] Your Rabb ordered you to leave your home *to fight* for justice, but some of the believers were reluctant.[5] They argued with you about the truth after it had been made clear, as if they were being driven to death with their eyes wide open.[6] Remember, Allah promised you victory over one of the two enemy parties and you wished for the one which was unarmed, but Allah intended to prove the truth to be true according to His words and to cut off the roots of the unbelievers,[7] so that truth should come out as truth and falsehood should be proved as false, even though the criminals wished otherwise.[8] When you prayed to your Rabb for help, He answered: "I will assist you with one thousand angels, one after another."[9] By this good news, Allah sought to comfort your heart, for victory comes only from Allah; surely, Allah is Mighty, Wise.[10] 8:[1-10]

Commandment relating to the spoils of war (booty)

Battle of Badr, a battle between truth and falsehood

SECTION: 2

Remember *(before the battle of Badr)* when He caused drowsiness to overcome you as an assurance from Himself, and sent down water from the sky to cleanse you and to remove from you the uncleanliness caused by Shaitân, to strengthen your hearts and to steady your footsteps.[11] Then your Rabb revealed His will to the angels: "I am with you, give courage to the believers. I will cast panic into the hearts of the unbelievers; therefore, smite their necks and beat every joint of their bodies."[12] This is because they defied Allah and His Rasool. Whoever defies Allah and His Rasool

Allah's help during the Battle of Badr

should know that Allah is strict in retribution.[13]   This is your *punishment,* so taste it, and there will also be the torture of hellfire for the unbelievers.[14]   O believers! When you encounter the unbelievers in a battle, never turn your backs to them;[15]   and whoever turns his back to them on such an occasion - unless it be a strategy of war, or to join another troop - shall incur the wrath of Allah and his abode shall be hell, and how awful shall be that dwelling![16]   *In fact*, it was not you who killed them, but it was Allah Who killed them; it was not you who threw the handful of sand, but it was Allah Who threw it so that He might pass the believers successfully through this excellent trial; surely, Allah is All-Hearing, All-Knowing.[17]   This is it; and Allah will surely frustrate the evil plots of the unbelievers.[18]   *O unbelievers!* You wanted a decision; lo! The decision, *in shape of the believers' victory,* has come to you. Now if you desist, it will be better for you, and if you repeat *your act of war against the believers,* so shall We repeat *the act of providing them assistance*, and your forces, however large in number they may be, shall avail you nothing, for verily Allah is with the believers.[19]   8:[11-19]

Allah's decision between Muslims and kuffâr

SECTION: 3

The worst people in the sight of Allah are those who do not use their common sense

O believers! Obey Allah and his Rasool and do not turn your back to him while you are hearing.[20]   Do not be like those who say: "We hear," but give no heed *to what they hear*.[21]   For the worst animals in the sight of Allah are the deaf and dumb: those devoid of reason.[22]   Had Allah perceived any virtue in them, He would have indeed endowed them with hearing. Had he made them *(those without virtue)* hear, they would have turned away and refused to listen.[23]   O believers! Respond to the call of Allah and His Rasool, when He calls you to that which gives you life; and know that Allah stands between man and his heart, and that it is He in Whose presence you shall all be assembled.[24]

Guard yourselves against temptations

Fear the affliction *(fitnah)* which will affect not only the wrongdoers among you *(but may affect good people as well)*; and know that Allah is strict in retribution.[25]   Call to mind how He gave you shelter when you were few in number and were oppressed in the land, fearing that the enemy would kidnap you. But He provided you a safe asylum, made you strong with His help, and gave you pure things for sustenance so that you may give thanks.[26]   O believers! Do not betray the trust of Allah and His Rasool, nor violate your trusts knowingly.[27]   You should know that your wealth and your children are, in fact, a test for you, and that Allah is He with Whom is a mighty reward.[28]   8:[20-28]

SECTION: 4

O believers! If you fear Allah, He will grant you a criterion *(to judge between right and wrong)*, do away with your sins and forgive you. Allah is the Lord of Mighty Grace.[29]   Remember, how the unbelievers plotted against you. They sought to take you captive, to kill you, or to exile you. They planned - and Allah also planned - Allah is the best planner of all.[30]   Whenever Our revelations are recited to them, they say: "Well, we have heard this. If we wanted we could fabricate the like. These are nothing but the tales of the ancients."[31]   Also remember how they said: "O Allah! If this is indeed the truth from You, then rain down stones on us from the sky or inflict some dreadful scourge to punish us."[32]   But Allah would not punish them while you are present in their midst. Nor does Allah punish people while they are asking His forgiveness.[33]   But now there is no reason why Allah should not punish them when they are blocking others from the Al-Masjid Al-Harâm *(in which Ka'bah is located)*, whereas they are not its lawful guardians. In fact, its only guardians are those who fear Allah, even though most of them do not understand.[34]   Their prayer at the House of Allah is nothing but whistling and clapping of hands: *whose only answer can be,* "Taste the punishment because of your denying the truth."[35]   Surely, the unbelievers spend their wealth to block the way of Allah and so will they spend it; but in the end it will become the cause of their regrets; and they will be defeated. *In the hereafter,* the unbelievers will be gathered together and driven to hell,[36]   in order that Allah may separate the filthy from the pure. He will heap the filthy one upon another, altogether, and then cast them into hell. Such are the ones who will be the losers.[37]

8:[29-37]

SECTION: 5

O Prophet, tell the unbelievers that if they desist *from unbelief,* their past shall be forgiven; but if they persist in sin, let them reflect upon the fate of their forefathers.[38]   *O believers,* fight them until there is no more oppression and until the whole Deen *(way of life)* is for Allah Alone; but if they cease *oppression,* then surely, Allah is All-Seer of what they do.[39]   If they give no heed, then you should know that Allah is your protector. He is the best to protect and the best to help.[40]   8:[38-40]

If you become Godfearing, He will grant you wisdom to judge between right and wrong

The lawful guardians of Ka'bah are those who have fear of Allah

For the unbelievers, who embrace Islam, their past is forgiven

JUZ (PART): 10

Rules about the distribution of spoils of war

Know that whatever war booty *(spoils of war)* you may gain, one-fifth is for Allah, His Rasool, close relatives *of the Rasool*, orphans, the needy and the wayfarer, if you do believe in Allah and in what We revealed to Our servant on the day of distinction *(between right and wrong)*, the day when the two armies met in combat *(at the battle of Badr)*. Allah has power over everything.[41]   Remember when you were on the nearer side of the valley and they were on the farther side, and the caravan was on lower ground than both of you. If you had made a mutual appointment to meet, you would have certainly failed; but Allah sought to accomplish what He has ordained, that those who were destined to perish might die by clear proof and those who were destined to live might survive by clear proof. Surely, Allah is He Who hears all and knows all.[42]   Also remember that Allah made them appear in your dream few in number; if He had shown them to you as many in number, you would surely have been discouraged and you would have disputed in your decision. But Allah saved you; surely, He knows the very secrets of the hearts.[43]   *Remember* when you met them *in the encounter*, He showed them to you few in number in your eyes and He made you appear few in number in their eyes so that Allah might accomplish what He had ordained: for ultimately all affairs return to Allah *for decision*.[44]　　　8:[41-44]

SECTION: 6

Order of Allah to remain firm during combat against enemy

O believers! When you encounter an enemy *in a combat*, be firm and frequently remember Allah so that you may be successful.[45]   Obey Allah and His Rasool and do not dispute with one another, lest you lose courage and weaken your strength. Show patience; surely, Allah is on the side of the patient.[46]   Do not be like those who started from their homes insolently, in order to be seen by everybody and debar others from the Way of Allah. Allah encompasses all their actions.[47]   *Remember* when Shaitân made their actions seem attractive to them, and said: "No one from mankind can overcome you today *(at the battle of Badr)*, for I will be at hand to help you." Yet, when the two armies came within sight of each other, he turned upon his heels saying: " I am done with you, for I can see what you cannot. I fear Allah, for Allah is severe in punishment.[48]　　　8: [45-48]

SECTION: 7

At that time the hypocrites and all those who had a disease in their hearts, said: "Their religion has deceived them." *But you should know that* anyone who puts his trust in Allah, Allah is indeed Mighty, Wise.[49]   If you could only see the angels when they were taking away the souls of the unbelievers! They were smiting their faces and their backs *saying*: "Taste the torment of the blazing fire![50]   This is *the punishment* for what your hands have sent forth, for Allah is never unjust to His servants."[51]   Their behavior is similar to that of the people of Fir'aun *(Pharaoh)* and to those that had gone before them. They also rejected the revelations of Allah and Allah seized them for their sins. Surely, Allah is Mighty and severe in punishment.[52]   8:[49-52]

Victory of the believers and the painful death of the unbelievers

That is because Allah will never change the blessings which He has bestowed on a people until they themselves change what is in their souls; verily Allah hears all and knows all.[53]   Their behavior is similar to that of the people of Fir'aun and those who have gone before them; they rejected the revelations of their Rabb, so We destroyed them for their sins, and We drowned the people of Fir'aun; they were all wrongdoers.[54]   8:[53-54]

Allah does not change His blessings unless people change themselves

Surely, the worst of animals in the sight of Allah are those who reject the truth and do not become believers,[55]   those who make treaties with you and time after time violate their treaties, and have no fear *of Allah*.[56]   If you encounter them in combat, make them a fearsome example for others who would follow them so that they all may learn a lesson.[57]   If you fear treachery from any of your allies, you may *fairly retaliate* by breaking off *the treaty* with them *(through properly notifying them to that effect) to be on equal terms*, for Allah does not love the treacherous.[58]   8:[55-58]

Treaties must be honored unless broken with proper notification

SECTION: 8

Let not the unbelievers think that they have won the game; surely, they can never frustrate *Allah*.[59]   Muster against them all the military strength and cavalry that you can afford so that you may strike terror into the hearts of your enemy and the enemy of Allah, and others besides them who are unknown to you but known to Allah. *Remember* that whatever you spend in the cause of Allah, shall be paid back to you in full and you shall not be treated unjustly.[60]   If the enemy is inclined towards peace, do make

Order to remain prepared for war against the unbelievers

Make peace, if the enemy is inclined towards peace

peace with them, and put your trust in Allah. He is the One Who hears all , knows all.[61]   Should they intend to deceive you, verily Allah is All-Sufficient for you. He is the One Who has strengthened you with His help and with the believers,[62]   uniting their hearts. If you had spent all that is in the earth, you could not have so united their hearts; but Allah has united them. He is Mighty, Wise.[63]   O Prophet! Allah is all-sufficient for you and for the believers who follow you.[64]   8:[59-64]

SECTION: 9

O Prophet! Rouse the believers to   prepare for combat. If there are twenty steadfast men among you, they shall defeat two hundred: if there are one hundred, they shall defeat one thousand of the unbelievers, for they are a people who lack understanding.[65] Now, Allah has lighten your burden, because He knows that there is still weakness in you, so, if there are one hundred steadfast men among you, they shall defeat two hundred and if there be one thousand, they will defeat two thousands with the leave of Allah; for Allah is with those who are steadfast.[66]   It is not fit for a Prophet that he should take prisoners of war until he has thoroughly subdued the land. Do you, *O followers of Muhammad,* desire the temporal goods of this world, while Allah desires for you the hereafter? Allah is Mighty, Wise.[67]   Had there not been a previous sanction from Allah *to take booty and ransom*, you should have been sternly punished for what you have taken.[68]   But now, enjoy the booty which you have taken; for it is lawful and pure, but *in the future* fear Allah. Allah is Forgiving, Merciful.[69]   8:[65-69]

SECTION: 10

O Prophet! Tell the captives in your custody: "If Allah finds goodness in your hearts He will give you even better than what has been taken from you, as well as forgive you. Allah Is Forgiving, Merciful." [70]   But if they have treacherous designs against you, *O Prophet*, they have already shown treason against Allah. That is why, He made them your captives. Allah is Knowledgeable, Wise.[71]   8: [70-71]

Those who believed *(embraced Islam)*, migrated and made Jihad *(exerted their utmost struggle)* with their wealth and their persons in the cause of Allah; as well as those who gave them asylum and help, are indeed the protecting friends of one another.

Allah's promise to make the believers victorious over armies 2 to 10 times larger than the believers

Treatment of prisoners of war who embrace Islam

Duties and obligations of the Islamic State towards

As to those who believed *(embraced Islam)* but did not emigrate *(to Dar-al-Islam, the Islamic State)*, you are under no obligation to protect them until they emigrate; yet, it is your obligation to help them in the matters of faith if they ask for your help, except against people with whom you have a treaty. Allah is observant of all your actions.[72] The unbelievers are protectors of one another. If you fail to do likewise, there will be disorder in the land and great corruption.[73] Those who believed *(embraced Islam)*, migrated and made Jihad *(exerted their utmost struggle)* in the cause of Allah, and those who gave them asylum and help - they are the true believers. They shall have forgiveness and honorable provisions.[74] Those who believed *(embraced Islam)* afterwards, migrated and joined you in Jihad - they too are your *brothers*; but blood relatives, in the Book of Allah, have greater rights on one another. Indeed Allah knows everything.[75]   8: [72-75]

Muslims living in non-Muslim countries

9: AT-TAUBA

Period of Revelation

This Sûrah was revealed in the 9th year of Hijrah in three different discourses. The first discourse (vv. 1-37) was revealed in Zil-Q'adah and set a new policy towards the mushrikeen. The second discourse (vv. 38-72) was revealed in Rajab and dealt with the Campaign of Tabûk. The third discourse (vv. 73-129) was revealed upon the Prophet's return from the Campaign of Tabûk. There are some pieces in this discourse that were sent down on different occasions during the same period and were afterwards consolidated by the Prophet into this Sûrah in accordance with the inspiration from Allah.

Major Issues, Divine Laws and Guidance:

* Policy towards the mushrikeen.
* Commandments relating to participation in Jihâd.
* Regulations relating to hypocrisy, weak faith, and negligence.
* Campaign of Tabûk.
* Establishment of a Dar-al-Islam (an Islamic state).
* Extending the influence of Islam to adjoining countries.
* Crushing the mischief of the hypocrites.
* Preparing the Muslims for a struggle in the cause of Islam.

 Now that the administration of the whole of Arabia had come into the hands of the believers, and all the opposing powers had become subservient, it was necessary to make a clear declaration of the policy which was to be adopted to make this newly formed Islamic state a perfect Dar-al-Islam. In order to accomplish this objective, the following measures were taken:

1. A declaration was made that all the treaties with the mushrikeen were abolished and the Muslims would be released from the treaty obligations with them after the expiration of four months notice.

2. A decree was issued that the guardianship of the Ka'bah should be taken away from the mushrikeen and placed permanently in the hands of the believers (vv. 12-18), that all the customs and practices relating to the era of "ignorance" should be abolished, and that the mushrikeen should not be allowed in the vicinity of the Ka'bah (v. 28). A decree was issued to crush the non-Muslim powers forcing them to accept the sovereignty of the

Islamic State. The object of Jihâd was not to coerce them to accept Islam, as they were free to accept or not to accept it. The object was to allow them the freedom to remain misguided, if they chose to be so, provided they paid Jizyah, the protection tax (v. 29), as a sign of their subjugation to the Islamic State.

3. To ensure the stability of the Islamic State, gangs of the hypocrites who were being tolerated despite their flagrant crimes, were crushed. The Muslims were enjoined to treat them openly as disbelievers (v. 73). Accordingly, the Prophet set on fire the house of Swailim, where the hypocrites used to gather for consultations in order to dissuade the people from joining the expedition of Tabûk. When the Prophet returned from Tabûk, he ordered that Masjid-e-Zirar, which was being used by the hypocrites as a place for hatching plots against the true believers, be pulled down and burned.

4. Those people who lagged behind in the Campaign of Tabûk or showed the least negligence, were severely taken to task if they had no plausible excuse for not fulfilling that obligation. For there could be no greater internal danger to the Islamic community than weakness of faith, especially at the time of a conflict with the whole non-Muslim world.

5. A declaration was made that in the future, the sole criterion of an individual's true faith would be the exertion that individuals make for spreading the Word of Allah and the role they play in the conflict between Islam and Kufr. Therefore, if anyone shows any hesitation in sacrificing his life, wealth, time, and energies, his faith shall not be regarded as genuine.

(vv. 81-96)

9: AT-TAUBA

This Sûrah, revealed at Madinah, has 16 sections and 129 verses.

(This is the only Sûrah that starts without the opening words "In the name of Allah, the Compassionate, the Merciful," since the Prophet did not dictate so.)

SECTION: 1

Proclamation to dissolve the "Treaty of Hudaibiya"

A *declaration* of immunity from Allah and His Rasool is hereby made to those of the mushrikeen with whom you have made a treaty:[1]   "You have four months to go around in the land *unmolested*; but you should know that you cannot frustrate Allah, and that Allah will humiliate the unbelievers."[2]   This is a public proclamation from Allah and His Rasool to the people on the day of the Great Hajj *(Pilgrimage)* that Allah and His Rasool do hereby dissolve *treaty* obligations with the mushrikeen. Therefore, if you repent, it will be better for you but if you turn away, then you should know that you cannot frustrate Allah. *O Prophet,* proclaim a painful punishment to those who are unbelievers,[3]   except *(this proclamation does not apply to)* those mushrikeen who honored their treaties with you in every detail and aided none against you. So fulfill your treaties with them to the end of their term; for Allah loves the righteous.[4]   When the forbidden months *(10,11,12 & 1 of the Islamic calendar)* are over, then fight the mushrikeen wherever you find them, seize them, besiege them, and prepare for them each and every ambush. But if they repent, establish Salah *(prayer)* and pay Zakah *(obligatory charity)*, then let them go their way. Surely, Allah is Forgiving, Merciful.[5]   If anyone from the mushrikeen asks you for asylum, grant it to him so that he may hear the Word of Allah, and then escort him to his place of safety: this should be done because these people do not know *the truth*.[6]

9:[1-6]

SECTION: 2

Commandment of Allah to honor the treaty so long as the unbelievers honor it

How can there be a treaty with the mushrikeen on the part of Allah and His Rasool - except for those with whom you ratified a treaty at the Al-Masjid Al-Harâm? So long as they honor it, you should also honor it too: for Allah loves the righteous.[7]   How *can you trust them*? If they prevail against you, they respect neither treaty nor ties of relationship. They just flatter you with their tongues, but their hearts reject you, and most of them are transgressors.[8]   They have sold the revelations of Allah for paltry worldly gain and they have hindered others from His way; indeed evil are the deeds that they have done.[9]   They neither honor the ties of relationship nor observe the obligations of treaties with the believers; it is they who are the transgressors.[10]   However, if they repent, establish Salah *(prayer)* and pay Zakah *(obligatory charity)*, then they shall be your brethren in Deen *(faith and way of life based on Divine guidance)*: thus do We spell out Our revelations for people of understanding.[11]   9:[7-11]

But if they violate their treaty once they have sworn it and insult your Deen, then fight with the ringleaders of unbelief - for their oaths are nothing to them - so that they may be stopped.[12]   Will you not fight against those people who have broken their oaths, conspired to expel the Rasool and were the first to attack you? Do you fear them? *Nay*, it is Allah Who is more deserving of your fear, if you are true believers.[13]   Fight them; Allah will punish them by your hands and humiliate them. He will grant you victory over them and soothe the hearts of believing people.[14]   He will take away all rancor from their hearts. Allah accepts the repentance of whom He pleases, and Allah is All-Knowledgeable, All-Wise.[15]   Do you think that you will be left alone *(without trial)* while Allah has not yet verified which of you had exerted your utmost struggle *(in the path of Allah)* and did not take any intimate friends other than Allah, His Rasool and the believers? Allah is well aware of all your actions.[16]   9:[12-16]

If the unbelievers violate the treaty, then fight against their ringleaders

SECTION: 3

It is not for the mushrikeen to maintain the mosques of Allah while they bear witness against themselves about their unbelief. It is they whose deeds are in vain and in the hellfire shall they live forever.[17]   The mosques of Allah should be maintained by those who believe in Allah and the Last Day, establish Salah *(prayers)*, and pay Zakah *(obligatory charity)* and fear none except Allah. It is they who are expected to follow the true guidance.[18]   9:[17-18]

Mushrikeen are forbidden to be the caretakers of Masâjid

Have you made those who provide water to the pilgrims and maintain the Al-Masjid-al-Harâm equal to those who believe in Allah, the Last Day and make Jihad *(strive in the cause of Allah)*? They are not equal in the sight of Allah, and Allah does not guide the wrongdoers.[19]   Those who believe *(embrace Islam)*, leave their homes *(migrate),* and make Jihad with their wealth and persons in the cause of Allah, have higher rank in the sight of Allah. It is they who will be truly successful.[20]   Their Rabb gives them good news of His mercy, His good pleasure, and paradise in which

Service to pilgrims is not equal to true belief in Allah, in the Last Day, and making Jihad

there is everlasting bliss for them.[21]   They will live therein forever. Surely, it is Allah with Whom is the greatest reward.[22]

9:[19-22]

Do not take your fathers and brothers as your friends if they prefer Kufr (unbelief) over Imân (belief)

O believers! Do not take your fathers and your brothers as your friends if they prefer Kufr (unbelief) over Imân (belief); for those who turn away from this *commandment* shall be *considered* wrongdoers.[23]   *O Prophet,* tell them: If your fathers, your sons, your brothers, your spouses, your relatives, the wealth that you have acquired, the business in which you fear a loss, and the homes which you like are dearer to you than Allah, His Rasool, and making Jihad *(struggle)* in His Way, then wait until Allah brings about His decision. Allah does not guide the transgressors.[24]   9:[23-24]

SECTION: 4

Allah's help is with the quality and not the quantity of the believers

Allah has indeed helped you in many battlefields and *(recently)* on the battle of Hunain: when you were proud of your great numbers, but the numbers availed you nothing. The earth, with all its vastness, seemed to close in upon you, and you turned your backs and fled.[25]   But Allah sent down His sakeenah *(peace and tranquility)* upon His Rasool and the believers, sent down to your aid those forces which you could not see, and punished the unbelievers. Thus was the recompense for the unbelievers.[26] Then after that, *you also witnessed that* Allah accepted the repentance of those whom He wanted; for Allah is Forgiving, Merciful.[27]

9:[25-27]

The prohibition of mushrikeen from entering Masjid-al-Harâm

O believers! *Know that* mushrikeen are unclean; therefore, do not let them come near the Al-Masjid-al-Harâm after this year's *pilgrimage.* If you fear poverty, Allah - if He so wills - will enrich you out of His bounty. Surely, Allah is All-Knowledgeable, All-Wise.[28]   Fight those people of the Book *(Jews and Christians)* who do not believe in Allah and the Last Day, do not refrain from what has been prohibited by Allah and His Rasool and do not embrace the religion of truth *(Al-Islam)*, until they pay Jizyah *(protection tax)* with their own hands and feel themselves subdued.[29]

9:[28-29]

SECTION: 5

The Jews and Christians, who call Ezra and Jesus

The Jews say: "Uzair *(Ezra)* is the son of Allah," and the Christians say: " Al-Maseeh *(Messiah, Christ)* is the son of Allah." That is what they say with their mouths, imitating the sayings of the former unbelievers. May Allah destroy them! How perverted they are![30]   They *(Jews and Christians)* have taken their rabbis and monks as their Lords beside Allah and *so they did with* Messiah *(Jesus),* the son of Maryam *(Mary),* although they were commanded *in the Torah and the Gospel* to worship none but One Ilâh *(Allah);* besides Whom there is none worthy of worship. Exalted be He above those whom they associate with Him.[31]   They desire to extinguish the light of Allah with their mouths but Allah *will not allow it to happen, for He* seeks to perfect His light even though the disbelievers may dislike it.[32]   It is He Who has sent His Rasool with guidance and true Deen *(faith)* to make it prevail over all other deens *(faiths)* even though the mushrikeen may hate it.[33]

9:[30-33]

> the sons of God, are mushrikeen

O believers! Indeed many of the rabbis and monks misappropriate the wealth of people and hinder them from the way of Allah. To those who hoard gold and silver and do not spend it in the way of Allah, announce unto them a painful punishment.[34] The Day *will surely come* when their treasure will be heated up in the fire of hell, and their foreheads, sides and backs branded with it. *They will be told*: "This is the treasure which you hoarded. Now taste what you were hoarding!" [35]   9:[34-35]

> Do not be like Rabbis and Priests who misappropriate the wealth of people

The number of months ordained by Allah is twelve in the Book of Allah since the day He created the heavens and the earth. Of these, four are sacred; that is the established *principle* of Deen. Therefore, do not wrong yourselves by *violating* them. But *you may* fight against the mushrikeen in all these *months* if they fight against you in all of them. Know that Allah is with the righteous.[36] Transposing a prohibited month is only an addition to unbelief, thereby the disbelievers are misguided. They make a certain month lawful one year and in another year they make the same a forbidden month, so that they make up for the months which Allah has sanctified, thus making lawful what Allah has forbidden. Their evil actions seem pleasing to them. Allah does not guide such disbelieving people.[37]   9:[36-37]

> The number of months in the book of Allah is 12, of which 4 are sacred

SECTION: 6

O believers! What is the matter with you that when you are asked to march forth in the way of Allah, you cling to the earth? Do you prefer the life of this world to the life of the hereafter? The comfort of this life is so little compared to that of the life of the hereafter.[38]   If you do not march forth, He will inflict on you a

> Allah's order to bear arms against the unbelievers, if necessary

painful punishment and replace you with other people, and you cannot harm Him at all, for Allah has power over everything.[39] If you do not help him *(the Prophet)*, *it does not matter*: Allah did help him when the unbelievers drove him out *of his town*, the second of two, while the two were in the cave and *(the enemy came to the opening of the cave)* he said to his companion *(Abu Bakr, first of the rightly-guided caliphs)*, "Do not worry, Allah is with us." So Allah sent down his serenity on him and strengthened him with forces which you could not see; thus, He made the word of the unbelievers lowest, while the word of Allah remained supreme. Allah is All-Mighty, All-Wise.[40]   March forth *whether you are equipped lightly or heavily* and make Jihad *(exert your utmost struggle)* in the way of Allah with your wealth and your persons. That is best for you if you understand.[41]   *As for the hypocrites,* if the gain would have been immediate and the journey short, they would have certainly accompanied you, but the long journey *(in Tabûk expedition)* was too hard for them. *To justify their not accompanying you,* they would even swear by Allah, "If we were able, we would certainly have marched with you." *By doing so,* they are destroying their own souls, for Allah knows that they are liars.[42] 9:[38-42]

SECTION: 7

Those who do not participate in Jihad are hypocrites

Allah forgives you! But why did you *(O Muhammad)* give them leave *to stay behind (You yourself should not have given them leave)* before it become clear to you which of them spoke the truth and which of them lied?[43]   Those who believe in Allah and the Last Day will never ask you for exemption from fighting with their wealth and their persons. Allah is aware of those who are righteous.[44]   Only those people ask for exemption who do not believe in Allah and the Last Day, whose hearts are filled with doubt and are wavering because of their doubts.[45]   If they had intended to march forth, they would certainly have made some preparation for it; but Allah did not like their going forth; so He made them lag behind and they were told, "stay behind with those who are staying."[46]   Had they gone with you, they would have added nothing but mischief, and they would have made efforts to create disorder among your ranks, and there were some among you who would have listened to them. Allah knows the wrongdoers.[47] Indeed they had plotted sedition before and created disturbance to make you unsuccessful until the truth came through and the decree of Allah prevailed, even though they disliked it.[48]   9:[43-48]

Among them there is someone *(Jâd-bin-Qais)* who said: "Grant me exemption and do not expose me to temptation *(of Roman women's beauty)*." Have they not fallen into temptation *(of telling lies, double dealings and hypocrisy)* already? Surely, hell has encircled these disbelievers.[49]   If you gain success, it grieves them, but if you face a setback, they say "We had taken our precautionary measures," and turn away, rejoicing.[50]   *O Prophet,* tell them: "Nothing will happen to us except what Allah has ordained for us; He is our protector;" and in Allah let the believers put their trust.[51]   *Further,* tell them: "Can you expect for us anything other than two glorious things *(victory or martyrdom)*? But we are waiting for Allah to afflict you with punishment either from Himself or by our hands. So wait if you will; we too are waiting."[52]   Say: "Whether you give willingly or with reluctance, it will not be accepted from you; for you are the people who are transgressors."[53]   The reasons which prevent their contributions from being accepted are: that they disbelieve in Allah and His Rasool, that they come to offer Salah *(prayer)* but reluctantly, and that they offer contributions but unwillingly.[54]   Let neither their wealth nor their children dazzle you: in reality, Allah intends to punish them with these things in this life and that their souls may depart while they are still unbelievers.[55]   They swear by Allah that they are indeed *believers* like you; yet, they are not of you; in fact, they are afraid *to appear to you in their true colors*.[56]   If they could find a place of refuge or a cave, or any hiding-place, they would certainly run to it with an obstinate rush.[57]   There are some among them who criticize you *(O Muhammad)* concerning *the distribution* of sadaqât *(donations)*. If they are given from it, they are pleased, and if they are not given from it, lo! They are full of rage.[58]   *It would have been better for them,* if they had only been pleased with what Allah and His Rasool had given them, and said: "Allah is all-sufficient to us! Soon Allah will give us of His bounty, and so will His Rasool. Indeed to Allah do we turn our hopes."[59]

9:[49-59]

Excuses of the hypocrites for not bearing arms against the unbelievers

SECTION: 8

In fact, the sadaqât *(Zakah - Obligatory Charity) collection* is for the poor, the helpless, those employed to administer the funds, those whose hearts need to be won over *to the truth*, ransoming the captives, helping the destitute who is in debt, in the Way of Allah and for the wayfarer. That is a duty enjoined by Allah; and Allah is All-Knowledgeable, All-Wise.[60]   9:[60]

Categories for the distribution of Zakah

Order of Allah not to molest the Prophet

There are some people among them who hurt the Prophet through saying: "He is all ears *(he listens to everyone)*." Say: "It is good for you that he listens to what is best for you; he believes in Allah, has faith in the believers, and is a blessing for those of you who are true believers." As for those who hurt the Rasool, they will have a painful punishment.[61] They swear to you by Allah in order to please you. But it is more fitting that they should please Allah and His Rasool if they are true believers.[62] Don't they know that anyone who opposes Allah and His Rasool shall live forever in the fire of hell? That surely is the worst humiliation.[63]   9:[61-63]

Punishment for those who make fun of the religion

The hypocrites are afraid lest a Sûrah should be sent down about them revealing *to the Muslims* what is in their hearts. Say: "Mock if you will, Allah will surely bring to light all that you fear."[64] If you ask them, *"what were you talking about?"* They will promptly say: "We were only jesting and having fun." Say: "What, then! Were you mocking at Allah, His revelations and His Rasool?"[65] Make no excuses now: you have rejected faith after your belief; even if We may pardon some of you *who were not serious in participating,* We will punish others amongst you, because they are criminals.[66]
9:[64-66]

SECTION: 9

Hypocritical actions and their punishment

The hypocrites, men and women, are all alike. They enjoin what is evil, forbid what is good, and tighten their hands *from spending in the cause of Allah.* They have forgotten Allah; so He has forgotten them. In fact, the hypocrites are transgressors.[67] Allah has promised the hypocrites, both men and women, and the unbelievers, the fire of hell to live therein forever, a sufficient recompense. Allah has cursed them and they shall have a lasting punishment.[68] *Your behavior is just* like those who have gone before you. They were mightier than you in power and more flourishing in wealth and children. They enjoyed their portion *of this worldly life*; thus have you enjoyed your portion as did those before you; and you have entered into vain discourses as they did. *Consequently* their deeds were fruitless in this world and in the Hereafter, and they are the ones who are the losers.[69] Have they not heard the news of those who have gone before them? The people of Nûh *(Noah)*, Ad and Thamûd; the people of Ibrâheem *(Abraham)*, the men of Madyan and the cities which were overthrown. Their Rasools came to them with clear proofs; *but they did not listen*, Allah did not wrong them, but they wronged their own souls.[70]
9:[67-70]

The true believers, both men and women, are protectors of one another. They enjoin what is good and forbid what is evil; they establish Salah *(prayers)*, pay Zakah *(obligatory Charity)*, and obey Allah and His Rasool. It is they on whom Allah will have His mercy; surely, Allah is Mighty, Wise.[71]　Allah has promised the believers, both men and women, gardens beneath which rivers flow, to live therein forever, and *they will have* beautiful mansions in these gardens of everlasting bliss. *Best of all*, they will have the good pleasure of Allah. Now that is the highest achievement.[72]

9:[71-72]

Believers' actions and their rewards

SECTION: 10

O Prophet! Make Jihad against the unbelievers and the hypocrites and be harsh against them. Hell shall be their home; and it is the worst of all homes.[73]　They swear by Allah that they said nothing, when in fact, they uttered the words of unbelief and they committed Kufr *(rejected faith)* after accepting Islam. They meditated a plot which they were unable to carry out. They had no reason to be revengeful, except that Allah and His Rasool had enriched them through His bounty. Therefore, if they repent, it will indeed be better for them; but if they turn back *(do not repent)*, Allah will punish them with a painful punishment in this life and in the Hereafter, and they shall have none on earth to protect or help them.[74]

9:[73-74]

Allah's order to make Jihad against hypocrites and unbelievers

There are some among them who made a covenant with Allah saying: "If He bestows on us His bounty, we will spend in charity and become truly of the righteous."[75]　But when He gave them of His bounty they became stingy, turned back *from their covenant* and became evasive.[76]　He put hypocrisy into their hearts to last till the Day wherein they shall meet Him as a consequence of their breach of covenant with Allah and the lies they told.[77]　Are they not aware that Allah knows their secret thoughts and their secret counsels, and that Allah knows fully well all that is hidden?[78]　As for those that taunt the believers who give freely and ridicule those who find nothing to give except the fruits of their labor; Allah will throw back their ridicule on them and they shall have a painful punishment.[79]　*O Prophet! It is the same,* whether you ask forgiveness for them or not; even if you ask for their forgiveness seventy times, Allah is not going to forgive them: because they have disbelieved Allah and His Rasool. Allah does not guide those who are transgressors.[80]

9:[75-80]

Behavior of the hypocrites relating to the bounties of Allah

SECTION: 11

The hypocrites did not join the war against the unbelievers

Those who remained behind *(did not join the Tabûk expedition)* were delighted to sit *inactive* behind Allah's Rasool, and they hated to make Jihad with their wealth and their persons in the cause of Allah. They said *to each other:* "Do not go forth in the heat." Say *to them*: "The fire of hell is much more severe in heat." If only they could understand![81]　Let them laugh a little; much will they weep as a recompense for what they have earned.[82]　*From* now *on*, if Allah brings you back to them and any of them asks your permission to go forth for Jihad, say: "You shall never be allowed to go forth with me nor fight an enemy in my company. You chose to sit *inactive* on the first occasion, therefore, you shall now stay with those who lag behind."[83]

The prohibition of offering Funeral prayer for the hypocrites

You shall never offer funeral prayer for any of them who dies, nor shall you attend their burial, for they have denied Allah and His Rasool and died while they were transgressors.[84]　Let neither their wealth nor their children dazzle you. Through these things Allah wants to punish them in this world and let their souls depart while they are still disbelievers.[85]　Whenever a Sûrah *(chapter)* is revealed, saying: " Believe in Allah and make Jihad along with His Rasool," capable people among them ask you for exemption, saying: "Please leave us with those who are to stay *at home*."[86]　They preferred to be with those who remain behind, *as a result,* a seal was set upon their hearts so that they do not understand.[87]　But the Rasool and those who believe with him, make Jihad with their wealth and their persons. They are the ones who will have all the goodness, and they are the ones who will be successful.[88]　Allah has prepared for them gardens beneath which rivers flow, to live therein forever: that is the greatest achievement.[89]

9:[81-89]

SECTION: 12

Genuine exemptions for staying behind from the battlefront

Some from among the bedouins also came with their excuses, begging exemption to stay behind; thus, those who lied to Allah and His Rasool sat *inactive*. Soon a painful punishment shall seize those of them who disbelieved.[90]　There is no blame on the disabled, the sick, and those lacking the means, to stay behind so long as they are sincere to Allah and His Rasool. There is no ground of *(blame)* against those righteous people. Allah is Forgiving, Merciful.[91]　Likewise, *there is no blame* on those who came to you and requested the conveyance *to the battlefront* and you said: "I am unable to provide you the conveyance," and they returned with their eyes streaming with tears; they were filled with sorrow that they had no resources of going forth *to the battlefield at their own expense*.[92] The ground of *(blame)* is only against those who begged exemption although they are rich. They preferred to be with those who remained behind. Allah has set a seal upon their hearts; so they do not know *what they missed*.[93]　　　　　　　　　　　　9:[90-93]

JUZ (PART): 11

Those who make excuses to avoid serving in armed struggle for the cause of Allah (when needed) are hypocrites

They will present to you *all sorts* of excuses when you return to them. Say: "Present no excuses: we shall not believe you: Allah has already revealed to us *the whole truth* about you. Now Allah and His Rasool will keep a watch over your conduct: in the end, you will return to Him Who knows what is hidden and what is open, and He will tell you all that you have been doing."[94] Soon they will swear to you by Allah when you return to them, so that you may leave them alone. So leave them alone: they are filth. Hell shall be their abode, a punishment for their misdeeds.[95] They will swear to you in order to please you, but even if you be pleased with them *(accept their excuses)*, Allah will never be pleased with these transgressors.[96] The Arabs of the desert are the worst in disbelief and hypocrisy, and are least inclined to acknowledge the limits that Allah has revealed to his Rasool. Allah is All-Knowledgeable, All-Wise.[97] Some of the desert Arabs look upon whatever they spend *in the way of Allah* as a penalty and wait for some misfortune to befall you. Misfortune may befall them! Allah hears all and knows all.[98] But some of the desert Arabs believe in Allah and the Last Day, and look on what they spend *in the way of Allah* as a means of bringing them close to Allah and receiving the prayers of the Rasool. Behold! That will bring them closer. Soon Allah will admit them to His mercy. Allah is Forgiving, Merciful.[99]

9:[94-99]

SECTION: 13

The categories of hypocrites

Commandment for the collection of Al-Zakah

As for the first pioneers *who accepted Islam* from the Muhâjireen *(immigrants)* and Ansâr *(supporters in Madinah)* and those who follow them in good deeds, Allah is well pleased with them and they are pleased with Him. He has prepared for them gardens beneath which rivers flow, wherein they shall live forever: that is the supreme achievement.[100] Some of the desert Arabs around you are hypocrites, and so are some of the residents of Madinah, who are adamant in their hypocrisy. You do not know them, but We do. Soon We shall give them double punishment: then they shall be turned to the most severe chastisement.[101] There are some who have confessed their sins: they have mixed records of good and bad deeds. It is quite possible that Allah may turn to them in mercy, for Allah is Forgiving, Merciful.[102] Take sadaqât *(here it means - Zakat-ul-Mall)* from their wealth, so that they may thereby be cleansed and purified, and pray for them; for your prayer will give them comfort. Allah hears all and knows all.[103] Do they not know that Allah accepts repentance from His servants and takes their sadaqât *(charity),* and surely, Allah is the One Who is the Accepter of Repentance, the Merciful?[104]   Tell them: "Do as you will. Allah, His Rasool and the believers will now keep a watch over your conduct; then you shall be brought to His court Who knows the hidden and the open, and He will inform you of all that you have done."[105]   There are yet others whose case is held in suspense for the decision of Allah. He will either punish them or turn to them in mercy; and Allah is Knowledgeable, Wise.[106] There are others who built a Masjid *(Masjid-al-Dirâr)* for mischievous motives, to spread disbelief and to disunite the believers, and an outpost for one *(Abu 'Amir)* who had made war against Allah and His Rasool before. They will indeed swear that their intentions are nothing but good; but Allah declares that they are liars indeed.[107] You should never stand *to offer Salah* in it. Certainly the Masjid founded on piety from the very first day is more deserving that you should stand *to offer Salah* in it; for in it there are men who love to be purified; and Allah loves those who purify themselves.[108] Who is a better person: he who lays the foundation of his building on piety to Allah and His good pleasure, or he who lays the foundation of his building on an undermined bank ready to crumble down, and it does crumble to pieces with him into the fire of Hell? Allah does not guide such wrongdoers.[109] The foundation of those who so build is never free from suspicion and shakiness in their hearts, until their hearts are cut to pieces. Allah is Knowledgeable, Wise.[110]   9:[100-110]

The hypocrites built a Masjid with mischievous motives

SECTION: 14

Indeed Allah has purchased from the believers their persons and their wealth, in return has *promised* them paradise; they fight in the cause of Allah and slay and are slain. This is a true promise which is binding on Him mentioned in the Tawrât *(Torah),* the Injeel *(Gospel)* and the Qur'an; and who is more true in fulfilling his promise than Allah? Rejoice, therefore, in the bargain which you have made, and that is a supreme achievement.[111] Those that turn *to Allah* in repentance, serve Him, praise Him, go out in the cause of Allah *(or fast),* make Rukû' *(bow down in prayer)* and Sujûd *(prostrate themselves in prayer),* enjoin what is good and forbid what is evil, and observe the limits *(permissions and prohibitions)* set by Allah *(they are the ones who make such a bargain with Allah).* O Prophet, proclaim the good news to such believers.[112]   9:[111-112]

Allah has purchased the persons and wealth of the Believers and in return has promised them paradise

Do not seek forgiveness for the mushrikeen

It is not proper for the Prophet and those who believe that they should beg forgiveness for the mushrikeen *(those who worship someone other than Allah)*, even though they be their relatives, after it has been explained to them that they are the inmates of hellfire.[113] Ibrâheem *(Abraham)* prayed for his father's forgiveness only to fulfill a promise he had made to him. But when it became clear to him that he was an enemy of Allah, he disassociated himself from him. Indeed, Ibrâheem used to invoke Allah with humility and was forbearing.[114] It is not the way of Allah to confound people after He has guided them, until He makes clear to them what they should guard against; surely, Allah has the knowledge of everything.[115] Surely, it is Allah to Whom belongs the kingdom of the heavens and the earth. He gives life and causes to die. You have none besides Allah to protect or to help.[116]

9:[113-116]

Allah forgave those three who lagged behind but were sincere

Allah forgave the Prophet and those Muhâjireen *(immigrants)* and the Ansâr who stood by him in the time of distress, when some were on the point of losing heart. He turned to them in mercy. Surely, to them He is Most Kind, Most Merciful.[117] *He also turned in mercy* to the three, *the decision of* whose case was deferred. So despondent were they that the earth, with all its vastness, and their own souls, seemed to close in upon them. They knew for certain that there was no refuge from Allah except with Him. Then He turned to them in mercy so that they could repent. Surely, Allah is the One Who is the Acceptor of Repentance, Most Merciful.[118]

9:[117-118]

SECTION: 15

Believers are only those who prefer the life of the Rasool over their own

O believers! Have fear of Allah and be with those who are truthful *in word and deed*.[119] It is not proper for the people of Madinah and the bedouins of the neighborhood to forsake the Rasool of Allah or to jeopardize his life so as to safeguard their own: because they do not suffer any thirst, fatigue or hunger for the sake of Allah, or take any step which may provoke the unbelievers, or inflict any injury upon an enemy, but shall be written down as a good deed to their account; for Allah does not waste the reward of the righteous.[120] *Likewise,* they do not spend anything *for the cause of Allah,* be it small or large, or cut across a valley *in Jihad,* but is written down to their credit; so that Allah may reward them based on the best of their deeds.[121] It is not proper that the believers should go forth all together. *Therefore,* why not a contin-

The requirement of obtaining understanding of religion

gent from each division stay behind so that they may obtain the understanding of the Deen *(Al-Islam),* and admonish the people when they return to them so that they may guard themselves *against un-Islamic conduct*![122]　　　　　　9:[119-122]

SECTION: 16

O believers! Fight the unbelievers who are near to you, and let them find firmness in you; you should know that Allah is on the side of the God-fearing.[123]　Whenever a Sûrah is revealed, some of them ask: "Which of you has had his faith increased by it?" As for the believers, it has certainly increased their faith and they do rejoice.[124]　But those whose hearts contain disease *of doubt and hypocrisy*, it has added filth to their existing filth, and they will die while they are still disbelievers.[125]　Do they not see that they are tested every year once or twice? Yet, they neither repent nor learn a lesson from this.[126]　Whenever a Sûrah is revealed, they look at each other, *saying,* "Is anyone watching?" Then they *silently* slip away. Allah has diverted their hearts *(from the guidance),* for they are a people who do not comprehend.[127]

9:[123-127]

Now, there has come to you, from among yourselves, a Rasool who grieves at your loss and who is excessively anxious for your success *in both worlds*, and who is kind and merciful towards the believers.[128]　Now, if they turn away from you, *(O Prophet)* say: "Allah is all-sufficient for me. There is none worthy of worship but He. In Him I have put my trust. He is the Rabb of the Mighty Throne."[129]　　　　　　　　9:[128-129]

Qur'anic verses do increase the faith of the believers

Character of the Prophet Muhammad (pbuh)

A Prayer taught by Allah

10: YÛNUS

Period of Revelation

This Sûrah was revealed during the last stage of the Prophet's residence at Makkah.

Major Issues, Divine Laws, and Guidance

* Allah is the only Creator of this universe.
* Deities whom the mushrikeen worship other than Allah, have no power to either benefit or harm anyone.
* Deities other than Allah are not even aware that they are being worshiped.
* To every nation Allah sent a Rasool for guidance.
* Al-Qur'an provides a cure for all the problems of mankind.
* Mushrikeen follow nothing but conjectures and preach nothing but falsehood.
* The story of the Prophet Nûh and his people.
* The story of the Prophet Musa, Fir'aun, and his chiefs.
* Belief after seeing the scourge did not benefit any nation except the nation of the Prophet Yûnus.
* Prohibition against forcing anyone to embrace Islam.

In the introductory verses of this Sûrah, an invitation towards the Right Way is extended to the people who were considering it a strange thing that Allah's message was being conveyed by a human being (Muhammad). They were charging the Prophet with sorcery, whereas in the Qur'an there was neither anything strange nor it had anything to do with sorcery or soothsaying. The prophet was simply informing mankind about two facts:

1. Allah, Who has created the universe, is, in fact, your Rabb, and He Alone is entitled to be worshipped.

2. That after the life in this world, there will be another life in the next world, where every one shall have to render full account of this world's life. They shall be rewarded or punished according to whether they adopted the righteous attitude required by Allah after acknowledging Him as their Rabb, or acted against His will.

Both of these facts are realities in themselves, whether you acknowledge them as such or not. If you accept them, you will have a very blessed end; otherwise you shall meet the evil consequences of your disbelief.

10: YÛNUS

This Sûrah, revealed at Makkah, has 11 sections and 109 verses.

In the name of Allah, the Compassionate, the Merciful.

SECTION: 1

Alif L'âm Râ. These are the verses of the wise Book.[1] Does it seem strange to the people that We revealed Our will to a man from among themselves, *saying:* "Warn mankind and give the good news to the Believers that they are on sound footing with their Rabb?" The disbelievers say: "This man is indeed an obvious magician!"[2]   10:[1-2]

Al-Qur'an is the book of wisdom

The fact is that your Rabb is the same Allah Who created the heavens and the earth in six Yaums *(days, time periods or stages)* and then established *Himself* on the Throne, *in a manner that suits His Majesty*, and is directing the affairs *of the universe.* None can intercede with Him, except the one who receives His permission. This is Allah your Rabb, so worship Him: will you not receive admonition?[3]   To Him you shall all return. Allah's promise is true. He is the One Who originates the *process of* Creation and repeats it *(will bring it back to life)* so that He may justly reward those who believed in Him and did righteous deeds. As for those who disbelieved, they shall have boiling fluids to drink and shall undergo a painful punishment because they rejected the truth.[4] He is the One Who gave the sun its brightness and the moon its light, established its phases that you may learn to compute the years and other such counts *(days, weeks, months).* Allah created them only to manifest the truth. He has spelled out His revelations for people who have knowledge.[5]   10:[3-5]

Allah is the One Who created this universe

He is the One Who originates creation and repeats it

Indeed in the alternation of the night and the day and what Allah has created in the heavens and the earth, there are signs for those who are Godfearing.[6]   As for those who do not hope to meet Us *on the Day of Judgement*, being well pleased and satisfied with this worldly life and those who give no heed to Our revelations,[7] they shall have the Fire as their abode because of what they had earned *(erroneous creed and wrong conduct).*[8]   In fact, those who believe *in the truth which is revealed in this Book* and do good deeds, their Rabb will guide them because of their faith and rivers will flow beneath their feet in the gardens of bliss.[9] Their way of request therein will be: "Glory to You O Allah!" Their greetings therein will be: "Peace *be upon you!*" And their closing remarks

There are signs of His manifestation in the creation of the heavens, earth, sun, moon, day and night

will be: "All praises are for Allah Alone, the Rabb of the Worlds!"[10]

10:[6-10]

SECTION: 2

If Allah were to hasten the punishment for their evil deeds as they hasten in asking good of this world, then the respite given to the people would have been terminated, *but this is not Our way.* We leave those people alone who do not entertain the hope of meeting Us, to blunder about in their rebellion.[11] Whenever affliction touches a man, he prays to Us, whether lying down on his side, sitting, or standing. But as soon as We relieve his affliction, he walks away as if he had never prayed to Us for removing that affliction which touched him! Thus the foul deeds which they do are made fair-seeming to the transgressors.[12] We have destroyed generations before your time when they adopted unjust attitudes: their Rasools came to them with clear signs but they would not believe! Thus, do We requite the criminals.[13] Then, We made you their successors in the land so that We may observe how you would conduct yourselves.[14] When Our clear revelations are recited to them, those who entertain no hope of meeting Us say to you: "Bring us a Qur'an different than this or make some changes in it." *O Muhammad,* tell them: "It is not possible for me to change it myself. I follow only what is revealed to me. Indeed, I cannot disobey my Rabb, for I fear the punishment of a Mighty Day."[15] Say: "If Allah wanted otherwise, I would have not recited this *(Qur'an)* to you, nor would I have made you aware of it. Indeed, a whole lifetime *(40 years)* I have lived among you before its revelation. Why do you not use your common-sense?"[16] Who can be more unjust than the one who himself forges a lie, then ascribes it to Allah or falsifies His real Revelations? Indeed, such criminals can never prosper.[17]

10:[11-17]

They worship *other deities* besides Allah, who can neither harm them nor benefit them, and they say: "These are our intercessors with Allah." *O Muhammad,* say to them: "Are you informing Allah of what He knows to exist neither in the heavens nor on the earth? Glory to Him! He is far above from having the partners they ascribe *to Him*!"[18] Mankind was once just one nation; later on they became divided *through inventing different creeds*. If your Rabb had not already given His word *(specified time for the life of mankind on Earth)*, the matters in which they differ would have certainly been decided.[19] *In regards to* their saying: "Why has not a sign been sent down to him *(Muhammad)* from his Rabb?"

Margin notes:

The behavior of the wrong doers towards Allah and His revelations

Deities other than Allah can neither harm nor benefit you

Mankind was one nation until they invented different creeds

Tell them: " Allah Alone has the knowledge of the unseen. Wait if you will: I too shall wait with you."[20]   10:[18-20]

SECTION: 3

When We show mercy to mankind after some calamity had afflicted them, they begin to plot against Our revelations! Tell them: "Allah is more swift in plotting than you; indeed Our messengers *(angels)* are recording all the plots you make."[21] He is the One Who enables you to travel through the land and by the sea; until when you are on board a ship, as the ship sails with a favorable wind and they feel happy about it; but when there comes a stormy wind and the waves reach them from all sides and they think they are being overwhelmed: then they pray to Allah with their sincere devotion, *saying*, "If You deliver us from this, we shall become your thankful *devotees*!"[22] Yet, when We deliver them, behold! The same people become unjustly rebellious in the land. O mankind! Your rebellion is against your own souls - *(you may enjoy)* the transitory pleasure of this world - in the end, you have to return to Us, then We shall inform you of what you have done.[23]
      10:[21-23]

> People call upon Allah when suffering but plot against Him when comfortable

The example of this worldly life *(which you love so much that you have even become neglectful of Our signs)* is like the water which We send down from the sky; it mingles *with the soil* and produces vegetation which becomes the food for men and animals. Then, at the very time when the crops are ripened and the land looks attractive, the people to whom it belongs think that they are able to cultivate it, there comes Our scourge upon it, by night or in broad day, and We mow it down thoroughly as if nothing existed there yesterday! Thus do We spell out Our signs for those who are thoughtful.[24]   10:[24]

> Example of this worldly life

Allah invites you to the Home of Peace and guides whom He pleases to the Right Way.[25] Those who do good deeds shall have a good reward and even more *(having the honor to see Allah)*! Neither blackness nor disgrace shall cover their faces. They will be the inhabitants of paradise; they will live therein forever.[26] As for those who have done evil deeds, they will be rewarded with like evil: disgrace will cover them - they shall have none to protect them from Allah - as if their faces were covered with patches of the dense darkness of night. They are the inmates of Fire *(Hell)*; they will live therein forever.[27] On the Day when We shall gather them all together, We shall say to those who committed shirk *(associated other deities with Us)*: "Stay where you are, you and those whom

> Allah invites you to the Home of Peace

Deities whom they worship are not even aware of being worshipped

you set as partners with Us." We will separate them from one another, then the shorakâ' *(partners they had set up with Us)* will say: "It was not us that you worshipped![28]   Allah is an all-sufficient witness between you and us, *(even if you worshipped us)* we were quite unaware of your worship."[29]   Thereupon, every soul shall know what it had sent forth, as they will be brought towards *the Court of* Allah, their true Patron, and their invented falsehoods will leave them in the lurch.[30]   10:[25-30]

SECTION: 4

Reasoning and truth about Allah vs. Other gods invented by the mushrikeen

Ask them: "Who provides your sustenance from the heaven and from the earth? Who has control over hearing and sight? Who brings forth the living from the dead and the dead from the living? Who regulates *the universe*?" They will soon reply: "Allah." Say: "Why do you not then fear *His punishment*?"[31]   The same Allah is your real Rabb: What is left after the truth except falsehood? How then can you turn away?[32]   Thus has the Word of your Rabb proved true in regards to the transgressors that they do not believe.[33]   Ask them: "Can any of your shorakâ' *(the deities you worship besides Allah)* create anything and then repeat its process?" *If they do not answer, then* tell them: "Well, Allah creates and then repeats the process. Then how is it that you are so misled?"[34]   *Again* ask them: "Is there any of your shorakâ' who can guide you to the truth?" *If they do not answer, then* tell them: "It is Allah Who guides to the truth. Then, who is more worthy to be followed: He that can guide to the truth, or he that cannot and is himself in need of guidance? What is the matter with you? What kind of judgement do you make?"[35]   The fact is that most of them follow nothing but mere conjecture and conjecture is in no way a substitute for the truth. Surely, Allah is well aware of all that they do.[36]   10:[31-36]

This Qur'an is the revelation from Allah

This Qur'an is not such as could be produced by anyone other than Allah; in fact, it is the confirmation of prior revelations *(Torah, Psalms and Gospel)* and fully explains the *Holy* Book; there is no doubt in this fact that it is *revealed* from the Rabb of the Worlds.[37]   Do they say: "He *(the Prophet)* has forged it?" Tell them: "If what you say is true; then produce one Sûrah like this, you may even call to your aid anyone you want other than Allah."[38]   Nay! They do not believe that which they cannot grasp, for they have not yet seen its prophecy fulfilled. Those who passed away before them disbelieved in the same way. But see what was the end of the wrongdoers![39]   Of these people there are some who will believe in it and some who will not: and your Rabb best knows the evil-doers.[40]   10:[37-40]

SECTION: 5

If they disbelieve you, say: "I am responsible for my actions and you are for yours! You are not accountable for my actions, nor am I responsible for what you do."[41] There are some among them who *pretend to* hear what you say: but can you make the deaf listen to you, incapable as they are of understanding?[42] Then there are some among them who *pretend to* look at you: but can you show the way to the blind, bereft as they are of sight?[43] The fact is that Allah does not do injustice to mankind in any way: but men are unjust to their own souls.[44] On that Day when He will gather them all together, *it will appear to them* as if they had not stayed *in this world* but an hour of a day to get to know each other. *At that time they will realize that*: in fact, the losers are those who denied the meeting with Allah and were not rightly guided.[45] Whether We show you *in your lifetime* some consequences of what We have promised them, or cause you to die *before that*, in any case they will have to return to Us: moreover Allah is watching all their actions.[46]   10:[41-46]

Every nation was sent a Rasool. Once their Rasool came, judgement was passed between them with all fairness and they were not wronged in the least.[47] They ask: "When will this promise be fulfilled, *tell us* if what you say be true?"[48] Say: "I have no control over any harm or benefit to myself, except what Allah wills. For every nation there is a deadline: when their deadline comes, it can neither be delayed for even a moment, nor can it be advanced.[49] Say: "Have you ever considered that if His scourge comes to you by night or by day, *you can do nothing to avert it*. What then is there that the criminals wish to hasten?[50] Would you believe it when it actually overtakes you? What! Now *you believe?* Even though it had been your own wish to hurry it on."[51] Then it will be said to the wrongdoers: "Taste the everlasting punishment! Should you not be rewarded according to your deeds?"[52] They ask you: "Is what you say really true?" Tell them: "Yes! By my Rabb, it is absolutely true! And you will not be able to avert it."[53]   10:[47-53]

SECTION: 6

If every person that has done injustice possessed all that the earth contains, he would be willing to offer it all in ransom *to redeem himself if he could*. They will regret in their hearts when

---

Those who disbelieve in this Qur'an shall be the losers in the hereafter

Every nation was sent a Rasool for their guidance

On the Day of Judgement, there

shall be no way out for the unbelievers

Al-Qur'an is a mercy, blessing, and cure for the problems of mankind

Whatever you do, Allah is a witness to it

The mushrikeen are wrong, they follow nothing but conjecture, preach nothing but falsehood

they see the punishment *of Hell*. The decision between them will be made with justice and no wrong will be done to them.[54] Be aware! All that is in the heavens and the earth belongs to Allah. Be aware! The promise of Allah is true, yet, most of them do not know.[55] He is the One Who gives life and causes death, and to Him you shall all return.[56]   10:[54-56]

O mankind! There has come to you an instruction from your Rabb, a cure for whatever *(disease)* is in your hearts, a guidance and a blessing for the true believers.[57] Say: "It is the grace and mercy of Allah *(that He has sent this Qur'an)*, so let the people rejoice over it, for it is better than *(the worldly riches)* they are collecting."[58] O Prophet, ask them: "Have you ever considered that out of the sustenance which Allah has given you, you yourselves have made some things halâl *(lawful)* and others harâm *(unlawful)*. Ask them: "Did Allah permit you to do so, or do you ascribe a false thing to Allah?"[59] What *treatment* do they think those people *will get*, who ascribe false things to Allah, on the Day of Resurrection? Indeed Allah is full of grace to mankind, but most of them are not grateful.[60]   10:[57-60]

SECTION: 7

No matter what affairs you may be engaged in, what portion from the Qur'an you may be reciting and whatever deeds you may be doing, We are your Witness thereof when you are deeply occupied with it: for there is not even an iota of anything in the earth or in the heaven that is hidden from your Rabb, neither anything smaller than that nor larger, but is recorded in a Clear Book.[61] Be aware! The friends of Allah has nothing to fear or to grieve.[62] Those who believe and *(constantly)* guard against evil,[63] for them there is good news in this life and in the hereafter - Allah's Words do not change - this is indeed the mighty achievement.[64] *O Prophet,* let not their remarks grieve you: surely, all honor belongs to Allah: He hears all and knows all.[65]   10:[61-65]

Be aware! Surely, whatever is in the heavens and in the earth belongs to Allah. Those who invoke other deities besides Allah, follow nothing but conjectures and preach nothing but falsehood.[66] He is the One Who has made the night for you to rest therein and the day so that you can see. Indeed, there are signs in this for those who listen *to His message*.[67] They *(Jews, Christians and Pagans)* say: "Allah has begotten a son!" Glory be to Him! He is Self-Sufficient! His is all that is in the Heavens and in the Earth! And you have no proof for what you say? Would you ascribe to Allah something about which you have no knowledge?[68] *O Prophet,* tell them: "Those who ascribe false things to Allah will never prosper."[69]   *Well, they may have* a little enjoyment in this world, but eventually they have to return to Us and then We will make them taste the severest punishment for their unbelief.[70]

10:[66-70]

SECTION: 8

Quote to them the story of Nûh *(Noah)* when he said to his people: "O my people! If it offends you that I should live among you and preach to you the revelations of Allah, *then you should know that* I have put my trust in Allah. Go ahead and muster all your shorakâ' *(deities you worship)* and come up with your firm decision. Plan it well so that you may not have any doubt about its being foolproof. Then execute it against me and give me no respite.[71]   If you have turned away from my message, *I did not lose any thing,* for I did not ask any reward from you *for my services*: my reward is only with Allah, I have been commanded to become a Muslim."[72]   But they disbelieved him. As a result, We saved him and those of them who were with him in the Ark and We made them successors *in the Earth* and drowned those who rejected Our revelations. You see what was the end of those who were warned *but did not believe*![73]

10:[71-73]

> The story of the Prophet Nûh and his people

Then after him We sent Rasools to their people. They came to them with clear signs but they would not believe what they had rejected before. Thus, do We set seals upon the hearts of those who *(intentionally)* exceed the limits.[74]   Then later on We sent Musa *(Moses)* and Haroon *(Aaron)* to Fir'aun *(Pharaoh)* and his chiefs with Our signs. But they showed arrogance, for they were a nation of criminals.[75]   When the truth did come to them from Us they said: "This is indeed sheer magic!"[76]   Musa replied: "Is this what you say of the Truth when it has come to you? Is this magic? Magicians do not prosper."[77]   They said: "Have you come to turn us away from the faith of our forefathers in order that you two *(Musa and Haroon)* may become the leaders in the land? We will never believe in you!"[78]   Fir'aun said: "Bring me every skillful magician."[79]   When the magicians came, Musa said to them: "Throw what you wish to throw!" [80]   So when they had thrown, Musa said: "The magic that you have brought, Allah will surely prove it wrong: for Allah does not promote the work of mischief makers.[81]   By His Words Allah

> Rasools were sent to the descendants of the Prophet Nûh - similarly the Prophets Musa and Haroon were sent to Pharaoh

vindicates the truth, much as the criminals may dislike it!"[82]

10:[74-82]

SECTION: 9

None but a few youth from his own people believed in Musa *(Moses)*, for fear of Fir'aun *(Pharaoh)* and his chiefs, lest they should persecute them; and certainly Fir'aun was mighty in the land and was one of those who did not hesitate to transgress any limit. [83] Musa said: "O my people! If you believe in Allah, then put your trust in Him, if you are really Muslims."[84] They replied: "In Allah do we put our trust. Our Rabb! Do not let us suffer at the hands of unjust people,[85] and deliver us through Your mercy, from the nation of unbelievers."[86] We revealed Our will to Musa and his brother, saying: "Take your people to dwell in Egypt, and make your houses as your Qiblah *(for worship)* and establish Salah *(prayer)* and give good news to the believers!"[87] Musa prayed: "Our Rabb! You have indeed bestowed on Fir'aun and his chiefs splendor and wealth in this worldly life. Our Rabb, have you done this so that they may mislead people from Your way? Our Rabb, destroy their wealth and harden their hearts, so that they may not believe until they see the painful punishment."[88] *Allah* replied: "Your prayer shall be answered! So remain steadfast and do not follow the path of those who have no knowledge."[89] We led the Children of Israel across the sea. Fir'aun and his hosts pursued them with wickedness and oppression, until when drowning, he cried out: "I believe that there is none worthy of worship but He *(Allah)* in Whom the Children of Israel believe, and I am one of the Muslims."[90] *In response, it was said to him*: "Now you *believe*! But a little while before you were disobedient and one of the mischief-makers![91] We shall save your body today, so that you may become a sign for the succeeding generations; indeed many among mankind are heedless of Our signs!"[92] 10:[83-92]

SECTION: 10

We settled the Children of Israel in a respectable dwelling and provided them with the good things of life. They did not cause dissension until after knowledge had come to them. Surely, your Rabb will judge between them in those matters in which they caused dissension on the Day of Resurrection.[93] If you are in doubt regarding what We have revealed to you, ask those who have been reading the Book before you. In fact, the truth has indeed come to you from your Rabb: therefore, do not be of those who doubt,[94] and do not join those who deny the revelations of Allah; otherwise you will become one of the losers.[95] 10:[93-95]

The story of Musa and Fir'aun

Children of Israel were delivered from the bondage of Fir'aun

Children of Israel were provided with good things of life

In fact, those against whom the Word of your Rabb has proved true, will not believe,[96] even if every sign should come to them, until they *themselves* see the painful punishment.[97] Was there any town which *seeing the scourge,* believed, and their belief profited them except the people of Yûnus *(Jonah)*? When they believed, We removed from them the disgraceful scourge and allowed them to enjoy their worldly life for a while.[98] 10:[96-98]

Belief after seeing the scourge did not benefit any nation except the nation of Yûnus

If it had been the will of your Rabb *that all the people of the world should be believers,* all the people of the earth would have believed! Would you then compel mankind against their will to believe?[99] It is not possible for anyone to believe except by the permission of Allah, and He throws filth on those who do not use their common-sense.[100] Say: "Look at whatever exists in the heavens and the earth." Signs and warnings do not benefit those people who do not believe.[101] Now are they waiting for *evil* days like the ones that befell the people who passed away before them? Say: "Wait if you will; I too will wait with you."[102] *When such a time comes,* We rescue Our Rasools and those who believe - this is *Our way*; it is but right that We rescue the believers.[103] 10:[99-103]

Forcing someone to convert to Islam is prohibited

SECTION: 11

Say: "O people! If you are in doubt about my Deen *(religion)*, then know that I will never worship those whom you worship besides Allah. I worship Allah, Who has the power to cause your death, and I am commanded to be one of the believers."[104] *I am further commanded*: "Dedicate yourself to the Deen *(religion)* in all uprightness and be not of the mushrikeen *(who associate other deities with Allah)*.[105] Do not invoke, beside Allah, others who can neither benefit nor harm you, for if you do, you shall certainly become one of the wrongdoers.[106] If Allah afflicts you with a calamity, none can remove it but He; and if He intends to bestow a favor upon you, none can withhold His bounty. He bestows it on whomsoever of His servants He pleases; He is the Forgiving, the Merciful."[107] 10:[104-107]

No one other than Allah can harm or benefit you

O Muhammad, declare: "O mankind! The truth has come to you from your Rabb! He that follows guidance *(Right Way)* follows it for his own good and he that goes astray does so at his own risk; for I am not a custodian over you."[108] *O Prophet,* follow what is revealed to you and be patient till Allah passes His judgement, for He is the best of all the Judges.[109] 10:[108-109]

Declare that guidance has come - now to follow or not to follow is your choice

11: HÛD

Period of Revelation

This Sûrah was revealed during the last stage of the Prophet's stay at Makkah, and most probably it was revealed immediately after Sûrah Yûnus.

Major Issues, Divine Laws, and Guidance

* Allah is the Provider and Sustainer of all creatures.
* Al-Qur'an is the pure Message of Allah and is not forged by the Prophet.
* Story of the Prophet Nûh and his people.
* Dialogue between the Prophet Nûh, his son and Allah.
* Prophets Hûd, Sâleh, Lût and Shu'aib's addresses to their people and consequences of their people's rejecting their messages.
* Divine law of virtues removing the evils.
* Allah has given freedom of choice to mankind (whether to believe or not to believe).

This Sûrah emphasizes invitation to the Message of Allah. It is an admonition and warning to the disbelievers. The **invitation** is to accept the Message of Allah, obey the Prophet of Allah, discard shirk, and worship Allah alone. Live your life in this world keeping in mind that you shall be held accountable for all of your actions on the Day of Judgement. The **admonition** is given through the example of those people who put their faith in and used their efforts for this worldly life and rejected the message of the Prophets. As a result, they met the evil consequences of their rejection. Therefore, people are advised to think seriously about whether or not they should follow the way of the arrogant, which history has proved to be the way to destruction. The **warning** is given to the disbelievers that they should not be deluded by the delay in the punishment for their misdeeds. The delay is only because of the respite that Allah has granted them, by His grace, to mend their ways. If they do not make use of this opportunity, they shall be inflicted with an inevitable punishment. Al-Qur'an has used the stories of the people of Nûh, Hûd, Sâleh, Lût, Shu'aib and Musa to achieve this purpose. The most prominent feature of these stories is to spell out how Allah passes His judgement on the people, He does not spare any disbeliever even if he/she may be a nearest relative of a Prophet of the time. The stories of Nûh and Lût clearly tell that even the Prophet's own son and wife were not spared for being disbelievers. Therefore, the believers should remember that real relationship is the relationship of faith.

11: HÛD

This Sûrah, revealed at Makkah, has 10 sections and 123 verses.

In the name of Allah, the Compassionate, the Merciful

SECTION: 1

Alif L'âm R'â. This Book, whose verses are perfected and issued in detail by the One Who is All-Wise, All-Aware,[1] *teaches* that you should worship none but Allah. Surely, I am a warner and bearer of good news from Him to you.[2]   You should seek forgiveness of your Rabb and turn to Him in repentance; He will grant you good provisions until an appointed term, and bestow His grace on everyone who has merit! But if you turn away *(pay no heed)*, I fear for you the punishment of a Great Day.[3]   To Allah you shall all return, He has power over everything.[4]   Behold! They cover up their chests to conceal their thoughts from Him! Beware! Even when they cover themselves with their garments, He knows what they conceal and what they reveal, for He knows even the inmost secrets of the chests.[5]   11:[1-5]

Teachings of the Qur'an

JUZ (PART): 12

Allah is the Sustainer of all creatures

There is no moving creature on Earth whose sustenance is not provided by Allah. He knows its living and its resting place, and all that is recorded in a Clear Book. [6]   He is the One Who created the heavens and the earth in six Yaume *(days, time period or stages)* - at the time when His Throne was resting on the water - so that He may test you *to find out* which of you is the best in deeds. Now if you tell them:" You shall indeed be raised up after death," the unbelievers would certainly say: "This is nothing but sheer magic!"[7]   And if We put off their punishment till an appointed time, they are sure to ask: "What is holding it back?" Beware! When the Day *of that punishment* comes, nothing will hold it back from them and they will be completely encircled by that which they are ridiculing.[8]   11:[6-8]

SECTION: 2

Man is ever ungrateful to Allah except believers

If We let man taste any mercy from Us, then withdraw it from him, he becomes despairing, ungrateful.[9]   But if We let him taste any favor after adversity has afflicted him, then he says: "All my sorrows are gone from me," and   he becomes jubilantly arrogant.[10]   Except those who show patience and do good deeds; they are the ones who will have forgiveness and a great reward.[11] *O Prophet, be on your guard* lest you omit to recite some things which are being revealed to you feeling distressed in your heart that they might say: "Why has no treasure been sent down to him, or why has no angel come with him?" *You should know* that you are but a warner! It is Allah Who is the Custodian of everything.[12]   Do they say: "He has made up *the Qur'an* himself." Say *to them*: "Make

Al-Qur'an is not forged by the Prophet

up ten Sûrahs like this and call to your aid whomsoever you can, *including your gods whom you worship* besides Allah, if what you say is true.[13]   But if they fail to answer you, then you should know that this *(Qur'an)* is revealed with the knowledge of Allah and that there is none worthy of worship but He! Will you then become Muslims?"[14]   11:[9-14]

Those who desire the life of this world and its splendors, they are given full reward of their deeds therein and shall not be diminished.[15]   They are the ones who will have nothing in the hereafter except Hellfire. *There they shall come to know that* their deeds were fruitless and their actions were worthless.[16]   Can they be like those who have clear revelations from their Rabb and to whom a witness from Himself recites it, and they have the Book of Musa *(Moses)* before them - a guidance and a blessing? *Can such people deny the revelation of Al- Qur'an? No, of course not, rather* such people will believe in this, but those factions who do not believe shall have their promised place in the Hellfire. So, *O Prophet,* do not be in any doubt about it; it is the Truth from your Rabb, even though most people do not believe so.[17] Who can be more wrong than the one who forges a lie against Allah? Such people will be brought before their Rabb and the witnesses will say: "These are the ones who lied against their Rabb." Beware! The Curse of Allah is on those wrongdoers[18] who hinder others from the path of Allah and seek to make it crooked, and who deny the hereafter.[19] They cannot frustrate Allah on earth and there is none to protect them besides Allah. Their punishment shall be doubled, for they could neither hear *others who speak the Truth* nor see *the Truth for themselves*.[20] They are the ones who have lost their own souls, and the *fancies* they invented have left them in the lurch.[21] No doubt they will be the greatest losers in the Hereafter.[22] As for those who believe and do good deeds and humble themselves before their Rabb, they will be residents of paradise to live therein forever.[23] The example of these two parties is like *two men, one of whom is* blind and deaf, and *the other who can* see and hear. Are they equal when compared? Will you not then learn a lesson *from this example*?[24]   11:[15-24]

The People of the Book (Jews and Christians) are of two kinds: those, who can see the Truth, and those who choose not to

SECTION: 3

We sent Nûh to his people. *Nûh said*: "I have come to warn you plainly,[25] not to worship anyone except Allah; *otherwise* I am fear for you the punishment of a painful Day."[26] *In answer to this,* the chiefs of the unbelievers among his people said: "We see you as no more than merely a human being like ourselves: and we see that no one has followed you except the meanest among us, whose judgement abilities are immature and we find nothing in you which gives you superiority over us: in fact, we think that you are liars."[27] He said: "O my people, look! If I am given clear proof from my Rabb, and He has bestowed on me His grace, although it be hidden from you, can I compel you to accept it against your will?[28] O my people! I do not ask you any wealth for this work, for I expect my reward from none but Allah. I am not going to drive away those who believe; for they will surely meet their Rabb. But I can see that you are acting out of ignorance.[29] And O my people! Who will save me from Allah, if I drive them away? Don't you

The Prophet Nûh's address to his people

understand *this simple thing*?[30]   I do not say that I possess the Treasures of Allah, nor do I say that I have knowledge of the unseen, nor do I claim to be an angel; nor do I say of those who are mean in your eyes, that Allah will not grant them any good - Allah knows best what is in their hearts - *for if I say any thing like this,* I will indeed become a wrongdoer."[31]   They said: "O Nûh! You have argued with us and argued too much, now bring upon us *the scourge* with which you threaten us, if what you say is true."[32]   He replied: " Allah will surely bring it on you if He pleases and then you will not be able to escape from it![33]   My counsel will not profit you, much as I desire to give you good counsel, if Allah wants to leave you astray; He is your Rabb and to Him you shall return." [34] Do *the pagans of Makkah* say: "He *(Muhammad)* has forged this *Qur'an*?" Say to them: "If I have indeed forged it, then its sin is on me! And I am clear of the sins which you are committing *for not believing it*."[35]   11:[25-35]

SECTION: 4

And it was revealed to Nûh: "None of your people will believe now, other than those who have already believed. So do not grieve at their evil deeds.[36]   Build an ark under Our Eyes in accordance with Our revelation, and beware not to plead with Me on behalf of those who are wrongdoers: for they are all to be drowned *in the flood*."[37]   So he started to build the ark; and whenever the chiefs of his people passed by him, they laughed at him. He said: "Laugh at us now if you will, *soon the time is going to come when* we too will laugh at you as you are laughing at us.[38] Soon you will come to know who will be seized by a humiliating scourge, and who will be afflicted with everlasting punishment."[39]   11:[36-39]

Finally when Our Command came and the water from Al-Tannûr *(a particular oven marked as a starting point to warn Nûh in order to get him ready to board the ark)* gushed forth! We said *to Nûh*: "Take into the Ark a pair from every species, your family - except those against whom the Word has already gone forth - and the believers; and those who believed with him were only a few."[40] Thus he said: "Embark on it; in the name of Allah is its course and its anchorage; surely, my Rabb is Forgiving, Merciful."[41]   11:[40-41]

As the *ark* floated with them on board over the mountainous waves and Nûh called out to his son, who stood apart: "O my

---

Sidebar notes:

Nûh's people challenged him and asked for the scourge of Allah

Allah commanded Nûh to build an ark

Allah commanded Nûh to embark and gather on board the believers and a pair from every species

son! Embark with us and be not with the unbelievers!"[42] He replied: "I will take refuge on some mountain, which will save me from the flood." *Nûh* said: "None shall be secure today from the judgement of Allah, except those on whom He has mercy!" And thereupon, a wave came between them and he *(Nûh's son)* became among one of those who drowned.[43] *Finally, Allah* said: "O earth! Swallow up your water," and "O sky! Cease your rain." The floodwater abated and the judgement was carried out. The *ark* rested on mount Al-Jûdi and it was said: "Gone are the wrongdoing people!"[44] Nûh called out to his Rabb saying: "O my Rabb! My son is of my family, and surely, Your promise is true and You are the most just of all Judges!"[45] *Allah* replied: "O Nûh! In fact, he is not of your family; for he is not of righteous conduct. So do not ask Me anything of which you have no knowledge! I admonish you, lest you become one of the ignorant!" [46] Nûh said: "My Rabb! I seek refuge in You from asking You that of which I have no knowledge; and unless You forgive me and have mercy on me, I shall surely be lost!"[47] It was said: "O Nûh! Disembark *(from the ark)* with Our peace and blessings on you and on the peoples who are with you. As for other people, We shall grant them the provisions of life for some time, *and if they do not behave righteously,* then they shall have a painful punishment from Us."[48] *O Muhammad,* these are some of the facts from the unseen *history* which We have now revealed to you: neither you nor your people knew about it before. So have patience; surely, the end is for the righteous.[49]   11:[42-49]

Dialogue between Nûh, his son, and Allah

SECTION: 5

To the people of 'Ad We sent their brother Hûd. He said: "O my people! Worship Allah, you have no god but Him; *otherwise* you are but inventing lies.[50] O my people! I do not ask you any reward for my services; for I expect my reward from none but my Creator. Will you not then use your common sense?[51] And O my people! Seek forgiveness from your Rabb and turn to Him in repentance. He will send you from the sky abundant rain and He will add strength to your strength. So do not turn away like criminals." [52] They said: "O Hûd! You have given us no clear proof. We are neither going to desert our gods just on your word, nor are we going to believe in you.[53] We believe that perhaps some of our gods have afflicted you with evil." He said: "Allah is my witness and let you also be my witness that I am done with your shirk of worshipping other deities besides Him.[54] So, let all of you

The Prophet Hûd's address to his people, their response, and its consequences

scheme against me if you will, and give me no respite.[55] I have put my trust in Allah, Who is my Rabb and your Rabb. There is no living creature whose destiny is not controlled by Him. Indeed, straight is the Way of my Rabb.[56] Now, even if you turn away, I have at least conveyed the message with which I was sent to you. *Since you have denied Him,* my Rabb will raise up some other people in your place and you cannot harm Him in any way. Indeed, my Rabb is watching over everything."[57] When Our judgement came to pass, We saved Hûd and those who believed with him through a special grace from Us - We did save them from a horrifying scourge.[58] Such were the people of 'Ad. They denied the revelations of their Rabb, disobeyed His Rasool, and followed the command of every stubborn oppressor. [59] They were followed by a curse in this world and cursed they shall be on the Day of Resurrection. Beware! 'Ad denied their Rabb. Beware! Gone are 'Ad, the people of Hûd.[60]   11:[50-60]

SECTION: 6

The Prophet Sâleh's address to his people, their response, and its consequences

To the Thamûd people, We sent their brother Sâleh. He said: "O my people! Worship Allah, you have none worthy of worship but He. It is He Who created you from the earth and made it a dwelling for you. So seek forgiveness from Him and turn to Him in repentance. Surely, my Rabb is very close, ready to answer."[61] They said: "O Sâleh! Till now you were the one in whom we had great expectations! Would you now forbid us the worship of what our forefathers worshipped? Indeed, we strongly doubt that to which you are calling us."[62] He said: "O my people! Tell me, if I have a clear proof from my Rabb and He has granted me mercy from Himself - who then will help me against Allah if I disobey Him? What would you add other than to make me lose even more?[63] And O my people! This she-camel of Allah is a sign for you. Leave her to pasture on Allah's earth and do not molest her lest a swift scourge should fall upon you!"[64] But, *even after the warning,* they hamstrung her. So he said: "You have but three days to enjoy your homes, that is a promise which will not be repudiated!"[65] When Our Judgement came to pass, We saved Sâleh and those who believed with him, through a special mercy from Us, and *save them* from the disgrace of that Day. Indeed, your Rabb is All-Strong, All-Mighty.[66] A terrible blast overtook the wrongdoers and by the morning they were laying dead, with their faces down in their homes,[67] as if they had never flourished there. Beware!

Thamûd denied their Rabb. Gone are the people of Thamûd.[68]

11:[61-68]

SECTION: 7

Our Messengers *(angels)* came to Ibrâheem *(Abraham) with* good news. They said "Peace be upon you." He answered: "Peace be upon you too," and hastened to entertain them with a roasted calf.[69]   But when he saw that their hands were not extended towards it, he felt uneasy with them and started to be afraid of them. They said: "Do not fear. We have been sent to the people of Lût."[70]   His wife, who was standing there, laughed when We gave her good news of *Allah's giving her a son* Ishâq *(Isaac)* and after him a *grandson* Ya'qoob *(Jacob)*.[71] She said: "O wonder! *(An expression to indicate surprise)* Shall I bear a child now when I have become an old woman and my husband has become well advanced in age? This is indeed a strange thing!"[72]   They said: "Do you wonder at Allah's decree? May Allah's mercy and His blessings be upon you, O residents of the household; for He is indeed worthy of all praise, full of all glory."[73] When the fear of Ibrâheem was gone as the good news *(of his son and grand son)* came to him, he began to plead with Us for the people of Lût.[74]   Indeed Ibrâheem was forbearing, used to invoke Allah with humility and repentant.[75]   *The angels said*: "O Ibrâheem! Leave this topic. The decree of your Rabb has already been issued, now there must come to them a punishment that cannot be averted!"[76]

11:[69-76]

When Our messengers, *in the form of beautiful young men,* came to Lût, he became upset about them, for he felt helpless to offer them protection *against his nation's many violent homosexual men.* He said: "This is a critical day."[77]   *No sooner did the guests come to him than* his people, long addicted to evil practices, came rushing towards him. He said: "O my people! Here are my daughters - they are purer for you. Now, fear Allah and do not humiliate me by *insulting* my guests. Is there not even one good man among you?"[78]   They said: "Well you know, we have no need of your daughters. You know fully well what we want."[79]   He said: "I wish I had power to suppress you or could find some powerful support."[80]   *The messengers* said: "O Lût! We are the messengers of your Rabb. They will not be able to harm you. Now, take your family and get out *of this town* while yet a part of the night remains - and let none of you turn back - except your wife, *who should be left behind.* She will face the same fate as they. Their scheduled

---

Good news for Prophet Ibrâheem: that he will be given a son (Isaac) and beyond him a grandson (Jacob)

The Prophet Lût's address to his people, their response, and its consequences

time *of doom* is the morning. Is not the morning very close?"[81] When Our Judgement came to pass, We turned their city upside down and rained down on them brimstones of baked clay, layer upon layer,[82] specially marked by your Rabb. Such *scourge* is not far off from the wrongdoers![83]   11:[77-83]

SECTION: 8

The Prophet Shu'aib's address to his people who were cheating in their business transactions

To the people of Madyan We sent their brother Shu'aib. He said: "O my people! Worship Allah, you have none worthy of worship but He. Do not give short measure and weight. Although I see you in prosperity today, I fear for you the scourge of a Day that will encircle you.[84] O my people! Give full measure and weight in all fairness. Do not defraud people of their goods and do not spread mischief in the land.[85] What remains from Allah *(through a lawful transaction)* is better for you if you are true believers, and I am not set up as a guardian over you."[86] They said: "Oh Shu'aib! Does your Salah *(prayer)* command you that we give up all those deities whom our forefathers worshipped or that we have no right of doing what we like with our own goods? For sure, you are the only forbearing and right-minded! *(They said this sarcastically)*."[87] He said: "O my people! You see, if I have a clear sign from my Rabb and He has given me good sustenance from Himself, *how can I, then, be a party to your evil and unlawful practices*? It is not my intention to forbid something for you, while I do the same forbidden thing. I desire nothing but to reform so far as I can manage. I cannot succeed except with the help of Allah; in Him do I trust and to Him do I turn for everything.[88] O my people! Let not my dispute with you bring upon you the doom similar to that of the people of Nûh or of Hûd or of Sâleh, nor are the people of Lût far off from you;[89] seek forgiveness of your Rabb and turn to Him in repentance; for my Rabb is indeed Merciful, Affectionate."[90]   11:[84-90]

Their negative response and its consequences

They said: "O Shu'aib! We do not comprehend much of what you say. In fact, we see that you are a powerless person among us. Were it not for your family, we certainly would have stoned you, for you are not strong enough to prevail against us."[91] He said: "O my people! Do you regard my family to be more powerful than Allah, that you have disregarded Him totally as a thing cast behind your back? Surely, my Rabb encompasses all that you do.[92] O my people! You keep on doing your way, and I shall keep up mine: soon you will find out who receives the disgraceful punishment and who is a liar! Wait if you will; I too am waiting with you!"[93]   When Our judgement came to pass, We delivered Shu'aib and those who believed with him through Our special mercy. A mighty blast seized the wrongdoers and they lay dead with their faces down in their homes,[94]   as if they had never flourished there. Behold! Like Thamûd, gone are the people of Madyan![95]   11:[91-95]

SECTION: 9

We sent Musa with Our signs and clear authority[96]   to Fir'aun *(Pharaoh)* and his chiefs; but they followed the command of Fir'aun, and the command of Fir'aun was not right.[97]   He will be in front of his people on the Day of Resurrection, and will bring them down to Hell. How awful will be the place to which they will be brought?[98]   A curse followed them in this life, and *a curse* will follow them on the Day of Resurrection. What an evil reward for one to receive.[99]   These are the stories of the towns which We relate to you; of them some have survived and some have ceased to exist.[100]   We were not unjust to them, but they were unjust to themselves. The deities they invoked beside Allah did not avail them when the judgement of your Rabb came to pass; they added nothing to their lot but perdition.[101]   Such is the scourge of your Rabb when He seizes a town of wrongdoers; indeed, His seizure is terrible and painful.[102]   In fact, there is a sign in this for those who fear the punishment of the hereafter; that is a Day in which mankind will be gathered together and that is a Day when all will be present.[103]   We do not delay it but to the appointed deadline.[104] When the Day will come, no one shall dare to speak except with His permission. Of them, some will be damned and some will be blessed.[105]   Those who are damned shall be in the fire; in there, they will have only sighs and sobs.[106]   They will dwell therein as long as the heavens and the earth shall last, unless your Rabb ordains otherwise; surely, your Rabb is the mighty doer of what He intends.[107]   As for those who are blessed, they shall be in paradise. They will dwell therein as long as the heavens and the earth shall last, unless your Rabb ordains otherwise; an award which shall never be taken away.[108]   Therefore, have no doubt concerning the deities they worship, for they *blindly imitate the* worship *of those deities* whom their forefathers used to worship before them; and surely, We shall give them their share *of punishment* in full without any abatement.[109]   11:[96-109]

Fate of Fir'aun and his chiefs who were given the warning but they gave no heed

SECTION: 10

Differences arose about the book given to Musa because of his followers' lack of belief

We certainly gave the Book to Musa *(Moses)*, but differences arose about it; had not a Word gone forth from your Rabb, the matter would have been decided between them *regarding those differences*. It is a fact that they are in suspicious doubt about this,[110] and it is also a fact that your Rabb will give them full measure for their deeds, for He is fully aware of what they do.[111] Therefore, stand firm *on the Right Way* as you are commanded, together with those who have turned *from unbelief to belief in Allah*, and do not transgress; surely, He is watching all that you do.[112] Do not be inclined to those who are unjust, lest you be seized by the fire; and you will not have any protector besides Allah, nor shall you be helped.[113]   11:[110-113]

Virtues remove evils and Allah does not let the reward of the righteous be wasted

Establish Salah *(prayers)* at the two ends of the day and in the early part of the night. Indeed virtues remove evils. This is a reminder for the mindful.[114] Be patient; for sure Allah does not let the reward of the righteous be wasted.[115] Why were there not among the generations before you, good persons who could forbid the people from making mischief in the land, except a few of those whom We delivered from among them? The wrongdoers, however, pursued the worldly pleasure they were provided, and became *confirmed* criminals.[116] It is not possible that your Rabb would destroy the towns unjustly while their inhabitants were reformers *(likely to mend their ways)*.[117]   11:[114-117]

Freedom of choice given to mankind is the Will of Allah

If your Rabb had so willed, He would have certainly made mankind one single nation *but that is not what He wants*, so they will not cease to differ[118] except those on whom He has bestowed His mercy; and that *very freedom of choice and action* is the whole purpose of their creation. *That is how* the Word of your Rabb, that He will fill Hell with jinns and human beings all together, will be fulfilled.[119] All these stories of the prior Rasools that We relate to you *(O Muhammad)* are to strengthen your heart therewith; through these there has come to you the truth, and an admonition and a reminder for the believers. [120] As for those who are unbelievers, say to them: "Do whatever you want, and so shall we.[121] Wait if you will! Surely, we too shall wait."[122] Allah Alone has the knowledge of what is hidden in the heavens and the earth, and everything shall ultimately return to Him *for decision*; Therefore, worship Him and put your trust in Him, and your Rabb is not unmindful of what you do.[123]   11:[118-123]

12: YÛSUF

Period of Revelation and Why Revealed

This Sûrah was revealed during the last stage of the Prophet's residence at Makkah. It was a time when the Quraish were considering the question of killing, exiling, or imprisoning him. The Jews instigated the unbelievers to test the Prophet Muhammad (peace be upon him) by asking him: "Why did the Israelites go to Egypt?" The history of the Israelites was not known to the Arabs, and the Prophet had no means of knowing their traditions. Therefore, they thought that the Prophet would not be able to give a satisfactory answer, and thus, would be totally exposed. But, contrary to their expectations, the tables were turned on them, when Allah revealed the whole story of the Prophet Yûsuf (Joseph) then and there. To their astonishment, the Prophet recited it to them on the spot. This put the Quraish in a very awkward position because, it not only ruined their scheme, but also warned them by applying the example of Yûsuf's brothers to their case, as if to say, "As you are behaving towards this Prophet, exactly in the same way the brothers of the Prophet Yûsuf behaved towards him; therefore, you should expect to meet with the same end."

Major Issues, Divine Laws, and Guidance

* All Rasools were human beings.
* Yûsuf's prayer to live and die as a Muslim.
* The faith of Prophets Ibrâheem (Abraham), Ishâq (Isaac), Ya'qoob (Jacob) and Yûsuf (Joseph), may Allah's peace be upon them all, was the same as that of the Prophet Muhammad (peace be upon him) and they invited the people to the same Message to which Muhammad (peace be upon him) was inviting them.
* Characters molded by Islam (based on the worship of Allah and account-ability in the hereafter) are compared to characters molded by disbelief and ignorance (based on the worship of false gods and the material world). Then the addressees are asked to decide for themselves between these two patterns.
* It is made clear that whatever Allah wills, happens, and no one can defeat His plan or prevent it from happening.
* The believers are advised to remain within the limits prescribed by Divine Law while pursuing their aims, because success and failure are entirely in the hands of Allah.
* The believers are advised to exert their efforts towards the Truth and put their trust in Allah. This will help them face their opponents with

confidence and courage.

* Allah taught the believers through this story that one who possesses true Islamic character can conquer the world with the strength of his character. The marvellous example of the Prophet Yûsuf shows how a man of high and pure character comes out successful even under the most adverse circumstances.

Moreover, the revelation of this Sûrah accomplished the following two objectives:

1. It provided proof of Muhammad's (peace be upon him) Prophethood, and that his knowledge was not based on mere hearsay, but was gained through revelation.

2. It applied the theme of this story to the Quraish and warned them that ultimately the conflict between them and the Prophet would end in his victory over them. As is stated in verse 7: "Indeed there are signs in this story of Yûsuf and his brothers for the inquirers (from among the Quraish)."

In fact, by applying this story to the conflict between the Prophet and the Quraish, the Qur'an had made a bold and clear prophecy which was fulfilled literally by the events that happened in the succeeding ten years. Hardly two years had passed after its revelation when the Quraish, like the brothers of the Prophet Yûsuf, conspired to kill the Prophet and forced him to emigrate from Makkah to Al-Madinah, where he gained power similar to that gained by the Prophet Yûsuf in Egypt. Again, in the end, the Quraish had to humble themselves before him just as the brothers of the Prophet Yûsuf humbly requested, "Show mercy to us for Allah rewards richly those who show mercy," (Verse 88) and the Prophet Yûsuf generously forgave them - though he had complete power to inflict his vengeance upon them. He said: "Today no penalty shall be inflicted on you. May Allah forgive you. He is the greatest of all those who forgive." (Verse: 92) The same story of mercy was repeated when, after the conquest of Makkah, the defeated Quraish stood meekly before the Prophet Muhammad (peace be upon him), who had full power to inflict his vengeance upon them for each and every cruelty committed by them. But instead, he merely asked them: "What treatment do you expect from me?" They replied, "You are a generous brother and the son of a generous brother." At this, the Prophet Muhammad (peace be upon him) forgave them very generously, saying: "I am giving the same answer to your request that Yûsuf gave to his brothers: "Today, no penalty shall be inflicted upon you: you are forgiven."

12: YÛSUF

This Sûrah, revealed at Makkah, has 12 sections and 111 verses.

In the name of Allah, the Compassionate, the Merciful.

SECTION: 1

Alif L'âm Râ. These are the verses of the Book that makes things clear.[1]   We have revealed this Qur'an in the Arabic language so that you *(Arabs)* may understand.[2]   We relate to you the best of stories through this Qur'an by Our revelation to you *(O Muhammad)*, though before this you were one of those who did not know.[3]   12:[1-3]

This is the narrative of that time, when Yûsuf *(Joseph)* said to his father: "O my father! In a dream I saw eleven stars, the sun and the moon - I saw them prostrate themselves before me!"[4]   He replied: "O my son! Do not say any thing about this dream to your brothers, lest they plot an evil scheme against you; for Shaitân is an open enemy to human beings.[5]   It will happen, *as you have seen in your dream,* that you will be chosen by your Rabb *for His work.* He will teach you how to interpret visions, and will perfect His favor upon you and the children of Ya'qoob *(Jacob)*, as He perfected it upon your forefathers Ibrâheem *(Abraham)* and Ishâq *(Isaac)* before you. Surely, your Rabb is Knowledgeable, Wise.[6]   12:[4-6]

SECTION: 2

Indeed in the *story* of Yûsuf and his brothers, there are signs for inquirers.[7]   *This is how the story begins: his step brothers held   a meeting and* said to one another: "Yûsuf and his brother *(Benjamin)* are loved more by our father than us, even though we are a group *of   ten and can help him more than them.* In fact, our father is clearly mistaken.[8]   Let us kill Yûsuf or throw him out to some far-off land so that the attention of our father turns exclusively towards us, after that, we may again become righteous people!"[9]   At this one of them said: "Do not kill Yûsuf, but if you must, throw him into the dark depths of some well, so that he may be picked up by some passing caravan."[10]   12:[7-10]

After this meeting, they asked their father: "O our father! Why is it that you do not trust us with Yûsuf, though we are his sincere well-wishers?[11]   Send him with us tomorrow, that he may play and enjoy himself. We shall take good care of him."[12]   *Their father* said: "I will be worried if you take him away, for I fear lest

The Qur'an   is revealed   in   the Arabic   language

Story   of   the Prophet   Yûsuf (Joseph)

In this story there are lessons for the inquirers

The stepbrothers of Yûsuf asked their father to send him with them on a hunting trip and threw him in a dark well

a wolf should eat him up while you are off guard."[13]　They said: "If a wolf could eat him despite our number, then surely we would be worthless people!"[14]　When *after such persistence* they were able to take him away, they resolved to throw him into a dark well. We revealed this *(to Yûsuf)* : "A time will come that you will admonish them about this act of theirs, when they do not know *your identity*."[15]　　　　12:[11-15]

They told their father that Yûsuf was eaten by a wolf

At nightfall they returned to their father, weeping.[16]　They said: "O our Father! We went off to compete in racing with one another, and left Yûsuf by our belongings, and a wolf ate him ! But you will not believe us even though we are telling the truth."[17]　*As proof,* they brought his shirt stained with false blood. "No!" He cried, "Your souls have tempted you to evil. *I need* good patience! Allah Alone can help me against that which you assert."[18]　　　　12:[16-18]

A caravan kidnapped him, brought him to Egypt, and sold him

On the other side, a caravan passed by, and sent a water carrier who let down his bucket *into the well. Seeing Yûsuf in it,* he shouted with joy: "Good news! I found a young boy." They concealed him like trade merchandise. Allah knew what they did.[19]　　　They sold him for a petty price, a few dirhams *(silver coins)*, they had such a low estimation of him.[20]　　　12:[19-20]

SECTION: 3

The Egyptian who bought him was a good man

The Egyptian who bought Yûsuf said to his wife: "Be kind to him. He may prove useful to us, or we may adopt him as a son." Thus We established Yûsuf in the land and arranged to teach him the interpretation of dreams. Allah has full power over His affairs, though most people do not know.[21]　When he reached maturity, We bestowed on him wisdom and knowledge. Thus do We reward the righteous.[22]　　　　12:[21-22]

His master's wife tried to seduce him but Allah saved him

Now, the lady of the house *(his master's wife)* attempted to seduce him. She bolted the doors and said: "Come!" He replied: "May Allah protect me from this! My lord has provided me with good residence. *Should I betray his trust*? Surely, wrongdoers do not prosper."[23]　She advanced toward him, and he *would have* advanced towards her had he not seen a sign from his Rabb. Thus did We shield him from indecency and immodesty, for he was one of Our sincere servants.[24]　They both rushed to the door. *In order to stop him she caught his shirt, and as a result* she ripped his shirt from behind. At the door they met her husband. *Seeing him* she cried: "What punishment does someone who intended evil against your wife deserve except imprisonment or a painful punishment?"[25] *Yûsuf* said: "It was she who attempted to seduce me." *At this - one accusing the other* - one member of her own family bore witness saying: "If his shirt is ripped from the front, then she is speaking the truth and he is lying.[26]　　But if it is ripped from behind, then he is speaking the truth and she is lying."[27]　So when he *(her husband)* saw that Yûsuf's shirt was ripped from behind, he said *to her*: "It is one of the scam of you women! Your scam was mighty indeed! [28] O Yûsuf, say no more about this, and you *(O my wife)* seek forgiveness for your sins, for you were indeed the wrongdoer."[29]

2:[23-29]

SECTION: 4

The women of the city *began to talk about this incident,* saying: "The wife of Al-'Aziz has seduced her young slave, for she has fallen madly in love with him. In fact, we see her in manifest error."[30]　When she heard about these remarks, she invited them and prepared for them a banquet, and gave each of them a knife. *When they were engaged in cutting foodstuff,* she asked *Yûsuf* to come out before them. When they saw him, they were so amazed that they cut their hands and exclaimed *spontaneously*: "Good Lord! He is no human being; he is but a noble angel."[31]　She said: "Well, this is he about whom you blamed me. No doubt I seduced him, but he refused. And now if he refuses to obey my order, he will certainly be thrown into prison and be disgraced."[32]　*Yûsuf* said: "O my Rabb! Prison is more to my liking than to which they invite me; and unless You ward off their cunning scam from me, I may, *in my youthful folly,* feel inclined towards them and become one of the ignorants."[33]　Thereupon, his Rabb answered his prayer and warded off their cunning scam from him; surely, He hears all and knows all.[34]　*Still,* even after all the evidence they had seen *(of his innocence and the guilt of their women)*, they thought it proper to send him to prison for a while.[35]　　　　12:[30-35]

SECTION: 5

Two young men also entered the prison along with him. One day one of them said: "I saw in a dream that I was pressing wine." The other said: "I saw in a dream that I was carrying bread on my head, of which birds were eating." Tell us the interpretation of these dreams, for we see that you are a man of virtue.[36]　*Yûsuf*

The women of the town started pointing fingers at the wife of Al-'Aziz. As a result, she invited them to a banquet and asked Yûsuf to appear before them

Yûsuf was sent to prison

Two prison inmates had dreams and asked Yûsuf for interpretation replied: "I will, *with Allah's permission,* tell you the interpretation of these dreams before the food that is provided for you, comes to you, this is part of the knowledge which my Rabb has taught me. In fact, I have forsaken the faith of those people who do not believe in Allah and even deny the hereafter.[37]   I follow the faith of my forefathers Ibrâheem *(Abraham)*, Ishâq *(Isaac)* and Ya'qoob *(Jacob)*. It is not fitting that we attribute any partners with Allah. It is the grace of Allah on us and on mankind *(that He has not made us the servants of anyone else other than Himself)*, yet, most of the people are not grateful. [38]   O my fellow inmates! Tell me what is better; many different lords or Allah, the One, the Irresistible?[39] Those whom you worship besides Him are nothing but mere names which you and your forefathers have invented, for which Allah has revealed no sanction. The Command belongs to none but Allah, Who has ordained that you worship none but Him. That is the true faith, yet, most of the people do not know.[40]   O my fellow inmates! *(Here is the interpretation of your dreams)*, one of you will *be released* and serve wine to his lord *(the king of Egypt)*; and the other will be crucified and the birds will eat from his head. That's how the cases about which you inquired will be decided."[41]   Then, to the one who he thought would be released, he said: "Mention me to your lord." But Shaitân made him forget to mention *(Yûsuf)* to his lord, so he remained in the prison a few more years.[42]

12:[36-42]

SECTION: 6

One day the king *of Egypt* said: "I saw seven fat cows in my dream which were eaten up by seven lean cows, likewise, *I saw* seven green ears of corn and *seven* others that were dried up. O chiefs! Tell me the meaning of my dream if you can interpret the dreams."[43]   They replied: "Confused nightmares! We are not skilled in the interpretation of dreams *(such as this)*."[44]   *Thereupon* one of the two *inmates* who was released remembered *Yûsuf* after all that time, and he said: "I will tell you its interpretation; just send me *to Yûsuf in the prison.*"[45]   *He came to Yûsuf in the prison and said:* "O Yûsuf the truthful one! Tell us the meaning of the dream of seven fat cows which are eaten up by seven lean ones and of seven green ears of corn and *seven* others dried up: so that I may return to the people and let them know the meaning of this dream."[46]   He replied: "You will cultivate for seven consecutive years. During this time you should leave the corn you reap in the ear, except what may be sufficient for your food.[47]   Then, after that

Yûsuf's address to his fellow inmates

The King of Egypt had a dream and asked for its interpretation

Yûsuf's interpretation of the King's dream

period, there will come upon you seven hard years which will eat away all that you had stored except a little which you may have specifically set aside. [48] After that *period* will come a year of abundant rain, in which the people will press *(olives, grapes etc.).*"[49]   12:[43-49]

SECTION: 7

        The king said: "Bring him to me." When the messenger came to *Yûsuf, he* said: "Go back to your lord and ask him about the case of those women who cut their hands. Indeed my Rabb has full knowledge of their scam."[50] *The king* questioned *those women,* saying: "What do you say about the incident when you attempted to seduce Yûsuf?" They replied: "God forbid! We know of no evil on his part." The 'Aziz's wife said: "Now that the truth has come to light, it was I who attempted to seduce him. In fact, he is *absolutely* truthful."[51] *Yûsuf said,* "I asked for this *inquiry* in order that he *(Al-'Aziz)* may know that I did not betray him in his absence, and that Allah does not let the scam of the treacherous succeed."[52]   12:[50-52]

The King of Egypt heard the case of the women and found that Yûsuf was innocent

JUZ (PART): 13

Yûsuf's appointment as a King's cabinet member

"Not that I am free from sin - man's soul is prone to evil, except the one to whom my Rabb has shown mercy, certainly my Rabb is Forgiving, Merciful".[53] The king said: "Bring him to me; I will take him for my special service." When *Yûsuf* had a talk with *the King,* he said: "From now on, you have *an honorable* place with us, and *you will enjoy our* full confidence."[54] *Yûsuf* said: "Place me over all the resources of the land. Certainly I know how to manage; I have the *necessary* knowledge."[55] Thus, We established Yûsuf in the land to live therein any where he wished. We bestow Our mercy on whom We please and We do not let the reward of good people be lost.[56] Yet, the reward in the hereafter will be even better for those who believe and are righteous.[57]

12:[53-57]

SECTION: 8

Yûsuf's brothers came to Egypt to get food and grain

Several years later when the famine started and there was no food available outside of Egypt, Yûsuf's brothers came *to Egypt for food* and entered his office. He recognized them but they did not recognize him.[58] When he had given them their due provisions *and they were about to leave,* he said: "Bring your half brother to me *next time.* Do you not see that I give full measure and provide the best hospitality?[59] But if you do not bring him, you shall have no grain, nor shall you even come near me again."[60] They replied: "We shall certainly try our best to get permission from his father. This we will surely do."[61] *Yûsuf* told his servants to put *his brothers'* trading stock into their saddlebags *secretly so that* they should know about it only when they reach their family, so that they might come back."[62]

12:[58-62]

Yûsuf asked them to bring Benjamin (Yûsuf's younger brother)

They asked their father to send Benjamin with them in order to get more grain

When *Yûsuf's brothers* returned to their father, they said: "Father! Grain is henceforth denied us *unless we take our step-brother with us*; please send our brother with us so that we may get our measure; we take full responsibility for his safety."[63] He said: "Should I trust you with him as I once trusted you with his brother? Allah is the best protector and He is the Most Merciful of those who show mercy."[64] When they opened their baggage, they discovered that their money had been returned to them. "Father!" They cried with joy, "What more can we ask for? Here is our trading stock returned to us. We will bring more food for our family, we will take good care of our brother and obtain an extra camel load of grain. This way, it will be easy to add another camel load *of grain*."[65]

Ya'qoob (Jacob) replied: "I will never send him with you until you pledge in the name of Allah that you will surely bring him back to me unless you become helpless." And when they had given their pledge, he said: "Allah is the Witness over the pledge you made."[66] Then he said; "My sons! Do not enter through one gate, enter through different gates. I can not avail you against Allah*'s decree*; *this advice is just a precaution*, because decision lies with Allah Alone. In Him do I put my trust and in Him let all those that trust, put their trust in Him."[67] When they entered *the city* as their father had advised them, it did not avail them against the will of Allah. It was just a concern in Ya'qoob's heart, which he satisfied. Indeed he possessed the knowledge which We had given him, but most people do not know.[68]   12:[63-68]

SECTION: 9

When they entered upon Yûsuf, he called his brother *(Benjamin)* alone to himself, and said: "In fact, I am your brother *(Yûsuf)*, now you need not grieve at what they had been doing." [69] While *Yûsuf* was arranging the loads of their provisions, he put the *royal* drinking cup into his brother's pack. Later on a crier called out: "O people of the caravan! You must be thieves."[70] They turned back and asked: "What have you lost?"[71] The *royal servants* said: "We have lost the King's drinking cup. The one who brings it will be awarded a camel-load of food." *Their leader said:* "I guarantee it."[72] *Yûsuf's brothers* said: "By Allah! You should know, *by our behavior during our stay here,* that we did not come here to make mischief in the land and we are no thieves."[73] *The royal servants* said: "What should be the punishment *of the thief,* if you are liars?" [74] They replied: "The punishment is: he in whose pack you find the royal cup will be *to make him* your bondsman, that's how we punish wrongdoers."[75] After this *Yûsuf* first began to search the packs of his stepbrothers before the pack of his own brother *(Benjamin)*. Finally he took it out of his brother's pack. Thus did We plan for Yûsuf. He could not seize his brother under the King's law; but Allah willed otherwise. We exalt in ranks whom We please, He is the One Whose knowledge is far greater than the knowledge of all others.[76] *At this accusation, his brothers* remarked: *"This is not strange* if he has committed a theft - for his brother also committed a theft before him." Hearing this, Yûsuf suppressed his feelings and did not reveal anything to them - he simply whispered to himself: "You are far worse in this respect.

Ya'qoob's advice to his sons

Yûsuf introduced himself to his brother Benjamin and schemed to retain him

Benjamin was accused of stealing so that he could be retained

Allah knows best the truth of what you assert."[77]   - They said: "O 'Aziz *(exalted one)*! He *(Benjamin)* has a very aged father *who may not be able to survive without him*, so please take one of us instead of him. We see that you are one of those who do good to others."[78] *Yûsuf* replied: "God forbid that we should seize other than the one with whom we found our property: *if we did so* then indeed we would be unjust."[79]   12:[69-79]

SECTION: 10

Yûsuf's brothers went back and told their father about the incident of Benjamin's stealing and retention

        When they lost their hope *of moving Yûsuf,* they went aside to confer in private. The eldest of them said: "You know that your father had taken from you a solemn pledge in the name of Allah, and you also know how you fell short of your duty with respect to Yûsuf. Therefore, I am not going to leave this land until my father gives me permission or Allah decides for me, and He is the best of all judges.[80]   Go back to your father and tell him, "father, your son committed theft. *We did not see him stealing, however, we saw the stolen cup being brought out of his pack.* We testify only to what we know, and we could not guard the unseen."[81]   You may enquire from the people of the city where we have been and the caravan in which we travelled that we are indeed telling the truth."[82]   *When they went back and told all this to their father, " No!" Cried their father,"* Your souls have contrived a story for you. Well, I will bear this too with good   patience. May be Allah will bring them all back to me; indeed He is the Knowledgeable, the Wise."[83]   He turned his face away from them, crying: "Alas for Yûsuf!" His eyes became white with grief, and he became sorely oppressed.[84] They said: "By Allah! *It appears that* you will not cease to remember Yûsuf until you ruin your health or kill yourself."[85]   He said: "I

Their father sent them back

complain of my distress and grief to Allah Alone and I know from Allah what you do not know.[86]   O my sons! Go and search for Yûsuf and his brother. Never give up hope of Allah's mercy; in fact, none despairs of Allah's mercy except the unbelieving people."[87]
                                                    12:[80-87]

They came to Yûsuf and begged for food and some charity

        When they *went back to Egypt and* entered *Yûsuf's* office, they said: "O 'Aziz *(Exalted one)*! We and our family are in great distress, and we have brought poor capital, please give us full quota and treat it as charity to us. Surely, Allah rewards the charitable."[88] *Hearing this, Yûsuf, who could contain himself no longer,* replied: "Do you know what you did to Yûsuf and his brother while acting out of ignorance?"[89]   *This took them by surprise,* and they said:

"What! Are you really Yûsuf?" He replied: "Yes! I am Yûsuf and this is my brother. Allah has indeed been gracious to us. Verily, he who fears Allah and is patient, then indeed, Allah does not let the reward of the good-doers be wasted."[90]   They said: "By Allah! Certainly Allah has preferred you over us. We have indeed been guilty."[91]   Yûsuf said: "There is no blame on you today. May Allah forgive you! He is the most Merciful of those who show mercy! [92]   Go, take this shirt of mine and cast it over the face of my father, he will recover his sight. Then come back to me with all the members of your family."[93]   12:[88-93]

Yûsuf disclosed his identity

He forgave his brothers and sent for his family

SECTION: 11

When the caravan started *(from Egypt)* their father *(who was in Ken'ân)* said: "Certainly I feel the scent of Yûsuf, even though you may think I am out of my mind."[94]   The people, *who heard him,* said: "By Allah! You are still suffering from your old illusion."[95]   But when the bearer of the good news arrived, he cast *the shirt of Yûsuf* over his face and he regained his sight. Then he said: "Didn't I tell you that I know from Allah what you do not know?"[96]   They said: "Father! Pray for the forgiveness of our sins. We have indeed done wrong."[97]   He replied: "Soon I will ask forgiveness for you from my Rabb; surely, He is the One Who is the Forgiving, the Merciful."[98]   12:[94-98]

Ya'qoob got the good news of his son Yûsuf

When they came to Yûsuf, he took his parents to himself, and said: "Welcome to Egypt. If Allah so wills, you will live here in peace."[99]   Then, he raised his parents to the throne, and they all fell down in prostration before him. Yûsuf said, "O my father! This is the interpretation of my old dream. My Rabb has really made it come true. It was His grace that He took me out of prison and brought you all here from bedouin life, after Shaitân had stirred up strife between me and my brothers. Surely, my Rabb is gracious to whom He wills. Surely, He is the One Who is the Knowledgeable, the Wise.[100]   O my Rabb! You have indeed given me sovereignty and taught me the interpretation of dreams. O, the Creator of the heavens and the earth, You are my Protector in this world and in the hereafter, make me die as a Muslim and admit me among the righteous."[101]   *O Muhammad,* this story, which We have revealed to you is a news of the unseen; for you were not there with *(the brothers of Yûsuf)* when they conspired and put together their plan against him.[102]   Yet, strive as you may, most men are not going to become believers,[103]   even though you do not demand any

Thus his family was relocated from Ken'ân to Egypt

Yûsuf's prayer to live and die as a Muslim

recompense for this information. *This Qur'an* is nothing but a reminder for all the worlds.[104]   12:[99-104]

SECTION: 12

Many people who believe in Allah, also commit shirk

There are many signs in the heavens and the earth which they pass by; yet, they pay no attention to them! [105]   *As a result,* most of them believe in Allah but still commit shirk.[106]   Do they feel secure that Allah's scourge will not fall on them, or that the Hour of Doom will not come upon them suddenly while they do not suspect it?[107]   Tell them *plainly*: "This is my way. I invite you to Allah with sure knowledge which I and my followers possess. Glory be to Allah, and I am not one of the mushrikeen."[108]

12:[105-108]

All the Rasools were human beings

We did not send *Rasools* before you, *O Muhammad,* but men, to whom We sent Our Revelations *after choosing them* from the people of their towns. Have *these unbelievers* not traveled through the land and seen what was the end of those who passed away before them? *From their destiny you should know that* the home of the hereafter is better for those who are righteous. Why don't you understand?[109]   *Respite was granted* until the Rasools gave up hope *of their people* and realized that they were being treated as liars, Our help came to them and We delivered those whom We pleased; and Our scourge was not averted from the criminal people.[110]   There is a lesson in these stories *of former people* for the men of common sense. This *story of Yûsuf revealed in the Qur'an* is not an invented tale, but a confirmation of previous scriptures - a detailed exposition of all things, and is a guidance and blessing for the people who believe.[111]   12:[109-111]

The story of Yûsuf is confirmation of previous scriptures

13: AR-RA'D

Period of Revelation

This Sûrah was revealed in the last stage of the Prophet's residence at Makkah and during the same period in which Sûrahs Yûnus, Hûd and Al-A'râf were revealed.

Major Issues, Divine Laws, and Guidance

* The Qur'an is the revelation of Allah.
* Trees, fruit, and vegetables are among the signs of Allah.
* Allah never changes the condition of a people unless they try to change themselves.
* Those who do not respond to the call of Allah will have no way to escape from the fire of hell.
* It is the remembrance of Allah that provides tranquility to hearts.
* Rasools have no power to show any miracle except by the leave of Allah.

The main theme of this Sûrah is to declare that the Message of Allah is the Truth and it will be a serious and fatal mistake to reject it. The arguments in the whole Sûrah turn around this theme, and the basic components of the Message which are Tawheed (God is One), Risâlat (Prophethood) and Resurrection. These arguments are repeated over and over again. People are invited to believe in these facts for their own good and if they don't, they are warned about incurring their own ruin. This Sûrah not only provides reasoning to satisfy the mind, but also appeals the heart to accept the faith. It puts forward logical arguments in support of the True Message and against the people's wrong notions. It makes frequent use of sympathetic advice to win over the hearts of disbelievers by warning them about the consequences of Kufr (unbelief) and the good results and rewards of having True Faith.

This Sûrah also answers the objections and clear the doubts of the disbelievers which appeared to be a hindrance in accepting the Divine Message. It also provides comfort, hope, and courage to the believers who were passing through a long and hard ordeal.

13: AR-RA'D

This Sûrah, revealed at Makkah, has 6 sections and 43 verses.

In the name of Allah, the Compassionate, the Merciful.

SECTION: 1

Al-Qur'an is revealed by Allah, the Creator of the heavens and the earth

　　　　Alif L'âm M'eem Râ. These are the Verses of the Book *(Qur'an)* and what has been revealed to you, *O Muhammad,* from your Rabb is the Truth, but most of the people do not believe in this.[1]　Allah is the One Who raised the heavens without any pillars as you can see, then firmly established Himself on the throne *of authority* and subjected the sun and the moon to His law - each one pursuing its course for an appointed time. He regulates all affairs. He spells out His revelations so that you may believe in meeting your Rabb.[2]　He is the One Who spread out the earth and placed thereon mountains and rivers, created fruits of every kind in pairs, two and two, and makes the night cover the day. Certainly in these things there are signs for those who use their common sense.[3]

13:[1-3]

Trees, fruit, vegetables and their tastes are the signs of Allah

　　　　In the earth there are tracts side by side: gardens of grapes, crops and palm trees growing singly or in cluster. They are all watered with the same water, yet, We make some of them excel others *in taste* as food. Surely in this, there are signs for people who use their common sense.[4]　Now, if there is anything that seems strange, then strange is their saying: "What! When we will become dust, could we then be raised to a new life again?" They are the people who have denied their Rabb, they are the ones who will have chains around their necks and they are the ones who will be the inmates of Hellfire to live therein forever.[5]　They ask you to hasten on the evil *(Allah's scourge)* rather than the good, although there have been instances of exemplary punishments before them. In fact your Rabb is the Lord of Forgiveness to the people, notwithstanding their wrongdoing; and verily your Rabb is also stern in retribution.[6]　The unbelievers say: "Why is not a sign sent down to him *(Muhammad)* from his Rabb?" You are nothing but a Warner and every nation was assigned a guide.[7]

For every nation Allah sent a guide (Rasool)

13:[4-7]

SECTION: 2

　　　　Allah knows what every female bears in her womb. He is fully aware of what decrease or increase *(miscarriage or a long wait)* takes place in the womb. Everything has a due measure with Him.[8]   He has perfect knowledge of both the visible and the invisible. He is the Great, the Most High.[9]   It is the same *to Him* whether any of you speak in secret or aloud, whether anyone hides under the darkness of night or walks about in broad daylight.[10] Each person has been assigned guardian angels before him and behind him, who watch him by the command of Allah. The fact is that Allah never changes the condition of a people until they change what is in themselves. If Allah wants to afflict a people with misfortune, none can ward it off, nor can they find any protector besides Him.[11]   He is the One Who shows you lightning, which causes fear and hope, and brings up heavy clouds *(with rain)*.[12] The thunder declares His glory with His praises and so do the angels in awe of Him. He *is the One Who* sends thunderbolts and smites with them whomever He wants. Yet these *unbelievers* dispute concerning Allah;   He is Mighty in strength and Severe in punishement.[13]   Praying to Him Alone is the right thing. The other deities they pray to, besides Him, cannot answer their prayers. They are like a man who stretches forth his hands to the water and asks it to reach his mouth. It cannot reach his mouth this way; likewise the prayer of the unbelievers is nothing but a fruitless effort.[14] Whatever is in the heavens and the earth do prostrate before Allah Alone willingly or unwillingly, and so do their shadows in the mornings and evenings.[15]   13:[8-15]

> Allah never changes the condition of a people unless they strive to change themselves

> Pray to Allah Alone

Ask them: "Who is the Rabb of the heavens and the earth?" *If they hesitate to respond,* say: "Allah." Then ask them: *"When this is the fact,* why do you take other deities, besides Him, who do not control any benefit or harm even to themselves, as your protectors?" Say: "Are the blind and the seeing equal? Or can darkness and light be equal?" *If that is not so, then,* have their shorakâ' *(other deities they worship)* created any thing like His creation which has made the matter of creation doubtful for them? Say: "Allah Alone is the Creator of everything and He is the One, the Irresistible."[16]   He sends down water from the skies and each channel starts flowing according to its measure, and then the torrent bears a swelling foam - like the scum which appears from metals which are melted *in the furnace* for making ornaments and utensils. By such examples Allah depicts truth and falsehood. As for the scum, it is thrown away, being worthless, but that which is useful for mankind remains behind on the earth. In this way Allah cites examples *to make His message clear*.[17]   There is an

> Deities besides Allah do not have any control over harm or benefit

> Those who do not respond to the call of their Rabb will have no way to escape

excellent reward for those who respond to the call of their Rabb. As for those who do not respond to Him - even if they had all that is in the earth, and as much besides, to offer as a ransom *in order to save themselves from punishment, it would be of no use.* They are the ones who will have a terrible reckoning; their abode will be hell - what an evil resting place.[18]   13:[16-18]

SECTION : 3

Those who fulfill their pledge with Allah will have an excellent abode in the Hereafter

Is he who knows that which has been revealed to you from your Rabb is the Truth, like the one who is blind *to this fact*? Only those who use their common sense benefit from this reminder:[19] those who fulfill their covenant with Allah and do not break their pledge; [20] who join together what Allah has commanded to be joined, who fear their Rabb and are afraid of the terrible reckoning;[21] who for the sake of Allah's pleasure keep their patience, establish Salah, spend secretly and openly out of the sustenance which We have provided for them, and repel evil with good - they are the ones for whom there is the home of the hereafter,[22] the Paradise of perpetual bliss: which they will enter together with the righteous among their forefathers, their spouses and their descendants. The angels will come to welcome them from every side,[23] saying: "Peace be upon you for all that you steadfastly endured in the world. How excellent is the home of the hereafter!"[24] As for those who break their covenant with Allah after confirming it and cut asunder what Allah has commanded to be joined and create mischief in the land, a curse shall be laid upon them and they shall have a terrible home.[25] Allah grants abundantly His provisions to whom He wills and sparingly to whom He pleases. *The unbelievers* rejoice in the life of this world: but brief indeed is the comfort of this worldly life as compared to the life of the hereafter.[26]

Those who break their pledge will have the curse and a terrible home

13:[19-26]

SECTION: 4

It is the remembrance of Allah that provides tranquility to hearts

The unbelievers say: "Why has no sign been sent down to him *(Muhammad)* from his Rabb?" Say: "In fact Allah lets go astray whom He wills, and guides to Himself those who turn to Him,[27] those who have believed and whose hearts find comfort in the remembrance of Allah. Indeed, in the remembrance of Allah do hearts find comfort.[28] Those who believe and do good deeds, blessed be they and blessed be their place of final return."[29]

13:[27-29]

O Muhammad! We have sent you among a nation before whom other nations have passed away, so that you may recite to them Our revelations which We have sent down to you; yet they are rejecting the Compassionate *(Allah)*. Say: "He is my Rabb! There is none worthy of worship but He. In Him I have put my trust and to Him I shall return."[30]   Even if there were a Qur'an that could move mountains, cleft the earth asunder or make the dead speak *(do you think the result would have been different?)* Surely all things are subject to Allah's command. Have not yet the believers been satisfied that if Allah wanted, He would have certainly guided the whole of mankind? As for the unbelievers, the disaster will not cease to afflict them *every now and then* or to crouch at their very doorsteps because of their misdeeds, until the promise of Allah is fulfilled; surely Allah will not fail His promise.[31]   13:[30-31]

> There is no God but Him, all things are subject to His command

SECTION: 5

Rasools have been mocked before you *(O Muhammad)*, but I always gave respite to the unbelievers and finally I seized them, so see how terrible was My requital![32]   Is He Who watches over each and every soul and knows all that it does *like any other*? Yet, they ascribe partners to Allah. *Say:* "then, name them!" Do you mean to inform Him of something new that He Himself does not know on this earth, or do you merely utter empty words?" Nay! Indeed their foul devices seem fair to the unbelievers, for they have been debarred from the Right Way; and there is none to guide those whom Allah has let go astray.[33]   They shall be punished in the life of this world, still more grievous is the punishment of the hereafter, and there is none to protect them from Allah.[34]   13:[32-34]

> Allah watches minutely each and every soul

The example of the paradise which the righteous have been promised in one beneath which rivers flow; eternal are its fruits, and eternal are its shades; such is the reward of the righteous. But the reward of unbelievers is the fire.[35]   *O Prophet, some of* those to whom We have given the Book rejoice at what is revealed to you, while there are some factions who deny a part of it. Tell them: "I am commanded to worship Allah and to associate none with Him. To Him I invite people and to Him I shall return."[36]   Thus We have revealed it: a legislation in the Arabic language. Now, if you follow their vain desires after real knowledge has come to you, there will be none to help or protect you against *the wrath of* Allah.[37]

13:[35-37]

> The Qur'an is revealed in Arabic for easy understanding

SECTION: 6

A Rasool has no power to show any miracle without the sanction of Allah

We have sent forth other Rasools before you and given them wives and children and it was never in the power of a Rasool to show any miracle without the sanction of Allah. For each period there was a Book:[38]　Allah abrogates and confirms what He pleases - with Him is the Master Copy of the Book.[39]　*O Muhammad!* Whether We let you see, *within your lifetime, a* part of what We threaten them with or cause you to die *before We smite them*, your mission is only to deliver the Message and it is for Us to take accountability.[40]　Do they not see that We are gradually reducing the land *in their control* through curtailing its borders?

When Allah commands, there is none to reverse it - Allah is the Master of all planning

When Allah commands, there is none to reverse His command and He is swift in taking accountability.[41]　Those *unbelievers* who have passed before them also devised plots; but Allah is the Master of all plots. He knows the actions of every soul. Soon the unbelievers will come to know who will get the home *of paradise* in the hereafter.[42]　The unbelievers say: "You are no Rasool." Say: "Allah is all-sufficient witness between me and you, and so are those who have knowledge of the Book."[43]　13[38-43]

14: IBRÂHEEM

Period of Revelation

This Sûrah also belongs to the group of Sûrahs revealed during the last period of the Prophet's residence at Makkah when the persecution of the Muslims was at its worst stage.

Major Issues, Divine Laws, and Guidance

* Allah never sent a Rasool for the guidance of a nation except one who spoke the language of those people.
* If every human being becomes a disbeliever, it makes no difference to Allah.
* Allah has based the creation of the heavens and the earth on Truth.
* Shaitân has no power except to seduce human beings.
* Greeting in paradise will be "Assalâm-u-Alaikum" which means: "peace be upon you."
* A quotation from the prayers of the Prophet Ibrâheem which the Prophet Muhammad (pbuh) made a part of Muslims' daily Salah (prayers).

This Sûrah is an admonition and a warning to the disbelievers who were rejecting Allah's Message and devising cunning schemes to defeat the mission of the Prophet.

14: IBRÂHEEM

This Sûrah, revealed at Makkah, has 7 sections and 52 verses.

In the name of Allah, the Compassionate, the Merciful.

SECTION: 1

This Book is revealed to bring mankind out of darkness into light

Alif L'âm Râ. *O Muhammad! This is* a Book which We have revealed to you so that you may bring mankind out of utter darkness *(ways of ignorance)* to the light, by the leave of their Rabb, to the Way of the Mighty, the Praiseworthy,[1]   Allah, the One to Whom belongs all that is in the heavens and the earth. Woe to the unbelievers, for they will be sternly punished,[2]   Those who love the life of this world more than the hereafter, who debar others from the Way of Allah and seek to make it crooked: they have gone far astray into error.[3]   14:[1-3]

All Rasools speak the language of their own people

We have not sent any Rasool except that he spoke the language of his own people, so that he could explain to them clearly. Then Allah leaves in error whom He wills and guides whom He pleases: He is the Mighty, the Wise.[4]   14:[4]

The Prophet Musa was sent to lead his people out of darkness into light

We sent Musa *(Moses)* with Our signs, saying: "Lead your people out of utter darkness into light, and remind them of the Days of Allah *(their history and Allah's favors)*." Surely, there are signs in this for every steadfast, thankful person.[5]   Recall! When Musa said to his people: "Remember Allah's blessings upon you when He delivered you from the people of Fir'aun *(Pharaoh)*, who subjected you to cruel afflictions, putting your sons to death and sparing your females, and in this there was a tremendous trial from your Rabb."[6]   14:[5-6]

SECTION: 2

If all the dwellers of Earth become nonbelievers, it makes no difference to Allah

Remember that your Rabb had forewarned: "If you are grateful, I will bestow abundance upon you, but if you are ungrateful *(then you should know that)* My punishment will be terrible indeed."[7]   Musa said: "If you and all the dwellers of the earth become unbelievers, *you should know that He does not stand in need of any of you*, surely, Allah is the Self-sufficient, Praiseworthy."[8]   Have you not heard the news of those who passed away before you, the people of Nûh *(Noah)*, 'Ad and Thamûd, and those who came after them? Allah Alone knows them. Their Rasools came to them with clear signs; but they put their hands in their mouths and said: "Certainly we reject the Message with which you have been sent and certainly we strongly doubt *the faith* to which you invite us."[9]   Their Rasools responded: "Are you doubting the existence of Allah, Who is the Creator of the heavens and the earth? *He is the One* Who invites you, so that He may forgive your sins and give you respite till your appointed term." They said: "You are nothing but humans like us! You only wish to turn us away from *the worship of those deities* whom our forefathers used to worship. Bring us some clear sign."[10]   Their Rasools said to them: "It is true that we are human like yourselves, but Allah bestows His grace of *appointing a Rasool* on such of His servants as He pleases. It is not in our power to bring you any sign except by Allah's permission, and in Allah let the believers put their trust.[11]   What reason do we have not to put our trust in Allah, when He has already guided us to the ways of our lives? We shall certainly endure your persecution patiently, and those who want to put their trust, should put their trust in Allah."[12]   14:[7-12]

> Let the believers put their trust in Allah

SECTION: 3

Finally, the unbelievers said to their Rasools: "Return to our religion or we will expel you from our land." But their Rabb revealed His will to them: "We shall destroy the wrongdoers[13] and give you the land to dwell in after they are gone! This is *the reward* for the ones who dread his standing before Me *on the Day of Judgment* and fear My threats."[14]   *The Rasools* called for judgement, *(and when the judgement was passed)* every tyrant opposer *of the Truth* was destroyed.[15]   Hell is next for him wherein he will be given festering water to drink;[16]   he will sip this water, but he will hardly swallow it. Death will surround him from all sides, yet, he will not die; beyond that there will be horrible punishment.[17]   14:[13-17]

> Allah punishes the wrongdoers and blesses those who dread His eminence

The parable of the deeds of those who deny their Rabb is like ashes, on which the wind blows furiously on a stormy day; they will gain nothing from their deeds, and that will be straying far away *from the goal of getting back to paradise*.[18]   Do you not see that Allah has based the creation of the heavens and the earth on Truth? That He can remove you if He wills and bring in your place a new creation?[19]   That is not at all difficult for Allah.[20]   When all people appear before Allah, those who were weak *in the world* will say to those who thought themselves mighty: "We were your followers. Now! Can you do anything to relieve us from the punishment of

> Allah has based the creation of heavens and earth on Truth

Allah?" They will reply: "Had Allah given us guidance, we would have guided you. Now it makes no difference whether we panic or bear it with patience, for there is no escape for us."[21]

14:[18-21]

SECTION: 4

Shaitân has no power over human beings - he only invites and people follow him

Once the matter has been decided, Shaitân will say: "In fact, the promises which Allah made to you were all true; I too made some promises to you but failed to keep any of them. However, I had no power over you. I just invited you, and you accepted my invitation. Now! Do not blame me, blame yourselves. I cannot help you, nor you can help me. I reject your former act of associating me with Allah. Certainly, such wrongdoers will have a painful punishment."[22]

14:[22]

Greetings in Paradise will be "Peace"

Those who believe and do good deeds will be admitted to Paradise, beneath which rivers flow, to live therein forever with the permission of their Rabb, and their greetings therein will be: "Peace!"[23]

14:[23]

Examples of a "good word" and a "bad word"

Do you not see how Allah gave the example of comparing a good word with a good tree, whose roots are firm and its branches high in the sky?[24] It yields its fruits in every season by Allah's leave. Allah cites these examples for people so that they may learn a lesson from them.[25] But the example of an evil word is that of an evil tree which is torn out from the earth and has no stability.[26] With firm words, Allah makes the believers steadfast in the life of this world and in the hereafter; but Allah lets the wrongdoers go astray. Allah does what He pleases.[27]

14:[24-27]

SECTION: 5

Those who show ingratitude towards Allah's favors shall be cast into Hell

Have you not seen those people who the grace of Allah with disbelief and drive their people into the House of Perdition? [28] Which is hell! Wherein they shall burn, an evil place to live.[29] They set up equals with Allah to mislead people from His Way. Tell them: "*Well,* you may enjoy yourself for a while, but your final destination is going to be hellfire."[30] *O Prophet,* tell My devotees who have believed, to establish Salah *(regular five times daily prayers)* and spend *in charity* openly and secretly out of the sustenance which We have given them, before the coming of that Day in which there will neither be trading nor any friendship.[31] It is Allah , Who has created the heavens and the earth. He sends down water from the sky with which He brings forth fruits for your sustenance. He has made the ships subservient to you, that they may sail through the sea by His command; and likewise, the rivers are made for your benefit.[32]   The sun and the moon are assigned for your service, which steadfastly pursue their courses, and has made the night and the day for your benefit.[33]   He has given you all that you could ask for; and if you want to count the favors of Allah, you will never be able to count them. In fact, man is unjust, thankless.[34]

14:[28-34]

Allah has given you countless favors

SECTION: 6

Remember when Ibrâheem *(Abraham)* said: "My Rabb! Make this city a city of peace and save me and my sons from the worship of idols.[35]   O my Rabb! They have indeed led many people astray *(and they might lead my descendants astray as well)*. Therefore, only those who follow my ways belong to me and *as for those* who disobey me; surely, You are Forgiving, Merciful.[36]   Our Rabb! I have settled some of my offspring in a barren valley near Your Sacred House. Our Rabb! *I have done this in the hope* that they would establish Salah *(prayer)*, therefore, turn the hearts of some people toward them and provide them with fruits so that they may give thanks.[37]   Our Rabb! Certainly You know what we conceal and what we reveal. *In fact*, nothing in the earth or in heaven is hidden from Allah.[38]   Praise be to Allah who has given me Isma'il *(Ishmael)* and Ishâq *(Isaac) in* my old age. Indeed, my Rabb hears all prayers.[39]   O my Rabb! Make me one who establishes Salah and *also* from my descendants . Our Rabb! Accept my prayer.[40]   Our Rabb! Forgive me and my parents and all believers on the Day when the accountability will take place."[41]

14:[35-41]

The prayer of Prophet Ibrâheem for the city of Makkah and its residents

The prayer of Prophet Ibrâheem which is made a part of a Muslims' five daily prayers

SECTION: 7

Never think that Allah is unaware of what these unjust people are doing. He is only deferring their case to that Day when their eyes will be fixedly open,[42]   they will be running in terror with their heads uplifted, staring but seeing nothing and their hearts utterly vacant.[43]   *O Muhammad* forewarn mankind of the Day when Our punishment will overtake them; when the wrongdoers will say: "Our Rabb! Give us a little more respite: we will answer Your call and follow the Rasools!" *But it will be said to them,* "Are you not the same people who once swore that you would suffer no decline?[44]   And you lived among the dwellings of those who had

Never think that Allah is unaware of the unjust, or that He will ever break His promise made to His Rasools

wronged their souls, and it had become clear to you how We dealt with them and We even described for you *many* examples."[45] They hatched their plots but their plots were well within the sight of Allah, even though their plots were such which could move mountains.[46]   Never think that Allah will break the promise which He made to His Rasools: surely, Allah is Mighty in power, the Lord of Retribution.[47]   *Warn them of* the Day when the earth will be changed to a different earth and the heavens as well, and all of them will stand before Allah, the One, the Irresistible;[48]   and on that Day you will see the criminals bound together in chains,[49]   their garments will be made of tar and their faces will be covered with flames.[50]   Allah will requite each soul according to its deeds; surely, Allah is swift in taking the account.[51]   14:[42-51]

Allah is the one and Only God

This is a proclamation for mankind: let them take warning therefrom; let them know that He is the One and Only - worthy of worship - and let the people of understanding learn a lesson.[52]

14:[52]

15: AL-HIJR

Period of Revelation

This Sûrah was revealed at about the same time as that of Sûrah Ibrâheem, which was during the last period of the Prophet's residence at Makkah. It appears from the repeated warnings in this Sûrah that the people in general had not accepted the Message; rather, they had become more obdurate and stubborn in their antagonism, enmity, and ridicule.

Major Issues, Divine Laws, and Guidance

* The Qur'an is a Divine Book.
* On the Day of Judgement, the disbelievers will wish that they had become Muslims.
* Allah Himself has taken the responsibility of preserving and safeguarding Al-Qur'an.
* Admonition is given through the story of Adam's creation, prostration of the angels before him, and refusal of Shaitân to prostrate.
* The Prophet Ibrâheem was given the good news of having a son by the same two angels who were assigned to destroy the nation of the prophet Lût (Lot).
* Al-Fâtiha is also named, "seven verses worthy of oft-recitation."
* Divine order to proclaim the commandments of Allah publicly and turn away from the mushrikeen.

This Sûrah also contains brief arguments for Tawheed on the one hand, and admonition to the disbelievers on the other.

15: AL-HIJR

This Sûrah, revealed at Makkah, has 6 sections and 99 verses.

In the name of Allah, the Compassionate, the Merciful.

SECTION: 1

Alif Lâm Râ. These are the verses of the *Divine* Book, the Glorious Qur'an which makes the things clear.[1]   15:[1]

JUZ (PART): 14

On the Day of Judgement, the unbelievers will wish that they were Muslims

The Day will come when the unbelievers will wish that they were Muslims.[2]   Leave them alone to eat and enjoy themselves and be deluded by false hopes, for soon they will find out the *Truth*.[3]   Never did We destroy a town whose term of life was not ordained beforehand.[4]   No people can forestall their doom, nor can they postpone it.[5]   They say: "O you to whom the reminder *(the Qur'an)* is being revealed! You are surely insane.[6] Why don't you bring us the angels, if you are of the truthful ones?"[7]   *O Muhammad, tell them:* "We do not send down the angels except for just cause *(to execute Our scourge)*, and when they come,   people are not given respite.[8]   Surely, We have

Allah Himself has taken the responsibility of preserving The Qur'an

revealed this reminder *(the Qur'an);* and We will surely preserve it Ourself.[9]   Certainly, We sent Rasools before you among the early nations;[10]   but whenever a Rasool came to them, they mocked him.[11]   Thus do We let *doubt* creep into the hearts of the criminals;[12]   that they do not believe in it, while there has already occurred the precedent of the former people.[13]   Even if we had opened a gate in Heaven and they ascend through it and keep on ascending,[14]   still they would have said, 'Our eyes have been dazzled; rather we have been bewitched.'"[15]   15:[2-15]

SECTION: 2

Allah created and decorated the heavens and also created everything suitable for human life on earth

It is We who have put constellations in the heaven, decked it *with stars* and made it fair-seeming for the beholders;[16]   and We have guarded them from every accursed shaitân.[17]   Any *shaitân* that steals a hearing, there follows him a bright flaming fire.[18]   We have spread out the earth and set mountains upon it; and caused to grow every suitable thing therein,[19]   and We provided therein means of sustenance for you and *many other creatures* to whom you do not provide.[20]   There is nothing which is not in Our *inexhaustible* treasure and sent down in appropriate measure.[21]   We send the fertilizing winds and send down water from the sky for you to drink; it is not you who hold the storage of this wealth.[22]   Certainly, it is We Who give life and cause to die, and We are the inheritors *of all*.[23]   Certainly We have full knowledge of those who have gone before you and certainly We know those who will come later.[24] Surely, your Rabb will gather them together; surely, He is Wise, Knowledgeable.[25]   15:[16-25]

SECTION: 3

We created man from sounding clay of altered black mud;[26]   while before him We had created Jinn from smokeless fire.[27]   *Remember* when your Rabb said to the angels: "I am about to create a man from sounding clay of altered black mud;[28]   when I complete his moulding and breathe into him My *created* soul, kneel down and prostrate before him."[29]   Accordingly, the angels prostrated altogether,[30]   except Iblees *(the Satan)*; he refused to join those who prostrated.[31]   *Allah* asked: "O Iblees! What is the matter with you that you did not join those who prostrated?"[32]   He replied: "It does not behoove me to prostrate myself to this man whom You have created from sounding clay of altered black mud."[33]   *Allah* said: "Get out of here, you are accursed.[34]   The curse will remain on you till the Day of Judgment."[35]   *At this Iblees* requested: "O my Rabb! Give me respite till the Day of Resurrection."[36]   *Allah* said: "*All right!* You are given the respite[37]   till the Day of appointed time."[38]   *Iblees* said: "O my Rabb! Since You let me go astray, I will make evil fair-seeming to them on earth and I will seduce them all[39]   except those of them who are Your sincere devotees."[40]   *Allah* said: "This course *of action* is all right with Me[41]   - you will not have any authority over My devotees except those misguided ones who follow you.[42]   Surely, hell shall be the promised place for them all,[43]   which has seven gates, each gate will be assigned to a separate group from among them."[44]   15:[26-44]

SECTION: 4

The righteous will be in the midst of the gardens and fountains *of paradise*[45]   *and it will be said to them*: "Enter into these in peace and security."[46]   We shall remove all hatred from their hearts - *they will become* like brothers and sit on couches face to face.[47]   No fatigue will touch them in there, nor will they ever be asked to leave.[48]   *O Prophet!* Tell My devotees that I am indeed the Forgiving, the Merciful;[49]   but at the same time My punishment is also the most painful punishment.[50]

15:[45-50]

Tell them about the guests of Ibrâheem *(Abraham)*.[51] They entered upon him and said: "Peace be upon you!" But he replied: "Surely, we are afraid of you."[52]   They answered: "Do not be afraid of us! We have come to you with good news of a son endowed with knowledge."[53]   He said: "Are you giving me the

Story of Adam's creation; prostration of the angels before him and the refusal of shaitân to prostrate

Shaitân and his followers are destined for hell

The righteous will be awarded paradise

The Prophet Ibrâheem is given the good news of a son by two angels

good news *of a son* when I have become old? What kind of good news you are giving?"[54] They replied: "We are giving you true good news; you should not be of those who despair."[55] He said: "Who would despair of the mercy of his Rabb except those who are astray?"[56] *Then* he asked: "On what expedition you have been sent, O emissaries *of Allah*?"[57] They replied: "We have been sent to *punish* the nation of criminals,[58] with the exception of Lût's *(Lot's)* family; we will certainly rescue them all[59] except his wife, who, *Allah says,* has been destined to remain with those who will stay behind."[60]   15:[51-60]

SECTION: 5

The same angels came to Prophet Lût and executed Allah's decree of stoning to death the nation of homosexuals

So when the emissaries came to the family of Lût,[61] he said: "You appear to be strangers."[62] They said: "We have come to you *with that scourge* concerning which these people had doubts.[63] We have come to you with the Truth of *Allah's decree* and we are telling you the truth.[64] You should, therefore, depart with your family during a part of the night and you yourself should follow them at their rear; let no one of you look back, keep on going where you are commanded to go."[65] We informed him about this decree of Ours that the roots of the sinners *of his city* would be cut off by the morning.[66] The people of the town came rejoicing *at the news of the young men's arrival*.[67] Lût said: "They are my guests, so do not disgrace me.[68] Have fear of Allah and do not put me to shame."[69] They said: "Have we not forbidden you from protecting other people?"[70] He said: "Here are my daughters, if you must act."[71] By your life, *O Prophet Muhammad,* they were madly blundering in their intoxication *of lust*![72] So the mighty blast overtook them at sunrise.[73] Thus We turned the town upside down and rained down on them brimstones of baked clay.[74] Surely, there are signs *(lessons)* in this for those who investigate,[75] and this *smitten town* still lies right on the permanent highway *on which the unbelievers travel during their business trips*.[76] Indeed, there is a sign in this for the true believers.[77] The people of Al-Aikah *(the nation of Prophet Shu'aib)* were also wrongdoers.[78] So We inflicted retribution on them. The ruined towns of these two nations are lying on an open road.[79]   15:[61-79]

SECTION: 6

Punishment to the people of Hijr for their disbelief

The people of Hijr also denied the Rasools.[80] We gave them Our signs, but they ignored them.[81] They hewed their homes in the mountains for safety.[82] But the mighty blast seized them early morning[83] and all their labor *of building their homes through carving the rocks* did not avail them.[84]　　We have not created the Heavens and the Earth, and all that lies between them but to manifest the Truth.　　The Hour *of Doom* is sure to come, so overlook *their misbehavior* in a gracious manner.[85]　　Surely, your Rabb is the All-Knowing Creator.[86]　　　　　　15:[80-86]

　　　　We have given you the Seven Verses that are worthy of recitation *over and over again (Sûrah Al-Fâtiha)* and the Glorious Qur'an.[87]　Do not look at the worldly wealth which We have given to different people among them, nor grieve at their condition. *Leave them alone,* attend to the believers in kindness,[88]　and tell *the unbelievers*: "Surely, I am only a plain warner."[89]　*This warning is like* the warning which We sent down to the schismatics,[90]　those who divided the Qur'an into separate parts, *believing in some and denying others.*[91]　　So by your Rabb! We will question them all[92]　about their doings.[93]　Therefore, proclaim publicly what you are commanded and turn away from the mushrikeen.[94]　　Surely, We Ourself will suffice you against the scoffers;[95]　those who place other deities alongside Allah, will soon come to know *their folly.*[96]　We know that your heart is distressed by what they say *against you.*[97]　*The cure of your heart's distress is that you should* celebrate the praises of your Rabb and be of those who prostrate themselves before Him,[98]　and worship your Rabb until there comes to you that which is certain *(death).*[99]　　　　　　15:[87-99]

Al-Fâtiha is also called: "Seven verses worthy of oft-recitation"

Proclaim the commandments of Allah publicly and turn away from the mushrikeen

16: AN-NAHL

Period of Revelation

This Sûrah was revealed during the last period of the Prophet's residence at Makkah. The seven years of famine, which had stricken Makkah, had come to an end and the persecution from the unbelievers had forced some Muslims to migrate to Habsha.

Major Issues, Divine Laws, and Guidance

* Proof of Tawheed and refutation of shirk.
* The mountains have been set on the earth to stabilize its balance.
* Allah has sent the Rasools to warn against the unbeliever's excuse: "If Allah wanted we would have not worshipped anyone else."
* Allah's promise to provide a good abode for those who migrate for His sake.
* If Allah were to punish people for their wrong doings, He would not have left even an animal around them.
* As water gives life to dead land so does the Qur'an to the human soul.
* Allah has provided signs in the lives of the bees, birds and animals.
* Allah commands to do justice, be good to others, and give to near relatives; and He forbids indecency, wickedness, and rebellion.
* Seek Allah's protection against Shaitân before starting to recite the Qur'an.
* Halâl (lawful) and Harâm (unlawful) are only from Allah.
* Ibrâheem was a nation in himself.
* Call towards the Way of Allah with wisdom; advise and reason in a courteous manner.

This Sûrah presents very convincing proofs of Tawheed and refutation of shirk based on plain signs in the universe and in man's own creation. It answers the objections of the disbelievers, refutes their arguments and removes their doubts. It gives warning about the consequences of persisting in false ways. It presents moral changes needed in practical human life. It tells the mushrikeen that the belief in Allah, which they also professed, demands that it should not be confined merely to lip service, but be exhibited in moral and practical life. Finally, it provided guidance to the Prophet and his companions about the attitude that they should adopt in facing antagonism and persecution by the disbelievers.

16: AN-NAHL

This Sûrah, revealed at Makkah, has 16 sections and 128 verses.

In the name of Allah the Compassionate, the Merciful.

SECTION: 1

Allah's commandment has come, so do not seek to hasten it. Glory be to Him and Exalted be He above the shirk *(associating other gods with Allah)* that they practice! [1] He sends down His angels with inspiration of His Command to whom He pleases of His servants, saying: "Warn the people that there is no god except Me, therefore, fear Me."[2] He has created the heavens and the earth to manifest the Truth; Exalted be He above the shirk that they practice.[3] He created man from a drop of semen, yet, he is an open contender.[4] He created cattle, which provide you with warm clothing, numerous benefits and some of them you eat.[5] How pleasant they look to you when you bring them home in the evening and drive them to pasture in the morning.[6] They carry your heavy loads to far-off towns that you could not otherwise reach without painful toil; indeed your Rabb is Kind and Merciful.[7] *He has created* horses, mules, and donkeys for you to ride and put on show, and He also creates other things which are beyond your knowledge.[8] It is up to Allah to show the Right Way, when there exist some crooked ways. If Allah wanted, He could have guided you all.[9] 16:[1-9]

Allah has sent down His revelations to warn people that there is no god but Him

He has created cattle for the benefit of human beings

SECTION: 2

It is He Who sends down water from the sky, which provides drinking water for you and brings forth fodder to pasture your cattle.[10] With it He grows for you crops, olives, date-palms, grapes, and every kind of fruit: surely, there is a great sign in this for those who think.[11] He has subjected to your service the night and the day, the sun and the moon: and *likewise* the stars also serve you by His command: surely, there are signs in this for people who use their common sense.[12] And *He has subjected* whatever He multiplied for you on the earth of different colors: surely, there is a sign in this for those who want to get reminded.[13] It is He Who has subjected the sea to your service, that you may eat fresh meat therefrom and that you may bring out of it ornaments to wear; and you see that ships plough their course through it. *He has done all this* so that you may seek His bounty and so that you may pay thanks

It is He Who sends down water from the sky for drinking and agriculture

He set mountains to stabilize the earth

to Him.[14]   He has set mountains on the earth - lest it should sway with you. *He also made* rivers and roads so that you may find your way;[15]   *and likewise made* landmarks and the stars for your guidance.[16]   Is then, He, Who has created all this, like the one who cannot create? Why don't you get admonition?[17]   If you want to count the favors of Allah, you will never be able to count them; surely, Allah is Forgiving, Merciful,[18] and Allah knows what you conceal and what you reveal.[19]   Those whom they invoke besides Allah have created nothing, but are themselves created.[20]   They are dead, not living; they do not even know when they will be raised to life again.[21]   16:[10-21]

Allah has bestowed so many favors, you cannot even count them

SECTION: 3

Your God is One God *(Allah - none has the right to be worshipped but He)*; as for those who do not believe in the hereafter, they have faithless hearts and are puffed up with arrogance.[22]   Allah surely knows what they conceal and what they reveal; certainly He does not love the arrogant.[23]   When they are asked: "What is it, that your Rabb has revealed?" They say: "Fictitious stories of the ancients!"[24]   On the Day of Resurrection, they will bear their own burden in full and some of the burden of those whom they misled without knowledge. Alas! Evil is the burden which they bear.[25]   16:[22-25]

The unbelievers are arrogant and they will be held responsible for that attitude

SECTION: 4

Those before them also plotted *against the Truth*, but Allah shook their edifice through its foundation, and its roof caved in on them; and the torment came at them from where they did not even suspect.[26]   Then on the Day of Judgment He will humiliate them and say: "Where are those deities you associated with Me concerning whom you used to dispute *with the true believers?*" Those who have been given knowledge will say: "Today there will be shame and sorrow for the unbelievers,"[27]   - those whom the angels cause to die while they were still engaged in doing injustice to their own souls. *At the time of death* they offer submission: "We were not doing anything wrong." *They will be replied:* "O Yea! *How dare you deny!* Certainly Allah is well aware of what you were doing.[28] Now, *go ahead and* enter the gates of Hell, there you will abide forever." In fact, very awful will be the abode of the arrogant.[29] *On the other hand* when the righteous people are asked: " What is it that your Rabb has revealed?" They say: "*That which is* the best."

On the Day of Judgment, Allah will humiliate the arrogant and cast them into hell while the righteous will be awarded paradise

Good is the reward for such righteous people in this world and the home of the hereafter will be even better. How splendid will be the home for the righteous[30] - Gardens of eternal abode will they enter, beneath which rivers flow, having therein all that they wish to have. Thus shall Allah reward the righteous,[31] - when the angels cause to die such pious people, they greet them: "Peace be upon you! Enter the paradise for the good deeds you used to do."[32] These *unbelievers* are only waiting for the angels to come down *to take their lives* or the commandment of your Rabb to come to pass *for their doom?* So did those who went before them. It was not Allah who was unjust to them, but they were unjust to themselves.[33] *At the end,* the evil results of their deeds overtook them, and the very scourge at which they mocked, hemmed them in.[34]   16:[26-34]

SECTION: 5

The mushrikeen say: "If Allah wanted, neither we nor our forefathers would have worshipped any one else but Him, nor made anything unlawful without His will." Such excuses were put forward also by those who went before them. Yet, Rasools have no more responsibility than to convey the Message clearly.[35] Indeed, We raised in every nation a Rasool, *saying*: "Serve Allah and keep away from Tâghoot *(false deities ₋ Shaitân)*." After that, Allah guided some of them while straying proved true against the others. So travel through the earth and see what was the end of those who denied *Our Message*.[36] *No matter* how eager you may be for their guidance, *you should know that* Allah does not guide those whom He let go astray and such people will have no helpers.[37] They solemnly swear their strongest oaths by Allah: "Allah will never raise the dead to life." Why not? It is a promise which He has made binding on Himself, though most among mankind may not know it.[38] *It will be fulfilled* so that He may manifest to them the Truth about which they differ, and so that the rejecters of Truth may know that they were indeed liars.[39] *As for its possibility,* when We intend to do anything which We want, We need only say, "Be," and it is.[40]   16:[35-40]

SECTION: 6

For those who migrated for the sake of Allah after persecution, We will certainly provide them a good abode in this life and the reward of the hereafter will be much greater, if they but knew *what a happy end awaits*[41]   those who bear *ills* with

Allah has sent the Rasools to warn against the unbeliever's excuse: "If Allah wanted, we would have not worshipped anyone else"

Allah has promised a good abode for those who migrate for His sake patience and put their trust in their Rabb.[42]　We have not sent any Rasool before you, *O Muhammad*, but were men, whom We revealed Our Message. You *(O people of Makkah)*, may ask those who have the Reminder *(the People of the Book)*, if you don't know *this fact yourselves*.[43]　*We sent those Rasools* with clear signs and scriptures; and now We have sent down the reminder to you *(O Muhammad)*, so that you may explain clearly to mankind as to what was sent to them so that they may think about it.[44]　16:[41-44]

Do the unbelievers feel secure against the wrath of Allah?

Do those who plot evil deeds feel secure that Allah will not cave in the earth beneath them or that the scourge will not come to them from directions that they did not suspect?[45]　Or that He may not seize them in the course of their journey leaving no way for their escape?[46]　Or that He may seize them after alerting them about the danger? Yet, your Rabb is Kind, Merciful.[47]　Do they not see how every object that Allah has created casts its shadow right and left, prostrating itself to Allah in all humility?[48] To Allah prostrate all the moving creatures of the heavens and the earth, including the angels; and they are not arrogant:[49]　they fear their Rabb Who is above them, and they do whatever they are commanded to do.[50]
16:[45-50]

SECTION: 7

Whenever unbelievers are in distress, they call upon Allah Alone. But no sooner does He relieve them that they start committing shirk

Allah has said: "Do not take two *or more* gods for worship: there exists only One God *(Allah)*, I am the One Whom you should fear."[51]　To Him belongs whatever is in the heavens and the earth, and perpetual sincere devotion is always for Him Alone - would you then fear any one other than Allah?[52]　Whatever blessings you enjoy are from Allah, and when touched by distress, He is the One to Whom you cry for help.[53]　Yet, no sooner does He relieve you from the distress than some of you begin to associate others with Him,[54]　as if to show their ingratitude for *the favors* that We bestow on them! Enjoy yourselves; soon you will come to know *the consequences.* [55]　They set aside a portion of what We have provided them with, for those deities about whom they know nothing. By Allah! You shall most certainly be questioned about the lies you fabricate.[56]　They ascribe daughters to Allah - Glory be to Him! - But for themselves, *they would like to have* what they desire *(sons)*.[57]　Whenever the news of a female child is announced to any one of them, his face darkens and he chokes with inward gloom.[58]　He hides himself from his people because of the bad news he has heard, *asking himself* whether he should retain her with disgrace or bury her in the dust. Beware! Evil is the Judgment they make *about Allah*.[59]   To those who do not believe in the hereafter, applies an evil similitude, while to Allah applies the highest attribute, for He is the Mighty, the Wise.[60]   16:[51-60]

SECTION: 8

If Allah were to punish mankind for their wrongdoing, He would not leave a single living creature on the face of the earth, but He gives them respite for an appointed time. So when their appointed time comes, they can neither stay behind for a moment nor can they go before it.[61]   They attribute to Allah what they themselves hate. Their tongues mouth the lie that they will have a good reward. Let there be no doubt: the only thing they will have is hell, to which they will be driven ahead of the others and left therein neglected.[62]   By Allah! We sent Rasools before you *(O Muhammad)* to other nations; but shaitân made their deeds seem fair to them *so they did not believe,* he is their patron today, and they shall have a painful punishment.[63]   We have revealed to you the Book *(the Qur'an)* so that you may clearly explain to them the reality of those things in which they differ - it is a guidance and blessing for those people who believe.[64]   Allah sends down water from the sky, and with it gives life to the land after it has been dead *(similarly this Qur'an is being sent to serve a similar purpose).* Surely, in this *example* there is a sign for those who listen.[65]

16:[61-65]

SECTION: 9

Surely, there is a lesson for you in cattle. We give you to drink of what is in their bellies, between bowels and blood - pure milk - pleasant for those who drink it.[66]   *Likewise, in* the fruits of the date-palms and the grapes, from which you derive intoxicants *(this was revealed before the prohibition of intoxicants)* and wholesome food, certainly in this, there is a sign for those people who use their common sense.[67]   *Behold!* Your Rabb inspired the bees to build their hives in the mountains, in the trees, and in anything which men may build *for beekeeping*,[68]   and feed on every kind of fruit and follow the smooth ways of your Rabb. From its belly comes forth a syrup of different colors, which contains a healing for mankind. Certainly in this there is a sign for those who think.[69]   Allah is the One Who created you, then He causes you to die; there are some amongst you whose lives are prolonged to an abject old age so that they know nothing after having known

If Allah were to punish mankind for wrongdoings, He would not leave even an animal around the wrong-doers

As water gives life to dead land so does The Qur'an to the human soul

There is a lesson for mankind in the lives of animals i.e., milk-producing animals and the honeybee

much. In fact, Allah is the All-Knowing, Almighty.[70]   16:[66-70]

SECTION: 10

Allah has made some of you excel in sustenance over the others; those who are so favored, do not give away their sustenance to their slaves so as to make them their equals. *How can you think that Allah will allow other deities to be His equals*? Would they refuse to acknowledge the favors of Allah?[71]   It is Allah Who has made for you mates from your own species and He is the One Who gives you sons and grandsons through your wives, and provides for you good things to eat: will they then, *after knowing all that,* believe in false deities and deny the favors of Allah?[72]   They worship those deities other than Allah, who neither provide them anything for sustenance from the heavens or the earth, nor have any power to do so?[73]   Therefore, compare none with Allah. Surely, Allah knows and you do not know.[74]   Allah gives you another example *of two men*: one of them is a slave, the property of the other, and has no power over anything; and the other man is one on whom We have bestowed Our bounty, from which he freely spends secretly and openly. *Ask them*: "Are those two men equal?" Praise be to Allah - most of them do not understand *this simple thing*.[75] *Well!* Allah gives you another example of two men: one of them is dumb and has no ability to do anything - a burden on his master - whenever he sends him on an errand, he does nothing useful. Can he be equal to the one who enjoins justice and follows the Right Way?[76]   16:[71-76]

SECTION: 11

Allah Alone has knowledge of the unseen things of the Heavens and the Earth. As for the advent of the Hour *of Judgment,* it will be like a twinkling of an eye or even quicker: surely, Allah has power over everything.[77]   Allah brought you forth from the wombs of your mothers when you knew nothing, and He gave you hearing, sight and intelligence so that you may give thanks to Him.[78]   Do they not see the birds, that wing their flight in the air towards the sky? Who holds them up but Allah? Surely, in this there are signs for the true believers.[79]   Allah has made your homes the places for your rest, and from animal skins tents for dwelling so that you may find them light when you travel and easy to pitch when you stop; while from their wool, fur, and hair, *He has provides you with* household items and articles of convenience for

---

There is a lesson in the process of your own creation

Why believe in deities who have no power to create anything and disbelieve in Allah, the Creator?

There are also signs of Allah in the lives of the birds and the animals

your prescribed term *of life*.[80] Allah has provided you shades *from the sun* out of what He has created. He has granted you resorts in the mountains, has granted you garments to protect yourselves from heat *and cold*; and coats of armor to protect you during your wars. Thus He completes his favors to you, so that you may surrender yourselves to Him *(become Muslims)*.[81] If they still give no heed to you *O Muhammad, you need not worry*, for your duty is only to convey the message clearly.[82] They recognize the favors of Allah, yet, they deny them; most of them are *ungrateful* disbelievers.[83]   16:[77-83]

SECTION: 12

Do they realize what will happen on that Day when We shall call a witness from every nation? Then the unbelievers will neither be allowed *to put forward any excuse* nor will they be allowed to repent.[84] When the wrongdoers face the punishment, it will neither be lightened for them nor will they be granted a delay.[85] When the mushrikeen see their deities whom they associated with Allah, they will say: "Our Rabb! Here are our 'associate gods' whom we used to invoke besides You." At this their deities will toss their statement back at them saying: "You are liars!"[86] They shall tender their submission to Allah that Day: and the gods of their own inventions will leave them in the lurch.[87] *As for* those who disbelieve and debar others from the Way of Allah, We shall punish them all the more for their mischief.[88] *O Muhammad, warn them about* that Day when We shall call a witness from every nation to testify against it, and We shall call you *O Muhammad* to testify against them: *that is why* We have sent down to you this Book *(the Qur'an)* to explain everything - a guide, a blessing and good news for those who surrender themselves to Allah (become Muslims).[89]   16:[84-89]

On the Day of Judgment a witness will be called from each nation and the unbelievers will face the reality of their invented false gods

SECTION: 13

Allah commands justice, good conduct, and giving to near relatives, and He forbids indecency, injustice, and rebellion: He admonishes you so that you may take heed.[90] Fulfill the covenant of Allah when you have pledged to do so, and do not break your oaths after you have sworn them; for *swearing in His name* you have made Allah your surety; surely, Allah has knowledge of all that you do.[91] Do not behave like that woman who had spun her yarn strongly and then broke it into pieces herself; nor take your

Allah commands justice, good conduct and giving to near relatives; He forbids indecency, injustice and rebellion

oaths as means of deceit between you so that your group may become greater in number and more powerful than the other, for Allah puts you to trial by these *oaths*; and on the Day of Resurrection He will certainly make clear to you *the truth* about which you differed.[92]   If Allah wanted, He could have made you all one nation, but He lets go astray whom He wants and guides whom He pleases: but most certainly you will be questioned about all your actions.[93]   *O believers!* Do not take oaths to deceive each other, lest your foot slip after being firmly fixed *upon guidance*; and taste the evil consequences for debarring others from the Way of Allah and incur a mighty punishment.[94]   16:[90-94]

What is with you is transitory; and what is with Allah is everlasting

Do not sell the covenant of Allah for a petty price. Certainly Allah's reward is far better than all your gain, if you but knew it.[95]   Whatever is with you is transitory and what is with Allah is everlasting. We will certainly reward those who are patient according to the noblest of their deeds.[96]   Whoever does righteous deeds, whether male or female, provided he is a believer, We shall surely grant him to live a good life, and We will certainly reward such people according to the noblest of their deeds *in the hereafter*.[97]   When you recite the Qur'an, seek Allah's protection from the accursed Shaitân,[98]   surely, he has no authority over those who believe and put their trust in their Rabb.[99]   His authority is only over those who befriend him and commit shirk with Him.[100]

When you recite The Qur'an, seek Allah's protection against Shaitân

16:[95-100]

SECTION: 14

Unbelievers accused Muhammad (pbuh) of being taught Al-Qur'an by a certain man, but the man they allude to is a non-Arab, while The Qur'an is in eloquent Arabic

When We substitute one verse in favor of another - and Allah knows best what He reveals *in stages* - they say: "You are but a forger." The fact is that most of them do not understand.[101]   Say, "The Holy Spirit *(Gabriel)* has brought it down piecemeal with truth from your Rabb to strengthen the faith of the believers, and to give guidance and good news to the Muslims."[102]   We know very well what they say *about you, O Muhammad*: "A certain man teaches him." But the man they allude to speaks a foreign language while this *(The Qur'an)* is in eloquent Arabic.[103]   In fact, Allah does not guide to those who do not believe in His revelations and they will have a painful punishment.[104]   Surely, those who do not believe in the revelations of Allah, are the ones who forge the falsehood and they are the ones who are liars![105]   Anyone who is forced to deny faith after its acceptance, while his heart remains loyal to the faith, shall be absolved; but any who denies faith *willingly after its acceptance* and opens his breast to unbelief, shall incur the wrath of Allah and shall be sternly punished.[106]   This is because such people love the life of this world more than the hereafter, and that Allah does not guide such unbelievers.[107] Such are those whose hearts, ears and eyes are sealed by Allah; and they are the ones who are heedless.[108]   There is no doubt that in the hereafter they will be the losers.[109]   On the other hand, Allah is most surely forgiving and compassionate towards those who had to leave their homes after being persecuted *because of their faith*, fought *for the cause of Allah* and remained patient.[110]

16:[101-110]

SECTION: 15

On the Day *of Judgment* every soul will come pleading for itself and every soul will be paid in full for what it has done, and they shall not be dealt with unjustly.[111]   Allah gives you an example of a town which was enjoying security and peace, receiving its provisions in abundance from every quarter, but it became ungrateful to the favors of Allah. As a result, Allah made its residents taste the consequences of their doings, through inflicting upon them misfortunes of hunger and fear.[112]   A Rasool was sent to them from among themselves, but they denied him; so the punishment overtook them because they were wrongdoers.[113]   So eat of the good and lawful things which Allah has provided for you; and be grateful to Allah for His favors, if you are sincere in His worship.[114]   He has only forbidden you to eat carrion *(meat of a dead body)*, blood, flesh of swine *(pig meat)* and that over which any name other than Allah's has been invoked. But if one is forced by necessity, intending neither to break the Divine Law nor to transgress limits, then surely, Allah is Forgiving, Merciful.[115] You shall not falsely declare with your tongues: "This is lawful, and that is forbidden," in order to ascribe false things to Allah, for those who forge lies against Allah will never prosper.[116]   Brief is their enjoyment *of this life*, and they shall have a painful punishment.[117]   To the Jews, We prohibited those things which We have already mentioned to you, We were not unjust to them but they were unjust to themselves.[118]   Yet, your Rabb is forgiving and merciful towards those who do something wrong through ignorance, but later repent and mend their ways.[119]

16:[111-119]

SECTION: 16

Surely, Ibrâheem *(Abraham)* was an Ummah *(a nation, an*

On the Day of Judgment, every soul will be paid in full for what it has done

Do not declare with your tongue what is halâl (lawful) and what is harâm (unlawful) - halâl and harâm are from Allah

Ibrâheem was an Ummah (a nation, a model)

exemplary leader, or a model), an upright man obedient to Allah, and he was not of the mushrikeen.[120]   He was always grateful for the favors of Allah, Who chose him and guided him to the Right Way.[121]   We gave him a good *life* in this world, and in the hereafter he will be among the righteous.[122]   And now We have revealed to you *Our will, saying*: "Follow the faith of Ibrâheem the upright, who was not of the mushrikeen."[123]   *As for* the Sabbath, it was ordained for those who differed about its *observance*. Surely, your Rabb will judge between them on the Day of Resurrection about that over which they differ.[124]   16:[120-124]

Call towards the Way of Allah with wisdom; advise and reason, if you have to, in a courteous manner

Call *people* to the Way of your Rabb with wisdom and best advice, and reason with them, *if you have to,* in the most courteous manner: for your Rabb knows best who strays from His Way and He knows best who is rightly guided.[125]   If you have to retaliate, let your retaliation be commensurate with the wrong which was done to you; but if you endure with patience, the best *reward* indeed is for those who endure with patience.[126]   Be patient - for your patience is not but with the help of Allah - do not grieve over them and do not distress yourself because of their plots,[127]   for Allah is with those who fear Him and adopt the righteous attitude.[128]   16:[125-128]

JUZ (PART): 15

17: AL-ISRÂ'

Period of Revelation

This Sûrah was revealed one year before Hijrah (migration to Madinah) on the occasion of the M'irâj (Ascension) during the last period of the Prophet's residence at Makkah.

Major Issues, Divine Laws, and Guidance

* Isrâ' and M'irâj (Allah gave the Prophet a tour of the universe).
* Divine Commandments:
  1. Worship none but Allah
  2. Be kind and obedient to parents
  3. Give to relatives and the needy
  4. Do not be a miser or a spendthrift
  5. Do not kill your children for fear of poverty
  6. Do not commit adultery
  7. Do not slay without just cause
  8. Do not say anything without knowledge
  9. Do not walk arrogantly on earth
  10. Safeguard the property of orphans
* Allah does not beget children and those who say this, utter a monstrous lie.
* There is surely a life after death.
* The obligation of Five Daily Prayers and the prayer of Tahajjud (special late night prayer).
* Humans are sent as Rasools to human beings.
* Perform Salah in a voice which is neither too loud nor too soft.

This Sûrah is a wonderful combination of warning, admonition, and instruction, which have been blended together in balanced proportion. The disbelievers of Makkah are admonished to take a lesson from the miserable end of the Israelites and other communities and mend their ways. The Israelites, with whom Islam was going to come in direct contact in the near future at Al-Madinah, have also been warned that they should learn a lesson from the chastisements which were inflicted upon them. They are warned to take advantage of the Prophethood of Muhammad (peace be upon him) since it is the last opportunity being given to them.

It is made clear that human success or failure, gain or loss, depends upon the true understanding of Tawheed (Oneness of God), Risâlat (Prophethood) and Life after death. Convincing arguments are provided to prove that the Qur'an is the Book of Allah and its teachings are true and genuine.

JUZ (PART): 15

17: AL-ISRÂ'

This Sûrah, revealed at Makkah, has 12 sections and 111 verses.

In the name of Allah, the Compassionate, the Merciful

SECTION: 1

Allah took Muhammad (pbuh) on a tour of the universe

Glory be to Him Who took His devotee *(Muhammad)* one night from Al-Masjid-al-Harâm *(in Makkah)* to Al-Masjid-al-Aqsa *(in Jerusalem)*, whose vicinity We have blessed, so that We may show him some of Our signs: surely, He is the One Who is the All-Hearer, the All-Seer.[1]　　　　　　17:[1]

Allah fulfilled the prophecy made in the Holy Book of the Israelites that they will create mischief in the land twice and each time they will be punished

We gave Musa *(Moses)* the Book and made it a guide for the Children of Israel, saying: "Do not take any other protector besides Me.[2]　You are the descendents of those whom We carried *in the Ark* with Nûh, and he was indeed a grateful devotee."[3] Besides this, We forewarned the Children of Israel in their *Holy Book* that you will do mischief in the land twice through becoming arrogant transgressors *and each time you will be punished.*[4] When the promise for the first of the two *forewarnings* came to be fulfilled, We sent against you Our servants who gave you a terrible warfare: so they rampaged through your homes and thus the promise was fulfilled.[5]　Then after this, We afforded you an opportunity to overpower them and helped you with wealth and sons, and granted you more manpower.[6]　If you did good, it was to your own benefit; but if you did evil, it was for your own-selves. Then, when the promise for your second *forewarning* came to be fulfilled, *We sent another army* to sadden your faces and to enter your masjid *(their temple in Jerusalem)* as the former had entered it before, and they utterly destroyed all that they laid their hands on.[7]　Now your Rabb may again be merciful to you; but if you repeat the same behavior, We will repeat *the punishment, and in the hereafter,* We have made hell a prison for such unbelievers.[8]

The Qur'an guides to the perfectly Straight Way

Surely, this Qur'an guides to the Way which is perfectly straight and gives the good news to the believers who do good that they shall have a great reward;[9]　and *at the same time it gives warnings* to those who do not believe in the hereafter, that We have prepared for them a painful punishment.[10]　　　　　　17:[2-10]

SECTION: 2

Yet, man prays for evil, *when angry,* as he pray for good, and mankind is ever hasty.[11]   We have made the night and the day as two signs. We enshrouded the night with darkness and gave light to the day, to enable you to seek the bounty of your Rabb, and that you may compute the years and count the numbers. Thus, We have set forth all things in detail.[12]   We have fastened the destiny of every man to his own neck, and on the Day of Resurrection We shall bring out for him a book spread wide open,[13] *saying:* "Read your book *of deeds.* Today you yourself are sufficient to take your own account."[14]   17:[11-14]

On the Day of Judgment, each individual shall be given the book of his own deeds

He that seeks guidance, that guidance shall be for his own soul, but he that goes astray does so to his own loss. No bearer shall bear the burden of another *on the Day of Judgment. And during your worldly life*, We do not inflict punishment until We send forth a Rasool *to make truth distinct from falsehood.*[15]   Whenever We have intended to destroy a town, *it was because* We sent Our commandments to its people who were leading easy lives but they showed disobedience; as a result Our Judgment was passed, and We razed that city to the ground.[16]   How many generations have We destroyed since Nûh's time? Sufficient is your Rabb to note and see the sins of His servants.[17]   17:[15-17]

He that seeks guidance, does so to his own good and he who goes astray, does so to his own loss

He that desires the transitory things *of this life,* We readily grant him such things as We please to whomsoever We want, then We condemn him to hell, where he will burn, blameworthy and rejected.[18]   He who desires the life of the hereafter and strives for it as best as he can provided he is a believer, the endeavor of every such person will be accepted.[19]   We bestowed on all - these as well those - out of the bounties of your Rabb; the bounties of your Rabb are not confined.[20]   See how We have exalted some over others, and certainly the hereafter is more exalted and greater in excellence.[21]   Do not associate another deity with Allah, lest you sit back, condemned, forsaken.[22]   17:[18-22]

He that desires the transitory things of this life, is given it here, but in the hereafter he shall be condemned to hell

SECTION: 3

Your Rabb has decreed to you that: You shall worship none but Him, and you shall be kind to your parents; if one or both of them live to their old age in your lifetime, you shall not say to them any word of contempt nor repel them and you shall address

Commandments of Allah to the believers that: You shall not worship any except Him, you shall be obedient to your parents, nice to your relatives and the community at large

them in kind words.[23]　You shall lower to them your wings of humility out of mercy *for them* and pray: "O my Rabb! Bestow on them Your blessings just as they cherished me when I was a little child."[24]　Your Rabb knows best what is in your hearts. If you have good intention, certainly He is most forgiving to those who turn to Him in repentance.[25]　You shall give to your relatives their due and to the needy, and to the wayfarers. You shall not be a spendthrift[26] - as spendthrifts are the brethren of shaitân and shaitân is ever ungrateful to His Rabb.[27]　You shall speak courteously *to needy persons* if you are waiting for your Rabb's bounty and you lack the means to assist them.[28]　You shall neither tie your hands to your neck *(be miserly)* nor stretch them forth to their utmost reach *(be prodigal)*, lest you sit back, blameworthy, destitute.[29]　Surely, your Rabb gives abundantly to whom He pleases and sparingly *to whom He wills*, for He is aware *of the condition* of His servants and observes them closely.[30]　　　　　　　17:[23-30]

SECTION: 4

Do not kill children for fear of want, nor commit adultery, do not kill anyone nor consume the property of orphans. Fulfill the pledges, give full measures, do not follow anyone blindly, do not walk arrogantly and do not associate other deities as an object of worship along with Allah

You shall not kill your children for fear of want, for it is We Who provide sustenance for them as well as for you; surely, killing them is a great blunder.[31]　You shall not go near the unlawful sex; surely, it is a shameful deed and an evil way *(opening the door to other evils)*.[32]　You shall not kill anyone whose killing Allah has forbidden, except for just cause *under the Islamic law*. If anyone is killed unjustly, We have granted the right of retribution to his heir, but let him not carry *his vengeance* too far in killing the culprit, as he is supported *by the law*.[33]　You shall not go near the property of an orphan, except with the good intention *of improving it*, until he attains his maturity. You shall fulfill your pledges; surely, you shall be held accountable for your pledges.[34]　You shall give full measure, when you measure, and weigh with even scale; this is the best way and will prove to be the best in the end.[35]　You shall not follow *anyone blindly in those matters* of which you have no knowledge, surely, the use of your ears and the eyes and the heart - all of these, shall be questioned *on the Day of Judgment*.[36]　You shall not walk arrogantly on the earth, for you can neither rend the earth asunder nor attain the height of the mountains.[37]　All these, their evil aspects are hateful in the sight of your Rabb.[38]　This is but a part of the wisdom which your Rabb has revealed to you. Do not associate with Allah other deities *as object of worship,* lest you should be cast into hell, blameworthy rejected.[39]　What! Has your

Rabb preferred to give you sons and adopted angels as daughters for Himself? Certainly you are uttering a monstrous statement.[40]

17:[31-40]

SECTION: 5

We have indeed explained things in various ways in this Qur'an so that they may receive admonition, yet, it has only added to their aversion.[41]   Tell them: If there were other gods besides Him as the *mushrikeen* say, they would have certainly tried to find a way to *dethrone* the Master of the Throne.[42]   Glory be to Him! He is far above the things that they say *about Him*.[43]   The seven heavens, the earth and all beings therein declare His glory. There is not a single thing but glorifies Him with His praise, but you do not understand their hymns of His glory. The fact is that He is very Forbearing, Forgiving.[44]   17:[41-44]

> If there were other gods besides Allah, they would have tried to dethrone Him

When you recite the Qur'an, We put a hidden barrier between you and those who do not believe in the hereafter.[45]   We cast a veil upon their hearts and make them hard of hearing, so they do not comprehend it. When in the Qur'an you mention His Oneness, they turn their backs in disgust.[46]   We are quite aware what they really wish to hear when they listen to you, and what they say when they converse in private. These wrongdoers say to one another: "The man you follow is surely bewitched"[47]   See what sort of examples they make up about you! They have surely gone astray and cannot find the Right Way.[48]   They say: "What! When we are reduced to bones and dust, shall we really be raised up again into a new creation?"[49]   Tell them: "*(Yes, most certainly you shall be brought back to life)*, even if you be stones or iron[50]   or even something harder than this that you may think of." Then they will ask: "Who will restore us?" Say: "The One Who created you the first time." Then they will shake their heads at you and ask: "Well, when will this be?" Say, "It may be quite soon!"[51]   It will be on the Day when He will call you and you will rise up in response to it, with His praise, and you will think that you remained in the state *of death* but a little while."[52]   17:[45-52]

> Belief in the hereafter is necessary to understand The Qur'an

> There is a life after death

SECTION: 6

Tell My servants that they should speak only what is the best. Surely, shaitân stirs up trouble among them. The fact is that shaitân is an open enemy to mankind.[53]   Your Rabb is fully aware of your *circumstances*. He may be merciful to you if He wants, or

> Believers should speak only good words

He may punish you if He wills. *O Prophet,* We have not sent you to be their guardian.[54]   Your Rabb is fully aware of all that is in the heavens and in the earth. We have exalted some prophets above the others and gave Zaboor to Daûd.[55]   17:[53-55]

Invented gods have no power to relieve you from any distress

Say: "Pray if you will to those whom you assert besides Him; they have neither the power to relieve you from any distress nor to change it."[56]   Those to whom they pray, themselves seek the means of access to their Rabb - trying as to who can be nearer - they hope for His Mercy and fear His punishment, for the punishment of your Rabb is terrible indeed.[57]   17:[56-57]

The reason for not sending the signs to Muhammad (pbuh) as were sent to prior prophets

There is not a town *(population)* but We shall destroy it before the Day of Resurrection or punish it with a severe punishment; this fact has been recorded in the Book of Records.[58]   We refrain from sending signs *(miracles)* only because the men of former generations treated them as false. *For example,* We sent the she-camel to the people of Thamûd - a manifest sign - but they wronged her. We send the signs only by way of warning, *and if people reject the sign after receiving it, they are doomed.*[59] Remember, *O Muhammad!* We told you that your Rabb encompasses mankind. We have made the Vision *(Al-Isrâ')* which We showed you *(as an eye witness and not as a dream)*, and the cursed tree *of Zaqqûm* which is mentioned in the Qur'an, a test for mankind. We are giving them warning to be fearful but it only increases their inordinate transgression.[60]   17:[58-60]

SECTION: 7

Shaitân, his enmity with human beings, and his vow to seduce them

Recall the occasion when We said to the angels: "Prostrate yourselves before Adam." They all prostrated except Iblees *(Shaitân)*, who replied: "Should I prostrate to the one whom You have created from clay?"[61]   Then he asked: "Tell me, is this the one whom You have honored above me? If You give me respite till the Day of Resurrection, I will certainly lead astray all but a few of his descendants."[62]   *Allah* said: "Go away! Hell is your reward, and the reward of those who follow you, an ample reward it shall be.[63] You may try to allure whomsoever you can with your *seductive* voice, muster against them all your cavalry and infantry, be their partner in their riches and their children, and promise them what you will - the promises of shaitân are nothing but deception[64]   - as for My servants, you shall have no authority over them. Your Rabb is sufficient as their Guardian."[65]   17:[61-65]

Your Rabb is the One Who drives your ships across the ocean, so that you may seek His bounty; indeed He is ever Merciful to you.[66] Whenever any adversity strikes you at sea, you forget all those whom you pray besides Him *(Allah)*, and invoke only Him; yet, when He brings you safe to the land, you turn your backs *upon Him*. Indeed, man is ever ungrateful.[67] Are you confident that He will not cave in the land beneath you, or let loose a deadly tornado upon you? Then you may not find anyone to protect you.[68] Or, are you confident that when again you go back *to sea* He will not smite you with a violent tempest and drown you for your disbelief? *If that happens*, then you will not find anyone who can question Us *regarding this end of yours*.[69] Indeed, We have honored the children of Adam, blessed them with conveyances on land and sea, provided them with good and pure things, and exalted them above many of Our creatures.[70] 17:[66-70]

Allah has provided conveyance for you on land and sea

SECTION: 8

Just imagine the scene of that Day when We shall call every community with their respective Imams *(leaders):* then those who will be given their 'book of deeds' in their right hand will read it *with pleasure* and they will not be wronged in the least.[71] But those who have played blind *(to the Truth)* in this world will be blind in the hereafter, and go even further astray from the Way *to Salvation*.[72] 17:[71-72]

Accountability of every community and its leaders

O Muhammad! These people have tried to entice you from Our revelations, hoping that you might fabricate something in Our name. *Had you done that*, they would have made you their friend.[73] Had We not strengthened your faith, you might have made some compromise with them.[74] In such a case We would have given you double punishment in this life and in the life hereafter. Then you would have found no helper against Our *wrath*.[75] They almost scared you off the land in order to expel you from it. If they do so, they will not be able to stay here much longer after you.[76] *This has always been* Our Sunnah *(course of action)* with regards to those Rasools whom We sent before you, and you will find no change in Our Sunnah *(course of action)*.[77] 17:[73-77]

No compromise is allowed in matters of Islamic law and principles

SECTION: 9

Establish Salah from the decline of the sun till the darkness of the night *(Zûhr, 'Asr, Maghrib and 'Isha)* and read the Qur'an at Fajr *(dawn)*; for the reading the Qur'an at Fajr is witnessed *(by the*

Five times daily Salah (prayers)

and an extra prayer (called Tahajjud) for the Prophet

angels).[78] During a part of the night, pray Tahajjud with this *Qur'an*, an additional prayer for you *(O Muhammad)*, that your Rabb may exalt you to 'Maqâman Mahmûda' *(a station of great glory)*.[79] And say: "O my Rabb! Make my entrance *(to the city of Al-Madinah)*, the entrance with truth and make my exit *(from the city of Makkah)*, the exit with truth and grant me a supporting authority from Yourself;"[80] and declare, "The Truth has come and falsehood has vanished, for falsehood by its nature is bound to perish."[81] We have sent down in the Qur'an that which is a healing

The Qur'an is a healing and mercy for the believers

and a mercy for the believers, while to the wrongdoers it adds nothing but loss.[82] *Man is a strange creature*: when We bestow Our favors on man, he turns his back and drifts off to one side *(instead of coming to Us)* and whenever evil touches him, he gives himself up to despair.[83] *O Prophet* say to them: "Everyone acts according to his own disposition; but only your Rabb knows best who is on the Right Way."[84]   17:[78-84]

SECTION: 10

Ar-Rûh (Spirit) is at the command of Allah

They put you questions about Ar-Rûh *(the Soul)*. Tell them: "The Soul is of the commands of my Rabb and the knowledge you are given is but very little."[85] If We want, We can definitely take away all that which We have revealed to you *(this Qur'an)*: then you will find none to help you in getting it back from Us.[86] But your Rabb has blessed you *with this knowledge*; surely, His blessings upon you have been great indeed.[87] Declare: "Even if

No one can produce a Qur'an like this

all human beings and Jinns combined their resources to produce the like of this Qur'an, they would never be able to compose the like thereof, even if they backed up each other *as best as they could*."[88]   17:[85-88]

Allah has used different methods in the Qur'an to make people understand His Message

In this Qur'an We have used different methods to make the people understand the Message, yet, the majority of them persist in unbelief.[89] They say: "We will not believe in you until you cause a spring to gush forth from the earth for us,[90] or until a garden of date-palms and grapes be created for you and cause rivers to flow in it;[91] or until you cause the sky to fall upon us in pieces as you have threatened us; or you bring Allah and the angels before us face to face,[92] or a house made with gold comes into being for you; or you ascend to the sky - we shall not even believe in your ascension until you bring down to us a book that we can read." *O Muhammad,* tell them: "Glory be to my Rabb! Have I ever claimed to be anything more than a human Rasool?"[93]   17:[89-93]

SECTION: 11

Nothing prevented people from belief when guidance came to them except the excuse: "What! Has Allah sent a man like us to be a Rasool?"[94]   *O Muhammad,* tell them: "Had there been in the earth angels walking about as settlers, We would certainly have sent down to them an angel from heaven as a Rasool."[95]   Say: "Sufficient is Allah as a witness between me and you. He is the One Who is Aware and Observant of His servants."[96]   Those whom Allah guides are rightly guided; and those whom He lets go astray, shall find no protector besides Him. On the Day of Resurrection We shall gather them all, prone on their faces, blind, dumb and deaf. Hell shall be their abode: whenever its flames die down, We will rekindle for them the fierceness of the fire.[97]   Thus shall they be rewarded: because they rejected Our revelations and said: "When we are reduced to bones and decayed particles, shall we really be raised to life in a new creation?"[98]   Can they not see that Allah Who has created the heavens and the earth has power to create people like them? He has set a deadline for their lives, there is no doubt about it: yet, the wrongdoers refuse to do anything except to disbelieve. [99]   Say *to them:* "If you had all the treasures of my Rabb's mercy at your disposal, you would have held them back for fear of spending. Man is ever so stingy!"[100]   17:[94-100]

Allah has sent a human Rasool to human beings; if the dwellers of earth had been Angels, Allah would have sent an angel as a Rasool

Only disbelievers can doubt life after death

SECTION: 12

To Musa *(Moses)* We gave nine clear signs. Ask the Children of Israel, when he came to them and Fir'aun told him: "O Musa! I think that you are bewitched".[101]   *Musa* replied: "You know it very well that no one except the Rabb of the heavens and the earth has sent down these signs as clear evidence, and O Fir'aun *(Pharaoh)*, surely, I think that you are doomed to destruction."[102] So *Fir'aun* resolved to remove *Musa and the Israelites* from the land *of Egypt,* but We drowned him and all who were with him.[103] Thereafter We said to the Children of Israel: "Settle down in the land and when the time of final promise shall come to pass, We shall assemble you all together."[104]   17:[101-104]

Musa was given nine signs; people still did not believe him

We have revealed the *Qur'an* in Truth, and with the Truth it has come down: and *O Muhammad,* We have sent you only to give good news *to the believers* and to warn *the unbelievers.*[105]   We have divided the Qur'an into sections so that you may recite to the people with deliberation, and We have sent it down in gradual

The Qur'an is revealed in truth and with the truth it

has come down in sections to suit each occasion; for easy deliberation

Offer Salah neither too loud nor in too low a voice, adopt the middle course

revelations *to suit particular occasions.*[106]   Say: "Whether you believe in it or not, it is true that those who were endowed with knowledge before its revelation *(Jews and Christians like Abdullah Bin Salâm and Salmân Al-Fârsi)* - when it is recited to them, they fall upon their faces in prostration,[107]   and say, 'Glory be to our Rabb! Our Rabb's promise has been fulfilled.'[108]   They fall down upon their faces, weeping as they listen, and this increases their reverence."[109]   *O Prophet,* say to them: "Whether you call Him Allah or call Him Rahmân; it is all the same by whichever name you call Him because for Him are all the Finest names. Offer your Salah neither in too loud a voice nor in too low a voice but seek a middle course[110]   and say: "Praise be to Allah, the One Who has begotten no son and Who has no partner in His Kingdom; nor is He helpless to need a protector, and glorify His greatness in the best possible way."[111]   17:[105-111]

18: AL-KAHF

Period of Revelation

This is the first of those Sûrahs which were revealed in the third stage (from the fifth to the tenth year) of Prophethood at Makkah. The persecutions of Muslims were severe but migration to Habsha had not yet taken place.

Major Issues, Divine Laws, and Guidance

* Story of the Companions of the Cave who were wakened up from their sleep after hundreds of years.
* Whenever you promise to do something in the future, always say "Insha Allah (If Allah so wills)."
* Similitude of this worldly life and its relationship with the life after death.
* Story of the Prophet Musa as a student of Khidr.
* Story of King Zul-Qarnain.
* The favors of Allah are countless and cannot be recorded even if all the oceans were to be used as an ink and other such oceans are brought to replenish this ink.
* Muhammad (peace be upon him) is but a human being like you.

This Sûrah was revealed to answer the following three questions which the mushrikeen of Makkah, in consultation with the Jews, had put to the Prophet in order to test him:

1. Who were "Companions of the Cave?"
2. What is the real story of Khidr?
3. Who was Zul-Qarnain?

These three questions and the stories involved concerned the history of the Jews, and were unknown in Arabia. These questions were intended to test whether the Prophet was really Divinely guided or would try to avoid the questions. Allah not only provided a complete answer to their questions but also explained the three stories to the disadvantage of the opponents of Islam.

The questioners were told that the Companions of the Cave believed in the same doctrine of Tawheed (Oneness of God) which was being put forward in the Qur'an and that their condition was similar to the condition of the persecuted Muslims of Makkah. On the other hand, the persecutors of the Companions of the

Cave had behaved in the same way towards them as the disbelieving Quraish were behaving towards the Muslims. Besides this, the Muslims have been taught that even if a believer is persecuted by a cruel society, he should not bow down before falsehood, rather he should migrate from that place if needed. The disbelievers of Makkah were told that the story of the 'Companions of the Cave' was a clear proof about the life hereafter. Allah has the power to put the people to sleep for hundreds of years and bring them back to active life after that long sleep or death as He did in case of the Companions of the Cave.

The story of the Companions of the Cave is also used to warn the chiefs of Makkah who were persecuting the newly formed Muslim community. At the same time, the Prophet is being instructed that he should in no case make a compromise with the persecutors nor should he consider them to be more important than his poor followers. This story is also meant to comfort and encourage the oppressed Muslims and relate to them how righteous people in the past saved their Faith. On the other hand, the chiefs of Quraish are admonished that they should not be puffed up with this transitory life that they are enjoying; rather they should seek the excellence of the hereafter which will be permanent and eternal.

Similarly the story of Khidr and Moses not only provides an answer to disbelievers but also provides comfort to the Believers. The believers are told: "You should have full faith in the wisdom of what is happening in the world according to the will of Allah. As the reality is hidden from you, sometimes it appears that things are going against you, in fact they may not be. If the curtain is removed from the "unseen", you would yourselves come to know that not only it is happening for the best but most of the times it is also producing good results for you."

The same is true of the story of Zul-Qarnain. It also admonishes the questioners, as if to say, "O chiefs of Makkah you should learn a lesson from Zul-Qarnain. Though he was a great ruler, a great conqueror and the owner of great resources, yet he always surrendered to Allah, whereas you are rebelling against Him even though you are insignificant as compared to him. Besides this, though Zul-Qarnain built one of the strongest walls, yet his real trust was in Allah and not in the 'wall'. He believed that the wall shall stay as long as it was the will of Allah, whereas you who possess only insignificant dwellings in comparison to him, consider yourselves to be permanently safe and secure against all sorts of calamities."

18: AL-KAHF

This Sûrah, revealed at Makkah, has 12 sections and 110 verses.

In the name of Allah, the Compassionate, the Merciful.

SECTION: 1

Praise be to Allah Who has revealed the Book to His servant and made it free from any crookedness.[1]   *He has made it* straight so that He may warn about the terrible punishment *for the unbelievers* from Him and give good news to the believers who do good deeds that they shall have a goodly reward *(paradise)*,[2]   wherein they will live forever.[3]   Further to warn those who say "Allah has begotten a son."[4]   They have no knowledge about it, nor did their forefathers; this is a monstrous word that comes from their mouths. They utter nothing but a lie.[5]   *O Muhammad!* You probably will kill yourself in grief over them, if they do not believe in this Message *(the Qur'an)*.[6]   18:[1-6]

> Those who say Allah has begotten a son are uttering a monstrous lie

We have decked the earth with all kinds of ornaments to test the people and to see which of them do the best deeds.[7]   In the end, We shall reduce all that is on it to a barren wasteland.[8]   Do you think that the Companions of the Cave and of Ar-Raqeem *(this may refer to the name of their dog, or the tablet on which their names were inscribed or the mountain in which the cave is situated)* were a wonder among Our signs?[9]   When those young men took refuge in the cave, they said "Our Rabb! Have mercy on us from Yourself and facilitate for us the right way."[10]   So We put upon their ears a cover *(put them into a deep sleep)* for a number of years in the cave,[11]   and then awakened them to find out which of the two parties *(believers and nonbelievers who were arguing about the fact of life after death)* could best tell the length of their stay.[12]   18:[7-12]

> Story of the Companions of the Cave

SECTION: 2

Now We tell you their real story. They were young men who believed in their Rabb, and We increased them in guidance.[13]   We put courage in their hearts when they stood up and declared: "Our Rabb is the Rabb of the heavens and the earth, we shall never call upon any other deity except Him, for if we do, we shall be uttering blasphemy.[14]   These people of ours have taken for worship other gods besides Him; *if they are right,* why do they not bring forth any convincing proof *of their divinity*? Who is more wicked than the one who invents a lie about Allah?"[15]   *The young men said to one another*: Now that you have withdrawn from them

> They were young men who declared the truth about the Oneness of Allah

and denounced those deities whom they worship beside Allah, let us take refuge in the cave; your Rabb will extend to you His mercy and provide you a means of safty."[16]   If you could look *at them in the cave, it would appear to you that* the rising sun declines to the right from their cave, and as it sets, passes them on the left, while they lay in an open space in between. This is from the signs of Allah. He whom Allah guides is rightly guided; but he whom He lets go astray, you will find no guardian to lead him to the Right Way.[17]

18:[13-17]

SECTION: 3

If you could see them, you might have thought them awake, though they were asleep. We turned them about to their right and left sides, while their dog lay stretched out with his forepaws at the entrance. Had you looked at them, you would have certainly turned away from them and flee in terror.[18]   In the same *miraculous* way, We woke them up from sleep so that they could question one another. One of them asked: "How long have you been here?" The others answered: "Maybe we have been here for a day or part of a day." *Finally* they concluded: "Our Rabb knows best how long we have stayed here. Anyhow, let one of us go to the city with this silver coin, and let him find who has the purest food and bring us something to eat. Let him behave with caution and let him not disclose our whereabouts.[19]   For, if they find you out, they will stone you to death, or force you back into their faith and in that case, you will never attain felicity."[20]   18:[18-20]

Thus did We reveal their secret to the people so that they might know that the promise of Allah is true and that there is no doubt about the coming of the Hour *of Judgment. (But what a pity that instead of considering the Hour of Judgment)* they started arguing among themselves about their case. Some said: "Erect a building over them." Their Rabb knows them best. Those who finally prevailed over their matter said: "We shall indeed erect a place of worship over them."[21]   Some will say: "They were three and their dog was the fourth." Others, guessing the unknown, will say: "They were five and their dog was the sixth," and still others will say: "They were seven and their dog was the eighth." Say: "My Rabb Alone knows their number. None but a few really know their *correct number."* Therefore, do not enter into discussion with them about their number except in a cursory way, nor ask any of them *(the speculators)* about the *companions of the cave*.[22]   18:[21-22]

Marginal notes:

They had to run away and take refuge in a cave

They were in a state of sleep

They were awakened by Allah after hundreds of year

Their identity was disclosed to resolve the disputed issue of life after death: What a shame that, instead of getting the point, people were disputing about their numbers

SECTION: 4

Never say of anything "I will certainly do it tomorrow"[23] provided you add: "If Allah wills!" And if you forget *to say this,* then call your Rabb to mind and say: "I hope that my Rabb shall guide me and bring me ever closer than this to the Right Way."[24] They stayed in their cave three hundred years plus an addition of another nine.[25] *O Prophet*, say: "Allah knows best how long they stayed; He is the One Who knows the secrets of the heavens and the earth; sharp is His sight and keen is His hearing! They have no protector besides Him and He does not let anyone share in His command.[26]

18:[23-26]

O Prophet! Recite what has been revealed to you from the Book of your Rabb: no one is authorized to change His Words and *if you dare*, you will find no refuge to protect you from Him.[27] Keep yourself content with those who call on their Rabb morning and evening seeking His good pleasure; and let not your eyes turn away from them desiring the attraction of Worldly Life; nor obey the one whose heart We have permitted to neglect Our remembrance, who follows his own desires and whose deeds were all in vain.[28] *O Prophet* proclaim: "This is the Truth from your Rabb. Now let him who will, believe in it, and him who will, deny it." *As for those who reject it*, for such wrongdoers, We have prepared a Fire whose flames, like walls, will hem them from all sides. When they cry for help, they will be showered with hot water like boiling oil, which will scald their faces. What a dreadful drink and what a horrible residence![29] As for those who believe and do good deeds, rest assured that We do not waste the reward of him who does good work.[30] They are the ones for whom there will be the gardens of eternity, beneath which rivers flow; they will be adorned therein with bracelets of gold; they will wear green garments of fine thick silk and recline on soft couches. What an excellent reward and what a beautiful residence![31]   18:[27-31]

SECTION: 5

O Prophet! Give them this parable. *Once there were* two men. To one of them We had given two gardens of grapevines surrounded with palm-trees and put between them land for cultivation.[32] Both of those gardens yielded abundant produce and did not fail to yield its best. We had *even* caused a river to flow between the two *gardens*.[33] And because he had abundant produce, he said to his companion while conversing with him: "I am richer than you

---

Whenever you promise to do something in the future, always say: "Insha Allah (If Allah wills)."

No one is authorized to change the Word of Allah

Proclaim: "Truth from Allah has come - choice is yours: believe it or disbelieve."

Parable of a believer and a disbeliever

and my clan is mightier than yours."[34]   When, having wronged his soul, he entered his garden and said: "I do not think that this *garden* will ever perish![35]   Nor do I believe that the Hour *of Judgment* will ever convene. And if ever if I am returned to my Rabb, I will surely find even a better place than this."[36]   His companion replied while still conversing with him: "Do you disbelieve in Him Who created you from dust, then from a drop of semen, and then fashioned you into a perfect man?[37]   *As for myself*, Allah is the One Who is my Rabb and I do not associate anyone with Him.[38]   When you entered your garden, why did you not say: 'It is as wonderful as Allah wanted it to be; no one has power except Allah!' Though you see me poorer than yourself in wealth and children,[39]   yet, my Rabb may give me a garden better than yours, and may send down thunderbolts from the sky upon your garden, turning it into a barren wasteland.[40]   Or its water may sink so deep *into the ground* that you may not be able to pump it out."[41]   *It so happened* that all his fruitful garden was utterly destroyed and there he stood wringing his hands with grief over all that he had spent on it, while it lay waste *before his eye*s, he could only say: "I wish I had not associated anyone with my Rabb!"[42]   *He was so helpless that* he could neither find anyone to help him besides Allah, nor could he himself avert *that catastrophe*[43] - it was then *that he realized* that the real protection comes only from Allah. His is the best reward and His is the best requital.[44]   18:[32-44]

SECTION: 6

Similitude of worldly life and its relationship with the life of the here-after

O Prophet! Give them the similitude of the life of this world. It is like the vegetation of the earth that flourishes with the rain from the sky, but afterwards *the same vegetation* turns into dry stubble which is blown away by the winds. Allah is the One Who has power over everything.[45]   *Likewise*, wealth and children are an attraction of this worldly life; yet, honorable deeds that last forever are better rewarded by your Rabb and hold for you a better hope *of salvation.*[46]   *You should prepare for* that Day when We will set the mountains in motion and you will see the earth as a barren waste; when We shall assemble *mankind* all together, leaving not even a single soul behind.[47]   They all will be brought before your Rabb standing in rows and *He will say*: "Well! You have returned to Us as We created you at first: even though you claimed that We had not fixed any time for *the fulfillment of* this promise *of meeting with Us!*"[48]   Then the book of their deeds will be placed before them. *At that time* you will see the sinners in great terror because of what is *recorded* therein. They will say: "Woe to us! What kind of a book is this? It leaves out nothing small or large: all is noted down!"   They will find all that they did, recorded therein. Your Rabb will not be unjust to anyone in the least.[49]   18:[45-49]

SECTION: 7

When We said to the angels: "Prostrate yourself before Adam," so they all prostrated themselves except Iblees *(Shaitân),* who was one of the Jinns and chose to disobey the command of his Rabb. Would you then take him and his children as your protectors rather than Me, even though they are your enemies? What a bad substitute the wrongdoers have chosen![50]   I did not call them to witness the creation of the heavens and the earth, nor their own creation, nor do I take those who lead mankind astray as My supporters.[51]   On the Day *of Judgment Allah* will say to them: "Call on those whom you thought to be My partners." They will call them but will receive no answer; and We shall put enmity between them.[52]   The criminals will see the fire and realize that they are going to fall into it, and they will find no place to escape.[53]

                                                18:[50-53]

SECTION: 8

We have given all kinds of examples in this Qur'an for the people *to understand its Message*, but man is exceedingly contentious.[54]   And nothing has prevented people from believing and seeking the forgiveness of their Rabb now that Guidance has come to them, except that they are waiting for the fate of former people to overtake them or the scourge to be brought to them face to face.[55] We send the Rasools only as bearers of good news and as warners, but the unbelievers seek to defeat the Truth with false arguments and they mocked at My revelations and My warnings.[56]   Who is more unjust than the one who, when reminded of the revelations of his Rabb, turns away from them and forgets what his own hands have done? *In regards to such people*, We have cast veils over their hearts, so they do not understand this *Qur'an*, and have made them hard of hearing. Call them as you may towards the guidance, they will never be guided.[57]   Had it been the Will of your Rabb, the Most Forgiving and Most Merciful, to seize them for their sins, He would have hastened their punishment, but for that they have an appointed time, beyond which they will find no escape.[58]   All those nations whom We destroyed for their wrongdoings were

Fate of those who follow the Shaitân and commit shirk

Allah has given all kinds of examples in the Qur'an, so that the people may understand His Message

given *respite and* an appointed time for their destruction.[59]

18:[54-59]

SECTION: 9

The Prophet Musa travelled to find Khidr to learn some of the knowledge given to him by Allah Almighty

Now tell them about the story of Khidr to whom Allah has given special knowledge. The Prophet Musa (Moses) was asked to go to him and learn from him. When *Musa set out to meet him at an appointed place,* he said to his young servant: "I will not give up my journey until I reach the junction of the two seas, even if I have to spend ages in travel."[60]   *It so happened that* when at last they reached the junction of the two *seas* they forgot about the fish *they were carrying,* which made its way into the sea, and disappeared.[61] When they had passed on some distance, Musa *(Moses)* asked his young servant: "Let us have our meal, really we have suffered much fatigue at this *stage of* our journey."[62]   He replied: "You know! I forgot to tell you about the fish, which made its way miraculously into the river, when we were resting beside that rock. It was Shaitân who made me forget to mention this incident to you."[63]   *Musa* said: "That is the place we were looking for," so they went back retracing their footsteps.[64]   There they found one of Our servants *(Khidr)* whom We had blessed with special favor from Ourselves and whom We had given special knowledge of Our own.[65]   Musa requested of him: "May I follow you so that you may teach me from that True Knowledge which you have been taught?"[66]   He answered: "Surely, you will not be able to bear with me,[67]   for how can you have patience about that which is beyond your knowledge?"[68]   *Musa* said: "If Allah wills, you shall find me patient and I shall not disobey you in any way."[69]   He said: "If you want to follow me, then do not question me about anything until I tell you about it myself."[70]

Khidr warned Musa that he would not be able to bear with him

18:[60-70]

SECTION: 10

The Prophet Musa could not resist questioning Khidr about making a hole in a boat

So they set forth, but when they embarked in a boat *to cross the river,* Khidr made a hole in it. Musa said: "Did you make a hole in it to drown its passengers? You have done a weird thing!"[71]   He said: "Didn't I say that you would not manage to have patience with me?"[72]   *Musa* said: "Pardon my forgetfulness, *please* do not be hard in dealing with me on account of this mistake." [73]   So they journeyed on until they met a boy, and *Khidr* killed him. Musa said: "You have killed an innocent person though he had killed nobody. Surely, you have done a horrible thing!"[74]   18:[71-74]

JUZ (PART): 16

Khidr said: "Did I not tell you that you will not be able to bear with me?"[75]   *Musa* replied: "If ever I ask you about anything after this, you may not keep me in your company; for then *I should deserve it because* you will have an excuse in my case."[76]   They travelled on until they came to the people of a town. They asked them for some food, but they refused to receive them as their guests. There they found a wall on the point of falling down, so he restored it. *Musa* said: "If you wanted you could have taken some wages for it!"[77]   *Khidr* replied: "That's it; this is the parting between you and me. But first I will explain to you those acts of mine which you could not bear to watch with patience.[78]   As for the boat, it belonged to some poor fishermen who toiled on the sea. I intended to damage it because there was a king after them who was seizing every boat by force.[79]   As for the youth, his parents are true believers, and we feared lest he would oppress them by rebellion and disbelief.[80]   It was our wish that our Rabb should grant them another in his place, a son more righteous and better in affection.[81]   As for the wall, it belonged to two orphan boys in the city and beneath it their treasure was buried. Since their father was a righteous man, your Rabb desired that these children should attain their maturity and take out their treasure. *All this was done* as a mercy from your Rabb. What I did was not done by my own will. That is the interpretation *of those actions* which you could not bear to watch with patience."[82]   18:[75-82]

The story of the Prophet Musa and Khidr

SECTION: 11

O Muhammad, they ask you about Dhul-Qarnain. Say "I will recite to you some of his story."[83]   Indeed We established his power in the land and We gave him all kinds of ways and means.[84]   So one time he followed a certain expedition *towards the West and he marched on*[85]   till he reached where the Sun was setting *(the west)*; he noted that it was setting in a murky spring and near it he found a people. We said: "O Dhul-Qarnain! You have the option to either punish them or to show them kindness."[86]   He said: "Anyone Who will do wrong shall be punished; then will he return to his Rabb and be sternly punished by Him.[87]   As for him who believes and does good deeds, he will have a good reward and will be assigned an easy task by our command."[88]   Then he set out on another expedition *towards the East and marched on*[89]   till he came to the rising of the

The Story of King Dhul-Qarnain

Sun *(the east)* ; he noted it rising on a people for whom We had not provided any shelter from it.[90]   *He left them* as they were: We had full knowledge of what was before him.[91]   Then he set out on another expedition *and marched on*[92]   till he reached between two mountains where he found a people who could hardly understand his language.[93]   They requested: "O Dhul-Qarnain! The people of Ya'jûj (Gog) and Ma'jûj (Magog) ravage this land; should we pay you tribute in order for you to build a wall-barrier between us and them?"[94]   *Dhul-Qarnain* said: "That which my Rabb has granted me is more than enough, just help me with workers and I will erect a fortified barrier between you and them.[95]   Bring me panels of iron." Finally when he dammed up the space between the two mountains, he said: "Ply your bellows." They did so until *the iron wall* became red hot, then he said: "Bring me some molten brass to pour over it."[96]   *This became such a barrier that Gog and Magog* could not scale it or dig through it.[97]   He said: "This is a blessing from my Rabb. But *you should know that* when the promise of my Rabb shall come to pass, He will level it to the ground, for the promise of my Rabb is ever true."[98]   On that Day, We shall let the people loose to surge like waves on one another. The trumpet will be blown and We shall assemble them all together.[99]   We shall spread Hell out on display before the unbelievers,[100]   who had turned a blind eye to My admonition and a deaf ear to My warning.[101]

18:[83-101]

SECTION: 12

Do the unbelievers think that they can take my servants as protectors, *to save themselves from Hell,* instead of Me? Certainly We have prepared Hell for the entertainment of such unbelievers.[102]   *O Muhammad* tell them: "Should we tell you the worst kind of losers relating to their deeds?[103]   Those whose efforts in this worldly life had gone astray from the Right Way, but all along they were under the delusion that they were doing good deeds;[104]   they are the ones who are disregarding the revelations of their Rabb and the fact that they will meet Him *for accountability of their deeds in the Hereafter*, so their deeds will become null and will not have any weight on the Day of Resurrection.[105]   Thus the reward of such people will be Hell; because they had no faith and because they took My revelations and My Rasools as a joke.[106]   *However,* those who believe and do good deeds, will be entertained with the Gardens of Paradise[107]   to live therein for ever and they will never desire to go anywhere else.[108]   18:[102-108]

Fates of the mush-rikeen and the believers on the Day of Judgement

O Muhammad tell them: "If the water of the ocean were ink with which to write the Words of my Rabb, the ocean would surely be consumed before the words of my Rabb are finished, even if We brought *another ocean of* similar quantity to replenish it.[109]

18:[109]

Words of Allah are countless and can not be recorded

O Muhammad, tell them: "I am but a human being like you; the revelation is sent to me to declare that your God is One God *(Allah)*; therefore, whoever hopes to meet his Rabb, let him do good deeds and join no other deity in the worship of his Rabb."[110]

18:[110]

Muhammad (pbuh) is but a human being like you

19: MARYAM

Period of Revelation

This Sûrah was revealed before the migration to Habasha (Abyssinia) during the third stage of the Prophet's residence at Makkah. Authentic traditions indicate that Sayyidunâ J'afar recited vv. 1-40 of this Sûrah in the court of Negus, the king of Habasha, when he called the immigrants to his court upon the extradition request of the Quraish.

Major Issues, Divine Laws, and Guidance

* Story of Zakariyya (Zacharia) and the birth of Prophet Yahya (John).
* Story of Maryam (Mary) and the miraculous birth of Prophet Isa (Jesus).
* Prophet Isa's address to his people from his cradle.
* The fact that Isa (Jesus), pbuh, is not the son of Allah (God), and that it is not befitting to the Majesty of Allah that He needs a son.
* Story of Prophet Ibrâheem (peace be upon him) and his mushrik father.
* All Prophets of Allah were divinely guided and chosen people.
* Life of the believers and the nonbelievers in this world and in the Hereafter.
* Those who say, "Allah has begotten a son," preach such a monstrous lie that if they could hear it, the heavens would crack, the earth would split and the mountains would crumble to pieces.
* Allah has made the Qur'an easy for mankind.

The Muslims' First Migration and its Historical Background

The chiefs of the Quraish had failed to suppress the Islamic movement through ridicule, sarcasm, and threats, so they resorted to persecution and economic pressure. They persecuted, starved, inflicted physical torture, and co-erced the Muslims to give up Islam. The most pitiful victims of their persecution were the poor people and the slaves. Not only were they not paid by the Quraish for labor and professional work but they were beaten, imprisoned, kept thirsty and hungry and were even dragged on the burning sands.

The condition of the Muslims had become so unbearable that in the fifth year of the Prophet's mission, he advised his followers in the following words: "You may migrate to Habasha, for there is a king who does not allow injustice to anyone. You should remain there till Allah provides a remedy for your affliction."

Taking advantage of this permission, eleven men and four women immedi-ately left for Habasha. The Quraish pursued them to the coast but fortunately they escaped by getting on a boat leaving for Habasha at the seaport of Shu'aibah. After a few months, other people followed suit and their number rose to eighty-three men and eleven women from the Quraish and seven from other tribes. Only forty Muslims were left with the Prophet at Makkah. This migration caused a great hue and cry in Makkah, for there was hardly any family of the Quraish which did not lose a son, a son-in-law, a daughter, a brother or a sister. These included the near relatives of Abu Jahl, Abu Sufyân and other chiefs of the Quraish who were notorious for their persecution of the Muslims. As a result, some of them became more bitter in their enmity toward Islam, while others were so moved by this that they embraced Islam.

The Quraish held a meeting and decided to send Abdullah bin Abi Rabiy'ah, the half brother of Abu Jahl, and Amr bin A's with some precious gifts to the king of Habasha to persuade him to send the immigrants back to Makkah. Sayyidah Umme Salmah, who became a wife of the Prophet later on and was among the migrants, related their story in detail. She says: "When these two clever statesmen of the Quraish reached Habasha, they distributed the gifts among the courtiers of the king and persuaded them to support their request to send the immigrants back. Then they approached Negus, the king of Habasha, presented the expensive gifts, and said: "Some headstrong brats of our city have come to your land so our chiefs have sent us to you with the request that you kindly send them back. These brats have forsaken our faith, have not embraced yours, and have invented a new faith." As soon as they made their request, all the courtiers supported their case, saying: "We should send such people back. It is not proper for us to keep them here." At this the king, who got annoyed, said: 'I am not going to send them back without proper enquiry. Since those people have put their trust in us through coming and taking shelter in my country rather than going to some other country, I will not betray them. I will send for them and investigate the allegations these people have made against them. Then I will make the decision.'" So the king sent for the immigrants to come to his court.

When the immigrants received the summons from the king, they held a meeting and after lengthy discussions decided: 'We shall present the teachings of the Prophet to the king without adding anything to or withholding anything from it regardless of whether he lets us remain here or turns us out of his country.' When they came to the court, the king put this question abruptly: 'I understand that you have given up the faith of your own people and have neither embraced my faith nor any other existing faith but have invented a new faith. I would like to know what your new faith is.' At this, J'afar bin Abi Tâlib responded on behalf of the immigrants, in these words: 'O king! We were sunk deep in ignorance and had become very corrupt; then Muhammad (peace be upon him) came to us as a Messenger of Allah and reformed us, but these Quraish began to persecute us, so we have come to your *country in the hope that here we will be free from persecution.' Hearing this statement, the king asked: 'Please recite a piece of the Revelation which your Prophet has received from Allah.' (In response, Sayyidunâ J'afar recited a portion of this Sûrah which relates to the story of Prophets Yahya (John) and Isa (Jesus), may peace be upon them.) When the king listened, he started weeping and wept so much that his beard became wet with tears. When Sayyidunâ J'afar finished the recital, he said: 'Most surely this Revelation and the Message brought by Jesus have come from the same source. By God, I will not put you in the hands of these people.'*

Next day Amr bin A's made another attempt. He went to the king and said: 'Please send for them again and ask them concerning the belief they hold about Jesus, for they say a horrible thing about him.' The king again sent for the immigrants, who had already learned about the scheme of Amr. They again held a meeting to discuss the answer they should give to the king if he should ask about the belief that they hold about Prophet Jesus. It was a very critical situation and all of them were uneasy about it; however, they decided that they would just say what Allah and His Rasool had said about Jesus. The next day, when they went to the King's court, he asked them the question that had been suggested by Amr bin A's. Sayyidunâ J'afar bin Abi Tâlib stood up and answered without any hesitation: 'Jesus was a Servant of Allah and His Messenger. He was a Spirit and a Word of Allah which had been sent to virgin Mary.' At this the king picked up a straw from the ground and said, 'By God, Jesus was no different (even as much as this straw) than what you have said about him.' After this the king returned the gifts of the Quraish, saying: 'I do not accept bribes.' Then he addressed the immigrants: 'You are welcome in my country and you can stay here in peace.'

These incidents indicate that Allah sent this Sûrah as a "provision" to the immigrants for their journey to Habasha. Following the story of Prophets Yahya and Isa, the story of the Prophet Ibrâheem is also related for the benefit of the immigrants as he was also forced to leave his country by the persecution of his father, his family and his countrymen like them. On the one hand, it was intended to console the immigrants that by migrating they would be following the tradition of Prophet Ibrâheem, so they could expect a good end similar to his. On the other hand, it was intended to warn the disbelievers of Makkah that they were similar to those cruel people who persecuted their forefather and leader, Ibrâheem, while the Muslims were in a position similar to that of Prophet Ibrâheem.

19: MARYAM

This Sûrah revealed, at Makkah, has 6 sections and 98 verses.

In the name of Allah, the Compassionate, the Merciful.

SECTION: 1

Kâf Hâ' Yâ' 'Ayn Sâd.[1]   This is a reminder of blessings that your Rabb bestowed on His servant Zakariyya,[2]   when he invoked his Rabb in secret,[3]   saying: "O my Rabb! Surely, my bones have weakened and the hair of my head glisten with grey, while I have never been disappointed in my prayer to You, O my Rabb![4]   Surely, I fear about my relatives after me, for my wife is barren, grant me an heir from Yourself[5] - who should inherit me and inherit the posterity of Ya'qoob, and make him, O my Rabb, a desirable person!"[6]   *We answered his prayer saying:* "O Zakariyya! Surely, We give you the good news of a son, his name shall be Yahya *(John)*: a name that We have not given to anyone before him."[7]   He asked: "O my Rabb! How shall I have a son when my wife is barren and I have reached an extreme old age?"[8]   The answer came: "So shall it be. Your Rabb says: 'It shall not be a difficult task for Me, just as I created you before, when you were nothing at all!"[9]   *Zakariyya* said "O my Rabb! Give me a Sign". He said: "Your sign is that for three nights you shall not be able to speak to the people even being sound in health."[10]   After this *Zakariyya* came out of the Mihrâb *(prayer chamber)* and asked his people, *through sign language,* to glorify Allah in the morning and in the evening.[11]   *To his son when he became old enough, We said:* " O Yahya, hold firmly to the Book." We granted him wisdom, while he was yet a boy,[12]   and also granted him kindness and purity from Us, and he grew up a pious man;[13]   dutiful to his parents - he was neither arrogant nor disobedient.[14]   Peace be on him the day he was born, the day of his death and the Day he will be raised to life again![15]   19:[1-15]

The story of Zakariyya and the birth and youth of Yahya (John)

SECTION: 2

O Muhammad, relate to them the story of Maryam in the Book *(the Qur'an)* when she withdrew from her family to a place in the East.[16]   She chose to be secluded from them. We sent to her Our angel and he appeared before her as a grown man.[17]   She said: "I seek Rahmân's *(Allah's)* protection against you, *leave me alone* if you are Godfearing."[18]   He said: "*Don't be afraid*, I am merely a messenger from your Rabb to tell you about the gift of a

The story of Maryam and the miraculous birth of Isa (Jesus)

righteous son."[19] She said: "How shall I bear a son, when no man has ever touched me nor am I unchaste?"[20] *The angel* replied: "So shall it be - Your Rabb says: 'It is easy for Me. We wish to make him a Sign for mankind and a blessing from Us' - and this matter has already been decreed."[21] So she conceived the child and she retired with him to a remote place.[22] The pains of childbirth drove her to the trunk of a palm-tree. She cried *in her anguish*: "Ah! Would that I had died before this, and been long forgotten!"[23] *An angel* from beneath consoled her, saying: "Do not grieve! Your Rabb has provided a brook at your feet.[24] If you shake the trunk of this palm-tree, it will drop fresh ripe dates upon you.[25] So eat, drink and refresh yourself. If you see any human being, say: `I have vowed a fast for Rahmân *(Allah)*, so I will not speak to any human being today'."[26]   19:[16-26]

Maryam brought her baby (Jesus) to her people and the baby spoke to his people in the cradle to defend his mother and proclaim his assignment to be their Prophet

Carrying the baby, she came back to her people. They said: "O Maryam! You have brought something hard to believe![27] O sister *(a woman from the noble family)* of Haroon! Your father was not a bad man nor your mother an unchaste woman."[28] *In response,* she merely pointed towards the baby. They said: "How can we talk to a babe in the cradle?"[29] *Whereupon the baby* spoke out: "I am indeed a servant of Allah. He has given me the Book and made me a Prophet.[30] He has made me blessed wherever I may be. He has commanded me *to establish* Salah *(prayer)* and *give* Zakah *(obligatory charity)* as long as I live.[31] *He has exhorted me* to honor my mother and has not made me arrogant, disobedient.[32] Peace be upon me the day I was born, the day I shall die and the Day I shall be raised to life again."[33] Such was Isa *(Jesus)* the son of Maryam, and this is the true statement about him concerning which they are in doubt.[34]   19:[27-34]

Isa (Jesus) is not the son of God, it is not befitting to the Majesty of God that He needs to beget a son

It is not befitting to *the majesty of* Allah that He Himself should beget a son! He is far above this; for when He decrees a matter He need only say: "Be" and it is.[35] *Isa declared,* Verily Allah is my Rabb and your Rabb: therefore, serve Him. This is the Right Way.[36] Inspite of this, the sects from among them are divided *concerning Jesus*. So woe to the disbelievers *who say Jesus is the son of Allah* - from the meeting of a Great Day *(the Day of Judgement)*.[37] They will be able to see and hear very clearly on that Day when they will appear before Us! But today these wrong-doers, *neither want to hear nor see the Truth and,* are in manifest error.[38] *O Muhammad,* forewarn them about the Day of intense regret when this matter will be decided, *even though at present they* are paying no heed and do not believe.[39]   Ultimately, *all things will perish and* it is We, Who will inherit the earth and all that is on it, and to Us shall they return.[40]   19:[35-40]

SECTION: 3

Relate to them the story of Ibrâheem from the Book *(the Qur'an)*, he was a truthful Prophet.[41]   Remember, when he said to his father: "O my father! Why do you worship something that can neither hear nor see, nor profit you in any way?[42]   O my father! I have been given some knowledge which has not come to you, so follow me: I'll guide you to the Right Way.[43]   O my father! Do not worship Shaitân: for Shaitân is disobedient to the Compassion-ate *(Allah)*.[44]   O my father! I fear that a punishment of the Compassionate may afflict you, and you may become a friend of the Shaitân."[45]   *His father* replied: "How dare you renounce my gods O Ibrâheem? If you do not stop this folly, I will indeed stone you *to death*: so be gone *from my house* before I punish you!"[46] *Ibrâheem* said: "Peace be upon you: I will pray to my Rabb for your forgiveness, surely, He is ever Kind to me.[47]   I am leaving you and those whom you invoke besides Allah: I will call upon my Rabb and I am hopeful that my prayers to my Rabb will not be ig-nored."[48]   So when he left them and the deities whom they worshipped besides Allah, We granted him descendants like Ishâq and Ya'qoob, and We made each of them a Prophet.[49]   We bestowed on them Our Mercy and We granted them the honor of being mentioned with true high respect.[50]   19:[41-50]

The story of Ibrâheem and his idol worshipping father

SECTION: 4

Relate to them *the story* of Musa in the Book; surely, he was a chosen man and was a Rasool, a Prophet.[51]   We called him from the right side of Mount Tûr and honored him to come closer for *exclusive* conversation.[52]   We made his brother Haroon a Prophet with Our blessing and assigned him *as his assistant*.[53] Also relate to them *the story of* Isma'il in the Book; he was a man of his word and was a Rasool, a Prophet.[54]   He commanded his people *to establish* Salah and *give* Zakah, and was the one with whom his Rabb was well pleased.[55]   Also relate to them *the story of* Idrees in the Book; he was a Truthful man, a Prophet,[56]   whom We raised to a lofty place.[57]   19:[51-57]

The Prophethood of Musa, Isma`il and Idrees

These are some of the Prophets on whom Allah bestowed His favors from among the descendants of Adam and of those

All prophets of Allah were Divinely Guided and chosen

whom We carried in the Ark with Nûh, and of the descendants of Ibrâheem and Israel, and from among those whom We guided and chose. Whenever the Revelations of the Compassionate *(Allah)* were recited to them, they fell in tears prostrating *to their Rabb.*[58] But the generations who succeeded them abandoned the Salah and started following their lusts; so they will soon face the consequences of their deviation.[59] However, those who repent, become believers and do good deeds, will be admitted to Paradise and will not be wronged in the least.[60] *They will be granted* the gardens of eternity which the Merciful has promised to His servants, *even though they have* not seen them, and His promise shall be fulfilled.[61] There, they will hear no nonsense, but only the words of peace; and they will be provided their sustenance day and night.[62] Such is the Paradise which We shall give as an inheritance to those of Our Servants who lead a pious life.[63] *The angel Gabriel who brought this revelation after a long interval said:* "We do not descend from heaven except by the command of your Rabb; to Him belongs whatever is before us and whatever is behind us and all that lies in between. Your Rabb is never forgetful.[64] He is the Rabb of the heavens and the earth, and of all that lies in between, so worship Him, be steadfast in His worship. Do you know any other god who is worthy the same Name as His?"[65]   19:[58-65]

SECTION: 5

Believers and unbelievers' life in this world and their life in the Hereafter

Man says: "What! Once I am dead, shall I be raised to life again?"[66] Does not man remember that We created him before out of nothing?[67] By your Rabb, We will gather them all together along with their shaitâns and set them on their knees around the fire of hell;[68] then from every sect, We will certainly drag out its stoutest rebels against the Compassionate *(Allah)*.[69] Certainly We know best who deserves most to be burned therein.[70] There is not a single one of you, who shall not pass over it. This absolute decree of your Rabb is unavoidable;[71] then We will deliver those who were pious *during their life on earth* and leave the wrongdoers therein humbled on their knees.[72] When Our Clear Revelations are recited to them, the unbelievers say to the believer: "Which one, of the two of us, have fine dwelling and better companions?"[73] *Don't they see,* how many generations have We destroyed before them, who were far greater in riches and in splendor?[74] Tell them: "Anyone who has gone astray, the Compassionate *(Allah)* prolongs his respite until he sees about which he was warned; - be it a worldly scourge or the Hour *of Doom* - then he will realize whose is the worst dwelling and whose are the weak companions?[75] *In fact,* Allah increases in guidance those who seek guidance; the righteous good deeds that last, are better in the sight of your Rabb to earn you a better reward and yield you the best fruit?"[76] Have you noticed the words of that person who rejects Our Revelations; yet, boasts: "I shall always be given wealth and children."[77] Has he gained knowledge of the Unseen or has he been awarded a contract by the Compassionate *(Allah)*?[78] By no means! We write down what he says and We will make his punishment long and terrible.[79] We will inherit all that he boasts of, and he will come back to Us all alone *leaving all these things behind.*[80] They have taken other deities for worship instead of Allah, so that they should be a source of strength to them.[81] By no means! Those very deities will renounce their worship and turn against them *on the Day of Judgment.*[82]   19:[66-82]

SECTION: 6

Don you not see that We have sent down to the unbelievers shaitâns who incite them to do evil?[83] Therefore, be not in haste against them, their days are numbered.[84] The Day will surely come, when We will gather the righteous like honored guests before the Compassionate *(Allah),*[85] and drive the criminals to Hell in a thirsty state, *like thirsty cattle are driven to water.*[86] None shall have the power to intercede except the one who may receive the sanction of the Compassionate *(Allah).*[87] They say: "The Compassionate *(Allah)* has begotten a son."[88] You have indeed uttered something so monstrous,[89] that the very heavens might crack, the earth might cleave asunder and the mountains might crumble to pieces[90] - at their ascribing a son to the Compassionate *(Allah),*[91] It is not befitting to the Compassionate *(Allah)* that He should beget a son.[92] There is none in the heavens and in the earth but comes to the Compassionate *(Allah)* as a servant.[93] He has comprehensive knowledge and has kept strict count of all His creatures,[94] and every one of them will come to Him individually on the Day of Resurrection.[95] Surely, the Compassionate *(Allah)* will bring about love for those who believe and do good deeds.[96] We have made this *Qur'an* easy in your own language so that you may give good news to the righteous and warn the headstrong contentious folk.[97] How many generations have We destroyed before them! Can you see any of them, or hear even a whisper of them?[98]   19:[83-98]

No god other than Allah will be able to save you on the Day of Judgement

Those who say Allah has begotten a son, preach such a monstrous lie that even the Heavens may crack, earth split and mountains crumble to pieces

Allah has made the Qur'an easy for mankind to understand

20: TÂ-HÂ

Period of Revelation

The period of this Sûrah's revelation is the same as that of Sûrah Maryam. It is just possible that it was sent down during the migration to Habasha or just after it. Some authentic traditions indicate that this Sûrah was revealed before Umar bin Khattâb embraced Islam.

Major Issues, Divine Laws and Guidance

* The Qur'an is but a reminder for those who fear Allah.
* In the Hereafter, the life of this world shall appear to be no more than a day or a part of a day.
* Story of the Prophet Musa (peace be upon him) as a Rasool towards Fir'aun and his chiefs.
* Famous prayer of the Prophet Musa (peace be upon him) before starting his mission.
* Dialogue between the Prophet Musa (peace be upon him) and Fir'aun.
* Confrontation of the Prophet Musa (peace be upon him) and Fir'aun's magicians, who after witnessing the miracles accepted Islam.
* A scene from the Day of Judgement.
* The Qur'an is sent in the Arabic language for easy understanding, so read it and say: "O Rabb increase my knowledge."
* The story of Adam's creation and Shaitân's temptations.
* Those who do not read the Qur'an and follow its directions shall be raised to life as blind persons on the Day of Resurrection.
* Do not envy others for their worldly riches.

This Sûrah begins with the object of the Qur'an's revelation that it is an admonition and guidance to the Right Way for those who fear Allah and want to save themselves from His punishment. This Qur'an is the Word of Allah Who is the Creator of the heavens and the earth and Godhead belongs to Him alone. These are the facts whether one believes or not. After this introduction, the story of the Prophet Musa (peace be upon him) is related to admonish the people of Makkah who knew about Musa (peace be upon him) as a Prophet of Allah due to their relations with Jews and neighboring Christian kingdoms. This story has verified the following facts:

1.   The fundamental principles of Tawheed and the Hereafter which are being

presented by the Prophet Muhammad, are the same as were conveyed by the Prophet Musa (peace be upon him) to his people.

2. *The Prophet Muhammad (peace be upon him) has been made a Rasool to convey Allah's Message to the people of Quraish without worldly means, just as the Prophet Musa (peace be upon him) was made a Rasool without worldly means to convey Allah's Message to a tyrant king, Fir'aun.*

3. *The people of Makkah were employing the same devices against the Prophet Muhammad (peace be upon him) as Fir'aun did against the Prophet Musa (peace be upon him), i.e., frivolous objections, accusations, and cruel persecutions. Just as the Prophet Musa (peace be upon him) came out victorious over Fir'aun, so shall the Prophet Muhammad (peace be upon him) over the Quraish, for the mission which is supported by Allah always comes out victorious in the end.*

4. *The Muslims are advised to follow the excellent example of the magicians, who remained steadfast in their faith, though Fir'aun threatened them with horrible vengeance.*

After this the story of Adam is related, as if to tell the Quraish, "the way you are following is the way of Shaitân, whereas the Right Way for a man is to follow his forefather Adam, who was seduced by Shaitân, but when he realized his error, he confessed, repented and returned to the service of Allah."

20: TÂ-HÂ

This Sûrah, revealed at Makkah, has 8 sections and 135 verses.

In the name of Allah, the Compassionate, the Merciful.

SECTION: 1

The Qur'an is a reminder for those who fear Allah, the Creator of the heavens and the earth

Tâ-Hâ.[1] We have not sent down this Qur'an to put you to trouble,[2] but as a reminder to those who fear *Allah.*[3] This is revealed from Him Who has created the earth and the lofty heavens,[4] the Compassionate *(Allah)* Who established *Himself on the Throne in a manner that suits His Majesty,*[5] to Him belongs whatever is in the Heavens and in the earth, and all that lies between them, and all that is beneath the soil.[6] The One to Whom you need not speak aloud; for He knows what is said in secret and what is yet more hidden.[7] He is Allah! There is no deity worthy of worship except Him! To Him belongs the most beautiful Names.[8] 20:[1-8]

The Prophet Musa went to the sacred valley of 'Tuwa' at mount Tûr

Have you heard the story of Musa?[9] When he saw a fire, he said to his family: "Wait! I saw a fire. I may be able to bring some fire or find someone beside the fire to guide us *towards the right direction."*[10] When he reached there, he was called: "O Musa![11] In fact, I am your Rabb! Take off your shoes, you are in the sacred valley of Tuwa.[12] I have chosen you, so listen to what I am about to reveal.[13] It is Me, Allah; there is none worthy of worship except Me, so worship Me and establish Salah *(prayers)* for My remembrance.[14] The final Hour is sure to come, I choose to keep it hidden, so that every soul may be rewarded according to its efforts.[15] Therefore, let not any, who does not believe in this fact and who follows his own desires, turn you away from believing in it, lest you should perish."[16] 20:[9-16]

Allah chose him as His Rasool and assigned him towards Fir'aun (Pharaoh)

"O Musa what is in your right hand?"[17] *Musa* replied: "It is my staff; I lean on it, I beat down fodder with it for my flocks and I have also other uses for it."[18] *Allah* said "Toss it down O Musa."[19] So he tossed it down and saw that it became a snake active in motion.[20] *Allah* said: "Catch it and do not be afraid, We shall change it to its original shape.[21] Now put your hand under your armpit, it shall become shining white without hurting you, this will be another Sign.[22] *These miracles are given to you*, in order to show you some of Our Great Signs.[23] Now go to Fir'aun *(Pharaoh)* for he has indeed transgressed all bounds."[24] 20:[17-24]

SECTION: 2

Musa prayed: "O my Rabb! Open my heart,[25]　ease my task[26]　and remove the impediment from my speech[27]　so that people may understand what I say[28]　and grant me a minister from my family;[29]　Haroon my brother.[30]　Grant me strength through him[31]　and let him share my task,[32]　so that we may glorify You frequently[33]　and mention You often;[34]　for You are the One Who has always been watching over us."[35]　*Allah* responded: "Your request is granted, O Musa.[36]　We had indeed bestowed a favor on you before,[37]　when We inspired your mother saying:[38]　'Put your child into the chest and throw the chest into the river. The river will cast him on to the bank and he will be picked up by one who is an enemy to Me and an enemy to him.' I made you an object of love and so arranged things that you may be brought up under My eye *(observation and care)*.[39]　Recall when your sister went to them and said: 'May I tell you of the one who can take care of this child?' Thus did We return you back to your mother to comfort her eyes and that she might not grieve. *Again when* you killed a man, We saved you from great distress and We tested you through various trials. You stayed a number of years with the people of Madyan. Now you have come here per Our pre-ordainment, O Musa.[40]　I have chosen you for My message.[41]　You and your brother should go with My Signs and do not neglect to mention Me.[42]　Go both of you to Fir'aun, for he has indeed transgressed all bounds.[43]　Speak to him in gentle words; perhaps he may take heed of the reminder or fear *Our punishment."*[44]　*Musa and Haroon* said: "Our Rabb! We fear that he may hasten to punish us or may cross all bounds."[45]　*Allah* said: "Do not be afraid, I shall be with you both. I hear everything and see everything.[46]　So go to him and say 'Surely, we both are Messengers of your Rabb. Let the Children of Israel go with us and oppress them no more. We have brought you a Sign from your Rabb; may peace be upon him who follows the guidance.[47]　Indeed it has been revealed to us that the scourge will fall on those who deny this fact and turn away'."[48]

20:[25-48]

When Musa and Haroon went to Fir'aun and delivered this message , he said: "Well, who is your Rabb O Musa?"[49]　*Musa* replied: "Our Rabb is He Who has given a distinctive form to all creatures and then rightly guided them."[50]　*Fir'aun* asked: "What do you say about the condition of previous generations?"[51]　*Musa* replied: "That knowledge is with my Rabb, duly recorded in a

---

The Prophet Musa prayed to Allah to open his heart, ease his task and remove the impediment from his speech so that people may understand what he says. Allah granted his request and reminded him about His favors

Dialogue between Musa and Fir'aun

Book. He neither makes a mistake nor does He forget."[52]   He is the One Who has made the earth a cradle for you, traced the roads on it for you to walk on; and sends down water from the sky with which We produce pairs of various kinds of vegetation[53] - eat from these yourselves and pasture your cattle. Surely, there are Signs in it for the people of understanding.[54]   20:[49-54]

SECTION: 3

Human life cycle

Fir'aun disbelieved Musa by calling his miracles a magician's trick and challenged him to confront his magicians in public - Musa accepted the challenge

We have created you from the *earth,* into it We shall return you and from it We shall bring you back to life once again.[55]   We showed *Fir'aun* all kinds of Our Signs, but he denied them and gave no heed.[56]   He said: "Have you come to drive us out of our land with your magic O Musa?[57]   Well, we will confront you with magic to match yours! Let us fix a day when both of us should meet, neither we nor you shall fail to keep it, in a place where both shall have even chances."[58]   Musa replied: "Let it be the Day of Festival and let the people be assembled before noon."[59]   Fir'aun then withdrew, concerted his plan and came back.[60]   Musa addressed them saying: "Woe to you *for this challenge!* Do not forge a lie against Allah *by calling it a magic,* lest He destroy you by a scourge; for whosoever forges a lie will indeed be disappointed."[61] *Hearing this,* they debated their case among themselves, whispering to one another.[62]   Finally they said: "These two *(Musa and Haroon)* are certainly expert magicians who intend to drive you out from your land with their magic and to do away with your best traditions.[63]   Therefore, muster up all devices and face them with a united front." *Finally when the day of confrontation came, Fir'aun said: "* Whoever comes out victorious this day shall prevail."[64]   20:[55-64]

The confrontation of Musa and Fir'aun's magicians

After witnessing Musa's miracle, the magicians accepted Islam

The magicians said: "O Musa! Will you throw down first or shall we?"[65]   *Musa* replied: "Go ahead, throw down first." Suddenly it appeared to *Musa* as if their cords and staffs were moving about because of their magic,[66] and Musa conceived fear within himself.[67]   We said: "Do not be afraid! You will surely come out on top.[68]   Throw that which is in your right hand. It will swallow up all that they have produced. What they have produced is nothing but a magician's trick, and a magician will never succeed *against a miracle* no matter how skillful he may be."[69]   *When the magicians saw the serpent of Musa swallowing all their display, being professionals they knew that it was not magic,* so the magicians humbled themselves by prostrating and said: "We believe in the Rabb of Haroon and Musa."[70]   *Fir'aun* said: "How do you dare to believe in Him without my permission? Surely, he must be your master, who taught you witchcraft. Well, I will cut off your hands and feet on alternate sides and crucify you on trunks of palm-trees; then you will know which one of us can give a more terrible and more lasting punishment."[71]   *The magicians* replied: "We can never prefer you over the miracle which we have witnessed and Him Who has created us. Therefore, do whatever you will; you can only punish us in this worldly life.[72]   As for us, we have believed in our Rabb so that He may forgive us our sins and the magic you have forced us to practice. Allah's *reward* is better and *His punishment is* more lasting *than yours (Fir'aun).*"[73] Surely, he who will come to his Rabb as a sinner shall be consigned to hell - wherein he shall neither die nor live.[74]   While he who will come to Him as a believer and has done good deeds shall have the highest ranks[75]   - gardens of eternity, beneath which rivers flow, to live therein forever; such is the reward of those who purify themselves from evil.[76]   20:[65-76]

Dialogue between the magicians and Fir'aun

SECTION: 4

We sent Our revelation to Musa,   *saying:* "Set forth with my servants at night and strike a dry path for them through the sea without fear of being overtaken *by Fir'aun* and without any fear *while passing through the sea.*"[77]   Fir'aun followed them with his armies but the waters completely overwhelmed them and covered them up.[78]   Thus Fir'aun misled his people instead of guiding them aright.[79]   O Children of Israel! We delivered you from your enemy, We fixed a time *to grant you the Tawrât* on the right side of Mount Tûr and We sent down to you Mannâ *(sweet dish)* and Salwâ *(quail meat)*[80] - *saying:* "Eat of the good things We have   provided for your sustenance and do not transgress, lest you should incur My wrath, and whoever incurs My wrath, is surely bound to perish,[81] but the one who repents, becomes a believer, does good deeds and follows the Right Way shall certainly be forgiven."[82]   20:[77-82]

Deliverance of the Children of Israel from the bondage of Fir'aun

When Musa came to mount Tûr, Allah said: "But, why have you come with such a haste ahead of your people, O Musa?"[83]   He replied: "They are close behind me, I hastened to You O my Rabb so that You may be pleased."[84]   *Allah* said: "Well, listen! We tested your people after you and the As-Sâmiriy *(Samaritan)* has led them astray."[85]   So Musa returned to his people in a state of anger and sorrow. He said: "O my people! Did your Rabb not make a gracious promise to you? Did my absence seem too long to you?

When the Prophet Musa went to Mount Tûr for communion with Allah - Israelites started worshipping the calf in his absence

Or was it to incur the wrath of your Rabb that you broke your promise with me?"[86] They replied: "We broke the promise through no fault of ours. We were made to carry the weight of the ornaments of *Fir'aun's* people and cast them *into the fire*, and that was what As-Sâmiriy suggested.[87] Then he forged a calf in the shape of a body which produced the mooing sound. Then said: 'This is your god and the god of Musa, but *Musa* forgot *to mention it to you*."[88] *What!* Could they not see that it did not respond to them and that it could neither harm them nor help them?[89] 20:[83-89]

SECTION: 5

Musa's inquiry about idol worshipping, his decision about Sâmiriy, Golden Calf and his address to his people

Haroon had already told them: "O my people! This is but a test for you; for verily your Rabb is the Rahmân *(Allah)*: so follow me and do as I command you."[90] They had replied: "We will not abandon its worship until Musa's return."[91] Then *Musa* addressed Haroon: " O Haroon! What prevented you from following me, when you saw them going astray?[92] Why did you disobey me?"[93] *Haroon* replied: "O son of my mother! Do not seize me by my beard nor pull the hair of my head. In fact, I was afraid lest you might say: 'You have caused a division, *through civil war*, among the Children of Israel and did not respect what I said, '*to keep peace*'."[93] Then *Musa* addressed *As-Sâmiriy*: "Now, what do you have to say about this, O Sâmiriy?"[94] He replied: "I saw what they did not see, so I took a handful *of dust* from the track of the Rasool *(angel Gabriel)* and threw it into the casting *of the calf*: thus did my soul prompt me."[95] *Musa* cursed him: "Get out of here! Now through out your life, you will say to other people: 'Touch me not'; and you will not escape your appointed doom. Behold this god to whom you had become a devoted worshipper: we will burn it and scatter its ashes into the sea."[96] *Then he addressed his people:* "O my people! Your God is only Allah, there is none worthy of worship but He. His knowledge encompasses every thing."[97] 20:[90-98]

The Qur'an is but a reminder and the life of this world shall appear to be no longer than one day in the hereafter

Thus do We relate to you, *O Muhammad*, some information of the past events; and indeed We have sent you this Reminder *(the Qur'an)* from Our Own Self.[99] Those who reject it, shall bear a heavy burden on the Day of Resurrection.[100] For ever shall they bear it, and it will be indeed a very evil burden to bear on the Day of Resurrection.[101] The Day, when the Trumpet will be blown and We shall assemble all the criminals, their eyes will turn blue *with terror*.[102] They shall murmur among themselves: "You hardly lived ten days on earth."[103] We know fully well what they will say; the most careful estimator among them will say: "No, you stayed no longer than a day."[104]   20:[99-104]

SECTION: 6

They ask you as *to what will happen* to the mountains. Tell them: "My Rabb will crush and scatter them like a fine dust.[105]   He will turn *the earth* into a plain leveled ground,[106]   wherein you will see neither any curve nor crease."[107] - On that Day the people will follow the Caller, no one will dare show any crookedness; their voices hushed before the Beneficent   *(Allah),* and you shall hear nothing but the sound of the marching feet.[108]   On that Day, no intercession will avail except the one to whom the Compassionate *(Allah)* shall grant permission and whose word is acceptable to Him.[109]   He knows what is before them and what is behind them while they do not encompass any knowledge about Him.[110]   Their faces shall be humbled before the Ever-Living, the Sustainer of all existence *(Allah).* The one who is carrying the burden of iniquity will be doomed:[111]   but the one who is a believer and does good deeds shall fear no injustice or curtailment *of his reward.*[112]
                    20:[105-112]

A scene from the Day of Judgement

Thus have we sent down the Qur'an in Arabic and clearly proclaimed in it some of the warnings so that they may take heed or that it may serve as a reminder to them.[113]   High and exalted be Allah, the True King! Do not hasten to recite the Qur'an before its revelation is completely conveyed to you, and say: "O my Rabb! Increase my knowledge."[114]   We had taken a covenant from Adam before, but he forgot. We did not find in him firm determination.[115]   20:[113-115]

The Qur'an is sent in Arabic to teach and to remind, so read and say: "O Rabb increase me in knowledge".

SECTION: 7

When We said to the angels "Prostrate yourselves before Adam," they all prostrated themselves except Iblees *(Shaitân),* who refused.[116]   Then We said: "O Adam! This *Shaitân* is a real enemy to you and to your wife. Do not let him get you both out of Paradise and get you in trouble.[117]   Here in *Paradise* you shall go neither hungry nor naked;[118]   you shall neither suffer from thirst nor from the heat of sun."[119] - But Shaitân seduced him saying: "O Adam! Should I show you the Tree of Immortality and an everlasting kingdom?"[120]   They both ended up eating the fruit of the forbidden tree. As a result their private parts became apparent to them and they both began to cover themselves with the leaves from the Garden. Thus did Adam disobey His Rabb and went astray.[121]

Story of Adam's creation and Shaitân's temptation

Allah forgave Adam's sin, chose him and guided him to the right Way

Later on *Adam repented and* his Rabb chose him, accepted his repentance and gave him guidance,[122] saying: "Get down from here all of you *(Adam, Eve and Iblees)*; you will remain enemies to one another, whenever there comes to you guidance from Me and whosoever will follow My guidance will neither go astray nor get into trouble;[123] but the one who will turn away from My reminder shall live a meager life and We shall raise him back to life as a blind person on the Day of Resurrection."[124] He will say: "O my Rabb! Why have you raised me up blind here, while I was clear-sighted before?"[125] *Allah* will say: "Just as Our revelations came to you and you disregarded them *(played blind)*; so are you neglected *(blind)* today."[126] Thus do We reward the one who is a transgressor and does not believe in the revelations of his Rabb. The punishment of the hereafter is more terrible and more lasting.[127] Have these people not learned a lesson that We have destroyed before them many generations in whose ruins they walk through? Certainly in these *ruins* there are Signs for people of understanding.[128]   20:[116-128]

Those who do not read The Qur'an and follow its guidance shall be raised as blind on the Day of Resurrection

SECTION: 8

Had it not been already decreed by your Rabb and a term for respite been appointed, they would have been punished.[129] Therefore, be patient with what they say. Glorify your Rabb with His praise before sunrise and before sunset, glorify Him during the hours of the night as well as at both ends of the day, so that you may find satisfaction.[130] Do not strain your eyes in longing for the worldly benefits We have bestowed on some among them, for with these We seek to test them. The *lawful* provision of your Rabb is better and more lasting.[131] Enjoin Salah *(prayers)* on your family and be patient in its observance. We demand nothing of you; instead We provide you sustenance. Good shall be the end of the Righteous.[132]   20:[129-132]

Do not envy others in worldly benefits, rather seek Allah's pleasure if you want to attain the blessed end

The Qur'an is a sign from Allah so there can be no excuse for the unbelievers on the Day of Judgement

They say: "Why does he *(Muhammad)* not bring us a Sign from His Rabb?" Has not a clear Sign *(the Qur'an)* come to them containing all *the teachings* of the former Scriptures?[133] Had We destroyed them as punishment before its revelation, they would have said: "Our Rabb! If only You had sent us a Rasool, we would certainly have followed Your revelations before being humiliated and disgraced." [134] Say: "All are waiting: so wait if you will. Very soon you shall find out, who is following the Right Way and who has been rightly guided."[135]   20:[133-135]

JUZ (PART): 17

21: AL-ANBIYÂ'

Period of Revelation

Both the subject matter and the style of the Sûrah indicate that it was sent down in the third stage of the Prophet's residence at Makkah.

Major Issues, Divine Laws, and Guidance

* The main issue for the people to consider is the Message of Allah rather than disputing about whether a human can be a Rasool.
* The creation of heaven and earth is not a game.
* If there were more than one God, the heavens and earth would have been in a state of disorder.
* The skies and earth once were one mass; Allah split them asunder and created the different planets.
* Allah has created all living beings from water.
* Allah has not granted immortality to any human being.
* Humans' invented gods cannot even defend themselves; how can they defend their worshippers.
* Prophet Musa (peace be upon him) was given Al-Furqân, so is this Al-Qur'an (the Qur'an) given to the Prophet Muhammad (peace be upon him).
* Prophet Ibrâheem (peace be upon him) was not an idol worshipper but an idol breaker.
* Mankind is but a single brotherhood.
* Whoever will do good deeds provided he is a believer, his endeavor shall not be rejected.
* Allah has sent the Prophet Muhammad (peace be upon him) as a blessing for all the worlds (humans, jinns, and others).

The objection of the disbelievers that a human being could not be a Rasool of Allah, and that they could not accept Muhammad (peace be upon him) as a Prophet, has been refuted. Examples have been cited from the life stories of the various Prophets to show that all the prophets who were sent by Allah were human beings. They had no share in godhead and they had to implore Allah to fulfill each and every necessity of their lives. All the prophets had to pass through distress and affliction; their opponents did their best to thwart their mission, but in spite of this, they came out successful with the help of Allah. Finally, all the prophets had one and the same Deen (way of life) Al-Islam, which is being presented by Muhammad (peace be upon him), and that is the only Right Way, while all other ways invented by human beings are utterly wrong.

JUZ (PART) : 17

21: AL-ANBIYÂ'

This Sûrah revealed at Makkah has 7 sections and 112 verses.

In the name of Allah, the Compassionate, the Merciful.

SECTION: 1

The Day of Accountability is getting closer, but the disbelievers are still heedless to the admonition and dispute as to how a human being can be a Rasool

The Day of Accountability for mankind is getting closer and closer, yet, they are heedless and are turning away *from the admonition.*[1]   They listen *with ridicule* to each fresh warning that comes to them from their Rabb and remain engaged in pleasure.[2] Their hearts are preoccupied *with worldly affairs;* these wrongdoers say to each other in private: "Is this man *(Muhammad)* not a human being like yourselves? Would you follow witchcraft with your eyes open?"[3]   Say: "My Rabb has knowledge of every word which is spoken in the heavens and the earth, and He hears all and knows all."[4]   "Rather," *some of them* say, "this *Qur'an* is jumble of dreams!" *Others say*: "He has made it all up!" *And yet, others say*: "He is a poet!" Let him bring to us a sign as did the former Rasools."[5]   *The fact, however, is that even though We showed Signs to the prior people,* not a single nation before them, which We destroyed, ever believed. Will they believe?[6]   The Rasools which We sent before you, *O Muhammad,* were also human to whom We sent revelation. *If you, O objectors,* do not know this, then ask the people of the Reminder *(Jews and Christians).*[7]   We did not give them bodies which could survive without food, nor were they immortal.[8]   Then We fulfilled Our promise with them: We saved them and those whom We pleased, and destroyed the transgressors.[9]   Now, O mankind, We have sent down to you a Book *(the Qur'an)* which deals with matters concerning yourselves; why don't you understand?[10]   21:[1-10]

SECTION: 2

Prior nations were destroyed due to similar iniquities

How many nations have We destroyed who were wrongdoers and replaced them by other nations![11]   When they felt that Our punishment was coming, they took to their heels and fled.[12]   *They were told:* "Do not run away. Return to your luxuries of life and to your homes, so that you may be asked questions."[13]   They replied: "Woe to us! Indeed we were wrongdoers."[14]   They kept on repeating *that statement* till We mowed them down, leaving no spark of life in them.[15]   21:[11-15]

Our creation of the heavens and the earth and all that lies between them is not a game.[16]   Had We intended to indulge in a pastime, We would surely have done it by Ourself - if such had been Our Will at all.[17]   Nay! We give falsehood a violent blow with the Truth to knock it out and behold! Falsehood vanishes away. Woe be to you, for that which you ascribe (*that Allah has a wife and a son*).[18]   21:[16-18]

The creation of the heavens and earth is not a game

To Him belongs all that exists in the heavens and in the earth; and *the angels*, who are in His very presence, are not too proud to serve Him, nor are they weary *of His service*.[19]   They glorify Him night and day; and do not slacken.[20]   Do the earthly deities, that they have taken for worship, have the power to raise the dead?[21]   Had there been, *in the heavens or in the earth*, other gods besides Allah, both *the heavens and earth* would have been in a state of disorder. Glory be to Allah, the Lord of the Throne, *absolutely* free is He *from the falsehood* that they attribute to Him.[22]   He is accountable to none about what He does, but they are accountable to Him.[23]   Even then, have they taken other deities for worship other than Him? Ask them: "Show us your proof." This (*Al-Qur'an*) is a reminder for those with me and also the reminder for those before me. But most of them have no knowledge of the Truth, so they are averse.[24]   21:[19-24]

If there were more than One God, the heavens and earth would have been in a state of disorder

The fact is that to every Rasool whom We sent before you, We revealed the same Message: "There is none worthy of worship but Me, so worship Me Alone."[25]   *In spite of receiving that message*, they still say: "The Beneficent (Allah) has begotten a son!" Glory be to Him! *The angels* are but His honored servants.[26] They do not precede Him in speaking and they act according to His commandment.[27]   He knows what is before them and what is behind them and they do not intercede except for the one whom He approves, and for fear of Him they tremble.[28]   If any of them were to say: "I am also a deity besides Him," We would send him to hell, thus shall We reward the wrongdoers.[29]   21:[25-29]

All Rasools were sent with the same Message: "There is no god but Allah, so worship Him Alone."

SECTION: 3

Have not the unbelievers ever considered that the skies and the earth were once one mass, then We split them asunder? And We

Once the skies and the earth were one

mass; Allah split them asunder, and He created all living things from water

Allah has not granted immortality to any human being. If Rasools are doomed to die, how are disbelievers going to live forever?

Invented gods cannot even defend themselves; how will they defend the unbelievers against Allah?

The scale of justice shall be set up on the Day of Judgment

have created every living thing from water. Will they still not believe?[30] And We have planted mountains on earth lest it should tilt *to one side* with them and We left between them open passages so that they may find their way.[31] And We have made the sky a safe canopy: yet, they are heedless to these signs.[32] He is the One Who has created the night and the day, and the sun and the moon: all *(the celestial bodies)* turning around in orbits of their own.[33]

21:[30-33]

O Muhammad, We have not granted immortality to any human before you: so if you are to die, will these *unbelievers* live forever?[34] Every soul is bound to have the taste of death. We are putting all of you to a test by passing you through bad and good conditions, and finally you shall return to Us.[35] When the unbelievers see you they do not take you but for one to be scoffed at, saying: "Is this the one who talks against your gods?" And they themselves deny the mention of the Compassionate *(Allah)*.[36] Man is a creature of haste *(impatience)*. Soon I will show you My signs, therefore, you need not be impatient.[37] They ask: "When will this promise be fulfilled if you are telling the truth?"[38] *They would not have asked this question* if only the unbelievers knew the Day when they will be able to protect neither their faces from the fire of hell nor their backs, nor will they be helped![39] Nay, it will come to them all of a sudden and overpower them so abruptly that they shall neither be able to avert it nor shall they get any respite.[40] *As for their scoffing,* the Rasools before you were also scoffed at; but their scoffers were hemmed in by the very thing at which they used to scoff.[41]

21:[34-41]

SECTION: 4

Ask them, "Who is there to protect you by night and by day from *the wrath of* the Compassionate?" Yet, they turn away from the admonition of their Rabb.[42] Do they have such gods, other than Us, who can help them? Their *gods can* neither help themselves, nor can they be protected from Us.[43] The fact is that We gave the good things of this life to them and their forefathers until *they got used to these things because of* their prolonged lives; can they not see how We gradually reduce the land *which was in their control* and curtail it from all sides? Do they still expect to be victorious *against Us*?[44] Tell them, "I am warning you on the authority of Revelation," but the deaf *(who follow their leaders blindly)* do not hear the call *even* when they are warned![45] Yet, even if a breath from the Wrath of your Rabb was to touch them, they will certainly say, "Woe to us! No doubt we were wrongdoers."[46]   On the Day of Judgement We shall set up scales of justice so that no one will be dealt with unjustly in any way; even if *someone has an act* as small as a grain of mustard seed, We will bring it to account, and sufficient are We to settle the accounts.[47]   21:[42-47]

Certainly, We granted Musa *(Moses)* and Haroon *(Aaron)* the Criterion *of right and wrong,* a light and a reminder for those righteous people[48]   who fear their Rabb though they have not seen Him, and dread the Hour *of Judgment*.[49]   And now We have revealed this blessed Reminder *(the Qur'an)*. Will you then deny it?[50]   21:[48-50]

Musa was given Al-Furqân (the criterion of right and wrong), so is this The Qur'an

SECTION: 5

Even before that We blessed Ibrâheem *(Abraham)* with rectitude, for We knew him well.[51]   Remember that occasion when *Ibrâheem* asked his father and his people, "What are these images to which you are so devoted?"[52] They replied, "We found our forefathers worshipping them."[53]   He said "Then certainly both you and your forefathers have been in manifest error."[54] They asked, "Have you brought us the Truth or are you one of the triflers?"[55]   He replied, "Nay! Your Rabb is the Lord of the heavens and the earth. It is He Who has created them; and I am of those who bear witness to this.[56]   By Allah! I will certainly plan against your idols when you turn and go away."[57]   So he broke them all in pieces, except the biggest of them, so that they might turn to it.[58]   *(On their return when they saw the plight of their idols),* some asked, "Who has done this to our gods? He must surely be a wicked person!"[59]   Others replied, "We heard a youth, called Ibrâheem, talking about them."[60]   They said, "Then bring him here before the eyes of the people, so that they may witness *how severely he is punished.*"[61]   *When Ibrâheem came,* they asked, "O Ibrâheem, are you the one who has done this to our gods?"[62]   He replied, "It is rather this chief of theirs who did it. Ask them, if they can speak!"[63]   Thereupon, they turned to *search* their own consciences, and said to themselves, "Surely, you yourselves are the wrongdoers!"[64]   *Confounded as they were,* lowering their heads, they said, "You know fully well that they cannot speak."[65] *At this Ibrâheem* said, "Do you then worship these deities, instead of Allah, who can neither benefit nor harm you?[66]   Shame on you and on those deities you worship besides Allah! Have you no sense

Ibrâheem questioned the idol worshipping of his father and his people

Ibrâheem broke all their idols to show that the gods who cannot even defend themselves, cannot be of any benefit to them

They decided to burn him alive but Allah commanded the fire to be cool and comfortable for Ibrâheem

at all?"[67]　　They said, "Burn him alive and avenge your gods, if you want to take any action."[68]　　*When they threw him in the fire*, We commanded, "O fire! Be cool and comfortable for Ibrâheem."[69] They sought to harm him, but We made them the big losers.[70]　　We delivered him and *his nephew* Lût *(Lot)* and directed them to the land which We have blessed for all the people of the world.[71]

21:[51-71]

Allah blessed Ibrâheem with a son (Ishâq) and then a grandson (Ya'qoob) and made each of them prophets

We gave him *a son* Ishâq *(Isaac)* and then a grandson Ya'qoob *(Jacob);* and We made each of them a righteous man.[72] We made them leaders who guided other people by Our command and We sent them revelations to do good deeds, establish Salah *(prayers) and* pay Zakah *(obligatory charity)*. Us Alone did they serve.[73]　　To Lût *(Lot)* We gave judgment and knowledge, and We delivered him from the town which practiced abominations - surely, its inhabitants were very wicked transgressors[74] - and We admitted him to Our mercy: for he was of the righteous people.[75]

21:[72-75]

SECTION: 6

Allah accepted the prayer of Nûh against the unbelievers

Before them Nûh *(Noah)* prayed to Us, We accepted his prayer and delivered him and his family from the great calamity.[76] We helped him against those people who had denied Our revelations; surely, they were an evil people, so We drowned them all *in the Great Flood*.[77]　　　　　　　　　　　　21:[76-77]

Allah blessed Prophets Daûd and Sulaimân with wisdom, knowledge, and kingdoms

And *remember* Daûd *(David)* and Sulaimân *(Solomon)*: when the two were judging a case regarding the field into which the sheep of certain people had strayed by night, and We were watching them to arrive at judgment,[78]　　at that time We gave Sulaimân insight *to arrive at the right decision*, although We had given judgment and knowledge to both of them. We caused the mountains and the birds to celebrate Our praises with Daûd; it was We Who made this happen.[79]　　We taught him the armor's craft, so that they might protect you in your wars: yet, are you ever grateful?[80]　　We made the raging winds *subservient* to Sulaimân, pursuing its course by his command to the land which We had blessed; and We have knowledge of everything.[81]　　And *We had subjected to him* many of the shaitâns who dived for him *into the sea* and performed other duties besides this; and We were the One Who had control over them *for him*.[82]　　　　　　　　　　　　21:[78-82]

Similarly We blessed Ayyûb, when he prayed to his Rabb

saying, "I am badly afflicted with distress: but of all those who show mercy You are the most Merciful."[83]   We accepted his prayer and relieved his affliction, and restored not only his family but also as many more with them as a favor from Us so that it may serve as a reminder to Our worshippers.[84]   21:[83-84]

Allah accepted the Prophet Ayyûb's prayer and removed his affliction

     Likewise, We blessed Isma'il *(Ishmael)*, Idrees and Dhul-kifl, for all of them practised patience.[85]   We admitted them to Our Mercy, for they were of the righteous people.[86]   *We blessed* Dhun-Nûn *(Yûnus / Jonah)*, when he departed in anger, thinking We would not take him to task for this, but later he prayed to Us from the depths of darkness, "There is none worthy of worship but You, glory be to You! Indeed I was the one who committed wrong."[87] We accepted his prayer and delivered him from distress; thus do We deliver the believers.[88]   *We also blessed* Zakariyya, when he prayed to his Rabb, "O my Rabb! Do not let me remain childless even though You are the best of inheritors.[89]   We accepted his prayer and gave him Yahya *(John)*, curing his wife for him *to bear a child*. They were ever quick in doing good deeds and called on Us with hope, fear, and to Us they had humbled.[90]   And *We blessed* the woman *(Maryam)*, who guarded her chastity, We breathed into her of Our *created* Spirit and We made her and her son a sign for the whole world.[91]   21:[85-91]

Allah accepted the prayers and blessed Prophets Isma'il, Dhul-kifl, Yûnus, and Zakariyya and also blessed Maryam

     Verily this religion of yours is a single religion and I am your only Rabb, therefore, worship Me Alone.[92]   But the people have divided their religion *into sects* between them - to Us they shall all return.[93]   21:[92-93]

Mankind is but one community

SECTION: 7

     Whoever shall do good deeds, provided he is a believer, his endeavor will not be rejected: We are recording it all for him.[94]   It is not possible that a nation which We have destroyed may return again.[95]   Until, when Gog and Magog will be let loose and they will swiftly swarm from every height,[96]   and the time for the fulfillment of the True Promise will draw near, then behold! The eyes of the unbelievers will fixedly stare in horror: "O woe to us! We were indeed heedless of this warning; nay, we were wrongdoers."[97]   21:[94-97]

Whoever does good deed, provided he is a believer, his endeavor will not be rejected

     Surely, you *(O mushrikeen)* and your deities that you worship besides Allah shall be the fuel of hell; therein you shall all

The Day of Judgment and the fate

of the disbelievers
and the believers

enter.[98] If those deities would have been true gods, they would not have gotten there *in hell*; but therein they shall abide forever.[99] In there, sobbing will be their lot, and they will not be able to hear anything else.[100] Certainly those for whom the good *reward* has preceded from Us, they will be kept far away from it.[101] They shall not hear even its slightest sound, and they shall dwell forever in the midst of whatever their souls desire.[102] The time of Great Terror *(Day of Judgement)* will not grieve them, and the angels will receive them with greetings: "This is your Day that you were promised."[103] On that Day We shall roll up the heavens like a scroll of writings; just as We originated the first creation, so shall We produce it again - that is Our promise, and We will fulfill it.[104] We wrote in The Zaboor *(Psalms xxxvii, 29)* after the reminder *(Torah given to Musa)*: that land shall be inherited by My righteous servants.[105] Surely, in this is great news for those people who worship Us.[106] 21:[98-106]

Allah has sent
M u h a m m a d
(pbuh) as a bless-
ing for all the
worlds (humans,
jinns, and others)

O Muhammad, We have not sent you but as a blessing for all the worlds.[107] Tell them: "It has been revealed to me that your god is but One God *(Allah)* - will you then become Muslims?"[108] If they turn away, tell them: "I have warned you all alike in complete fairness; now I do not know whether what you are threatened with is near or far.[109] It is He Who knows your spoken words and hidden thoughts.[110] I do not know whether *this delay* is a trial for you or you are being given respite for an appointed time."[111] *Finally the Prophet* said: "O my Rabb! Pass Your Judgment in Truth. *And O People!* Our Rabb is most Compassionate, Whose help we seek against the blasphemies you utter."[112] 21:[107-112]

22: AL-HAJJ

Period of Revelation

As this Sûrah contains the characteristics of both Makki and Madani Sûrahs, the commentators have differed as to its period of revelation. From its style it appears that a part of it (vv. 1-24) was sent down in the last stage of the Prophet's residence at Makkah, shortly before migration and the rest (vv. 25-78) after migration, most probably in the month of Zul-Hijjah, during the first year of his residence at Madinah. That is why this Sûrah combines the characteristics of both Makki and Madani Sûrahs.

Major Issues, Divine Laws, and Guidance

* A scene from the Hour of Doom.
* Human life cycle: life in this world and life in the Hereafter.
* Behavior of those individuals who were standing at the verge of faith is identified.
* Allah always helps His Rasools.
* Divine law granting equal rights to all Muslims in Al-Masjid-al-Harâm, whether they are natives or foreigners.
* Allah Himself identified the site and asked Prophet Ibrâheem (peace be upon him) to build the Ka'bah and call mankind to come for Hajj (Pilgrimage).
* Someone who commits Shirk is like someone who falls from the sky and his body is snatched away by birds.
* The fact that it is not the blood or the flesh of a sacrificed animal which reaches Allah but the piety of the individual who is offering the sacrifice.
* The Commandment of Allah granting permission to the believers to defend themselves and fight against the unbelievers and mushrikeen.
* On the Day of Judgement, Allah Himself will be the Judge for all.
* Allah's promise to those who migrate for His sake that He will reward them generously.
* The fact that Allah called the believers, Muslims, in the prior scriptures and also in the Qur'an.

It appears that after the migration, when the month of Zul-Hijjah arrived, it brought to the immigrants the memories of their homes in Makkah, and naturally they must have thought about the Ka'bah and the Hajj congregation. These memories grieved them to think that the mushrikeen Quraish had debarred them from visiting the Sacred Mosque. Therefore, they might have been praying for and expecting Divine permission to wage war against those tyrants who had expelled them from their homes and prevented them from visiting the House of Allah. This

Sûrah specifies the purpose for which the Ka'bah was built and clearly states that Hajj (pilgrimage) was enjoined for the worship of the One God (Allah). But it is an irony that it had been dedicated to the rituals of shirk, the worship of 360 idols and the real worshippers of One God (Allah) had been debarred from visiting it. Through this Sûrah, Allah also granted the Muslims permission to wage war against the tyrant mushrikeen in order to oust them and establish the righteous way of life. According to Ibn Abbâs, Mujâhid, Urwah bin Zubair, Zaid bin Aslam, Muqatil bin Hayyan, Qatadah and other great commentators, v. 39 is the first verse that granted the Muslims permission to wage war.

This Sûrah has also addressed the mushrikeen of Makkah, the wavering Muslims, and the true believers as follows:

The mushrikeen *are warned in a forceful manner in these words: "You have persisted in your ignorance and trusted your deities instead of Allah, though they possess no power to protect you." They are also admonished time and again for their creed of shirk through providing sound arguments in favor of Tawheed (Oneness of God) and the Hereafter.*

The wavering Muslims, *who had embraced Islam but were not prepared to endure any hardship in its way, have been admonished in these words: "What is this faith of yours? You are ready to believe in Allah and become His servants provided you are given peace and prosperity, but if you meet with afflictions and hardships in His Way, you discard Allah and cease to remain His servants. You should bear in mind that this wavering attitude of yours cannot avert those misfortunes and losses which Allah has ordained for you."*

The true believers *are told that the mushrikeen of Makkah have no right to debar them from visiting the Ka'bah. They have no right to prevent anyone from performing Hajj because the Ka'bah is not their private property. This objection acted as an effective political weapon against the Quraish because it posed this question: "Are the Quraish mere attendants of the Ka'bah or its owners?" This question implied that if the Quraish succeeded in debarring the Muslims from Hajj without any protest from others, they would feel encouraged in the future to debar others who happened to have strained relations with the Quraish. In order to emphasize this point, the history of the Ka'bah's construction is cited to show that it was built by the Prophet Ibrâheem (peace be upon him) according to the commandment of Allah and he had invited all of mankind to perform Hajj. That is why people coming from outside Makkah had enjoyed equal rights with the local people from the very beginning. It is also made clear that the House had not been built for the rituals of shirk but for the worship of One Allah. Thus it was sheer tyranny that the worship of Allah was being forbidden there while the worship of idols enjoyed full license.*

22: AL-HAJJ

This Sûrah, revealed at Madinah, has 10 sections and 78 verses.

In the name of Allah, the Compassionate, the Merciful.

SECTION: 1

O mankind! Have fear of your Rabb; the catastrophic quaking of the Hour *of Doom* will be terrible indeed.[1]   On that Day, you shall see that every nursing mother will forget her nursing-babe and every pregnant female will miscarry, and you will see people as if they were drunk, though not drunk: such will be the horror of Allah's chastisement.[2]   Yet, there are among people some who, in their ignorance, argue about Allah and follow every rebellious devil,[3]   for whom it is decreed that whoever will take him as his friend, he will mislead him and drive him to the punishment of burning fire.[4]   22:[1-4]

A scene from the Hour of Doom

O mankind! If you doubt about the life after death, remember that We first created you from dust, then from a sperm, then from a leech- like mass, then from a morsel of flesh, some formed and some unformed, so that We may manifest to you *Our power*. We cause to remain in the womb whom We wish for an appointed term, and then We bring you forth as infants; then We *nourish you so that* you may reach your age of full strength. There are some of you who die young and some who live on to their abject old age when all that they once knew they know no more. You sometimes see the land dry and barren; but no sooner do We pour down rain upon it then it begins to stir and swell, putting forth every kind of beautiful growth.[5]   This is because Allah is the Ultimate Truth: it is He Who gives life to the dead and it is He Who has power over everything,[6]   and that the Hour *of Doom* is sure to come - there is no doubt about it; and that Allah will raise up those who are in the graves.[7]   22:[5-7]

Life cycle, life in this world and life in the Hereafter

Yet, there are, among people, others who wrangle about Allah, though they neither have knowledge nor guidance, nor an enlightening Book,[8] twisting his neck *in arrogance* to lead others astray from the Path of Allah - for such people there is disgrace in this life, and on the Day of Resurrection we shall make them taste the punishment of burning fire,[9]   saying: "This is what you prepared and sent forth with your own hands." Rest assured that Allah is not unjust to His servants.[10]   22:[8-10]

People invoke other deities besides Allah, without knowledge and guidance

SECTION: 2

Behavior of those who are standing at the verge of faith

There are some people who worship Allah standing on the verge of faith *and disbelief*. When such a person is blessed with good fortune he is content; but if he encounters a trial he turns back headlong; thus losing both this world and the hereafter, which is a clear-cut loss.[11]   Then instead of Allah, he starts calling those deities who can neither harm nor help him; now that is going too far off in deviation *from the Right Way*.[12]   He is calling upon those who are more likely to harm than help; what an evil master and what an evil friend he chooses *for help!*[13]   As for those who believe and do good deeds, Allah will admit them to gardens beneath which rivers flow. Surely! Allah does what He wants.[14]

22:[11-14]

Allah always helps His Rasools

If anyone thinks that Allah will not help *His Rasool* in this world and in the Hereafter, let him stretch out a rope to the sky if he can and cut *a hole to peep* through and see for himself whether his device can avert that which irritates him.[15]   Thus have We revealed this *Qur'an* in clear verses; and verily Allah gives guidance to whom He wants.[16]   Surely, as for those who are true believers *(the Muslims)*, the Jews, the Sabians, the Christians, the Magians and the ones who commit shirk *(polytheists)* - Allah will judge between them on the Day of Resurrection; for Allah is a witness over everything.[17]   Do you not see how all who dwell in the heavens and the earth prostrate themselves in worship to Allah, including the sun, the moon, the stars, the mountains, the trees, the animals and a large number of people. But there are many who deserve the punishment. He who is disgraced by Allah has none who can raise him to honor; surely, Allah does what He pleases.[18]

All the dwellers of the heavens and the earth prostrate before Allah

(As-Sajdah)

22:[15-18]

The disbelievers will have garments of fire, boiling water, lashes with maces of iron

These are the two adversaries *(the believers and disbelievers)* who dispute with each other about their Rabb: as for the disbelievers, garments of Fire will be cut out for them, boiling water will be poured over their heads,[19]   which will not only melt their skins but also the inner parts of their bellies,[20]   and there will be maces of iron to lash them.[21]   Whenever, in their anguish, they try to escape therefrom, they will be forced back therein, *and will be told*: "Taste the punishment of conflagration!"[22]

22:[19-22]

SECTION: 3

As for those who have faith and do good deeds, Allah will

certainly admit them to gardens beneath which rivers flow. They shall be decked with pearls and bracelets of gold, and their garments will be of silk.[23] *This is because during their life on earth*, they were guided to accept the pure words *of Allah* and they were shown the Way of the All-Praiseworthy.[24] As for those who are unbelievers and debar others from the Way of Allah and from the Masjid-al-Harâm, to which We have assigned all mankind with equal rights whether they are natives or foreigners, and whoever intends to deviate from righteousness to wrongdoing in its vicinity, We will make him taste a painful punishment.[25]

Allah has given equal rights to all believers at Masjid-al-Harâm, whether they are natives or foreigners

22:[23-25]

SECTION: 4

Remember! We identified the site of the Sacred House to Ibrâheem *(Abraham)*, *saying*, "Worship none besides Me, sanctify My House for those worshippers who make Tawâf *(walking counterclockwise around it as part of the Umrah or Hajj rituals)*, stand in prayer, bow, and prostrate themselves;[26] and *O Ibrâheem* make a proclamation of Hajj *(Pilgrimage)* to mankind: they will come to you on foot and on lean camels from every distant quarter,[27] so that they may witness the benefits which are made available here for them, and pronounce the name of Allah over the cattle which We have provided as food for them, on the appointed days: eat then of their meat yourselves and feed the indigent having a very hard time.[28] Then they should accomplish their needful acts *of shaving or cutting their hair and taking a bath*, fulfill their vows and go for Tawâf of the Ancient House.[29] This was *the object for which the Ka'bah was built,* and whoever honors the sacred rites of Allah, it is good for him in the sight of his Rabb. The meat of cattle is lawful to you, except what has already been mentioned to you; therefore, shun the abomination of idols and shun all false statements.[30] 22:[26-30]

Allah identified the site of the Sacred House to Ibrâheem, and commanded him to build the Ka'bah, then call mankind to come for Hajj (Pilgrimage)

Dedicate yourselves to Allah and do not commit shirk with Him: for anyone who commits shirk, it is as though he had fallen from the sky; then his body is either snatched away by birds or carried away by the wind to some far-off place;[31] so it is; and he who honors the rites of Allah, surely, shows the piety of his heart.[32] You may benefit *(by using their milk or ride in case of camels)* from the cattle *dedicated for sacrifice,* until the time *of their slaughter,* then their place of sacrifice is near the Ancient House.[33]

Committing shirk is like falling from the sky, then body being snatched away by birds

22:[31-33]

SECTION: 5

It is not the meat or the blood of the sacrificed animals that reaches Allah, it is your piety that reaches Him

For every nation We prescribed a way of sacrifice so that they may pronounce the name of Allah over the cattle which He has given them for food, *but the object is one and the same: to remember that* your god is only One God; so submit yourselves to Him as Muslims, and *O Prophet*, give good news to the humble,[34] whose hearts tremble at the mention of Allah; who endure adversity with patience, who establish Salah *(prayers)* and spend in charity out of what we have provided for them.[35] We have made the sacrifice of camels and cows among the rites of Allah, for there is much good for you in them. Therefore, pronounce the name of Allah over them while standing, and when they fall down on their sides *after slaughter, when their movement completely stops,* then eat of their meat, feed the contented *(poor who do not ask)* and the beggars *(poor who ask)*. Thus We have subjected them to you so that you may be grateful.[36] It is neither their meat nor their blood that reaches Allah; it is your piety that reaches Him. Thus, He has subjected these animals to you so that you may glorify Allah for giving you guidance, and *O Prophet,* give good news to the doers of good.[37] Surely, Allah wards off evil from those who are true believers: for certainly Allah does not love anyone who is treacherous, ungrateful.[38]   22:[34-38]

SECTION: 6

Permission is granted to the believers to fight in self defense, and for the cause of Allah

Permission *to fight back* is hereby granted *to the believers* against whom war is waged and because they are oppressed *(before this revelation, Muslims were not allowed to fight even for self defense)*; certainly Allah has power to grant them victory[39] - those who have been unjustly expelled from their homes only because they said, "Our Lord is Allah." Had not Allah repelled some people by the might of others, the monasteries, churches, synagogues, and mosques in which Allah's praise is daily celebrated, would have been utterly demolished. Allah will certainly help those who help His cause; most surely, Allah is Mighty, Powerful.[40] These are the people who, if We give them authority in the land, will establish Salah *(prayers)* and pay Zakah *(obligatory charity)*, enjoin justice and forbid evil; the final decision of all affairs is in the hands of Allah.[41]   22:[39-41]

O Muhammad, you are not the only

If they deny you *O Muhammad,* remember that before them the people of Nûh *(Noah)*, 'Ad and Thamûd;[42] the people of

Ibrâheem *(Abraham)* and that of Lût *(Lot);*[43] as well as the residents of Madyan had denied their Prophets. Likewise, Musa *(Moses)* was also denied. Initially, I gave respite to all those unbelievers and then I seized them: see how *terrible* was My reproach![44]   How many townships, teeming with wrong doings, have We utterly destroyed! Today they lie with their roofs fallen in, their wells abandoned, and their lofty castles deserted.[45]   22:[42-45]

one being denied, all Prophets were denied before you

Have they not traveled through the land? Have they no hearts to learn wisdom, or ears to hear *the Truth*? Certainly, it is not their eyes which have become blind, but it is the hearts in their breasts which are blind.[46]   These people ask you to hasten the threatened punishment. Well, Allah will never go back on His promise. In fact, a day of your Rabb is equal to a thousand years of your calculation.[47] There have been many townships teeming with wrong doings, to whom at first I gave respite and at the end I smote them. Towards Me is the destination of all.[48]   22:[46-48]

A day of your Rabb is equal to one thousand years of your calculation

SECTION: 7

O Muhammad, tell them: "O mankind! I am merely a plain Warner to you;[49]   Those who accept the true faith and do good deeds shall be forgiven and provided honorable sustenance;[50] but those who strive against Our revelations, shall be the inmates of flaming fire."[51]   22:[49-51]

Acceptors of Truth shall be forgiven, while others punished

Never have We sent a Rasool or a Prophet before you, *O Muhammad,* in whose reciting of the Revelations shaitân did not threw *some falsehood*; but Allah abolishes that which shaitân throws in and confirms His own Revelations, for Allah is All-Knowing, All-Wise.[52]   He makes what is thrown in by shaitân a trial for those whose hearts suffer from the disease *of hypocrisy* and whose hearts are hardened - *that's why* the wrongdoers are in *such* an extreme dissension[53]   - so that those who are endowed with knowledge may realize that this *(Qur'an)* is the Truth from your Rabb and thus believe in it and humble their hearts towards Him, and surely, Allah will guide the believers to the Right Way.[54]   As for the unbelievers, they will never cease to doubt *the revelation*, until the Hour *of Doom* overtakes them suddenly or there comes on them the punishment of the Day of Disaster.[55]   On that Day the Sovereignty will be that of Allah's; He will judge between them; so those who have embraced the true faith and done good deeds shall enter the gardens of delight;[56]   but the unbelievers who have

Shaitân tampered with the wishes of all Rasools, but Allah abrogated such interjection

On the Day of Judgement, Allah Himself shall be the Judge for all

denied Our revelations shall receive a disgraceful punishment.[57]

　　　　　　　　　　　　　　　　　　22:[52-57]

SECTION: 8

Those who migrated for the sake of Allah shall be generously rewarded. Allah is the only One Who is Real, all other deities are false

　　　　As for those who migrated for the sake of Allah and *afterwards* were killed or died, Allah will make a good provision for them; certainly Allah is the One Who is the best Provider.[58] He will admit them to a place with which they shall be well pleased; for Allah is All-Knowing, Most Forbearing.[59] Thus shall it be! He that retaliates equal to the infliction he received and then is wronged again, will most certainly be helped by Allah; surely, Allah is the One Who is All-Forbearing, Most Forgiving.[60] That is because it is Allah Who causes the night to pass into the day, and the day into the night, Allah is indeed All-Hearing, All-Seeing.[61] That is because Allah is the Ultimate Truth; and all those deities besides Him, whom they invoke, are falsehood; indeed, it is Allah Who is the Supreme, the Great.[62] Do you not see that Allah sends down water from the sky so the land becomes green? Surely, Allah is the Benignant, the All-Knowing.[63] To Him belongs all that is in the heavens and the earth; surely, Allah is the One Who is the Self-sufficient, the Praiseworthy.[64]　　　　22:[58-64]

SECTION: 9

Allah is the One Who has given you life, causes you to die and will bring you back to life for passing on His Judgement

　　　　Do you not see that Allah has subdued to you all that is in the earth and the ships that sail through the sea by His command? He is withholding the sky in a way that it cannot fall down on the earth without His permission; surely, Allah is very kind and merciful to mankind.[65] He is the One Who has given you life, will cause you to die and then will bring you back to life again - yet, man is indeed very ungrateful.[66] To every nation We have prescribed the rites of worship which they observe, therefore, let them not dispute with you concerning this matter - keep calling them to the Way of your Rabb; for most surely, you are rightly guided.[67]　　　　22:[65-67]

Allah will judge between you concerning those matters in which you differ

　　　　If they argue with you, say: "Allah knows best all that you do."[68] Allah will judge between you on the Day of Resurrection concerning the matters in which you differ.[69] Do you not know that Allah is aware of all that is in heaven and the earth? Certainly all of this is recorded in a Book and it is very easy for Allah to do so.[70] Yet, they worship besides Allah those deities for which He has revealed no sanction, nor they themselves have any knowledge about them; certainly the wrongdoers shall have no helper.[71] When Our revelations are recited to them with all their clarity, you can notice a denial on the faces of the unbelievers. They can barely restrain themselves from assaulting those who recite Our revelations. Say to them: "Should I tell you something which is far worse than that? It is the fire *of hell*, which Allah has promised to those who reject the truth; what an evil abode it will be!"[72]

22:[68-72]

SECTION: 10

O mankind! Here is an example *for your understanding,* so listen to it carefully. Those deities whom you call besides Allah, cannot create a single fly, even if they all combined their forces, rather, if a fly snatches away anything from them, they cannot even get it back; how feeble are the suppliants and how powerless are those whom they supplicate![73]　　They do not render to Allah the homage due to Him; in fact, Allah is the One Who is All-Powerful, All-Mighty.[74]　　　　　22:[73-74]

Gods besides Allah have no power to create even a creature like a fly

Allah chooses His messengers from among the angels and from among the human beings, for surely, Allah is All-Hearing, All-Seeing.[75]　　He knows what is before them and what is behind them, and to Allah shall all matters return *for decision*.[76]　　O believers! Bow down, prostrate yourselves, worship your Rabb and do good deeds so that you may attain salvation.[77]　　Strive in the Way of Allah as you ought to strive *with sincerity and discipline;* He has chosen you and has not laid upon you any hardship in the observance of your faith - the faith of your father Ibrâheem *(Abraham)*. He named you Muslims before *in prior scriptures* and in this *(Qur'an)*, so that the Rasool (Muhammad) may testify against you and you yourselves may testify against the rest of mankind. Therefore, establish Salah *(prayers)*, pay Zakah *(obligatory charity) and* hold fast to Allah, Who is your Protector - what an excellent Protector and a splendid Supporter![78]　　22:[75-78]

Allah named the believers Muslims in the prior scriptures and also in this (The Qur'an)

JUZ (PART): 18

23: AL-MU'MINÛN

Period of Revelation

This Sûrah was revealed during the middle stage of the Prophet's residence at Makkah. It was the climax of the famine in that region (vv. 75-76). From the contents of this Sûrah, it appears that a bitter conflict had begun between the Prophet Muhammad and the disbelievers though the persecution had not yet begun.

Major Issues, Divine Laws, and Guidance

* Characteristics of "true believers."
* Stages of human creation.
* Story of the Prophet Nûh (peace be upon him) and the great flood.
* Story of the Prophet Hûd (peace be upon him) and the blast which destroyed the unbelievers.
* Allah has not charged any soul with more than it can bear.
* Guidance to repel evil with good and to seek the protection of Allah against the temptations of Shaitân.
* On the Day of Judgement it will appear as if the life of this world was less than one day.
* The fact that the disbelievers will never get salvation.

This Sûrah invites the people to accept and follow the Message of the Prophet Muhammad, the whole Sûrah revolves around this theme. According to an authentic tradition related by Urwah bin Zubair, Sayyidunâ Umar, who had embraced Islam by that time, said, "This Sûrah was revealed in my presence and I observed the state of the Prophet during its revelation. When the revelation ended, the Prophet remarked, 'On this occasion ten such verses have been sent down to me that the one who measures up to them will most surely go to paradise.' Then he recited the first ten verses of this Sûrah."

JUZ (PART): 18

23: AL-MU'MINÛN

This Sûrah, revealed at Makkah, has 6 sections and 118 verses.

In the name of Allah, the Compassionate, the Merciful

SECTION: 1

Indeed! Successful are those believers[1] who are humble in their Salah *(prayers)*,[2] who avoid vain talk,[3] who are punctual in the payment of Zakah *(charity)*,[4] who guard their private parts[5] except from their spouses or those who are *legally* in their possession, for in that case they shall not be blamed[6] - however those who seek to go beyond that *in lust* are the ones who are the transgressors[7] - who are true to their trust and covenants,[8] and who are diligent about their Salah *(prayers)*.[9] These are the heirs[10] who will inherit paradise; and live therein forever.[11]

23:[1-11]

Indeed! We have created man from an extract of clay,[12] then placed him as a drop of semen in a firm resting place,[13] then changed the semen into a leechlike mass, then the leechlike mass into a fetus lump, then the fetus lump into bones, then clothed the bones with flesh, and then We brought him forth as quite a different creature *from the embryo* - so blessed is Allah, the best of all creators![14] Then after *living for* a while you shall all die,[15] then most surely, you shall be raised to life again on the Day of Resurrection.[16]

13:[12-16]

We have made seven avenues *(heavens)* above you; and We are never unmindful of Our creation.[17] We send down water from the sky according to a due measure, then We cause it to settle in the soil - *you should know that if We please,* We are certainly able to take it away[18] - then with it We cause to grow gardens of palm trees and grapes for you; yielding abundant fruit of which you eat,[19] and also a tree which grows from Mount Sinai which produces oil and relish as *a food for those* who like to eat it.[20] In cattle, too, there is a lesson for you: from within their bodies We produce *milk* for you to drink, besides this you gain numerous other benefits; some of them you eat,[21] yet, on others as well as on ships you ride.[22]

23:[17-22]

Marginal notes:

Characteristics of true believers

Stages of human creation

Allah has made the heavens, vegetation, trees and animals for the benefit of human beings

SECTION: 2

The Prophet Nûh was sent to guide his people - they disbelieved him and as a result Allah drowned all disbelievers in the great flood

We sent Nûh *(Noah)* to his people. He said, "O my people! Worship Allah, you have none worthy of worship but He, are you not afraid of Him *for committing shirk?"*[23]   The chiefs of the unbelievers among his people said, *"Nûh* is but a human like you; he desires to assert his superiority over you. If Allah wanted *to send Rasools,* He could have sent down angels; we have never heard such a thing as he says from our forefathers."[24]   *Some of them said:* "He is just a madman, so bear with him for a while."[25]   *Nûh* said, "O my Rabb! Help me against their calling me a liar."[26]   So We revealed Our will to him, saying: "Build an ark under Our Eyes and Our inspiration; and when Our judgement comes to pass and water wells out from At-Tannûr *(oven),* take aboard a pair *(a male and a female)* from every species and take your family, except those of them against whom the judgement has already been passed; and do not plead with Me in favor of the wrongdoers, for they are *doomed* to be drowned *in the flood.*[27]   Then when you have embarked on the ark with your companions, say: "Praise be to Allah Who has delivered us from the nation of wrongdoers,"[28]   and pray, "O my Rabb! Bless my landing from this Ark, for You are the best to make my landing safe."[29]   There are many signs in this story, and surely, We do test people.[30]   23:[23-30]

After the Prophet Nûh, Allah sent Hûd to guide his people

Then We raised after them a new generation *(the people of 'Ad),*[31]   and sent them a Rasool *(Hûd)* from among themselves, *who said to them:* "Worship Allah! You have none worthy of worship but He. Will you not fear Him *for committing shirk?*"[32]   23:[31-32]

SECTION: 3

They called the Prophet Hûd an imposter; as a result, Allah destroyed them all in a mighty blast

But the chiefs of his people - who disbelieved the message and denied the Meeting in the hereafter, - on whom We had bestowed affluence in this worldly life, said: "This person is but a human like you; he eats of what you eat and drinks of what you drink.[33]   If you obey a human like yourselves, you shall indeed be lost.[34]   What! Does he claim that when you are dead and turned into dust and bones, you will be brought to life *out of your graves*?[35]   Impossible! Just impossible is that with which you are being threatened![36]   There is no other life but our life of this world: we live here and die here, and shall never be raised to life again.[37]   This man is but an impostor, forging a lie against Allah, and we are not going to believe him."[38]   *At this the Rasool* prayed: "O my

Rabb! Help me against their calling me a liar."[39] *Allah* responded: "After a short time they will surely be sorry."[40]   So the Blast overtook them in all justice and We swept them away *like the rubbish of dead leaves* - so gone is the nation of wrongdoers.[41] After them We raised other generations[42] - no people can hasten their term nor can they postpone it[43]   - and sent forth Our Rasools one after another: every time a Rasool came to his people, they disbelieved him, so We *punished them* one after another and made them mere tales; so gone is the nation of disbelievers.[44]

23:[33-44]

Then We sent Musa *(Moses)* and his brother Haroon *(Aaron)* with Our signs and clear authority,[45]   to Fir'aun *(Pharaoh)* and   his chiefs: but they behaved arrogantly, for they were very haughty people.[46]   They said: "What! Should we believe in two human beings like ourselves, and whose people are our slaves?"[47]   So they disbelieved both of them and became among those who were destroyed.[48]   And We gave Musa the Book, so that his people might be rightly guided.[49] And We made the son of Maryam *(Jesus)* and his mother a sign for mankind, and gave them a shelter on a peaceful lofty ground, furnished with flowing steams.[50]   23:[45-50]

SECTION: 4

O Rasools! Eat of pure things and do good deeds, certainly, I have knowledge of all your actions.[51]   In fact, your Ummah *(religion)* is one Ummah *(religion)*, and I am your only Rabb: so fear Me Alone.[52]   Yet, people have divided themselves into factions and each faction rejoices in its own doctrines[53]   - well! Leave them in their heedlessness for an appointed time.[54] Do they think that, in giving them wealth and children,[55]   We are eager for their welfare? By no means! They do not understand *the reality of the matter*.[56]   Surely, those who live cautiously for fear of their Rabb,[57] who believe in the revelations of their Rabb;[58]   who do not commit shirk with their Rabb,[59]   who give to charity whatever they can give, and their hearts are full of fear *by the very idea* that they shall have to return to their Rabb,[60]   it is they who rush in doing good deeds and try to be the first in attaining them.[61]

23:[51-61]

We charge no soul with more than it can bear; We have a Book of record which shall clearly tell the truth, and they shall not be treated unjustly.[62]   But their hearts are blind to all this; and

---

After Hûd, Allah sent Rasools to other people; those people also denied and faced a similar punishment

Musa was sent to Fir'aun and his chiefs; they also disbelieved and faced destruction

Allah has said: "In fact, your religion is one religion; I am your Rabb, so fear Me Alone."

Allah has not charged any soul

with more than it can bear

their deeds are also different *from the believers*. They will continue doing their misdeeds[63]   until when We seize those of them who live in comfort with punishment; lo! Then they start crying for help *in supplication*.[64]   *We shall say*: "Do not cry for help this Day, for surely, from Us you shall receive no help.[65]   My revelations were recited to you, but you used to turn back on your heels[66]   in arrogance, talking nonsense about *the Qur'an* like one telling fables by night.[67]   Do they not ponder over the Word *of Allah* or has anything new come to them which did not come to their forefathers?[68]   Or is it because they do not recognize their Rasool, *who is a member of their own community,* that they deny him?[69]   *Or are they really convinced about what* they say that he is a madman? Nay! In fact, he has brought them the Truth and most of them dislike the Truth.[70]   - Had the Truth followed their appetites, the heavens, the earth and everything therein would have been disrupted. Nay! We have brought them their reminder *(the Qur'an)*, but they are heedless to their reminder.[71]   Or is it that you are asking them for some recompense? But the recompense of your Rabb is the best, for He is the best provider of sustenance.[72]   As a matter of fact, you *(O Muhammad)* are calling them to the Right Way;[73]   and surely, those who do not believe in the hereafter are deviating from the Right Way.[74]   If We show them mercy and relieve them of their affliction, they would obstinately persist in their rebellion, blindly wandering to and fro;[75]   for even now, when We have inflicted punishment on them, they have neither submitted to their Rabb nor did they humbly supplicate.[76]   Until when We open upon them a gate of severe punishment, you will see that they are plunged in utter despair.[77]

23:[62-77]

Those who do not believe in the hereafter will ever stray away from the Right Path

SECTION: 5

It is *Allah* Who has given you ears, eyes and hearts - yet, seldom you show gratitude[78]   - it is He Who has muliplied you on the earth and before Him you shall all be assembled *on the Day of Judgement*.[79]   It is He Who gives life and cause you to die, and in His control is the alternation of the night and the day: then why don't you understand?[80]   On the contrary said what *their forefathers* said before them;[81]   they said: "What! After death when our bodies become dust and bones, could we really be raised to life again?[82]   We have heard many such promises and so did our forefathers before us. These are nothing but legends of prior people."[83]

23:[78-83]

Allah has given you ears, eyes and hearts but you seldom show gratitude

Say: "To whom belongs the earth and everything therein? Tell me if you know?"[84] They will promptly reply: "to Allah!" Ask them: "Then why you do not use your common sense *and believe in Him*?"[85] Say: "Who is the Rabb of the seven heavens and the Rabb of the Great Throne?"[86] Right away they will say: "Allah." Ask them: "Then why you do not fear Him?"[87] Say: "In whose hands is the sovereignty of all things, protecting all, while against Him there is no protection? *Tell me* if you know."[88] Quickly they will reply: "Allah." Ask them: "Then how are you deluded?"[89] The fact of the matter is that We have brought them the Truth, and undoubtedly these people are liars.[90]

23:[84-90]

Even the disbelievers recognize the existence of Allah

Never has Allah begotten a son, nor is there any god along with Him. Had it been so, each god would govern his own creation, and each would have tried to overpower the others. Exalted be Allah, above the sort of things they attribute to Him![91] He knows what is hidden and what is open: far above is He from the shirk of these people.[92]   23:[91-92]

Allah has never begotten a son, nor is there any other god besides Him

SECTION: 6

Pray: "O my Rabb! If You show me *in my lifetime that punishment* with which they are being threatened,[93] then O my Rabb, do not include me amongst these unjust people."[94] Surely, We have the power to let you see the punishment with which they are being threatened.[95] Repel evil with good, We are fully aware of all their slanders.[96] Say, "O my Rabb! I seek refuge in You from the prompting of the shaitâns,[97] and O my Rabb! I seek refuge in You even from their presence."[98] 23:[93-98]

Repel evil with good and seek refuge with Allah against the temptations of shaitân

These people will never refrain from wrongdoing until when death comes to anyone of them, he will say: "O my Rabb! Send me back,[99] so that I may do good deeds in the world that I have left behind." Never! This is just a statement which carries no value, *it will be too late because* there will be a barrier *between them and the world they have just left* till the Day they are raised to life again.[100] On the Day when the Trumpet will be blown, they will neither have any relations among them, nor will they ask about each other.[101] Then only those whose weight *of good deeds* is heavy, will attain salvation.[102] As for those whose weight *of good deeds* is light, they will be the ones who have lost their souls to live in hell forever.[103] The Fire will burn their faces and they will grin therein

The wrongdoers will wish that they could be sent back to this world to adopt the Right Way, but it will be too late with their lips displaced.[104]   *We shall say to them:* "Were My revelations not recited to you, and did you not deny them?"[105] They will say: "O our Rabb! Our misfortune overwhelmed us and we became erring folk.[106]   Our Rabb! Get us out of here; if we ever return to sin, then we shall indeed be wrongdoers."[107]   *In answer to this Allah* will say: "Stay here in shame and do not plead with Me![108]   For you are the same people, *who used to make fun* of some of My worshippers who prayed: 'Our Rabb, We believe in You; please forgive us and have mercy on us, for You are the Best of those who show mercy!'[109]   But you ridiculed them so much, that you even forgot My very existence, and went on laughing at them.[110]   Today, I have rewarded them for their fortitude, and they are the ones who are successful."[111]   23:[99-111]

They will be asked: "How many years did you live on earth?"[112]   They will reply: "We lived there a day or part of a day; You may ask those who kept the count."[113]   It will be said: "Well, *now you know that* your stay was just a little while - *what a pity,* if you had only realized!"[114]   Did you think that We had created you without any purpose and that you would never return to Us *for accountability?*"[115]   23:[112-115]

Therefore, exalted be Allah, the Real King; there is none worthy of worship but He, the Lord of the Honorable Throne.[116] Whoever invokes any other god besides Allah - about whose divinity he has no proof - he will have to give an account to his Rabb. Surely, such unbelievers will never attain salvation.[117] Say: "O my Rabb! Forgive, have Mercy; You are the Best of those who show mercy!"[118]   23:[116-118]

On the Day of Judgement it will appear as if the life of this world was less than one day

The unbelievers will never attain salvation

24: AN-NÛR

Period of Revelation

The consensus of opinion among the commentators of the Qur'an is that this Sûrah was sent down after the campaign against Bani Al-Mustaliq which took place after the Battle of the Trench in 6 A.H., at the occasion of slander against the wife of the Prophet Muhammad (peace be upon him), Sayyidah 'Aisha (Allah be pleased with her), who accompanied him in this campaign.

Major Issues, Divine Laws, and Guidance

* Laws relating to
     a) the punishment for rape, fornication and adultery.
     b) the punishment for bearing false witness relating to any of these crimes.
     c) Li'ân (bearing witness against one's own wife when there is no other witness in a case of adultery).
* Slander against the wife of the Prophet Muhammad (peace be upon him), Allah's declaration of her innocence, and admonition to those who were involved in that scandal.
* Regulations relating to entering houses other than your own.
* Regulations relating to mixed gatherings of males and females.
* Allah's commandment for singles to get them married.
* Allah's commandment to help slaves in getting their freedom.
* Allah is the Light of the heavens and the earth.
* Allah has created every living creature from water.
* True believers are those who, when called towards Allah and His Rasool, say: "We hear and we obey."
* Regulations relating to:
     a) entering the room of a married couple.
     b) eating at houses other than one's own.
* Allah's commandment for attending meetings which are called for discussions and decisions about taking collective actions.

Social Reforms enacted in this Sûrah and their background:

After the victory at the battle of Badr, the Islamic movement began to gain strength and at the Battle of Trench, it had become clear that the united forces of the unbelievers, numbering over ten thousand, could not crush the Islamic movement. Jews, Hypocrites and Mushrikeen understood well, that the war of aggression which the unbelievers had been waging against Muslims for several years, had come to an end. On that occasion the Prophet himself said to the believers: "After this year, the Quraish will not be able to attack you; you will take the offensive against them."

After the defeat in the Battle of the Trench the unbelievers realized that the Muslims could not be defeated on the battlefield and that the rise of Islam was not due to the numerical strength of the Muslims nor to their superior arms and material resources, since the Muslims were fighting against fearful odds on all these fronts, their success was due to their moral superiority. The pure and noble qualities of the Prophet and his followers were capturing the hearts of the people, and were also binding them together into a highly disciplined community. As a result, they were defeating both the mushrikeen and the Jews therefore, they chose the moral front to carry on the conflict.

They got the first opportunity when in Dhul-Qa'dah 5 A.H. the Prophet married Zainab (abph), the divorced wife of his adopted son, Zaid bin Hârithah (abph). The Prophet married Zainab in accordance with the commandment of Allah to put an end to a custom of ignorance, which had given the same status to the adopted son as that of his real son. The hypocrites, the Jews, and the mushrikeen considered it a golden opportunity to exploit the situation to vilify the Prophet and to ruin his high reputation with a malicious slander through concocting a story in the following words: "One day Muhammad (peace be upon him) happened to see the wife of his adopted son and fell in love with her; he maneuvered her divorce and married her." Though this was an absurd fiction, it was spread with such a skill and cunning that it succeeded in its purpose to the extent that some Muslim commentators also have cited some parts of it in their writings, and the orientalists have wilfully exploited it to vilify the Prophet. The fact is that Zainab (abph) was never a stranger to the Prophet. She was his first cousin, being the daughter of his real paternal aunt, Umaimah, daughter of Abdul Muttâlib, his real grand father. He had known her from her childhood to her youth. Just one year before this incident, he himself had persuaded her to marry Zaid (abph), who was a slave and whom the Prophet had freed and then adopted as his son, this was to demonstrate that in Islam, even a freed slave has rights equal to that of Quraish. But Zainab (abph) could not reconcile her psychological reservation about marriage with a liberated slave. Therefore, she and her husband could not continue together for long, which inevitably led to their divorce.

The second slander was made on the honor of Sayyidah 'Aisha (abph), a wife of the Prophet, in connection with an incident which occurred while he was returning *from the Campaign against the Bani Al-Mustaliq. This attack was even more severe than the first one and was the main reason for the revelation of this Sûrah. The mischief that was engineered by Abdullah bin Ubayy through this slander was to attack the honor of the Prophet and Sayyidunâ Abu Bakr Siddeeq (abph), who was the father of Sayyidah 'Aisha (abph), to undermine the high moral superiority which was the greatest asset of the Islamic Movement and to ignite civil war between the Muhâjireen and the Ansâr, and between Aus and Khazraj, the two clans of the Ansâr.*

This Sûrah was revealed to strengthen the moral fibre of the Muslim society, which had been shaken by the slander against Sayyidah 'Aisha (abph). The following laws and guidance are given to reform the Muslim community:

1. *Rape, adultery and fornication which had already been declared to be social crimes in Sûrah Al-Ahzâb (vv. 15,16) are now made criminal offences and the one proven guilty is to be punished.*
2. *Muslims are enjoined to boycott adulterous men and women and are forbidden to have any marriage relations with them.*
3. *One who accuses another of adultery but fails to produce four witnesses, is to be punished with eighty lashes.*
4. *The law of Li'ân is enacted to provide the method for a husband to bear witness against his own wife in a case of adultery when there are no other witnesses, and also provides the wife a method to refute his testimony.*
5. *The Muslims are enjoined to learn this lesson from the incident of the slander against Sayyidah 'Aisha. The Muslims are advised that they should be very cautious about the charges of adultery against people of good reputation, and instead of spreading such a rumor, they should refute and suppress them immediately." In this connection, a general principle is enunciated that the proper spouse for a pure man is a pure woman, for he cannot get along with a wicked woman for long, and the same is the case with a pure woman. The Muslims are admonished as follows: "When you know that the Prophet is the purest of all human beings, how could you believe that he could live with a wicked woman and exalt her as the most beloved of his wives? For it is obvious that an adulterous woman could not have been able to deceive a pure man like the Prophet. You should have considered the fact that the accuser is a mean person while the accused is a pure woman. This should have been enough to convince you that the accusation is not worth your attention."*
6. *Those who spread evil rumors and propagate wickedness in the Muslim community deserve punishment and not encouragement.*
7. *Relations in the Muslim community should be based on good faith and*

not on suspicion: everyone is innocent unless he/she is proven guilty.

8. People are forbidden to enter houses other than their own without seeking permission.

9. Both men and women are instructed to lower their gaze when they come in contact with each other.

10. Women are enjoined to cover their heads and breasts, not to display their beauty before other men except their servants or such relatives with whom their marriage is prohibited, hide their charms and not to put on jingling ornaments when they go out of their homes.

11. Marriage is encouraged and enjoined even for slaves, because unmarried people are more prone to indecency.

12. The institution of slavery is discouraged. Slave owners and other people are enjoined to give financial help to slaves to earn their freedom under the law of Mukatabat (contract).

13. Prostitution by slave girls is forbidden, for prostitution in Arabia was confined to this class alone.

14. Respect of privacy is enjoined even for servants and children, including one's own. They are enjoined not to enter the private rooms of married couple without permission; especially in the early morning, at noon and at night.

16. Elderly women are given the concession that they can set aside their head covers when they are inside their homes but should refrain from display of adornments.

17. The Muslims are encouraged to develop close relationships by taking their meals together. Close relatives and intimate friends are allowed to take their meals in each other's home without any formal invitation.

18. Clear differences between believers and hypocrites are clarified to enable every Muslim to discriminate between the two. At the same time the community is strengthened through adopting the disciplinary measures in order todiscourage the enemies from creating mischief in it.

The most conspicuous thing about this Sûrah is that it is free from the bitterness which inevitably follows such shameful and absurd attacks as the lies circulated about the wife of the Prophet. Instead of showing any wrath at this provocation, it prescribes laws and regulations. It contains reformative commandments and wise instructions that were needed at that time for the education and training of the newly formed Muslim community.

24: AN-NÛR

This Sûrah revealed, at Madinah, has 9 sections and 64 verses.

In the name of Allah, the Compassionate, the Merciful.

SECTION: 1

This is a Sûrah which We have revealed and made *its legislation* obligatory; in it we have revealed clear verses, so that you may take heed.[1]   *As for* the fornicatoress and fornicator *(female and male guilty of illegal sexual intercourse),* flog each of them one hundred lashes and do not take pity in enforcing the law ordained by Allah, if you believe in Allah and the Last Day, and let a party of the believers witness their punishment.[2]   24:[1-2]

Punishment for rape or fornication

The fornicator shall not marry any but a fornicatoress or a mushrikah, and none marries her *(fornicatoress) except* a fornicator or a mushrik: such *marriages* are forbidden to the believers.[3] Those who accuse a chaste woman *of fornication* and do not produce four witnesses *to support their allegation,* shall be flogged with eighty lashes and their testimony shall not be accepted ever after, for they are the ones who are wicked transgressors[4] - except those who repent thereafter and mend their conduct; for Allah is surely Forgiving, Merciful.[5]   24:[3-5]

Punishment for false witness

Those men who accuse their own wives but have no witness except themselves, each one of them shall be made to swear four times by Allah that his charge is true,[6] and the fifth time calls for the curse of Allah upon himself, if he is lying.[7] *As for the wife,* the punishment shall be averted from her if she swears four times by Allah that his *(her husband's)* charge is false[8] and the fifth time calls for the wrath of Allah upon herself, if his charge is true.[9] If it were not for Allah's grace and mercy upon you, *you would have no method of handling these situations.* Allah is the Acceptor of Repentance, All-Wise.[10]   24:[6-10]

Li'ân (accusing wife when there is no other witness in a case of adultery)

SECTION: 2

Surely, those who concocted the slander *(against 'Aisha - a wife of the Prophet)* are from a clique among you. Do not regard this incident as only an evil, for it also *contains* a good *lesson* for you. Whoever took any part in this sin, has earned his share

Slander against a wife of the Prophet

accordingly, and the one who took on himself the leading part, shall have a terrible punishment.[11]   Why did not the believing men and believing women, when they heard *of this slander*, think well of their own people, and say: "This is clearly a false accusation?"[12] Why did they not produce four witnesses? If they cannot produce the required witnesses, they are the liars in the sight of Allah.[13] Were it not for the grace and mercy of Allah towards you in this world and the Hereafter, you would have been severely punished for your involvement in this scandal;[14]   when you passed on with your tongues and uttered with your mouths that about which you had no knowledge. You took it lightly while it was a very serious offence in the sight of   Allah.[15]   Why did you not, when you heard about it, say: "It is not befitting for us to talk about it, Glory be to You, *O Allah*! This is a monstrous slander?"[16]   Allah admonishes you never to repeat a mistake like this, if you are true believers.[17]   Allah has made His revelations clear to you, Allah is All-Knowing, All-Wise.[18]   Those who love to spread such slanders among the believers will have a painful punishment in this life and in the Hereafter. Allah knows and you do not know.[19] Were it not for the grace and mercy of Allah towards you, *this scandal would have produced very bad results for you.* Allah is indeed very Kind, most Merciful.[20]   24:[11-20]

SECTION: 3

O believers! Do not follow the footsteps of Shaitân: because anyone who follows the footsteps of Shaitân is seduced by him to commit acts of indecency and wickedness. If there had not been the grace and mercy of Allah upon you, none of you would have ever been purified *from that sin*, for it is Allah Alone Who purifies whom He pleases, and Allah is All-Hearing, All-Knowing.[21]   Let not those among you who are endowed with grace and amplitude of means swear to withhold their help from their relatives, the indigent and those who migrated for the cause of Allah - rather let them forgive and overlook - do you not wish that Allah should forgive you? Allah is Forgiving, Merciful.[22]   Those who accuse chaste and believing women who are, in good faith, unaware *of what is plotted against them,* are cursed in this life, and in the hereafter they shall have a grievous punishment.[23]   *Such people should not forget* that Day when their own tongues, their own hands and their own feet will testify against their misdeeds.[24]   On that Day, Allah will give them the full reward they deserve, then they will realize that it is Allah Who is the Manifest Truth *(perfect in*

Allah cleared the Prophet's wife to be innocent

Allah commanded the believers not to follow shaitân and not take part in false accusations and slanders

justice).[25]   Impure women are for impure men, and impure men are for impure women; pure women are for pure men, and pure men are for pure women. They are free from the *slanderer's* accusations; for them there shall be forgiveness and honorable provision *from Allah.*[26]   24:[21-26]

SECTION: 4

O believers! Do not enter houses other than your own until you have sought permission and said greetings of peace to the occupants; this is better for you, so that you may be mindful.[27]   If you do not find anybody therein, still, do not enter until permission is given to you; and if you are asked to go back, then go back; this is more fitting for you; and Allah is cognizant of what you do.[28] There is no blame on you if you enter houses which are not used for dwelling and in which you have something belonging to you; and Allah knows what you reveal and what you conceal.[29]

24:[27-29]

Enjoin the believing men to lower their gaze and guard their modesty; that is chaster for them. Surely, Allah is well aware of their actions.[30]   *Likewise,* enjoin the believing women to lower their gaze and guard their modesty; not to display their beauty and ornaments except what normally appears thereof; let them draw their veils over their bosoms and not display their adornment except to their husbands, their fathers, their fathers-in-law, their own sons, their stepsons, their own brothers, their nephews on either brothers' or sisters' sides, their own womenfolk, their own slaves, male attendants who lack sexual desires or small children who have no carnal knowledge of women. Also enjoin them not to strike their feet in order to draw attention to their hidden trinkets. And O believers! Turn to Allah in repentance, all of you, *about your past mistakes,* so that you may attain salvation.[31]   24:[30-31]

Get the singles among you married as well as those who are fit for marriage among your male slaves and female slaves. If they are poor, Allah will make them free from want out of His grace: for Allah has boundless *resources* and is All-Knowing.[32]   And let those who do not find means to marry keep themselves chaste until Allah enriches them out of His bounty. As for those of your slaves who seek writing *to buy out their liberty*, execute the deed *of liberty* with them if you find them deserving, and give them some of the wealth which Allah has given you. Do not force your slave-girls

---

Etiquettes for entering the houses other than your own

Required behavior in mixed gatherings of males and females

Allah's order for single people to get married

Allah's order to grant liberty to those slaves who seek to buy their freedom

into prostitution for your own worldly gains, if they wish to preserve their chastity; and if anyone forces them into it, then surely, after such a compulsion Allah will be forgiving and merciful to them *(the slave girls)*.[33] We have already sent down to you revelations giving you clear guidance and cited examples of those people who passed away before you and an admonition for the righteous.[34]   24:[32-34]

SECTION: 5

Allah is the Light of the heavens and the earth

Allah is the Light of the heavens and the earth. The parable of His Light is as if there were a niche, in which there is a lamp, the lamp is enclosed in crystal, the crystal is of a starlike brilliance, it is lit with the olive oil from a blessed olive tree which is neither eastern nor western, its very oil would almost be luminous though no fire touched it - *as though all the means of increasing* Light upon Light *are provided* - Allah guides to His Light whom He pleases. Allah cites such parables *to make His message clear* to the people; and Allah has knowledge of everything.[35]   24:[35]

Allah's Light is found in the places of worship which are built for his remembrance by His devotees

His Light is found in those houses which Allah has sanctioned to be built for the remembrance of His name; where His name is glorified in the mornings and in the evenings *again and again*,[36] by such people whom neither business nor business profit can divert from the remembrance of Allah, nor from establishing Salah *(prayers)* and nor from paying Zakah *(obligatory charity)*, for they fear the Day *of Judgement* when hearts and eyes will be overturned,[37] so that Allah may reward them according to the best of their deeds and add for them even more out of His grace: for Allah gives without measure to whom He pleases.[38]   24:[36-38]

Deeds of the unbelievers are like a mirage in a sandy desert

As for the unbelievers, their deeds *will disappear* like a mirage in a sandy desert, which the thirsty *traveller* thinks to be water, but when he comes near, he finds it to be nothing, instead he finds Allah to settle his account - Allah is swift in settling accounts.[39] Or *another parable of an unbelievers* is like the darkness in a bottomless ocean overwhelmed with billows, one over the other, overcast with dark clouds - layers of utter darkness, one above another - *so much so that* if he stretches out his hand, he can hardly see it. The one to whom Allah does not give light, will have no light![40]   24:[39-40]

SECTION: 6

Do you not see that Allah is the One Who is praised by all those who are in the heavens and in the earth? The very birds praise Him as they wing their flight. Each one knows its prayers and how to praise Him, and Allah has full knowledge of all their actions.[41] To Allah belongs the kingdom of the heavens and the earth; and towards Allah lies the final goal.[42] Do you not see that Allah makes the clouds move gently, then joins them together, then piles them up in masses, then you see the rain coming from inside them? He also sends down hail from the clouds that look like mountains in the sky, afflicting therewith whom He wills and turning it away from whom He pleases; the flash of His lightning almost takes away sight.[43] Allah alternates the night and the day; there is indeed a lesson in it for those who possess insight.[44] Allah has created from water every living creature: of them there are some that creep upon their bellies, some that walk on two legs, and yet, some that walk on four; Allah creates what He pleases; surely, Allah has power over everything.[45]   24:[41-45]

Everything in the heaven and earth glorifies and praises Allah

Allah has created every living creature from water

We have indeed sent down very clear revelations, and Allah guides to the Right Way whom He pleases.[46] They say: "We believe in Allah and the Rasool and we obey," but *no sooner do they utter these words than* some of them turn their backs; these are no believers.[47] When such people are called to Allah and His Rasool that he may judge between them, behold! A party of them declines to come.[48] However, if they have the truth on their side, they come to him voluntarily.[49] Is there a disease in their hearts? Either they are skeptical, or else they fear that Allah and His Rasool will deny them justice. Nay! In fact, they are the ones who are the wrongdoers.[50]   24:[46-50]

Those who claim to be believers but do not demonstrate their belief through actions are not true believers

SECTION: 7

The response of the true believers, when they are called to Allah and His Rasool to judge between them, is only to say: "We hear and we obey." Such are the ones who will attain felicity.[51] Only those who obey Allah and His Rasool, have fear of Allah and be careful not to incur His displeasure, are the ones who will be the successful.[52] They solemnly swear by Allah that if you command them, they will go forth *leaving their homes. O Muhammad* tell them: "Do not swear; your obedience *not your oaths* will count;

True believers are those who, when called towards Allah and His Rasool, say: "We hear and we obey."

surely, Allah is fully aware of what you do."[53] Say: "Obey Allah and obey the Rasool. If you do not, he *(the Rasool)* is only responsible to fulfill his duty, as you are responsible to fulfill yours; and if you obey him, you shall be rightly guided. *Note it well, that* the responsibility of the Rasool is only to deliver *Allah's* message clearly."[54] Allah has promised those of you who believe and do good deeds that He will most surely make them successors *of the present rulers* in the earth as He made their ancestors before them, and that He will establish for them their religion, the one which He has chosen for them, and that He will change their present state of fear into peace *and security.* Let them worship Me Alone and not to commit shirk with Me; and if anyone rejects *faith* after this, it is they who are the transgressors.[55] Therefore, establish Salah *(prayers)*, pay Zakah *(obligatory charity)* and obey the Rasool, so that you may be shown mercy.[56] Never think that the unbelievers can escape in the land. *As for them,* the fire shall be their home, and that is an evil abode.[57]   24:[51-57]

SECTION: 8

Etiquette of seeking permission to enter the room of married couples

O believers! Let those whom your right hands possess *(your servants)* and those children who have not yet attained puberty ask your permission before coming in to see you on three occasions: before Fajr Salah *(dawn prayer)*, at noon when you put off your clothes, and after the 'Isha Salah *(night prayer)*. These are your three times of privacy. At other times, there is no blame on you if you, or they, go around attending each other. Thus Allah makes His revelations clear to you, for Allah is All-Knowing, All-Wise.[58] And when your children reach the age of puberty, let them ask your permission as their elders do. Thus Allah makes His revelations clear to you, for Allah is All-Knowing, All-Wise.[59]

24:[58-59]

Etiquette of eating at houses other than your own

There is no blame on such elderly women who have no interest in getting married, if they lay aside their cloaks without displaying their adornment, but it is better for them if they do not discard. Allah is All-Hearing, All-Knowing.[60] There is no blame on the blind, nor is there a blame on the lame, nor is there a blame on the sick, nor on yourselves, to eat in your houses or the houses of your fathers, or your mothers, or your brothers, or your sisters, or your paternal uncles, or your paternal aunts, or your maternal uncles, or your maternal aunts, or in houses with the keys of which you are entrusted, or your sincere friends. There is no blame on you whether you eat together or apart; however, when you enter the houses, you should greet one another with the greeting of peace prescribed by Allah blessed and pure. Thus Allah makes His revelations clear to you, so that you may grow in understanding.[61]

24:[60-61]

SECTION: 9

The true believers are only those who believe in Allah and His Rasool, and who, when gathered with him on a matter requiring collective action, do not depart until they have obtained his permission - only those who ask your permission are the ones who truly believe in Allah and His Rasool - so when they ask your permission to leave for their private business, you may give permission to those of them whom you deem appropriate and implore Allah to forgive them; surely, Allah is Forgiving, Merciful.[62] Do not consider the summoning of the Rasool in the same manner, as you consider the summoning of one another among yourselves. Allah knows those of you who slip away, concealing *themselves behind others*. Let those who disobey his orders beware, lest some trial befall them or a painful punishment be inflicted on them.[63] Beware! Whatever is in the heavens and in the earth belongs to Allah. He knows all your thoughts and actions. On the Day *of Judgment* when they will be brought back to Him, He will tell them all that they have done. Allah has the knowledge of everything.[64] 24:[62-64]

Requirement to attend meetings which require collective action

25: AL-FURQÂN

Period of Revelation

It appears from its style and subject matter that, like Sûrah Al-Mu'minûn, this Sûrah was revealed during the third stage of the Prophet's residence at Makkah.

Major Issues, Divine Laws, and Guidance

* The Qur'an is the criterion to distinguish right from wrong.
* Wrongdoers are those who reject the Truth, disbelieve the Rasool, deny the Day of Judgement and life after death.
* On the Day of Judgement, those deities whom the mushrikeen invoke beside Allah will deny any claim of divinity and hold the mushrikeen responsible for their shirk.
* On the Day of Judgement, the disbelievers shall regret for not adopting the Right Way.
* The wisdom of sending the Qur'an through a piecemeal revelation is explained.
* Allah's commandment of making Jihâd against unbelief with this Qur'an.
* Characteristics of true believers are described.

Subject matter and topics of this Sûrah include the doubts and objections that were being raised by the disbelievers of Makkah against the Qur'an, the Prophethood of Muhammad (peace be upon him) and his teachings. Appropriate answers to those objections are given and the people are warned about the consequences of rejecting the Truth.

At the end of the Sûrah a description of the character of a true believer is given. This description might be summarized as follows: "Here is the criterion for distinguishing the genuine from the counterfeit: Look at the noble character of those people who have believed in and followed the teachings of the Prophet and the kind of people that the Prophet is trying to produce through his training. You may compare these believers with those Arabs who have not yet accepted the Message, who are clinging to their ignorance and doing their utmost to defeat the Truth. Now decide for yourselves which of the two is better."

25: AL-FURQÂN

This Sûrah, revealed at Makkah, has 6 sections and 77 verses.

In the name of Allah, the Compassionate, the Merciful

SECTION: 1

Blessed is the One Who has revealed   Al-Furqân *(the criterion to distinguish right from wrong: The Qur'an)* to His servant, that he may be a Warner to the worlds;[1]   He is the One to Whom belongs the kingdom of the heavens and the earth, has begotten no son and has no partner in His kingdom; He has created everything and ordained them in due proportions.[2]   Yet, *the unbelievers* have taken besides Him other gods that created nothing but are themselves created, and can neither harm nor help even themselves, and posses no power of *causing* death or of *giving* life, or of raising the dead.[3]   Those who deny the Truth say: "This *Qur'an* is but a forgery which he *(Muhammad) himself* has devised and some other people have helped him." Unjust is what they do and falsehood is what they utter![4]   And they say: "These are the stories of the ancients which he has copied down from what is read to him day and night."[5]   Tell them: "This *(Qur'an)* is revealed by Him Who knows the secrets of the heavens and the earth; surely, He is Ever-Forgiving, Merciful."[6]   And they say: "What sort of Rasool is he who eats food and walks about in the markets? Why has no angel been sent down with him to threaten *the disbelievers*?[7]   Why has he not been given a treasure or at least a garden from which he could eat?" And these wicked people further say: "You are only following a man who is bewitched."[8]   See what sort of examples they apply to you! Because they are lost and cannot find the way *to refute the truth of Tawheed and life after death.*[9]   25:[1-9]

SECTION: 2

Blessed is He, Who, if He wills, could give you much better things than what they propose for you: *not one but* many gardens beneath which rivers flow; and make for you palaces too.[10]   But in fact, they deny the Hour - and for the one who denies the coming of the Hour, We have prepared a blazing fire.[11]   When it sees them from a distant place, they will hear its raging and roaring.[12]   And when, chained together, they are flung into some narrow space, they will fervently plead for death.[13]   *But they will be told*: "Do not plead for one death today, but plead for many deaths."[14]

Blessed is Allah Who revealed this Qur'an, the criterion to distinguish right from wrong

The wrongdoers are those who reject the truth and disbelieve a Rasool because he is a human being

Those who deny the Hour and life after death will be cast in the blazing fire

Ask them: "Which is better, this hell or the eternal paradise which the righteous are being promised, which will be the reward *of their good deeds* and also their final destination;[15] wherein they will live forever and get everything that they wish for: and this is the promise worth praying for, from your Rabb."[16] 25:[10-16]

On that Day, He will gather all these people together along with *the deities* whom they worshipped besides Allah, and ask: "Were it you who misled these servants of Mine, or did they choose to go astray themselves?"[17] Those *deities* will answer: "Glory be to You! It was not befitting for us that we could take any guardian besides You, but You let them and their forefathers enjoy the comforts of worldly life until they forgot the Reminder, and thereby became worthless people."[18] Thus *your gods* will deny all that you profess today. Then you shall neither be able to avert *your punishment* nor shall you get any help *from anywhere*; and everyone among you who is guilty of wrongdoing, We shall make him taste the mighty punishment.[19] We have sent no Rasool before you, who did not eat or walk through the streets. In fact, We have made you a trial for one another. Now, will you show patience, for your Rabb is Ever-Seeing.[20] 25:[17-20]

On the Day of Judgement, those deities whom the mushrikeen invoke, will deny any claim of divinity and hold the mushrikeen responsible for their shirk

JUZ (PART): 19

SECTION: 3

Those who do not expect to meet Us *on the Day of Judgement* say: "Why are not the angels sent down to us or why do we not see our Rabb?" Certainly they have become arrogant within themselves and are scornful with that great arrogance.[21]   On the Day when they see the angels, it will not be a Day of rejoicing for the criminals; rather they will cry: "May there be a stone barrier *between us and the angels of punishment*."[22]   Then We shall turn to the deeds which they did, *based on their wrong opinions*, and render them vain like blown dust.[23]   *In contrast*, the heirs of paradise shall have the best residence and finest lodging on that Day.[24]   25:[21-24]

The unbelievers who ask for angels today will ask for a stone barrier between them and the angels of punishment

On that Day when the heavens shall burst asunder with clouds and the angels will be sent down ranks after ranks,[25]   the real Kingdom on that Day will belong only to the Compassionate *(Allah)*, a hard Day shall it be for the unbelievers.[26]   On that Day the wrongdoer will bite his hands saying: "Oh! Would that I had only taken the pathway alongside the Rasool!"[27]   Oh! Would that I had never chosen so-and-so as my friend.[28]   He was the one who led me astray from the admonition even after it had reached me." Shaitân is ever treacherous to man.[29]   The Rasool will say: "O my Rabb! Surely, my people deserted this Qur'an *(neither learned nor acted upon its guidance)*."[30]   That is how We made for every Rasool an enemy among the criminals, but your Rabb is sufficient for you *(O Muhammad)* as a Guide and Helper.[31]
                                                25:[25-31]

Disbelievers shall regret on the Day of Judgement for not adopting the Right Path

The unbelievers ask: "Why is not the Qur'an revealed to him all in a single revelation?" This method of slow, well arranged, piecemeal revelations is adopted to strengthen your heart.[32]   *The other reason for this method is that* any time they come to you with an argument, We reveal to you the Truth and properly explain it.[33] Those who will be dragged headlong into hell shall have an evil place to dwell in, for they had lost the Way *by taking an utterly wrong stand.*[34]   25:[32-34]

Allah explains the wisdom behind revealing the Qur'an piecemeal rather than all at once

SECTION: 4

We gave Musa *(Moses)* the Book and appointed his brother Haroon *(Aaron)* as a deputy with him,[35]   and said to them: "Both

All nations which rejected Allah's revelations and His Rasools were utterly destroyed

of you should go to the people who have denied Our Revelations." *But those people rejected Our Rasools, as a result,* We destroyed them utterly.[36]   As for the people of Nûh *(Noah)* We drowned them when they rejected the Rasools and made them an example for mankind; and We have prepared a painful punishment for such wrongdoers.[37]   The nations of 'Ad and Thamûd were also destroyed, and so were the dwellers of Ar-Rass, and many generations between them.[38]   We admonished each of them by citing examples *of those who were destroyed before them, even then they rejected Our revelations,* so We exterminated each one of them.[39] These unbelievers must have passed by that town which was destroyed by a fatal rain; had they not seen its ruins? But *the fact of the matter is* they do not believe in the life hereafter.[40] Whenever they see you, they scoff at you, saying: "Is this the man whom Allah has sent as a Rasool?[41]   Had we not stood firm, he *(Muhammad)* would have turned us away from our gods." Very soon, when faced with punishment, they will realize who actually

Those who have taken their desires as their gods are nothing but animals

went off the Right Way.[42]   Have you ever seen the one who has taken his own desires as his god? Would you take the responsibility of guiding him?[43]   Or do you think that most of them listen or try to understand? They are nothing but like animals - nay, they are even further off the track![44]   25:[35-44]

SECTION: 5

Allah has made the night a mantle, sleep to rest, and the day to work

Have you not seen how your Rabb extends a shadow? If He wanted, He could make it constant. Then We made the sun an indication of it;[45] *as the sun climbs up*, We withdraw it gradually towards Ourselves.[46]   He is the One Who has made the night a mantle for you, and sleep a rest, and made the day to rise up again.[47]   He is the One Who sends the winds as heralds announcing His Mercy and sends down pure water from the sky,[48] so that with it We may give life to a dead land, and quench the thirst of countless animals and men that We have created.[49]   We distribute this water among them so that they may glorify Us, yet most people refuse to do anything except show ingratitude.[50]
25:[45-50]

Do not yield to the unbelievers; make Jihad against them with the Qur'an

Had it been Our Will, We could have sent a Warner to every town,[51]   therefore, do not yield to the unbelievers, and make Jihad *(strive)* against them with this *Qur'an*, a mighty Jihad *(strenuous striving)*.[52]   He is the One Who has released the two seas *(bodies of water)*, the one sweet and pleasant, the other salty and bitter, and set a rampart between them, an insurmountable barrier.[53]   He is the One Who has created man from water, then made for him blood relationships and of marriage relationships, your Rabb is indeed All-Powerful.[54]   Yet they worship those deities besides Allah which can neither help nor harm them, *over and above this*, the unbeliever has become a helper *of every rebel* against his own Rabb.[55]   But *O Muhammad*! We have sent you only to proclaim good news and to give warning.[56]   Say: "I ask of you no recompense for this work except that he who wants, may take the Right Way to his Rabb."[57]   Put your trust in the Ever-Living *(Allah)* Who never dies: celebrate His praise, for He Alone is sufficient to be aware of the sins of His servants.[58]   The One Who created the heavens and the earth and all that is between them in six Yaume *(days, time periods or stages)*, and then established *Himself* on the Throne *in a manner that suits His majesty*; the Compassionate *(Allah): as to His Glory*, ask the one who knows.[59] When it is said to them, "Prostrate yourselves before the Most Compassionate," they ask: "Who is that Most Compassionate? Are we to prostrate just because you order us to?" It merely increases their disdain.[60]   25:[51-60]

SECTION: 6

Blessed is the One Who has decked the sky with constellations and placed in it a lamp *(the sun)* and a shining moon.[61]   He is the One Who has caused the night and the day to succeed each other, for him who desires to learn a lesson or desires to render thanks.[62]   True servants of the Compassionate *(Allah)* are those who walk on the earth in humility and when the ignorant people address them, they say: "Peace;"[63]   who pass the night prostrating before their Rabb and standing in prayers;[64]   who say: "Our Rabb! Ward off the punishment of hell from us, for its punishment is atrocious[65] -   certainly it is an evil abode and an evil resting place;"[66]   who, when they spend, are neither extravagant nor stingy, but keep the balance between those *two extremes*;[67]   who do not invoke any other god besides Allah, nor kill any soul which Allah has made sacred, except for a just cause, nor commit fornication - he that does this shall be punished for his sin,[68]   and his punishment shall be doubled on the Day of Resurrection and in disgrace he shall abide forever,[69]   except the one who repents, becomes a true believer, and starts doing good deeds, for then Allah will change his evil deeds into good, and Allah is Most Forgiving,

Put your trust in Ever-Living (Allah), Who will never die

Characteristics of the True Servants (believers) of Allah

Most Merciful.[70]   He that repents and does good deeds, has truly turned to Allah in good faith.[71]   Those are the ones who do not bear witness to falsehood and, if they ever pass by futility, pass with dignity.[72]   Who, when reminded about the revelations of their Rabb, do not turn a blind eye and a deaf ear to them.[73]   Who pray: "Our Rabb! Make our wives and children the comfort of our eyes, and make us leaders of the righteous."[74]   Such are the ones who will be rewarded with the lofty places *in paradise* for their patience, wherein they shall be welcomed with greetings and salutations.[75] They shall live forever in that excellent dwelling and excellent resting place![76]   *O Muhammad!* Say: "My Rabb would not have any care for, but for your invocation to Him. Now that you have rejected *His revelations*, soon you will face the inevitable *punishment.*"[77]   25:[61-77]

26: ASH-SHU'ARÂ

Period of Revelation

This Sûrah was revealed during the middle stage of the Prophet's residence at Makkah. According to Ibn Abbâs, Sûrah Tâ-Hâ was revealed first, then Sûrah Al-Wâqi'a, and then Sûrah Ash-Shu'arâ. (Rûh-ul-Ma'âni, Vol. 19, p. 64). About Sûrah Tâ-Hâ it is well known that it was revealed before Sayyidunâ Umar embraced Islam.

Major Issues, Divine Laws, and Guidance

*   Allah's address to the Prophet Muhammad (peace be upon him) that he should not fret himself to death with grief for the people's disbelief.
*   Story of Musa, Fir'aun, and deliverance of the children of Israel.
*   Story of Ibrâheem and his arguments against idol worshipping.
*   The mushrikeen and their gods will both be toppled into hell.
*   Stories of Prophets Nûh, Hûd, Sâleh, Lût, Shu'aib (pbut) and their people.
*   The Qur'an is revealed in the Arabic language and is not brought by shaitâns; as it is neither in their interest nor in their power to do so.
*   The shaitâns descend on those slandering sinners who listen to hearsay and are liars.

This Sûrah begins with words of consolation to the Prophet, as if to say: "Why do you fret for their sake? If these people have not believed, it is not because they have not seen any sign, but because they are obstinate. The whole earth is full of signs that can guide a seeker of truth to reality, but stubborn and misguided people have never believed even after seeing the signs, whether these were the signs of natural phenomena or the miracles of the prophets. Such people always stick to their erroneous creeds until the Divine scourge actually overtakes them." Then the discussion is summed up, saying "O disbelievers, if you really want to see signs, why do you insist on seeing those horrible signs that visited the doomed nations of the past? Why don't you appreciate the Qur'an which is being presented in your own language? Why don't you appreciate Muhammad (peace be upon him) and his companions? Can the revelations of the Qur'an be the work of a Shaitân or a Jinn? Does the recipient of the Qur'an appear to be a sorcerer? Are Muhammad (peace be upon him) and his companions no different from a poet and his admirers? Why don't you give up disbelief and search your hearts for the Truth? When in your hearts, you yourselves believe that the revelations of the Qur'an have nothing in common with sorcery and poetry, then you should know that you are wrong and unjust."

26: ASH-SHU'ARÂ

This Sûrah, revealed at Makkah, has 11 sections and 227 verses.

In the name of Allah, the Compassionate, the Merciful

SECTION: 1

Dedication of the Prophet Muhammad (pbuh) to the guidance of mankind

Tâ Seen M'eem.[1]   These are verses of the Manifest Book.[2]   *O Muhammad,* you will perhaps fret yourself to death with grief because they do not believe.[3]   If We wanted, We could send down upon them a sign from the heaven before which they would bend their necks in submission, *but that is not what We want.*[4]   They have been turning their backs on each fresh warning that comes to them from the Compassionate *(Allah).*[5]   But now that they have rejected the warning, they will soon come to know the reality of what they have been mocking at.[6]   Have they not looked at the earth to see how We have caused all kinds of noble plants to grow in it?[7]   Surely, in this, there is a sign; yet, most of them do not believe.[8]   Surely, your Rabb is the All-Mighty, the Most Merciful.[9]   26:[1-9]

SECTION: 2

The assignment of Musa as a Rasool and his dialogue with Fir'aun

Remind them of the story when your Rabb called Musa *(Moses)* and said: "Go to the wicked people[10]   the people of Fir'aun *(Pharaoh).* Have they no fear?"[11]   *Musa submitted,* saying: "My Rabb! I fear that they will reject me.[12]   *As a result of which* my breast may feel cramped, while my tongue is not eloquent; *therefore,* send Haroon *(Aaron)* with me.[13]   They have a charge *of manslaughter* against me and I fear they may put me to death."[14]   *Allah* said: "Indeed not! Proceed, both of you, with Our signs; surely, We are with you, listening.[15]   Go to Fir'aun and tell him: "We are the Rasools from the Rabb of the Worlds.[16]   You should send with us the Children of Israel."[17]   *When they went to Fir'aun and conveyed the Message of Allah, he* said: "Did we not cherish you when you were a child? Did you not stay several years of your life among us?[18]   Then you did what you did; you are so ungrateful!"[19]   *Musa* replied: "I did that when I was a misguided *youth.*[20]   I fled from you all because I feared you; but now my Rabb has granted me judgment *(wisdom)* and appointed me as one of His Rasools.[21]   Is it a favor with which you taunt me, that you have enslaved the Children of Israel?"[22]   Fir'aun said: "Who is this Rabb of the Worlds?"[23] *Musa* replied: "He is the Rabb of the heavens and the earth and all that lies between them, if you really care to believe."[24] *Fir'aun* said to those around him, "Do you hear that?"[25] *Musa* continued: "He is your Rabb and the Rabb of your forefathers."[26] *Fir'aun* interjected: "This Rasool of yours, who has been sent to you, is crazy."[27] *Musa* continued:" He is the Rabb of the east and west, and all that lies between them. If you would only *care and try* to understand." [28] *At this, Fir'aun, who did not want to listen any more* said: "If you serve any other god besides me, I shall have you thrown into prison."[29] *At this, Musa* said: "What if I show you a convincing sign?"[30] *Fir'aun* said: "Go ahead, show it if you are of the truthful."[31] *Hearing this, Musa* threw down his staff, and thereupon it changed into a veritable serpent.[32] Then he drew forth his hand and it became shining bright for the spectators.[33]   26:[10-33]

SECTION: 3

     After witnessing both the miracles, Fir'aun (Pharaoh) said to the chiefs around him: "This fellow is certainly a skilled magician,[34] who seeks to drive you out from your land by the force of his magic. Now what is your advice?"[35] They submitted: "Put him and his brother off for a while, and dispatch collectors to the various cities[36] to bring you every skilled magician."[37] So the magicians were brought together at the appointed time on a fixed day.[38] The people were *motivated* through saying: "Would you come to the gathering?[39] So that we may follow the magicians if they are dominant."[40] When the magicians arrived, they asked Fir'aun: "Shall we get a reward if we are dominant?"[41] *Fir'aun* replied: "Yes *of course*! You will be made my courtiers."[42] Musa said to them: "Cast down what you are going to cast."[43] Thereupon, they cast down their ropes and staffs, saying: "By the might of Fir'aun, we shall be the winners."[44] Then Musa threw down his staff, and lo! It swallowed what they produced.[45] At this, all the magicians fell in prostration,[46] saying: "We believe in the Rabb of the Worlds,[47] the Rabb of Musa *(Moses)* and Haroon *(Aaron)*."[48] Fir'aun shouted: "How dare you believe in him before I give you permission? He must be your master who taught you witchcraft. But soon you shall find out. I will cut off your hands and your feet on opposite sides and crucify you all."[49] They replied: "We don't care! We are going to return to our Rabb anyway.[50] We only desire that our Rabb may forgive us our sins, as we are the first to believe."[51]   26:[34-51]

The miracles of the Prophet Musa

Fir'aun took the Prophet Musa's miracles as magic and summoned the magicians to compete with him

After witnessing a miracle, all the magicians embraced Islam

SECTION: 4

Deliverance of the Children of Israel and the destruction of Fir'aun and his chiefs

We revealed to Musa *(Moses)*, saying: "Set off with my servants by night and beware that you will be pursued."[52]   Fir'aun *(Pharaoh)* sent collectors to all the cities,[53]   *and to mobilize his people he said*: "These Israelites are but a handful of people,[54] who have provoked us much;[55]   while we have a large army, well prepared."[56]   Thus did We make them leave their gardens and their water springs,[57]   their treasures and sumptuous dwellings.[58] This is how *they were made to lose,* while on *the other hand* We made the Children of Israel inheritors of such things.[59]   At sunrise *the Egyptians* pursued them.[60]   When the two hosts came face to face, the companions of Musa cried out: "We are surely overtaken."[61]   *Musa* said: "Not at all! My Rabb is with me; He will show me a way out."[62]   Then We revealed Our will to Musa: "Strike the sea with your staff," and the sea was cleft asunder, each part stood like a mighty mountain.[63]   We made the other party *(Fir'aun and his army)* follow them.[64]   We delivered Musa and all who were with him;[65]   and drowned the others.[66]   Surely, there is a lesson in this: yet, most of these people do not *learn this lesson to* become believers.[67]   Surely, your Rabb is the All-Mighty, the Most Merciful.[68]   26:[52-68]

SECTION: 5

The story of the Prophet Ibrâheem and his arguments against idol worshipping

Narrate to them the story of Ibrâheem,[69]   when he asked his father and his people: "What is that which you worship?"[70] They replied: "We worship idols, and sit beside them with all devotion."[71]   *Ibrâheem* asked: "Do they hear you when you call on them?[72]   Can they help you or harm you?"[73]   They replied: "No! But we found our forefathers doing so."[75]   *Ibrâheem* said: "Have you ever seen *with open eyes* these which you have been worshipping[74] - you and your forefathers?[76]   They are all enemies to me; except the Rabb of the Worlds,[77]   Who created me, then He gave me guidance.[78]   He is the One Who gives me food and drink,[79] Who gives me health when I get sick,[80]   Who will cause me to die and then bring me back to life,[81]   Who, I hope, will forgive me my mistakes on the Day of Judgment."[82]   *After this, Ibrâheem prayed:* "O my Rabb! Bestow wisdom upon me and admit me among the righteous,[83]   grant me a reputation of truthfulness on the tongue of later generations,[84]   count me among the inheritors of the paradise of Bliss;[85]   forgive my father, for he is from among those who have gone astray,[86]   do not hold me up in shame on the Day

The prayer of the Prophet Ibrâheem for this life and the life hereafter

when everybody will be raised back to life[87]   - the Day when neither wealth nor sons will avail anyone,[88]   *and when none shall be saved* except him who will come before Allah with a pure heart,[89]   when paradise shall be brought in the sight of the righteous;[90]   while hell shall be spread open to the straying[91]   and they will be asked: "Now, where are those whom you worshipped[92]   besides Allah? Can they help you or even help themselves?"[93]   Then they will be toppled into it, both they and those who misled them,[94]   together with all the armies of Iblees *(shaitân)*,[95]   wherein they will argue with one another[96]   saying: " By Allah, we were indeed in manifest error,[97]   when we made you equals with the Rabb of the Worlds.[98]   It was the criminals, who led us astray.[99]   Now we have no intercessors,[100]   and no loving friends.[101]   If we could but once return *to our worldly life*, we would be of the true believers."[102]   Surely, in this narration there is a great lesson, but most of these people do not *learn a lesson to* become believers.[103]   Surely, your Rabb is the All-Mighty, the Most Merciful.[104]   26:[69-104]

The mushrikeen and their gods both will be toppled into hell

SECTION: 6

The people of Nûh, also, rejected the Rasools.[105]   Remember when their brother Nûh asked them: "Have you no fear *of Allah*?[106]   Rest assured that I am a trustworthy Rasool *of Allah* towards you,[107]   so fear Allah and obey me.[108]   I do not ask you for any reward for my services, for my reward will be given by the Rabb of the Worlds,[109]   so fear Allah and obey me."[110]   They replied: "Should we believe in you, whereas your followers are but the lowest of the low?"[111]   He said: "I have no knowledge as to what they have been doing;[112]   their account is the concern of my Rabb, if you could use your common sense![113]   I am not going to drive away any believer.[114]   I am nothing but a plain Warner."[115] They said: "O Nûh! If you do not stop, you shall be stoned to death."[116]   *Nûh* prayed: "O my Rabb! My people have denied me.[117]   Decide the case between me and them openly. Deliver me and the believers who are with me."[118]   So We *granted his prayer,* delivered him and those with him in the laden ark,[119]   and drowned the rest *in the flood.*[120]   Surely, in this story there is a great lesson, but most of these people do not *learn a lesson and* become believers.[121]   Surely, your Rabb is the One Who is the All-Mighty, the Most Merciful.[122]   26:[105-122]

The story of the Prophet Nûh, his dialogue with his people, and the destruction of the disbelievers

SECTION: 7

The people of 'Ad, too, disbelieved the Rasools.[123] Remember when their brother Hûd asked them: "Have you no fear *of Allah*?[124] Rest assured that I am a trustworthy Rasool *of Allah* towards you.[125] So fear Allah and obey me.[126] I do not ask you any reward for my services, for my reward will be given by the Rabb of the Worlds.[127] Are you erecting a monument on every high place for fun?[128] Are you building strong fortresses as if you are going to live here forever?[129] Whenever you lay your hands on anyone, you act like cruel tyrants.[130] Have fear of Allah and obey me.[131] Fear the One Who has given you all the things that you know.[132] He has given you flocks and children,[133] gardens and fountains.[134] Truly, I fear for you the torment of a dreadful Day."[135] They replied: "It is the same to us whether you preach to us or you are not one of the preachers.[136] This is nothing but the custom of the former people,[137] and we are not going to be punished."[138] So they disbelieved him and We *utterly* destroyed them. Surely, in this story there is a great lesson, but most of these people do not *learn a lesson and* become believers.[139] Surely, your Rabb is the One Who is the All-Mighty, the Most Merciful.[140]

26:[123-140]

SECTION: 8

The people of Thamûd also disbelieved the Rasools.[141] Remember when their brother Sâleh asked them: "Have you no fear *of Allah*?[142] Rest assured that I am a trustworthy Rasool *of Allah* towards you.[143] So fear Allah and obey me.[144] I do not ask you for any reward for my services, for my reward will be given by the Rabb of the Worlds.[145] Will you be left in peace to enjoy all that you have here *forever*?[146] Gardens and fountains,[147] crops and palm-trees laden with juicy fruit,[148] carving your dwellings in the mountains and leading a happy life?[149] Have fear of Allah and obey me.[150] Do not follow the bidding of the extravagant,[151] who create corruption in the land and reform nothing."[152] They replied: "You are but one of the bewitched![153] You are no more than a human being like us. Bring forth a sign if you are one of the truthful."[154] *Sâleh* said: "Well, here is the she-camel *(the sign that you asked for)*. She shall have her share of water as you all have yours, each drinking on an *alternate* appointed day.[155] Do not touch her with evil, lest the punishment of a dreadful Day may overtake you."[156] Yet, they hamstrung her, and then became full of regrets;[157]   so the punishment overtook them. Surely, in this story there is a great lesson, but most of these people do not *learn a lesson and* become believers.[158]   Surely, your Rabb is the One Who is the All-Mighty, the Most Merciful.[159]   26:[141-159]

SECTION: 9

The people of Lût *(Lot)*, also, disbelieved the Rasools.[160] Remember when their brother Lût asked them: "Have you no fear *of Allah*?[161]   Rest assured that I am a trustworthy Rasool *of Allah* towards you.[162]   So fear Allah and obey me.[163]   I do not ask you for any reward for my services, for my reward will be given by the Rabb of the Worlds.[164]   Will you fornicate with males from among the creatures of the worlds[165]   and leave those whom your Rabb has created for you to be your mates? Nay! You are a people who have transgressed all limits."[166]   They replied: "If you do not stop, O Lût, you shall become one of the expelled."[167]   *Lût* said: "I am certainly one of those who abhor your actions.[168]   O my Rabb! Deliver me and my family from their wicked deeds."[169]   So We delivered him and all his family[170]   except an old woman who was left among those who remained behind.[171]   Then We utterly destroyed the rest.[172]   We rained down on them the rain *of brimstones:* and evil was the rain which fell on those who were forewarned.[173]   Surely, in this story there is a great lesson, but most of these people do not *learn a lesson and* become believers.[174]   Surely, your Rabb is the One Who is the All-Mighty, the Most Merciful.[175]   26:[160-175]

SECTION: 10

The people of Aiykah, also, disbelieved the Rasools.[176] Remember when Shu'aib asked them: "Have you no fear *of Allah*?[177]   Rest assured that I am a trustworthy Rasool *of Allah* towards you.[178]   So fear Allah and obey me.[179]   I do not ask you for any reward for my services, for my reward will be given by the Rabb of the Worlds.[180]   Give full measure and be not of those who cause losses to others *by fraud*.[181]   Weigh with even scales[182] and do not cheat your fellow men of what is rightfully theirs: nor spread evil in the land.[183]   Fear Him Who has created you and the generations before you."[184] They replied: "You are surely one of those who are bewitched.[185]   You are no more than a human being like us and we think that you are lying.[186]   Let a fragment fall out of the sky on us if you are telling the Truth."[187]   *Shu'aib*

The story of the Prophet Lût, his address to his people, and the destruction of disbelievers

The story of the Prophet Shu'aib, his address to his people, and the destruction of disbelievers

said: "My Rabb has full knowledge of all your actions."[188] So they disbelieved him, and the torment of the day of shadow *(dark clouds carrying Allah's scourge)* seized them, and indeed, it was the torment of an extremely dreadful day.[189] Surely, in this story there is a great lesson, but most of these people do not *learn a lesson and* become believers.[190] Surely, your Rabb is the One Who is the All-Mighty, the Most Merciful.[191] 26:[176-191]

SECTION: 11

Surely, this *Qur'an* is a revelation from the Rabb of the Worlds.[192] The trustworthy Spirit *(Angel Gabriel)* brought it down[193] upon your heart so that you may become one of those who *are appointed by Allah to* warn the people[194] in a plain Arabic language.[195] This fact was foretold in the scriptures of the former people.[196] Is it not sufficient proof for the people that the learned men of the children of Israel knew about it?[197] *Even so that* if We had revealed it to a non-Arab,[198] and he had recited it to them in fluent Arabic, they would still not have believed in it.[199] We have thus caused unbelief in the hearts of the criminals.[200] They are not going to believe in it until they see the painful scourge[201] which, in their heedlessness, will come to them suddenly.[202] Then they will ask: "Can we be given some respite?"[203] Do they wish to hurry on Our scourge?[204] *Just think*! If We let them enjoy this life for many years,[205] and then the scourge with which they are threatened falls upon them,[206] of what avail will their past enjoyments be to them?[207] 26:[192-207]

Never have We destroyed a population to whom We did not send Warners;[208] they were forewarned, and We have never been unjust.[209] This *Qur'an* is not brought down by the shaitâns:[210] it is neither in their interest nor in their power *to produce such a masterpiece.*[211] They are kept too far off to even hear it.[212] So do not call on other gods besides Allah, lest you become one of those who incur His punishment.[213] Admonish your close relatives[214] and lower your wings of kindness to those of the believers who follow you,[215] but if they disobey, tell them: "I am not accountable for what you do."[216] Put your trust in the All-Mighty, the Merciful,[217] Who observes you when you get up[218] and your movement among those who prostrate themselves *in worship*.[219] He is the One Who is the All-Hearing, the All-Knowing.[220] 26:[208-220]

The Qur'an is revealed in plain Arabic by Allah through angel Gabriel; those people who do not want to believe will not believe

The Qur'an is not brought down by shaitâns: it is neither in their interest nor in their power

Shall I tell you, *O people,* on whom the shaitâns descend?[221]   They descend on every slandering sinner,[222]   those who pass on what is heard - and most of them are liars[223] - and the poets are followed by those who go astray.[224]   Do you not see, how they wander in every valley *(speak about every subject - right or wrong - in their peotry),*[225]   and they say what they do not do?[226]   *However,* an exception is made for those *(poets)* who believe, do good deeds, engage much in the remembrance of Allah and defend themselves when wronged. The unjust oppressors will soon find out what vicissitudes their affairs will take.[227]

26:[221-227]

Shaitâns descend on slandering sinners, who listen to hearsay and are liars

27: AN-NAML

Period of Revelation

This Sûrah was revealed during the middle stage of the Prophet's residence in Makkah. According to the traditions narrated by Sayyidunâ Ibn Abbâs and Sayyidunâ Jâbir bin Zaid, "First, Sûrah Ash-Shu'arâ was sent down, then Sûrah An-Naml, and then Sûrah Al-Qasas".

Major Issues, Divine Laws, and Guidance

* The Qur'an is a guide and good news to the believers.
* Prophet Musa's (peace be upon him) nine miracles, which were shown to Fir'aun and his people.
* Story of Prophet Sulaimân (Solomon) and the Queen of Sheba.
* Stories of Prophets Sâleh, Lût (pbut) and their people.
* The disbelievers actually doubt Allah's power of creation.
* A sign from the signs, and a scene from the scenes of Doomsday.
* Those who accept guidance do so to their own good and those who reject and go astray, do so to their own peril.

This Sûrah contains of the following two discourses.

The theme of the **first discourse** is that the only people that can benefit from the guidance of the Qur'an and become worthy of the good promises made in it, are those who accept the realities of the universe presented in this Book, and then show obedience and submission in their practical lives. But the greatest hindrance for man to follow this way, is the denial of the Hereafter. For it makes him irresponsible, selfish, and greedy in this worldly life, which in turn, makes it impossible for him to submit to the Will of Allah and to accept the moral restrictions on his lusts and desires.

After this introduction, three types of characters have been presented: Examples of the first type are Fir'aun (Pharaoh), his chiefs, the nation of Thamûd and the people of Prophet Lût (peace be upon him) who were all heedless of the Hereafter and consequently had become the slaves of their desires. That's why they did not believe even after seeing miracles. Rather, they turned against those who invited them to goodness and piety. They persisted in their evil ways, which were abhorred by every sensible person. They did not heed the admonition even moments before they were overtaken by the scourge of Allah.

An example of the second type is Prophet Sulaimân (Solomon) (peace be upon him), who had been blessed by Allah with wealth, kingdom and grandeur far greater than the chiefs of the disbelievers of Makkah. But, since he regarded himself answerable before Allah and recognized that whatever he had was only due to Allah's bounty, he adopted righteousness and the attitude of obedience.

An example of the third type is the Queen of Sheba, who ruled over the most wealthy and well-known people in the history of Arabia. She possessed all those means of life which could cause a person to become proud and arrogant. Her wealth and possessions far exceeded the wealth and possessions of the Quraish. She professed shirk, which was not only an ancestral way of life for her, but she had to follow it in order to maintain her position as a ruler. Therefore, it was much more difficult for her to give up shirk and adopt the way of Tawheed than it could be for a common mushrik. But when the Truth became evident to her, nothing could stop her from accepting it. Her deviation was, in fact, due to her being born and brought up in a polytheistic environment, not because of her being a slave to her lusts and desires. Her conscience was not devoid of the sense of accountability before Allah.

The theme of the **second discourse** is to draw the attention of the people to some of the most glaring and visible realities of the universe by asking questions such as: "Do the realities of the universe testify to the creed of shirk which you are following, or to the truth of Tawheed to which the Qur'an invites you?" After this the real malady of the disbelievers is pointed out, saying, "The thing which has blinded them and made them insensitive to every reality, is their denial of the Hereafter. This same thing has rendered every matter and affair of life non-serious for them. Because, according to them, if ultimately everything has to become dust, and the whole struggle of existence is to enjoy this worldly life then the truth and falsehood are equal and alike. Therefore, the question of whether one's system of life is based on right or wrong becomes meaningless."

In conclusion, the invitation of the Qur'an to serve One God (Allah) is presented in a concise but forceful manner, and the people are admonished to accept this invitation because accepting it, is to their advantage and rejecting it, will be to their disadvantage. For if they deferred their faith till they saw those signs of Allah, after the appearance of which they would be left with no choice but to believe and submit, then it will be too late to gain any benefit from it.

27: AN-NAML

This Sûrah, revealed at Makkah, has 7 sections and 93 verses.

In the name of Allah, the Compassionate, the Merciful

SECTION: 1

The Qur'an is a Guide and Good News to the Believers

Tâ Seen. These are verses of the Qur'an, the Book *that makes the things* clear;[1]   a guide and good news for the believers,[2] who establish Salah *(prayer)* and pay Zakah *(obligatory charity)* and firmly believe in the hereafter.[3]   As for those who do not believe in the hereafter, We make their deeds seem fair to them, therefore they blunder about *in their folly.*[4] They are the ones for whom there is an evil punishment, and in the hereafter, they will be the greatest losers.[5] And *O Muhammad,* most surely you are receiving this Qur'an from the One Who is wise and All-Knowing.[6]   27:[1-6]

The story of the Prophet Musa's selection as a Rasool

Relate to them the story of Musa *(Moses)*, when he said to his family: "I have seen a fire; soon I may either bring you some information *about the right direction* from there or a lighted torch to warm yourselves with."[7] When he came to it, a voice called out to him: "Blessed be He Who is in this fire and all around it! Glory be to Allah, the Rabb of the Worlds![8] O Musa, this is I, Allah, the All-Mighty, the Wise.[9]   Throw down your staff." When he saw it moving like a snake, he turned back and fled without even looking back. "O Musa, do not be afraid," *said Allah,* "My Rasool need not be afraid in My presence,[10]   except him, who is guilty of wrongdoing; even then, if he replaces that wrongdoing with a good deed, I am indeed Forgiving, Merciful.[11] Now put your hand into your pocket, it will come out shining white without any harm. These *two signs* are from the nine signs *that you will be given during your mission* to Fir'aun *(Pharaoh)* and his people; for truly,

Nine signs were shown to Fir'aun but he still disbelieved and incurred Allah's punishment

they are a nation of transgressors."[12]   But, when our signs were shown to them, they said: "This is clear sorcery."[13]   They were convinced in their hearts about the truth *of those miracles*, yet, they denied those signs in their wickedness and pride. So you see, what was the end of those transgressors.[14]   27:[7-14]

SECTION: 2

The story of the Prophet Sulaimân, to whom Allah

We bestowed knowledge on Daûd *(David)* and Sulaimân *(Solomon)*. They both said: "Praise be to Allah Who has exalted us above many of His believing servants."[15]   Sulaimân succeeded Daûd. He said: "O people! We have been taught the language of birds and given all sorts of things. This is indeed an evident grace *from Allah."*[16]   An army put together for Sulaimân was comprised of Jinns, men and birds; they all were kept under strict discipline.[17]   *Once in an expedition, he was marching with his army* when they came across a valley of ants, one of the ants said: "O ants, get into your habitations lest Sulaimân and his army crush you *under their feet* without even noticing it."[18]   So *Sulaimân* smiled, laughing at its statement, and said: "O my Rabb! Inspire me to render thanks for Your favors, which You have bestowed on me and on my parents, to do such good deeds that will please You; and admit me, by Your mercy, among Your righteous servants."[19]   27:[15-19]

gave rule over jinns, men, birds and winds

He took a roll call of the birds and said: "I do not see the hoopoe, where is he? How could he be absent?[20]   I will certainly punish him severely or even slay him, if he does not offer me a strong reason *for his absence*."[21]   The *hoopoe*, who did not take long in coming, said: I have just found out that which you do not know. I have brought you reliable information about *the people of Saba' (Sheba)*.[22]   I found a woman ruling over them; she has been given everything and she possesses a magnificent throne.[23]   Further, I found that she and her people prostrate themselves before the sun instead of Allah. Shaitân has made their deeds fair-seeming to them and thus turned them away from the Right Way, so they have no guidance[24]   to prostrate themselves before Allah, the One Who brings to light all that is hidden in the heavens and the earth and knows exactly what you hide and what you reveal.[25]   Allah! There is none worthy of worship but He. He is the Lord of the Mighty Throne."[26]   *Sulaimân* said: "Soon we shall find out whether what you say is true or false.[27]   Go and deliver to them this letter of mine, then turn aside and wait for their answer." [28]   The Queen said: "O my chiefs! A very important letter has been delivered to me;[29]   it is from Sulaimân, and it begins with the name of Allah, the Compassionate, the Merciful.[30]   *It reads*: Do not be arrogant against me and come to me in complete submission *(as Muslims)*."[31]   27:[20-31]

The hoopoe brought him the news about the Queen of Sheba

A letter from King Sulaimân to the Queen of Sheba

SECTION: 3

Then she asked: "O chiefs! Let me hear your advice, for I make no decision without your counsel."[32]   They replied: "We are a valiant and mighty nation. You are the commander. So consider what you will command."[33]   *The queen* said: "When the kings invade a town, they ruin it and debase its honorable people; and thus

Communications between the Queen of Sheba and Sulaimân

they always do.[34] Therefore, I shall send them a present and see with what reply my envoys will return."[35] When the *envoys of the queen* came to Sulaimân, he said: "Do you want to provide me wealth? What Allah has given me is far more than what He has given you. Rather, it is you who exult in your present.[36] Go back to your people: *if your people do not submit,* we will march against them with such an army which they shall never be able to face, and we shall drive them out *of their land* humbled and disgraced."[37]

27:[32-37]

A man who had the 'Knowledge of the Book' brought the Throne of the Queen to king Sulaimân in twinkling of an eye

Later on when Sulaimân (Solomon) heard that the Queen of Sheba was coming in submission, he asked: "O my chiefs! Which of you can bring to me her throne before they come to me in submission?"[38] An powerful one from the Jinns said: "I will bring it to you before you adjourn *your court*; and most surely I have the necessary strength and I am trustworthy."[39] One person who had knowledge of the Book said: "I can bring it to you in the twinkling of an eye." As soon as Sulaimân saw *the throne* placed before him, he exclaimed: "This is by the grace of my Rabb to test me whether I am grateful or ungrateful. Anyone who is grateful, surely his gratitude is a gain for his own soul, and anyone who is ungrateful *should know that* surely, my Rabb is Free of all needs and Generous."[40] Then he said: "Disguise her throne for her so that we may see whether she recognizes it or she is of those who cannot recognize the Truth."[41] So when *the queen* arrived, she was asked: "Is your throne like this?" She replied: "It is just the same; even before *witnessing this miracle of bringing my throne here* we had been given the knowledge *that Sulaimân was not only a king but also a Prophet of Allah,* and we had become Muslims."[42] - Other deities whom she worshiped besides Allah had prevented her *from believing,* for she belonged to an unbelieving folk.[43] - Then she was asked to enter the palace. When she saw its *floor,* she thought it was a pool of water, so she *tucked up her skirts* uncovering her legs. *Sulaimân* said: "it is a palace *whose floor is* smoothly paved with glass." *At this* she exclaimed: "O my Rabb! I have indeed wronged my soul, now I submit myself *in Islam* with Sulaimân to Allah, the Rabb of the Worlds."[44]

27:[38-44]

Queen of Sheba and her people embraced Islam

SECTION: 4

The story of the Prophet Sâleh and his people

To *the people of* Thamûd, We sent their brother Sâleh, *saying*: "Worship Allah," but they divided themselves into two discordant factions.[45] Sâleh said: "O my people! Why do you wish to hasten towards evil rather than good? Why do you not ask forgiveness of Allah so that you may be shown mercy?"[46]　They said: "We consider you and your companions a sign of bad luck." He said: "Your luck is with Allah; in fact, you are a people under trial."[47] There were nine ringleaders in the city who created mischief in the land and reformed nothing.[48]　They said to one another: "Let us pledge, on oath by Allah, that we shall make a secret night attack on him and his family, then we shall tell his guardian that we were not even present at the time his family was killed, and that we are telling the truth."[49]　Thus they plotted a plan, and We too devised a counter plan which they did not perceive.[50]　Just see what was the outcome of their plot! We annihilated them completely, together with all their people.[51]　There lie their houses in desolate ruins as a result of their wrongdoings. Verily in this *story* there is a lesson for those people of knowledge.[52]　Yet, We delivered the true believers who were righteous.[53]　　　　　　　　27:[45-53]

Also mention to them the story of Lût *(Lot)*, when he said to his people: "Do you commit indecency though you see *its iniquity*?[54]　Do you approach men for your sexual desires instead of women? The fact is that you are a people steeped in ignorance."[55]　But his people had no answer except to say: "Drive out the family of Lût from your city. Surely, they are people who would keep chaste."[56]　So, We delivered him and his family except his wife - about whom We had decreed that she shall be of those who will remain behind[57] - and We rained down on them a shower *of brimstones*; and evil was the rain which fell on those who were forewarned.[58]　　　　　　　　27:[54-58]

SECTION: 5

Say: "Praise be to Allah and peace be on His servants whom He has chosen *to deliver His message. Ask them*: " Who is better? Allah or the deities they associate with Him?"[59]　27:[59]

His people plotted to kill him, but Allah saved him and destroyed the disbelievers

The Prophet Lût admonished his people but they paid no heed so they faced the scourge of Allah

Praise to Allah and peace be on His Rasools

JUZ (PART): 20

Just think, is there any god besides Allah Who has created anything in the universe, answers the oppressed or guides to the Right Way?

Is not He *(Allah),* Who has created the heavens and the earth, sends down rain from the sky and with it brings forth the beautiful gardens *not better than the false gods that they worship*? It is not in your ability to cause the growth of trees *for those gardens.* Is there another god besides Allah *who could do that*? No doubt they are people who *have swerved from justice in* ascribing equals *to Him*.[60] *Just think* who has made the earth a place for your residence, caused in it the rivers to flow, set mountains upon it and placed a barrier between the two seas? Is there another god besides Allah? Nay, most of them have no knowledge.[61]   *Just think* who answers the oppressed person when he cries out to Him and relieves his affliction, and makes you, *O mankind,* inheritors of the earth? Is there another god besides Allah? How little do you reflect![62] *Just think* who guides you in darkness on the land and the sea, and who sends the winds as heralds of good news of His mercy? Is there another god besides Allah? Exalted be Allah above what they associate with Him![63]   *Just think* who originates creation and then repeats its production, and who gives you sustenance from the heavens and the earth? Is there another god besides Allah? Say: "Show us your proof if you are telling the truth!"[64]   Say: No one in the heavens or in the earth has the knowledge of the unseen except Allah and they do not know when they shall be raised to life again.[65]   Nay, they have no knowledge of the hereafter. Nay, they are in doubt about it. Rather, they are blind about it![66]

27:[60-66]

SECTION: 6

The disbelievers doubt Allah's power of creation

The unbelievers say: "What! When we and our fathers have become dust, shall we really be raised *from the dead*?[67] This promise which is made to us was also made to our forefathers before us; these are nothing but the legends of prior people."[68] Say: "Travel through the earth and see what has been the end of the criminals."[69]   *O Prophet,* do not worry about them nor feel distressed because of their plots.[70]   They also ask: "When will this promise be fulfilled if what you say is true?"[71]   Say: "It may be that a part of what you wish to hasten is near at hand."[72]   Surely, your Rabb is very gracious to mankind: yet, most of them are ungrateful.[73]   Indeed your Rabb knows what their breasts conceal and what they reveal.[74]   Nor is there any secret in the heaven and the earth which is not recorded in a clear Book.[75]   In fact, this Qur'an clarifies for the Children of Israel most of those matters in which they differ.[76]   It is certainly a guide and blessing to true believers.[77]   Surely, your Rabb will decide between them by His judgement, He is the All-Mighty, the All-Knowing.[78]   Therefore, put your trust in Allah, for you are certainly on the manifest Truth.[79]   The fact is that you cannot make the dead hear you, nor can you make the deaf hear the call especially when they turn their backs and pay no heed,[80]   nor can you guide the blind people to prevent them from straying; none will listen to you except those who believe in Our revelations and become Muslims.[81]   When the time to fulfill Our word comes to pass, We will bring out from the earth a strange creature which will speak to them *about this* that the people did not believe in Our revelations.[82]   27:[67-82]

The Qur'an clarifies those matters in which the Israelites differ

A sign from the signs of Doomsday

SECTION: 7

On that Day We shall gather from every nation a multitude of those who disbelieved Our revelations; then they shall be arranged *in classifications according to their merits*,[83]   until when they have all arrived, *their Rabb* will ask: "Did you deny My revelations without gaining their comprehensive knowledge? If not, what else were you doing?[84]   The sentence will be carried out against them for the consequence of their wrongdoings and they will not be able to utter a word.[85]   Do they not see that We have made the night for them to rest in, and the day to give them light? Surely, there are signs in this for the true believers.[86]

27:[83-86]

Do not deny Allah's revelations without gaining their comprehensive knowledge

On the Day, when the trumpet shall be blown and all who dwell in the heavens and the earth shall be terrified except those whom Allah will choose to spare, and all shall come to Him in utter humiliation.[87]   You shall see the mountains, which you think are firmly fixed, pass away like clouds. Such is the artistry of Allah, Who has perfected all things. He is aware of what you do.[88]   Those who have done good deeds shall be rewarded with what is better and shall be secure from the terror of that Day.[89]   And those who have done evil deeds, shall be flung upon their faces in the Hellfire.

A scene from the Doomsday

Those who accept guidance do so to their own good and those who go astray do so to their own peril

Should you not be rewarded according to your deeds?[90] *O Muhammad,* say to them: "I have been commanded to worship the Rabb of this city *(Makkah)*, the One Who has sanctified it and Who is the Owner of all things; and I am commanded to be of those who are Muslims,[91]　and that I should recite the Qur'an. Now, whoever follows this guidance will be guided for his own good, and to him who goes astray, say: "I am merely one of the Warners."[92] Then proclaim: "Praise be to Allah, very soon He will show you His signs and you will recognize them. Your Rabb is not unaware of what you do."[93]　　　　27:[87-93]

28: AL-QASAS

Period of Revelation

As mentioned in the introduction to Sûrah An-Naml, according to Ibn Abbâs and Jâbir bin Zaid, Sûrahs Ash-Shu'arâ, An-Naml and Al-Qasas were revealed one after the other during the middle stage of the Prophet's residence at Makkah.

Major Issues, Divine Laws, and Guidance

*   The story of Fir'aun (Pharaoh) who plotted to kill all the male children of the Israelites. How Allah saved Musa (peace be upon him) and arranged for him to be brought up in Fir'aun's own household.
*   Youth of Prophet Musa (peace be upon him), his folly of killing a man, his escape to Madyan, his marriage, his seeing a fire at Mount Tûr, and his assignment as a Rasool towards Fir'aun.
*   The stories of prior generations are related in the Qur'an as an eye opener for the disbelievers to learn a lesson.
*   Unbiased Jews and Christians - when they hear the Qur'an, can recognize the Truth and feel that they were Muslims even before hearing it.
*   Guidance is not in the hands of the Prophets; it is Allah Who gives guidance.
*   The fact that on the Day of Judgement, disbelievers will wish that they had accepted guidance and become Muslims.
*   Allah has not allowed the mushrikeen to assign His powers to whom they want.
*   The story of Qaroon, the legendary rich man.
*   Allah says that the revelation of the Qur'an is His mercy; a believer should let no one turn him away from it.

This Sûrah removes the doubts and objections that were being raised against the Prophethood of the Prophet Muhammad (peace be upon him) and invalidates the excuses which the unbelievers had for not believing in him. Then the story of the Prophet Musa (peace be upon him) is related to emphasize that Allah is All-Powerful and can provide the means for whatever He wills to do. He arranged for the child (Musa), through whom Fir'aun was to be removed from power, to be brought up in Fir'aun's own house and he did not know whom he was fostering.

The unbelievers wondered about the Prophet Muhammad (peace be upon him) - how he could be blessed with the Prophethood all of a sudden. This is explained through the example of the Prophet Musa (peace be upon him) who was given the Prophethood unexpectedly during a journey, while he himself did not know what he was going to be blessed with. In fact, he had gone to bring a piece of fire, but returned with the gift of Prophethood.

The unbelievers were wondering why Allah would assign the Prophet Muhammad (peace be upon him) this mission without any special help or supernatural forces to aid him. Again, the example of the Prophet Musa (peace be upon him) is used to explain that a person from whom Allah wants to take some service always appears without any apparent helper or force behind him, yet he can put up with much stronger and better-equipped opponents. The contrast between the strengths of Musa (peace be upon him) and that of Fir'aun is far more extreme than that between Muhammad (peace be upon him) and the Quraish; yet the whole world knows who came out victorious in the end and who was defeated.

The unbelievers were referring to the Prophet Musa (peace be upon him) again and again, saying: "Why has Muhammad not been given the same which was given to Musa (peace be upon him)?" That is to say, the miracles of the Staff and the Shining Hand; as if to suggest that they would readily believe only if they were shown the kind of the miracles that Musa (peace be upon him) showed to Fir'aun. The disbelievers are admonished, that those who were shown those miracles did not believe even after seeing the miracles. Instead they said: "This is nothing but magic," for they were full of stubbornness and hostility to the Truth just like the disbelievers of Makkah. Then a warning is given by citing the fate of those who disbelieved after witnessing those miracles. This was the background against which the story of the Prophet Musa was narrated and a perfect analogy is made in every detail between the conditions then prevailing in Makkah and those which were existing at the time of the Prophet Musa (peace be upon him).

In conclusion, the disbelievers of Makkah are admonished for mistreating those Christians who came to Makkah and embraced Islam after hearing the verses of the Qur'an from the Prophet. Instead of learning a lesson from their acceptance of Islam, the Makkan's leader, Abu Jahl, humiliated them publicly. Then the real reason for not believing in the Prophet is mentioned. The disbelievers were thinking, "If we give up the polytheistic creed of the Arabs and accept the doctrine of Tawheed (Oneness of God), it will be an end to our supremacy in the religious, political and economic fields. As a result, our position as the most influential tribe of Arabia will be destroyed and we shall be left with no refuge anywhere in the land." This was the real motive of the chiefs of the Quraish for their antagonism towards the Truth, and their doubts and objections were only a pretense invented to deceive the common people.

28: AL-QASAS

This Sûrah, revealed at Makkah, has 9 sections and 88 verses.

In the name of Allah, the Compassionate, the Merciful

SECTION: 1

Tâ Seen M'eem.[1] These are the verses of the Book that makes things clear.[2] In all truth, We narrate to you some information about Musa *(Moses)* and Fir'aun *(Pharaoh)* for *the instruction of* the believers.[3] 28:[1-3]

It is a fact that Fir'aun *(Pharaoh)* elevated himself in the land and divided its residents into groups, one group of which he oppressed, putting their sons to death and sparing only their females. Indeed he was one of the mischief-makers.[4] But We wanted to favor those who were oppressed in the land, to make them leaders, to make them the heirs,[5] to establish them in the land and to show Fir'aun, Hâmân and their warriors at their hands the same which they feared.[6] So We inspired the mother of Musa: "Suckle him, and when you feel any danger to his *life*, cast him into the river without any fear or grief; for We shall certainly restore him to you and make him one of Our Rasools."[7] *We made* Fir'aun's family pick him up *from the river: it was intended that Musa* may become their adversary and a cause of their sorrow; surely, Fir'aun, Hâmân and their warriors were all sinners.[8] The wife of Fir'aun said: "This child may become the comfort of the eyes for me and for you. Do not kill him. He may prove useful to us or it may be that we will adopt him as our son." They were unaware *of the result of what they were doing.*[9] *On the other hand*, the heart of Musa's mother was sorely troubled. She would have disclosed as to who he was, had We not strengthened her heart so that she might become one of the true believers.[10] She said to *Musa's* sister: "Go, and follow him." So she *(Musa's sister)* watched him from a distance in such a way that the others did not notice it.[11] We had already ordained that he would refuse to suck *any foster mother*. His sister *came to Fir'aun's wife and* said: "Shall I point out to you a house whose people will take care of him for you and they will be sincere to him?"[12] Thus did We restore him to his mother that her eye might be comforted, that she might not grieve and that she might know that the promise of Allah is true. Yet, most of them do not understand.[13] 28:[4-13]

Story of the Prophet Musa

Fir'aun plotted to kill the sons of the Israelites to save his kingship, while Allah planned to bring up one of them in Fir'aun's own household

SECTION: 2

The Prophet Musa's youth, his folly of killing a man, and his escape from Fir'aun's retribution

When he reached maturity and became full-grown, We bestowed on him wisdom and knowledge. Thus do We reward the righteous.[14]   One day he entered the city at a time when its people were not yet active, he found two men reaching each others throats; one was from his own race and the other of his foes. The man of his own race appealed for his help against his foe, whereupon Musa gave his foe a blow that killed him. *On seeing what he has done* he said: "This is from the work of Shaitân; surely, he is a sworn misleading enemy."[15]   Then he prayed: "O my Rabb! I have indeed wronged my soul, please forgive me." So *Allah* forgave him, surely, He is the Forgiving, the Merciful.[16]   *Musa* said: "O my Rabb! After this favor that You have bestowed on me, I shall never be a helping hand to the criminals."[17]   Next morning as he was walking in the city in fear and caution, suddenly he saw the same man whom he had helped the day before cried out to him again for help. Musa told him: "You are certainly a misguided person."[18] Then when *Musa* was about to lay his hands on a man who was an enemy to both of them, he cried out: "O Musa! Do you intend to kill me as you killed a person yesterday? You only want to become a tyrant in the land and have no intention of reforming anything."[19] *At that time,* there came a man running from the other end of the city and said: "O Musa! The chiefs are plotting to kill you, therefore, run away, surely, I am your well wisher."[20]   Hearing this, Musa left that place in fear and caution, praying: "O my Rabb! Deliver me from the nation of wrongdoers."[21]   28:[14-21]

SECTION: 3

His arrival at Madyan, acceptance of a ten year term of employment, and marriage

As he made his way towards Madyan, he said: "Soon my Rabb shall guide me to the Right Way."[22]   When he arrived at the well of Madyan, he saw a multitude of men watering *their flocks*, and besides them two women who were keeping *their flocks* back. He asked: "What is the problem?" They replied: "We cannot water *our flocks* until the shepherds take away *their flocks from the water, because we are weak* and our father is a very old man."[23]   So he watered *their flocks* for them and went back to the shade and prayed: "O my Rabb! Surely, I am in desperate need of whatever good that You may send down to me."[24]   Soon after that, one of the two women came to him walking bashfully and said: "My father is calling you. He wishes to reward you for watering *our flocks* for us." When *Musa* came to him and narrated his story, the *old man* said: "Have no fear. You have escaped from those wicked people."[25] One of them said: "Father, hire him. The best that one can hire is a man who is strong and trustworthy."[26] *The old man* said *to Musa*: "I am willing to give you one of my daughters in marriage if you stay in my service for eight years; but if you make it ten if would be gracious of you; for I do not want to impose any hardship on you; Allah willing, you will find me one of the righteous."[27] *Musa* replied: "So be it *an agreement* between me and you. Whichever of the two terms I complete, let there be no compulsion on me. Allah is the surety over what we have agreed upon."[28]   28:[22-28]

SECTION: 4

After completing the term *of his agreement*, when Musa *(Moses)* was travelling with his family, he saw a fire in the direction of Mount Tûr. He said to his family: "Stay here, I saw a fire and I hope to bring some information from there or a lighted torch with which you may warm yourselves."[29] But when he reached there, a voice called out to him from the right side of the valley of the blessed spot from the tree , saying: "O Musa, surely, I am Allah, the Rabb of the Worlds."[30] *Then Allah commanded,* "Throw down your staff." When *Musa* saw that *the staff* was writhing like a snake, he turned his back and fled, and did not even look back. *Allah said,* "O Musa, come back and do not fear; you are quite safe.[31] Now put your hand into your pocket: it will come out shining white without any harm to you - draw your hand towards yourself to ward off fear - these are two credentials from your Rabb towards Fir'aun and his chiefs, surely, they are wicked people."[32] *Musa* submitted: "O my Rabb! I have killed one of them: I fear that they will put me to death.[33] My brother Haroon *(Aaron)*, is more eloquent in speech than I: send him with me as a helper to confirm my words; I fear that they will treat me as a liar."[34] *Allah* replied: "We will certainly strengthen you with your brother and give both of you such authority that they shall not be able to harm you. With Our signs you two as well as those who follow you will surely triumph."[35]   28:[29-35]

His arrival at Mount Tûr, seeing a fire, conversation with Allah, and his appointment as a Rasool to Fir'aun and his chiefs

When Musa *(Moses)* came to them *(Fir'aun and his chiefs)* with Our clear signs *and invited them to Islam*, they said: "This is nothing but baseless sorcery; we never heard such a thing in the

Fir'aun and his chiefs disbelieved;

as a result, Allah destroyed them but saved the Children of Israel

time of our forefathers."[36]　　Musa stated: "My Rabb knows best who it is that comes with guidance from Him and who will gain the reward of the hereafter; surely, the wrongdoers will not attain felicity."[37]　　Fir'aun said: "O Chiefs! You have no other god that I know of, except myself. O Hâmân! Bake for me bricks from clay and build me a high tower so that I may climb it to see the God of Musa; most surely, I think him to be one of the liars."[38]　　He and his warriors were arrogant in the land without any right; they thought that they would never be brought back to Us.[39]　　So We seized him and his warriors, and flung them into the sea. See what was the end of wrongdoers?[40]　　We made them leaders who started calling people to hellfire, but on the Day of Resurrection they will not get any help.[41]　　We laid a curse on them in this world, and on the Day of Resurrection they will be of the despised.[42]

28:[36-42]

SECTION: 5

Information about the destruction of prior generations is given to teach a lesson

We gave Musa *(Moses)* the Book　*(Torah),* after We had destroyed the former generations, an eye opener, a guide, and a blessing so that they may be reminded.[43]　　*O Muhammad,* you were not present on the western side *of the mountain* when We gave Musa the Law, nor did you witness that event.[44]　　But We raised many generations and a long time has passed over them; you were not living among the people of Madyan, reciting to them Our revelations; but it is We Who are sending to you *the news of that time.*[45]　　Nor were you at the side *of the mountain* of Tûr when We called out *to Musa*, but it is your Rabb's mercy *that you are being given this information* so that you may forewarn a nation to whom no Warner had come before you. Maybe they will take heed,[46]　　so that they may not be able to say, when a disaster befalls them on account of their misdeeds: "Our Rabb, had You sent us a Rasool, we would have followed Your revelations and would have been among the believers."[47]　　Now that the Truth has come to them from Us, they are saying: "Why is he *(Muhammad)* not given the like of what was given to Musa?" Have they not rejected that which was given to Musa before? They claim: "These *(Torah and Qur'an)* are the two works of sorcery complementing each other!" And they say: "We disbelieve in both."[48]　　Ask them: "Bring a Book from Allah which is a better guide than these two, I will follow it, if what you say be true!"[49]　　So, if they do not meet this demand, you should know that they only follow their own desires. And who is more misguided than the one who follows his own desires without any guidance from Allah? In fact, Allah does not guide such wrongdo-ing people.[50]   28:[43-50]

SECTION: 6

We have conveyed Our Word to them over and over again in order that they may take heed.[51]   Those to whom the scriptures were given before this *(Jews and Christians)*, they do *recognize the Truth and* believe in this *(Qur'an)*.[52]   When it is recited to them they say: "We believe in it, surely, this is the Truth from our Rabb: indeed we were Muslims even before this."[53]   They are the ones who will be given their reward twice, because they have endured with fortitude, repelling evil with good and giving in charity out of what We have given them.[54]   When they hear vain talk, they withdraw from it saying: "Our deeds are for us and yours for you; peace be on you: we do not desire the way of the ignorant."[55]
           28:[51-55]

Righteous Jews and Christians can recognize the truth of The Qur'an and feel that they were Muslims even before hearing it

O Prophet, you cannot give guidance to whom you wish, it is Allah Who gives guidance to whom He pleases, and He is quite aware of those who are guided.[56]   *Those who do not wish to be guided* say: "If we go along with you and accept this guidance, we shall be driven out from our land." But have We not given them a secure sanctuary to which are brought the fruits of all kinds as a provision from Us? But most of them have no knowledge.[57]   How many towns have We destroyed which once flourished in their economy? Just see those dwellings of theirs, only a few of which have been inhabited after them; at last We Alone became *their* inheritors.[58]   Your Rabb would never destroy the towns until He had sent in their mother town a Rasool, reciting to them Our revelations; and We would not destroy towns except when their dwellers had become wrongdoers.[59]   The things which you have been given are but the provisions and adornments of this worldly life; and that which is with Allah is better and more lasting. Have you no common sense?[60]   28:[52-60]

Prophets cannot give guidance; it is Allah who gives guidance

SECTION: 7

Can a person to whom We have made an excellent promise and he is sure to receive it, be like the one to whom We have only given the provisions of this world and he is scheduled to be presented on the Day of Resurrection *for punishment*?[61]   *Let them*

On the Day of Judgement, the disbelievers will wish that they had

accepted Guidance

not forget that Day when We shall call them and ask: "Where are those whom you deemed to be My associates?"[62]   Those who are proven guilty as charged, will say: "Our Rabb! These are the ones whom we led astray; we led them astray as we were astray ourselves. However, we declare our innocence *from them* before You; it was not us that they worshipped."[63]   Then they will be told: "Call your shorakâ' *(associate gods),"* so they will call them, but will get no answer. They will see the punishment and wish if only they had followed the guidance.[64]   *Let them also not forget that,* on that Day, He will call them and ask: "How did you answer Our Rasools?"[65]   They will be so confused on that Day that they will not even ask one another.[66]   However, the one who has repented in this life, and believed, and done good deeds may hope to be among those who will achieve salvation.[67]   28:[61-67]

Allah has not allowed the mush-rikeen to assign His powers to whom-ever they want

Your Rabb creates whatever He wills and chooses *for His work* whom He pleases. It is not for them *(mushrikeen)* to choose *and assign the powers of Allah to whom they want.* Glory be to Allah! He is far above the shirk that these people commit.[68]   Your Rabb knows all that they conceal in their hearts and all that they reveal.[69]   He is Allah; there is no god but He. Praise belongs to Him in this world and in the hereafter: His is the Judgement and to Him you all shall be brought back.[70]   *O Prophet,* ask them: "Have you ever considered that if Allah makes the night perpetual till the Day of Resurrection, which deity other than Allah could bring you light?" Will you not listen?[71]   Ask them again: "Have you ever considered that if Allah makes the day perpetual till the Day of Resurrection, which deity other than Allah could bring you the night in which you could rest? Will you not see?[72]   It is out of His mercy that He has made for you the night during which you may rest, and the day during which you may seek His bounty, and that you may render thanks.[73]   *They should be mindful of* that Day when He will call them and ask: "Where are those deities whom you deemed My associates?"[74]   And We shall bring forth a witness from every nation and ask: "Bring your proof *about other deities besides Me.*" Then they shall come to know that in reality *there is only One God*, Allah, and *that the gods of* their own inventions have left them in the lurch."[75]   28:[68-75]

SECTION: 8

It is a fact is that Qaroon *(Korah)* was one of Musa's people, but he rebelled against them. We had given him such treasures that their very keys were a heavy burden to a band of strong men. When his people said to him: "Do not exult, for Allah does not love the exultant.[76]   Rather seek, by means of what Allah has given you, to attain the abode of the hereafter, while not neglecting your share in this world. Be good to others as Allah has been good to you, and do not seek mischief in the land, for Allah does not love the mischiefmongers."[77]   He replied: "All that I have been given is by virtue of the knowledge that I possess." Did he *(Qaroon)* not know that Allah had destroyed many people before, who were mightier in strength and greater in riches than him? But the criminals will not be asked about their sins *because Allah knows them well*.[78] *One day* he came out before his people in his worldly glitter, those who sought the life of this world said: "Ah! Would that we had the like of Qaroon's fortune! He is indeed a very lucky man."[79]   But those who were endowed with knowledge said: "Alas for you! Better is the reward of Allah for him that has faith and does good deeds; but none shall attain it except those who endured with fortitude."[80] Then We caused the earth to swallow him, together with his dwelling, and he had no host to help him against Allah; nor was he able to defend himself.[81]   Now the same people who wished for a position like his, the day before, began to say: "Alas! *We had forgotten that* it is indeed Allah Who enlarges the provision for whom He wills of His servants and restricts it *from whom He pleases*. If Allah had not been gracious to us, He could have caused the earth to swallow us too. Alas! *We did not remember that* the disbelievers never attain felicity."[82]   28:[76-82]

Story of Qaroon, the rich man, who was from the people of Musa but he rebelled against the guidance of Allah

SECTION: 9

As for the abode of the Hereafter, We have reserved it for those who seek neither exaltation nor corruption in the earth; the ultimate good is for the righteous.[83]   Anyone who brings a good deed shall have something even better; while anyone who brings an evil deed *will find* that those who perform evil deeds will be punished only to the extent of their deeds.[84]   O Prophet, rest assured that He Who charged you with the Qur'an, will bring you back to the best end. Say: "My Rabb best knows him who has brought guidance and him who is in manifest error."[85]   You *(O Muhammad)* never expected that the Book would be revealed to you. Only through your Rabb's mercy *has it been revealed to you*: therefore do not be a helper in any way to the unbelievers.[86]   Let no one turn you away from the revelations of Allah now that they

Revelation of the Qur'an is the mercy of Allah, let no one turn you away from it

have been revealed to you. Invite people to your Rabb and be not of the mushrikeen *(who join other deities with Allah).*[87] Invoke no other god besides Allah. There is none worthy of worship but He. Everything will be destroyed except His Face. To Him belongs the judgement and to Him will you all be returned.[88]

28:[83-88]

29: AL-'ANKABÛT

Period of Revelation

This Sûrah was revealed shortly before the Muslims' migration to Habash, the middle stage of the Prophet's residence at Makkah, when there was extreme persecution of the Muslims.

Major Issues, Divine Laws, and Guidance

* Allah tests the Believers to see who is truthful and who is a liar.
* Be kind to parents but do not obey them in the matters of shirk (associating anyone else with Allah).
* Those who say: "Follow us, we will bear your burden on the Day of Judgement," are liars.
* The Prophet Nûh admonished his people for 950 years not to commit shirk.
* The Prophet Ibrâheem admonished his people not to commit shirk, for which they tried to burn him alive, but Allah saved him.
* The Nations of 'Ad, Thamûd, Madyan and Fir'aun rejected the Rasools of Allah, as a result Allah destroyed them all.
* Parable of those who take protectors other than Allah, is that of the dwelling of a spider and in fact the weakest of all the dwellings is the dwelling of a spider.

This Sûrah strengthens the faith of sincere Muslims and admonishes those who were showing weakness in their faith. This Sûrah also addresses those questions which some young men were facing in those days, whose parents were urging them to abandon Islam and return to their ancestral religion.

The Muslims are instructed: "If you feel that the persecution has become unbearable for you, you should give up your homes instead of giving up your faith. Allah's earth is vast: seek a new place where you can worship Allah with full peace of mind."

The disbelievers are urged to understand Islam. The realities of Tawheed (Oneness of God) and the Hereafter are presented with rational arguments, shirk is refuted, and their attention is drawn towards the signs in the universe; they are told that all these signs conform to the teachings of the Prophet Muhammad (peace be upon him).

29: AL-'ANKABÛT

This Sûrah, revealed at Makkah, has 7 sections and 69 verses.

In the name of Allah, the Compassionate, the Merciful

SECTION: 1

Allah tests the believers to see, who is truthful and who is a liar?

Alif Lâm M'eem.[1]　Do people think that they will be left alone on saying "We believe," and that they will not be tested?[2] We did test those who have gone before them. Allah has to see *(for the purpose of reward and punishment)* who are the truthful and who are the liars.[3]　Or do the evildoers think that they will escape from Our reach? How bad is their judgment![4]　He that hopes to meet Allah must know that Allah's appointed time is sure to come and He hears all and knows all.[5]　He that strives, does that for his own soul; for Allah is certainly transcendent and beyond any need of the worlds.[6]　As for those who believe and do good deeds, We shall cleanse them of their sins and We shall reward them according to the best of their deeds.[7]　　　　29:[1-7]

Be kind to your parents but do not obey them in the matter of shirk

We have enjoined man to show kindness to his parents; but if they *(your parents)* force you to commit shirk with Me, of which you have no knowledge, do not obey them. To Me is your return and I will inform you of what you have done.[8]　Those who have accepted the true faith and do good deeds shall be admitted among the righteous.[9]　There are some among people, who say: "We believe in Allah;" yet, when they suffer in the cause of Allah they confuse the persecution of people with the punishment of Allah. But when there comes help *in the shape of a victory* from your Rabb, they are sure to say: "We have always been with you." Is not Allah fully aware of what is in the hearts of the people of the world.[10]　Most surely, Allah will make known those who believe, and those who are the hypocrites.[11]　The unbelievers say to the

Those who say, "Follow us we will bear your burden," are liars

believers: "Follow us, and we will bear the burden of your sins." But they will not bear any burden of their sins; they are surely lying.[12]　Of course, they shall bear their own burdens as well as the burdens of others in addition to their own; and on the Day of Resurrection they shall be questioned about their invented lies.[13]

29:[8-13]

SECTION: 2

We sent Nûh *(Noah)* to his people and he lived among them

a thousand years less fifty. Then because of their wrongdoings the flood overtook them.[14]   But We delivered him and all who were in the ark and We made that *ark* a sign for the peoples of the world.[15]   *Likewise* Ibrâheem *(Abraham)*, when he said to his people: "Worship Allah and fear Him; this is better for you if you understand.[16]   You worship idols besides Allah and fabricate falsehood. In fact, those whom you worship besides Allah have no power to give you your sustenance; therefore, seek your sustenance from Allah, worship Him, and give thanks to Him; to Him you shall be returned.[17]   If you deny *the Message*, then nations have denied before you . The only duty a Rasool has is to deliver *Allah's Message* clearly."[18]   Do they not see how Allah originates creation then repeats its process? Surely, it is easy for Allah.[19] Say *to them*: "Travel through the earth and see how Allah originated the creation; then will recreate life. Surely, Allah has power over everything.[20]   He punishes whom He wills and shows mercy to whom He pleases; and to Him you shall be turned back.[21] You can neither make *Him* helpless in the earth nor in the Heaven; nor have you any protector or helper besides Allah."[22]

29:[14-22]

SECTION: 3

As for those who disbelieve Allah's revelations and deny that they will ever meet Him, they are the ones who shall despair of My mercy and they are the ones for whom there shall be a painful punishment.[23]   The people *of Ibrâheem (Abraham)* had no answer except to say: "Kill him!" Or "Burn him!" But Allah saved him from the fire *when they tried to burn him.* Surely, in this incident, there are signs for those who believe.[24]   *Ibrâheem* addressed them: "Today you have made idols, instead of Allah, a means of affection among yourselves in this worldly life, *but,* on the Day of Resurrection you shall disown and curse one another. Fire shall be your abode and you shall have no helper."[25] *Witnessing this whole incident,* Lût *(Lot)* believed in him *(Ibrâheem). Finally Ibrâheem* said: "I will migrate towards my Rabb *(go where my Rabb has bidden me).* He is the One Who is the Mighty, the Wise."[26]   We gave him Ishâq *(Isaac - a son)* and Ya'qoob *(Jacob - a grandson),* and placed the Prophethood and the Book in his progeny - thus We gave him his reward in this life, and in the hereafter he will surely be among the righteous.[27]

29:[23-27]

When Lût *(Lot)* said to his people: "Surely, you are

Nûh admonished his people for 950 years not to commit shirk. Likewise, Ibrâheem admonished his people not to commit shirk.

The people of Ibrâheem even tried to burn him alive but Allah saved him

Ibrâheem's nephew Lût was the only one who affirmed his belief with him

The Prophet Lût was appointed as a Rasool towards the nation of homosexuals

committing such sexual misconduct as no one in the worlds has ever attempted before you.[28]   Do you lust after males, cut off the highway and commit evil deeds even in your assemblies?" His people had no answer except to say: "Bring us the scourge of Allah if you are truthful."[29]   *Lût* prayed: "O my Rabb! Help me against this corrupt nation."[30]   29:[28-30]

SECTION: 4

They rejected Allah's guidance; as a result Allah destroyed them all

When Our Messengers *(angels)* came to Ibrâheem *(Abraham)* with the good news *(the birth of a son in his old age)*, they said: "We are to destroy the people of that township, for its people are indeed wrongdoers."[31]   *Ibrâheem* said: "But Lût is in there." The *angels* replied: "We know who is in there: we shall certainly save him and his family, except his wife, who will remain behind!"[32]   And when Our Messengers *(angels)* came to Lût, he became sad and anxious on their account, for he felt powerless *to protect them*. But they said "Do not fear nor grieve *(we are the angels assigned for their torment)*: we shall save you and your family except your wife; she will be of those who will remain behind.[33] We are going to bring down a scourge from heaven upon the people of this town on account of their transgression."[34] Surely, We have left a clear sign from it *(the ruins of this town)* for people who care to understand.[35]   29:[31-35]

Likewise the Nations of 'Ad, Thamûd, Madyan and Fir'aun rejected the Rasools of Allah, which resulted in their destruction

To *the people of* Madyan, *We sent* their brother Shu'aib, who said: "O my people! Worship Allah and look forward to the Last Day, and do not transgress in the land wickedly."[36]   But they denied him, so a severe earthquake seized them and they lay dead, prostrate in their dwellings.[37]   *Likewise, We destroyed the people of* 'Ad and the Thamûd: you have seen the traces of their dwellings. Shaitân had made their foul deeds fair-seeming to them and diverted them from the *Right* Way, though they were intelligent people.[38]   *Also remember* Qaroon *(Korah)*, Fir'aun *(Pharaoh)* and Hâmân. Indeed Musa *(Moses)* came to them with clear signs but they remained arrogant in the land; yet, they could not overreach *(escape Our punishment)*.[39]   We seized all of them for their sinfulness: against some We sent a violent tornado full of stones, some were seized by a mighty blast, some were swallowed up by the earth, and yet, some We drowned. It was not Allah Who was unjust to them, but they were unjust to their own souls.[40]

29:[36-40]

The parable of those who take protectors other than Allah is that of a spider who builds for itself a dwelling, and surely, the weakest of all dwellings is the dwelling of a spider - if they only knew.[41]   Surely, Allah knows whatever they invoke besides Him; He is the All-Mighty, the Wise.[42]   These are the parables that We cite for mankind; but none will grasp them except those who have knowledge.[43]   Allah has created the heavens and the earth to manifest the Truth. Surely, in this there is a sign for the believers.[44]

29:[41-44]

The parable of those who take protectors other than Allah

JUZ (PART): 21

SECTION: 5

Salah (Prayers) keeps one away from shameful deeds

Recite from this Book *(the Qur'an)* which has been revealed to you and establish Salah *(Islamic prayers)*. Surely, Salah keeps one away from shameful and evil deeds; and surely, the remembrance of Allah *(in response Allah's mention of your name in front of the angels)* is the greatest indeed, Allah knows what you do.[45]   Do not argue with the People of the Book except in good manner - except with those who are wicked among them - and say:

Do not argue with the People of the Book except in good taste

"We believe in that which is sent down to us and that which is sent down to you; our God and your God is the same One God *(Allah)*, to Him we submit *as Muslims.*"[46]   O Prophet, We have sent down this Book to you *(similar to that of Musa and Isa)*. So the People of the Book believe in it, and so do some of these *(people of Arabia)*: and none but unbelievers deny Our revelations.[47]   *O Muhammad*, you have never read a book before this nor have you ever transcribed one with your right hand. In that case, the quibblers could suspect it.[48]   Rather, these are clear signs in the breast of those who are endowed with knowledge: and none deny Our signs except the wrongdoers.[49]   They ask: "Why have the signs not been sent down to him from his Rabb?" Tell them: "The signs are in the hands of Allah. I am only a plain Warner."[50]   Is it not enough for them that We have sent down to you this Book *(the Qur'an)* which is recited to them; surely, in it is a blessing and a reminder for those who believe.[51]   29:[45-51]

SECTION: 6

Those who believe in falsehood and disbelieve Allah shall be the losers

Tell them: "Allah is sufficient as a witness between me and you - for He knows all that is in the heavens and the earth - those who believe in falsehood and disbelieve Allah, it is they who shall be the losers."[52]   They challenge you to hasten the scourge on them. Had a time not been fixed for it, the scourge would have already come to them. It is going to come suddenly and catch them unawares.[53]   They challenge you to hasten the scourge, whereas hell will surely encircle the unbelievers.[54]   On that Day the punishment shall cover them from above and from beneath their feet, and *Allah* will say: "Now taste the reward of your deeds."[55] O My servants who have believed! Surely, My earth is spacious *to migrate if needed,* therefore, worship Me *and Me Alone*.[56]   Every soul shall taste death, then to Us you shall all return.[57]   Those who embrace true faith and do good deeds shall be lodged in the mansions of paradise beneath which rivers flow, to live therein forever. What an excellent reward for the doers *of good deeds*;[58] the ones who have shown patience and put their trust in their Rabb.[59]   How many creatures are there that do not carry their provisions with them? Allah provides for them as He provides for you, and He is All-hearing, All-knowing.[60]   If you ask the disbelievers as to who has created the heavens and the earth, and subjected the sun and the moon *to His laws*? They will certainly say: "Allah!" How are they then being deluded away *from the truth?*[61]   Allah gives abundantly to whom He pleases and sparingly to whom He wills;   surely, Allah has knowledge of all things.[62]   And if you ask them who sends down rainwater from the sky and thereby raises the dead land back to life?" They will certainly say: "Allah!"   Say, "Praise be to Allah!"   Yet, most of them do not use their common sense.[63]   29:[52-63]

SECTION: 7

The life of this world is nothing but a pastime and play! It is the life of the hereafter that is the real life, if they but knew it.[64]   If they embark on a ship, *and the ship gets into trouble,* they call upon Allah, being sincerely obedient to Him; but when He brings them safely to land, they start committing shirk *(giving credit for their safe arrival to others);*[65]   so that they may show ingratitude for the blessing that We have bestowed on them and enjoy *the life of this world*! They will soon come to know *the result of this behavior.*[66]   Do they not see that We have made *Makkah* a secure sanctuary for them, while the people are being snatched away from all around them? Do they still believe in falsehood and deny the blessings of Allah?[67]   And who is more wicked than the one who forges a lie against Allah or rejects the Truth when it reaches him? Is not the hell a fitting abode for such disbelievers?[68]   As for those who strive in Our cause, We will surely guide them to Our ways; surely, Allah is with the righteous.[69]   29:[64-69]

How many creatures are there who do not carry their provisions with them?   Allah provides them as He provides you

The life of this world is nothing but pastime, the real life is the life hereafter

Those who strive in Our cause, We do guide them to Our Way

30: AR-RÛM

Period of Revelation

This Sûrah was revealed in 615 CE, the year when the Romans were completely overpowered by the Persians, during the time of the Prophet's residence at Makkah. This was the same year in which the Prophet gave permission to the oppressed Muslims to migrate to Habsha.

Major Issues, Divine Laws and Guidance:

* The Roman's (Christian's) defeat at the hands of Persians (pagans) was considered by Makkan's a sign of the Muslim's defeat at the hands of Arab unbelievers.
* Prophecy of the Roman's victory against Persians and the Muslims victory against the disbelievers.
* Allah has originated the creation and He will resurrect the dead for final judgement.
* Creation of Man, his Consort, Heaven, Earth, Language, Colors, Sleep, Quest for work, Lightning, Rain and Growth of vegetation - all are signs from Allah.
* Wrongdoers are those who are led by their own desires without real knowledge.
* True Faith vs. Sects and shirk.
* Commandment to give relatives their due and take care of the poor and travellers in need.
* Mischief in the land is due to Man's own misdeeds.
* Allah tells the Prophet: "O Prophet! You can not make the dead hear you."

Condition of Human Society at that time:

The prediction made in the initial verses of this Sûrah is one of the most outstanding evidences of the Qur'an being the Word of Allah. Research scholar Abul A'lâ Maudûdi narrated the historical background relevant to this Sûrah as follows:

"Eight years before the Prophet's advent as a Prophet, the Byzantine Emperor Maurice was overthrown by Phocus, who captured the throne and became king. Phocus first had the Emperor's five sons executed in front of him, and then had the Emperor killed and hung their heads in a thoroughfare in Constantinople. A few days after this, he had the empress and her three daughters also put to death. This *event provided Khusrau Parvez, the Sassâni king of Persia; a good moral excuse to attack Byzantine. Emperor Maurice had been his benefactor; with his help he had got the throne of Persia. Therefore, he declared that he would avenge his godfather's and his children's murder upon Phocus. So, he started a war against the Byzantine in 603 CE and within a few years, putting the Phocus armies to rout in succession, he reached Edessa (presently known as Urfa) in Asia Minor, on the one front, and Aleppo and Antioch in Syria, on the other. When the Byzantine ministers saw that Phocus could not save the country, they sought the African governor's help, who sent his son, Hercules, to Constantinople with a strong fleet. Phocus was immediately deposed and Hercules was made emperor. He treated Phocus as he had treated Maurice. This happened in 610 CE, the year the Prophet was appointed to the Prophethood.*

The moral excuse for which Khusrau Parvez had started the war was no more valid after the deposition and death of Phocus. Had the object of his war really been to avenge the murder of his ally on Phocus for his cruelty, he would have come to terms with the new Emperor after the death of Phocus. But he continued the war, and gave it the color of a crusade between Zoroastrianism and Christianity. The sympathies of the Christian sects (i. e. Nestorians and Jacobians, etc.) which had been excommunicated by the Roman ecclesiastical authority and tyrannized for years also went with the Magian (Zoroastrian) invaders, and the Jews also joined hands with them; so much so that the number of Jews who enlisted in Khusrau's army rose to 26,000.

Hercules could not stop this storm. The very first news that he received from the East after ascending the throne was that of the Persian's occupation of Antioch. After this, Damascus fell in 613 CE. Then in 614, the Persians occupying Jerusalem, played havoc with the Christian world. Ninety thousand Christians were massacred and the Holy Sepulchre was desecrated. The Original Cross on which, according to Christian beliefs, Jesus had died, was seized and carried to Mada'in. The chief priest Zacharia was taken prisoner and all the important churches of the city were destroyed. How puffed up was Khusrau Parvez at this victory can be judged from the letter that he wrote to Hercules from Jerusalem. He wrote: "From Khusrau, the greatest of all gods, the master of the whole world: To Hercules, his most wretched and most stupid servant: 'You say that you have trust in your Lord. Why didn't then your Lord save Jerusalem from me?"

Within a year after this victory, the Persian armies overran Jordan, Palestine and the whole of the Sinai Peninsula and reached the frontiers of Egypt. In those very days, another conflict of a far greater historical consequence was going on in Makkah. The believers in One God, under the leadership of the Prophet

Muhammad (may Allah's peace be upon him), were fighting for their existence against the followers of shirk under the command of the chiefs of the Quraish, and the conflict had reached such a stage that in 615 CE, a substantial number of the Muslims had to leave their homes and take refuge with the Christian kingdom of Habsha, which was an ally of the Byzantine Empire. In those days the Sassâni victories against Byzantine were the talk of the town, and the pagans of Makkah were delighted and were taunting the Muslims to the effect: "Look the fire worshippers of Persia are winning victories and the Christian believers in Revelation and Prophethood are being routed everywhere. Likewise, we, the idol worshippers of Arabia, will exterminate you and your religion."

These were the conditions when this Sûrah of the Qur'an was sent down, and in it, a prediction was made, saying: "The Romans have been vanquished in the neighboring land and within a few years after their defeat, they shall be victorious. And it will be the day when the believers will rejoice in the victory granted by Allah." It contained not one but two predictions: First, the Romans shall be Victorious; and second, the Muslims also shall win a victory at the same time. Apparently, there was not a remote chance of the fulfillment of either prediction in the next few years. On the one hand, there were a handful of the Muslims, who were being beaten and tortured in Makkah, and even till eight years after this prediction there appeared no chance of their victory and domination. On the contrary, the Romans were losing more and more ground every day. By 619 CE the whole of Egypt had passed into Sassâni hands and the Magian armies had reached as far as Tripoli. In Asia Minor they beat and pushed back the Romans to Bosporus, and in 617 CE they captured Chalcedony (modern, Kadikoy) just opposite Constantinople. The Emperor sent an envoy to Khusrau, praying that he was ready to have peace on any terms, but he replied, "I shall not give protection to the emperor until he is brought in chains before me and gives up obedience to his crucified god and adopts submission to the fire god." At last, the Emperor became so depressed by defeat that he decided to leave Constantinople and shift to Carthage (modern, Tûnis). In short, as the British historian Gibbon says, even seven to eight years after this prediction of the Qur'an, the conditions were such that no one could even imagine that the Byzantine Empire would ever gain an upper hand over Persia, not to speak of gaining domination. No one could hope that the Empire, under the circumstances, would even survive.

When these verses of the Qur'an were sent down, the disbelievers of Makkah made great fun of them, and Ubayy bin Khalaf bet Sayyidunâ Abu Bakr ten camels that the Romans would not be victorious within three years. When the Prophet came to know of the bet, he said, "The Qur'an has used the words bid-i-sineen, and the word bid in Arabic applies to a number up to ten. Therefore, make *the bet for ten years and increase the number of camels to one hundred." So, Sayyidunâ Abu Bakr spoke to Ubayy again and bet a hundred camels for ten years.*

In 622 CE, when the Prophet migrated to Madinah, the Emperor Hercules set off quietly for Trabzon from Constantinople via the Black Sea and started preparations to attack Persia from the rear. For this he asked the Church for money, and Pope Sergius lent him the Church collections on interest, in a bid to save Christianity from Zoroastrianism. Hercules started his counter attack in 623 CE from Armenia. Next year, in 624 CE, he entered Âzerbaijân and destroyed Clorumia, the birthplace of Zoroaster, and ravaged the principal fire temple of Persia. Great are the powers of Allah, this was the very year when the Muslims achieved a decisive victory at Badr for the first time against the mushrikeen (Quraish). Thus, both the predictions made in Sûrah Rum were fulfilled simultaneously within the stipulated period of ten years.

The Byzantine forces continued to press the Persians hard and in the decisive battle at Nineveh, (627 CE) they dealt them the hardest blow. They captured the royal residence of Dast-Gerd, and then pressing forward, reached right opposite to Ctesiphon, which was the capital of Persia in those days. In 628 CE, in an internal revolt, Khusrau Parvez was imprisoned and 18 of his sons were executed in front of him and a few days later, he himself died in prison. This was the year when the peace treaty of Hudaibiyah was concluded, which the Qur'an has termed as "the supreme victory," and in this very year Khusrau's son, Qubâd II, gave up all the occupied Roman territories, restored the True Cross and made peace with Byzantine. In 628 CE, the Emperor himself went to Jerusalem to instal the "Cross" in its place, and in the same year the Prophet entered Makkah for the first time after the Hijrah to perform the Umrah-tul-Q'adah.

After this, no one could have any doubt about the truth of the prophecy of the Qur'an, with the result that most of the Arab polytheists accepted Islam. The heirs of Ubayy bin Khalaf lost their bet and had to give one hundred camels to Sayyidunâ Abu Bakr Siddeeq. He took them before the Prophet, who ordered that they be given away in charity, because the bet had been made at a time when gambling had not yet been forbidden by the Qur'an; but now it had been forbidden. Therefore, the bet was allowed to be accepted from the belligerent disbelievers, but instructed to be given away in charity and should not be brought in personal use."

30: AR-RÛM

This Sûrah revealed at Makkah, has 6 sections and 60 verses.

In the name of Allah, the Compassionate, the Merciful

SECTION: 1

The Roman's (Christians') defeat at the hands of the Persians (Pagans) was taken as a sign of the Muslims' defeat at the hands of Arab unbelievers, so Allah gave good tidings for the Roman victory as well as the Muslim victory in a few years

Alif Lâm M'eem.[1]　The Romans have been defeated *(by the Persians, in Syria - A.D. 615; the Prophet Muhammad's sympathies were with the Romans who were Christians, while the pagan Arabs were on the side of the Persians who were idol worshippers)*[2]　in the nearer land *(Syria, Iraq, Jordan and Palestine)*, but after this defeat, they will soon be victorious[3]　within a few years. The decision *of all matters* lies with Allah before and after *these events*. On that day the believers will rejoice[4]　for *the victory of the Romans as well as their own victory against the pagans with* the help of Allah. He helps whom He pleases and He is the All-Mighty, the Most Merciful.[5]　This is the promise of Allah and Allah never breaks His promise; but most people do not know.[6]　They only know the outward show of this world's life, but they are heedless about the life to come.[7]　Have they not considered in their own creation and that Allah created the heavens and the earth and all that lies between them for a just reason, and for a specified time? But *the truth is that* many among mankind do not believe in the meeting with their Rabb *(the Day of Resurrection)!*[8] Have they not traveled through the earth and seen what was the end of those before them? They were superior in strength than these; they tilled the soil and populated it more than these *pagans* have done. There came to them their Rasools with clear signs *(but they rejected them at the expense of their own destruction)*: it was not Allah Who wronged them, but they wronged their own souls.[9]　Then evil was the outcome for those who committed evil for they rejected the revelations of Allah and kept ridiculing them![10]　　　　　30:[1-10]

SECTION: 2

It is Allah Who originates creation and then repeats it and to Him everyone will be brought for the final Judgement

It is Allah Who originates creation; then repeats it, and then to Him you shall be brought back.[11]　On the Day when the Hour *of Judgement* will be established, the criminals shall be in despair.[12] None of their shorakâ' *(gods which they had set up besides Allah)*, will be there to intercede for them and they themselves will disown their shorakâ'.[13]　　On that Day when the Hour *of Judgement* will be established, *mankind* will be sorted out.[14]　Those who have embraced the faith and have done good deeds shall be made happy in a garden *of paradise.*[15]　　And those who have rejected Faith, denied Our revelations and the meeting of the hereafter shall be presented for punishment.[16]   Therefore, glory be to Allah in the evening and in the morning[17] - all praise is due to Him in the heavens and the earth - so *glorify Him* in the late afternoon and when the day begins to decline.[18] He brings out the living from the dead and the dead from the living, and gives life to the earth after its death. Likewise you shall be brought forth *to life after your death.*[19]   30:[11-19]

SECTION: 3

Of His signs is that He created you from dust and there you are: people scattered *throughout the earth.*[20]   And of His signs is that He created for you mates from among yourselves that you may find comfort with them, and He planted love and mercy *for each other* in your hearts; surely, there are signs in this for those who think about it.[21] And also of His signs are the creation of the heavens and the earth, and the difference of your languages and colors; surely, there are signs in this for the knowledgeable.[22]   And among His signs is your sleep at night and quest for His bounty during the day; surely, there are signs in this for those who listen.[23]   And of His signs is the showing of lightning, in which there is fear as well as hope; and He sends down rainwater from the sky and with it gives life to the earth after its death; surely, there are signs in this for those who use their common sense.[24] And of His signs are the firmly standing heaven and earth by His command; then as soon as He summons you out of the earth, you shall come forth *at one call.*[25]   To Him belongs everything that is in the heavens and the earth; all are obedient to Him.[26]   He is the One Who originates creation, then repeats it; and this is ever easier for Him. To Him belongs the highest attribute in the heavens and the earth, and He is the All-Mighty, the All-Wise.[27]   30:[20-27]

SECTION: 4

We give you an example from your own lives. Do you let your slaves be equal partners in the wealth which We have given you? Do you fear them as you fear each other? Thus do We spell out Our revelations for those who use their common sense.[28]   Nay! The wrongdoers are led by their own desires, without real knowledge. So who can guide those whom Allah leaves astray? They will have no helpers.[29]   Therefore, stand firm in your devotion to the upright faith - the nature made by Allah, the one on which mankind is created - and never should you try to change Allah's creation *(or religion)*. That is the standard of true faith, but most among mankind do not know.[30]

The creation of man, his consort, heavens, earth, language, colors, sleep, quest for work, lightning, rain and growth of vegetation - all are signs of Allah

The wrongdoers are led by their own desires without real knowledge

True faith and the nature of sects

Turn in repentance to Him, fear Him, establish Salah *(regular five times daily prayers)* and do not be of the mushrikeen[31] - those who divide their religion *into sects* and become separate groups, each group rejoicing in its own circle.[32]   30:[28-32]

When an affliction befalls people they call upon Allah, but when He relieves them, lo! They start committing shirk

When an affliction befalls the people, they turn in prayer to their Rabb in repentance. But when He let them taste a blessing from Him, lo! Some of them start committing shirk,[33] showing ingratitude for What We have given them. Enjoy yourselves; soon you will find out *your folly*.[34] Have We sent down to them an authority, that speaks of the shirk which they are committing?[35] When We give mankind a taste of blessing, they rejoice, but when some evil afflicts them because of their own misdeeds, lo! They are in despair.[36] Do they not see that it is Allah Who gives abundantly to whom He pleases and sparingly to whom He wills? Surely, there are signs in this example for those who believe.[37]   30:[33-37]

Commandment to give ones relatives their due and likewise to the poor and the travellers in need

O believers, give what is due to your relatives, the needy and the traveller in need. That is best for those who seek the pleasure of Allah and it is they who will attain felicity.[38] That usury which you give so that it may increase through the wealth of other people, does not increase with Allah: but the Zakah *(obligatory charity)* that you give to seek the pleasure of Allah, shall be repaid to you many times over.[39] It is Allah Who has created you, then provides you your sustenance, then He causes you to die, and then He will bring you back to life. Is there any of your shorakâ' *(gods you have set up besides Allah)* who can do any of these things? Glory be to Him, and exalted be He above the shirk these people commit.[40]   30:[38-40]

SECTION: 5

Mischief in the land is the result of Man's own misdeeds. That is how Allah let them taste the fruit of their deeds

Corruption has appeared in the land and the sea in consequence of man's own misdeeds. *Through such evil, Allah* makes people taste a part of that which they have done, so that they may turn back *from evil*.[41] *O Prophet,* tell them: "Travel through the earth and see what was the end of those who have passed away before you: most of them were mushrikeen *(worshipped other gods besides Allah)*."[42] Therefore, stand firm in your devotion to the true faith before that Day arrives on which there will be no chance of averting it. On that Day, they shall be divided *in two groups*.[43] Those who disbelieved will bear the burden of their disbelief, and those who have done good deeds will prepare a good place *in paradise* for themselves,[44] so that He may, out of His mercy, reward those who have believed and done good deeds. Surely, He does not like the disbelievers.[45]   30:[41-45]

Of His signs is that He sends the winds as bearers of good news, giving you a taste of His blessing, and your ships may sail by His command, and that you may seek of His bounty, and that you may be grateful.[46] We sent before you Rasools to their respective people, and they brought them clear signs. *Some rejected them while others believed,* then We subjected the guilty ones to Our retribution and *We aided the believers -* for We made it incumbent on Us to help the believers.[47] It is Allah Who sends the winds to raise the clouds, then He spreads them in the sky and breaks them into fragments as He pleases, then you see raindrops falling from their midst. When He showers this rain upon those of His servants whom He pleases, lo! They are filled with joy,[48] though before its coming they may have lost all hope.[49] Just look at the traces of Allah's Mercy! How He gives life to the earth after its death. Surely, the same way He will give life to the dead; for He has power over all things.[50] And if We send a wind which turns *their crops* yellow, behold they will become even more firm in their disbelief.[51] *O Prophet,* you cannot make the dead hear you, nor can you make the deaf hear your call especially when they have turned their backs and run away;[52] nor can you guide the blind out of their error. None will hear you save those who believe in Our revelations and submit themselves as Muslims.[53]   30:[46-53]

Allah sent His Rasools for the guidance of people; some believed while others rejected, Allah subjected the guilty to His retribution and helped the Believers

SECTION: 6

It is Allah Who has created you in a state of helplessness *(as a baby)*, then gave you strength to come out of helplessness *(in youth)*, then after strength again helplessness and grey hair *(in old age)*. He creates whatever He wills and it is He Who is the All-knowing, the All-Mighty.[54] On the Day when the Hour *of Judgement* will be established, the criminals will swear that they did not stay *in this world* more than an hour; thus are they ever deluded.[55] But those who are given knowledge and faith will say: "In fact, you have stayed, according to the Book of Allah, till the Day of Resurrection and this is the Day of Resurrection: but you were not aware."[56] On that Day, no excuse of theirs will avail the wrongdoers, nor will they be allowed to seek forgiveness.[57] *The fact is that* We have set forth every kind of example for men in this Qur'an, but whatever sign you may bring, the unbelievers are sure to say: "You are preaching falsehood."[58] Thus Allah has set a seal on the hearts of those who do not acknowledge *the truth.*[59] So *O Prophet*, have patience: surely, the promise of Allah is true; and do not let those, who themselves have no certainty of faith, shake your firmness.[60]   30:[54-60]

O Prophet, you cannot make the dead to hear you

It is Allah Who has created you and shall bring you to justice on the Day of Judgement

31: LUQMÂN

Period of Revelation

This Sûrah was revealed in the last years of middle stage of the Prophet's residence at Makkah. Its subject matter indicates that it was revealed in the same period when Sûrah 'Ankabût was revealed.

Major Issues, Divine Laws and Guidance:

* The Qur'an is the Book of wisdom and a blessing for the righteous.
* Luqmân's advise to his son, not to commit Shirk (to associate any one else with Allah in worship).
* Rights of mother and parents.
* Not to obey parents if they ask you to commit shirk.
* Islamic moral behavior and human interaction.
* The main reason of misguidance is the blind following of one's forefathers.
* If all trees were pens and oceans ink, Allah's words could not be put to writing.
* Allah is the only reality, all others whom people invoke besides Him are false.
* O Mankind, fear that Day when neither a father shall avail his son, nor a son his father, let not Shaitân deceive you concerning this fact.

This Sûrah also advises the young converts to Islam that even though the rights of parents are paramount, they are not to supersede the rights of Allah. They should not listen to the parents if they prevent them from accepting Islam, or compel them to revert to the creed of Polytheism.

This Sûrah also points out that Islam is not a new teaching which is being presented for the first time. The learned and wise people of the past ages said and taught the same message which the Qur'an is presenting today. In other words, it says, "O People of Makkah: In your own area there lived a wise man, named Luqmân, whose wisdom has been well known among you, whose proverbs and wise sayings are cited in your daily conversation and who is often quoted by your poets and orators. Now you should see precisely what creed and what morals he used to teach."

31: LUQMÂN

This Sûrah revealed at Makkah, has 4 sections and 34 verses.

In the name of Allah, the Compassionate, the Merciful

SECTION: 1

Alif Lâm M'eem.[1] These are verses of the Book of wisdom,[2] a guide and a blessing for the righteous:[3] who establish Salah *(Islamic Prayers)*, give Zakah *(obligatory Charity)* and firmly believe in the hereafter.[4] These are on true guidance from their Rabb and these are the ones who will attain felicity.[5] Among the people there are some who purchase idle talks so that they may lead people away from the Way of Allah, without any knowledge, and take *the invitation to the Right Way* as a mockery. For such people there will be a humiliating punishment.[6] When Our revelations are recited to such a person, he turns his face away in arrogance as if he did not hear them or as if his ears were sealed: announce to him the news of a painful punishment.[7] As for those who believe and do good deeds, there will be gardens of delight,[8] wherein they shall live forever. The promise of Allah is true: He is the All-Mighty, the All-Wise.[9] He created the heavens without visible pillars; He set mountains on the earth lest it should shake with you; and scattered through it all kinds of moving creatures. We send down rain from the sky with which We grow every type of noble plants.[10] This is Allah's creation; now, show Me what is there that others *(gods)* besides Him have created? - In fact, the wrongdoers are in manifest error.[11]

31:[1-11]

The Qur'an is the Book of Wisdom, a Guide and a Blessing for the Righteous

SECTION: 2

We gave wisdom to Luqmân saying: "Give thanks to Allah," and the one who pays thanks, does so for his own good; and the one who denies His favors, *should know that* Allah is certainly free of all wants, worthy of all praise.[12] When Luqmân, while advising his son, said to him: "O my son! Do not ever commit shirk *(associating anyone else with Allah)*; surely, committing shirk is the worst iniquity."[13]

31:[12-13]

Luqmân advised his son not to commit Shirk

We have enjoined man concerning his parents - his mother carries him in her womb while suffering weakness upon weakness and then weans him in two years - *That's why We commanded him:* "Give thanks to Me and to your parents, *and keep in mind that,* to

Rights of the mother and parents

Obey your parents but not in the matters of Shirk

Me is your final goal.[14]   If they argue with you to commit shirk, of which you have no knowledge, then do not obey them; however you should still treat them kindly in this world, but follow the way of that individual who has turned to Me. *After all,* to Me is your return; then I will inform you about *the reality of* all that you have done."[15]   31:[14-15]

Advice of Luqmân about moral behavior and interaction

Luqmân further said: "O my son! Allah will bring all things *to light,* be they as small as a grain of a mustard seed, be they hidden inside a rock or *high above* in the heavens or *deep down* in the earth. Allah knows the finest mysteries and is well aware of all things.[16]   O my son! Establish Salah *(prayers)*, enjoin good and forbid evil. Endure with patience whatever befalls you, surely, all that is of the matters requiring determination.[17]   Do not speak to the people with your face turned away *with pride*, nor walk proudly on earth; for Allah does not love any self-conceited boaster.[18]   Be moderate in your pace and lower your voice; for the harshest of voices is the braying of a donkey."[19]   31:[16-19]

SECTION: 3

Main reason for misguidance is the blind following of one's forefathers

Do you not see that Allah has subjected *to your benefit* all that is in the heavens and in the earth, and has lavished on you His evident and hidden favors? Yet, there are some people who still argue about Allah without knowledge,   without guidance or an enlightening Book.[20]   When they are asked to follow what Allah has revealed, they reply: "Nay, we shall follow the ways upon which we found our forefathers." What! *Will they still follow them* even though Shaitân invites them to the punishment of the blazing fire.[21]   He who surrenders himself to Allah and leads a righteous life has indeed grasped the most trustworthy hand-hold; as the ultimate disposal of affairs rests with Allah.[22]   *As for* he who disbelieves, let not his disbelief grieve you. To Us is their return and We shall inform them the reality of their deeds; surely, Allah knows the secrets of the breasts.[23]   We let them enjoy for a while *this life*, then *in the hereafter* We shall drive them to an unrelenting punishment.[24]   31:[20-24]

Mushrikeen admit that Allah is the Creator of the heavens and the earth

If you ask them: "Who has created the heavens and the earth?" They will certainly say: "Allah." Say: "Praise be to Allah!" But most of them do not *use their common sense* to understand.[25]   To Allah belong all that is in the heavens and earth; surely, Allah is the One Who is free of all wants, worthy of all praise.[26]   If all the trees on earth were pens, and the ocean *were ink*, replenished by seven more oceans, *the writing of* Allah's Words would not be exhausted; surely, Allah is Mighty, Wise.[27]   Neither your creation nor your resurrection is anything but as simple as *the creation and resurrection* of a single soul; surely, Allah is All-Hearing, All-Seeing.[28] Do you not see that Allah causes the night to pass into the day and the day into the night, that He has subjected the sun and the moon *to follow His law*, each pursuing its course for an appointed term, and that Allah is well aware of all your actions?[29]   This is because Allah is the Truth and because all those whom people invoke besides Him, are false, and because Allah is the One Who is the Most High, the Great.[30]   31:[25-30]

If all the trees were pens and the oceans were ink, the writing of Allah's words could not be exhausted

Allah is the only reality, all others to whom people invoke besides Him are false

SECTION: 4

Do you not see how the ships sail through the ocean by the grace of Allah so that He may show you some of His signs? Surely, there are signs in this for every patient, thankful person.[31]   When any giant wave covers them like a canopy, they pray Allah with all devotion making their faith pure for Him. But when He delivers them safely to land, some of them falter *between belief and unbelief.* None reject Our revelations except the treacherous and the ungrateful.[32]   O mankind! Have fear of your Rabb and fear that Day when no father shall avail his son nor a son his father. Surely, the promise of Allah is true. Let not the life of this world deceive you, nor let the Deceiver *(Shaitân)* deceive you concerning Allah.[33]   Surely, Allah Alone has the knowledge of the Hour, He is the One Who sends down rain and He knows what is in the wombs. No one knows what he will earn the next day; and no one knows in what land he will die. Surely, Allah knows all these and is aware of everything.[34]   31:[31-34]

O mankind, fear that Day when no father shall avail his son nor a son his father. Let not the Shaitân deceive you concerning this fact

32: AS-SAJDAH

Period of Revelation

This Sûrah was revealed during the initial stage of the middle period of the Prophet's residence at Makkah.

Major Issues, Divine Laws and Guidance

* Al-Qur'an is beyond all doubts, a revelation from Allah, sent to warn those people to whom no Warner had come before.
* On the Day of Judgement, the disbelievers shall believe, but that belief will be of no benefit to them.
* There is a special reward for those who forsake their beds, invoke their Rabb with fear and hope, and spend in charity.
* Al-Qur'an is similar to the Book which was given to the Prophet Musa (Moses).

The main theme of this Sûrah is to remove the doubts that the people had concerning Tawheed (God is One and Only), the Hereafter and the Prophethood, and to invite them to these three realities. The disbelievers are asked to use their common sense and judge for themselves as to which of the things presented by the Qur'an are strange and novel: "Look at the administration of the heavens and the earth: consider your own creation and structure. Don't these things testify to the teaching which this Prophet is presenting before you in the Qur'an? Does the system of the universe point towards Tawheed or towards shirk? Does your intellect testify that the One Who has given you your present existence will not be able to give you life again?" Then a scene of the Hereafter has been depicted, the fruits of belief and the evil consequences of disbelief have been mentioned and the people exhorted to give up disbelief before they meet their doom, and accept the teaching of the Qur'an, which will be to their own advantage in the Hereafter. They are told that it is Allah's supreme mercy that He does not seize man immediately for his errors to punish him. Instead, He warns man beforehand by afflicting him with small troubles, hardships, calamities, losses and strokes of misfortune so that he may wake up and take admonition. Then they are told: "This is not the first novel event of its kind that a Book has been sent down upon a man from Allah. Before this, the Book was sent to Musa (Moses), whom you all know.

In conclusion, the Prophet is asked to say: " When the time for final Judgement regarding you and us will come, believing then will be of no benefit to you at all. Believe now, if you want to save yourselves from punishment on the Day of Judgement."

32: AS-SAJDAH

This Sûrah revealed at Makkah, has 3 sections and 30 verses.

In the name of Allah, the Compassionate, the Merciful

SECTION: 1

Alif Lâm M'eem.[1]   This Book *(the Qur'an) is* - no doubt - revealed by the Rabb of the worlds.[2]   Do the people say: "He *(Muhammad)* has forged it?" Nay! It is the Truth from your Rabb, so that you may warn a people to whom no Warner has come before you: so that they may receive guidance.[3]   It is Allah Who has created the heavens, the earth and all that is between them in six Yaums *(days, time period or stages)*, then established Himself on the Throne *in a manner that suits His Majesty*. You have no guardian or intercessor besides Him. Will you not then take heed?[4] He plans all affairs from the heavens to the earth: then each affair ascends to Him in a yaum *(time period)* which, to your calculations, is one thousand years.[5]   Such is He, the Knower of all the hidden and the open, the All-Mighty, the Merciful.[6]   It is He Who has given the best form to everything that He has created. He originated the creation of man from clay;[7]   then *automated the creation of* his progeny by an extract of a paltry fluid;[8]   then He fashioned him in due proportion and breathed into him of His spirit. He gave you ears, eyes and heart; yet, you are seldom thankful.[9]   They say: "What! Once we are lost in the earth, shall we be created afresh?" Nay! They deny the fact that they will ever meet their Rabb.[10] Say: "The angel of death *('Azrâ'il)* who is assigned for you, will carry off your souls and bring you back to your Rabb."[11]

32:[1-11]

The Qur'an which there is no doubt, is revealed by Allah to Muhammad, so that he may warn those people to whom no Warner had come before

SECTION: 2

If only you could visualize when the criminals will lower their heads *(ashamed and humiliated)* before their Rabb *saying:* "Our Rabb! We have seen and we have heard; please send us back *to the world* and we will do good deeds: we are now convinced."[12] Had We so willed, We could have given every soul its guidance. But My word which I had said has been fulfilled, that: "I shall fill hell with jinns and men all together."[13]   Now taste the reward for your forgetting the meeting of this Day - We too have forgotten you *(left you in punishment)* now - taste the everlasting punishment in consequence of your misdeeds."[14]   32:[12-14]

On the Day of Judgement, the unbelievers shall believe but that belief will be of no benefit to them

There is a special reward for those who forsake their beds and invoke their Rabb with fear and hope and spend in charity

Only those people believe in Our revelations, who, when they are reminded of them, prostrate themselves in adoration and celebrate the praises of their Rabb and are not puffed up with pride.[15] Who forsake their beds and invoke their Rabb with fear and hope; and they spend *in charity* out of the sustenance which We have given them.[16] No one knows what delights of the eye have been kept hidden for them as a reward for their *good* deeds.[17] Can he who is a believer be like the one who is a transgressor? *Of course,* they are not alike.[18] As for those who believe and do good deeds, they shall be awarded the gardens of paradise as an entertainment for their good deeds.[19] But those who transgress shall be cast into the fire. Whenever they try to escape from it, they shall be pushed back into it, and it will be said to them: "Taste the punishment of the fire which you used to deny."[20] We shall certainly make them taste the lighter torment *in this life* before the greater punishment *of the hereafter*, so that they may return to *the Right Way.*[21] Who could be more unjust than the one who is reminded of the revelations of his Rabb and he turns away from them? Surely, We shall take vengeance on such criminals.[22]

32:[15-22]

SECTION: 3

The Qur'an is similar to the Book which was given to the Prophet Musa

We gave the Book to Musa *(the Torah)* - so be not in doubt for receiving this *Book (Al-Qur'an) which is similar to that* - and We made it *(the Torah)* a guide for the Children of Israel.[23] We appointed from among them leaders giving guidance under Our command so long as they showed patience and firmly believed in Our revelations.[24] Surely, your Rabb will decide between them, on the Day of Resurrection, concerning those matters wherein they differ among themselves.[25] Do they not learn a lesson *from the historical events* of how many generations We have destroyed before them in whose dwelling-places they move about? Surely, there are signs in this. Do they not listen?[26] Do they not see how We drive the rain to the parched lands and therefrom bring forth crops of which they and their cattle eat? Have they no vision?[27] Still they say: "When will this judgement take place, if you are telling the truth?"[28] Tell them: "On the Day of Judgement it will be of no benefit to the unbelievers even if they believe, *since at that time* they will not be granted a respite."[29] Therefore, pay no heed to them, and wait as they are waiting.[30] 32:[23-30]

33: AL-AHZÂB

Period of Revelation

This Sûrah was revealed during the 5th year after Hijrah (migration) of the Prophet to Madinah. During that year, three important events took place: the Battle of the Trench or Al-Ahzâb, the raid on Bani Quraizah (a Jewish tribe) and the Prophet's marriage with Sayyidah Zainab (the divorced wife of his adopted son Zaid bin Hârith).

Major Issues, Divine Laws and Guidance

*   Fear Allah, do not obey the unbelievers and the hypocrites.
*   Laws relating to:
    Divorce
    Status of an adopted son
*   By word of mouth, neither your wives become your real mothers nor your adopted sons your real sons.
*   Prophet's wives are declared to be the mothers of all believers.
*   Blood relations have greater claims than others in the Book of Allah.
*   Battle of the Trench (Al-Ahzâb):
    - Favors of Allah
    - Attitudes of the hypocrites
    - Non participants in the war against unbelievers are declared to have no faith at all and that all their deeds are void.
*   The life of Prophet Muhammad (peace be upon him) is declared to be a model for all.
*   Admonition to the wives of the Prophet.
*   It is not befitting for the believers to have options in what has been decided by Allah and His Rasool.
*   Allah's commandment to the Prophet to marry the divorced wife of his adopted son.
*   The Prophet Muhammad (peace be upon him) is not the father of any of your men but a Rasool of Allah and Seal of the Prophethood.
*   The Prophet Muhammad (peace be upon him) is given special permission to marry more than four wives along with restriction of neither to marry any more nor to divorce any for marring another in her place after this commandment.
*   Etiquettes concerning the visits to the Prophet's household.
*   Allah Himself and His angels send blessings on the Prophet, and the believers are commanded to do the same.
*   Laws of Hijâb (dress code) for women.

* *The trust of Allah was presented to the heavens, the earth and the mountains: they refused to take that responsibility but man took it.*

The Battle of the Trench - Al-Ahzâb

Background

Soon after the battle of Uhud, Bani Asad started making preparations for a raid on Madinah. The Prophet sent 150 warriors under the command of Sayyidunâ Abu Salmah (the first husband of Sayyidah Umme Salmah). This army took Bani Asad by surprise and made them run in a panic leaving all their possessions behind. After this, Bani An-Nadheer, a Jewish tribe, plotted to kill the Prophet but their plot was discovered in time. The Prophet ordered them to leave Madinah within ten days and warned that anyone who remained behind after that would be put to death. Abdullah bin Ubayy, the chief of the hypocrites of Madinah, encouraged them to defy the order and refuse to leave Madinah. He even promised to help them with 2,000 men, and assured them that Bani Ghatfân from Najd also will come to their aid. As a result, Bani An-Nadheer refused to follow the order and said that they would not leave Madinah no matter what. As soon as the time limit of ten days came to an end, the Prophet laid siege to their quarters, but none of their supporters had the courage to come to their rescue. At last, they surrendered on condition that every three of them would be allowed to load a camel with whatever they could carry and go away leaving the rest of their possessions behind. Thus, the suburbs of the city, which were inhabited by the Bani An-Nadheer, their gardens, their fortresses and other properties fell into the hands of Muslims.

After this, the Prophet received information that the tribe of Bani Ghatfân was preparing for a war against Madinah. He marched against them with 400 Muslims and overtook them by surprise. As a result, they fled their houses without any struggle and took refuge in the mountains.

After this in the month of Sh'abân A. H. 4, the Prophet went to the place of Badr with 1500 Muslims to fight against Abu Sufyân, who had challenged the Prophet and the Muslims at the end of the Battle of Uhud, saying: "We shall again meet you in combat at Badr next year." The Prophet accepted his challenge. From the other side, Abu Sufyân left Makkah with an army of 2,000 men, but did not have the courage to march beyond the town of Marr-Az-Zahrân, now known as Wadi Fâtimah. The Prophet waited for him at Badr for eight days; the Muslims during these days did profitable business with a trading caravan. This incident helped in restoring the image of the Muslims that had been tarnished at Uhud. It also made the whole of Arabia realize that the Quraish alone could no longer resist Muhammad (peace be upon him).

The Battle

The leaders of the Bani an-Nadheer, who had settled in Khaiber after their banishment from Madinah, went to the Quraish, Ghatfân, Hudhail and many other tribes requesting them to gather all their forces and attack Madinah jointly. Thus, in Shawwâl, A. H. 5, a very large army of the Arab tribes marched against the small city of Madinah. From the north came the Jews of Bani An-Nadir and Bani Qainuqah. From the east advanced the tribes of Ghatfân, Bani Sulaima, Fazarah, Murrah, Ashja, S'ad, Asad, etc. and from the south the Quraish along with a large force of their allies numbering from ten to twelve thousand warriors. Had it been a sudden attack, it would have been disastrous. Before the enemy could reach Al-Madinah, the Prophet got a trench dug on the northwest of Madinah in six days and took up defensive positions with 3,000 warriors. Mount Salat was at their back, and thick palm tree gardens on their south, therefore, the enemy could not attack from those sides. The same was the case on the east side where there were lava rocks, which were impossible for a large army to cross. The same was the case with the south- western side. The attack, therefore, could be made only from the eastern and western sides of the Uhud mountain, which the Prophet had secured by digging a trench. The disbelievers were not at all aware that they would have to encounter a trench outside Madinah. This kind of a defensive stratagem was unknown to the Arabs. Thus, they had to lay a long siege during winter for which they were not prepared.

The only alternative that remained for the disbelievers was to incite the Jewish tribe of Bani Quraizah, who were living in the southeastern part of the city to rebel. The Prophet had a treaty with them that in case of an attack on Madinah they would defend the city along with them. As a result, the Prophet had made no defensive arrangement in that area and had even sent Muslim families to take shelter in the forts situated on that side of the city. The invaders perceived this weakness in the defenses of the Muslim army. They sent a Jewish leader of Bani An-Nadheer to Bani Quraizah and induced them to break the treaty and join the war against the Muslims. In the beginning, they refused saying that they had a treaty with Muhammad (peace be upon him) who had faithfully abided by it and given them no cause for complaint. But, when Ibn Akhtab said to them, "Look, I have summoned a united force of entire Arabia against him. This is a perfect opportunity to get rid of him, if you lose it, you will never have another opportunity," thus, the anti-Islamic mind prevailed over every moral consideration and they agreed to violate the treaty.

When the Prophet received this news, he at once asked the chiefs of the Ansâr, to go and find out the truth. He advised them that if they found Bani Quraizah still loyal to the treaty, they should return and say so openly before the Muslim army; however, if they found that they were bent upon treachery, they should only inform him so that the common Muslims would not panic. When inquired, Bani Quraizah openly told the chiefs: "There is no agreement and no treaty between us and Muhammad." At this they returned and submitted their report to the Prophet.

After ascertaining verification, the Prophet, at that critical moment, initiated peace negotiations with the warrior tribe of Bani Ghatfân offering them one third of the fruit harvest of Madinah in lieu of their withdrawal. But when he asked S'ad bin Ubâdah and S'ad bin Muâdh, chiefs of the Ansâr for their opinion about the conditions of peace, they asked, "O Rasool of Allah: Is it your personal wish that we should agree on these conditions, or is it Allah's Command that we have no option but to accept it, or, are you proposing this only to save us from the enemy?" The Prophet replied, "I am proposing this only to save you: I see that the whole of Arabia has formed a united front against you. I want to divide the enemy." At this, the two chiefs protested saying, "Your honor, if you want to conclude this pact for our sake, please forget it. These tribes could not subdue us under tribute when we were polytheists. Now that we have the honor of believing in Allah and His Rasool, will they make us sink to this depth of ignominy? Let the sword be the arbiter till Allah passes His judgement between them and us." With these words, they tore up the draft for the treaty which had not yet been signed.

In the meantime Nu'aim bin Mas'ud, a member of the Ashja branch of the Ghatfân tribe, became a Muslim and came before the Prophet and submitted, "No one as yet knows that I have embraced Islam: You can take from me whatever service you please." The Prophet replied: "Go and sow the seeds of discord among the enemy." So, first of all, Nu'aim went to the tribe of Quraizah with whom he was on friendly terms, and said to them, "The Quraish and the Ghatfân can become wearied of the siege and go back, and they will lose nothing, but you have to live here with the Muslims. Just consider what your position will be if the matter turns out that way. Therefore, I would advise you not to join the enemy until the outsiders should send some of their prominent men as hostages to you." This had the desired effect upon the Bani Quraizah and they decided to demand hostages from the united front of the tribes. Then he went to the chiefs of the Quraish and the Ghatfân and said to them, "The Bani Quraizah seem to be slack and irresolute. They may demand some men as hostages from you and then hand them over to Muhammad (peace be upon him) to settle their affair with him. Therefore, be very firm and cautious in your dealing with them." This made the leaders of the united front suspicious of Bani Quraizah, and they sent them a message, saying, "We are tired of the long siege; let there be a decisive battle; let us, therefore, make a general assault simultaneously from both *the sides." The Bani Quraizah sent back the word, saying, "We cannot afford to join the war unless you hand over some of your prominent men to us as hostages." The leaders of the united front became convinced that what Nu'aim had said was true. They refused to send hostages. And the Bani Quraizah, on the other side, also felt that Nu'aim had given them the correct counsel. Thus, the strategy worked: it divided the enemy.*

Victory granted by Allah without fight

The siege was prolonged for more than 25 days. It was winter, and supply of food, water and forage was becoming more and more scarce. Division in the camp was also a great strain on the morale of the besiegers. Then, suddenly one night, a severe windstorm accompanied by thunder and lightning hit the camp. It added to the cold and darkness. The wind blew over the tents and put the enemy in disarray. They could not withstand this severe blow of nature. They left the battleground during the night and returned to their homes. In the morning, there was not a single enemy soldier to be seen on the battlefield. The Prophet, finding the battlefield completely empty, said: "The Quraish will never be able to attack you after this: now you will take the offensive." This was a correct assessment of the situation. Not only the Quraish but the united front of all the enemy tribes had made their final assault against Islam and had failed. They could no longer dare invade Madinah; now the Muslims were on the offensive.

Raid on Bani Quraizah

When the Prophet returned from the Trench, angel Gabriel came to him in the early afternoon with the Divine Command; the Muslims should not lay aside their arms without dealing with the Bani Quraizah. On receipt of this Command, the Prophet made the announcement: "Everyone who is steadfast in obedience should not offer his 'Asr Prayer till he reaches the locality of the Bani Quraizah." Immediately after this, he despatched Sayyidunâ Ali with a contingent of soldiers as vanguard towards the Quraizah. When they reached there, the Jews climbed on to their roof tops and started hurling abuses on the Prophet and the Muslims, but their invectives could not save them from the consequences of their treachery. They had committed a breach of treaty at the most critical moment of the war, joined hands with the invaders and endangered the entire population of Madinah. When they saw the contingent of Sayyidunâ Ali, they thought that they had come only to overawe them. But when the whole Muslim army arrived under the command of the Prophet himself and laid siege to their quarters, they were very frightened. They could not stand the severity of the siege for more than two or three weeks. At last, they surrendered themselves to the Prophet on the condition that they would accept whatever decision Sayyidunâ S'ad bin Muâdh, the chief of the Aus, would give. They had accepted Sayyidunâ S'ad as their judge, because, in the pre-Islamic days, the Aus and the Quraizah had been confederates. They hoped that in view of their past ties, Sayyidunâ S'ad would treat their previous allies leniently. But Sayyidunâ S'ad had just experienced and seen how the two Jewish tribes, who had been allowed to leave Madinah previously, had instigated the other tribes living around Madinah and summoned a united front of ten to twelve thousand men against the Muslims. He was also aware how treacherously this Jewish tribe had behaved on the occasion when the city was under attack threatening the safety of its entire population. He, therefore, decreed that all the male members of the Quraizah should be put to death, their women and children taken prisoners and their properties distributed among the Muslims. The sentence was carried out. When the Muslims entered their strongholds they found that this treacherous tribe had collected 1,500 swords, 300 coats of mail, 2,000 spears and 1,500 shields in order to join the war. If Allah had not helped the Muslims, all this military equipment would have been used to attack Madinah from the rear at a time when the polytheists were making preparations for a general assault on the Muslims after crossing the Trench. After this disclosure, there remained no doubt that the decision of Sayyidunâ S'ad concerning those people, was perfectly the right decision.

Social Reforms

In this Sûrah, the Islamic laws pertaining to marriage and divorce were complemented; the law of inheritance was introduced, drinking and gambling were prohibited, and new laws and regulations concerning economic and social life were enacted.

Status of adopted children

The question concerning adoption was also addressed in this Sûrah. An adopted son was regarded as their own offspring by the Arabs at that time: he was entitled to inheritance; he was treated like a real son and real brother by the adopted mother and the adopted sister; he could not marry the daughter of his adopted father or his widow after his father's death. And the same was the case if the adopted son died or divorced his wife. The adopted father regarded that woman as his real daughter-in-law. This custom clashed in every detail with the laws of marriage, divorce and inheritance enjoined by Allah in Sûrahs Al-Baqarah and An-Nisâ'. It made a person who could get no share in inheritance, entitled to it at the expense of those who were really entitled to it. It prohibited marriage between the *men and the women who could enter into the contract of marriage. And, above all, it helped spread the immoralities which the Islamic Law wanted to eradicate. For a real mother, a real sister and a real daughter cannot be like the adopted mother, the adopted sister and the adopted daughter. When artificial relations endowed with customary sanctity are allowed to mix freely like the blood relations, evil is often the result. That is why the Islamic law of marriage and divorce, the law of inheritance and the law prohibiting adultery, require, that the concept and custom of regarding the adopted son as a real son should be corrected. This concept, however, could not be uprooted by merely passing a legal order, because centuries old prejudices and superstitions could not be changed by mere word of mouth. Therefore, a little before the Battle of the Trench, the Prophet was asked by Allah to marry Sayyidah Zainab, the divorced wife of his adopted son, Zaid bin Hârithah (may Allah be pleased with him). The Prophet acted on this Commandment during the siege of Bani Quraizah.*

Defamatory remarks by the Jews, Pagans and Hypocrites

As soon as the marriage was contracted, there arose a storm of propaganda against the Prophet. The polytheists, the hypocrites and the Jews all were burning with jealousy at the Prophet's triumphs which followed one after the other. The way they had been humbled within two years after Uhud, in the Battle of the Trench, and in the affair of the Quraizah, had made them sore at heart. They had also lost hope that they could ever subdue Muslims on the battlefield. Therefore, they seized the opportunity of this marriage as a godsend blessing for them and thought they would put an end to the Prophet's moral superiority, which was the secret of his power and success. Therefore, stories were concocted that Muhammad (peace be upon him), God forbid, had fallen in love with his daughter-in-law, and when his son came to know of this, he divorced his wife, and the father married his daughter-in-law. The propaganda, however, was absurd on the face of it. Sayyidah Zainab was the Prophet's first cousin. He had known her from childhood to youth. So, there could be no question of his falling in love with her at first sight. Then, he himself had arranged her marriage with Sayyidunâ Zaid (his adopted son) under his personal influence, although her whole family had opposed it. They did not like that a daughter of the noble Quraish should be given in marriage to a freed slave. Sayyidah Zainab herself was not happy at this arrangement. But everyone had to submit to the Prophet's command. The marriage was solemnized and a precedent was set in Arabia that Islam had raised a freed slave to the status of the Quraishite nobility. If the Prophet had in reality any desire for Sayyidah Zainab, there was no need in marrying her to Sayyidunâ Zaid. He himself could have married her.

The Laws of Hijâb

The fact that the tales invented by the enemies of Islam also became topics of conversation among the Muslims, was a clear sign that the element of sensuality in society had crossed all limits. If this malady had not existed, it was not possible that people would have paid any attention whatever to such absurd stories about such a righteous and pure person like the Prophet. This was precisely the occasion when the reformative Commandments pertaining to the law of Hijâb (women's dress code) were first introduced in the Islamic society. These reforms were introduced in this Sûrah and complemented a year later in Sûrah An-Nûr, when slandering remarks were made on the honor of Sayyidah 'Aisha, a wife of the Prophet Muhammad, peace be upon him.

33: AL-AHZÂB

This Sûrah revealed at Madinah, has 9 sections and 73 verses.

In the name of Allah, the Compassionate, the Merciful

SECTION: 1

O Prophet! Fear Allah and do not obey the unbelievers and the hypocrites: certainly Allah is All-Aware, All-Wise.[1] Follow that which is revealed to you from your Rabb: for Allah is well aware of what you do.[2] Put your trust in Allah: for Allah is your all-sufficient protector.[3]   33:[1-3]

> Fear Allah and do not obey the unbelievers and hypocrites

Allah has not put two hearts in a person's body: nor does He regard your wives whom you *divorce* through Zihâr *(divorcing a wife saying: from now on you are as my mother. Depriving her conjugal rights, yet, keeping her like a slave and not letting her marry anyone else)* as your mothers: nor does He regard your adopted sons as your sons. These are mere words which you utter with your mouths; but Allah declares the Truth and guides you to the Right Way.[4] Call *your adopted sons* by their fathers *names*; that is more just in the sight of Allah, and if you don't know who their fathers are, then *call them* your brothers in faith and your friends. There is no blame on you for an unintentional mistake, but *you will be held responsible for* what you do with the intention of your hearts; Allah is Forgiving, Merciful.[5]   33:[4-5]

> By word of mouth neither your wives become your mothers nor adopted sons become your real sons

The Prophet is closer to the believers than their own selves and his wives are as their mothers. Blood relatives have a greater claim on one another *(regarding inheritance)* than the other believers and the Muhâjireen *(early Muslims who migrated from Makkah to Madinah)* in the Decree *of Allah*: although you are permitted to some good *(through leaving bequests)* for your friends. This has been written in the Book of Allah.[6] *O Muhammad,* remember the Covenant which We took from all the Prophets - from you as well as from Nûh *(Noah)*, Ibrâheem *(Abraham)*, Musa *(Moses)* and Isa *(Jesus)* son of Maryam *(Mary)*- We took that solemn Covenant from all of them,[7] so that He may question the truthful concerning the Truth *(that they were entrusted with)*: as for the unbelievers, He has prepared a painful punishment.[8]   33:[6-8]

> The Prophet's wives are the believers' mothers

> Blood relations have greater claims than others in the Book of Allah

SECTION: 2

Favors of Allah during the battle of Trench

O believers! Remember the favor of Allah, which he bestowed on you, when you were attacked by your enemy's army *(during the battle of the Trench / Confederates)* and We unleashed against them violent winds and invisible forces. Allah has seen all that you were doing.[9] When they *(enemy)* came upon you from above and from below; when your eyes were petrified *due to fear* and your hearts leaped up to your throats, and you began to entertain all sorts of doubts about Allah;[10] there and then were the believers put to test, and were terribly shaken.[11]   33:[9-11]

The attitude of the Hypocrites during the battle of Trench

Remember, when the hypocrites and those in whose hearts there was a disease were openly saying: "Allah and His Rasool promised us nothing but delusion!"[12] And a party of them said: "O people of Yathrib *(Madinah)*! You cannot stand the attack much longer. Go back *to your city.*" And yet, another party of them sought leave of the Prophet saying: "In fact, our houses are insecure," whereas they were not insecure. They intended nothing but to run away *from the battlefront.*[13] Had the city been entered from all sides, and had they been incited to sedition *(disbelief)*, they would have had little hesitation to become partners in it.[14] Even though they had made a covenant with Allah not to show their backs, and the covenant with Allah must surely be answered for.[15]   33:[12-15]

Those who discourage others from participating in the fight against the unbelievers and don't participate in such a war themselves have no faith and all their deeds will be null and void

Tell them: "If you are ran away from death or being killed, running away will not do you any good - for you would enjoy this life only for a little while."[16] Ask them: "Who can protect you from Allah if He intends to harm you or *who can prevent Him* if He intends to show you mercy?" They will find none besides Allah to protect or help them.[17] Allah is well aware of those among you who hold others back and those who say to their brethren: "Join us," and seldom take part in the fighting themselves.[18] They are ever reluctant to assist you. Whenever they are in danger, they look towards you with their eyes rolling as though they were at the point of death, but when they are out of danger, they will lash you with their sharp tongues, in greed for gain. Such people have no faith. Allah has made all their deeds null and void, and this is easy for Allah.[19] They thought that the confederates would never withdraw. Indeed, if the confederates should come again, they would wish to be among the bedouins and seek news about you *from a safe distance*; and if they happened to be with you, they would take but a little part in the fighting.[20]   33:[16-20]

SECTION: 3

You have indeed, in the life of Allah's Rasool, the 'Best Model' for him whose hope is in Allah and the Day of the Hereafter, and who engages himself much in the remembrance of Allah.[21] When the true believers saw the confederate forces they said: "This is what Allah and His Rasool had promised us: Allah and his Rasool were absolutely true." This increased them all the more in their faith and their zeal in obedience.[22]   Among the believers there are men who have been true to their covenant with Allah: of them some have completed their vow *through sacrificing their lives,* and some others are waiting for it, and have not changed *their commitment* in the least.[23]   *All this happens* so that Allah may reward the truthful for their truth and punish the hypocrites or accept their repentance if He wills: for Allah is Forgiving, Merciful.[24]   33:[21-24]

The Life of Rasool Allah (Muhammad) is the best Model for you

Allah turned back the unbelievers; they retreated in their rage without gaining any advantage, and Allah was sufficient to fight on behalf of the believers; for Allah is All-Powerful, All-Mighty.[25]   And brought down, from their fortresses, those people of the Book *(the Jews of Bani Quraizah)* who supported *the invaders*, and cast terror into their hearts. As a result, some of them you slew and some you took as prisoners.[26]   Thus He made you heirs of their lands, their houses and their goods, and also the land on which you had never set your foot before. Truly, Allah has power over all things.[27]   33:[25-27]

Allah helped the Muslims gain victory over the unbelievers and the Jewish tribes in Madinah and Khaiber

SECTION: 4

O Prophet! Say to your wives: "If you desire the life of this world and its glitter, then come, I shall give you of these and let you go in an honorable way."[28]   But if you seek Allah and His Rasool and the home of the hereafter, then you should rest assured that Allah has prepared a great reward for those of you who are good.[29] O wives of the Prophet! If any of you commits an open indecency, her punishment will be increased to double and this is easy for Allah.[30]   33:[28-30]

Admonition to the wives of the Prophet Muhammad (pbuh)

JUZ (PART): 22

Allah's command-
ment to the wives
of the Prophet
Muhammad

Those of you *(O wives of the Prophet Muhammad)* who obey Allah and His Rasool and practice righteousness, shall be granted double reward, and for them We have prepared a generous provision.[31] O wives of the Prophet! You are not like the other women: if you fear *Allah*, then you should not be complaisant while talking *to the men who are not closely related to you,* lest the one in whose heart there is a disease may thereby be encouraged; and speak using suitable good words.[32] Stay in your homes and do not display your finery as women used to do in the days of ignorance *(pre-Islamic days)*; establish Salah *(Prayers)*, pay Zakah *(obligatory charity)*, and obey Allah and His Rasool. O members of the household *of Rasool,* Allah only intends to remove unclean- liness from you and to purify you completely.[33] Remember the revelations of Allah which are recited in your homes and wise sayings (As-Sunnah), surely, Allah is Most Courteous and Well- Aware of all things.[34]   33:[31-34]

SECTION: 5

It is not fitting for
believers to have
option in what has
been decided by
Allah and His
Rasool

Surely, the Muslim men and the Muslim women, the believ- ing men and the believing women, the devout men and the devout women, the truthful men and the truthful women, the patient men and the patient women, the humble men and humble women, the charitable men and the charitable women, the fasting men and the fasting women, the men who guard their chastity and the women who guard their chastity, and the men who remember Allah much and the women who remember Allah much - for all of them, Allah has prepared forgiveness and a great reward.[35] It is not fitting for a believing man or a believing woman to have an option in their affairs when a matter has been decided by Allah and His Rasool; and whoever disobeys Allah and His Rasool has indeed strayed into a clearly wrong path.[36]   33:[35-36]

Allah commanded
the Prophet
Muhammad to
marry the divorced
wife of his adopted
son

O Prophet, remember when you said to the one *(Zaid, Prophet's adopted son)* whom Allah as well as you had favored: "Keep your wife in wedlock and fear Allah." You sought to hide in your heart what Allah intended to reveal; you were afraid of the people whereas it would have been more appropriate to fear Allah. So when Zaid fulfilled his desire *(divorced his wife)*, We gave her to you in marriage, so that there remains no hindrance for the believers to wed the wives of their adopted sons if they divorced them. And Allah's Command had to be carried out.[37] There can be no blame attached to the Prophet for doing what is sanctioned for him by Allah. Such has been the way of Allah with those who have gone before; and the decrees of Allah are preordained.[38]   Those who are charged with the mission of conveying the message of Allah, who fear Him alone and fear none but Allah; for Allah is sufficient to settle the account.[39]   Muhammad is not the father of any of your men *(he is not going to leave any male heirs),* but is the Rasool of Allah and the Seal of the Prophets. Allah has the knowledge of all things.[40]   33:[37-40]

SECTION: 6

O you who have believed, remember Allah with much remembrance,[41]   and glorify Him morning and evening.[42]   It is He Who sends His blessings on you *(believers)* and so do His angels, that He may bring you out of darkness into light, for He is Merciful to the believers.[43] On the Day of their meeting with Him, their greeting shall be: "Salaam *(peace)*!": and He has prepared for them a generous reward.[44]   O Prophet! Surely, We have sent you as a witness, as a bearer of good news and as a Warner,[45]   and to call the people towards Allah by His leave and a lamp spreading light *(guidance)*.[46]   Give good news to the believers that they shall have great blessings from Allah.[47]   Do not obey the unbelievers and the hypocrites, disregard their annoyances and put your trust in Allah; for Allah is sufficient as a disposer of affairs.[48]   33:[41-48]

O believers! If you marry believing women and divorce them before the marriage is consummated, you have no Iddat *(waiting period)* to count concerning them, so give them some present and relieve them gracefully.[49]   O Prophet! We have made lawful to you the wives to whom you have given their dowers; and those ladies whom your right hands possess *(from the prisoners of war)* whom Allah has assigned to you; and the daughters of your paternal uncles and aunts, and the daughters of your maternal uncles and aunts, who have migrated with you; and the believing woman who gave herself to the Prophet if the Prophet desires to marry her - this permission is exclusively for you and not for the other believers; We know what restrictions We have imposed on the other believers concerning their wives and those whom their right hands possess. *We have granted you this privilege as an exception* so that no blame may be attached to you. Allah is Forgiving, Merciful.[50]   You may put off any of your wives you please and take *to your bed* any of them you please, and there is no blame on you if you call back any of them you had temporarily set aside.

Muhammad is not the father of any of your men but a Rasool and Seal of the Prophethood

The Prophet is sent as a bearer of good news, as a Warner and as a lamp spreading light

Divorce when no Iddat (waiting period for remarriage) is required

Special permission for the Prophet Muhammad to marry more than four wives

Restriction on the Prophet to marry or exchange the present wives after this commandment

This is most proper, so that their eyes may be cooled and they may not grieve, and that they will remain satisfied with what you give them. *O believers!* Allah knows all that is in your hearts; for Allah is All-Knowing, Most Forbearing.[51] It shall be unlawful for you, *O Muhammad,* to marry more women after this or to change your present wives *with other women*, though their beauty may be pleasing to you, however those *ladies* whom your right hands possess *are an exception.* Allah keeps watch over all things.[52] 33:[49-52]

SECTION: 7

Do not enter the houses of the Prophet without permission, and if invited, do not seek long conversation

O believers! Do not enter the houses of the Prophet without permission, nor stay waiting for meal time: but if you are invited to a meal, enter; and when you have eaten, disperse and do not seek long conversation. Such behavior annoys the Prophet, he feels shy in asking you to leave, but Allah does not feel shy in telling the truth. If you have to ask his wives for anything, speak to them from behind a curtain. This is more chaste for your hearts and for theirs. It is not proper for you to annoy the Rasool of Allah, nor ever to marry his wives after him; this would be a grievous offence in the sight of Allah.[53] Whether you reveal anything or conceal it, surely, Allah has full knowledge of all things.[54] There is no blame on *the ladies if they appear before* their fathers, their sons, their brothers, their brothers' sons, their sisters' sons, their own women and those whom their right hands possess *(slaves). O Ladies!* Have fear of Allah: for Allah is a witness to all things.[55] 33:[53-55]

Do not marry the Rasool's wives after his death

Allah Himself and His angels send blessings on the Prophet, O believers do the same

Indeed Allah and His angels send blessings on the Prophet. O believers, call for *Allah's* blessings on him and salute him with all respect.[56] Surely, those who annoy Allah and His Rasool, are cursed by Allah in this world and in the hereafter. He has prepared for them a humiliating punishment.[57] And those who annoy believing men and believing women, for no fault of theirs, shall bear the guilt of slander and an evident sin.[58] 33:[56-58]

SECTION: 8

Commandment of Hijâb (dress code) for women

O Prophet! Enjoin your wives, daughters and the believing women that they should draw their gowns over themselves. That is more proper, so that they may be recognized and not bothered. Allah is Forgiving, Merciful.[59] 33:[59]

If the hypocrites, those in whose hearts is malice and the scandal mongers of Madinah do not desist; We shall rouse you against them, and their days in the city - as your neighbors - will be numbered.[60] They shall be cursed wherever they are found and they shall be seized and killed mercilessly.[61] This has been the Way of Allah *regarding such people* among those who lived before you, and you will never find any change in the Way of Allah.[62]   33:[60-62]

Punishment for the Hypocrites and scandal mongers

People ask you about the Hour *of Doom*. Tell them: "Allah Alone has the knowledge of it. Who knows? It may be that the Hour is near at hand."[63] Surely, Allah has laid a curse on the unbelievers and has prepared for them a blazing fire;[64] to live therein forever and they shall find no protector or helper.[65] That Day, when their faces will roll about in the fire, they will say: "Woe to us! Would that we had obeyed Allah and obeyed the Rasool."[66] They will *further* say: "Our Rabb! We obeyed our chiefs and our great ones and they misled us from the Right Way.[67] Our Rabb! Give them double punishment and lay on them a mighty curse."[68]   33:[63-68]

The unbelievers shall ask double punishment for their leaders

SECTION: 9

O believers! Be not like those who slandered Musa *(Moses)*, but Allah cleared him of what they said - for he was honorable in the sight of Allah.[69] O believers! Fear Allah and always say the right thing;[70] He will bless your works and forgive your sins - for he that obeys Allah and His Rasool, has indeed achieved the highest achievement.[71] The fact is that We offered the Trust *("khilâfat or freedom of choice," and voluntarily using this option to abide by all what Allah has prescribed)* to the heavens, to the earth and to the mountains, but they refused to undertake it and were afraid, but man undertook it. He was indeed unjust and ignorant.[72] *(The inevitable result of bearing the burden of Allah's Trust is)* that Allah will punish the hypocrite men, the hypocrite women, the mushrik men and the mushrik women, and that Allah will turn in mercy to the believing men and the believing women: for Allah is Forgiving, Merciful.[73]

O believers! Fear Allah and always say the right thing

The heavens, earth and mountains refuse to take the Trust (freedom of choice) but man took it

33:[69-73]

34: SABÂ

Period of Revelation

The exact period of its revelation is not known from any reliable tradition. It appears to be the early Makkan period when persecution had not yet become tyrannical and the Islamic movement was being suppressed only by ridicule, rumor-mongering, false allegations and casting of evil suggestions in the people's minds.

Major issues, Divine Laws and Guidance

* The Day of Resurrection is sure to come for Allah's Judgement to reward the believers and punish the disbelievers.
* Those who do not believe in the hereafter are doomed.
* The mountains and birds used to sing Allah's praises with the Prophet Dawôôd (pbuh).
* Allah subjected the winds and Jinns to the Sulaimân (Solomon), pbuh.
* Intercession before Allah can not avail anyone except for whom He permits.
* Muhammad (peace be upon him) is sent as a Rasool for the whole of mankind.
* Wealth and children are a test to whom they are given.
* Whatever you spend in charity, Allah will pay you back in full.
* The truth has come, falsehood neither originates nor restores anything.
* On the Day of Judgement disbelievers will wish that they were believers.

This Sûrah deals with those objections of the disbelievers which they were raising against the Prophet's message of Tawheed, the Hereafter and his Prophet-hood, mostly in the form of allegations, taunts and mockery. Those objections have been answered in the form of instructions, admonition and warning about the evil consequences of their stubbornness. The stories of the Sabians and the Prophets Daûd (David) and Sulaimân (Solomon), peace be upon them, have been cited, as if to say: "You have both these historical precedents before you. On the one hand, there were the Prophets David and Solomon, who had been blessed by Allah with great powers and such grandeur and glory as had never been granted to any one before them. In spite of this, they were not proud and arrogant, but remained grateful servants of their Rabb. On the other hand, were the people of Sabâ, who, when blessed by Allah, became proud and were consequently destroyed. They were remembered only in myths and legends. With these precedents in view, you may see and judge for yourselves as to which type of life is better: the one which is based on belief in Tawheed, the Hereafter and the attitude of gratefulness to Allah, or the one which is based on disbelief, denial of the Hereafter and shirk (worshipping someone else beside Allah)."

34: SABA'

This Sûrah, revealed at Makkah, has 6 sections and 54 verses.

In the name of Allah, the Compassionate, the Merciful

SECTION: 1

Praise be to Allah to Whom belongs all that is in the heavens and the earth! To Him be the praise in the hereafter. He is the Wise, the Aware.[1] He has the knowledge of all that goes into the earth and that which comes out of it; and all that comes down from heaven and that which ascends to it. He is the Merciful, the Forgiving.[2] The unbelievers say: *"The Hour of Doom will never come to us."* Tell them: "Nay! By my Rabb, the Knower of the unseen, it shall certainly come upon you. Nothing, even equal to an atom, in the heavens or the earth is hidden from Him; nor is there anything smaller or greater than that, but is recorded in the Clear Book.[3] *The Hour is going to come and the Day of Judgement shall be established,* to reward those who have believed and done good deeds; it is they for whom there is forgiveness and an honorable sustenance."[4] As for those who strive to discredit Our revelations, there will be a humiliating painful punishment.[5] 34:[1-5]

The Hour is surely going to come and Judgement shall be established to reward the believers and punish those who discredit Allah's revelations

Those to whom knowledge has been given can see that the revelation sent down to you from your Rabb is the Truth and it guides to the Way of the Almighty, the Praise-Worthy.[6] The unbelievers say *to the people*: "Shall we point out to you a man who claims that when your body will disintegrate *and crumble* into dust, you shall be raised to life again?[7] Has he forged a lie against Allah or is he mad?" Nay! In fact those who do not believe in the Hereafter are doomed, for they are in gross error.[8] Do they not see the sky and the earth that surrounds them from front and from behind? If We want, We can cave in the earth to swallow them up or let the fragments of the sky fall upon them. Surely, there is a sign in this for every devotee that turns *to Allah* in repentance.[9]

34:[6-9]

Those who do not believe in the hereafter are doomed

SECTION: 2

We bestowed Our blessings on Daûd and commanded: "O mountains! Join him in glorifying My praise," and *a similar command was given* to the birds. We made iron soft for him[10] *saying*: "make coats of armor measuring out the links in mail and *O people of Daûd*, do good deeds; surely, I am watching over all of

The mountains and birds used to sing Allah's praise with the Prophet Daûd

Allah subjected the winds and Jinns to the Prophet Sulaimân

your actions."[11]   And *We made* the winds *subservient* to Sulaimân, which made a month's journey in the morning and a month's journey in the evening; and We made a fountain of molten copper to flow for him; and subdued Jinns for him who worked in front of him by the leave of his Rabb; and if any of them turned aside from Our command, We made Him taste the punishment of the blazing fire.[12]   They worked for him as he desired: making elevated chambers, images, basins as large as reservoirs and built-in cooking cauldrons. *We said*: "O Family of Daûd! Work grate-fully." Only a few of My servants are truly grateful.[13]   When We decreed Sulaimân's death, *he was leaning on his staff.* They *(Jinns)* did not know that he was dead until the earthworm *(termite)* ate away his staff and he fell down. Thus it became clear to the Jinns that if they had known the unseen, they would not have continued in the humiliating punishment of their task.[14]   34:[10-14]

Claim of people that Jinns know the unseen is wrong

The people of Saba' rejected Allah's blessings and disbelieved in the hereafter, so Allah made them merely a tale of the past

For the people of Saba' *(Sheba)* there was indeed a sign in their dwelling place: two gardens - one to the right and one to the left. *It was said to them:* "Eat of what your Rabb has given you and render thanks to Him. Pleasant is your land and forgiving is your Rabb."[15]   But they gave no heed. So We let loose upon them the waters of the dam and We converted their two gardens into the gardens producing bitter fruit, tamarisks and a few lote bushes.[16] Thus did We requite them for their disbelief; and never do We punish any but the ungrateful![17]   Between them and the towns which We had blessed *(Syria and Palestine)*, We placed other towns in prominent positions so that they could journey to and back in measured stages. *We said:* "Travel through them by day and night in complete security."[18]   But they prayed: "Our Rabb! Make our journeys longer." Thereby they wronged their souls and We made them merely a tale that is told and dispersed them in scattered fragments. Surely, there is a sign in this for every patient, grateful person.[19]   *In their case*, Iblees' *(Satan's)* suspicions proved true, as they all followed him except a *small* group of the believers,[20] even though he had no authority over them. *It all happened* because We wanted to see who *among them* believed in the hereafter and who is in doubt concerning it. Your Rabb is watching over all things.[21]   34:[15-21]

SECTION: 3

O Prophet, say *to the mushrikeen:* "Call on those deities whom you pray besides Allah - they do not have power over an atom's weight of anything in the heavens or in the earth, nor have they any share in either, nor is any of them a helper to Allah."[22] No intercession before *Allah* can avail anyone except him who has been given His permission. Until when terror will be removed from their *(angels)* hearts, they shall ask: "What has your Rabb ordained?" They will answer: "The Truth," He is the Most High, the Great.[23] *O Prophet*, ask them: "Who provides your sustenance from the heavens and the earth?" *If they do not answer, then* say: "It is Allah! *Certainly one of us; either* we or you are rightly guided or in manifest error."[24] Further, tell them: "You shall not be questioned about our errors nor shall we be questioned about your actions."[25] Say: "Our Rabb will bring us all together, then He will rightly judge between us. He is the Judge Who knows everything."[26] Say: "Show me those whom you have made associate gods with Him. Nay! By no means *can you do it.* Allah Alone is the Almighty, the Wise."[27] *O Prophet,* We have sent you to the entire mankind, to give them good news and forewarn them, but most men do not know.[28] They ask you: "When will this promise *of resurrection* be fulfilled, if you are telling the truth?"[29] Tell them: "For you the appointment of a day is fixed, which you can neither postpone for a moment nor bring it early."[30] 34:[22-30]

SECTION: 4

The disbelievers say: "We shall never believe in this Qur'an, nor in the scriptures which came before it." If you could only see when these wrongdoers will be made to stand before their Rabb, tossing accusing words on one another! Those who had been despised as weaklings will say to the arrogant: "If it had not been for you, we would certainly have been believers."[31] The arrogant will say to those despised weaklings: "Did we block you off from guidance when it came to you? Nay! Rather you yourselves were guilty."[32] Those despised weaklings will say to the arrogant: "No! It was you who plotted day and night, bidding us to disbelieve in Allah and to set up equals with Him," - They will *feel ashamed, therefore,* conceal their regrets, once they see the punishment, and We shall put yokes on the necks of those disbelievers; can there be any other reward except for what they did?[33] Whenever We have sent a Warner to a town, its wealthy residents have said: "We surely disbelieve in what you are sent with."[34] They say: "We have more wealth and children, *which indicates that our gods are happy with us so* we shall never be punished."[35] *O Prophet* tell them: "Surely,

---

No intercession before Allah can avail anyone except for whom He permits it

The Prophet Muhammad is sent for the entire mankind

Those who disbelieve in the Qur'an and prior scriptures, will have yokes placed around their necks before being tossed into hell

Wealth and children are not the

indications of
Allah's pleasure

my Rabb gives abundantly to whom He wills and sparingly *to whom He pleases*, but most people do not understand this."[36]

34:[31-36]

SECTION: 5

It is belief that
brings you close to
Allah, not the
wealth or children

It is neither your wealth nor your children which bring you closer to Us even one jot, but those who believe and do good deeds; for them, there will be a double reward for their deeds and they shall reside in high mansions, safe and secure.[37] *As for* those who strive in opposing Our revelations, they shall be brought for punishment.[38] *O Prophet* tell them: "Surely, my Rabb gives abundantly to whom He pleases and sparingly to whom *He wills*. Whatever you spend *in charity,* He will pay you back. He is the best of those who provide sustenance.[39] One Day He will gather them all together and ask the angels: "Was it you that these people used to worship?"[40] They will respond: "Glory be to You! Our tie is with You - as a protector - not with them; but they used to worship the Jinns and it was them in whom most of these people believed."[41] On that Day you will be helpless to profit or harm one another. To the wrongdoers We shall say: "Taste the punishment of the fire which you persistently denied."[42] *Today* when Our clear revelations are recited to them, they say: "This man only wants to turn you away from those *gods* whom your forefathers have been worshipping." *Others* say: "This *Qur'an* is nothing but an invented falsehood." *While yet, others,* who deny the truth when it comes to them, say: "This is nothing but plain magic."[43] *In fact,* neither had We given them books to study, nor had We sent to them any Warner before you.[44] Those who have gone before them also denied - these *Arabs* have not received one tenth of what We had granted them - yet, when they denied My Rasools, see how terrible was My scourge.[45]

34:[37-45]

Whatever you
spend in charity,
Allah will pay you
back

Unbeliever's state-
ments about the
Prophet and
Al-Qur'an

SECTION: 6

The unbelievers are
asked to ponder
upon their wrong
statements

O Prophet say: "I would ask you one thing. For Allah's sake! Think individually or consult one another and ponder whether your companion *Muhammad* is really crazy? *You yourselves will come to the conclusion that* he is nothing but a Warner to you before a severe punishment."[46] Tell them: "I do not ask you for any compensation, it is all in your interest. My reward is only due from Allah and He is a witness over everything."[47] Say: "In fact my Rabb reveals *to me* the truth, and He is the Knower of all hidden *realities*."[48] Say: "The truth has arrived and falsehood neither

The truth has come,
falsehood neither

originates nor restores anything."[49] Say: "If I am in error, the loss is surely mine and if I am right, it is because of what my Rabb has revealed to me. Surely, He hears all and is very close."[50]

34:[46-50]

If you could only see *the disbelievers on the Day of Judgement* when they will be terrified! *On that Day* there will be no escape; and they will be seized from a nearby place.[51] Then they will say: "We believe in it *(the Truth brought by the Prophet)*": but how could they attain *the Faith* from such a far distant place.[52] They had disbelieved in it before - and they had engaged in conjecture about the unseen when they were far away *during their life on earth'?*[53] A barrier will be placed between them and what they desired to have, as was done with the similar people before them; for they were indeed involved in a misleading suspicion.[54]

34:[51-54]

originates nor restores anything

On the Day of Judgement the un-believers will want to believe but it will be of no avail to them

35: FÂTIR

Period of Revelation

This Sarah was revealed in the middle of Makkan period when antagonism had grown quite strong and every sort of mischief was created by the disbelievers to frustrate the mission of the Prophet.

Major Issues, Divine Laws and Guidance

* None can award or withhold blessings besides Allah.
* Shaitân is your enemy, so take him as such.
* The person who considers his evil deeds to be good deeds cannot be guided to the right path.
* Real honor is in being obedient to Allah.
* Mankind is in need of Allah while He is not in need of anyone.
* None can make those who are buried in the grave hear you.
* Those who recite Al-Qur'an, establish Salah (Prayers) and give Zakah (Obligatory Charity) may hope for Allah's blessings and reward.
* Allah has not sent any Book which has a provision of shirk (worshipping anyone else besides Allah).
* Plotting evil recoils none but the author of it.
* If Allah was to punish people for their wrong doing, He would not have left even an animal around them.

This discourse warns and admonishes the people of Makkah and their chiefs for their antagonistic attitude towards the Prophet's message of Tawheed, as if to say: "O foolish people, the way to which this Prophet is calling you is for your own benefit. Your anger, your tricks, your conspiracies and designs to frustrate the message or him, are against your own interest. If you do not listen to him, you will be harming your own selves, not him. Just consider and ponder over what he preaches:

1. He repudiates shirk (worshipping someone else beside Allah). If you look around carefully, you yourself will realize that there is no basis for shirk.

2. He presents the Doctrine of Tawheed (God is One and Only). If you use your common sense, you will come to the conclusion that there is no being beside Allah, the Creator of the Universe, which might possess divine attributes, powers and authority.

3. *He tells you that you have not been created to be irresponsible in this world and that you have to render an account of your deeds before your God.*

4. *He tells you that there is life after the life of this world, when everyone will meet the consequences of what he has done here. If you do not think so, you will find that your doubts about it are absolutely baseless. Don't you see the phenomenon of creation and reproduction, the alteration of day and night? How can then your own recreation be impossible for Allah Who created you from an insignificant sperm?*

5. *Doesn't your own intellect testify that good and evil cannot be alike? Think and judge for yourselves as to what is reasonable: should good and evil meet with the same fate and end up as dust, or should good be rewarded and evil be punished?*

Now, if you do not admit and acknowledge these rational and reasonable arguments, and do not abandon your false gods, the Prophet will not lose anything, rather, it is you who will suffer the consequences. The Prophet's responsibility is only to make the truth plain to you, which he has done."

35: FÂTIR

This Sûrah revealed at Makkah, has 5 sections and 45 verses.

In the name of Allah, the Compassionate, the Merciful

SECTION: 1

None can withhold or award blessings besides Allah

Praise be to Allah, the Originator of the heavens and the earth! Who appoints the angels having two, three and four wings as His messengers. He adds to His creation as He pleases; for Allah has power over all things.[1] None can withhold the blessings which He bestows on people, and what He withholds, none can award it thereafter. He is the Mighty, the Wise.[2] O mankind! Call to mind the favors of Allah on you; is there any creator other than Allah who provides for you from the heavens and the earth? There is no god but He. How then are you turning away *from Him*?[3] *O Prophet!* If they deny you, so were the Rasools denied before you. All affairs shall ultimately be presented before Allah.[4] O mankind! Certainly the promise of Allah is true, therefore, let not the life of this world deceive you nor let the chief deceiver *(Satan)* deceive you *about Allah*.[5]

Shaitân is your enemy: so take him as such

Surely, Shaitân *(Satan)* is your enemy: so take him as an enemy. He is inviting his adherents towards his way so that they may become companions of the blazing fire.[6] Those who disbelieve shall have a terrible punishment, and those who believe and do good deeds shall have forgiveness and a magnificent reward.[7]   35:[1-7]

SECTION: 2

That person who considers his evil deeds to be good, cannot be guided to the Right Path

Can that person whose evil deeds are so fair seeming to him that he considers them good *be like the one who is rightly guided*? The fact is that Allah leaves to stray whom He wills and guides whom He pleases. Therefore, *O Prophet,* let not your soul expire in sorrow on their account. Allah is aware of all their actions.[8] It is Allah Who sends forth winds to raise up the clouds, then drives them to a dead land and therewith revives the earth after its death. Similar will be the resurrection of the dead.[9]

       35:[8-9]

The real honor is in the obedience of Allah

If anyone is seeking honor, *let him know* that all honor belongs to Allah Alone. Good words ascend to Him and good deeds are exalted by Him. *As for* those who plan evil deeds, they shall have severe punishment and their plots will be brought to nothing.[10] It is Allah Who created you from dust, then from a sperm-drop, then He made you pairs. No female conceives or delivers without His knowledge. No long-lived man grows old or has his life cut short but is written in a Book; surely, all this is easy for Allah.[11]

35:[10-11]

The two bodies of water, of which one is sweet and pleasant to drink and the other is salty and bitter, are not alike. Yet, from each kind of water you eat fresh meat and extract ornaments which you wear; and you see the ships plough their course through them that you may seek His bounty, and that you may be grateful.[12] He causes the night to pass into the day and the day into the night, and He has made the sun and the moon to serve you; each one follows its course for an appointed term. Such is Allah, your Rabb; His is the kingdom; and those to whom you pray besides Him do not even own a thread of a date-stone.[13] If you pray to them, they cannot hear your prayers and even if they could hear you they could not answer you. On the Day of Resurrection they will deny your associating *them with Allah. O mankind!* None can inform you about all this like the One Who is All-Aware.[14] 35:[12-14]

> Allah has created water, day, night, the sun and moon for man's benefit. Deities besides Allah can neither hear, nor response nor own even a thread of a date-stone

SECTION: 3

O mankind! It is you who stand in need of Allah, and it is Allah Who is Free of all wants, Worthy of all praise.[15] If He wants, He can destroy you and replace you with a new creation;[16] and this is not at all difficult for Allah.[17] No bearer of a burdens will bear another's burden, and if a heavily laden person cries out for help, none will come forward to share the least of his burden, even though he be a close relative. *O Prophet!* You can only admonish those who fear their Rabb - though they cannot see Him - and establish Salah *(prayers)*. He that purifies himself does so for his own good. To Allah is the destination of all.[18] 35:[15-18]

> Mankind is in need of Allah, while He is not in need of anyone

The blind and the seeing are not alike;[19] nor the darkness and the Light;[20] nor the shade and the heat;[21] nor the living and the dead. Certainly Allah can make anyone hear if He so wills; but, *O Prophet*, you cannot make those who are in the graves hear you.[22] You are nothing but a Warner.[23] Certainly We have sent you *O Muhammad)* with the Truth as a bearer of good news and as a Warner, for there has not been a nation which has not had a Warner.[24] If they disbelieve you, know that their predecessors also disbelieved their Rasools who came to them with clear signs,

> The living and the dead are not alike. You cannot make those who are buried in the grave hear you

scriptures and the light-giving Book.[25] But in the end, I seized the disbelievers, and behold, how terrible was My disapproval![26]

35:[19-26]

SECTION: 4

Do you not see that Allah sends down rain from the sky with which We bring forth fruits of various colors? Similarly, in the mountains there are streaks of various shades including white, red, jet-black rocks.[27] Likewise, men, beasts and cattle have their different colors. In fact, only those among His servants who possess knowledge fear Allah; surely, Allah is All-Mighty, All-Forgiving.[28] Surely, those who recite the Book of Allah, establish Salah *(prayers)*, spend out of what We have given them, secretly and openly, hoping for imperishable gain.[29] That He may pay them back their full reward and give them even more out of His grace; surely, He is Forgiving and Appreciative *of His devotees*.[30] O *Prophet,* what We have revealed to you of the Book is the Truth, which confirms the previous scriptures. Surely, with respect to His servants, Allah is well Aware and fully Observant.[31] The We gave the Book *(the Qur'an)* as an inheritance to those of Our servants *(Muslims)* whom We have chosen; among them there are some who wrong their own souls, some who follow a middle course and some who, by Allah's leave, excel in good deeds. That is indeed the supreme grace.[32] They shall enter the gardens of eternity, where they shall be decked with bracelets of gold and pearls; and their dress therein will be of silk.[33] They will say: "Praise be to Allah Who has removed all sorrow from us; Our Rabb is indeed Forgiving and appreciative *of His devotees*,[34] Who, out of His bounty, has admitted us to this Eternal Home where we shall experience neither toil nor weariness."[35] As for the disbelievers, there shall be the fire of hell, no term shall be determined for them so that they could die nor shall its punishment ever be lightened for them. Thus shall We reward every disbeliever.[36] Therein they shall cry for help: "Our Rabb! Get us out, from now on we shall do good deeds and shall not repeat the ones we used to do". *The response will be:* "Did we not give you lives long enough so that he who would, could take a warning? *Besides,* someone did come to warn you. Now taste *the fruit of your deeds*, here there is no helper for the wrongdoers."[37]

35:[27-37]

SECTION: 5

Surely, Allah knows the unseen of the heavens and the

Margin notes:

Those who recite the Qur'an, establish Salah and give charity may hope for Allah's blessings and rewards

Those who disbelieve, shall have a painful punishment in the hellfire forever

earth, He even knows the secrets of the breasts *(hidden thoughts of people)*.[38]　It is He Who has made you successors upon the earth. Whoever disbelieves, bears the burden of his disbelief; and for the disbelievers, their disbelief does not increase anything except the wrath of their Rabb and the disbelievers do not gain anything except an increase in their loss.[39]　*O Prophet,* say: Have you ever considered your shorâka' to whom you call upon besides Allah. *Can you* show me anything that they have created in the earth? Or what is their share in *the creation of* the heavens? Or have We given them a Book from which they derive a provision *of shirk*? Nay, in fact, the wrongdoers promise each other nothing but delusions.[40] It is Allah Who keeps the heavens and the earth from slipping out of their places. Should they ever slip, none can hold them back besides Him; certainly He is Most Forbearing, Oft-Forgiving.[41]

35:[38-41]

Allah has not sent any Book which has a provision of Shirk (worshipping anyone else besides Allah)

These *very people used to* swear on solemn oaths by Allah that if a Warner ever comes to them, they would be better guided than any other nation *of the world*; yet, when a Warner has come to them they have increased in nothing but aversion,[42]　behaving arrogantly in the land and plotting evil, whereas the plotting of evil recoils none but its authors. Are they waiting but for that end which overtook the former nations? If so, you will never find any change in the ways of Allah, and you will never find any alteration in the ways of Allah.[43]　Have they not traveled through the land and seen what was the end of those who went before them, who were far superior in strength than these people? There is nothing in the heavens or in the earth which can frustrate Allah; surely, He is All-Knowing, All-Powerful.[44]　If it was Allah's will to punish people for their misdeeds, He would have not left any living creature on the surface *of the earth*, but He is giving them respite for an appointed time; when their appointed time comes, *they will realize that* in fact, Allah has been watching His servants all along.[45]　35:[42-45]

Plotting evil recoils none but the author of it

If Allah was to punish people for their wrong doings, He would not have left even an animal around them

36: YÂ-SÎN

Period of Revelation

This Sûrah was revealed during the last stage of the Prophet's residence at Makkah.

Major Issues, Divine Laws and Guidance

* Al-Qur'an is revealed by Allah to warn people and establish a charge-sheet against the disbelievers.
* Allah has created all things in pairs.
* The day, night, sun and moon, all are being regulated by Allah.
* Scenes from the Day of Judgement:
    - Allah's greetings to the residents of Paradise.
    - Allah's address to the criminals / sinners.
    - Hands and feet shall bear witness.
* All human beings shall be raised to life again on the Day of Judgement for accountability of their deeds.

The object of this discourse is to warn the unbelievers about the consequences of not believing in the Prophethood of Muhammad (may Allah's peace and blessings be upon him) and of resisting and opposing it with tyranny, ridicule and mockery. Arguments are also given about Tawheed (the Oneness of God), Risâlat Prophethood) and the Hereafter from the signs of the universe and the use of common sense.

Imam Ahmed, Abu Daûd, Nasâi, Ibn Mâjah and Tabarâni have related on the authority of Sayyidunâ Ma'qil bin Yâsar that the Prophet said: "Sûrah Yâ-Sîn is the heart of the Qur'an." This is similar to describing the Sûrah Al-Fâtiha as the Umm-al-Qur'an (the essence or core of the Qur'an), because Al-Fâtiha contains the sum and substance of the teaching of the whole Qur'an. Sûrah Yâ-Sîn has been called the throbbing heart of the Qur'an because it presents the message of the Qur'an in a most forceful manner which breaks the inertia and stirs the spirit of man to action. Imam Ahmed has also related that the Prophet said: "Recite Sûrah Yâ-Sîn to the dying ones among you." The objective is to refresh the dying person's memory about Islam and also bring before him a complete picture of the Hereafter so that he may know what stages he will have to pass after crossing the stage of this worldly life. In view of this, it would be desirable, that, along with the recitation of the Sûrah Yâ Sîn, its translation is also read for the benefit of the person who does not know Arabic so that the purpose of the admonition is duly fulfilled.

36: YÂ-SÎN

This Sûrah, revealed at Makkah, has 5 sections and 83 verses.

In the name of Allah, the Compassionate, the Merciful

SECTION: 1

Yâ Sîn.[1]   *I swear* by the Qur'an which is full of Wisdom[2] that you are indeed one of the Rasools *who are sent*[3]   on a Right Way.[4]   This *Qur'an* is revealed by the Almighty, the Merciful.[5] So that you may warn a people whose forefathers were not warned, hence they are unaware.[6]   In fact, the Word has been proven true against most of them *who are arrogant;* so they do not believe.[7] *Since they have chosen to neglect Our revelations,* We have thus put on their necks iron collars reaching to chins, so that their heads are forced up,[8]   and We have put a barrier in front of them and a barrier behind them, and We have covered them up, so that they cannot see.[9]   It is the same for them whether you warn them or warn them not, they will not believe.[10]   You can only warn those who follow the Reminder *(the Qur'an)* and fear the Compassionate *(Allah)*, though they cannot see Him. To such people give good news of forgiveness and a generous reward.[11]   Surely, We shall resurrect the dead; We are recording all that they are sending ahead and that they are leaving behind. We have recorded everything in an open ledger.[12]   36:[1-12]

The Qur'an is revealed by Allah to warn people

The Prophet is told that he could warn only those who have the fear of Allah

SECTION: 2

Narrate to them the example of the people of a certain town to whom the Rasools came.[13]   At first, We sent to them two Rasools, but when they rejected both, We strengthened them with a third and they all said: "Surely, we have been sent to you as Rasools."[14]   They replied: "You are but humans like us. The Compassionate *(Allah)* has revealed nothing; you are surely lying."[15]   They said: "Our Rabb knows that we have indeed been sent as Rasools to you[16]   and our only duty is to convey His message plainly."[17]   They replied: "We regard you as an evil omen for us. If you do not stop, we will stone you or you will receive from us a painful punishment."[18]   They said: "Your evil omens be with you!. *Do you call it "evil omen" because* you are being admonished? Indeed you are a nation of transgressors."[19]   In the meantime, a man came running from the remote part of the City and said: "O my people! Follow these Rasools.[20]   Follow the ones who ask no payment of you and are *rightly* guided."[21] 36:[13-21]

The example of three Prophets who were sent to one town; all the people denied them except one man who came from across the town

JUZ (PART): 23

Allah blessed the believer with paradise and destroyed the disbelievers

It would not be justifiable on my part if I do not worship Him Who has created me and to Whom you shall be brought back.[22] Should I take other gods besides Him? If the Compassionate *(Allah)* should intend to harm me, their intercession will avail me nothing, nor will they be able to save me.[23] If I do so, I would indeed be in manifest error.[24] Surely, I believe in your Rabb, so listen to me."[25] *Consequently they killed that man and* it was said to him: "Enter paradise." He exclaimed: "Would that my people knew *what I know!*[26] How my Rabb has granted me forgiveness and included me among the honored ones."[27] After him We did not send any army against his people from heaven, nor was it necessary to do so.[28] It was nothing but a single blast and they all became extinct.[29] Alas bondsmen! Whenever there comes to them a Rasool, they mock at him.[30] Do they not see how many generations We have destroyed before them who will never return to them?[31] While each one of them will be brought before Us *on the Day of Judgment.*[32]   36:[22-32]

SECTION: 3

Allah has created all things in pairs

The dead land may serve as a sign for them; We give it life and produce from it grain for them, which they eat.[33] We also produce from it gardens with date-palms and vines, and We cause springs to gush forth from it,[34] so that they may enjoy the fruits thereof. It was not their hands that made all this; should they not then give thanks?[35] Glory be to Allah Who created all things in pairs: the plants of the earth, mankind themselves and other living things which they do not know.[36]   36:[33-36]

The day, night, sun and moon; all are being regulated by Allah

Another sign for them is the night; when We withdraw the daylight from it, and behold they are in darkness.[37] The sun runs its course, this *course* is predetermined for it by the Almighty, the All-Knowing.[38] As for the moon, We have designed phases for it till it again becomes like an old dried curved date stalk.[39] It is neither possible for the sun to overtake the moon, nor for the night to outstrip the day: each floats along in its own orbit.[40]   36:[37-40]

Another sign for them is how We carried their race through the flood in the laden ark;[41] and similar vessels We have made for them on which they ride.[42] If We want, We can drown them, and they will have no helper *to save them*, nor can they be rescued,[43] except through mercy from Us and as an enjoyment of life for a while.[44] When it is said to them: "Have fear of that which is before you and that which is behind you, so that you may receive mercy," *they pay no heed*.[45] Whenever any sign from the signs of their Rabb comes to them, they turn away from it.[46] Whenever they are asked: "Spend out of what Allah has given you." The disbelievers say to the believers: "Should we feed those whom Allah can feed Himself if He so chooses? You are quite obviously in error!"[47] Further, they say: "When will this promise *of resurrection* come to pass, if what you say is true?"[48] In fact, what they are waiting for is a single blast, which will seize them while they are yet disputing among themselves *in their worldly affairs*.[49] Then, they will neither be able to make a will, nor will they be able to return to their families.[50]   36:[41-50]

The disbelievers' attitude towards spending in the way of Allah

SECTION: 4

Then a trumpet shall be blown and, behold, they will rise up from their graves and hasten to their Rabb.[51] They will say: "Oh, Woe to us! Who has raised us up from our graves? *They will be told:* "This is what the Compassionate *(Allah)* had promised and true was the word of the Rasools."[52] It will be no more than a single blast, and then they will all be gathered before Us.[53] On that Day no soul will suffer the least injustice and you shall be rewarded according to your deeds.[54]   36:[51-54]

A scene from the Day of Judgement

Surely, on that Day, the residents of paradise will be busy with their joy;[55] they and their spouses will be in shady groves reclining on soft couches.[56] They will have all kinds of fruit and they will get whatever they call for;[57] they will be greeted with the word "Salaam *(Peace)*" from the Lord of Mercy *(Allah)*.[58]   36:[55-58]

Allah's greeting to the residents of paradise

While to the sinners, He will say: "Get aside today, you criminals![59] Did I not enjoin you, O children of Adam, not to worship Shaitân, who is your open enemy,[60] and that you should worship Me, which is the Right Way?[61] Yet, in spite of this, he *(Shaitân)* has led a great number of you astray. Didn't you have common sense?[62] This is the hell, of which you were repeatedly warned.[63] Now! Burn in it this Day because you persistently rejected the truth."[64] On that Day, We shall seal their mouths while their hands will speak to Us and their feet will bear witness

Allah's address to the criminal sinners

On the Day of Judgement, the hands and feet of the wrongdoers shall testify

to all their misdeeds.[65]   Had it been Our Will, We could surely have blotted out their eyes; and let them run about groping for the way, then how could they see?[66]   And had it been Our Will, We could have deformed them *(paralyzing them)* in their places, then neither could they move forward nor retrace their steps.[67]

36:[59-67]

SECTION: 5

The Qur'an is to warn those who are alive and establish charge against the disbelievers

Those to whom We grant long life, We reverse their nature. Do they not understand anything *from this*?[68]   We have not taught him *(Muhammad)* poetry, nor does it behoove him. This is nothing but a reminder and a plain Qur'an[69]   to warn those who are alive and to establish the charge against the disbelievers.[70]   Do they not see that among the other things which Our hands have fashioned, We have created cattle which are under their domination?[71]   We have subjected these animals to them, that they may ride on some and eat *the meat* of others;[72]   in them there are other advantages and drinks *(milk)* for them. Should they not then be grateful?[73]   Yet, they have taken other gods besides Allah hoping to get their help.[74]   But they do not have the ability to help them, yet, *their worshippers* stand like warriors ready to defend them.[75]   Let not their words grieve you *(O Muhammad)*. Surely, We have knowledge of all that they conceal and all that they reveal.[76]

36:[68-76]

Allah, Who has created man, shall give him life again for accountability on the Day of Judgement

Does not man see that We have created him from a sperm? Yet, he stands up as an open adversary.[77]   He starts making comparisons for Us and forgets his own creation. He says: "Who will give life to bones that have been decomposed?"[78]   Tell them: "He Who has created them for the first time, will give them life again, He is well-versed in every kind of creation.[79]   It is He Who produces for you the spark from the green tree to kindle fire therewith.[80]   Does He Who has created the heavens and the earth, no power to create the likes of them?" Of course He does! He is the All-Knowing Supreme Creator.[81]   Whenever He intends a thing, He needs only to say: "Be," and it is.[82]   Glory be to Him in Whose hands is the Kingdom of all things; and to Whom you shall all be brought back.[83]

36:[77-83]

37: AS-SÂFFÂT

Period of Revelation

This Sûrah was revealed in the last stage of the middle Makkan period when the Prophet and his Companions were passing through very difficult and discouraging circumstances.

Major Issues, Divine Laws and Guidance

* Allah Himself testifies that your God is one and the shaitâns do not have any access to the exalted assembly of angels.
* Life in the hereafter and the Day of Judgement are real.
* Scenes from the Day of Judgement:
    - Dialogue between the followers and the leaders who mislead them.
    - A scene from the scenes of Paradise.
    - A sample of conversation between the residents of Paradise.
    - A scene from the scenes of Hell.
* Prayer of the Prophet Nûh and Allah's response.
* The Story of the Prophet Ibrâheem (Abraham):
    - He questioned his people for worshipping idols.
    - His people threw him in the furnace, but Allah saved him.
    - He prayed for a son and Allah granted him a son.
    - Allah tested him by asking to offer the sacrifice of his only son and he passed the test.
* Risâlat (Prophethood) of Musa (Moses), Haroon (Aaron), Ilyâs (Elias) and Lût (Lot), peace be upon them all.
* Story of the Prophet Yûnus (Jonah), peace be upon him.
* Allah has promised to help His Rasools and His devotees.

The disbelievers of Makkah have been severely warned for their attitude of mockery, ridicule towards the Prophet's message of Tawheed, the Hereafter, and their utter refusal to accept and acknowledge his claim of Prophethood. In the end, they have been plainly warned that the Prophet, whom they are mocking and ridiculing, will overwhelm them in spite of their power in the very courtyards of their houses. Brief and impressive arguments have been given about the validity of the doctrines of Tawheed and the Hereafter. Criticism has been made of the creed of the Mushrikeen (those who worship other deities beside Allah) showing the absurdity of their beliefs; they have been informed of the evil consequences of their deviations, which have been contrasted with the splendid results of the faith and righteous acts.

Then, in continuation, precedents from the past history have been cited to show how Allah had treated His Prophets and their followers, how He has been favoring His faithful servants and punishing their deniers and rejecters.

The most instructive of historical narratives presented in this Sûrah is the importance of the pious life led by the Prophet Ibrâheem (Abraham), who became ready to sacrifice his only son as soon as he was asked by Allah to do so. In this, there was a lesson not only for the disbelieving Quraish who were proud of their blood relationship with him, but also for the Muslims who had believed in Allah and His Messenger. By narrating this event, they were told about the essence and the real spirit of Islam, and how a true believer should be ready to make sacrifices for the pleasure of Allah. The believers are given the good news that they should not be disheartened at the hardships and difficulties that they had to encounter in the beginning, for in the end, they will be successful. The bearers of falsehood, who appeared to be dominant at the time, would be overwhelmed and vanquished at the hands of the Muslims. A few years later, the turn of events proved that it was not an empty consolation but an inevitable reality of which the believers were foretold in order to strengthen their hearts.

37: AS-SÂFFÂT

This Sûrah revealed at Makkah, has 5 sections and 182 verses.

In the name of Allah, the Compassionate, the Merciful

SECTION: 1

I swear by those who arrange themselves in ranks,[1]   by those who drive away *devils,*[2]   and by those who proclaim the message *of Allah,*[3]   that surely, your God is One *(Allah)*,[4]   the Rabb of the heavens and of the earth, and all that lies between them, and the Rabb of the easts *(every point of the sun rising)*.[5]   We have indeed decked the worldly heaven with beautiful stars[6]   and to secure it against all obstinate rebellious shaitâns.[7]   They cannot even hear the words of the exalted assembly *of angels* and they are darted at from every side *if they try to get closer;*[8]   they are repulsed and are under a constant chastisement.[9]   Eavesdroppers are pursued by a flaming fire of piercing brightness.[10]   Ask them: "What is more difficult - their creation or the rest of Our creation? - Them We have created out of a sticky clay.[11]   37:[1-11]

Allah testifies that your God is one God and that shaitâns do not have excess to the exalted assembly of angels

You marvel *at their insolence*, while they mock *at you and the Qur'an*.[12]   When they are admonished, they pay no heed.[13]   When they see a sign, they mock at it,[14]   and say: "This is nothing but plain sorcery.[15]   What! When we are dead and have become dust and bones, shall we be raised to life again[16]   - we and also our forefathers of the ancient time?"[17]   Tell them: "Yes, and you shall then be humiliated."[18]   It will be just a single shout, and they will see it all with their own eyes.[19]   "Ah, woe to us!" They shall exclaim, "this is the Day of Judgement!"[20]   *It will be said: "Yes,* this is the same Day of Judgement which you used to deny."[21]
          37:[12-21]

Life in the hereafter and the Day of Judgement are real

SECTION: 2

It will be commanded: "Gather all the wrongdoers, their companions and those whom they used to worship[22]   besides Allah and show them the way to hell.[23]   *When they will all be gathered and angels will start pushing them towards hell, Allah shall say:* "Stop for a while, they have to be questioned:[24]   "What is the matter with you today that you do not help each other?"[25]   Nay! On that Day they shall all be submissive.[26]   Some of them will step forward to question one another.[27]   *The followers will say to their leaders:* "It was you who used to come at us from the

A scene from the Day of Judgement and a treat for the wrongdoers

A dialogue between the followers and the leaders who mislead them

right hand *(right hand is a symbol of authority) and forced us towards the wrong way.*"[28] They will reply: "Nay! But it was you who had no faith.[29] We had no power over you; the fact is that you were rebellious people;[30] true is the verdict which Our Rabb has passed upon us; we shall indeed taste *the punishment of our sins*:[31] We misled you, for we ourselves were astray."[32] So on that Day they shall all be partners in the punishment.[33] Thus, shall We deal with the criminals;[34] for when they were told: "There is none worthy of worship but Allah," they used to puff themselves up with pride[35] and say: "What! Should we give up our gods for the sake of a mad poet?"[36] Whereas he had come with the truth and had confirmed *the message of* prior Rasools.[37] You are surely going to taste the painful punishment:[38] and this reward is nothing except for what you had done.[39] 37:[22-39]

A view from the scenes of paradise

But the sincere devotees of Allah[40] shall have familiar sustenance[41] - fruits, and shall be honored[42] in the gardens of delight.[43] Reclining face to face upon soft couches,[44] they shall be served with goblets filled at a fountain of wine,[45] a crystal-white drink, delicious to those who drink it.[46] It will neither have bad effect nor will it make them drunk.[47] And beside them there will be chaste and beautiful dark-eyed virgins,[48] as if they were delicate eggs closely guarded.[49] Some of them will be asking questions to others.[50]

An example of conversation from a resident of paradise

One of them will say: "I had a friend[51] who used to ask: 'Are you really of those who accept *(the Resurrection after death)*?[52] When we are dead and turned to dust and bones, shall we ever be brought to judgement?'"[53] He will say: "Would you like to see him?"[54] He will look down and see *his friend* in the midst of hellfire.[55] Then he will say: "By Allah! You had almost ruined me.[56] Had it not been for the grace of my Rabb, I should certainly have been among those who are brought there.[57] Is it not so that we shall not die[58] after our first death and that we shall not be chastised?"[59] Most surely, it is a mighty achievement.[60] For such an end, let every one strive who wishes to strive.[61] 37:[40-61]

A scene from the scenes of hell

Is this a better entertainment or the tree of Zaqqum?[62] Surely, We have made this tree a trial for the wrongdoers.[63] Surely, it is a tree that grows in the bottom of the hellfire,[64] bearing fruits as if they were heads of shaitâns;[65] on it they shall feed and with it they shall fill their bellies.[66] Then on top of that, they will be given a concoction made from boiling water.[67] Then to hellfire they shall be returned.[68] In fact, they found their fathers on the wrong path,[69] and they are eagerly following their footsteps.[70] Most of the ancients went astray before them,[71] though We had sent Warners to them.[72] See what was the end of those who had been forewarned: *they all perished,*[73] except the sincere devotees of Allah.[74]   37:[62-74]

SECTION: 3

Nûh prayed Us; see how excellent was Our response to his prayer![75] We delivered him and his people from the mighty distress,[76] and made his progeny to be the only survivors,[77] and We left his good name among the later generations.[78] Salutation to Nûh among the people of the worlds.[79] Thus do We reward the righteous.[80] Surely, he was one of Our believing devotees.[81] Then the rest We drowned *in the great flood*.[82]   37:[75-82]

> The Prophet Nûh prayed and Allah respond to his prayers

Surely, Ibrâheem belonged to the first group *(who followed Nûh's way),*[83] when he came to his Rabb with a pure heart.[84] Behold, he said to his father and to his people: "What are these that you worship?[85] Would you serve false gods instead of Allah?[86] What is your idea about the Rabb of the worlds?"[87] Then he looked at the stars one time[88] and said "I am feeling sick."[89] So his people left him behind and went away *to their national fair.*[90] He *sneaked into the temple,* turned to their gods and said: "Why don't you eat *from these offerings before you*?[91] What is the matter with you that you do not speak?"[92] Then he fell upon them, smiting them with his right hand.[93] The people came running to the scene.[94] "Would you worship that which you have carved with your own hands," he said,[95] "when Allah is the One Who created you and that which you have carved?"[96] They said to one another: "Prepare for him a furnace and throw him into the blazing flames."[97] Thus did they scheme against him: but We humiliated them in their scheme.[98]   37:[83-98]

> The story of the Prophet Ibrâheem, "The Friend of Allah"

Ibrâheem said: "I am going to take refuge with my Rabb, He will surely guide me.[99] O my Rabb! Grant me a righteous *son.*"[100] So We gave him the good news of a clement son.[101] When he reached the age to work with him, *Ibrâheem* said to him: "O my son! I have seen a vision that I should offer you as a sacrifice, now tell me what is your view." He replied: "O my father! Do as you are commanded: you will find me, if Allah so wills, of the patient."[102] And when they both submitted to Allah and *Ibrâheem*

> The Prophet Ibrâheem was asked to offer his only son in sacrifice as a test and he fulfilled it

laid down his son prostrate upon his forehead for sacrifice,[103]   We called out to him: "O Ibrâheem *stop*![104]   You have fulfilled your vision." Thus do We reward the righteous.[105]   That was indeed a manifest test.[106]   We ransomed his son for a great sacrifice[107] and We left his good name among the later generations.[108]   Salutation to Ibrâheem.[109]   Thus We reward the righteous.[110]   Surely, he was one of Our believing devotees.[111]   We gave him the good news of *his son* Ishâq - a prophet - one of the righteous.[112]   We blessed him and Ishâq both. Among their progeny there are some who are righteous and some who clearly wrong their own souls.[113]

37:[99-113]

SECTION: 4

Allah bestowed His favors on Prophets Musa and Haroon

We bestowed Our favor on Musa and Haroon.[114]   We delivered them with all their people from the mighty distress.[115]   We helped them, so they became victorious.[116]   We gave them the explicit Book *(Torah)*,[117]   and guided them both to the Right Way.[118]   We left their good names among the later generations.[119]   Salutation to Musa and Haroon.[120]   Thus do We reward the righteous.[121]   Surely, they were two of Our believing devotees.[122]

37:[114-122]

Ilyâs (Elias) was one of the Rasools of Allah

Ilyâs *(Elias)* was surely one of Our Rasools.[123]   "Behold," he said to his people, "Have you no fear *of Allah*?[124]   Would you invoke Bâ'l *(their invented god)* and forsake the best of the Creators[125] - Allah - Who is your Rabb and the Rabb of your forefathers?"[126]   But they denied him, so they will certainly be called to account,[127] with the exception of the sincere devotees of Allah.[128]   We left his good name among the later generations.[129]   Salutation to Ilyâs.[130]   Thus do We reward the righteous.[131]   He was surely one of Our believing devotees.[132]   37:[123-132]

Lût was also a Rasool of Allah

Lût was one of Our Rasools.[133]   Behold, We delivered him and his whole family[134] except an old woman who was among those who remained behind,[135]   and We destroyed the others.[136]   Surely, you pass by their ruins in the morning[137] and at night. Will you not use your common sense?[138]   37:[133-138]

SECTION: 5

Story of the Prophet Yûnus (Jonah)

Yûnus *(Jonah)* was surely one of Our Rasools.[139]   He ran away to the laden ship;[140] and when he took part in the casting of lots, he lost *and was then thrown into the sea*.[141]   A whale swallowed him, for he had become blameworthy.[142]   Had he not *repented and became* of those who glorify Allah,[143]   he would certainly have remained inside its belly till the Day of Resurrection.[144]   Then We cast him upon a desolate shore in a state of serious illness[145]   and caused a gourd plant to grow over him.[146] We sent him to a nation of one hundred thousand people or more.[147]   They believed in him, so We permitted them to enjoy their life for a while.[148]   37:[139-148]

Just ask *the unbelievers*: *Does it make any sense that* their Rabb should have daughters while they choose to have sons?[149] Or is it that We created the angels as females and they were present at their creation?[150]   Surely, they invent a lie when they say: [151] "Allah has children. They are utter liars."[152]   Would He choose daughters rather than sons?[153]   What is the matter with you? How do you judge?[154] Will you not take heed?[155] Or do you have any proof *of what you are saying*?[156]   Show us your scriptures if you are truthful![157]   They assert blood-relationship between Him and the jinns; and the jinns know quite well that they will be called *to account*.[158]   Glory be to Allah! He is free from what they ascribe to Him,[159]   except Allah's sincere devotees *who do not attribute such things to Him*.[160] Therefore, neither you nor those whom you worship[161] can deceive anyone about Allah[162]   except him who is destined for hell.[163]   *In fact, the angels say:* "We each have our appointed place.[164]   We arrange ourselves in ranks for His service[165]   and we are surely those who declare His glory."[166]
37:[149-166]

Mushrikeen's claim of Angels being daughters of Allah and Jinns having blood relations with Allah are utterly false

Before this, *the same disbelievers* used to say:[167]   "If we had received a reminder which the earlier people had received,[168] We certainly would have been sincere devotees of Allah."[169]   But *now that the Qur'an has come,* they reject it: soon they will find out *the consequences of this attitude*.[170]   We have already promised Our servants whom We sent as Rasools[171]   that they would certainly be helped,[172]   and that Our forces will surely be victorious.[173] So turn away from them for a while[174] and watch them; soon they will it for themselves.[175]   Do they wish to hurry on Our punishment?[176]   But dreadful will be that morning, when it will descend in the courtyards of those who have been forewarned.[177]   So turn away from them for a while[178]   and watch them; soon they will it for themselves.[179] Glory be to your Rabb, the Lord of Honor, *Who is free* from what they ascribe to Him![180] Peace be on the Rasools,[181]   and praise be to Allah, the Rabb of the Worlds.[182]   37:[167-182]

Allah has promised to help His Rasools and His devotees

38: SÂD

Period of Revelation

According to some traditions this Sûrah was revealed in the 4th year of the Prophethood after Sayyidunâ Umar embraced Islam which happened after the migration to Habsha. Yet, other traditions indicate that it was revealed during the last illness of Abu Tâlib, the uncle of the Prophet, i.e. the 10th or 11th year of the Prophethood.

Major Issues, Divine Laws and Guidance

* Al-Qur'an is full of admonition. The disbelievers are in sheer arrogance for calling the Prophet a liar.
* Story of the Prophet Dawôôd (David):
    - The mountains and birds used to sing the rhymes of Allah with him.
    - The two litigants, who came to him for a decision.
* Allah has not created the heavens and earth in vain.
* Story of the Prophet Sulaimân:
    - His inspection of steeds which were used in Jihâd.
    - His prayer to grant him a kingdom, similar of which may not be granted to any one.
* Story of the Prophet Ayûb, his sickness, patience and relief.
* The mission of the Prophet:
    - To warn the people
    - To declare that there is no divinity except Allah.
* Story of the creation of Adam and disobedience of Iblees (Shaitân).

Here is a narration of the traditions related by Imam Ahmed, Nasâi, Tirmidhi, Ibn Jareer, Ibn Abi Shaibah, Ibn Abi Hâtim, Muhammad bin Ishâq and others:

When Abu Tâlib fell ill, and the Quraish chiefs knew that the end of his life was near, they held consultations and decided to approach the old chief with the request that he should solve the dispute between them and his nephew. They feared that if Abu Tâlib died and then they subjected Muhammad (peace be upon him) to harsh treatment after his death, the Arabs would taunt them, saying, "They were afraid of the old chief as long as he lived, now that he is dead, they have started mistreating his nephew." At least 25 of the Quraish chiefs including Abu Jahl, Abu Sufyân and Umayyah bin Khalaf went to Abu Tâlib. First, they put before him their *usual complaints against the Prophet, then said, "We have come to present before you a just request and it is: let your nephew leave us to our religion, and we shall leave him to his. He may worship whomever he pleases: we shall not stand in his way in this matter; but he should not condemn our gods and should not try to force us to give them up. Please ask him to make terms with us on this condition." Abu Tâlib called the Prophet and said, "Dear nephew, these people of your tribe have come to me with a request. They want you to agree with them on a just matter so as to put an end to your dispute with them." Then he told him about the request of the chiefs of the Quraish. The Prophet replied, "Dear uncle: I shall request them to agree upon one thing, which, if they accept, will enable them to conquer the whole of Arabia and subject the non-Arab world to their domination. "Hearing this the people were first confounded; they did not know how they should turn down such a proposal. Then, after they had considered the matter, they replied: "You speak of one thing: we are prepared to repeat ten others like it, but please tell us what it is." The Prophet said: Lâ-Ilâh-ill-Allah. At this they got up all together and left the place saying what Allah has quoted in the first section of this Sûrah.*

The Sûrah begins with a review of the aforesaid meeting and the discourse is based on the dialogue between the Prophet and the disbelievers. Allah says that the actual reason for their denial is not because of any flaw in the message of Islam, but their own arrogance, jealousy and insistence on following their ancestors blindly. They are not prepared to believe in a man from their own clan as a Prophet of Allah and follow him. After describing the stories of nine Prophets, one after the other, Allah has emphasized the point that His law of justice is impartial and that only the people of right attitude are acceptable to Him, that He calls to account and punishes every wrongdoer whoever he may be. He likes only those people who do not persist in wrongdoing and repent as soon as they are informed about it, they live their lives in this world keeping in mind their accountability to Allah in the Hereafter.

In conclusion, reference has been made of the story of Adam and Iblees (Shaitân), which is meant to tell the disbelieving Quraish that the same arrogance and vanity which was preventing them from accepting Muhammad (peace be upon him) had prevented Iblees also from bowing before Adam. Iblees felt jealous of the high rank that Allah had given to Adam and was cursed when he disobeyed His Command. Likewise, "You, O people of Quraish, are feeling jealous of the high rank that Allah has bestowed on Muhammad (peace be upon him) and are not prepared to obey him whereas Allah has appointed him as His Rasool. Therefore, if you do not follow him you will be doomed ultimately to the same fate as that of Shaitân."

38: SÂD

This Sûrah, revealed at Makkah, has 5 sections and 88 verses

In the name of Allah, the Compassionate, the Merciful

SECTION: 1

The Qur'an is full of admonition.

The unbelievers are in sheer arrogance for calling the Prophets as liars

Sâd.[1]   By the Qur'an which is full of admonition![1] Surely, the unbelievers are in sheer arrogance and perverseness.[2] How many generations have We destroyed before them? *When their doom approached*, they all cried out *for mercy*, but it was no longer the time to be saved.[3]   They wonder that a Warner has come to them from among themselves, and the disbelievers say: "He is a sorcerer telling lies![4]   Does he claim that there is only One God in place of all other gods? Surely, this is a strange thing."[5]   Their leaders go about saying: "Pay no heed, stand firm in the service of your gods; this *slogan of One God* is designed *against you*.[6]   We have not heard such a thing from anyone of the people of latter days *(Jews and Christians)*: it is nothing but a fabrication.[7]   Is he the only fit person among us to whom the admonition is revealed?" But in fact, they doubt My admonition, for they have not yet tasted My punishment.[8]   Do they have the treasures of the mercy of your Rabb, the All-Mighty, the Munificent One.[9]   Or do they have sovereignty over the heavens and the earth and all that lies between them? If so, let them ascend by any means *to be in a position of dictating to Allah according to their wishes*.[10]   They are no more than a faction of soldiers who will certainly be defeated.[11]   Before them the people of Nûh, `Ad and Fir'aun, the man of stakes, denied *their Rasools*,[12]   So did Thamûd, the people of Lût and those of Aiykah *(the people of Median)* - all divided themselves into factions;[13]   all denied their Rasools, so just was my torment *that had befallen them*.[14]   38:[1-14]

SECTION: 2

The story of the Prophet Daûd, with whom mountains and birds used to sing the rhymes of Allah

These people also await nothing but a single mighty Blast *(the blowing of the trumpet)* - the one which none may retard.[15] They say: "Our Rabb, hasten our doom for us before the Day of Reckoning."[16]   *O Prophet,* have patience at what they say, and remember Our servant Daûd, the man of strength, who was frequent in turning *to Allah*.[17]   We made the mountains join him in Our praises at evening and the sunrise.[18]   And the birds, too, with all their flocks, join in glorifying *Allah* with him.[19]   We strengthened his kingdom and gave him wisdom and sound judgment in speech *and decision.*[20]   Have you heard the story of the two litigants who made an entry into his prayer chamber through climbing over the wall?[21]   When they entered in upon Daûd and he became terrified, they said: "Have no fear, we are two litigants, one of whom has wronged the other. Judge rightly between us and do not be unjust, and guide us to the Right Way.[22]   This man is my brother; he has ninety nine ewes while I have only one ewe. Yet, he says: 'Turn her over to me' and overpowered me in speach."[23]   *Without listening to the other litigant, Daûd* said: "He has certainly wronged you in seeking to add your ewe to his flock: in fact, many partners are unjust to one another; except those who believe and do good deeds, and they are few indeed." - *While saying this,* Daûd realized that We had tested him. So he sought forgiveness of his Rabb and fell down prostrating himself and turned *to Allah* in repentance.[24]   So We forgave his error. He will enjoy a place of nearness with Us and an excellent abode![25]   *We said:* "O Daûd! We have made you a vicegerent in the earth, so rule among the people with justice and do not follow your own desires lest they mislead you from the Way of Allah. *As for* those who go astray from the Way of Allah, they shall surely have a severe punishment because of forgetting the Day of Reckoning.[26]   38:[15-26]

SECTION: 3

We have not created the heaven and the earth and all that lies between them in vain. That is the fancy of the unbelievers. So woe to the disbelievers from the hellfire.[27]   Should We treat those who believe and do good deeds like those who create mischief in the earth? Should We treat the righteous like the sinners?[28]   This Book *(Al-Qur'an)* which We have sent down to you *(O Muhammad)* is highly blessed, so that they may ponder upon its verses and the men of understanding may learn a lesson from it.[29]

38:[27-29]

To Daûd We gave Sulaimân *(Solomon)*, an excellent devotee! Who was frequent in returning to Us.[30]   *Worthy of mention is the incident* when, one afternoon, excellent-bred steeds *to be used in Jihad,* were presented before him;[31]   and he said: "Surely, I have adopted the love of these good things with a view to glorify my Rabb." *In testing race of the steeds,* when they disappeared from sight,[32]   *he commanded*: "Bring them back to me." Then he began to pass his hand over their legs and necks *with affection.*[33]   Behold, We also put Sulaimân to test and placed a

---

The story of the two litigants who came to Daûd for a decision

Allah has not created the heavens and the earth in vain

The story of Sulaimân's inspection of steeds to be used in Jihad

mere body on his throne, then he turned to Us in repentance,[34] and said "O my Rabb! Forgive me and grant me a kingdom similar to which may not be given to anyone after me. Surely, You are the Bountiful Giver."[35] *We accepted his prayer and* subjected the wind to his power, which blew gently in whichever direction he wanted;[36] and the shaitâns *(Jinns) including* all kinds of builders, divers[37] and others fettered in chains.[38] *We said to him:* "This is Our gift: you may give or withhold to whomever you want, without any accountability."[39] Surely, he has a place of nearness to Us and will have an excellent place of final abode.[40] 38:[30-40]

SECTION: 4

Mention Our devotee Ayyûb *(Job)*, when he called upon his Rabb saying: "Shaitân has afflicted me with distress and suffering,"[41] *and We told him:* "Strike your foot on the ground. A cool spring *will gush forth.* Wash and drink *to refresh your-self.*"[42] And We restored to him his family and similar to them more as a grace from Ourselves and a reminder for the people of understanding.[43] *Then, to fulfill his oath of giving his wife one hundred strikes which he made during his sickness, We said:* "Take a bunch of twigs and strike with it and do not break your oath." Certainly We found him full of patience. *He was* an excellent devotee, who turned to Us over and over again.[44] And mention Our devotees Ibrâheem *(Abraham)*, Ishâq *(Isaac)* and Ya'qoob *(Jacob)*: men of power and vision.[45] Surely, We chose for them a special quality of keeping in mind the abode of the hereafter.[46] Certainly they are with Us; among the best chosen.[47] Also mention Isma'il, Al-Yas'â *(Elisha)* and Dhul-Kifl; all of them were among the best.[48]   38:[41-48]

This *Qur'an* is but a reminder. Surely, the righteous shall return to an excellent resort.[49]   The gardens of eternity, whose gates shall be wide open to receive them.[50]   They shall recline there, calling for abundant fruit and delicious drinks;[51] and beside them there shall be chaste virgin companions of equal age.[52] These are the things which you are being promised on the Day of Reckoning;[53]   this will be Our provision which will never finish.[54]   Such will be *the reward for the righteous*. But for the rebellious, there will be an evil resort[55] - hell, that is! In which they will burn - the worst abode.[56]   Such will it be *the reward for the wrongdoers*.   So they will taste scalding water, festering blood *(pus)*[57]   and other things of the same sort.[58]   *It will be said to the ringleaders:* "Here are your troops being thrown headlong with you. No welcome for them; for they are going to burn in the hellfire.[59]   *The followers* shall say *to their misguided leaders:* "But you! There is no welcome for you either! It was you who have brought us to this end. Such an evil abode."[60]   *Then* they will pray: "Our Rabb, inflict on those who brought this fate upon us double punishment in the fire."[61]   Then they will say *to one another*: "But why do we not see those whom we deemed wicked[62]   and whom we used to ridicule? Or has our eyesight failed to notice them?"[63] Surely, this is the very truth: the people in the hellfire will argue just like that.[64]   38:[49-64]

SECTION: 5

O Prophet, tell them: "My mission is only as a Warner; there is no divinity except Allah, the One, the Irresistible,[65]   the Rabb of the heavens and the earth and all that lies between them, the Almighty, the Oft-Forgiving."[66]   Say: "This is a supreme message:[67]   yet, you turn away from it."[68]   *Also say:* "I had no knowledge of the exalted assembly *of angels* when they were disputing *(the creation of Adam)* among themselves.[69]   It has only been reveled to me, and I am but a clear Warner."[70]   38:[65-70]

The mission of the Rasools is to warn people and declare that there is no divinity except Allah

Behold when your Rabb said to the angels: "I am about to create a man from clay:[71]   then when I have fashioned him and breathed of My *created* spirit into him, fell down and prostrate yourselves before him."[72]   Accordingly all the angels prostrated themselves,[73]   except Iblees; he acted arrogantly and became one of the disbelievers.[74]   *Allah* said: "O Iblees *(Shaitân)*! What prevented you from prostrating yourself to the one whom I have created with My own hands? Are you too arrogant, or do you think that you are one of the exalted ones?"[75]   *Iblees* said: "I am better than he: You created me from fire while You created him from clay."[76]   *Allah* said: "Get out of here: for you are accursed,[77]   and My curse shall be on you till the Day of Judgment."[78]   *Iblees* said: "O my Rabb! Then give me respite till the Day of Resurrection."[79] *Allah* said: "Well, you are given respite[80]   till the Day of Appointed Time."[81]   *Iblees* said: "I swear by Your Honor, I will mislead them all[82]   except your chosen sincere devotees among them."[83]   *Allah* said: "The Truth is, and the Truth I say:[84]   that I shall fill hell with you and all of those who follow you among them."[85]   *O Prophet,* tell them: "I do not ask you any compensation for conveying *this Message*, nor do I pretend to be what I am not.[86] This *Qur'an* is nothing but a Reminder to all the Worlds;[87]   and before long, you will certainly know its truth."[88]   38:[71-88]

The story of the creation of Adam and disobedience of Iblees (Shaitân)

39: AZ-ZUMAR

Period of Revelation

This Sûrah was revealed in the early stage of the Prophet's mission and before permission was granted to the Muslims, who were being persecuted, to migrate to Habsha. Some traditions provide the explanation that this verse was revealed for Sayyidunâ Ja'far bin Abi Tâlib and his companions when they made up their mind to emigrate to Habsha. (Rûh al-Maani, vol. XXII, p. 226).

Major Issues, Divine Laws and Guidance

* The mushrikeen (those who worship someone else beside Allah) try to justify their worship of saints saying: "It brings us closer to Allah."
* On the Day of Judgement no one shall bear the burden of others.
* Believers who cannot practice their faith should migrate to other places where they can.
* The real losers are those who lose their souls and families on the Day of Judgement.
* No one can rescue the one against whom Allah's sentence of punishment has been decreed.
* Al-Qur'an is consistent yet it repeats the teachings in different ways.
* Allah has cited every kind of example in the Qur'an so that people may clearly understand.
* Who can be more wicked than the one who invents a lie against Allah?
* Those who have transgressed against their souls should not despair of Allah's mercy, they should repent while they can.
* On the Day of Judgement, everyone's Book of Deeds shall be laid open and justice shall be done with all fairness.

The entire Sûrah is a most eloquent and effective address which was given before some Muslims migrated to Habsha, from an environment filled with tyranny and persecution, ill-will and antagonism at Makkah. The disbelievers are told that they should not pollute their worshipping of Allah with the worship of any other deity. The truth of Tawheed and the excellent results of accepting it, the falsehood of shirk and the evil consequences of following it, have been explained in a very forceful way so that the people might give up their wrong ways of life and return to the mercy of their Rabb. The believers are also instructed: "If a place has become constrictive for the worship and service of Allah, His earth is vast; you may emigrate to some other place in order to save your faith; Allah will reward you for your patience."

39: AZ-ZUMAR

This Sûrah, revealed at Makkah, has 8 sections and 75 verses.

In the name of Allah, the Compassionate, the Merciful

SECTION: 1

The revelation of this Book *(the Qur'an)* is from Allah, the Almighty, the Wise.[1] Certainly We have revealed to you the Book with the Truth: therefore worship Allah, offering Him your sincere obedience.[2] Beware! Sincere true obedience is due to Allah Alone! *As for* those who take other guardians *(protectors)* besides Him *and justify their conduct, saying:* "We worship them only that they may bring us nearer to Allah." Surely, Allah will judge between them concerning all that in which they differ. Allah does not guide him who is a liar and a disbeliever.[3] If Allah had intended to take a son, He could have chosen anyone He pleased out of His creation: Glory be to Him! *(He is above such things.)* He is Allah, the One, the Irresistible.[4] He created the heavens and the earth to manifest the Truth. He causes the night to succeed the day and the day to overtake the night. He has subjected the sun and the moon to His law, each one following a course for an appointed term. Beware! He is the All-Mighty, the All-Forgiving?[5] He created you all from a single person, then from that person He created his mate. He also created for you eight head of cattle in pairs. He creates you in the wombs of your mothers in stages, one after another, in three layers of darkness. This is Allah, your Rabb. To Him belongs the sovereignty. There is none worthy of worship but He. How can you then turn away from Him?[6] 39:[1-6]

The mushrikeen try to justify their worship of saints saying: "they bring us closer to Allah."

If you disbelieve, *then you should know that* Allah does not need you. He does not like disbelief from His servants. *Therefore,* if you are grateful, He is pleased with you. *On the Day of Judgement,* no bearer of burdens will bear the burden of another. Ultimately, all of you have to return to your Rabb. Then He will tell you the truth of all that you did *in this life.* Surely, He knows even the secrets of your hearts.[7] When some trouble befalls man, he cries to his Rabb and turns to Him in repentance; but no sooner does He bestow on him His favor than he forgets whom he had prayed before and sets up rivals to Allah, thus misleading others from His Way. Tell *such people*: "Enjoy your unbelief for a little while; certainly you will be of the inmates of hellfire."[8] Can he who is

On the Day of Judgement, no bearer of burden shall bear the burden of another

obedient, pass the hours of night prostrating *in worship* or standing *in adoration*, fearing the hereafter and hoping to earn the Mercy of his Rabb, *be compared to the man who does not? Are those who know equal to those who do not know? In fact, none will take heed except the people of understanding.*[9]   39:[7-9]

SECTION: 2

Believers who cannot practice their faith should migrate to other places where they can

      Say: "O My servants who have truly believed, fear your Rabb; those who will do good deeds in this world shall receive a good reward. *If it has become difficult to follow the Right Way where you live, then migrate, you will find that* Allah's earth is spacious. Those who endure with patience will be rewarded without measure."[10]   Say: "I am commanded to worship Allah and serve none but Him[11] and I am commanded to be the first of those who submit *to Allah* as Muslims."[12]   Say: "Surely, I fear - if I disobey my Rabb - the punishment of a mighty Day."[13]   Say: "Allah Alone I worship, and Him Alone I serve.[14]   As for yourselves*, I have conveyed to you the Truth and if you do not believe, then* worship what you want besides Him." Say: "The real

The real losers are those who shall lose their souls and their families on the Day of Judgement

losers are those who will lose their souls as well as their families on the Day of Resurrection. Ah! That will indeed be an open Loss."[15] There shall be layers of fire above them and layers of fire beneath them. This the doom of which Allah frightens His servants: "O My servants, avoid My wrath."[16]   As for those who refrain *from worshipping* Tâghoot *(false deities)* and turn to Allah in repentance, there is good news. So, *O Prophet,* give good news to My servants,[17]   who listen to the Words and follow the best thereof. Such are the ones whom Allah has guided and such are the ones who are endowed with understanding.[18]   39:[10-18]

No one can rescue the one against whom the sentence of punishment has been decreed

      Is the one against whom the sentence of punishment has been decreed *equal to the one who refrains from evil?* Can you rescue the one who is in the fire? *Of course not.*[19]   As for those who truly fear their Rabb, they shall be lodged in lofty mansions, built with one story upon another, beneath which the rivers flow; this is the promise of Allah; Allah does not fail in His promise.[20] Do you not see how Allah sends down water from the sky which penetrates the earth and comes out through springs? With it He brings forth a variety of crops with different colors, then they wither and you see them turning yellow, and then finally He crumbles them *to pieces.* Surely, in this *example,* there is a lesson for the people of understanding.[21]   39:[19-21]

SECTION: 3

Is the one whose heart Allah has opened to Islam and is walking in the light from his Rabb, *like the one who has learned no lesson and is still a non-Muslim.* So woe to those whose hearts are hardened against the remembrance of Allah! They are clearly in error.[22]   Allah has revealed the most beautiful message, a Book consistent in its verses yet, repeating *its teachings in different ways.* Those who fear their Rabb are filled with awe when they hear it; then, their skins and their hearts become pliant to the remembrance of Allah. Such is the guidance of Allah: He guides with it whom He pleases. But he whom He lets go astray shall have none to guide him.[23]   Is the one who will have to confront the terrible punishment of hell fire with his face on the Day of Resurrection *like the one who shall enter paradise*? To such wrongdoers it will be said: "Now taste *the fruits* of your labor."[24]   Those who have gone before them also disbelieved, consequently, the punishment overtook them from the directions they least expected.[25]   So Allah made them taste humiliation in this worldly life, and the punishment in the life to come shall be even more terrible, if they but knew it.[26]   We have cited for mankind every kind of parable in this Qur'an, so that they may learn a lesson.[27]   This Qur'an is revealed in Arabic, which is free from any crookedness, so that they may learn to be righteous.[28]   Allah cites you a parable - there is a *slave* man who is shared by many masters, each pulling this man to himself *(like the man who worships other deities besides Allah)*, and *there is another slave* man who belongs entirely to one master *(like the man who worships Allah Alone)*- are the two alike in comparison? Praise be to Allah! But most of them do not know.[29] *O Prophet,* you shall die and they too shall die.[30]   Then on the Day of Resurrection, your disputes shall be settled in the presence of your Rabb.[31]   39:[22-31]

The Qur'an is consistent in its verses yet repeats its teachings in different ways

Allah has cited every kind of parable in the Qur'an so that people may clearly understand

JUZ (PART): 24

SECTION: 4

Who can be more wicked than the one who invents a lie against Allah?

Who could be more unjust than the one who invents a lie against Allah and rejects the truth when it comes to him? Is there not an abode in hell for such unbelievers?[32] And the one who comes with the truth and the one who confirms it - they are the ones who are the Godfearing.[33] They shall have from their Rabb all that they wish for. Thus shall the righteous be rewarded.[34] Allah will do away from their account their worst deeds and reward them according to their best deeds.[35] Is Allah not all-sufficient for His servant? Yet, they try to frighten you with others besides Him! For such whom Allah lets go astray, there can be no guide.[36] But the one whom Allah guides, none can lead him astray. Is not Allah All-Mighty, the Lord of retribution?[37] If you ask them: "Who created the heavens and the earth?" They will surely say: "Allah." Ask them: "Do you think then, that if Allah intends to harm me, can they *(your goddesses)* - whom you invoke besides Allah - save me from His harm or if He wants to bestow on me His blessings, can they withhold His blessings?" Tell them: "Allah is all-sufficient for me. On Him do the reliants rely."[38] Say: "O my people! *If you do not believe me, then* do whatever you want in your positions and so shall I. Soon you will find out[39] as to whom shall come the disgraceful scourge and who shall get the everlasting punishment."[40] *O Prophet,* surely, We have revealed to you the Book with the truth, for *the instruction of* Mankind. He who follows the Right Way shall follow it for his own good; and he who goes astray shall do so at his own peril. You are not *set up as* a guardian over them.[41]　　39:[32-41]

If Allah intends to harm you, no one can save you and if He intends to bestow His blessings upon you, no one can withhold them

SECTION: 5

It is Allah Who recalls the souls of people upon their death and the living people during their sleep

It is Allah Who recalls the souls at the time of their death, and of the living during their sleep. He withholds the souls of those on whom He has passed the decree of death, and restores the rest till an appointed term. Surely, there are signs in this for those who think.[42] Have they taken others besides Allah to intercede for them? Ask them: *"How can they intercede,* if they have neither control over anything nor do they understand?"[43] Say: "Intercession is wholly in the hands of Allah. To Him belongs the dominion of the heavens and the earth, and to Him you shall all be brought back."[44] When Allah's Oneness is mentioned, the hearts of those who deny the hereafter shrink with aversion; but when other *deities* than He are mentioned, they are filled with joy.[45] Say: "O Allah! Creator of the heavens and the earth, Who has the knowledge of the unseen and the seen! You Alone can judge the disputes of your servants concerning those matters in which they differ."[46]   39:[42-46]

If the wrongdoers possessed all the treasures of the earth and as much more besides it, they would gladly offer it to redeem themselves from the painful punishment on the Day of Resurrection. For there will become apparent to them from Allah what they would never have imagined.[47]   The evil result of their deeds will become manifest to them and they will be completely encircled by what they used to mock at.[48]   Man is such that when he is in trouble he appeals to Us; but when We bestow Our favor upon him, he says: "This has been given to me because of certain knowledge *I possess*." Nay! It is but a test, yet, most of them do not know.[49]   The same was said by those who passed before them, but they gained no benefit from what they had earned,[50]   and the evil consequences of their deeds overtook them. Very soon, the wrongdoers among these people will also be overtaken by the evil consequences of their misdeeds and they will not be able to escape.[51]   Do they not know that Allah   enlarges the provision for whom He pleases and restricts it *from whom He wills?* Surely, there are signs in this for those who believe.[52]   39:[47-52]

If the wrongdoers possess all the treasures of the earth and much more besides it, they will gladly offer it as a ransom to redeem themselves on the Day of Judgment

SECTION: 6

Say: "O My servants who have transgressed against their souls, do not despair of Allah's mercy, for Allah forgives all sins. It is He Who is the Forgiving, the Merciful.[53]   Turn in repentance to your Rabb, and submit to Him before there comes to you the scourge: for then, there shall be none to help you.[54]   Follow the best way that is revealed to you by your Rabb before the scourge comes to you all of a sudden while you do not perceive it.[55]   Lest someone should say: 'Alas! I neglected my duty towards Allah and I was one of those who mocked *at His revelations*.'[56]   Or lest he should say: 'If Allah had guided me, I would have been one of the righteous.'[57] Or lest he should say upon seeing the punishment: 'I wish I had another chance, I would certainly be among the doers of good.'"[58]   *Then Allah will say to him:* "My revelations did come to you; but you denied them; you were arrogant and you were among the unbelievers."[59]   On the Day of Judgment you shall see that the faces of those who uttered falsehood against Allah shall be turned black. Is there not an abode in hell for such arrogant?[60]   *On the contrary*, Allah will deliver the righteous to their place of salvation. No harm shall touch them, nor shall they ever grieve.[61]   Allah is the Creator of all things and of all things He is the Guardian.[62]   To Him belong the keys of the heavens and the earth.

Those who have transgressed against their souls should not despair of Allah's mercy, they should repent while they can

Those who deny the revelations of Allah, it is they who will be the losers.[63]   39:[53-63]

SECTION: 7

Worship Allah and be among His thankful servants

O Prophet say *to the mushrikeen:* "O ignorant! Do you bid me to worship someone other than Allah?"[64]   *Tell them plainly because* it has already been revealed to you as it was revealed to those before you that if you commit shirk, all your deeds will become fruitless and you will surely be among the losers."[65]   Therefore, worship Allah and be among *His* thankful servants.[66]   They have not appraised Allah with true appraisal, while on the Day of Resurrection the whole earth shall be in His grasp and all the heavens shall be rolled up in His right hand. Glory be to Him! Exalted be He above what they associate with Him.[67]   The Trumpet shall be blown, and all that is in the heavens and the earth will fall dead except those whom Allah will please *to exempt*. Then the Trumpet will be blown for the second time and behold! They shall all stand up, looking around.[68]   The earth will be shining with the light of her Rabb, the Book of record will be laid open, the Prophets and other witnesses will be brought in, and justice shall be done between people with all fairness: none shall be wronged.[69] Every soul will be paid in full according to its deeds, for He knows fully well as to what they did.[70]   39:[64-70]

On the Day of Judgment, the Book of Deeds will be laid open and justice will be done with all fairness

SECTION: 8

After Judgment, the unbelievers will be driven to hell and the righteous will be led to paradise

After the Judgment, the Unbelievers will be driven to hell in groups. When they reach there, its gates will be opened and its keepers will say: "Did there not come to you Rasools from among yourselves, who recited to you the revelations of your Rabb and forewarned you about the meeting of this Day?" "Yes," they will answer. But at that time the sentence of punishment would have been already announced against the unbelievers."[71]   They will be told: "Enter the gates of hell to live therein forever." Evil shall be the abode of the arrogant."[72]   As for those who fear their Rabb, they shall be led towards paradise in groups. When they reach there, its gates will be opened, and its keepers will say: "Peace be upon you! You have done well, now enter it to live therein forever."[73]   They will say: "Praise be to Allah Who has truly fulfilled His promise and has given us this land to inherit, now we can live in paradise wherever we like." How excellent will be the reward for the righteous![74]   You will see the angels surrounding the Divine Throne, glorifying their Rabb with His praises. The Judgment between the people will be made with perfect justice, and it will be proclaimed: "Praise be to Allah the Rabb of the worlds!"[75]   39:[71-75]

40: AL-MU'MIN / GHÂFIR

Period of Revelation

This Sûrah was revealed after Sûrah Az-Zumar and according to Ibn 'Abbâs and Jâbir bin Zaid, its present position in the order of the Sûrahs in the Qur'an is the same as its chronological order of revelation.

Major Issues, Divine Laws and Guidance

* The angels who bear the throne of Allah pray for those humans who repent and follow the Right Way.
* A scene from the Day of Judgement.
* Allah knows the furtive looks and secret thoughts.
* Story of the Prophet Musa, Fir'aun, Hâmân and Qaroon.
* An excellent speech of one of the relatives of Fir'aun in favor of the Prophet Musa.
* Fir'aun plotted against that relative, who was a believer, but Allah saved him and destroyed the people of Fir'aun. They are being presented before the fire of Hell every morning and evening.
* Allah says; "Call me, I will answer your prayers."
* No one has the right to be worshipped except Allah, the Creator and the Rabb of the worlds.
* Those who argue about the revelations of Allah will soon find out the Truth.
* Allah has sent many Rasools before Muhammad (peace be upon him): of them some are mentioned in the Qur'an and some are not.
* Belief after seeing the scourge of Allah is of no avail to the disbelievers.

The disbelievers were creating every kind of suspicion in the minds of the people about the teachings of the Qur'an, the message of Islam and the Prophet. They were also preparing the groundwork for the assassination of the Prophet Muhammad (peace be upon him).

As an admonition to the conspirators of assassination, the story of a Believer from the people of Fir'aun (Pharaoh) has been cited. The disbelievers are warned that if they do not desist from wrangling against the Revelations of Allah, they will be doomed to the same fate as the nations of the past and they shall be given worse torment in the Hereafter. At that time, they shall repent, but it will be too late.

40: AL-MU'MIN / GHÂFIR

This Sûrah, revealed at Makkah, has 9 sections and 85 verses.

In the name of Allah, the Compassionate, the Merciful

SECTION: 1

Hâ M'eem.[1] The revelation of this Book is from Allah, the Almighty, the All-Knowledgeable,[2] the Forgiver of sins, the Acceptor of repentance, the Stern in punishment and the Lord of bounty; there is none worthy of worship but He, to Whom all shall return.[3] None dispute the revelations of Allah but those who disbelieve; so let not their affluent activities in the land deceive you.[4] Before them the people of Nûh denied *the Message* and so did other groups after them. Every nation plotted against its Prophet, to seize him and sought to refute the truth through falsehood; but I seized them, and how terrible was My retribution![5] Thus shall the Word of your Rabb be proved true against the disbelievers; they are the inmates of hellfire.[6] Those *angels* who bear the Throne *of Allah* and those who stand around it glorify their Rabb with His praises, believe in Him and implore forgiveness for the believers, saying: "Our Rabb! You embrace all things with your mercy and knowledge. Forgive those who repent and follow Your Way, and save them from the punishment of the blazing fire.[7] O our Rabb, admit them to the gardens of eternity which You have promised them together with all the righteous among their fathers, their spouses and their descendants. You are the All-Mighty, All-Wise.[8] Protect them from the evil consequences of their deeds. He from whom You ward off evil consequences that Day will surely earn Your mercy, and that will surely be the highest achievement.[9]   40:[1-9]

SECTION: 2

On the Day of Judgement it will be said to the disbelievers: "Allah's hatred towards you was far greater - *during your worldly life* when you were called to the Faith and you used to refuse - than your hatred of yourselves."[10] They will say: "Our Rabb! Twice have You made us die and twice have You given us life. We now confess our sins. Is there any way out?"[11] *They shall be answered: "You are facing this fate* because when you were asked to believe in Allah, the One and Only, you disbelieved; but when you were asked to commit shirk *(associate other partners with Him),* you believed. Today judgement rests with Allah, the Most

---

Side notes:

No one disputes the revelations of Allah except the unbelievers

The angels who bear the Throne of Allah pray for those humans who repent and follow the Right Way

A scene from the Day of Judgement

High, the Most Great."[12]   It is He Who shows you His signs and sends down sustenance from the heavens for you. Yet, none learns a lesson, *from the observation of these signs,* except those who turn to Him.[13]   So invoke Allah with sincere devotion to Him *(worship none but Him)* however much the unbelievers may dislike it.[14] Possessor of the Highest Rank, the Master of the Throne, sends down the inspiration by His command on those of His servants whom He chooses, that he *(the Prophet who received the revelations)* may warn *mankind* of the Day when they shall meet Him.[15]   The Day when they all shall come forth *from their graves* with nothing hidden from Allah. *It will be asked:* "Whose is the Kingdom today?" *No one shall dare to speak, and Allah Himself will say:* "It is Allah's, the One, the Irresistible.[16]   Today every soul shall be rewarded for whatever it has earned; today there shall be no injustice; surely, Allah is swift in settling accounts."[17]   *O Prophet,* warn them of the Day that is drawing near, when the hearts will leap up to the throats with grief; when the wrongdoers will have neither friend nor intercessor who could be listened to.[18]   Allah knows the furtive looks and the secret thoughts,[19]   and Allah will judge with all fairness. *As for* those whom the unbelievers invoke besides Him, they will not *be in a position* to judge at all. Surely, it is Allah Alone Who hears all and sees all.[20]   40:[10-20]

Allah knows the furtive looks and the secret thoughts

SECTION: 3

Have they not travelled through the land and seen what was the end of those who have gone before them? They were far greater in power than these and *left greater* traces in the land: but Allah seized them for their sins and there was none to protect them from Allah.[21]   That was because there came to them their Rasools with clear revelations but they denied: so Allah seized them. Mighty is He indeed and stern is His retribution.[22]   40:[21-22]

Those who denied the Prophets and Allah's revelations were all destroyed

Indeed, We sent Musa with Our signs and a clear authority,[23]   to Fir'aun *(Pharaoh)* Hâmân and Qaroon *(Korah)*; but they called him 'a sorcerer, a liar'.[24]   Then, when he brought them the truth from Us, they said: "Kill the sons of those who share his faith and spare only their females." But futile were the schemes of the unbelievers.[25]   *Finally* Fir'aun said: "Let me kill Musa; and let him invoke his Rabb! I fear that he may change your religion or that he may cause mischief to appear in the land."[26]   Musa said: "I have indeed taken refuge in my Rabb and your Rabb from every arrogant one who does not believe in the Day of Reckoning."[27]

40:[23-27]

The Prophet Musa was sent to Fir'aun, Hâmân and Qaroon, and Fir'aun intended to kill the Prophet Musa

An excellent speech of one of the relatives of Fir'aun in favor of the Prophet Musa

At this, a believer from among the relatives of Fir'aun, who had kept his faith hidden, said: "Will you kill a man merely because he says: 'My Rabb is Allah,' and who has brought you clear signs from your Rabb? If he is lying, may his lie be on his head; but if he is speaking the truth, then some of the dreadful things he is threatening you with may very well fall on you. Surely, Allah does not guide the one who is a lying transgressor."[28]　O my people! You are the rulers and are dominant in the land today: but who will help us against the scourge of Allah, should it befall us?" Fir'aun said: "I am pointing out to you only what I see and I am guiding you only towards the right way."[29]　Then the person who was a true believer said: "O my people! In fact, I fear for you the day *of disaster* like what befell prior parties,[30] such as the people of Nûh, 'Ad and Thamûd and those who came after them, and Allah does not intend to wrong His servants.[31]　And O my People! I fear for you the Day of calling,[32] when you will turn your backs and flee, when there will be none to protect you from Allah. The one whom Allah lets go astray, shall have none to guide him.[33]　Do you remember that a long time before this, Yûsuf came to you with clear signs, but you always remained in doubt concerning what he brought; and when he died you said: 'After him, Allah will never send another Rasool.' Thus Allah lets go astray the ones who are the doubting transgressors,[34]　who dispute the revelations of Allah having no authority vouchsafed to them. Such an attitude is disgusting in the sight of Allah and of the believers. Thus Allah seals up the heart of every arrogant tyrant."[35]　*After hearing this,* Fir'aun said: "O Hâmân! Build me a high tower that I may attain the means of access,[36]　an access to the heavens, so that I may see the God of Musa, I think he is a liar." Thus Fir'aun's evil deeds were made fair-seeming to him and he turned away from the Right Way. The schemes of Fir'aun led him to nothing but destruction.[37]

40:[28-37]

SECTION: 5

The man who was a *true* believer, said: "O my people! Follow me, I shall guide you to the Right Way.[38]　O my people! The life of this world is only temporary enjoyment, while the abode of the hereafter is everlasting.[39]　The one who does evil shall be recompensed to the extent of the evil done; and the one who is a believer and does good deeds, whether man or woman, shall enter the paradise and therein receive sustenance without measure.[40]

And O my people! How is it that I call you to salvation, while you call me to the fire?[41]   You invite me to deny Allah and commit shirk with Him *(worship other gods),* of which I have no knowledge; while I bid you to *worship* the All-Mighty, the All-Forgiving.[42]   No doubt you call me towards those who can neither grant my request in this world nor in the hereafter. In fact, we all have to return back to Allah and the transgressors are the ones who shall go to hell.[43]   Soon you will remember what I have told you, I am entrusting my affairs to Allah, surely, Allah is ever watchful over *His* servants."[44]   So Allah saved *that believer* from all those evil plots that the people devised against him, and the people of Fir'aun were overtaken by a horrible scourge.[45]   It is the fire of hell before which they are presented morning and evening *(from the time of their death until the Day of Resurrection)*, and on the Day when the Hour *of their Judgment* will come, *it will be commanded:* "Make the people of Fir'aun *(Pharaoh)* enter the severest punishment."[46] *Then imagine that time* when these people will start arguing with each other in the fire, and the weak *followers* will say to the arrogant *leaders*: "We were your followers: can you now save us from some of these flames?"[47]   The arrogant *leaders* will reply: "We are all in it together! Allah has already judged between *His* servants."[48] *Also imagine* when the dwellers of fire will ask the Keepers of hell: "Pray to your Rabb for relieving our punishment at least for one day!"[49]   *The Keepers of hell* will ask: "Did there not come to you Rasools with clear revelations?" "Yes," they will answer. *The Keepers of hell* will say: "Then pray yourselves." But vain shall be the prayer of the disbelievers.[50]   40:[38-50]

SECTION: 6

     We surely will help Our Rasools and the believers *both* in this world's life and on the Day when the witnesses will take a stand to testify.[51]   On that Day, no excuses shall avail the wrongdoers. The curse shall be their lot and the worst place will be their home.[52] Indeed We gave Musa *the Book of* Guidance and made the Children of Israel inherit that Book,[53]   which was a guide and an admonition to the people of understanding.[54]   So be patient, the promise of Allah is true. Implore forgiveness for your sins and celebrate the praises of your Rabb evening and morning.[55]   Those who dispute the revelations of Allah with no authority bestowed on them; they nurture in their hearts arrogant ambitions which they shall never attain. Therefore, seek refuge with Allah; It is He Who hears all and sees all.[56]   Certainly, the creation of the heavens and

Allah saved that believer from the plots of Fir'aun and destroyed the people of Fir'aun; now they are presented before the fire of hell morning and evening (punishment of the graves)

Allah does help His Rasools and the believers in this world's life and will help them in the life hereafter

the earth is a greater task than the creation of men; yet, most people do not know.[57]   The blind and those who can see are not alike, nor are the believers who do good deeds *equal* to the wicked; yet, you seldom think.[58]   The hour *of Doom* is sure to come, there is no doubt about it; yet, most people do not believe it.[59]   And your Rabb says: "Call Me, I shall answer *your prayers*. Surely, those who are too arrogant to worship Me shall soon enter hell in utter humiliation."[60]   40:[51-60]

SECTION: 7

It is Allah Who has made for you the night to rest in and the day to see your way around. Surely, Allah is bountiful to mankind, yet, most of the people are not thankful.[61]   Such is Allah your Rabb, the Creator of all things. There is no god but Him. *None has the right to be worshipped except Him,* so how are you being deluded?[62]   Thus were deluded those who denied the revelations of Allah.[63]   It is Allah Who has made the earth a resting place for you, and the sky a canopy. He has molded your bodies and molded them well, and has provided you with good things. Such is Allah, your Rabb. So blessed is Allah, the Rabb of the worlds.[64]   He is the Ever-Living. There is none worthy of worship but He. There-fore, call upon Him with your sincere devotion. Praise be to Allah, the Rabb of the worlds.[65]   *O Prophet*, tell them: "I have been forbidden to worship those whom you invoke besides Allah. *How can I do this* when clear revelations have come to me from my Rabb, and I have been commanded to submit myself to the Rabb of the worlds."[66]   It is He Who has created you from dust, then from a sperm, then from a leechlike mass, then He delivers you *from the womb of your mother* as a child, then He makes you grow to reach the age of full strength, then He makes you *grow to* reach an old age - though some of you die earlier - so that you may complete your appointed term and grow in wisdom.[67]   It is He Who gives you life and causes you to die. *It is He Who* when He decides to do something, needs only to say: "Be," and it is.[68]   40:[62-68]

SECTION: 8

Do you not see how those who argue about the revelations of Allah turn away *from the Right Way*?[69]   Those who have denied the Book *and the Message* which We have sent through Our Rasools shall soon come to know the truth *when they will be cast into the fire of hell*:[70]   when, with yokes around their necks, and chains *in their legs*, they shall be dragged[71]   through scalding fluid

---

Your Rabb says: "Call on Me, I will answer your prayers"

No one has the right to be worshipped except Allah, the Creator and the Rabb of the worlds

Those who argue about the revela-tions of Allah, will soon find out the truth

and burned in the fire of hell.[72]   Then they shall be asked: "Where are those gods whom you invoked in worship[73]   besides Allah?" They will answer: "They have forsaken us, *now we have come to know that* those whom we used to invoke, were in fact nothing." Thus Allah lets the disbelievers go astray.[74]   *It will be said:* "You have met this fate because during your life on earth, you took delight in things other than the truth and behaved insolently.[75] Now enter the gates of hell to live therein forever. What an evil abode will it be for the arrogant!"[76]   So be patient, *O Prophet,* Allah's promise is true. Whether We let you witness the evil consequences with which they are being threatened, or We cause you to die *before We smite them*, in any case, they shall all return to Us.[77]   *O Prophet,* We have sent many Rasools before you; of them there are some whose stories We have relayed to you and others whose stories We have not relayed to you. It was not possible for any of those Rasools to bring a sign except by the leave of Allah. Then when the command of Allah comes, the matter will be decided with justice, and then the wrongdoers will surely suffer the loss.[78]   40:[69-78]

> Allah has sent many Rasools before Muhammad; some are mentioned in The Qur'an and some are not

SECTION: 9

It is Allah Who has provided you with cattle, that you may use some for riding and some for food;[79]   and there are also other advantages in them for you; they take you where you wish to go, *carrying you* on their backs as ships carry you *by the sea*.[80]   Thus, He shows you His signs; then, which of the signs of Allah will you deny?[81]   Have they never travelled through the earth and seen what was the end of those who have gone before them? They were more in number and superior in strength than these and they have left behind greater traces *of their power* in the land; yet, all that they did was of no avail to them.[82]   When their Rasools came to them with clear revelations, they proudly boasted about the *worldly* knowledge they had; but *the very forewarned scourge* at which they mocked, hemmed them in.[83]   When they saw Our scourge, they cried out: "We believe in Allah, the One and Only, and we reject *all those deities* whom we used to associate with Him."[84]   But after seeing Our scourge, their professing the faith *(Islam)* was of no use to them; such was the practice of Allah in dealing with His servants in the past, and *thus* the disbelievers were lost.[85]   40:[79-85]

> Cattle are the signs of Allah for people of understanding

> Belief after seeing the scourge of Allah is of no avail to the disbelievers

41: HÂ M'EEM AS-SAJDAH / FUSSILÂT

Period of Revelation

According to authentic Traditions, this Sûrah was revealed after Sayyidunâ Hamzah embraced Islam and before Sayyidunâ Umar embraced Islam during the early stages of the Prophet's residence at Makkah.

Major Issues, Divine Laws and Guidance

* The Qur'an is revealed to give admonition.
* Woe to those who deny the Hereafter and do not pay Zakah (charity).
* Story of the creation of earth, mountains, seas, skies and heavens.
* Allah's scourge upon the nations of 'Ad and Thamûd.
* On the Day of Judgement, man's own ears, eyes and skin will bear witness against him relating to his misdeeds.
* Those who say their God is Allah and stay firm on it, angels are assigned for their protection.
* The best in speech is the one who calls people towards Allah, does good deeds and says, "I am a Muslim."
* The message which is revealed to the Prophet Muhammad (peace be upon him) is the same message which was revealed to the prior Prophets.
* The Qur'an is a guide and healing for the believers. It is similar to the Book given to the Prophet Musa (Moses).
* On the Day of Judgement, all those gods whom people worshiped besides Allah, shall vanish.
* Have you even considered that if the Qur'an is really from Allah and you deny it, what will happen to you!

The disbelievers had given clear notice to the Prophet to the effect, "You may continue your mission of inviting the people to Allah, but we will go on opposing you as hard as we can to frustrate your mission." To accomplish this objective, they had devised a plan that whenever the Prophet or one of his followers would try to recite the Qur'an before the people, they would make so much noise that no one could hear anything.

The unbelievers were saying: "If an Arab presents a discourse in Arabic, what could be the miracle in it? Arabic is his mother tongue. Anyone could compose anything that he pleased in his mother tongue and then make the claim that he had received it from Allah. A miracle would be if the person would suddenly arise and make an eloquent speech in a foreign tongue which he did not know. Then only could one say that the discourse was not of his own composition, but a revelation from Allah."

In response to this, this Sûrah has clearly stated: "This Qur'an is an unchangeable Book and you can not defeat it by your noise and falsehoods. Whether falsehood comes from the front or makes a secret and indirect attack from behind, it cannot succeed in refuting it. Now that the Qur'an is being presented in your own language so that you may understand it, you say that it should have been revealed in some foreign language. But had We sent it in a foreign language, you yourselves would have said: What a joke! The Arabs are being given guidance in a non-Arabic language, which nobody understands. In fact you have no desire to obtain guidance. You are only inventing new excuses for not affirming the faith. Have you ever considered that if this Qur'an is really from Allah, then what fate you would meet by denying and opposing it?"

41: HÂ-M'EEM AS-SAJDAH / FUSSILÂT

This Sûrah, revealed at Makkah, has 6 sections and 54 verses.

In the name of Allah, the Compassionate, the Merciful

SECTION: 1

The Qur'an is a giver of good news and an admonition

Hâ M'eem.[1] This is revealed by the Compassionate, the Merciful *(Allah)*:[2] a Book whose verses are well explained, a Qur'an in the Arabic language for people who understand.[3] A giver of good news and an admonition: yet, most of the people turn their backs and do not listen.[4] They say: "Our hearts are concealed in veils *from the faith* to which you call us, there is deafness in our ears and there is a barrier between you and us: so you work *your way* and we keep on working *our way.*"[5] *O Prophet* say: "I am but a human being like you. It is revealed to me that your God is but One God, therefore, take the Right Way towards Him and implore His forgiveness. Woe to the mushrikeen *(those who associate other gods with Allah);*[6] those who do not pay Zakah *(obligatory charity) and* deny the hereafter.[7] As for those who believe and do good deeds, they will have a never ending reward.[8]

Woe to those who deny the hereafter and do not pay Zakah

41:[1-8]

SECTION: 2

The Story of the creation of the earth, mountains, seasons, skies and heavens

Ask them: "Do you really deny the One Who created the earth in two Yaums *(days, time periods, stages)* and do you set up rivals in worship with Him while He is the Rabb of the worlds.[9] He set upon it mountains *towering high* above its surface, bestowed blessings upon it, provided it with sustenance *according to the needs* of all its dwellers, in four Yaums *(days, time periods, stages)* equal in length - for *the information of* those who ask.[10] Then He turned towards the sky, which was but smoke, He said to it and to the earth: 'Come forward both of you, willingly or unwillingly,' and they submitted: 'We shall come willingly.'[11] So, from this creation, He formed the seven heavens in two Yaume *(days or stages)* and to each heaven He ordained its laws. We adorned the lowest heaven with brilliant lamps as well as for protection. Such is the design of the All-Mighty, the All-Knowing."[12] 41:[9-12]

Warning to the disbelievers

Now if they turn away, say to them: "I have given you warning of a thunderbolt, like the thunderbolt which struck 'Ad and Thamûd."[13] When their Rasools came to them from before and from behind, saying: "Worship none but Allah," they replied: "If our Rabb wanted *to send us a message*, He would certainly have sent down angels, so we *categorically* deny the message with which you are sent."[14]   As for 'Ad, they conducted themselves with arrogance in the land without any justification and said: "Who is stronger than us in might?" Could they not see that Allah Who created them, was mightier than them? Yet, they continued to reject Our revelations.[15]   So, over a few ill-omened days, We let loose on them a furious hurricane to make them taste a shameful scourge in this life, but more shameful still will be the punishment of the hereafter, and they shall have none to help them.[16]   As for Thamûd, We offered them Our guidance, but they preferred to remain blind rather than to receive guidance *towards the Right Way*; so the thunderbolt of humiliating scourge seized them for their misdeeds,[17]   but We saved those who believed and had the fear *of Allah*.[18]   41:[13-18]

The example of Allah's scourge upon the nations of 'Ad and Thamûd

SECTION: 3

Imagine that Day when the enemies of Allah will be brought together and marched to the hellfire in ranks.[19]   Finally when they will reach there, their ears, their eyes, and their skins will testify to what they used to do.[20]   And they will ask their skins: "Why did you testify against us?" Their *skins* will reply: "Allah Who gives the faculty of speech to everything, has made us speak. He is the One Who created you to begin with, and now to Him you are being brought back.[21]   *During your life on earth* you never thought it necessary to hide yourselves *while committing crimes, you never even thought* that your own ears, your own eyes and your own skins would testify against you. Rather you thought that even Allah had no knowledge of many things that you do.[22]   This thought of yours, which you entertained concerning your Rabb, has brought you to destruction and now you have become of those who are utterly lost."[23]   So *even* if they are patient, the fire will still be their home, and if they beg for pardon, it shall not be granted to them.[24]   We have assigned intimate companions, *of like nature,* for them Who made attractive to them what was before them *(evil deeds during their worldly life)* and what was behind them *(disbelief in the life after death)*; and the same word *(sentence of punishment)* proved true against them, which overtook generations of jinn and men who have gone before them. Indeed, they *all* were losers.[25]   41:[19-25]

On the Day of Judgment people's own ears, eyes and skins will bear witness against them relating to their misdeeds

SECTION: 4

Those who do not listen to the Qur'an shall be sternly punished

The disbelievers say: "Do not listen to this Qur'an and make noise *when it is recited* so that you may gain the upper hand."[26]   We will certainly cause those who disbelieve to taste a severe punishment, and requite them for the worst of their misdeeds.[27]   The reward of the enemies of Allah is hell, which will be their eternal home: a reward for their denying Our revelations.[28]   Wherein, the disbelievers will say: "Our Rabb! Show us those among jinns and mankind who misled us: we shall trample them under our feet so that they become the lowest."[29]   Surely, those who say: "Our Rabb is Allah," and then stay firm on it, the angels will descend on them, *at the time of their death, saying*: "Do not be frightened or grieved, but be delighted at the good news of paradise that you have been promised.[30]   We are your protectors in this life and in the hereafter. There you shall find all that your souls desire and all that you can ask for:[31]   A hospitable gift from the All-Forgiving, All-Merciful."[32]   41:[26-32]

Those who say our God is Allah and then stay firm on it, angels are assigned for their protection

SECTION: 5

The best in speech is the one who calls people towards Allah, does good deeds and says: "I am a Muslim".

Example of Allah's signs

Who is better in speech than the one who calls *people* towards Allah, does good deeds and says: "I am a Muslim?"[33]   Good deeds are not equal to the evil ones. Repel *other's* evil deeds with *your* good deeds. You will see that he with whom you had enmity, will become as if he were your close friend.[34]   But none will attain this quality except those who patiently endure and none will attain this quality except those who are truly fortunate.[35]   If any time you are tempted by Shaitân, seek refuge with Allah. It is He Who hears all and knows all.[36]   Among His signs are the night and the day and the sun and moon. Do not prostrate yourselves before the sun or the moon; rather prostrate yourselves before Allah, Who created them, if you truly are His worshippers.[37]   So if *the unbelievers* disdain *His worship*, let them remember that *the angels* who are nearest to your Rabb, glorify Him day and night, and never feel tired.[38]   And among His other signs is the earth that you see barren; but when We send down rain upon it, it stirs to life and its yield increases. Surely, He Who gives it life, will raise the dead to life. Surely, He has power over all things.[39]   Those who pervert Our revelations are not hidden from Us. *Just consider* who is better? The one who is cast into the fire or the one who emerges safe on the Day of Resurrection? Do as you like; surely, He is watching all your actions.[40]   Those who reject this reminder when it comes to them *shall be punished*. And indeed, it is a mighty Book.[41]   No falsehood can approach it from before or from behind. It is a revelation from the One Who is Wise and Praiseworthy.[42] Nothing is said to you *(O Muhammad)* except what was said to the Rasools before you: that surely your Rabb is the Lord of forgiveness, and *at the same time* the Lord of painful retribution.[43]   Had We revealed this Qur'an in a foreign language, they *(the same people)* would have said: "Why have not its verses been made clear *in our language*? Why a foreign language, *while the audience and the Prophet are* Arabs?" Say *O Prophet*: "To the believers, it is a guide and a healing; and to the ones who do not believe, it is merely their deafness and their blindness; *because they act as if* they are being called from a far-off place, *so they neither hear nor understand.*"[44]   41:[33-44]

Nothing is said to Muhammad which was not said to the prior Prophets; the Qur'an is a guide and healing for the believers

SECTION: 6

Before this Qur'an, We had given the Book to Musa and it was *similarly* disputed. If your Rabb had not already given a word, the Judgment would have been passed between them; grave though their suspicions are about it.[45]   He who does good deeds, does it for his own soul; and he who commits evil, does so at his own peril: Your Rabb is never unjust to His servants.[46]   41:[45-46]

The Book given to the Prophet Musa was similar to The Qur'an

JUZ (PART): 25

On the Day of Judgment all other gods to whom people worship besides Allah shall vanish

To Him *Alone* is referred the knowledge of the Hour *of Doom.* No fruit comes out of its sheath, no female conceives or gives birth but with His knowledge. On the Day *of Judgment* when *Allah* will ask *the unbelievers*: "Where are those partners that you associated with Me?" They will answer: "We confess to you that none of us can vouch for them."[47]   Those deities whom they used to invoke will vanish from them and they shall realize that there is no escape.[48] Man is never tired of praying for good, but when any evil befalls him, he loses hope and is in despair.[49]   And if, after affliction, We vouchsafe him a favor from Ourselves, he is sure to say: "I deserve this, I do not think that the Hour will ever come; and even if I am brought back to my Rabb, I would still get good treatment from Him." *The fact, however, is that* We shall tell the disbelievers the truth of all that they had done and We shall make them taste a severe punishment.[50]   When We bestow favors on man, he turns away and drifts off to another side; and when an evil befalls him, he comes with lengthy supplications.[51]

41:[47-51]

Have you ever considered that if The Qur'an is really from Allah and you deny it, what will happen to you

O Prophet, ask them: "Have you ever considered: if this *Qur'an* is really from Allah and you deny it, who can be more astray than you who have gone too far in defying Him?"[52]   Soon shall We show them Our signs in the universe and in their own souls, until it becomes clear to them that this *Qur'an* is indeed the truth. Is it not enough that your Rabb is a witness over everything?[53] Still they are in doubt about meeting their Rabb! Yet it is He Who encompasses everything.[54]   41:[52-54]

42: ASH-SHURÂ

Period of Revelation

This Sûrah's period of revelation is not known from any authentic tradition, however, it appears from its subject matter that it was revealed after Hâ-M'eem As-Sajdah / Fussilât, for it seems to be, in a way, a supplement to it. In Sûrah Hâ-M'eem As-Sajdah the Quraish chiefs were taken to task for their deaf and blind opposition, in order to show those who live in Makkah and in its outskirts, how unreasonable those chiefs were in opposing Muhammad (peace be upon him). Yet, how serious the Prophet was in everything he said, how rational was his standpoint and how noble was his character and conduct? Immediately after that warning this Sûrah was sent down to provide teaching and instruction, and made the truth of the Prophet's message plain in such an impressive way that anyone who loves the truth can not help but to accept His message.

Major Issues, Divine Laws and Guidance

* The Heaven might have broken apart from above those who elevate Allah's creatures to His level if angels were not begging forgiveness for the residents of Earth.
* Islam is the same religion which was enjoined on Nûh (Noah), Ibrâheem (Abraham), Musa (Moses), and Isa (Jesus). They were all ordained to establish Deen-al-Islam and not to create divisions in it.
* He who desires the harvest in the Hereafter shall be given manyfold and he who desires it in this life shall be given a portion here but shall have no share in the Hereafter.
* Whatever inflictions befall upon people, are the result of their own misdeeds.
* True believers are those who establish Salah (Prayer), give charity and defend themselves when oppressed.
* The real losers are those who will lose on the Day of Resurrection.
* It is Allah who gives daughters and sons as He pleases.
* It is not vouchsafed for any human being that Allah should speak to him face to face.

This discourse, as described in Tafheem-ul-Qur'an, begins in a way as if to say: "Why are you expressing surprise and amazement at what Our Prophet is presenting before you? What he says is not new or strange, nor it is something which is being presented for the first time in history that Revelation have come down to a man from God and he is being given instructions for the guidance of mankind!

Allah has been sending similar Revelations with similar instructions to former Prophets. It is not surprising that the Owner of the Universe should be acknowledged as the God and Ruler, but the strange thing is that one should accept some one else as God in spite of being His subject and slave. You are angry with him who is presenting Tawheed (God is One and Only) before you, whereas the shirk that you are committing with regard to the Master of the Universe (associating some one else with Him) is such a grave crime as may cause the heavens to break asunder. The angels are amazed at this boldness of yours and fear that the wrath of Allah might descend on you any moment."

After this, the people have been told that a person's being appointed to the Prophethood and his presenting himself as a Prophet does not mean that he has been made master of people's destinies. Allah has kept all destinies in His own hands. The Prophet has come only to arouse the heedless and guide the strayed ones to the Right Way. To call to account those who do not listen to him and to punish or not to punish them is Allah's discretion and not a part of the Prophet's mission. Therefore, they should know that the Prophet has not come with a claim similar to those that are made by their so called religious guides and saints to the effect that he who would not listen to them, or would behave insolently towards them, shall face a terrible death. The people are told that the Prophet has not come to condemn them but he is their well wisher; he is warning them that the way they are following will only lead to their own destruction.

Then an answer is given to the question: Why didn't Allah make all human beings righteous by birth, and why did He allow the differences of viewpoint due to which people start following each other in thought and action? After this, it has been explained that the way of life presented by the Prophet Muhammad (peace be upon him) is that Allah Almighty is the Creator, Master and real Patron of the Universe and Mankind. He Alone is the man's Ruler, He Alone has the right to give man Faith (Deen), Law (system of belief and practice), judge the disputes and show what is right and what is wrong. No other being has any right to be his lawgiver. In other words, like natural sovereignty, the sovereignty with regard to lawmaking is also vested only in Allah. None else, apart from Allah, can be the bearer of this sovereignty. If a person does not recognize and accept this Divine rule of Allah, it is futile for him to recognize only the natural sovereignty of Allah.

Based on this principle, Allah has ordained a Deen (True Religion) for Man from the very beginning. It was one and the same Religion that was vouchsafed, in every age, to all the Prophets. No Prophet ever founded any new or separate religion of his own. The same one Religion has been enjoined by Allah for all Mankind since Adam, and all the Prophets have been following it and inviting others to follow it.

This Religion and Creed was not sent for man to rest contentedly only with believing in it. It was sent with the purpose and intention that it should be introduced, established and enforced in the world, and no man-made religion should prevail on Allah's earth except His Religion. The Prophets had not been appointed only to preach this Religion, but also to establish it in the world.

This same religion is the original religion of mankind, but after the death of the Prophets, selfish people created new creeds by creating schisms for vested interests due to self-conceit, vanity and ostentation. Actually all the different religions and creeds found in the world today have resulted from corruption of the original Divine Truth.

The Prophet Muhammad (peace be upon him) has been assigned to present before people the same original Religion, in place of the various practices and man-made creeds, and try to establish the same. Of this, if instead of being grateful, you feel angry and come out to fight him, it is your folly; the Prophet will not abandon his mission only because of your foolishness. He has been enjoined to adhere to his faith at all costs and to carry out the mission to which he has been appointed. Therefore, the people should not cherish any false hope that in order to please them, he would accommodate them and cater to the same whims and superstitions of ignorance which corrupted Allah's Religion before.

The Prophet has been chosen by Allah for this mission. You all know that he had no concept of the "Book" or the "True Faith" during the first forty years of his life and then his sudden emergence before the people with these two concepts, is a manifest proof of his being a Prophet. His conveying the teaching of Allah does not mean that he claims to have spoken to Allah, face to face, but that Allah has conveyed to him this Guidance, as in the case of all other Prophets:

- Through Revelation, or
- From behind a veil, or
- He sends an angel with the message.

These methods have been clarified so that the opponents of the message may not have an opportunity of accusing the Prophet of claiming to have spoken to God, face to face, and the lovers of the truth should know through what methods Allah gave instruction to Muhammad (peace be upon him), whom He had appointed to the mission of Prophethood.

42: ASH-SHÛRA

This Sûrah, revealed at Makkah, has 5 sections and 53 verses.

In the name of Allah, the Compassionate, the Merciful

SECTION: 1

Hâ M'eem.[1] 'Ain Sîn Qâf.[2] Thus, does Allah All-Mighty, the All-Wise send His revelation to you, *O Muhammad,* as He sent to those before you.[3] To Him belongs all that is in the heavens and the earth. He is the Most High, the Most Great.[4] The heavens might have almost broken apart from above those who are *elevating Allah's creatures to His rank,* and *it is not happening because* the angels glorify their Rabb with His praise and beg forgiveness for those on earth. Behold! Surely, it is Allah Who is the oft-Forgiving, most Merciful.[5] Those who take others as their guardians besides Him, Allah Himself is watching them; and *O Prophet,* you are not the disposer of their affairs.[6] Thus have We revealed to you this Qur'an in Arabic, so that you may warn the residents of the Mother City *(Makkah)* and its suburbs, and forewarn them of the Day of assembly about which there is no doubt: when some will go to paradise and others to the blazing fire.[7] If Allah wanted, He could have made all of them a single nation; but He admits to His mercy whom He pleases; as for the wrongdoers, they will have no protector nor helper.[8] Have they set up other guardians beside Him, while Allah Alone is the Guardian? It is He Who gives life to the dead and it is He Who has power over all things.[9]   42:[1-9]

The heavens might have broken apart from above those who elevate Allah's creatures to His rank if the angels were not begging forgiveness for the residents of earth

SECTION: 2

O Prophet, tell them: Whatever the subject of your dispute is, its Judgment belongs to Allah: Such is Allah, my Rabb; in Him I have put my trust, and to Him I turn *in all of my affairs and in repentance,*[10] the Creator of the heavens and the earth. He has made for you mates from among yourselves and also mates among the cattle *from their own kind*; by this means does He multiply you. There is no one like Him. He Alone hears all and sees all.[11] To Him belong the keys of the heavens and the earth. He gives abundantly to whom He pleases and sparingly to whom He wills. He is the Knower of everything.[12] He has ordained for you the same Deen *(way of life - Islam)* which He enjoined on Nûh *(Noah)* - and which We have revealed to you *O Muhammad* - and which We enjoined on Ibrâheem *(Abraham)* and Musa *(Moses)* and Isa *(Jesus)*: "Establish the Deen of Al-Islam and make no division *(sects)* in it." Intolerable for the mushrikeen is that to which you *O Muhammad* call them. Allah

Islam is the same Deen (way of life) which was enjoined on Nûh, Ibrâheem, Musa (Moses) and Isa (Jesus). They were all ordered to establish Deen-al-Islam and do not create division (sects) in it

chooses *for His service* whom He wills, and guides to Himself who turns to Him *in all of his affairs and in repentance*.[13] The people did not become divided into sects until after knowledge had come to them, out of iniquity among themselves. Had your Rabb not issued the word *to defer their punishment* till an appointed time, the matter would have already been settled between them. The fact is that those who were made to inherit the Book after them, are surely in disquieting doubt concerning it.[14] Therefore, call them *to the true Deen,* stay firm *on the Right Way* as you are commanded and do not follow their vain desires. Tell them: "I believe in whatever Allah has revealed of the Book and I am commanded to do justice between you. Allah is Our Rabb and your Rabb. We are responsible for Our deeds and you for yours. Let there be no dispute among us. Allah will bring us all together *on the Day of Judgment and decide,* and to Him is the final return.[15] Those who dispute concerning Allah after His religion *(Al-Islam)* has been accepted by the people, their dispute is futile in the sight of their Rabb, on them is His wrath and for them there will be a terrible punishment.[16] It is Allah Who has revealed this Book *(Al-Qur'an)* with the truth, and the Balance *(to distinguish between right and wrong).* What will make you realize that perhaps the Hour *of doom* is near at hand?[17] Only those who deny it seek to hasten it on; but the believers dread its coming and know that *its coming* is the truth. Behold! Those who dispute concerning the hour *of doom* are far astray.[18] Allah is very Gracious to His servants. He gives sustenance to whom He pleases. He is the Powerful, the Almighty."[19]

42:[10-19]

SECTION: 3

He who desires the harvest of the hereafter, shall be given *manifold* increase in his harvest; and he who desires the harvest of this world, a share of it shall be given to him: but in the hereafter he shall have no share at all.[20] Have they made shorakâ' *(partners with Allah)* who, in the practice of their faith, have made lawful to them what Allah has not allowed? Had a decree of *making the decision on the Day of* Judgment not been issued already, the matter would have certainly been decided between them; surely, the wrong-doers will have a painful punishment.[21] You will see that the wrongdoers will be fearing the bad consequences of their deeds which will surely befall them. While those who believe and do good deeds shall dwell in the luxurious gardens *of paradise*, and shall receive from their Rabb all that they wish for; that will surely be the magnificent blessing.[22] Such *a blessing* is the good news which Allah gives to His servants who believe and do good deeds.

He who desires the harvest in the here-after shall be given many folds, but he who desires it in this life shall be given a portion here but shall have no share in the hereaf-ter

O Prophet, say to them: "I do not ask you any compensation except your love for being close relative." He that does a good deed shall be repaid many times over. Surely, Allah is oft-Forgiving, most-Appreciative.[23]   Do they say: "He has forged a falsehood against Allah?" But if Allah so willed, He could have sealed your heart. In fact, Allah blots out falsehood and vindicates the truth by His words. Surely, He knows the secrets of all hearts.[24]   It is He Who accepts repentance from His servants and pardons their sins, and He knows whatever you do.[25]   He answers the prayers of those who believe and do good deeds and gives them even more out of His bounty. As for the unbelievers, they shall have severe punishment.[26]   Had Allah bestowed abundance upon His servants, they would have transgressed beyond bounds in the earth; *that's why* He sends down in due measure as He pleases; He is well aware and observant of His servants.[27]   It is He Who sends down rain even after they have lost all hope, and spreads His Mercy. He Alone is the Praiseworthy Guardian.[28]   Among His signs is the creation of the heavens and the earth, and the living creatures that He has spread in both of them: and He is capable of gathering them all together whenever He will.[29]

42:[20-29]

SECTION: 4

Whatever afflictions befall upon people are the result of their own misdeeds

Whatever affliction befalls you, is the result of what your own hands have done, even though for many *of your misdeeds* He grants forgiveness.[30]   You cannot escape from Allah in the earth and there is no protector or helper for you besides Allah.[31]   Among His signs are the ships which look like mountains upon the sea.[32]   If He wants, He can cause the wind to become still and leave them *(the ships)* motionless on the back *of the sea* - surely, in this example, there are signs for every such person who patiently endures and is grateful.[33]   - Or He may cause them to perish *(by drowning)* on account of what they have earned *(sins)*; yet, He forgives many sins.[34]   Those who dispute about Our revelations *should know that* there is no escape for them.[35]   Whatever you are given is nothing but a provision for the transitory life of this world, better and ever lasting is the reward which Allah has for those who believe, and put their trust in their Rabb,[36]   avoid major sins and shameful deeds, forgive even when they are angry;[37]   answer the call of their Rabb, establish Salah *(prayer)*, conduct their affairs with mutual consultation, spend out of the sustenance which We have given them,[38]   and when they are oppressed, help *and defend* themselves.[39]   The recompense for an injury is an injury proportionate to it; but if a person forgives and makes reconciliation, he shall be rewarded by Allah; He does not like

True believers are those who establish Salah, give charity and defend themselves when oppressed

the wrongdoers.[40]   Those who take revenge when wronged cannot be blamed.[41]   The blameworthy are those who oppress their fellow men and conduct themselves with wickedness *and injustice* in the land. It is they who will have a painful punishment.[42]   And whoever is patient and forgive others, that would truly be from the things requiring determination.[43]   42:[30-43]

SECTION: 5

He whom Allah lets go astray has no protector after Him. When they will face the punishment, you will see the wrongdoers exclaim: "Is there any way back *to the world*?"[44]   You will see them brought forward to it *(hell)* humbled with humiliation, looking at it with stealthy glances. The *true* believers will say: "The real losers indeed are those who have lost themselves and their families on the Day of Resurrection." Beware! Surely, the wrongdoers shall suffer everlasting punishment.[45]   They shall have no protectors who could help them besides Allah. The one whom Allah lets go astray has no way of salvation.[46]   Answer the call of your Rabb before that Day arrives which cannot be averted against the will of Allah. There shall be no refuge for you on that Day, nor shall you be able to deny *your sins*.[47]   Now if they give no heed, *they should* know that We have not sent you, *O Muhammad,* to be their keeper. Your only duty is to convey *My message*. Man is *such that* when We give him a taste of Our Mercy, he is very happy about it; but when, through his own fault, an evil afflicts him, he becomes utterly ungrateful."[48]   42:[44-48]

> The real losers are those who will lose on the Day of Resurrection

To Allah belongs the kingdom of the heavens and the earth. He creates whatever He pleases. He gives daughters to whom He pleases and gives sons to whom He pleases.[49]   To some He gives both sons and daughters, and makes barren whom He will; surely, He is All-knowledgeable, All-Powerful.[50]   42:[49-50]

> It is Allah Who gives daughters and sons as He pleases

It is not vouchsafed for any human being that Allah should speak to him face to face; He speaks either through inspiration, or from behind a veil, or through sending a messenger *(angel Gabriel)* authorized by Him to reveal His will; surely, He is Most High, Most Wise.[51] Thus, have We revealed to you *O Muhammad,* a Spirit *(inspired Book - the Qur'an)* by Our command: while you did not know what the Book and what the Imân *(faith) was*! But We have made it *(the Qur'an)* a light whereby We guide those of Our servants whom We please; and surely, you are guiding mankind to the Right Way:[52] - the Way of Allah, to whom belongs all that is in the heavens and the earth. Beware! All affairs will eventually return to Allah *for a decision*.[53]   42:[51-53]

> It is not vouchsafed for any human being that Allah should speak to him face to face

43: AZ-ZUKHRUF

Period of Revelation

This Sûrah's period of revelation is not known from any authentic tradition, however, it appears that it was revealed in the same period in which the Sûrahs Al-M'umin, As-Sajdah and As-Shurâ were sent down. The revelation of this series of the Sûrahs began when the disbelievers of Makkah were planning to assassinate the Prophet. They were holding consultations day and night in their assemblies relating to this issue. An attempt of assassination had also been made as is referred in the verses 79 and 80.

Major Issues, Divine laws and Guidance

* Al-Qur'an is a transcript from the Mother-Book which is in Allah's keeping
* Supplication before riding a conveyance.
* Creed of the mushrikeen, that angels are female divinities, is false.
* An example of the Prophet Ibrâheem who recognized the Oneness of Allah and rejected the shirk using merely his common sense and observing Allah's signs from nature.
* If it were not that all mankind will become one race of unbelievers, Allah would have given the unbelievers houses which were made of sterling silver.
* He who turns away from the remembrance of Allah, Allah appoints a Shaitân to be his intimate friend.
* Hold fast to the Qur'an if you want to be rightly guided.
* The Prophet Isa (Jesus) was no more than a mortal, whom Allah favored and made an example for the children of Israel.
* O Prophet tell the Christians: "If Allah had a son, I would have been the first one to worship him."

In this Sûrah, a forceful criticism has been made of the Quraish and other Arabs' creeds and superstitions. The disbelievers were admitting the fact that the Creator of the earth, the heavens, themselves and their deities is only Allah. They also knew and admitted that the blessings they were benefiting from, had been bestowed by Allah; yet they insisted on making others associates of Allah in His Godhead. They believed that the angels were goddesses; they had carved their images as females; they adorned them with female dresses and ornaments. They called them daughters of Allah, worshipped them and invoked them for the *fulfillment of their needs. They had no answer to the question as to how they knew that the angels were female? When they could not find the basis for their claims and superstitions, they presented the pretense of destiny and said: "Had Allah disapproved our practices, we could not have worshipped these deities." Whereas the means of finding out whether Allah had approved of something or not, are His Books and not those things which are happening in the world.*

When they were asked: "Have you any other authority, apart from this argument for the polytheism of yours?" They replied: "The same has been the practice of our forefathers." In other words, this, in their opinion, was a strong enough argument (daleel) for a creed to be right and true, whereas the Prophet Ibrâheem, peace be upon him, being the descendant of whom was the only basis of their pride and distinction, had rejected the religion of his elders, left his home, and had discarded every such blind imitation of his forefathers which did not have the support of any rational argument.

After criticizing each practice of ignorance of the disbelievers and rejecting it with rational arguments, this discourse has pointed out: " Allah has neither any offspring, nor are there separate gods for the earth or heavens, nor is there any intercessor who may be able to protect the disbelievers from Allah's punishment. Allah is far above from having a child. He Alone is the God of the whole universe: all others are His servants."

43: AZ-ZUKHRUF

This Sûrah, revealed at Makkah, has 7 sections and 89 verses.

In the name of Allah, the Compassionate, the Merciful

SECTION: 1

The Qur'an is a transcript from the Mother Book which is in Allah's keeping

Hâ M'eem.[1] By the Book that makes things clear.[2] We have revealed this Qur'an in the Arabic language so that you may understand *its meanings*.[3] Surely, it is in the Mother Book in Our keeping, which is sublime and full of wisdom.[4] Should We take this Reminder away from you and ignore you because you are a nation who has transgressed all limits?[5] And how many Prophets have We sent among the prior peoples?[6] Never did it happen that a Prophet came to his people and they did not mock at him.[7] So We destroyed them, though they were stronger in power than these people, and provided an example in the case of prior people.[8]

43:[1-8]

Even the mushrikeen believe that heavens, earth and all therein is created by Allah

If you ask them: "Who has created the heavens and the earth?" They will surely say: "They were created by the All-Mighty, the All-Knowledgeable."[9] The One Who has made the earth a resting place for you and has made routes therein so that you may find your ways.[10] The One Who sends down rain from the sky in due measure and thereby resurrects a dead land - that's how you shall be brought forth *(raised to life again)*.[11] The One Who has created all kind of things in pairs and made for you the ships and cattle on which you ride[12]

Supplication before riding a conveyance

so that you may firmly sit on their backs, then as you mount, recall the goodness of your Rabb and say: "Glory be to Him Who has subjected these to Our use, otherwise We could not have brought them under our control,[13] and to our Rabb we shall all return."[14] Yet, *in spite of recognizing all this*, they have made some of His servants to be a part of Him! Surely, man is clearly ungrateful.[15]

43:[9-15]

SECTION: 2

Some mushrikeen regard the angels to be the female divinities being the daughters of Allah

Would Allah choose daughters *(pagan Arabs believed that angels were the daughters of Allah)* for Himself out of what He Himself creates and gives you sons?[16] Yet, when *a new born-girl - the gender* that they ascribe to the Compassionate - is announced to one of them, his face darkens and he is filled with grief.[17] *Do they ascribe to Allah, the female* gender who is brought up in adornment and is unable to make herself clear in disputation?[18] They regard the angels, who are themselves servants of the Compassionate, as female *divinities*. Did they witness their creation? *They should know that* their testimony shall be noted down and they shall be called to account for it.[19] They say: "Had it been the will of the Compassionate, We should never have worshipped them." They have no knowledge about that; they are merely guessing.[20] Or have We given them before this a Book, which they hold as an authority *for their angel-worshipping*?[21] *The only argument* they *have is to* say: "We found our forefathers practicing this faith, and surely we are guided by their footsteps."[22] Even so, whenever We sent a Warner before you to forewarn a nation, its affluent people said: "We found our forefathers practicing this faith and surely, we are going to follow their footsteps."[23] *Each Warner* asked: "What if I bring you better guidance than that which your forefathers practiced?" But they replied: "Well! We reject the faith with which you have been sent."[24] *Consequently,* We inflicted Our retribution on them; then see what was the end of those who disbelieved?[25]   43:[16-25]

SECTION: 3

Behold! Ibrâheem said to his father and his people: "I renounce *the deities* that you worship,[26] except Him Who created me, for He will surely guide me."[27] And he left this statement *as an abiding precept* among his descendants, so that they should turn to it.[28] However, I kept on providing them and their forefathers with the comfort *of this life*, until there came to them the truth and a Rasool to expound it clearly.[29] But now when the truth has come to them, they say: "This is magic and we do not believe it."[30] They also say: "Why is this Qur'an not revealed to a man of great importance in the two towns *(Makkah and Ta'if)*"?[31] Is it they who distribute the blessings of your Rabb? It is We Who distribute the means of their livelihood in the life of this world, raising some in rank above others, so that one may take others into his service. But the blessing of your Rabb is far greater in value than *the wealth of this world* which they amass.[32] And were it not that all mankind might become one nation *of unbelievers*, We would have given those who disbelieve in the Compassionate *(Allah)* houses whose roofs and stairways, by which they go to upper chambers, all made with silver,[33] and also silver doors of their houses and couches on which they recline,[34] along with ornaments of gold, for all these are nothing but merely comforts of this worldly life. It is *the*

The Prophet Ibrâheem recognized the Oneness of Allah and rejected Shirk (Polytheism)

If it were not that all mankind will become one race of unbelievers, Allah would have given the unbelievers houses made with sterling silver

life of the hereafter which your Rabb has reserved for the righteous.[35]   43:[26-35]

SECTION: 4

He who turns away from the remembrance of the Compassionate *(Allah)*, We assign a shaitân for him, who becomes his intimate companion.[36] - and turns such people away from the Right Way, while they think that they are guided aright.[37] - Ultimately, when that person will come to Us *on the Day of Judgment*, he will say *to his shaitân companion*: "I wish that I was far apart from you as the east is from the west: you turned out to be an evil companion."[38] *Then it will be said to them*: "Well, you have already done wrong, *realizing* this *fact* today will avail you nothing, as you both are partners in the punishment.[39]   *O Prophet,* can you make the deaf hear, or give direction to the blind or those *who choose to remain* in manifest error?[40]   We shall surely inflict retribution on them, whether We take you away from this world,[41] or let you see their end, which We have promised them: surely, We have full power over them.[42]   Therefore, hold fast to *this Qur'an* which is revealed to you, surely, you are on the Right Way.[43]   In fact, this *Qur'an* is a reminder for you and your people; and you shall soon be questioned about it.[44]   Ask those of Our Rasools whom We sent before you if We ever appointed other gods to be worshipped besides the Compassionate *Allah*?[45]   43:[36-45]

SECTION: 5

We sent Musa with Our signs to Fir'aun and his chiefs. He said to them: "I am a Rasool of the Rabb of the worlds."[46]   When he showed them Our signs, they laughed at them.[47]   Yet, We showed them sign after sign each greater than the one preceding it, and We afflicted them with the scourge so that they might return *to the Right Way*.[48]   *Each time they were seized by a scourge,* they requested *Musa*: "O magician! Pray to your Rabb for us by virtue of the covenant He has made with you; we shall surely accept your guidance."[49]   But each time We lifted the scourge from them, they broke their pledge.[50]   *One day* Fir'aun made a proclamation among his people: "O my people! Is the kingdom of Egypt not mine? Are these rivers flowing beneath me not mine also? Can you not see?[51]   Am I not better than this despicable wretch, who can hardly express himself clearly?[52]   *If he is really a Rasool then* Why have no gold bracelets been given to him, or angels sent down

Sidebar notes:

He who turns away from the remembrance of Allah, Allah appoints a Shaitân to be his intimate friend

Hold fast to The Qur'an if you want to be rightly guided

The Prophet Musa was sent to Fir'aun and his chiefs with signs but they ridiculed him and the signs, as a result, Allah drowned them all

to accompany him?"[53]   Thus did he misled his people and they obeyed him; surely, they were a nation of transgressors.[54]   At last when they provoked Us, We inflicted retribution on them and drowned them all,[55]   and made them a lesson and an example for the later generations.[56]   43:[46-56]

SECTION: 6

When Maryam's son *Isa (Jesus)* is quoted as an example, your people raise a clamor at it,[57]   and say: "Are Our gods better or is he?" They cite this to you, merely for argument. Nay! They are quarrelsome people.[58]   He *(Jesus)* was no more than a mortal whom We favored and made an example to the Children of Israel.[59]   Had it been Our will, We could have replaced you with angels to succeed you on earth.[60]   He *(Jesus)* is, in fact, a sign for the coming of the Hour *(Day of Resurrection)*. Therefore, have no doubt about its coming, follow me; this is the Right Way.[61]   Let not shaitân restrain you, for he is your open enemy.[62]   When Isa *(Jesus)* came with clear signs, he stated: "I have come to you with wisdom *(Prophethood)*, and to clarify some of those things about which you have disputes: so fear Allah and obey me.[63]   Surely, it is Allah Who is my Rabb and your Rabb, so worship Him. This is the Right Way."[64]   *In spite of these teachings*, the factions disagreed among themselves; so woe to the wrongdoers *from the punishment of a painful Day*.[65]   Are they only waiting for the Hour *of Doom* - that it should come upon them suddenly, while they are unaware?[66]   On that Day, even friends will become enemies to one another with the exception of the righteous people.[67]

43:[57-67]

SECTION: 7

"O My devotees! Today you have nothing to fear or to grieve,"[68]   *it will be said to* those who believed in Our revelations and became Muslims,[69]   "Enter paradise, you and your spouses; you will be made happy."[70]   There they shall be served with golden dishes and golden goblets, and they shall have everything that their souls can desire and all that their eyes can delight in - *and it will be said to them*: "Now you shall abide therein forever.[71]   You have inherited this paradise by virtue of your *good* deeds.[72]   therein you shall have plenty of fruit to eat."[73]   But the criminals will abide in the punishment of hell.[74]   Their punishment will never be lightened, and they shall remain in despair therein.[75]   We did not wrong them, but it is they who wronged themselves.[76]   They will

The Prophet Isa (Jesus) was no more than a mortal whom Allah favored and made him an example for the Children of Israel

On the Day of Judgment believers will have no fear or regret. They will be awarded paradise and made happy

O Prophet, tell the Christians: if Allah had a son, I would have been the first one to worship him

cry: "O Mâlik *(the keeper of hell)*! Let your Rabb put an end to us." But he will answer: "Nay! You are going to live forever."[77] We have brought you the truth, but most of you hate the truth.[78] If they have devised a plan *to ruin you (O Muhammad)*, then surely, We too shall devise a plan *to ruin them*.[79] Do they think that We cannot hear their secret talks and their private conversation? Of course We do, and Our messengers *(angels)* who are assigned to them, record it all.[80] *O Prophet* tell *those who ascribe a son to Allah*: "If the Compassionate *(Allah)* had a son, I would be the first to worship him. *But, on the contrary, I am the first to deny that He has a son.*"[81] Glory be to the Rabb of the heavens and the earth, the Rabb of the Throne; He is above what they ascribe to Him.[82] So let them talk nonsense and play until they face their Day, which has been promised to them.[83] It is He *(Allah)* Who is the only God, *to be worshipped*, in the heavens and the only God, *to be worshipped*, on the earth; He is the All-Wise, the All-Knowledgeable.[84] Blessed be He to Whom belongs the dominion of the heavens and the earth and all that lies between them! He Alone has the knowledge of the Hour *of Doom*, and to Him you shall all be brought back.[85] And those whom they invoke besides Him, have no power to intercede for them except those who testify to the truth by virtue of knowledge.[86] If you ask them Who created them, they will certainly say: "Allah." How then are they deluded away *from the truth*?[87] *Allah has heard the Prophet's* cry: "O my Rabb! Surely, these are a people who would not believe."[88] *Therefore, O Prophet!* Bear with them and wish them peace. They shall soon come to know *the truth*.[89]   43:[68-89]

44: AD-DUKHÂN

Period of Revelation

This Sûrah's period of revelation could not be determined from any authentic tradition, but the internal evidence of the subject matter shows that this Sûrah was sent down during the same period in which Sûrah Zukhruf was revealed, when the whole of Arabia was overtaken by such a terrible famine that the people were sorely distressed. At last, some of the Quraish chiefs, including Abdullah bin Mas'ud and Abu Sufyân, came to the Prophet and requested him to pray to Allah to deliver his people from that calamity. This Sûrah was sent down at that occasion.

Major Issues, Divine Laws and Guidance

* Allah has revealed this Qur'an in the blessed night (Laila-tul-Qadr) in which all matters are decided wisely by His command.
* The Qur'an by itself bears the clear testimony that it is not the composition of a man but of Allah, Rabb of the worlds.
* Lessons to be learned from the story of the Prophet Musa (Moses) and the people of Fir'aun.
* Allah delivered the Children of Israel and chose them over the nations of the world in spite of their weaknesses.
* The Day of Sorting Out is the time appointed for the Resurrection of mankind.
* Food and drink for the sinners in Hell is compared to food and entertainment for the righteous in paradise.

This Sûrah was revealed for the admonition and warning of the people of Makkah stating: "The Hour when Allah, out of sheer mercy, decided to appoint a Rasool and send His Book to you was highly blessed. The fact that a Rasool has been raised and the Book sent down in that particular Hour when Allah decides their destinies, and Allah's decisions are not weak that they may be changed to the people's liking. The only argument that you have given to practice shirk is that it had been the practice of your forefathers, which is not any justification for such a heinous sin. If your forefathers had committed this folly, there is no reason for you to continue committing it blindly."

After this, the question of the famine, which was raging in Makkah at that time, is discussed. On the one hand, the Prophet is foretold that the people have not learned any lesson from this calamity, and on the other, the disbelievers are addressed so as to say : "You are lying when you say that you will believe as soon as the torment is removed from you. We shall remove it to see how sincere you are *in your promise." In this connection, reference of Fir'aun (Pharaoh) and his people is made that those people also met with the same trial, but after witnessing several signs one after the other, they did not give up their stubbornness till at last they met their doom.*

Then the theme of the Hereafter is stated which the disbelievers had denied saying: "We have never seen anyone rising back to life after death. Raise our forefathers back to life if you are true in your claim about the life hereafter." The response to this is provided in these words: "This cannot be done to meet the demand of individuals; Allah has appointed a time when He will surely resurrect all mankind simultaneously and will subject them to accountability in His Court. If one has to protect oneself there, one should think about it here. For no one will be able to save himself there by his own power, nor by the power of any one else."

In conclusion, a warning is given: "This Qur'an has been revealed in simple language in your own tongue so that you may understand it; yet if you do not understand it and insist on seeing your evil end, you may wait; Our Prophet too shall wait. Whatever is to happen, will happen at Allah's appointed time."

44: AD-DUKHÂN

This Sûrah, revealed at Makkah, has 3 sections and 59 verses.

In the name of Allah, the Compassionate, the Merciful

SECTION: 1

Hâ M'eem.[1] By the Book that makes things clear,[2] We revealed this Qur'an in a blessed night *(Laila-tul Qadr)*; for We wanted to forewarn *mankind*.[3]   In that *night* every matter is decided precisely[4] by a command from Ourself. Surely, We have been sending *the Rasools*,[5] as a blessing from your Rabb; it is He Who is All-Hearing, All-Knowing.[6] The Rabb of the heavens and the earth and all that lies between them, *mark this,* if you are true believers![7] There is no god but He. He gives life and death. He is your Rabb and the Rabb of your forefathers.[8] Yet, they play about in doubt.[9] Well! Wait for the Day when the sky will pour down visible smoke,[10] enveloping all the people; this will be a painful punishment.[11] *They will say*: "Our Rabb! Remove from us this punishment; surely, we shall become real believers."[12] But how can the admonition be beneficial to them *at that time*? A Rasool *(Muhammad)*, who makes things clear, has already come to them[13] yet, they deny him, saying: "He is a madman, taught by others!"[14] We shall remove the affliction *(famine from which they were suffering)* for a while, but you will revert *to the same old ways*.[15] One day We shall seize you with a mighty onslaught to exact Our retribution.[16]   44:[1-16]

Allah revealed this Qur'an in the Blessed Night (Laila-tul-Qadr) in which all matters are decided wisely by His command

Before them, We had put the people of Fir'aun *(Pharaoh)* to the same test, when an honorable Rasool came to them,[17] *saying:* "Hand over to me the servants of Allah. I am to you a Rasool worthy of all trust.[18]   Do not be arrogant against Allah; surely, I have brought to you a clear authority.[19] I have taken refuge with my Rabb and your Rabb against you stoning me.[20] If you do not believe me, then leave me alone."[21]   *But they became aggressive,* so *Musa* prayed to his Rabb: "These are indeed criminal people."[22] *The reply came:* "Set forth with My servants *(Israelites)* at night, surely, you shall be pursued.[23]   *When you have crossed the sea along with your people miraculously,* then leave the sea as it is *(calm and divided)*; for they are a host who are destined to be drowned."[24]   How many gardens and springs they left behind![25] And agriculture and grand palaces![26]   And means of luxury and comfort which they used to enjoy![27] Thus was their end! And We

Lessons to be learned from the story of the Prophet Musa and the people of Fir'aun

let other people inherit *what was once theirs*.[28]   Neither heaven nor earth shed tears for them; nor were they given a respite.[29]

44:[17-29]

SECTION:

We did deliver the Children of Israel from a humiliating chastisement[30]   *inflicted* by Fir'aun who was the most arrogant among such inordinate transgressors,[31]   and We chose them, knowingly, above the nations of the world *of their time*.[32]   We showed them signs in which there was a clear trial.[33]   As to these *(people of Quraish)* who say:[34]   "There is nothing beyond our first death and we shall not be raised again.[35]   Bring back our forefathers if you are truthful."[36]   Are these people better than the people of Tubba' and those who were before them? We destroyed them all, only because they had become criminals.[37]   It was not for a sport that We created the heavens, the earth and all that lies between them.[38]   We have not created them except with the Truth, but most of them do not understand.[39]   Surely, the Day of sorting out is the time appointed *for the resurrection of* them all.[40]   On that Day no one shall be able to protect his friend, nor shall they receive any help[41]   except those to whom Allah will show His Mercy: for it is He Who is the All-Mighty, the All Merciful.[42]   44:[30-42]

SECTION: 3

Surely, the Zaqqûm tree[43]   *shall be the* food of the sinners;[44]   it will be like the dregs of oil, *which shall* boil in the bellies,[45]   like the boiling of scalding water.[46]   *It will be said:* "Seize him and drag him into the depth of the hell,[47]   then pour scalding water over his head[48]   - Taste *this*! Verily, You were *pretending to be* the mighty noble![49] This is *the punishment* which you use to doubt."[50]

44: [43-50]

Surely, the righteous, will be in a secure place;[51]   among gardens and springs,[52]   dressed in fine silk and rich brocade, *sitting* face to face.[53]   Such shall be *their place*! And We shall wed them to Hourin-'Ain (*damsels with beautiful big and lustrous eyes*).[54]   There, in full peace, they shall call for every kind of fruit;[55]   and after having prior death *in this world*, they shall taste death no more; and He *(Allah)* will protect them from the torment of hell[56]   as a grace from your Rabb, and that will be the supreme achievement.[57]   Surely, We have made this *Qur'an* easy *by revealing* it in your own language so that they may take heed.[58]   *If they do not accept the admonition* then wait; surely, they *too* are waiting.[59]

44:[51-59]

45: AL-JÂTHIYA

Period of Revelation

The period of the revelation of this Sûrah has not been mentioned in any authentic tradition, however, its subject matter clearly shows that it was revealed consecutively after Sûrah Ad- Dukhân which is the middle stage of the Prophet's residence at Makkah. The close resemblance between the contents of the two Sûrahs makes them look like the twin Sûrahs.

Major Issues, Divine Laws and Guidance

* If the disbelievers do not believe in Allah and His revelations then in what report will they believe!
* Allah has subjected the seas and all that is between the heavens and the earth for human beings.
* Israelites made sects in their religion after the knowledge had come to them through the Torah.
* Allah is the protector of righteous people.
* He that makes his own desires as his god, Allah will let him go astray and set a seal upon his ears and heart.
* Allah's address to the disbelievers on the Day of Judgement.

It answers the doubts and objections of the disbelievers of Makkah about Tawheed (God is One and Only) and the Hereafter and warns them regarding the attitude that they had adopted against the message of the Qur'an.

This discourse begins with the arguments for Tawheed. In this connection, reference has been made to the countless signs that are found in the world, from man's own body, to the earth and heavens, and it is pointed out that everywhere around him, man finds things which testify to Tawheed, which he refuses to acknowledge. If man observes carefully the variety of animals, the day and night, the rainfall and the vegetation growing thereby, the winds and his own creation, then ponders over them intelligently, he will find these Signs sufficiently convincing of the truth that this universe is not Godless, nor under the control of many gods, but it has been created by One God, Whose name is Allah, and He Alone is its Controller and Ruler. The countless forces and agencies that are serving his interests in the universe have not come into being just accidentally, nor have they been provided by gods and goddesses, but it is One God Alone Who has supplied and *subjected them to man from Himself. If a person uses his mind properly and rightly, his own intellect will proclaim that God Alone is man's real Benefactor and He Alone deserves that man should be obedience to Him.*

About the Hereafter, Allah says: "It is utterly against reason and justice that the good and the bad, the obedient and the disobedient, the oppressor and the oppressed should be made equal. Just as you did not become living of your own accord, but became living by Our power, so you do not die of your own accord, but die when We send death. A time is certainly coming when you will all be gathered together. You may not believe in this because of your ignorance today, but the time will come when you will see it yourself. You will be presented before Allah and your whole book of conduct will be laid open bearing evidence against each of your misdeeds. Then you will come to know how dearly has your denial of the Hereafter and your mockery of it cost you."

45: AL-JÂTHIYA

This Sûrah, revealed at Makkah, has 4 sections and 37 verses.

In the name of Allah, the Compassionate, the Merciful

SECTION: 1

Hâ M'eem.[1] This Book is revealed from Allah, the All-Mighty, the All-Wise.[2] Surely, in the heavens and the earth there are signs for the *true* believers;[3] in your own creation and that of animals which are scattered through *the earth*, there are signs for those who are firm in faith;[4] in the alternation of night and day, in the sustenance that Allah sends down from heaven with which He revives the earth after its death and in the changing of the winds, there are signs for those who use their common sense.[5] These are the revelations of Allah, which We are reciting to you in all truth. Then, in what report after Allah and His revelations, will they believe?[6] Woe to each lying sinner![7] He hears the revelations of Allah recited to him, yet, he arrogantly persists as though he never heard them; announce to him a painful punishment.[8] And when something of Our revelations come to his knowledge, he takes them as a joke; for all such people, there will be a humiliating punishment.[9] Beyond them there lies hell, and nothing of what they have earned *in this world* will be of any benefit to them, nor those whom they have taken as their protectors besides Allah, and they shall have grievous punishment.[10] This *Qur'an* is the true Guidance. As for those who deny the revelations of their Rabb, there will be a terribly painful punishment.[11]   45:[1-11]

Food for thought to those who are seeking the signs of Allah

If they do not believe in Allah and His revelations then in what report will they believe?

SECTION: 2

It is Allah Who has subjected the sea to you, so that ships may sail upon it by His command, and that you may seek His bounty and be grateful to Him.[12] He also subjected to you whatever is in the heavens and the earth; all from Himself. Surely, there are signs in this for those who think.[13] *O Prophet*, tell the believers to forgive those who do not hope for the days of Allah *(His reward or His retribution)*, so that He may Himself recompense those people according to what they have earned.[14] He that does a righteous deed, does it for his own soul; and he that commits an evil, does so at his own peril. In the end, you all will be brought back to your Rabb.[15] We gave the Book to the Children of Israel and bestowed

Allah has subjected the seas and all that is between the heavens and the earth for human beings

The Israelites made sects in their religion after the knowledge had come to them through Torah

on them rulership and Prophethood. We provided them with good things of life, exalted them above the nations *of their time,*[16] and gave them clear instructions relating to the matters *of religion through revealing to them the Torah.* Then they did not differ among themselves, *until* after the knowledge had come to them, out of iniquity among themselves. Surely, your Rabb will judge between them on the Day of Resurrection concerning the matters in which they have set up differences.[17]   45:[12-17]

The Wrongdoers are protectors of one another while the protector of righteous is Allah Himself

O Prophet, We have put you on the Shari'ah *(Right Way)* of Our commandment, so follow it, and do not yield to the desires of ignorant people;[18] for they can avail you nothing against Allah. In fact, the wrongdoers are protectors of one another, while the protector of the righteous is Allah *Himself.*[19] These *(the Qur'an and Shari'ah)* are the eye openers for mankind; a guidance and a blessing to the true believers.[20] Do the evil doers think that We shall make them like those who believe and do good deeds - *make them* equal in their life and their death? Worst is the judgment that they make![21]   45:[18-21]

SECTION: 3

He who has made his own desires as his god, Allah lets him go astray and sets a seal upon his ears and heart

Allah has created the heavens and the earth with truth, in order to reward each soul according to its deeds, and none of them shall be wronged.[22] Have you considered *the case of such an individual* who has made his own desires as his god, and Allah, knowing *him as such,* lets him go astray, and sealed his hearing and heart and drew a veil over his sight? Who is there to guide him after Allah *has withdrawn His guidance*? Will you not learn a lesson?[23] *The disbelievers* say: "There is nothing but our life of this world. We live and die; nothing but time destroys us." *In fact,* they have no knowledge concerning this. They are merely guessing.[24] When Our clear revelations are recited to them, they have no other argument but to say: "Bring our forefathers back if what you say is true!"[25] *O Prophet* tell them: "It is Allah Who gives you life and later causes you to die; then it is He Who will gather you all on the Day of Resurrection, about which there is no doubt, yet, most people do not know."[26]   45:[22-26]

SECTION: 4

To Allah belongs the Kingdom of the heavens and the earth. On that Day when the Hour *of Judgment* will be established,

those who followed the falsehood, shall lose.[27]   You shall see
every nation on its knees. Every nation shall be summoned to its
book of record, *and Allah will say:* "Today you shall be rewarded
for your deeds.[28] This book of Ours speaks about you with the truth.
Surely, We were recording all your deeds."[29]   As for those who
believed and did righteous deeds, their Rabb will admit them into His
mercy. That will be a manifest achievement.[30]   But as to those who
disbelieved, *Allah will say*: "Were My revelations not recited to you?
But you showed arrogance and became a nation of criminals."[31]
When it was said, "the promise of Allah is true and there is no doubt
in coming the Hour *of Judgment.* You used to say, 'We do not know
what the Hour *of Judgment* is: we think it is just a conjecture, we
are not convinced.'"[32]   Then the evil of their deeds will become
manifest to them, and they will be completely encircled by that
which they used to mock at.[33]   It will be said: "Today We will
forget you as you forgot the meeting of this Day of yours! Hellfire
will be your home and none will be there to help you.[34]   This is
because you used to take Allah's revelations as a joke and you let
the worldly life deceive you." Therefore, on this Day neither shall
they be taken out of hell, nor shall they be given a chance for
amending *their ways to please their Rabb.*[35]   So, praise be to
Allah, the Rabb of the heavens, the Rabb of the earth and the Rabb
of the worlds.[36]   To Him belongs greatness throughout the
heavens and the earth, and He Alone is the All-Mighty, the All-
Wise.[37]   45:[27-37]

Allah's address
to the disbelievers
on the Day of
Judgment

JUZ (PART): 26

46: AL-AHQÂF

Period of Revelation

This Sûrah was revealed during the Prophet's return from Tâ'if to Makkah. According to all authentic traditions, he went to Tâ'if three years before Hijrah i.e. at the end of the 10th year or in the early part of the 11th year of the Prophethood.

Major Issues, Divine Laws and Guidance:

*   Those deities whom mushrikeen invoke are not even aware that they are being invoked.
*   The Qur'an is the word of Allah, not of the Prophet Muhammad (peace be upon him).
*   The Prophet is but a plain Warner.
*   The Qur'an confirms the revelation of the Torah given to the Prophet Musa.
*   Those who treat their parents with kindness shall be rewarded and those who rebuke their parents shall be punished.
*   No deity can save people from the wrath of Allah.
*   A group of Jinns embraced Islam after hearing the Qur'an.
*   Pass on the message of Allah, and bear with the disbelievers patiently.

The 10th year of the Prophethood was a year of extreme persecution and distress in the prophet's life. The Quraish and the other tribes had continued their boycott of the Bani Hashim and the Muslims for three years and the Prophet, his family and companions lay besieged in Shi'b Abi Tâlib. The Quraish had blocked up this area from all sides so that no supplies of any kind could reach the besieged people. Only during the Hajj season were they allowed to come out and purchase some articles of necessity. But even at that time, whenever Abu Lahab noticed any of them approaching the marketplace or a trading caravan, he would call out to the merchants exhorting them to announce forbidding rates of their articles for them, and would pledge that he himself would buy those articles so that they did not suffer any loss. This boycott which continued uninterrupted for three years had broken the backs of the Muslims and the Bani Hashim, so much so that at times, they were forced to eat grass and the leaves of trees. At last, when the siege was lifted, Abu Tâlib, the Prophet's uncle, who had been shielding him for ten long years, died. Hardly a month later, his wife, Sayyidah Khadijah, who had been a source of peace and consolation for him ever since the beginning of his mission, also passed away. Because of these tragic incidents which happened one after the other, the Prophet used to refer this year as the year of sorrow and grief.

After the death of Sayyidah Khadijah and Abu Tâlib, the disbelievers of Makkah became even bolder in their campaign against the Prophet. The Prophet decided to go to Tâ'if and approach the chiefs and nobles of the Bani Thaqeef. But, not only they refused to listen to him, they asked him to leave. When he was leaving, the chiefs of Thaqeef sent their slaves and scoundrels after him. They screamed at him, abused him and pelted him with stones for most of the way from both sides of the road until he broke down, wounded and bleeding. The degree of his injuries were such that his shoes were filled with blood. Wearied and exhausted, he took shelter in the shade of a wall of a garden outside Tâ'if, and prayed:

"O Allah, to You I complain of my weakness, little resource, and lowliness before men. O Most Merciful, You are the Rabb of the weak, and You are my Rabb. To whom will You confide me? To the one who will misuse me, or to an enemy to whom You have given power over me? If You are not angry with me, I care not. Your favor is wide for me. I take refuge in the light of Your countenance by which the darkness is illuminated, and the things of this world and the next are rightly ordered, lest Your anger descends upon me or Your wrath lights upon me. It is for You to be satisfied, until You are well pleased. There is no power and no might except Yours."

(Ibn Hisham: A. Guillaume's Translation, p. 193)

Grief stricken and heart broken, when he returned near Qarn al-Manazil, he felt as though the sky was overcast by clouds. He looked up and saw Gabriel in front of him, who called out: "Allah has heard the way your people have responded. He has, therefore, sent this angel in-charge of the mountains. You may command him as you please." Then the angel of the mountains greeted him and submitted: "If you like, I will overturn the mountains from either side upon these people." The Prophet replied : "No, but I expect that Allah will create from their seed those who will worship none but Allah, the One and Only." (Bukhâri, Dhikr al Mala'ikah; Muslim: Kitab al-Maghazi; Nasa'i: Al-Bauth). One night when he was reciting the Qur'an in prayer, a group of the jinn happened to pass by and listened to the Qur'an, believed in it, and returned to their people to preach Islam. Thus, Allah gave His Prophet the good news that, if people were running away from his invitation, there were many jinns, who have become believers, and are spreading the message among their own kind. Anyone who keeps this background in view, and studies this Sûrah will have no doubt left in his mind that this is not at all the composition of Muhammad (peace be upon him), but "a Revelation from the All-Mighty, All- Wise Allah." For nowhere in this Sûrah, from the beginning to the end, does one find even a tinge of the human feelings and reactions, which are naturally produced in a man who is passing through such hard conditions. Considering the Prophet's prayer that is cited above which contains his own language, one can clearly note that its every word is saturated with his feelings.

JUZ (PART) : 26

46: AL-AHQÂF

This Sûrah, revealed at Makkah, has 4 sections and 35 verses.

In the name of Allah, the Compassionate, the Merciful

SECTION: 1

Allah created the heavens, the earth and all that lies between them to manifest the truth

Hâ M'eem.[1]   This Book is revealed by Allah, the All-Mighty, the All-Wise.[2]   We have not created the heavens and the earth and all that lies between them but to manifest the truth, and to last for an appointed term. Yet, the disbelievers give no heed to Our warning.[3]   Ask them: "Have you pondered on those whom you invoke besides Allah? Show me anything that they have created in the earth, or do they have any share in *the creation* of the heavens? Bring me any Book revealed before this, or some remnant of *divine* knowledge *in support of your beliefs,* if you are telling the truth."[4]   And who could be more astray than the one who invokes

Those deities to whom mushrikeen invoke, are not even aware that they are being invoked

those *deities* besides Allah who cannot answer him till the Day of Resurrection - who are not even aware that they are being invoked?[5]   And when mankind shall be assembled *on the Day of Judgment*, they will become enemies of those who invoked them and deny their worship altogether.[6]   46:[1-6]

The Qur'an is the word of Allah, not of the Prophet

When Our revelations are recited to them, clear as they are, and the truth comes before them, the disbelievers say: "This is plain magic."[7]   Do they say that *the Prophet* has fabricated it himself? *O Prophet,* tell them: "If I have fabricated it myself, then there is nothing that you can do to protect me from *the wrath* of Allah. He knows fully well what you say about it. Enough is He as a witness between me and you. He is the Oft-Forgiving, the Most Merciful."[8] *O Prophet* tell them: "I am not the first among the Rasools; nor do I know what will be done with me or with you. I follow only what

The Prophet is but a plain Warner

is revealed to me, and I am no more than a plain Warner."*[9] *Further* say: "Think, if this *Qur'an* is from Allah and you reject it, when a witness *(a Jew)* from the Children of Israel has also testified to its similarity *with earlier scriptures* and has believed *(accepted Islam)*, while you are showing arrogance, *how unjust you are!* Surely, Allah does not guide the unjust people."[10]

46:[7-10]

SECTION: 2

　　　　The unbelievers say about the believers: "Had there been any good *to believe in the message of the Qur'an*, they would not have believed in it before us *(because the unbelievers were strong and wealthy whereas believers were weak and poor)*." And since they did not accept its guidance, they say: "This is an ancient falsehood."[11]　Yet before it, the Book of Musa was revealed which was a guide and blessing; and this Book *(Qur'an)* confirms it. It is revealed in the Arabic language to forewarn the wrongdoers and to give good news to those who have adopted the righteous conduct.[12]　Indeed those who say: "Our Rabb is Allah, and then remain firm, shall have nothing to fear or to grieve.[13]　They shall dwell in paradise forever as a reward for their good deeds.[14]

46:[11-14]

The Qur'an conforms the revelation of Torah given to the Prophet Musa

　　　　We have enjoined upon man to treat his parents with kindness. With much trouble his mother bore him, and with much pain did she give him birth. His bearing and his weaning took thirty months. When he reaches the age of full strength and becomes forty years old, he says: "My Rabb! Grant me the grace that I may thank you for the favors which You have bestowed on me and on my parents, and that I may do good deeds that will please You, and grant me good children. Surely, I turn to You in repentance　and surely, I am one of the Muslims."[15]　　Such are the people from whom We shall accept the best of their deeds and overlook their misdeeds. They shall be among the residents of paradise: true is the promise that has been made to them *in this life.*[16]　But he who rebukes his parents and says: "Uff *(as if to say, do not bother me)*! Do you threaten me with a resurrection, whereas many a generations have passed before me *and none has come back from among them*?" And they both *(father and mother)* cry for Allah's help and say: "Woe to you! Be a good believer. Surely, the promise of Allah is true." But he replies: "This is nothing but tales of the ancients."[17] Such are the people against whom the verdict *of torment* has proved true and they will be among the prior nations of the jinns and humans that have passed away before them. Indeed they will be the losers.[18]　For all, there will be ranks according to their deeds, so that He may reward them fully for what they have done and they shall not be wronged.[19]　On that Day when the disbelievers will be brought before the fire, *they will be told*: "You received your good things in your earthly life and you enjoyed them for a while.

Those who treat their parents with kindness shall be rewarded and those who rebuke their parents shall be punished

Today you shall be recompensed with a punishment of humiliation because you behaved with arrogance for which you had no right *during your life* on earth and because of the transgressions you committed."[20]   46:[15-20]

SECTION: 3

Nation of 'Ad rejected Allah's message, as a result she faced destruction

Remember *the story of* 'Ad's brother, *the Prophet Hûd,* when he warned his people, the residents of Ahqâf *(sand hills)* - in fact, Warners came to their respective people before him and after him - saying: "Worship none but Allah. Surely, I fear for you the torment of a mighty Day."[21] They replied: "Have you come to turn us away from our gods? Bring us *the torment* that you threaten us with, if you are telling the truth."[22] *The Prophet Hûd* said: "The Knowledge *of when it is going to come* is only with Allah. I am only conveying the Message with which I have been sent;) however, I can see that you are an ignorant people."[23] Then when they saw *the torment in the shape of* a cloud coming towards their valleys, they said: "This cloud will bring us rain." - "Nay! It is what you were asking to hasten, a fierce wind bringing you a woeful torment.[24] It is going to destroy everything by the command of its Rabb. So they became such that nothing could be seen except their dwellings. Thus do We reward the nation of criminals.[25] We had established them much better than We have established you, *O Quraish of Makkah,* and endowed them with *the faculties of* hearing, seeing, and intellect. Yet, their *faculties of* hearing, sight and intellect availed them nothing since they denied the revelations of Allah; and they were completely hemmed in by the same thing that they used to mock at.[26]   46:[21-26]

SECTION: 4

No deity can save people from the wrath of Allah

We have destroyed the towns which once flourished around you - and We repeatedly sent them Our revelations so that they may turn *to the Right Way.*[27] - Then Why did not those whom they had taken for gods besides Allah, as a means of access to Him, help them? But those *deities* utterly forsook them, because those were nothing but their lies and their false inventions.[28]   46:[27-28]

A group of jinns embraced Islam after hearing The Qur'an and became the preachers

Remember, when We sent towards you a group of jinns, who, when they reached *the place where you were reciting,* listened to the Qur'an, said to each other: "Be silent." When the recitation was over, they returned to their people as warners.[29] They said "O our people! We have just listened to a Book that has been revealed after Musa *(Moses)*, confirming that which came before it and a guidance to the truth and to the Right Way.[30]   O our people, answer the one who is calling you towards Allah and believe in him! *Allah* will forgive you your sins and save you from a painful punishment.[31]   He that does not answer the one who is calling towards Allah, shall neither escape in the earth, nor shall have any protector besides Him. Surely, such people are in manifest error."[32]   Do they not see that Allah, Who created the heavens and the earth and was not wearied by their creation, has the power to raise the dead to life? Yes! Surely, He has the power over everything.[33]   On the Day when the unbelievers will be brought before the fire, *Allah will ask:* "Is this not real?" "Yes, by our Rabb!" They will answer. "Well, then taste the punishment now," He will reply, "in consequence of your disbelief."[34]   46:[29-34]

Therefore, bear with them with patience, as did the Rasools endowed with firmness of purpose before you, and do not be in haste about them. On the Day when they shall see that which they are being threatened with, their life *on earth* will seem to them as if they had lived no more than an hour of a day. The Message *of forewarning* has been conveyed. Shall any be destroyed except the transgressors?[35]   46:[35]

Keep on passing the message of Allah and bear the disbelievers with patience

47: MUHAMMAD

Period of Revelation

The contents of this Sûrah indicate that it was sent down after the Hijrah to Madinah, after the revelation of Sûrahs Al-Hajj and Al-Baqarah in which fighting was enjoined, but before the battle of Badr.

Major Issues, Divine Laws and Guidance:

* Allah voids the deeds of the disbelievers.
* In war, thoroughly subdue the unbelievers before taking them as prisoners of war.
* If you help the cause of Allah, Allah will help and protect you.
* True believers do not follow their own desires in the matter of religion.
* Promise of obedience (Islam) and good talk which is not followed by action is cursed by Allah.
* Allah puts the believers to test to know the valiant and the resolute.
* In the case of war, Allah is on the side of the true believers.
* Do not be miserly, if you are asked to give in the cause of Allah.

The theme of this Sûrah is to prepare the believers for war through providing them instructions to that effect. That is why this Sûrah is also called Al-Qitâl. The two groups were confronting each other at that time, one which had refused to accept the Truth (disbelievers) and the other group which had accepted the Truth (believers) which had been sent down by Allah to His servant, Muhammad (peace be upon him). Allah, in His final decision, has rendered fruitless and vain, all the works of the disbelievers and set right the condition and affairs of the believers.

The believers (Muslims) have been given instructions relating to war and are reassured of Allah's help and guidance. They are given hope for the best rewards on offering sacrifices and struggle in the cause of Allah, both in this world and in the hereafter. Then the discourse turns towards the hypocrites, who were claiming to be sincere Muslims before the command to fight. They were confounded after this command. They began to conspire with the disbelievers in order to save themselves from the hazards of war. They are plainly warned that the acts and deeds of the hypocrites are not acceptable to Allah.

In conclusion, the Muslims are invited to spend their wealth in the cause of Allah, although at that time, they were economically very weak. They are clearly warned that anyone who adopts a miserly attitude would not harm Allah but would result in his own destruction, for Allah does not stand in need of help from men. If one group of men fail to make sacrifices in the cause of Allah, He would remove it and bring another group in its place.

47: MUHAMMAD

This Sûrah, revealed at Makkah, has 4 sections and 38 verses.

In the name of Allah, the Compassionate, the Merciful

SECTION: 1

Those who disbelieve and obstruct Allah's Way, He will render their deeds fruitless.[1] As for those who believe and do good deeds and believe in what is revealed to Muhammad - and that is the truth from their Rabb - He will remove from them their sins and improve their condition.[2] This is because the unbelievers follow falsehood, while the believers follow the truth from their Rabb. Thus, Allah cites their similitudes for mankind.[3]

47:[1-3]

Allah voids the deeds of the disbelievers

Therefore, when you meet the unbelievers *in the battlefield* smite their necks, until you thoroughly subdued them, then *take prisoners of war and* bind them firmly. Thereafter *you have the choice* whether you show them favor *(release them without ransom)* or accept ransom, until the war lays down its burdens. Thus *are you commanded*. If Allah wanted, He Himself could have punished them; but *He adopted this way* so that He may test some of you by means of others. As for those who are slain in the cause of Allah, He will never let their deeds be lost.[4] Soon, He will guide them, improve their condition[5] and admit them to the paradise which He has made known to them.[6]

47:[4-6]

In case of war, thoroughly subdue the unbelievers before taking prisoners of war

O believers! If you help *the cause of* Allah, He will help you and establish your feet firmly.[7] As for the unbelievers, they shall be consigned to perdition, and He will bring their deeds to nothing.[8] That is because they hate the revelations of Allah; therefore, He rendered their deeds fruitless.[9] Have they not travelled through the land and seen what the end of those who have gone before them was? Allah destroyed them utterly and a similar *fate awaits* these unbelievers.[10] This is because Allah is the Protector of the believers while the unbelievers have no protector.[11]

47:[7-11]

If you help the cause of Allah, Allah will help and protect you

SECTION: 2

Surely, Allah will admit those who believe and do good deeds to gardens beneath which rivers flow. While those who are unbelievers, they are to enjoy *only this life* and eat as cattle eat; but

The believers do not follow their own desires

in the hereafter, the fire shall be their abode.[12]   How many cities that were mightier than your city, which has driven you out, We have destroyed *for their disbelief,* and there was none to save them?[13]   Can he who follows the clear guidance from his Rabb be compared to the one who is led by his own desires and whose foul deeds seem fair to him?[14]   47:[12-14]

Parable of paradise and hell

Here is the description of the paradise which the righteous have been promised: it has rivers, the water of which will never change in taste or smell, rivers of milk whose taste never changes, rivers of wine, delicious to those who drink, and rivers of honey, pure and clear. In it, they will have all kinds of fruits, as well as forgiveness from their Rabb. *Can such people be compared to those* who shall dwell in hell forever, and they will be given scalding water which will cut their intestines into pieces?[15]
                                                          47:[15]

Hypocrites are those on whose heart Allah has set a seal

Some of them, listen to you but no sooner do they leave your presence than they ask those endowed with knowledge: "What was it that he said just now?" Such are the men upon whose hearts Allah has set a seal, and who follow their own desires.[16] As for those who follow the Right Way, Allah will increase their guidance and bestow on them their righteousness.[17]   Are they waiting for anything other than the Hour *of Doom* to overtake them suddenly? Its signs have already come; and when it actually overtakes them, what chance will they have to benefit by this admonition?[18]   Therefore, you should know that there is none worthy of worship but Allah; implore Him to forgive your sins and to forgive the believing men and believing women; for Allah knows your activities and your resting places.[19]   47:[16-19]

SECTION: 3

Promise of obedience (Islam) and good talk which is not followed by action is cursed by Allah

The believers were asking: "Why is not a Sûrah revealed *allowing us to fight*?" But when a decisive Sûrah, carrying the order to fight is revealed, you saw those in whose hearts was a disease, looking at you like the one under the shadow of death. Woe to them![20]   *On their tongues is the promise of* obedience and good talk, so if they would have proved their promise with Allah when the final command was given, it would have been better for them.[21] Would you then, if you turned away *from Islam,* cause corruption in the land and violate the ties of blood.[22]   Such are those whom Allah has cursed and made them deaf and blinded their sight.[23]

Will they not ponder upon the Qur'an? Or are there locks upon their hearts?[24] Those who turn back to unbelief after the guidance has become clear, are seduced by Shaitân *through false hopes* and He *(Allah)* has given them respite.[25] That is because they said to those who hate what Allah has revealed: "We shall obey you in some matters," and Allah knows their secret talks.[26] Then what will they do when the angels will carry off their souls, smiting their faces and their backs?[27] That is because they followed the way that called for the wrath of Allah and hated to adopt the way of His pleasure; therefore, He made all their deeds void.[28]

47:[20-28]

SECTION: 4

Do those in whose hearts is a disease *(of hypocrisy)* think that Allah will not reveal their malice?[29] Had We so pleased, We could have pointed them out to you and you would have recognized them *promptly* by their marks. But you will surely know them by the tone of their speech. Allah knows all of your actions.[30] We shall put you to test until We make evident those who strive their utmost and are patient among you, and test your words and deeds.[31] Surely, the unbelievers, who obstruct others from the Way of Allah and oppose the Rasool after the guidance has become clear to them, shall in no way harm Allah; and He will make their deeds fruiteless.[32] O believers! Obey Allah and obey His Rasool, and do not let your deeds come to nothing.[33] Those who disbelieve and obstruct the Way of Allah and die while they were still disbelievers, Allah will never forgive them.[34]

47:[29-34]

Allah put the believers to test in order to know the valiant and the resolute

Therefore, do not be fainthearted crying for peace, for you will surely gain the upper hand. Allah is on your side and will never let your deeds be wasted.[35] The life of this world is but a play and amusement. If you believe and follow the way of piety, He will grant you your rewards and will not ask you to give up your possessions.[36]

47:[35-36]

In case of war, Allah is on the side of the believers

If He were to demand all *of your possessions* and press you for it, you would grow stingy, and He would bring out all your malice.[37] Behold, you are those who are being asked to give in the cause of Allah. Yet, some of you are stingy, whereas whoever is stingy to His cause, is in fact, stingy to himself. Allah is self-sufficient. It is you who are needy. If you turn away, He will replace you by some other people, who will not be like you.[38]

47:[37-38]

Do not be stingy if you are asked to give in the cause of Allah

48: AL-FAT-H

Period of Revelation

This Sûrah was revealed in Dhil-Q'adah, A. H. 6, when the Prophet was on his way to Madinah after concluding the Treaty of Hudaibiyah with the disbelievers of Makkah.

Major Issues, Divine Laws and Guidance:

* Allah granted the Muslims a manifest victory through the treaty of Hudaibiyah.
* Swearing allegiance to the Prophet was considered swearing allegiance to Allah and Allah was well pleased with their actions.
* Those who do not participate in a war between Islam and Kufr are condemned by Allah.
* Only the blind, lame and sick are exempt from war between Islam and Kufr.
* A vision to conquer Makkah was shown to the Prophet.
* Characteristics of the Prophet Muhammad (peace be upon him) and his followers.

This Sûrah should be read keeping in mind the following historical background:

In 6th year After Hijrah (A.H.), the Prophet saw a dream that he went to Makkah with his Companions and had performed Umrah. Obviously, the Prophet's dream could not be a mere dream and fiction, for it is a form of Divine inspiration as Allah Himself has confirmed in verse 27, in which He says that He Himself had shown that dream to His Rasool. Since it was not merely a dream but a Divine inspiration, therefore, the Prophet had to obey and follow. The Prophet informed his companions about his dream and began to make preparations for the journey. Among the tribes living in the suburbs, he had the public announcement made that he was proceeding for Umrah and the people could join him. About 1,400 of the companions joined him on this highly dangerous journey.

They set off from Madinah in the beginning of Dhil Q'adah, A. H. 6. At a place called Dhul Hulaifah, they put on pilgrim robes with the intention of performing Umrah. They had taken 70 camels with collars around their necks indicating that they were sacrificial animals; and kept only a sword each in sheaths, which the pilgrims to the Ka'bah were allowed to carry according to the recognized custom of Arabia. They carried no other weapons. Thus, the caravan set out for the Ka'bah, the House of Allah, in Makkah, chanting the prescribed slogan of "Labbaik, Allahumma labbaik."

The Prophet sent a man of the Bani Ka'b as a secret agent so that he may keep him informed of the intentions and movements of the Quraish. When the Prophet reached Usfân, he brought the news that the Quraish had reached Dhi Tuwa with full preparations and they had sent Khâlid bin Waleed with two hundred cavalry towards Kura'al-Ghamim to intercept him. The Quraish wanted somehow to provoke the Prophet's companions to fight so that they could tell the Arabs that the Muslims had actually come to fight and had put on the pilgrim garments only to deceive others. Upon receiving this information, the Prophet immediately changed his route and following a very rugged, rocky track, reached Hudaibiyah, which was situated right on the boundary of the sacred Makkan territory. Here, he was visited by Budail bin Warqa, the chief of the Bani Khuza'ah along with some men of his tribe. They asked what he had come for. The Prophet replied that he and his companions had come only for pilgrimage to the House of Allah. The men of Khuza'ah went and told this to the Quraish chiefs and counselled them not to interfere with the pilgrims.

The Quraish sent Urwah bin Mas'ud Thaqafi who held lengthy negotiations with the Prophet and persuaded him to give up his intention to enter Makkah. But the Prophet gave him the same reply that he had given to the chief of the Khuza'ah. Urwah went back and said to the Quraish: "I have been to the courts of the Caesar, the Khosroes and the Negus but, by God, never have I seen any people so devoted to a king as are the companions of Muhammad. If Muhammad makes his ablutions, they would not let the water fall thereof on the ground but would rub it on their bodies and clothes. Now you may decide as to what you should do."

The Prophet sent Sayyidunâ Uthmân (may Allah be pleased with him) as his envoy to Makkah with the message that they had come only for pilgrimage and had brought their sacrificial camels along, and that they would go back after performing the rites of pilgrimage and offering the sacrifice. But the Quraish did not agree and withheld Sayyidunâ Uthmân in the city. In the meantime, a rumor spread that Sayyidunâ Uthmân had been killed. Since he did not return in time, the Muslims took the rumor to be true. Now they could show no more forbearance because their ambassador was killed. The Muslims had no alternative but to prepare for war. Therefore, the Prophet summoned all his companions and took a solemn pledge from them that they would fight to death. It was not an ordinary undertaking. The Muslims were only 1400 and had come without any weapons. They were camping at the boundary of Makkah, which was 250 miles away from their own city. The enemy could attack them in full strength and could surround them with its allies from the adjoining tribes as well. In spite of this, none from the caravan except one man, failed to give his pledge to fight to death, and there could be no greater proof of their dedication and sincerity to the cause of Allah. This pledge is well known in the history of Islam and is called the Ba'it-e-Ridwân.

Later on they came to know that the news about Sayyidunâ Uthmân was false. He returned with a deputation under the leadership of Suhail bin 'Amr from the Quraish to negotiate peace with the Prophet. The Quraish insisted no more in disallowing the Prophet and his companions to enter Makkah. However, in order to save face, they insisted only that they should return that year and come back the following year to perform Umrah. After lengthy negotiations, peace was concluded on the following terms:

1. War would be suspended for ten years, and no party would engage in any hostility, open or secret, against the other.

2. If anyone during that period from among the Quraish defected to Muhammad's camp, without his guardian's permission, he would be returned back to Makkah. But, if a companion of Muhammad were to defect to the Quraish, there will be no requirement for his return.

3. Every Arab tribe would have the option to join either side as its ally and enter the treaty.

4. Muhammad and his men would go back that year. They could come the following year for Umrah and stay in Makkah for three days, provided they bring only one sheathed sword each, and no other weapon of war. In those three days, the Makkans would vacate the city for them (so that there was no chance of conflict), but they would not be allowed to take along any Makkan on return.

The disbelieving Quraish looked at this treaty as a victory and the Muslims were upset considering this as a humiliation in accepting these conditions. When the document was finished, the Prophet asked his companions to slaughter their sacrificial animals at that very place, shave their heads and put off the pilgrim garments, but no one moved. The Prophet repeated the order thrice but the companions were so much in shock, depression and dejection that they did not comply. During his entire period of Risâlat (Prophethood), on no occasion had it ever happened that he (Prophet Muhammad, peace be upon him) commanded his companions to do something and they did not hasten to comply. This caused him a great shock. Returning to his tent, he expressed his grief to his wife, Sayyidah Umme Salamah. She said, "You shall quietly go and slaughter your own camel and call the barber to have your head shaved. After that, the people will automatically do what you did and will understand that whatever decision you have taken will not be changed." That suggestion worked and that is precisely what happened. The people slaughtered their animals, shaved their heads or cut their hair short and put off the pilgrim garb. Nevertheless, their hearts were still afflicted with grief.

Later, when this caravan was returning to Madinah, this Sûrah was revealed, telling the Muslims that the treaty that they were regarding as their defeat was in fact a great victory. The Prophet summoned the Muslims together and said: "Today such a thing has been sent down to me which is more valuable to me than the world and what it contains." Then he recited this Sûrah. The believers became satisfied when they heard this Divine Revelation. The advantages of this treaty began to appear one after the other which proved that this peace treaty indeed was a great victory. Salient features of this treaty were as follows:

1.   This treaty acknowledged the existence of the Islamic State in Arabia. Prior to this, the Arabs considered the Prophet Muhammad (peace be upon him) and his Companions as rebels and outlaws. By concluding this agreement, the Quraish themselves recognized the Prophet's sovereignty over the territories of the Islamic State and opened the way for the Arab tribes to enter into treaties of alliance with either one of the parties.

2.   The Quraish acknowledged the Muslim's right of pilgrimage to the House of Allah. They admitted that Islam was not an antireligious creed, and like the other Arabs, its followers also had the right to perform the rites of Hajj and Umrah. This diminished the hatred in the Arab's hearts caused by the propaganda made by the Quraish against Islam and its followers.

3.   The no-war pact for ten years provided full peace to the Muslims, and they were able to preach Islam in such a way that within two years after Hudaibiyah, the number of the people who embraced Islam far exceeded those of the past 19 years. It was due to this treaty that two years later, when in consequence of the Quraish's violating the treaty, the Prophet invaded Makkah. He was accompanied by an army of 10,000 , whereas on the occasion of Hudaibiyah, only 1,400 men had joined him in the march for Umrah.

4.   The suspension of hostilities provided the Prophet an opportunity to establish and strengthen Islamic rule and turn the Islamic society into a full-fledged civilization and way of life through practicing the Islamic law.

It was this great blessing about which Allah says in verse 3 of Sûrah Al-Mâ'idah: "Today I have perfected your Religion for you and completed My blessing on you and approved Islam as the Way of Life for you."

5. *The balance of power in Arabia changed within two years after this treaty was signed, the strength of the Quraish and other pagan tribes diminished and the domination of Islam became certain. One provision of this treaty which had disturbed the Muslims most was the condition about the fugitives from Makkah and Madinah, that the former would be returned and the latter would not be returned. But not much longer afterwards, this condition also proved to be disadvantageous for the Quraish. Sequence of events revealed, what far-reaching consequences the Prophet had foreseen and why he accepted it. A few days after the treaty a Muslim of Makkah, Abu Basir, escaped from the Quraish and reached Madinah. The Quraish demanded him back and the Prophet returned him to their men who had been sent from Makkah to arrest him. But while on the way to Makkah, he again fled and camped on the road by the Red Sea shore, the route of trade caravans of the Quraish to Syria. After that, every Muslim who succeeded in escaping from the Quraish would go and join Abu Basir instead of going to Madinah, until 70 men gathered there. They would attack any Quraish caravan that passed that way. At last, the Quraish themselves begged the Prophet to call those men to Madinah, and the condition relating to the return of the fugitives itself became null and void.*

6. *Being assured of peace from the south, the Muslims overpowered all the opposing forces in the north and central Arabia easily. Just three months after Hudaibiyah, Khaiber, the major stronghold of the Jews, was conquered and after it, the Jewish settlements of Fadak, Wad-al-Qura, Taima and Tabûk also fell in the hands of Muslims, one after the other. Later on, all other tribes of central Arabia, which were bound in alliance with the Jews and Quraish, came under the banner of Islam.*

48: AL-FATH

This Sûrah, revealed at Madinah, has 4 sections and 29 verses.

In the name of Allah, the Compassionate, the Merciful

SECTION: 1

O Prophet, Surely, We have granted you a manifest victory *in the shape of a Treaty concluded at Hudaibiyah,*[1] so that Allah may forgive your past as well as your future sins, perfect His blessings upon you and guide you to the Right Way,[2] and that Allah may bestow on you His mighty help.[3] It was He, Who sent down tranquillity into the hearts of the believers, so that they may add more faith to their Faith. To Allah belongs the forces of the heavens and the earth. Allah is All-Knowledgeable, All-Wise.[4] *He has caused you to do as you have done,* so that He may admit the believing men and believing women into the gardens beneath which rivers flow, to live therein forever and remove their ills from them; and that is the highest achievement *for them* in the sight of Allah.[5] And that He may punish the hypocritical men and the hypocritical women and the mushrik men and the mushrik women, who entertained an evil thought about Allah. A turn of evil shall befall them, for Allah's wrath is upon them. He has laid His curse on them and prepared for them the fire of hell, which is a very evil abode.[6] To Allah belong the forces of the heavens and the earth; and Allah is All-Mighty, All-Wise.[7] *O Prophet,* We have sent you as a witness, as a bearer of good news, and as a warner,[8] so that you, *O people,* may believe in Allah and His Rasool, and that you may help him, honor him and glorify Allah morning and evening.[9] Surely, those who swore allegiance to you *O Prophet*, indeed swore allegiance to Allah Himself. The Hand of Allah was above their hands. Now, the one who will breaks his pledge, will break it at his own peril, and the one who will keeps his pledge that he has made with Allah, will soon be given a great reward by Him.[10]   48:[1-10]

SECTION: 2

The bedouins who stayed behind will soon say to you: "Our goods and families kept us occupied, so please ask forgiveness for us." They say with their tongues what is not in their hearts. Say: "Who has the power *to intervene* on your behalf with Allah if it be His will to do you harm or to do you good? Allah is well

Allah granted the Muslims a manifest victory through the treaty of Hudaibiyah

Swearing allegiance to the Prophet is considered swearing allegiance to Allah

Bedouins who did not go with the Prophet for war between Islam and

Kufr are condemned for lagging behind

aware of what you do.[11] Rather you thought that the Rasool and the believers would never return to their families; this fancy seemed pleasing to your hearts. You conceived evil thoughts and thus became a people who incurred damnation."[12] He who does not believe in Allah and His Rasool, We have prepared a blazing fire for such unbelievers.[13] To Allah belongs the kingdom of the heavens and the earth: He forgives whom He pleases and He punishes whom He wills. Allah is All-Forgiving, Most Merciful.[14] When you set forth to take the spoils of war, those who stayed behind will say: "Let us come with you." They wish to change Allah's decree. Tell them *plainly*: "You shall not come with us. Allah has already said this before." Then they will say: "Nay! But you are jealous of us." *Whereas there is no question of jealousy,* but little do they understand *such things*.[15] Tell the bedouins who stayed behind: "You shall soon be called upon to fight against a mighty people then either you will fight them or they shall surrender. Then if you obey, Allah will grant you a good reward, but if you turn away as you have done before, He will inflict on you a painful penalty."[16]

Only the blind, lame and sick are exempt from war

There is no blame on the blind, the lame, and the sick, *if they stay behind*. He that obeys Allah and His Rasool shall be admitted to gardens beneath which the rivers flow, and he that turns away shall be punished with a painful punishment.[17]   48:[11-17]

SECTION: 3

Allah was well pleased with those who swore allegiance to the Prophet before the treaty of Hudaibiyah

Allah was well pleased with the believers when they swore allegiance to you under the tree. He knew what was in their hearts, so He sent down tranquillity upon them and He rewarded them with a speedy victory,[18] and many spoils which they will soon acquire. Allah is All-Mighty, All-Wise.[19] Allah has promised you many spoils which you shall acquire, and has given you these *spoils of Khaiber* with all promptness. He has restrained the hands of enemies from you, so that it may serve as a sign to the believers and that He may guide you to the Right Way.[20] *Besides, He promises you* other *spoils* as well, which are not yet within your reach but Allah has surely encompassed them. Allah has power over everything.[21] Even if the unbelievers had fought against you, they would have been put to flight, and would not have found any protector or helper.[22] Such has been the practice of Allah in the past; and you shall find no change in the practice of Allah.[23] It is He Who has restrained their hands from you and your hands from them in the valley of Makkah, *through the Peace Treaty of*

Hudaibiyah, after that He had given you victory over them, and Allah was watching all your actions.[24] They are the ones who disbelieved and obstructed you from the Al-Masjid-al-Harâm *(Sacred Mosque - Ka'bah)* and prevented your offerings from reaching their destination. Had there not been believing men and believing women *in the city of Makkah,* whom you did not know, and their possibility of being trampled *(killed)* by your army and thus incurring unwitting guilt on their account, *Allah would have allowed you to fight, but He held back your hands*, so that He may admit to His mercy whom He will. Had *the believers* stood apart from them, We would certainly have punished the disbelievers among them with painful punishment.[25] While the unbelievers set up in their hearts pride and haughtiness - the pride and haughtiness of the time of ignorance - Allah sent down His tranquillity upon His Rasool and the believers, and made the believers adhere to the word of piety; for they were most worthy and deserving of it. Allah has full knowledge of everything.[26] 48:[18-26]

Had there not been believers in Makkah, Allah would have allowed the Muslims to fight against Quraish

SECTION: 4

Indeed Allah did, in all truth, fulfil the vision which He had shown to His Rasool that - "you shall enter, Allah willing, Al-Masjid Al-Harâm *(Sacred Mosque - Ka'bah)* fearless and secure *to perform Umrah,* some having their heads shaved and others having their hair cut," for He knows what you do not know. So, besides that He granted you a near victory *before the fulfillment of that vision.*[27] It is He who has sent His Rasool with guidance and the religion of truth, so that He may exalt this *religion* over all other religions: and sufficient is Allah as a witness.[28] Muhammad, the Rasool of Allah, and those with him are strong against the unbelievers and kind *to each other* among themselves. When you see them, *you will find them* making Rukû' *(bowing down)* and Sujûd *(prostrate in prayers),* craving for the blessings from Allah and His good pleasure. They have the marks *of Sujûd (prostration)* on their foreheads, the traces of their prostration. This is their description in the Tawrât *(Torah)*; and their description in the Injeel *(Gospel)*: they are like the seed which puts forth its sprout, then strengthens it, then becomes thick and stands firmly on its stem, delighting the sowers *of the seed,* so that *through them* He may enrage the unbelievers. Yet, to those of them who will believe and do good deeds, Allah has promised forgiveness and a great reward.[29] 48:[27-29]

Vision to conquer Makkah is shown to the Prophet

Characteristics of Muhammad (pbuh) and his followers

49: AL-HUJURÂT

Period of Revelation

Traditions and the subject matter indicate that this Sûrah is a combination of the commandments and instructions revealed on different occasions. According to some traditions most of these commandments were revealed during the final stage of the Prophet's life at Madinah.

Major Issues, Divine Laws and Guidance:

* Allah's command to lower ones voice in the presence of the Prophet.
* If the believers fight among themselves make peace between them.
* Islamic etiquettes of moral behavior:
    - Do not laugh at someone to degrade him.
    - Do not defame someone through sarcastic remarks.
    - Do not call someone by offensive nicknames.
    - Avoid immoderate suspicions, for in some cases it is a sin.
    - Do not spy on one another.
    - Do not backbite one another.
    - All mankind is created from one man and one woman, therefore, no one has superiority over another, and noblest is he who is the most pious.
* True believer is he who believes in Allah, His Rasool and makes Jihâd with his wealth and person in the Way of Allah.

The subject matter of this Sûrah is to teach Muslims manners worthy of true believers. In the first five verses they are taught the manners that they should observe with regard to Allah and His Rasool. They are given the instruction, not to believe information without basis and not to act without careful thought. If information is received about a person, a group or a community, it should be evaluated carefully to see whether the source of information is reliable or not. If the source is not reliable, it should be tested and examined to see whether the news is authentic or not, before taking any action. Guidance is provided towards attitudes that Muslims should adopt in cases where groups of Muslims have conflict with each other.

Muslims are exhorted to safeguard against the evils, that corrupt collective life and spoil mutual relationships such as mocking and taunting each other, calling by offensive nicknames, creating suspicions, spying on each other and backbiting. All of these evils are declared as forbidden and unlawful. In addition, na-

tional and racial distinctions that cause universal corruption in the world are condemned. Nations, tribes and families with pride of ancestry tend to look down upon others as inferior to themselves. Nationalism historically promotes superiority complexes that have been the main cause of injustices, wars and tyranny in the world. In this Sûrah Allah has cut the root of this evil by stating that all men are descendants of the same pair of humans (Adam and Eve). Their division into tribes and communities is only for the sake of recognition, not for boasting and pride. There is no lawful basis of one man's superiority over the other except on the basis of moral excellence.

In conclusion, people are told that true Faith is not the verbal statement of believing in Allah and His Rasool, but to obey them in practical life and to exert sincere efforts with one's self and wealth in the cause of Allah. As for those who profess Islam orally without testifying by their hearts and actions, thinking that they had done someone a favor by accepting Islam, they may be counted among the Muslims in this world and may even be treated as Muslims in the society, but they are not believers in the sight of Allah.

49: AL-HUJURÂT

This Sûrah, revealed at Madinah, has 2 sections and 18 verses.

In the name of Allah, the Compassionate, the Merciful

SECTION: 1

Allah's commandment to lower one's voice in the presence of the Prophet

O believers! Do not put yourselves ahead of Allah and His Rasool. Fear Allah; surely, Allah hears all and knows all.[1]   O believers! Do not raise your voices above the voice of the Prophet, nor speak aloud when talking to him as you speak aloud to one another, lest your deeds should come to nothing while you do not even perceive it.[2]   Those who lower their voices and speak softly in the presence of Allah's Rasool are the ones whose hearts Allah has tested for piety; they shall have forgiveness and a great reward.[3]   Those who call out to you, *O Muhammad,* from outside the private apartments, most of them lack common sense.[4] If only they had patience until you could come out to them, it would certainly be better for them. Allah is Forgiving, Merciful.[5]   O believers, if an evildoer comes to you with some news, verify it *(investigate to ascertain the truth)*, lest you should harm others unwittingly and then regret what you have done.[6] And know that Allah's Rasool is among you. If he were to follow you in most affairs, you would certainly be in trouble. But Allah has endeared this faith to you and beautified it in your hearts, making unbelief, wrongdoing, and disobedience abhorrent to you. It is they who are rightly guided[7] through Allah's grace and blessing. Allah is All-Knowledgeable, All-Wise.[8]   If two parties among the believers

Make peace between the believers if they fall into fighting among themselves

fall into a fight, make peace between them. Then if either of them transgresses against the other, fight the transgressors until they returns to the commands of Allah. Then, if they return, make peace between them with justice and be fair; for Allah loves those who are fair and just.[9] The believers are brothers to one another, therefore, make reconciliation between your brothers and fear Allah, so that you may be shown mercy.[10]   49:[1-10]

SECTION: 2

Islamic etiquettes of moral behavior

O believers! Let no men laugh at other men who may perhaps be better than they are; and let no women laugh at other women, who may perhaps be better than they are. Do not defame *through sarcastic remarks about* one another, nor call one another by *offensive* nicknames. It is an evil thing to be called by a bad name after being a believer, and those who do not repent are the ones who are the wrongdoers.[11] O believers! Avoid immoderate suspicion, for, in some cases, suspicion is a sin. Do not spy on one another, nor backbite one another *(to say something about another behind ones back that if one hears it, dislikes it)*. Would any of you like to eat the flesh of his dead brother? Surely, you would abhor it. Fear Allah; for Allah is the Accepter of repentance, Merciful.[12] O mankind! We created you from a single *pair of a* male and a female, and made you into nations and tribes that you might get to know one another. Surely, the noblest of you in the sight of Allah, is he who is the most righteous. Allah is All-Knowledgeable, All-Aware.[13]

49:[11-13]

> Mankind is created from a single male and a female and noblest is he who is the most righteous

The bedouins say: "We have believed." Tell them: "You have not believed; rather say 'We have become Muslims;' for faith has not yet found its way into your hearts. If you obey Allah and His Rasool, He will not deny you the reward of your deeds; surely, Allah is Forgiving, Merciful."[14] The true believers are those who believe in Allah and His Rasool, then never doubt; and make Jihad with their wealth and their persons in the cause of Allah. They are the ones who are truthful *in their claim to be the believers*.[15] *O Prophet say to those who claim to have believed*: "Do you apprise Allah of your religion? Whereas, Allah knows all that is in the heavens and the earth and He has full knowledge of everything."[16] *They think* they have conferred upon you a favor by embracing Islam. Tell them: "You have conferred upon me no favor by accepting Islam. It was Allah Who has conferred a favor upon you in guiding you to the true faith; *admit this*, if you are truthful *in your claim of having faith*.[17] Surely, Allah knows the secrets of the heavens and the earth; and Allah is watching all your actions."[18]

49:[14-18]

> The difference between a true Believer and a Muslim

50: QÂF

Period of Revelation

This Sûrah was revealed in the second stage of the Prophet's residence at Makkah, i.e. from the third year of the Prophethood to the fifth year, when antagonism from disbelievers had become quite intense but had not yet become tyrannical.

Major Issues, Divine Laws and Guidance:

*   Life after death is a reality and there is nothing strange about it.
*   Allah has assigned two angels to each person, for noting down each word that he utters.
*   Every disbeliever will be thrown into the hell and the hell shall be asked, "Are you full." Hell will answer, "Are there some more?"
*   Admonish people with the Qur'an and bear them with patience.

Authentic traditions show that the Prophet used to recite this Sûrah, generally in the prayer on the Eid day. A woman named Umme Hisham bin Hârithah, who was a neighbor of the Prophet, said that she was able to commit Sûrah Qâf to memory only because she often heard it from the Prophet in the Friday sermons. According to some other traditions, the Prophet used to recite it during Fajr (morning) Prayer. This shows the importance of this Sûrah in the sight of the Prophet. That is why he made sure that its contents reached as many people as possible over and over again.

The reason for its importance can be easily understood by a careful study of the Sûrah. The theme of the entire Sûrah is the Hereafter. When the Prophet started preaching Allah's message in Makkah, what surprised the people most was the news that people would be resurrected after death, and they would have to render an account of their deeds. In this Sûrah, arguments are given for the possibility and occurrence of the hereafter in brief and short sentences, and the people are warned, as if to say: "Whether you express wonder and surprise, or you regard it as something remote from reason, or deny it altogether, in any case, it cannot change the truth. The absolute, unalterable truth is that Allah knows the whereabouts of each and every particle of your body that has decomposed in the earth, and knows where and in what state it is. Allah's one signal is enough to make all the decomposed particles gather together again and make you rise up once again as you had been created in your earthly life. Likewise, the idea that you have been *created alone in the world and that you are not answerable to anyone, is no more than a misunderstanding. The fact is that not only is Allah Himself directly aware of each act and word of yours, He is aware of even the ideas that pass in your mind. He has assigned angels to each one of you who are recording whatever you do and utter. On the Day of Judgment, you will come out of your graves at one call, just as the young shoots of vegetable sprout up from the earth after the first rain shower. Then, this heedlessness which obstructs your vision, will be removed and you will see with your own eyes all that you are denying today. At that time, you will realize that you have not been created to be irresponsible in this world but accountable for all your deeds, and that you will be awarded paradise as a reward or hell as a punishment. The paradise and the hell which you regard as impossible and imaginary things, will, at that time, become visible realities. In consequence of your enmity and opposition to the truth, you will be cast into the same hell which you deny today and those who fear Allah and adopt the path of righteousness, will be admitted to the same paradise at the mention of which you express wonder and surprise."*

P

50: QÂF

This Sûrah, revealed at Makkah, has 3 sections and 45 verses.

In the name of Allah, the Compassionate, the Merciful

SECTION: 1

Qâf. By the Glorious Qur'an, *We have sent you as a warner*.[1] But they wonder that there has come to them a warner *(Muhammad)* from among themselves. So the unbelievers say: "This is very strange[2] that after we are dead and have become dust, *we shall be raised to life again,* such a return is far from reason."[3] We know all that the earth consumes of their bodies, and We have a Book which keeps records of everything.[4] Nay! But these people deny the truth when it comes to them, and they are confused.[5] Have they not looked at the sky above them, *and marked,* how We have made it, adorned it, and that there are no flaws in it?[6] And the earth! We have spread it out and set upon it mountains and caused to grow in it every kind of beautiful vegetation.[7] *All these things are* eye-openers and a reminder for every servant returning *to Allah.*[8] We send down blessed water from the sky with which We bring forth gardens and the harvest grain,[9] and tall palm trees laden with clusters of dates, piled one over another,[10] a sustenance for the servants; thereby giving new life to dead land. That is how the resurrection will be *of the dead.*[11] Before, the people of Nûh and the dwellers of Ar-Rass denied *this truth* and so did Thamûd,[12] 'Ad, Fir'aun *(Pharaoh)* and the brethren of Lût,[13] the dwellers of the Al-Aiykah and the people of Tubba'; all of them disbelieved their Rasools and thus My threat war justly fulfilled.[14] Were We fatigued with the first creation that they are in doubt about a new creation?[15] 50:[1-15]

SECTION: 2

We created man, We know the prompting of his soul, and We are closer to him than his jugular vein.[16] *Besides this direct knowledge,* We have assigned to every one two scribes *(guardian angels),* one seated on his right and the other on his left,[17] not a single word does he utter but there is a vigilant guardian ready to note it down.[18] When the agony of death will bring the truth *before his eyes, they will say*: "This is what you were trying to escape!"[19] And the Trumpet shall be blown; that will be the Day of which you were threatened![20] Each soul will come forth; with it, there will be *an angel to* drive and *an angel to bear* witness.[21]

Life after death is a reality and there is nothing strange about it

Allah has assigned two angels to each person for noting each single word that he utters

It will be said: "You were heedless of this, but now We have removed your veil, so your eyesight is sharp today!"[22]   His companion *(angel)* will say: "Here is my testimony ready with me."[23]   *The sentence will be*: "Throw into hell, every stubborn disbeliever,[24]   opponent of good, and doubting transgressor[25] who set up other gods besides Allah. So, throw him into severe punishment."[26]   His companion *(shaitân)* will say: "Our Rabb! I did not mislead him. He himself had gone far astray."[27]   *Allah* will say: "Do not dispute with each other in My presence. I gave you warning beforehand.[28]   My words cannot be changed, nor am I unjust to My servants."[29]   50:[16-29]

> Every stubborn disbeliever will be thrown into hell

SECTION: 3

On that Day, We shall ask the hell: "Are you full?" And the *hell* will answer: "Are there any more?"[30]   Paradise shall be brought close to the righteous, which will no more be a distant thing,[31]   *and it will be said*: "Here is what you were promised. It is for every penitent faithful person,[32]   who feared the Compassionate *(Allah)* without seeing Him and will come before Him with a repenting heart."[33]   *Allah will say:* "Enter it in peace; this is the Day of Eternal Life!"[34]   There they shall have all that they wish, and We shall have yet more to give.[35]   50:[30-35]

> Hell shall be asked, "Are you full." Hell will answer, "Are there any more?"

How many generations, far stronger in power, have We destroyed before them! They searched the entire land: but could they find any refuge?[36]   Surely, in this, there is a lesson for every person who has a heart, and listens attentively.[37]   We created the heavens and the earth and all that lies between them in six Yaums *(days, time periods or stages)*, and no fatigue touched Us.[38]   So, *O Prophet*, bear with patience whatever they say, and glorify your Rabb with His praise before sunrise and before sunset.[39]   And glorify Him during a part of the night and after the prostration *(prayers)*.[40]   And listen! The Day when the Caller will call out from a place quite near,[41]   the Day when the people will hear the mighty blast in reality; that will be the Day of coming forth *(the dead will rise from their graves)*.[42]   Surely, it is We Who give life and death; and to Us shall all return.[43]   On that Day when the earth splits asunder and the people are rushing out of it, gathering them all will, then, be quite easy for Us.[44]   We know very well what these *unbelievers* say. You *(O Muhammad)* are not there to compel them to believe. So admonish with this Qur'an *every such person* who fears My warning.[45]   50:[36-45]

> Admonish the unbelievers and bear with them in patience

> Admonish them with The Qur'an

51: AZ-ZÂRIYÂT

Period of Revelation

This Sûrah was revealed in the 5th year of the Prophet's residence at Makkah when his invitation was being resisted and opposed with denial, ridicule and false accusations, but persecution had not yet started.

Major Issues, Divine Laws and Guidance:

* Surely the Day of Judgement shall come to pass, only the perverse persons turn away from this truth.
* The same angels who gave good news, of having a son, to Ibrâheem annihilated the nation of homosexuals.
* There is a lesson in the stories of Fir'aun, 'Ad, Thamûd and people of Nûh.
* Allah, Who built the heavens and spread out the earth, has assigned the Prophet Muhammad (peace be upon him) to be a Warner for mankind.

This Sûrah emphasizes the Hereafter , and extends an invitation of Tawheed (God is One and Only). The people are warned that refusal to accept the message of the Prophets and persistence in ignorance has proven to be disastrous for those nations who adopted this attitude in the past.

People's different and conflicting beliefs about the end of human life are themselves an express proof that none of these beliefs and creeds is based on knowledge; everyone has individually formed an ideology on the basis of conjecture, which has become his creed. Some thought that there would be no life-after-death; some believed in life- after-death, but in the form of the transmigration of souls; some believed in the life hereafter, but invented different sorts of props and supports to escape retribution. About a question of such vital and fundamental importance, a wrong view of which renders man's whole life-work wasted, ultimately ruining his future for ever. It would be a disastrous folly to build an ideology only on the basis of speculation and conjecture, and without knowledge. It would mean that man should remain involved in grave misunderstanding, his whole life passing in heedless error, and after death, should suddenly meet with a situation for which he had made no preparation at all. There is only one way of forming the right opinion about such a question, and it is through the knowledge that the Prophets of Allah have conveyed.

   The invitation to Tawheed (God is One and Only) is given in the following words: "Your Creator has not created you for the service of others, but for His own service. He is not like your false gods which receive sustenance from you and the godhead of which cannot function without your help. He is the All-Mighty God (Allah), Who is the Sustainer of all, Who does not stand in need of sustenance from anyone and Whose Godhead is functioning by His own power and might. Finally, the Prophet is instructed to ignore the rebels and keep on performing his mission of invitation and admonition, for it is useful and beneficial for the believers, although it may not be so, for the other people. As for the wicked people who still persist in their rebellion, they should know that their predecessors who followed the same way of life, have already received their shares of Allah's retribution.

51: ADH-DHÂRIYÂT

This Sûrah, revealed at Makkah, has 3 sections and 60 verses.

In the name of Allah, the Compassionate, the Merciful

SECTION: 1

Surely the Day of Judgment shall come to pass, only the perverse persons turn away from this truth

By the winds scattering dust;[1]   by the clouds heavy laden;[2]   by the *ships* smoothly gliding;[3]   by *the angels* who distribute *blessings* by *Allah's* command,[4]   that which you are being promised is surely true;[5]   and surely, the Day of Judgment shall convene.[6]   By the sky full of orbits,[7]   surely, you contradict *one another* in what you say *about the Qur'an and the Prophet Muhammad*.[8]   Deluded away from *the Qur'an and the Prophet Muhammad* is he who is deluded.[9]   Woe to those who tell lies,[10] those who are engulfed in *ignorance and* heedlessness.[11]   They ask: "When will the Day of Judgment be?"[12]   It will be the Day when they will be punished in the fire,[13]   *and it will be said:* "Taste your chastisement! This is what you were seeking to hasten."[14]   As for the righteous, they will be in the midst of gardens and springs,[15] joyfully receiving what their Rabb shall give them; for they were before that *(during their life on earth)* righteous people.[16]   They used to sleep but little in the night time,[17]   pray for forgiveness before dawn,[18]   and share their wealth with the needy who asked for it, and those who did not ask.[19]   In the earth, there are signs for the firm believers,[20]   and also in your own selves; can you not see?[21]   In heaven is your sustenance and all that you are promised.[22]   I swear by the Rabb of heaven and earth that this is true, *as certain* as you are speaking now![23]   51:[1-23]

SECTION: 2

Story of the Prophet Ibrâheem, when he was given the good news of having a son

Have you heard the story of Ibrâheem's honored guests?[24] When they entered upon him and said: Salaam (peace be upon you)." He replied: Salaam (peace be upon you)." And seeing that they were strangers,[25]   he went quietly to his family, brought a fat *roasted* calf,[26]   and placed it before them saying: "Will you not eat?"[27]   *When he saw them not eating,* he became afraid of them. They said: "Have no fear," and they gave him good news of a son endowed with knowledge.[28]   *Hearing this,* his wife came forward with a loud cry and she struck her face in astonishment saying: *"A son to* a barren old woman!"[29]   They replied: "Thus has said your Rabb: surely, He is the Wise, the Knowledgeable."[30] 51:[24-30]

JUZ (PART): 27

Ibrâheem (Abraham) asked: "*O Divine* Messengers, what is your errand?"[31] They replied: "We have been sent to a guilty nation *(people of Lût, who were homosexuals)*,[32] to shower upon them clay stones,[33] marked by your Rabb for the transgressors."[34] So We delivered all those who were believers in the town[35] - We found none but one household of true Muslims[36] - We left therein a sign for those who fear the painful punishment.[37]

51:[31-37]

There is also a sign for you in the story of Musa *(Moses)*: when We sent him to Fir'aun *(Pharaoh)* with clear authority,[38] but he turned his back along with his chiefs, saying: "He *(Moses)* is a sorcerer or a madman."[39] Consequently, We seized him and his warriors, and cast them into the sea. Indeed he deserved much blame.[40] *There is also a sign* in *the story of* 'Ad: when We let loose on them a blighting wind[41] which spared nothing that it reached and made everything rotten that it blew on.[42] *Likewise* in the *story of* Thamûd, when it was said to them: "Enjoy yourselves for a while *(three days)*,"[43] but they *did not repent and* disobeyed the commandment of their Rabb; consequently, they were overtaken by the thunderbolt even while they were looking on.[44] So they neither could stand up on their feet nor could they defend themselves.[45] And *We destroyed* the people of Nûh *(Noah)* before them, surely, they were a nation of transgressors.[46]

51:[38-46]

SECTION: 3

We have built the heaven with power, for We are able to extend the vastness *of space thereof.*[47] We have spread out the earth; how excellent a spreader We are![48] We have created everything in pairs, so that you may learn a lesson from it.[49] *O Prophet, say to mankind*: "Rush towards Allah, surely, I am assigned by Him as a plain Warner to you all.[50] Do not set up any other god besides Allah, surely, I am assigned by Him as a plain Warner to you all."[51] It has been the case that whenever a Rasool came to the peoples before them, they said *about him*: "He is a sorcerer or a madman."[52] Have they transmitted this statement *from one generation to the next*? Nay, but they are all rebellious people.[53] So, *O Prophet,* ignore them; you are not at fault.[54] But keep on admonishing them, for admonition is beneficial to the true

---

The same angels who gave good news to Ibrâheem annihilated the nation of homosexuals

There is a lesson in the stories of Fir'aun, 'Ad, Thamûd and people of Nûh

Allah, Who built the heavens and spread out the earth, has assigned the Prophet Muhammad to be a Warner for mankind

believers.[55] I *(Allah)* have not created jinns and mankind except to worship Me *(Alone)*.[56] I require no sustenance from them, nor do I ask that they should feed Me.[57] Surely, it is Allah Who is the giver of all sustenance, the Lord of Power, the Invincible.[58] Surely, those who are wrongdoers, shall have their portion *of torment* similar to the portion of their predecessors; so let them not *challenge Me to* hurry it on.[59] Woe then to the unbelievers, on that Day with which they are being threatened![60]   51:[47-60]

52: AT-TÛR

Period of Revelation

This Sûrah was revealed in the 5th year of the Prophet's residence at Makkah. During this period the Prophet (peace be upon him) was being targeted with objections and accusations but severe persecution of the Muslims had not yet started.

Major Issues, Divine Laws and Guidance:

* The reward for the righteous will be paradise, in which they will show gratitude for Allah's graciousness, while the deniers of truth will be put in hellfire.
* Mission of the Prophet is admonition.
* Response to the disbelievers' disbelief:
    - If they doubt the Qur'an, let them produce a scripture like this.
    - Were they created without a Creator?
    - Do they possess the treasures of Allah?
    - Do they have other means to hear the facts about Allah?
    - Do they have the knowledge of the unseen?

If so let them produce their proof.

Swearing by some realities and signs, which testify to the Day of Resurrection, a statement is made emphatically that it will surely take place, and none has the power to prevent its occurrence. Then, the statement goes on as to what will be the fate of those who deny it when it actually occurs, and how those who believe in it and adopt the way of righteousness will be blessed by Allah.

Then, the Quraish chiefs' attitude towards the message of the Prophet (peace be upon him) is criticized. They called him a sorcerer, a madman or a poet, and would thus mislead the common people against him so that they should not pay any serious attention to the message he is conveying.. They looked upon him as a calamity that had suddenly descended on them and would openly wish to get rid of him. They accused him of fabricating the Qur'an by himself and of presenting it in the name of Allah and thus it was a fraud that he was committing. They would often taunt him saying that Allah could not have appointed an ordinary man like him to the office of Prophethood. They expressed great disgust at his invitation and message, and would avoid him as if he was asking them a reward for it. They would sit and take counsel together to devise schemes in order to put an end to his mission. And while they did all this, they never realized what creeds of ignorance they were practicing, and how selflessly and sincerely was Muhammad (peace be upon him) exerting himself to deliver them from their error. While criticizing them for this attitude and conduct, Allah has put before them certain questions, one after the other, each of which is either an answer to some objection of theirs, or a criticism of some error. Then, it has been said that it would absolutely be of no avail to show them a miracle in order to convince them about the Prophethood of Muhammad (peace be upon him), for they were such stubborn people that they would misinterpret anything they were shown only to avoid affirming the faith.

The Prophet (peace be upon him) is given the instruction that he should persistently continue giving his invitation and preaching Allah message in spite of the accusations and objections of his opponents and enemies, and should endure their resistance patiently till Allah's judgement comes to pass. Besides, he has been consoled, as if to say "Your Rabb has not left you alone to face your enemies, after raising you as a Prophet, but He is constantly watching over you. Therefore, endure every hardship patiently till the Hour of His Judgement comes, and seek through praising and glorifying your Rabb, the power that is required for exerting your efforts in the cause of Allah under such conditions.

52: AT-TÛR

This Sûrah, revealed at Makkah, has 2 sections and 49 verses.

In the name of Allah, the Compassionate, the Merciful

SECTION: 1

By the *mount* Tûr *(where Moses was given the Torah)*,[1] and by the Book written[2] on an unfolded scroll,[3] and by the inhabited House,[4] and the elevated canopy *(sky)*,[5] and the surging sea,[6] the torment of your Rabb will surely come to pass![7] There shall be none to avert it.[8] On that Day, heaven will shake violently[9] and the mountain will travel around.[10] On that Day, woe be to the deniers of truth,[11] who are engaged in their useless sports.[12] On that Day they shall be driven to the fire of hell with violence,[13] *and it will be said to them:* "This is the fire which you denied.[14] Is this magic, or do you not see?[15] Now burn therein; it will be the same for you, whether you bear it patiently or not. You are being rewarded according to your deeds."[16] *As for* the righteous, they will be in Gardens and bliss,[17] rejoicing in what their Rabb has given them, and their Rabb shall shield them from the torment of hell.[18] *It will be said to them:* "Eat and drink to your hearts' content, this is the reward for your *good* deeds."[19] They shall recline on couches arranged in rows; and We shall wed them with beautiful Hûris *(damsels)* with beautiful big eyes.[20] We shall unite the true believers with those of their descendants who follow them in their faith, and shall not deny them the reward of their good deeds - everyone is held in pledge for his deeds[21] - and We shall provide them fruits, and such meats as they desire.[22] They will pass from hand to hand a cup of wine which shall cause no idle talk, nor sinful urge;[23] and there shall wait on them young boys, *exclusively appointed* for their service, who will be as handsome as treasured pearls.[24] They will converse with one another *about their worldly life*[25] and say: "When we were living among our kinfolk, we were fearing *Allah's displeasure.*[26] But Allah has been gracious to us; He has delivered us from the punishment of fire.[27] Indeed we used to pray only to Him. Surely, He is the Beneficent, the Merciful."[28]   52:[1-28]

Deniers of truth will be put in the fire of hell

The reward for the righteous will be paradise in which they will show gratitude for Allah's graciousness

SECTION: 2

Therefore, O *Prophet,* keep up *your mission of* admonition. By the grace of your Rabb you are neither a soothsayer nor a

The mission of the Prophet and the response to the disbelievers' argument

madman.[29]   Do they say: "He is but a poet! We are waiting for some misfortune to befall him."[30]   Tell them: "Wait if you will; I too shall wait with you."[31]   Do their faculties of reasoning prompt them to say this? Or is it merely that they are wicked people?[32]   Do they say: "This man has invented this *Qur'an* himself?" Nay! They do not want to believe.[33]   Let them produce a recital like this *(Qur'an)*, if what they say is true![34]   Were they created by no one? Or were they their own creators?[35]   Have they created the heavens and the earth? Nay! They will never be convinced.[36]   Do they possess the treasures of your Rabb? Or is it they who are in control?[37]   Do they have a stairway to heaven *by means of which* they overhear Him? If so, let any of them who overheard Him, bring clear proof.[38]   Is He to have daughters and you sons?[39]   Do you ask them compensation for your services, that they should fear to be overburdened by a debt?[40]   Do they have *the knowledge of* the unseen, and they write it down?[41]   Do they intend to devise a plot *against you*? If so, the disbelievers themselves will be trapped in their plot.[42]   Do they have a god other than Allah? Exalted is Allah, far above those deities they associate with Him.[43]   *They are such people that,* even if they will see a part of heaven falling down, they would say: "It is but a mass of clouds."[44]   So leave them alone until they encounter that Day of theirs wherein they shall sink into fainting *with terror*.[45]   The Day when their plotting will avail them nothing and none will help them.[46]   Surely, for such wrongdoers, there is another punishment besides that, even though most of them do not realize that.[47]   *Therefore*, wait for the Judgment of your Rabb with patience; surely, you are under Our Eyes *(loving care and protection).* Glorify your Rabb with His praises when you wake up,[48]   and glorify Him in a part of the night, and also as the stars fade away.[49]

52:[29-49]

53: AN-NAJM

Period of Revelation

This is the first Sûrah of the Qur'an, which the Prophet (peace be upon him) had publicly recited before an assembly of the Quraish (and according to Ibn Marduyah, in the Ka'bah) in which both the believers and the disbelievers were present. At the end, when he recited the verse requiring the performance of a Sajdah and fell down in prostration, the whole assembly also fell down in prostration with him, and even those chiefs of the polytheists who were in the forefront of the opposition to the Prophet (peace be upon him) could not resist falling down in prostration. Ibn Mas'ud (may Allah be pleased with him) says that he saw only one man, Umayyah bin Khalaf, from among the disbelievers, who did not fall down in prostration but took a little dust and rubbing it on his forehead said that it was enough for him. This Sûrah was revealed in Ramadân of 5th year of Prophet's residence at Makkah.

Major Issues, Divine Laws and Guidance:

* Scene of the First Revelation, that was brought by angel Gabriel to the Prophet Muhammad (peace be upon him).
* Allah gave Prophet Muhammad (peace be upon him) a tour of the Heavens, Paradise and other great signs.
* Lât, Uzza and Manât (goddesses of Arabs) are nothing but names invented by pagan Arabs.
* Angels have no share in divinity, nor can they even intercede without the permission of Allah.
* Do not claim piety for yourselves, Allah knows who is Godfearing and pious.
* No soul shall bear the burden of another, there shall be nothing for a person except what he strived for.

The theme of the Sûrah is to warn the disbelievers of Makkah about the error of their attitude that they had adopted towards the Qur'an and the Prophet Muhammad (peace be upon him). The discourse starts by saying: "Muhammad (peace be upon him) is neither deluded nor has gone astray, as you are telling others in your propaganda against him, nor has he fabricated this teaching of Islam and its message, as you seem to think he has. In fact, whatever he is presenting is nothing but Revelation which is sent down to him. The facts that he presents before you are not the product of his own imagination and speculation but realities of which he himself is an eye witness. He has himself seen the Angel through whom *this knowledge is conveyed to him. He has been directly made to observe the great Signs of Allah during his trip of M'irâj; whatever he says is not what he has imagined but what he has seen with his own eyes." After this, following three convincing arguments are presented:*

1. *The religion that you are following is based on mere conjecture and invented ideas. You have set up a few goddesses like Lât, Manât and Uzza, whereas they have no share in divinity. You regard the angels as the daughters of Allah. You think that these deities of yours can influence Allah in your favor, whereas the fact is that all the angels together, who are stationed closest to Allah, cannot influence Him even in their own favor. None of the beliefs that you have adopted is based on knowledge and reason, but are wishes and desires based on which you have taken some whims as realities. This is a grave error.*

2. *The final judgement will not depend on your desires or the claims that you make about your purity and chastity but on whether you are pious or impious, righteous or unrighteous in the sight of Allah. If you refrain from major sins, He, in His mercy, will overlook your minor errors.*

3. *A few basic principles of the true faith are reiterated which were stated in the Books of the Prophets Ibrâheem (Abraham) and Musa (Moses), to remove their misunderstanding that Prophet Muhammad (peace be upon him) has brought some new and novel religion, but are the same basic truths which the former Prophets of Allah had always presented in their respective ages. It is made clear that the destruction of the 'Ad, the Thamûd, the people of the Prophets Nûh (Noah) and Lût (Lot) was not the result of accidental calamities, but Allah has destroyed them in consequence of the same wickedness and rebellion from which the disbelievers of Makkah are not inclined to refrain and desist.*

This was such an impressive Sûrah, that even the most hardened deniers of the truth were completely overwhelmed, and when after reciting these verses of Divine Word the Prophet of Allah (peace be upon him) fell down in prostration, they too could not help falling down in prostration along with him.

53: AN-NAJM

This Sûrah, revealed at Makkah, has 3 sections and 62 verses.

In the name of Allah, the Compassionate, the Merciful

SECTION: 1

By the star when it sets,[1] your companion *(Muhammad)* is neither astray, nor is he misguided.[2] He does not speak out of his own desire,[3] but this *(Al-Qur'an)* is an inspired revelation.[4] He is being taught *(this Qur'an)* by one who is mighty in power *(angel Gabriel)*;[5] the one free from defects who became stable in the view.[6] He stood poised at the uppermost horizon;[7] then he drew near, coming closer[8] within the length of two bows or even closer,[9] and revealed to *Allah's* servant *(Muhammad)* that what he was supposed to reveal.[10] His *(Muhammad's)* own heart did not deny that which he saw.[11] How can you, *O unbelievers,* then question what he saw?[12] And he *(Muhammad)* saw him once again[13] near Sidra-tul-Muntaha *(the Lote-tree at the farthest end of the seven heavens, beyond which none can pass).*[14] Near it there is Janna-tul-M'awâ *(paradise of abode).*[15] When that Lote-tree was covered with what covered it,[16] his eyes did not turn aside nor did they exceed the limit:[17] and he did indeed see some of his Rabb's greatest signs.[18]   53:[1-18]

Scene of the first revelation, brought by Angel Gabriel to the Prophet Muhammad

Allah gave him a tour of heavens, paradise and other great signs

Have you ever seen Lât and Uzza[19] and another, the third, Manât *(names of Arabian idols, claimed by the pagans of Makkah to be the daughters of Allah)*?[20] Are you to have sons, and He the daughters?[21] This indeed is an unfair division![22] These *(Lât, Uzza and Manât)* are nothing but names which you and your forefathers have invented, for Allah has vested no authority in them. The unbelievers follow nothing but mere conjecture and the whims of their own souls, even though right guidance has already come to them from their Rabb.[23] Or should man have whatever he wishes?[24] Nay! To Allah belongs the last *(Hereafter)* and the first *(this world).*[25]   53:[19-25]

Lât, Uzza and Manât (goddesses of Arabs) are nothing but names invented by pagan Arabs

SECTION: 2

How many are the angels in the heavens; yet, their intercession can avail none unless Allah gives permission to whom He pleases, and *only* in favor of whom He wants and approves.[26] Those who do not believe in the Hereafter, give the angels the female names *of goddesses.*[27] But they have no knowledge of it. They follow mere conjecture; and surely, conjecture is not a substitute for truth.[28] Therefore, neglect those who ignore Our warnings and seek

Angels have no share in divinity, nor can they intercede without permission

only the life of this world.[29] This is the sum of their knowledge. Surely, your Rabb knows best who have strayed from His path, and who are rightly guided.[30] To Allah belongs all that is in the heavens and in the earth, so that He may requite the evildoers according to their deeds, and richly reward those who do good deeds.[31] Those who avoid the major sins and shameful deeds except the small offenses, surely, for them your Rabb will have abundant forgiveness. He knew you well when He created you from earth and when you were just embryos in your mothers' wombs; therefore, do not claim piety for yourselves. He knows best who is really Godfearing *(pious)*.[32]   53:[26-32]

> **Do not claim piety for yourselves, Allah knows who is Godfearing and pious**

SECTION: 3

Have you seen the one who *(Waleed bin Mugheerah, who was willing to embrace Islam, but upon someone's promise to take the responsibility of getting the punishment on his behalf in lieu of certain amount of money, he)* turned away.[33] He gave a little *from the promised amount* then stopped.[34] Does he possess the knowledge of the unseen that he could see the reality?[35] Or has he not been notified about what was in the scrolls of Musa *(Moses)*[36] and of Ibrâheem *(Abraham)*, who always kept his word:[37] "That no soul shall bear the burden of another,[38] that there shall be nothing for a man except what he strives for,[39] that his striving shall be scrutinized,[40] that he shall be fully rewarded for it,[41] that to your Rabb is the final goal,[42] that it is He Who grants laughter and tears,[43] that it is He Who ordains death and life,[44] that it is He Who has created in pairs, the male and the female,[45] from a drop of ejaculated semen,[46] that it rests upon Him to grant the second life *(the life of hereafter)*,[47] that it is He Who gives wealth and satisfaction,[48] that He is the Rabb of the Sirius *(dog star whom the pagans used to worship)*,[49] and that it is He Who destroyed the prior people of 'Âd,[50] then the people of Thamûd, sparing no one,[51] and before them the people of Nûh *(Noah)*, who were the most unjust and rebellious,[52] and that it is He Who destroyed the Mu'tafikah *(Overthrown Cities of Sodom to which the Prophet Lût was sent)*,[53] who were covered by *the scourge* that covered them."[54] Then which of your Rabb's blessings would you doubt?[55] This Warner *(Muhammad)* is just like the earlier warners.[56] The ever approaching *(the Day of Judgment)* is drawing near;[57] none besides Allah can avert it.[58] Do you then wonder at this revelation,[59] and laugh instead of weeping?[60] Rather you are wasting your time,[61] prostrate yourselves before Allah and worship Him *while you can*![62]   53:[33-62]

> **No soul shall bear the burden of another; there shall be nothing for a person except what he strived for**

54: AL-QAMAR

Period of Revelation

The incident of the shaqq-al-Qamar (splitting of the moon) that is mentioned in it, determines its period of revelation precisely. This incident took place at Mina in Makkah five years before the Prophet's migration to Madinah.

Major Issues, Divine Laws and Guidance:

* The Day of Judgment is drawing near yet the unbelievers are not paying heed to the signs of Allah.
* We have made the Qur'an easy to understand the admonition, so is there any who would take the admonition?
* The story of Thamûd and Lût who called their Prophet liars is related to show how terrible was Allah's scourge, and how clear was His warning.
* People of Fir'aun were seized for disbelieving Allah's warning. The same warning has come to you, will you not take admonition?

In this Sûrah, the disbelievers of Makkah have been warned about their stubbornness towards the message of the Prophet, peace be upon him. The amazing and wonderful phenomenon of the splitting of the Moon was a manifest sign of the truth that the Resurrection, of which the Prophet was giving them the news, could take place. The great sphere of the Moon had split into two distinct parts in front of their very eyes. The two parts had separated and receded so much apart from each other that, to the onlookers, one part had appeared on one side of the mountain and the other on the other side of it. Then, in an instant, the two had rejoined. This was manifest proof of the truth that the system of the Universe was neither eternal nor immortal; it could be disrupted. The disbelievers described it as a magical illusion and persisted in their denial. Such people neither believe in the admonition, nor learn a lesson from it, nor affirm faith after witnessing manifest signs with their own eyes. They would believe only when resurrection has taken place and they will be rushing out of their graves towards the Summoner on that Day. The stories of the people of Nûh (Noah), 'Ad, Thamûd, Lût (lot) and the Fir'aun (Pharaoh) have been related briefly, and they have been reminded of the terrible punishments that these nations suffered when they belied and disregarded the warnings given by the Prophets of Allah. .

54: AL-QAMAR

This Sûrah, revealed at Makkah, has 3 sections and 55 verses.

In the name of Allah, the Compassionate, the Merciful

SECTION: 1

The Day of Judgment is drawing near yet the unbelievers are not paying heed to the signs of Allah

The Hour *of Doom* is drawing near, the moon has split asunder; *which is a clear proof that the same thing can happen to the earth.*[1] Yet, when they see a sign, the unbelievers turn their backs and say: "This is an ingenious magic."[2] They deny this and keep on following their own fancies. Ultimately every matter shall be laid to rest.[3] There has already come to them the information *of former nations* containing enough deterrents[4] and *this Qur'an is* a profound wisdom *to serve as a warning,* but warnings are of no use to these people.[5] Therefore, *O Prophet,* turn away from them. On the Day when the caller will call them to a terrible event.[6] They shall come out from their graves, like swarming locusts, with downcast eyes,[7] rushing towards the caller, and the same unbelievers will cry: "This is indeed an awful Day!"[8]

54:[1-8]

We have made the Qur'an easy to understand the admonition, so is there any who would take the admonition?

Long before them, the people of Nûh *(Noah)* disbelieved. They rejected Our servant, called him a madman and repulsed him.[9] *After admonishing the people for 950 years,* finally he invoked his Rabb: "Help me, I have been overcome!"[10] So We opened the gates of heaven with pouring rain[11] and caused the earth to burst with gushing springs, and the waters met to fulfill the decreed end.[12] We carried him in *an Ark* built with planks and nails,[13] which drifted on under Our Eyes *(loving care and protection)*: a reward for him *(Noah)* who was denied *by the unbelievers.*[14] We have left that *Ark* as a sign, so is there any who would take admonition?[15] How terrible was My scourge and how clear My warning![16] We have indeed made the Qur'an very easy to read and remember, but is there any who would take admonition?[17] *Likewise the people of* 'Âd did not believe, then how terrible My scourge was and how clear My Warning![18] We let loose on them a furious wind, on a day of continuous misfortune,[19] which snatched them off like trunks of uprooted palm-trees.[20] How terrible was My scourge and how clear My warning![21] We have indeed made the Qur'an very easy to read and remember, so is there any who would take admonition?[22]

54:[9-22]

SECTION: 2

The people of Thamûd disbelieved Our warning,[23] say-ing: "Are we to follow a human who stands alone among us? That would surely be an error and madness.[24] Was he the only person among us to receive this warning? Nay! He is indeed an insolent liar."[25] *To Our Rasool Sâleh, We said:* "Tomorrow they shall find out who is an insolent liar.[26] We are going to send the she-camel as a trial for them. Therefore, watch them and have patience.[27] Tell them that the water must be shared between them *and the she-camel*, and each will come to the water at its own turn.[28] At last *the people of Thamûd* called out to one of their companions, who took the responsibility and hamstrung her.[29] Then how terrible was My scourge and how clear My warning![30] We let loose on them one mighty blast and they became like the trampled twigs that are used by one who pens cattle.[31] We have indeed made the Qur'an very easy to read and remember, so is there any who would take admonition?[32] *Another example is,* of the people of Lût *(Lot)* who disbelieved Our warning.[33] We let loose on them a stone-charged tornado which spared none except Lût's household, whom We saved before dawn[34] through Our grace. Thus do We reward those who give thanks.[35] *Lût* did warn them of Our scourge but they doubted the warnings.[36] They even demanded his guests from him but We blinded their eyes, *and said:* "Now taste My punishment and *the result of disbelieving* My warning."[37] At daybreak they were overtaken by a lasting punishment[38] *as if to say:* "Now taste My punishment and *the result of disbelieving* My warning."[39] We have indeed made the Qur'an very easy to read and remember, so is there any who would take admonition?[40]   54:[23-40]

The story of Thamûd and Lût who called their Prophet liars, to show how terrible was Allah's scourge and how clear was His warning?

SECTION: 3

My warnings also came to the people of Fir'aun *(Pharaoh)*.[41] They disbelieved all Our signs. Consequently, We seized them with a seizure of the All-Mighty, All-Powerful.[42] *O Quraish,* are your unbelievers better than they were, or have you been granted an immunity in the Divine Scriptures?[43] Or, do they say: "Acting together, we can defend ourselves?"[44] Soon will their multitude be routed and put to flight.[45] Nay! The Hour *of Judgment* is the time promised *to deal with them.* That hour will be the most grievous and bitter.[46] Yet, surely, the wicked people

People of Fir'aun were seized for dis-believing Allah's warning. The same warning has come to you, will you not take admonition?

persist in error and madness.[47] On that Day when they will be dragged into the fire with their faces downwards, *We shall say:* "Taste the touch of hell!"[48] Surely, We have created everything in perfect ordainment *(destiny and purpose)*.[49] We command but once and Our will is done in the twinkling of an eye.[50] *O disbelievers,* We have already destroyed many like you. Will you not take admonition?[51] All that they do is being added to their record books:[52] every action, small and big is being noted down.[53] Surely, the righteous will be in the midst of gardens and rivers,[54] a place of true honor, in the presence of the Almighty Sovereign.[55]   54:[41-55]

55: AR-RAHMÂN

Period of Revelation

This Sûrah was revealed during the early stage of the Prophet's residence at Makkah.

Major Issues, Divine Laws and Guidance:

* It is Allah Who created man, taught him the Qur'an and taught him how to convey his feelings and thoughts.
* Allah is the Rabb of the easts and the wests. It is He, Who made the laws to regulate the oceans: their products and ships.
* All that exists, will perish, except Allah.
* No one can run away from the jurisdiction of Allah.
* Sinners will be punished in hell and the righteous will be awarded paradise with lush gardens, springs, fruits and bashful virgins.

This is the only Sûrah of the Qur'an in which, besides men, the jinn are directly addressed. In this Sûrah both men and jinn are taught to realize the wonders of Allah's power, His countless blessings, their own helplessness and accountability before Him. They are warned of the evil consequences of being disobedient to Him and made aware of the best results of His obedience.

However at several other places in the Qur'an there are clear pointers that the jinn are a creation, who like men, are endowed with freedom of will and action and are therefore, accountable; who have been granted the freedom of belief and unbelief and of obedience and disobedience. Also among them are believers and unbelievers, the obedient and the rebellious, just as there are among human beings. Among them exist such groups as have believed in the Prophets sent by Allah and in the Divine Books. This Sûrah clearly points out that the message of the Prophet (peace be upon him) and the Qur'an is meant both for men and for jinn. The Prophethood of Muhammad (peace be upon him) is not restricted to human beings alone. The beginning of the Sûrah addresses human beings. But from verse 13 onward both men and jinn are addressed together, and one and the same invitation is extended to both.

55: AR-RAHMÂN

This Sûrah, revealed at Madinah, has 3 sections and 78 verses.

In the name of Allah, the Compassionate, the Merciful

SECTION: 1

It is Allah Who created man, taught the Qur'an and taught him how to convey his feelings and thoughts

The Compassionate *(Allah)*.[1] Who taught you the Qur'an,[2] created man[3] and taught him how to speak *and convey his feelings and thoughts*.[4] The sun and the moon move along their computed courses.[5] The shrubs and the trees prostrate in adoration.[6] He has raised the heaven on high and created the balance:[7] don't ever tamper with this balance.[8] *Therefore, you also* establish weight with justice and do not give less measure.[9] He laid out the earth for His creatures,[10] with all its fruits and palms having sheathed clusters,[11] and grain with husk and scented herbs.[12] So, *O jinns and men,* which of your Rabb's favors will both of you deny?[13] He created man from sounding clay similar to pottery,[14] and created jinns from smokeless fire.[15] So, *O jinns and men,* which of your Rabb's favors will both of you deny?[16]   55:[1-16]

Allah is the Rabb of the easts and wests and He puts the laws to regulate oceans, its products and ships

He is the Rabb of the two easts and the Rabb of the two wests.[17] So, *O jinns and men,* which of your Rabb's favors will both of you deny?[18] He has made the two oceans apparently meeting together,[19] yet, between them is a barrier which they cannot cross.[20] So, *O jinns and men,* which of your Rabb's favors will both of you deny?[21] He produces pearls and coral, from both of them.[22] So, *O jinns and men,* which of your Rabb's favors will both of you deny?[23] His are the ships looming up like mountains on the sea.[24] So, *O jinns and men,* which of your Rabb's favors will both of you deny?[25]   55:[17-25]

SECTION: 2

All that exists will perish except Allah, Who is busy in mighty tasks all the time

All that exists on the earth will perish,[26] but the Face of your Rabb will remain full of Majesty and Glory.[27] Then, *O jinns and men,* which of your Rabb's favors will both of you deny?[28] All who dwell in the heavens and the earth, implore Him for their needs, every day He is busy in some mighty task.[29] Then, *O jinns and men,* which of your Rabb's favors will both of you deny?[30] O you, the two burdens *(jinns and mankind)*! Soon We shall find the time to call you *to account*.[31]   Then, *O jinns and men,* which of your Rabb's favors will both of you deny?[32]

55:[26-32]

O you, the assembly of jinns and men! If you have the power to get away from the boundaries of the heavens and the earth (*to escape from His punishment*), then get away! You cannot get away except with Our authority.[33]   Then, *O jinns and men,* which of your Rabb's favors will both of you deny?[34]   The flames of fire and molten brass will be unleashed on you both, *jinns and men,* and you will not be able to defend yourselves.[35]   Then, *O jinns and men,* which of your Rabb's favors will both of you deny?[36] When the heaven splits asunder and reddens like red-oil.[37]   Then, *O jinns and men,* which of your Rabb's favors will both of you deny?[38]   On that Day neither man nor jinn will need be asked about his sins.[39]   Then, *O jinns and men,* which of your Rabb's favors will both of you deny?[40]   Because the sinners will be recognized by their faces and they shall be seized by their forelocks and their feet.[41]   Then, *O jinns and men,* which of your Rabb's favors will both of you deny?[42]   *It will be said to them:* "This is the hell which the criminals had denied."[43]   They shall wander to and fro between *fire* and hot boiling water.[44]   Then, *O jinns and men,* which of your Rabb's favors will both of you deny?[45]

55:[33-45]

SECTION: 3

For those who fear standing before their Rabb, there will be two gardens.[46]   Then, *O jinns and men,* which of your Rabb's favors will both of you deny?[47] Having *shady trees with* lush green branches.[48]   Then, *O jinns and men,* which of your Rabb's favors will both of you deny?[49]   In both of them there will be two flowing springs.[50]   Then, *O jinns and men,* which of your Rabb's favors will both of you deny?[51]   In both of them there will be two kinds of every fruit.[52]   Then, *O jinns and men,* which of your Rabb's favors will both of you deny?[53]   They will recline on couches lined with rich brocade while the fruit of the gardens will be within their easy reach.[54]   Then, *O jinns and men,* which of your Rabb's favors will both of you deny?[55]   Therein will be chaste virgins, whom neither man nor jinn has touched before.[56]   Then, *O jinns and men,* which of your Rabb's favors will both of you deny?[57]   *So beautiful* as though they were rubies and corals.[58]   Then, *O jinns and men,* which of your Rabb's favors will both of you deny?[59]

No one can run away from the jurisdiction of Allah

Sinners will be punished in hell

Righteous will be rewarded in paradise with lush gardens, springs, fruits, bashful virgins and much more

Could the reward for goodness be anything but goodness?[60] Then, *O jinns and men,* which of your Rabb's favors will both of you deny?[61]   And besides these two there shall be two other gardens.[62]   Then, *O jinns and men,* which of your Rabb's favors will both of you deny?[63]   Densely shaded with dark green trees.[64] Then, *O jinns and men,* which of your Rabb's favors will both of you deny?[65]   In both of them there will be two gushing springs.[66] Then, *O jinns and men,* which of your Rabb's favors will both of you deny?[67]   Each planted with fruit trees, dates and pomegranates.[68]   Then, *O jinns and men,* which of your Rabb's favors will both of you deny?[69]   In each of them, there will be chaste and beautiful *virgins.*[70]   Then, *O jinns and men,* which of your Rabb's favors will both of you deny?[71]   Hûris *(beautiful damsels)* sheltered in their tents.[72]   Then, *O jinns and men,* which of your Rabb's favors will both of you deny?[73]   Whom neither man nor Jinn has ever touched before.[74]   Then, *O jinns and men,* which of your Rabb's favors will both of you deny?[75]   Reclining on green cushions and beautiful fine carpets.[76]   Then, *O jinns and men,* which of your Rabb's favors will both of you deny?[77]   Blessed be the name of your Rabb, Owner of Majesty and Honor.[78]

55:[46-78]

56: AL-WÂQI'A

Period of Revelation

This Sûrah was revealed before the affirmation of the faith by Sayyidunâ Umar (may Allah be pleased with him). It has been established historically that Sayyidunâ Umar embraced Islam after the first migration to Habsha, in the fifth year of the Prophethood.

Major Issues, Divine Laws and Guidance:

*   Scene of the Doomsday when:
    -   Some will be abased and some exalted.
    -   The earth will be shaken up.
    -   The mountains will be crumbled to scattered dust.
    -   Mankind will be divided into three groups: the foremost in rank and position, the common righteous people and the disbelievers.
*   Admonition to the disbelievers with the examples of creation.
*   The testimony of Allah about the Qur'an.

The theme of this Sûrah is the Hereafter, Tawheed and response to the disbelievers' suspicions about the Qur'an. In regards to Tawheed and the hereafter convincing arguments are given, and man's attention is drawn to his own body, the food that he eats, the water that he drinks, and the fire on which he cooks his food. He is invited to ponder the question, "What right do you have to behave independently or serve any other deity than God Almighty (Allah), Whose creative power has brought you into being and Whose provisions sustain you? How can you entertain the idea that after having once brought you into existence, He has become so helpless and powerless that He cannot recreate you once again?"

In conclusion, man is warned that he may shut his eyes to the truth in his arrogance, but death is enough to open his eyes. When death comes he becomes helpless: he cannot save his own parents; he cannot save his own children; he cannot save his religious guides and beloved leaders. They die in front of his eyes while he looks on helplessly. If there is no supreme power ruling over him, and his assumption is correct that he is all in all in the world, and there is no God (Allah), then why can't he restore to the dying person his soul? Just as he is helpless in this, so it is beyond his power to stop Allah from calling the people to account and granting them rewards or punishment. He may or may not believe it, but every person will surely see his own end after death.

56: AL-WÂQI'A

This Sûrah, revealed at Makkah, has 3 sections and 96 verses.

In the name of Allah, the Compassionate, the Merciful

SECTION: 1

Scene of Dooms-day when mankind will be divided into three groups:

When the inevitable event will come to pass[1] - no one will be able to deny its coming [2] - then some shall be abased and some exalted.[3]   The earth shall be shaken with a terrible shake,[4]   and the mountains shall be made to crumble with awful crumbling[5] and shall become like scattered dust.[6]   Then you shall be divided into three groups:[7]   those on the right hand - how *blessed* shall be the people of the right hand;[8]   those on the left hand - how *damned* shall be the people of the left hand;[9]   and foremost shall be the foremost.[10]   They will be nearest to Allah,[11]   in the gardens of bliss.[12]   Most of them will be from the former[13]   and a few from the later generations.[14]   They shall have the jewelled couches,[15] reclining on them, facing each other,[16]   and they will be served by the eternal youths[17]   with goblets, beakers and cups of pure wine,[18] - which will neither pain their heads nor take away their senses.[19]   *They shall have* fruits of their own choice[20] and flesh of fowls that they may desire,[21]   and beautiful large-eyed Hûris *(damsels)*,[22]   as lovely as well guarded pearls[23]   as a reward for the *good* deeds that they had done.[24]   There they shall not hear any vain talk nor sinful words,[25]   but only the greetings of "Peace *be upon you*! Peace *be upon you!*"[26]   56:[1-26]

A. Reward for the foremost group

B. Reward for the right-hand group

Those of the right hand - who shall be those on the right hand![27]   They shall be among the thornless lote trees,[28]   clusters of bananas,[29]   extended thick shades,[30]   constantly flowing water,[31]   abundant fruits[32]   of unforbidden, never-ending supply,[33] and will be reclining on high raised couches.[34]   We shall create *their wives* of special creation[35]   and make them virgins[36]   beloved by nature, equal in age,[37]   for those of the right hand.[38]   56:[27-38]

SECTION: 2

C. Punishment for the left-hand group

Many of them will be from the former[39]   and many from the later *generations*.[40]   As for those of the left hand - how *unfortunate* will be the people of the left hand![41]   They will be in the midst of scorching winds and in boiling water:[42]   in the shade of a pitch-black smoke,[43] neither cool nor refreshing.[44] For they lived in comfort before meeting this fate.[45] They persisted in heinous sins[46] and used to say: "When we are dead and turned to dust and bones, shall we then be raised to life again?[47] And our forefathers, too?"[48] Tell them: "Surely, those of old and those of present age[49] shall certainly be brought together on an appointed time of a known Day.[50] Then, "O the erring rejecters,[51] you shall eat of the Zaqqûm tree,[52] and fill your bellies with it;[53] and drink on top of it scalding water;[54] yet, you shall drink it like a thirsty camel do."[55] Such will be their entertainment on the Day of Reckoning.[56]   56:[39-56]

We have created you; then why do you not believe *in the Resurrection*?[57] Have you ever considered the semen you discharge:[58] Is it you who create *the child* from it, or are We the Creator?[59] It is We Who have ordained death among you and We are not helpless[60] in replacing you by others like yourselves or transforming you into beings that you do not know.[61] You already know well your first creation, why then do you not take heed?[62] Have you ever considered the seed that you sow in the ground?[63] Is it you who cause it to grow or are We the grower?[64] If it be Our Will, We could crumble *your harvest* into chaff, and you would then be left lamenting:[65] "We are indeed left laden with debts;[66] indeed we have been deprived *from the fruits of our labor*!"[67] Have you ever considered the water which you drink?[68] Is it you who send it down from the clouds or are We the sender?[69] If it be Our Will, We could turn it salty. Why then do you not give thanks?[70] Have you ever considered the fire that you kindle?[71] Is it you who made the tree to grow *which feeds the fire* or are We the grower?[72] We have made it a reminder *(of the great fire of hell)*, and a provision *of life* for the travellers.[73] So glorify the name of your Rabb, Who is the Greatest.[74]   56:[57-74]

Admonition to the disbelievers with the examples of creation

SECTION: 3

I swear by the setting of the stars,[75] and it is indeed a mighty oath if you but knew it,[76] that this is indeed an Honorable Qur'an,[77] inscribed in a well-guarded Book,[78] which none can touch except the purified *(angels)*:[79] a revelation from the Rabb of the worlds.[80] Would you scorn a scripture such as this[81] and instead *of thanking Allah* for the provisions He gave you, you are denying *Him by disbelief*?[82] Why is it not then that when you see

Testimony of Allah about the Qur'an

a dying person's soul come up to his throat[83]   while you are helplessly watching[84] - and at that time We *(i.e., Our angels who take the soul)* are nearer to him than you, but you do not see.[85] Then why do you not - if you claim you are not subject to reckoning[86] - restore *to the dying person* his soul? *Answer this, if what you say be true!*[87] Then if the dying person is one of those near to Us,[88] for him there is comfort and bounty, and a garden of bliss.[89] And if he is of the companions of right hand,[90] he is greeted with salutation: "Peace be upon you," for being from the companions of the right hand.[91]   And if he is of the erring rejecters,[92] he is welcomed with scalding water,[93] and burning in hellfire.[94]   Surely, this is an absolute truth.[95]   Therefore, glorify the name of your Rabb, Who is the Greatest.[96]

56:[75-96]

57: AL-HADEED

Period of Revelation

This Sûrah, that was revealed at Madinah during the interval between the Battle of Uhud and the Truce of Hudaibiyah between the 4th and 5th year after Hijrah. It was revealed at the time when the tiny Islamic State of Madinah was hemmed in by the disbelievers and the handful of ill equipped Muslims were entrenched against the combined powers of entire Arabia. In such circumstances Islam not only stood in need of the sacrifice of life from its followers, but it also needed monetary help and assistance. In this Sûrah a forceful appeal has been made for the same.

Major Issues, Divine Laws and Guidance:

* Allah created the heavens and the earth in six Yôme (Days or Stages) and He has the knowledge of everything.
* On the Day of Judgment, the true believers will have their light shining before them while the hypocrites will have a fate similar to the disbelievers.
* Those who spend in charity will be repaid manifold and also be given a liberal reward besides it.
* The life of this world is but a play, amusement and illusion.
* Do not grieve for the things that you miss, nor overjoy at what you gain.
* Prophets Nûh (Noah), Ibrâheem (Abraham) and Isa (Jesus) were sent for guidance to the Right Way, as for the monasticism, people instituted it themselves.

This Sûrah persuades the Muslims to make monetary sacrifices in particular, and to make them realize that Islam is not merely verbal affirmation and some outward practices, but its essence and spirit is sincerity towards Allah and His Religion. The faith of the one who is devoid of this spirit and who regards his own self and wealth as dearer to himself than Allah and His Religion, is hollow and has no value in the sight of Allah. The attributes of Allah Almighty are mentioned in order to make the listeners realize, as to Who is addressing them. Then, the following guidance is provided:

1. The inevitable demand of the Faith is that one should not hesitate to spend one's wealth for the sake of Allah. In fact the wealth belongs to Allah, and man has been granted proprietary rights only as His vicegerent. Yesterday this wealth was in other people's possession, today it is with you, and tomorrow it will pass on to

someone else. Ultimately, it will go back to Allah, Who is the inheritor of every-thing in the universe. Only that portion of this wealth will be of any use to man, which he spends in the Cause of Allah during the period it is in his possession.

2.   Although making sacrifices for the sake of Allah is commendable in all cases, the true worth of these sacrifices is determined by the nature of the occasion. There was a state when the power of paganism was overwhelming and there was a danger that it might subdue and overcome Islam completely; there was another state when Islam was in a stronger position in its struggle against pagan-ism and the believers were attaining victories. Both these states were not equal in regards to their respective importance. Therefore, the sacrifices that were made in these different states would also not be equal. Those who sacrificed their lives and spent their wealth to further promote the Cause of Islam when it was already strong would not attain the rank of those who struggled with their lives and their wealth to promote and uphold the cause of Islam when it was weak.

3.   Whatever is spent for the Cause of Islam is a loan to Allah. Allah will not only return it manifold, but will also give from Himself an extra reward.

4.   In the Hereafter, the Light shall be bestowed only on those believers who spent their wealth in the Cause of Allah. As for the hypocrites who watched and served only their own interests in the world, and who were least bothered whether the Truth or falsehood prevailed, they will be segregated from the believers in the Hereafter. Not only will they be deprived of the Light, but will be counted among the disbelievers.

5.   The life of this world is like a crop which flourishes and blooms, then turns pale and finally reduced to chaff. The everlasting life is the life Hereafter, when the results of great consequence will be announced. Therefore, if one has to envy for something, it should be for Paradise.

6.   Whatever good a man gets and whatever hardship he suffers in this world, is preordained by Allah. A true believer is he who does not lose heart in affliction and is not puffed up with pride in good times.

7.   Allah sent His Messengers with clear signs, the Book and the Law of Justice so that the people may conduct their affairs in justice. He sent down iron so that its power may be used to establish the Truth and vanquish falsehood.

57: AL-HADEED

This Sûrah, revealed at Madinah, has 4 sections and 29 verses.

In the name of Allah, the Compassionate, the Merciful

SECTION: 1

All that is in the heavens and the earth glorifies Allah, and He is the All-Mighty, the All-Wise.[1]   To Him belongs the kingdom of the heavens and the earth; it is He Who gives life and causes death; and He has power over all things.[2]   He is the First *(nothing is before Him)* and the Last *(nothing is after Him)*, the Most High *(above Whom there is nothing)* and the Intimate *(nothing is nearer than Him)*, and He has the knowledge of all things.[3] It is He Who created the heavens and the earth in six Yaums *(days, time periods or stages)*, then established Himself on the throne *in a manner that suits His majesty*. He knows all that enters the earth and all that emerges from it, all that comes down from Heaven and all that ascends to it; and He is with you *(observing and witnessing)* wherever you are. Allah is watching all your actions.[4]   To Him belongs the kingdom of the heavens and the earth, and all affairs go back to Allah for decision.[5]   He causes the night to pass into the day and the day to pass into the night, and He has knowledge of the inmost secrets of your hearts.[6]   Believe in Allah and His Rasool and spend *in charity* out of what He has entrusted you with, for those of you who believe and spend *in charity* shall be richly rewarded.[7]   What is the matter with you that you do not believe in Allah, whereas the Rasool is inviting you to believe in your Rabb, Who has indeed taken your covenant, if you are true men of faith?[8] It is He Who sends clear revelations to His servant, so that He may lead you from the depths of darkness into the light. Surely, Allah is Most Kind and Most Merciful to you.[9]   What is the matter with you that you do not spend in the Way of Allah, whereas to Allah belongs the inheritance of the heavens and the earth? Those of you who spent and fought *in the Cause of Allah* before the conquest *of Makkah*, shall receive higher ranks of honor than the others who spent and fought thereafter. But to all, Allah has promised a good reward, and Allah is aware of all your actions.[10]   57:[1-10]

SECTION: 2

Who is the one that will give to Allah a goodly loan, so that

All that is in the heavens and earth glorifies Allah, Who created the heavens and earth in six periods and has the knowledge of everything

Those who spend in charity will be richly rewarded

On that Day the true believers will have their light shining before them while the hypocrites will have their fate no different than the disbelievers

He may increase it manifold to his credit and give him a liberal reward besides it.[11]　On the Day *of Judgment* you shall see the believing men and the believing women, with their light shining before them and on their right hands, *it will be said to them:* "Rejoice today, you shall enter the gardens beneath which rivers flow, in which you shall live forever, and that is the highest achievement."[12]　On that Day the hypocrites - both men and women - will say to the true believers: "Wait for us, that we may borrow some of your light." But they will be told: "Go away! Seek your light elsewhere." So a wall with a gate shall be set up between them. Inside, there shall be mercy, and outside all along there shall be punishment of hell.[13]　They will call to the believers, saying: "Were we not on your side?" "Yes," they will reply, "but you led yourselves into temptation, you looked forward for our destruction, you doubted *in faith*, and you were deceived by your vain desires until Allah's command came, while the arch-deceiver *(shaitân)* deceived you concerning Allah *till the last moment*."[14]　*They will be told,* "Today no ransom shall be accepted from you, or from the unbelievers. Your abode is the fire: which you have justly earned, and it is an evil refuge."[15]　Has not the time arrived for the believers to submit with submissive hearts to the remembrance of Allah and to the truth He has revealed, so that they may not become like those who were given the Book before this, *even though* their term was prolonged for them but their hearts became hardened? And most among them were transgressors.[16]　You should know that Allah　restores the earth to life after its death, *similarly you shall be brought back to life after your death.* We have spelled out Our revelations for you, so that you may understand.[17]　Surely, the charitable men and the charitable women, and those who give a goodly loan to Allah, shall be repaid manifold, and also be given a liberal reward besides it.[18]　Those who believe in Allah and His Rasools, they are the truthful and the true witnesses in the sight of their Rabb; they shall have their reward and their light. But those who disbelieve and reject Our revelations; they shall be the inmates of hellfire.[19]　　　　57:[11-19]

Those who spend in charity will be repaid manifold and also be given liberal reward besides it

SECTION: 3

Life of this world is but play, amusement and illusion

You should know that the life of this world is only play and amusement, a show and boasting among yourselves, a quest for greater riches and more children. Its similitude is that of vegetation *that flourishes after rain*: the growth of which delights the tillers, then it withers and you see it turn yellow, soon it becomes dry and crumbles away. In the hereafter, there will be either severe punishment or forgiveness from Allah and His good pleasure. The life of this world is nothing but an illusion.[20]   *Therefore,* rush towards the forgiveness of your Rabb and for the paradise which is as vast as the heaven and the earth, prepared for those who believe in Allah and His Rasools. Such is the grace of Allah, which He bestows on whom He pleases, and Allah is the Owner of mighty grace.[21]   No affliction can befalls the earth or your own souls, except that it is recorded in a Book, before We bring them *(the souls)* into existence; surely, that is easy for Allah.[22]   *This is done* so that you may not grieve for the things that you miss, or be overjoyed at what you gain; for Allah does not love any vainglorious boaster,[23]   those who, being stingy themselves, enjoin others to be stingy also. He that gives no heed *should know* that Allah is free of all needs, worthy of all praise.[24]   Surely, We have sent Our Rasools with clear signs, and sent down with them the Book and the Scales of Justice, so that people may conduct themselves with fairness. We *also* sent down Iron, with its mighty strength and many benefits for mankind, so that Allah may know those who will help Him, though unseen, and help His Rasools. Surely, Allah is All-Powerful, All-Mighty.[25]   57:[20-25]

Do not grieve for the things that you miss, nor overjoy at what you gain

SECTION: 4

We sent Nûh *(Noah)* and Ibrâheem *(Abraham)*, and bestowed among their descendants Prophethood and the Book. Some of them adopted the right guidance, but most of them were transgressors.[26]   After them We sent other Rasools, one after the other, and followed them with Isa *(Jesus),* the son of Maryam. We gave him The Injeel *(Gospel),* and put compassion and mercy into the hearts of his followers. As for monasticism, they instituted it themselves - for We did not enjoin it on them - in order to seek the good pleasure of Allah, but they did not observe it as it should have been observed. Yet, We rewarded those among them who were true believers, but most of them are transgressors.[27]   O believers! Fear Allah and believe in His Rasool *(Muhammad, peace be upon him)*. He will grant you a double share of His mercy, provide for you a light to walk with and forgive you your sins. Allah is Oft-Forgiving, Most Merciful.[28]   *You should adopt this way* so that the people of the Book may know that they do not have the sole right to the grace of Allah, and that His grace is entirely in His own hands, which He bestows on whomever He wills: and Allah is the Owner of mighty grace.[29]   57:[26-29]

Prophets Nûh, Ibrâheem and Isa (Jesus) were sent for guidance to the Right Path. As for monasticism, people instituted it themselves

JUZ (PART): 28

58: AL-MUJÂDALAH

Period of Revelation

There is no tradition to indicate when this incident of pleading and arguing (Mujâdalah) took place, but there is a hint in the subject matter of the Sûrah on the basis of which it can be said with certainty that it happened after the battle of the Trench (Shawwâl, 5 A. H.). In Sûrah Al-Ahzâb, Allah while negating that an adopted son could be one's real son, had just said; "And Allah has not made those of your wives, whom you divorce by Zihâr, your mothers." But in that Sûrah divorcing a wife through Zihâr (calling one's wife as one's mother) was not declared to be a sin or a crime, and no legal injunction was imposed concerning it. Contrary to it, in this Sûrah the whole law relating to Zihâr has been enacted, which shows that these detailed injunctions were revealed after a brief reference relating to this issue in Sûrah Al-Ahzâb.

Major Issues, Divine Laws and Guidance:

* * *Pagans practice of divorce through 'Zihâr (calling one's wife as one's mother)' is prohibited.*
* * *Penalty for practicing 'Zihâr.'*
* * *Allah is omnipresent, if three persons converse in secret, he is fourth of them.*
* * *Secret counsels are forbidden except about virtue and piety.*
* * *Conspiring in secret is the work of Shaitân.*
* * *Etiquettes of holding a meeting.*
* * *Order to spend in charity before consulting the Rasool in private.*
* * *Those who befriend those who are under the wrath of Allah will be severely punished.*
* * *True believers do not befriend those who oppose Allah and His Rasool.*

In this Sûrah instructions have been given to the Muslims about the different problems that confronted them at that time. From the beginning of the Sûrah to verse 6 legal injunctions about Zihâr are given. The Muslims are strictly warned that they should not persist in the practices of ignorance after they have accepted Islam.

In vv. 7-10 the hypocrites are taken to task for their secret consultations by which they conspired against the "Prophet (peace be upon him), and because of their hidden malice and grudge they used to greet him, like the Jews, in a manner as to wish him ill instead of well. In this connection, the Muslims are consoled: "These secret consultation of the hypocrites can do no harm to you; therefore, you should go on doing your duty with full trust in Allah". Besides, they are also taught: "The true believers, when they talk secretly together, should not talk of sin and transgression or disobedience to the Prophet, if they have to talk secretly together they should talk of goodness and piety."

In vv. 11-13 the Muslims are taught manners of social behavior and given instructions to correct social evils which were prevalent among the people then as they are today. If some people are sitting in an assembly, and more people arrive, they do not show even the courtesy to squeeze in to make room for others, with the result that the newcomers have to keep standing, sit in the doorway, go back, or seeing that there is some room inside, start jumping over the people to find room for themselves. This used to be the case in the Prophet's assemblies. Therefore, Allah gave the instruction: Do not behave selfishly and narrow-mindedly in your assemblies. Accommodate the newcomers also with an open heart.

From verse 14 to the end of the Sûrah, members of the Muslim society, which was a mixture of the sincere Muslims, the hypocrites and the waverers, have been told the criteria of sincerity in Islam through citing the example of two kinds of Muslims as follows:

*   *One kind of Muslims are those who keep the friendship with the enemies of Islam. They do not hesitate to be treacherous to Islam for the sake of their interests. They spread all sorts of doubts and suspicions against Islam and prevent the people from adopting the Way of Allah. But since they are part of the Muslim community their false profession of Faith serves them as a cover and shield.*
*   *The second kind of Muslims are those who, in the matter of Allah's Religion, do not tolerate even their own father, brother, children, and family, if they say anything against Allah or His Rasool. They do not cherish any feeling of love for the person who is an enemy of Allah, His Rasool and His Religion.*

In these verses Allah has explicitly stated that the people of the first kind, in fact, belong to Shaitân's party, however hard they may try to convince others of their Islam by swearing oaths. And the honor of belonging to Allah's party are the Muslims of the second kind. They are the true Muslims, they will attain true success, and with them is Allah well pleased.

JUZ (PART): 28

58: AL-MUJÂDALAH

This Sûrah revealed at Madinah, has 3 sections and 22 verses.

In the name of Allah, the Compassionate, the Merciful

SECTION: 1

The pagan practice of divorce through Zihâr (calling his wife as his mother) is prohibited

Allah has indeed heard the words of the woman *(Khawlah, daughter of Tha'labah, who had been divorced by calling her: "You are to me like my mother" which was an acceptable practice for divorce among pagan Arabs)*, who pleaded with you against her husband and made her complaint to Allah, Allah has heard what you said to each other. Allah hears all and sees all.[1]   Those of you who divorce their wives by Zihâr *(calling them to be like their mothers) should know* that they are not their mothers. Their mothers are only those who gave birth to them. Surely, the words they utter are absurd and false. *Allah could punish them for this but He forgave them,* surely, Allah is All-Pardoning, All-Forgiving.[2]   Those who divorce their wives by Zihâr, then wish to retract the words they uttered, shall have to free a slave before they touch each other. This is prescribed *as a penalty for doing so.* Allah is well-aware of all your actions.[3]   He who cannot afford *the funds to free a slave*, shall fast two consecutive months before they touch each other. He that cannot *fast*, shall feed sixty poor people. This is *enjoined* so that you may have faith in Allah and His Rasool. These are the limits set by Allah, and the violators shall have a painful punishment.[4]   Those who resist Allah and His Rasool, shall be humiliated as were those before them. We have sent down clear revelations; the disbelievers shall have a humiliating punishment.[5]   On the Day *of Judgment* Allah will raise them all *back to life*, then inform them about what they have done. Allah has kept full record *of their deeds* even though they may have forgotten, for Allah is a witness over all things.[6]

Penalty for practicing 'Zihâr'

58:[1-6]

SECTION: 2

Allah is Omnipresent, if three persons converse in secret, He is the fourth

Are you not aware that Allah knows all that is in the heavens and in the earth? It cannot be that three persons converse in secret and He is not the fourth of them; or five persons *converse in secret* and He is not the sixth of them - whether fewer or more, wherever they may be, He is with them *(observing and witnessing)*. Then on the Day of Resurrection, He will inform them of what they have done, surely, Allah has knowledge of all things.[7]   Have you not seen those, who, though forbidden to hold secret counsels, persistently do what was forbidden? They hold secret counsels among themselves for sin, hostility and disobedience to the Rasool. Yet, when they come to you, they greet you in words which Allah does not greet you with, and say to themselves: "Why does Allah not punish us for what we say?" Hell is enough for them, they shall burn in its flames, what an evil destination![8]   O believers! When you confer together in private, do not talk about sin, hostility and disobedience to the Rasool, but about virtue and piety; and fear Allah before whom you shall be brought together.[9]   Conspiring in secret is the work of shaitân, who means to grieve the believers; but he cannot harm them at all except as Allah permits; so in Allah let the believers put their trust.[10]   O believers! When you are asked to make room in your meetings, make room, Allah will make room for you *in the Hereafter*. And if you are told to rise up, then rise up: Allah will raise to higher ranks those of you who have faith and those who have been given knowledge. Allah is aware of all your actions.[11] O believers! When you want to consult the Rasool in private, offer something in charity *to the needy* before your consultation, that is best and purest for you. But if you lack the means, know that Allah is Oft-Forgiving, Most Merciful.[12]   Do you hesitate to give out in charity before your private consultation *with him*? If you cannot afford it - Allah will forgive you - so establish Salah *(prayer)* and pay Zakah *(obligatory charity)*, and obey Allah and His Rasool.   Allah is well aware of all your actions.[13]   58:[7-13]

Secret counsels are forbidden except about virtue and piety

Conspiring in secret is the work of Shaitân

Etiquettes of holding a meeting

The order to spend in charity before consulting the Rasool in private

SECTION: 3

Have you not seen the ones who have befriended those people who are under the wrath of Allah? They are neither on your side nor yet on theirs and they knowingly swear to falsehood.[14] Allah has prepared for them a severe punishment; evil indeed is what they were doing.[15]   They use their oaths as shields, and debar others from the Way of Allah. They shall have a humiliating punishment.[16] Neither their riches nor their sons shall avail them anything against Allah. They shall be the inmates of hell and live there forever.[17]   On the Day when Allah will raise them all to life, they will swear to Him as they now swear to you, thinking that their oaths will help them. By no means! Surely, they are the liars.[18] Shaitân has gained possession of them, and caused them to forget Allah's warning. They are the party of shaitân. Beware! Surely, it is the party of shaitân that shall be the loser.[19] Those who resist

People who befriend those who are under the wrath of Allah will be severely punished

True believers do not befriend those who oppose Allah and His Rasool

Allah and His Rasool will be among the most humiliated.[20] Allah has decreed: "It is I and My Rasools who will most certainly prevail." Surely, Allah is All-Powerful, All-Mighty.[21] You will never find any people who believe in Allah and the last Day on friendly terms with those who oppose Allah and His Rasool, even though they be their fathers, their sons, their brothers or their relatives. It is they in whose hearts Allah has inscribed faith and has strengthened them with true guidance from Himself. He will admit them to gardens beneath which rivers flow, to live therein forever. Allah will be well pleased with them, and they will be well pleased with Him. They are the party of Allah. Beware! Surely, it is the party of Allah that will be successful.[22]   58:[14-22]

59: AL-HASHR

Period of Revelation

This Sûrah was revealed after the battle of Bani An-Nadheer. All traditions agree that this battle took place after the incident of Bi'r Ma'unah, and historically it is also well known that the incident of Bi'r Ma'unah occurred after the Battle of Uhud.

Major Issues, Divine Laws and Guidance:

* The Jewish tribe of Bani An-Nadheer is given the order of exile for their mutiny against the Islamic State.
* Distribution of the belongings of Bani An-Nadheer.
* Jews and their background (See commentary in following pages).
* Good qualities of true Muhâjireen immigrants and good qualities of true Ansâr (the residents of Yathrib (Madinah).
* Hypocrites' conspiracy with the people of the Book (Jews).
* The parable of Shaitân and a disbeliever.
* Let each soul see what it is sending for the Hereafter.
* If the Qur'an was sent down upon a mountain it would have crumbled into pieces from the fear of Allah's disobedience.
* Sixteen attributes of Allah in three verses: the God, the Knower of the Seen and the Unseen, the Compassionate, the Merciful, the King, the Holy, the Giver of peace, the Grantor of security, the Guardian, the Almighty, the Irresistible, the Supreme, the Creator, the Evolver, the Modeler and the All-Wise.

The theme of this Sûrah is an appraisal of the battle against the Bani An-Nadheer which can be summarized as follows:

1. There is an admonition to take heed of, from the fate that they had just witnessed in the fall of Bani An-Nadheer: a major tribe which was as strong in numbers as the Muslims, whose people boasted of far more wealth and possessions, who were well-equipped militarily and whose forts were well-fortified, but could not stand siege even for a few days. They expressed their readiness to accept banishment from their centuries old, well-established settlement even though not a single man from among them was killed. Allah says that this happened not because of any power possessed by the Muslims but because the Jews had tried to resist and fight Allah and

His Rasool. Those who dare to resist the power of Allah always meet
with the same fate.

2. An exception to the law relating to war is enunciated: "The destruction
    caused in the enemy territory for military purposes does not come under
    spreading mischief in the earth."

3. Guidance is provided as to how the lands and properties which came
    under the control of the Islamic State, as a result of war or peace
    terms, are to be managed. It was the first occasion that the Muslims took
    control of a conquered territory, therefore, the law concerning it was laid
    down for their guidance.

4. The attitude of the hypocrites on the occasion of this battle is reviewed
    and the causes underlying their attitude are pointed out.

5. The last section is an admonition for all those people who had professed
    to have affirmed the faith and joined the Muslim community, but were
    devoid of the true spirit of the Faith. In it, they are told: what the real
    demand of the Faith is, what the real difference between piety and wicked-
    ness is? What the place and importance of the Qur'an, which they
    professed to believe in is? And what the attributes of Allah, in Whom they
    claimed to have believed, are?

Historical Background of Jews in Madinah

In order to understand the subject matter of this Sûrah, it is necessary to
know the history of the Jews residing in Madinah and Hijâz, otherwise, one cannot
understand the real causes behind the way the Prophet (peace be upon him) dealt
with their different tribes.

According to a well-known research scholar and mufassir Abul A'lâ
Maudûdi, no authentic history of the Arabian Jews exists in the world. They did
not leave any writings of their own in the form of a book or a tablet which might
shed light on their past, nor have the Jewish historians and writers of the non-
Arab world made any mention of them. The reason being that after their settlement
in the Arabian peninsula, they had detached themselves from the main body of the
Jewish nation, and the Jews of the world did not count them among themselves.
They had given up the Hebrew culture and language, even the names, and adopted
Arabism instead. In tablets that have been unearthed in archaeological research

in the Hijâz, no trace of the Jews is found before the first century of the Christian era, except for a few Jewish names. Therefore, the history of the Arabian Jews is based mostly on the verbal narrations prevalent among the Arabs, most of which had been spread by the Jews themselves.

The Jews of the Hijâz claimed that they had come to settle in Arabia during the last stage of the life of the Prophet Moses (peace be upon him). They said that the Prophet Moses had despatched an army to expel the Amalekites from the land of Yathrib (Madinah) and had commanded it not to spare even a single soul of that tribe. The Israelite army carried out the Prophet's command, but spared the life of a handsome prince of the Amalekite king and returned with him to Palestine. By that time the Prophet Moses had passed away. His successors took great exception to what the army had done, for, by sparing the life of an Amalekite, it had clearly disobeyed the Prophet and violated the Mosaic law. Consequently, they excluded the army from their community, and it had to return to Yathrib and settle there forever. (Kitab al-Aghani, vol. xix, p. 94). Thus the Jews claimed that they had been living in Yathrib since about 1200 B.C. But, this had in fact no historical basis. The Jews probably had invented this story in order to overawe the Arabs into believing that they were of noble lineage and the original inhabitants of the land.

The second Jewish immigration, according to the Jews, took place in 587 BCE, when Nebuchadnezzer, the King of Babylon, destroyed Jerusalem and dispersed the Jews throughout the world. The Arab Jews said that several of their tribes at that time had come to settle in Wadi al-Qura, Taima, and Yathrib. (Al-Baladhuri, Futuh al-Buldan). But this too has no historical basis. By this, they also might have wanted to prove that they were the original settlers of the area.

As a matter of fact, in CE 70 the Romans massacred the Jews in Palestine, and then in CE 132 expelled them from that land, many of the Jewish tribes fled to find an asylum in the Hijâz, a territory that was contiguous to Palestine in the south. There they settled wherever they found water springs and greenery, and then by intrigue and through money lending business gradually occupied the fertile lands. Areas of Ailah, Maqna, Tabûk, Taima, Wadi al Qura, Fadak and Khaiber came under their control during that period, and Bani Quraizah, Bani An-Nadheer, Bani Bahdal and Bani Qainuqa also came during the same period and occupied Yathrib .

Among the tribes that settled in Yathrib (Madinah) the Bani An-Nadheer and the Bani Quraizah were more prominent because they belonged to the Cohen or priest class. They were looked upon as of noble descent and enjoyed religious leadership among their tribes. When they came to settle in Yathrib, there were some other tribes already living there. They subdued them and became the owners of this green and fertile land. About three centuries later, in CE 450 or 451, the great flood of Yemen occurred which has been mentioned in vv. 16-17 of Sûrah Sabâ. As a result of this, different tribes of the people of Sabâ were compelled to leave Yemen and disperse to different parts of Arabia. Thus, the Bani Ghassân went to settle in Syria, Bani Lakhm in Hirah (Iraq), Bani Khuza'ah between Jeddah and Makkah, and the Aus and the Khazraj went to settle in Yathrib. As Yathrib was under Jewish domination, they did not allow the Aus and the Khazraj to gain a footing. As a result the two Arab tribes had to settle on lands that had not yet been brought under cultivation. There they could hardly produce enough to enable them to survive. At last, one of their chiefs went to Syria to ask for the assistance of their Ghassanide brothers; he brought an army from there and broke the power of the Jews. Thus, the Aus and the Khazraj were able to gain complete dominance over Yathrib, with the result that two of the major Jewish tribes, Bani An-Nadheer and Bani Quraiza were forced to take quarters outside the city. Since the third tribe, Bani Qainuqa, was not on friendly terms with the other two tribes, it stayed inside the city as usual, and had to seek protection of the Khazraj tribe. As a counter measure to this, Bani An-Nadheer and Bani Quraizah took protection of the Aus tribe so that they could live in peace in the suburbs of Yathrib.

Before the Prophet's arrival at Madinah and until his emigration, the following were the main features of the Jews' position in Hijâz, in general, and in Yathrib, in particular:

1. In the matters of language, dress, civilization and way of life they had completely adopted Arabism, even their names had become Arabian. Of the 12 Jewish tribes that had settled in Hijâz, none except the Bani Zaura retained its Hebrew name.

2. Because of this Arabism, the western orientalists have been misled into thinking that, perhaps, they were not really Israelites but Arabs who had embraced Judaism, or at least a majority of them were Arab Jews. But there is no historical proof to show that the Jews ever engaged in the propagation of Judaism in Hijâz, or that their rabbis invited the Arabs to embrace Judaism like the Christian priests and missionaries. On the contrary, they prided themselves upon their Israelite descent and racial prejudices. They called the Arabs, Gentiles, which did not mean illiterate or uneducated, but savage and uncivilized people. They believed that the Gentiles were not entitled to any human rights, these were reserved only for the Israelites, and therefore, it was lawful and right for the Israelites to defraud them of their properties.

3.   Economically they were much stronger than the Arabs. Since they had emigrated from the more civilized and culturally advanced countries of Palestine and Syria. They knew many arts that were unknown to the Arabs, they also enjoyed trade relations with the outside world. Hence, they had captured the business of importing grain in Yathrib and the upper Hijâz and exporting dried dates to other countries. Poultry farms and fisheries were mostly under their controls. They excelled at cloth weaving as well. The Jews had also set up wine shops in different areas, where they sold wine which was imported from Syria.

4.   They would not allow the Arabs to be united and, therefore, kept them fighting and entrenched against each other. They knew that whenever the Arab tribes will unite, they would not allow the Jews to remain in possession of their large properties, gardens and fertile lands, which they had come to own through their profiteering and money lending businesses.

Such were the conditions when Islam came to Madinah, and ultimately an Islamic State came into existence after the Prophet's (upon whom be Allah's peace) arrival there. One of the first things that he accomplished was unification of the Aus, the Khazraj and the Emigrants into a brotherhood. The second was that he concluded a treaty between the Muslims and the Jews on definite conditions, in which it was pledged that neither party would encroach on the rights of the other, and both would unite in a joint defense against the external enemies. Some important clauses of this treaty clearly show what the Jews and the Muslims had pledged to adhere to in their mutual relationship:

"The Jews must bear their expenses and the Muslims their expenses. Each must help the other against anyone who attacks the parties of this document. They must seek mutual advise and consultation, since loyalty is a protection against treachery. They shall sincerely wish one another well. Their relations will be governed by piety and recognition of the rights of others, and not by sin and wrongdoing. The wronged must be helped. The Jews must stay with the believers so long as the war lasts. Yathrib shall be a sanctuary for the parties of this document. If any dispute or controversy, likely to cause trouble, should arise, it must be referred to Allah and to Muhammad the Rasool of Allah; the Quraish and their helpers shall not be given protection. The contracting parties are bound to help one another against any attack on Yathrib. Every one shall be responsible for the defense of the portion to which he belongs."

(Ibn Hisham, vol. ii, pp. 147 to 150)

This was an absolute and definitive covenant, to the conditions of which the Jews themselves had agreed. But not very long after this, they began to show hostility towards the Prophet, peace be upon him, Islam and the Muslims. Their hostility and perverseness continued increasing day by day. There were three main causes:

First, they envisaged the Prophet (peace be upon him) merely as a chief of his people, who should be content to have concluded a political agreement with them and should only concern himself with the worldly interests of his group. But they found that he was extending an invitation to believe in Allah, His Rasool and the Book (which also included belief in their own Prophets and scriptures). He was urging the people to give up disobedience of Allah and adopt obedience to the Divine Commands and abide by the moral laws of their own prophets. This, they could not agree with. They feared that if this universal ideological movement gained momentum, it would destroy their rigid religiosity and wipe out their racial nationhood.

Second, when they saw that Aus, Khazraj and the Emigrants were uniting into a brotherhood and the people from the Arab tribes of the surrounding areas, who entered Islam, were also joining this Islamic Brotherhood of Madinah and forming a religious community, they feared that the selfish policy which they had been so far following of sowing discord between the Arab tribes for the promotion of their own well being and interests for centuries, would not work in the new system. They knew that they would inevitably face a united front of the Arabs against which their intrigues would not succeed.

Third, the work that the Prophet (peace be upon him) was carrying out, of reforming the society and civilization, included putting an end to all unlawful methods in business and mutual dealings. Moreover, he had declared the taking and giving of usury as impure and unlawful earning. This caused them the fear that, if his rule became established in Arabia, he would declare interest legally forbidden. In this, they saw their own economic disaster and death.

For the reasons stated above, they made, resistance and opposition to the Prophet (peace be upon him), their national goal. They would not hesitate to employ any trick, any device and cunning, to harm him. They spread every kind of falsehood so as to cause distrust against him in the people's minds. They created every kind of doubt, suspicion and misgiving in the hearts of the new converts so as to turn them back from Islam. They would resort to every kind of deceit and fraud in order to harm the Muslims economically. Whenever one with whom they had business dealings, would accept Islam, they would do whatever they could to cause him financial loss. If he owed them something, they would fret and harass him by making repeated demands, and if they owed him something, they would withhold the payment and would publicly say that, at the time the bargain was made, he professed a different religion, and since he had changed his religion, they were no longer under any obligation to repay him. Several instances of this nature are cited in the commentaries by Tabari, Nisaburi, Tabrizi and in Rûh al Ma'ani relating to verse 75 of Sûrah Âl-e-'Imrân.

They had adopted this hostile attitude against the covenant even before the Battle of Badr. But when the Prophet (upon whom be Allah's peace) and the Muslims won a decisive victory over the Quraish at Badr, they were filled with grief, anguish, malice and anger. Ka'b bin Ashraf, the chief of the Bani An-Nadheer, cried out: "By God, if Muhammad has actually killed these nobles of Arabia, the earth's belly would be better for us than its back." Then he went to Makkah and incited the people to vengeance by writing and reciting provocative elegies for the Quraish chiefs killed at Badr. Then he returned to Madinah and composed lyrical verses of an insulting nature about Muslim women. At last, enraged with Ka'b Bin Ashraf's mischief, the Prophet (peace be upon him) sentenced him to death.

(Ibn Sad, Ibn Hisham, Tabari)

The first Jewish tribe which, after the Battle of Badr, openly and collectively broke their covenant were the Bani Qainuqa. They lived in a locality inside the city of Madinah. As they practised the crafts of goldsmith, blacksmith and vessel maker, the people of Madinah visited their shops quite frequently. They were proud of their bravery and valor. Being blacksmiths by profession, even their children were well armed. They could instantly muster 700 fighting men from among themselves. They were also arrogantly aware that they enjoyed relations of con-federacy with the Khazraj and Abdullah bin Ubayy (the chief of the Khazraj), was their chief supporter. At the victory of Badr, they were so provoked that they began to trouble and harass the Muslims, particularly the Muslim women, who visited their shops. Gradually things came to such a pass that one day a Muslim woman was stripped naked publicly in their bazaar. This led to a brawl, in which a Muslim and a Jew were killed. The Prophet (upon whom be Allah's peace) himself visited the local Jewish tribe, got them together and counselled them on decent conduct. But the reply that they gave was; "O Muhammad, you perhaps think we are like the Quraish; they did not know fighting; therefore, you overpowered them. But, when you come in contact with us, you will see how men fight." This was in clear words a declaration of war. Consequently, the Prophet (peace be upon him) laid siege to their quarters in A. H. 2. The siege had hardly lasted for a fortnight when they surrendered and all their fighting men were taken prisoners. Abdullah bin Ubayy came up in support of them and requested that they should be pardoned. The Prophet conceded his request and decided to exile the Bani Qainuqa from Madinah leaving their properties, armor and tools of trade behind.

(Ibn Sa'd, Ibn Hisham, Târikh Tabari)

For some time after these punitive measures (i. e. the banishment of the Qainuqa and killing of Ka'b bin Ashraf), the Jews remained so terror stricken that they did not dare commit any further mischief. But later in Shawwâl, A. H. 3 the Quraish, in order to avenge for their defeat at Badr, marched against Madinah with great preparations. The Jews saw that only one thousand men had marched out with the Prophet (upon whom be Allah's peace) in comparison to three thousand men of the Quraish. To make matter worse, three hundred hypocrites who initially joined the Prophet, deserted and returned to Madinah. At this point, they committed the first and open breach of the treaty by refusing to join the Prophet in the defense of the city even though they were bound to it by the agreement. Then, when in the Battle of Uhud the Muslims suffered a set back, they were further emboldened. So much so that the Bani An-Nadheer made a secret plan to kill the Prophet (peace be upon him). The plan, however, failed before it could be executed.

As a result, there was no question of making any further concession for them. The Prophet (peace be upon him) at once sent to them the ultimatum that the treachery they had meditated against him had come to his knowledge. Therefore, they were to leave Madinah within ten days. If anyone of them was found staying behind in their quarters, he would be put to the sword. Meanwhile, Abdullah bin Ubayy sent them the message that he would help them with two thousand men and that the Bani Quraizah and Bani Ghatfân would also come to their aid. Therefore, they were to stand firm and not leave. On this false assurance, they responded to the Prophet's ultimatum saying that they would not leave Madinah and that he could do whatever was in his power. Consequently, in Rabi-al-Awwal, A. H. 4, the Prophet (peace be upon him) laid siege to them, and after a few days of the siege, they surrendered on the condition that they could take their personal property, except the armor, which could be carried on three camels. Thus, Madinah was rid of this second mischievous tribe of Jews. Only two persons of the Bani An-Nadheer embraced Islam and stayed behind, rest of the tribe went to Syria and Khaiber.

59: AL-HASHR

This Sûrah, revealed at Madinah, has 3 sections and 24 verses.

In the name of Allah, the Compassionate, the Merciful

SECTION: 1

All that is in the heavens and the earth glorifies Allah, and He is the Almighty, the All-Wise.[1]   It is He Who drove the disbelievers from among the People of the Book *(reference is to the Jewish tribe of Bani Al-Nadeer)* out of their homes at the first banishment. You did not think that they would ever go out; and they thought that their fortresses would defend them from Allah, but *the wrath of* Allah came to them from where they never expected - which cast such terror into their hearts - that they destroyed their homes by their own hands as well as by the hands of the believers. So learn a lesson *from this exampl*e! O people of insight.[2]   Had Allah not decreed exile for them, He would certainly have punished them in this world, and in the hereafter they shall have the torment of the Fire.[3]   That is because they set themselves up against Allah and His Rasool; and he that sets himself up against Allah *should know* that Allah is stern in retribution.[4]   Whatever palm-trees you cut down or left them standing on their stems, was by the leave of Allah, so that He might humiliate the transgressors.[5]

59:[1-5]

As for those spoils of theirs which Allah has bestowed on His Rasool, you spurred neither cavalry nor camelry to capture them: but Allah gives authority to His Rasools over whom He pleases, for Allah has power over all things.[6]   Whatever spoils from the dwellers of the township Allah has bestowed on His Rasool, shall belong to Allah, His Rasool, *Rasool's* relatives, and to the orphans, the needy and the travellers in need; so that it may not become the property of the rich among you. Whatever the Rasool gives you, take it and from whatever he forbids you, refrain from it. Fear Allah; for Allah is stern in retribution.[7]   *A share of the spoils shall be given* to the indigent Muhâjireen *(immigrants)* who were driven out of their homes and their possessions, and are seeking Allah's grace and His good pleasure and who *want to* help Allah and His Rasool, they are indeed the true believers.[8]   *A share of the spoils shall also be given* to those who had homes *in Madinah (the Ansâr)* and believed even before the arrival of the Muhâjireen and love those who migrated to them and entertain no jealousy in

---

Jewish tribe of Banu Al-Nadeer is given the order of exile for their mutiny against the Islamic State

Distribution of the belongings of Banu Al-Nadeer

Good qualities of true immigrants and good qualities of true Ansâr (the residents of Madinah)

their hearts for things given to them, and prefer those *Muhâjireen* over themselves, even though they themselves are poor. *In fact,* those who are saved from their own covetousness, are the ones who will achieve true success.[9]   And *it is also for* those who came after them and say: "Our Rabb! Forgive us and our brothers who embraced the faith before us and do not leave any malice in our hearts towards the believers. Our Rabb! Surely, You are the Kind, the Merciful."[10]   59:[6-10]

SECTION: 2

Hypocrites' conspiracy with the people of the Book

Have you not observed the hypocrites? They say to their fellow unbelievers among the people of the Book: "If they drive you out, we will go with you. We will never obey anyone against you. If you are attacked we will certainly help you." Allah bears witness that they are lying.[11]   If *the People of the Book* are driven out, they will never go with them, if *the people of the Book* are attacked, they will not help them; and even if they help them, they will turn their backs, leaving them with no help at all.[12]   In their hearts there is greater dread of you than of Allah, because they are a people devoid of understanding.[13]   They will never fight against you together except in fortified townships or from behind walls. Strong is their enmity amongst themselves; you think of them united, whereas their hearts are divided. This is because they are a people devoid of common sense.[14]   Their example is like those who have *(Jews of Bani Qainuqa)* tasted, a short while before them, the evil consequences of their deeds. They shall have a painful punishment.[15]

Parable of a shaitân vs. a disbeliever

Their parable is like the Shaitân who says to man: "disbelieve," and when he becomes a disbeliever, he says: "I am free of you; I fear Allah, the Rabb of the worlds."[16]   The end of both will be that they will be tossed in hell and remain there forever. Thus shall be the reward of the wrongdoers.[17]   59:[11-17]

SECTION: 3

Let each soul see what it is sending for the Hereafter

O believers! Fear Allah and let every soul see what it is sending for the morrow *(Hereafter)*. Fear Allah, surely, Allah is aware of all your actions.[18]   Be not like those who forgot Allah, as a result *Allah caused them to* forget themselves, it is they who are the transgressors.[19]   The companions of hell and the companions of paradise are not equal. The companions of paradise - they are the successful.[20]   59:[18-20]

If We had sent down this Qur'an on a mountain, you would have seen it humble itself and split asunder from the fear of Allah. We are citing these examples for mankind so that they may think *about it.*[21]   59:[21]

The Qur'an could even affect a mountain

Allah is He, besides Whom there is none worthy of worship, the Knower of the unseen and the seen. He is the Compassionate, the Merciful.[22]   Allah is He, besides Whom there is none worthy of worship, the King, the Holy, the Perfect *(free from all defects)*, the Bestower of Faith, the Guardian, the Almighty, the Irresistible, the Supreme: Glory be to Allah! He is far above the shirk they commit *(by associating other gods with Him).*[23]   He is Allah, the Creator, the Inventor, the Bestower of Forms. To Him belong the most beautiful names. All that is in the heavens and the earth declares His glory, and He is the All-Mighty, the All-Wise.[24]   59:[22-24]

Fifteen exclusive Attributes of Allah

60: AL-MUMTAHANAH

Period of Revelation

This Sûrah was revealed after the treaty of Hudaibiyah and before the conquest of Makkah.

Major Issues, Divine Laws and Guidance:

* Do not befriend those who are the enemies of Allah and the Muslims.
* The Prophet Ibrâheem (peace be upon him) and his companions are an excellent example for the believers.
* Exception to the prohibition of friendship is made with those unbelievers who had neither fought against the believers nor expelled them from their homes.
* For women that become believers, test their Imân, and if you find them truthful, do not return them to their unbelieving husbands.
* Women's Bai'ah (oath of allegiance) in Islam is based on their commitment that they will not commit shirk, they will not steal, they will not commit adultery, they will not kill their children, they will not give any cause for scandal and that they will not disobey the Prophet.

The detail of three issues on which this Sûrah provided guidance:

1.   A strong exception is taken to the act of Sayyidunâ Hâtib bin Abi Balta'a who, a little before the conquest of Makkah, had sent a secret letter to the Quraish chiefs informing them of the Prophet's intention to attack them. He had tried to inform the enemy of a very important war secret of the Prophet (peace be upon him) only for the sake of safeguarding his family. This would have caused great bloodshed at the conquest of Makkah had it not been made ineffective in time. It would have cost the Muslims many precious lives; many of the Quraish would have been killed, many of whom would have rendered great services to Islam afterward; the gains which were to accrue from conquering Makkah peacefully would have been lost. All of these serious losses would have resulted only because one of the Muslims had wanted to safeguard his family from the dangers of war. Administering a severe warning at this blunder Allah has

taught the believers that no believer should, under any circumstances and for any motive, have relations of love and friendship with the disbelievers who are actively hostile to Islam, and a believer should refrain from everything which might be helpful to them in the conflict between Islam and disbelief. However, there is no harm in dealing kindly and justly with those disbelievers who may not be practically engaged in hostile activities against Islam and the persecution of the Muslims.

2.   A very serious social problem is addressed which was agitating the minds of the Muslims at that time. There were many Muslim women in Makkah, whose husbands were pagans, but they were emigrating and reaching Madinah somehow. The second relates to the Muslim women who had started emigrating from Makkah to Madinah after the conclusion of the Truce of Hudaibiyah. The problem arose whether they also were to be returned to the disbelievers, like the Muslim men, according to the conditions of the truce. Likewise, there were many Muslim men in Madinah whose wives were pagans and had been left behind in Makkah. The question arose whether the marriage bond between them continued to be valid or not. Allah settled this problem forever, saying that the pagan husband is not lawful for the Muslim woman, nor the pagan wife lawful for the Muslim husband.

3.   The Holy Prophet (peace be upon him) has been instructed to ask the women who accept Islam to pledge that they would refrain from the major evils that were prevalent among the womenfolk of the pre-Islamic Arab society, and to promise that they would henceforth follow the ways of goodness which the Rasool of Allah may enjoin.

60: AL-MUMTAHANAH

This Sûrah, revealed at Madinah, has 2 sections and 13 verses.

In the name of Allah, the Compassionate, the Merciful

SECTION: 1

Do not befriend those who are the enemies of Allah and the Muslims

O believers! Do not make friendship with those who are enemies of Mine and yours. Would you show affection towards them, when they have denied the truth that has come to you and have driven the Rasool and yourselves out *of your homes*, simply because you believe in Allah, your Rabb? If it was indeed to strive in My way, and to seek My good pleasure that you left *your homes*, how can you befriend them in secret? I know all that you conceal, and all that you reveal. Any of you who does this has indeed has gone astray from the Right Way.[1]   If they overcome you, they would behave with you as enemies and stretch out their hands and their tongues towards you with evil, and they wish to see you become unbelievers.[2]   On the Day of Resurrection, neither your relatives nor your children shall avail you. Allah will judge between you, and He is observing all your actions.[3]   60:[1-3]

Ibrâheem and his companions are an excellent example for the believers

You have an excellent example in Ibrâheem *(Abraham)* and his companions. They said to their people plainly: "We are clear of you and *your gods*, whom you worship besides Allah. We renounce you. Enmity and hate shall reign between us forever until you believe in Allah, the One *and Only God*." The exception is what Ibrâheem said to his father: "I will pray for your forgiveness, although I have no power to get anything for you from Allah." *Their collective prayer was:* "Our Rabb! In You we have put our trust, to You we turn *in repentance* and to You is our final goal.[4]   Our

Prayer of Ibrâheem and his companions

Rabb! Do not make us a victim of the unbelievers. Forgive us, our Rabb! You are the All-Mighty, the All-Wise."[5]   Truly, in those there is an excellent example for everyone who puts his hopes in Allah and the Last Day. He that gives no heed *should know* that Allah is free of all wants, worthy of all praise.[6]   60:[4-6]

SECTION: 2

Exception to the prohibition of friendship with

It may well be that Allah will put love between you and those with whom you are now at odds *because of the order which is given to you*, for Allah is All-Powerful, and Allah is Oft-Forgiving, Most Merciful.[7]   Allah does not forbid you to be kind and equitable to those who had neither fought against your faith nor driven you out of your homes. In fact, Allah loves the equitable.[8] Allah only forbids you to make friendship with those who fought you on account of your faith and drove you out of your homes and backed up others in your expulsion. Those who will take them for friends are indeed the wrongdoers.[9]   60:[7-9]

unbelievers who had neither fought against the believers nor expelled them from their homes

O believers! When the believing women seek refuge with you as immigrants, test them. Allah best knows their faith. If you find them true believers, do not send them back to the unbelievers. They are not lawful to the unbelievers, nor are the unbelievers lawful to them. Return *to their unbelieving husbands* what they have spent on them. There is no blame on you if you marry such women, provided you give them their dowers. Do not hold on to your marriages with unbelieving women. Demand what you have spent on them and let the *unbelievers* ask back what they have spent. This is the order of Allah which He has decreed between you. Allah is All-Knowing, All-Wise.[10]   If you do not get back the demanded amount *that you have spent on your disbelieving wives* from the unbelievers, and you have an accession *by the coming over of women from the unbelievers side, you can offset the amount through* paying those whose wives have fled, the equivalent of the amount they have spent *on their disbelieving wives*. Fear Allah, in Whom you believe.[11]   60:[10-11]

As for women that become believers, test their Imân, and if you find them truthful do not return them to their unbelieving husbands

O Prophet! When the believing women come to you to take the oath of allegiance , *take their pledge*: that they will not commit shirk with Allah, that they will not steal, that they will not commit fornication, that they will not kill their children, that they will not give any cause for scandal which they may invent between either their hands or legs *(a woman accusing another woman of having an illicit relationship with a man and spreads such stories - or - a woman carrying an illegitimate child and makes her husband believe that it is his)*, and that they will not disobey you in any just matter, then accept their allegiance and pray to Allah for their forgiveness. Surely, Allah is Oft-Forgiving, most Merciful.[12]   60:[12]

Women's Bai'ah (oath of allegiance)

O believers! Do not befriend those who have incurred the wrath of Allah. Indeed they despair of the Hereafter, just as the unbelievers despair of those buried in the graves *that they will not be brought back to life on the Day of Resurrection*.[13]   60:[13]

Do not befriend any with whom Allah is angry

61: AS-SAFF

Period of Revelation

This Sûrah was sent down shortly after the Battle of Uhud.

Major Issues, Divine Laws and Guidance:

* Believers are commanded not to say something that they would not do.
* The Prophet Isa (Jesus) gave good news of a Rasool coming after him whose name will be Ahmed (Muhammad), peace be upon him.
* The bargain to save oneself from the hellfire is to believe in Allah, His Rasool and strive one's utmost (Jihâd) in the cause of Allah with one's wealth and person.
* Believers are commanded to be the helpers of Allah like the disciples of Isa (Jesus), peace be upon him.

This Sûrah exhorts the Muslims to adopt sincerity in Faith and to struggle with their lives in the cause of Allah. It is addressed to Muslims of weak faith as well as to those who entered Islam as a cover-up. The believers are warned; "Allah hates those people who say one thing and do another. He loves those who fight for the sake of Truth like a solid wall against the enemies of Allah."

Muslims attitude towards their Rasool and their Religion should not be like the attitude that the Israelites had adopted towards their Rasools - Moses and Jesus (peace be upon them). The proclamation is made with the challenge that the Jews, the Christians and the hypocrites, who are conspiring with the unbelievers, can try however hard they may, to extinguish this Light of Allah, but it will shine forth and spread in the world.

The believers are told that the way to success, both in this world and in the Hereafter, is only to believe in Allah and His Rasool sincerely, and to exert their utmost efforts in Allah's Way with their wealth and their persons.

Finally, the believers are exhorted to be like the disciples of the Prophet Isa (Jesus), peace be upon him, who helped him in the cause of Allah.

61: AS-SAFF

This Sûrah, revealed at Madinah, has 2 sections and 14 verses.

In the name of Allah, the Compassionate, the Merciful

SECTION: 1

All that is in the heavens and the earth glorifies Allah. He is the All-Mighty, the All-Wise.[1] O believers! Why do you preach what you not practice?[2] It is very hateful in the sight of Allah that you preach what you not practice.[3] Indeed Allah loves those who fight for His Cause in solid ranks as if they were a mighty edifice.[4] Remember, what Musa *(Moses)* said to his people: "O my people! Why do you hurt me while you know that I am the Rasool of Allah towards you?" *But in spite of this,* when they adopted perverseness, Allah let their hearts be perverted. Allah does not guide those who are transgressors.[5] And remember when Isa *(Jesus)* the son of Maryam said: "O children of Israel! I am the Rasool of Allah towards you, confirming the Torah which came before me, and giving you good news of a Rasool that will come after me whose name shall be Ahmad *(another name of the Prophet Muhammad)*." But when he *(Muhammad)* came to them with clear signs, they said "This is plain magic."[6] Who could be more wrong than the one who invents falsehoods against Allah while he is being called towards Islam? Allah does not guide those who are wrongdoers.[7] They seek to extinguish the Light of Allah with their mouths, but Allah will perfect His Light, much as the unbelievers may dislike it.[8] It is He Who has sent His Rasool with the guidance and the religion of truth to make it prevail over all religions, much as the Mushrikeen may dislike it.[9]   61:[1-9]

O believers, do not say something that you don't do

The Prophet Isa (Jesus) gave the good news of a Rasool coming after him whose name would be Ahmad (Muhammad)

SECTION: 2

O believers! Should I tell you of a bargain that will save you from a painful punishment?[10] It is to believe in Allah and His Rasool and strive your utmost in the cause of Allah with your wealth and your persons. That is best for you, if you but knew it.[11] He will forgive you your sins and admit you to gardens beneath which rivers flow, and will lodge you in beautiful mansions in the gardens of eternity, which will be a supreme achievement.[12] And yet, another blessing which you love: help from Allah and a speedy

A bargain to save oneself from the hellfire

Like the disciples of Isa (Jesus), believers are commanded to be the helpers of Allah

victory. So *O Prophet*, give this good news to the believers.[13]   O believers! Be the helpers of Allah, just as Isa *(Jesus)* the son of Maryam said to his disciples: "Who will be my helpers in the cause of Allah?" And the disciples responded: "We will be your helpers in the cause of Allah." Then a group from the children of Israel believed in him *(Isa)* and another group disbelieved. We aided the believers against their enemies, so they became victorious.[14]

61:[10-14]

62: AL-JUMU'AH

Period of Revelation

This Sûrah was revealed in two stages. Its first section was revealed in A.H. 7, probably on the occasion of the conquest of Khaiber, and the second section was revealed shortly after the Prophet's migration to Madinah when he established the Friday congregation prayer on the 5th day after his arrival.

Major Issues, Divine Laws and Guidance:

* Allah has appointed Muhammad (peace be upon him) as His Rasool.
* Allah has rebutted the claim of Jews, to be the favorites of Allah to the exclusion of others.
* Commandment relating to the obligation of 'Friday Prayers.'

The first section was revealed after the final defeat of the Jewish tribes at the Battle of Khaiber. Allah Almighty revealed this last and final address which was directed towards the Jews in the Qur'an. In this, Jews are reminded of three things:

1. Did you refuse to believe in Muhammad (peace be upon him) only because he was born among a people whom you considered 'gentiles'? You were under the false delusion that a Rasool must necessarily belong to your community only and that anyone who claimed to be a Prophet outside your own community must be an imposter. This is Allah's bounty, which He may bestow on any one He may please. You have not been granted a monopoly over it.

2. You were made the bearers of the Torah, but you did not undertake your responsibility and discharge it as you should have. Therefore, you are no better than that donkey who is loaded with books and does not know what burden he is bearing. You not only shirk your responsibility of being the bearers of Allah's book, but you did not even hesitate to deliberately deny Allah's revelations. Yet you consider yourselves as Allah's favorites!

3. If you really consider yourselves as Allah's favorites and were sure of having a place of honor and high rank with Him, you would not have feared

death and accepted a life of disgrace and subjugation. This condition itself is a proof that you are fully conscious of your misdeeds, and your conscience is aware that if you die with these misdeeds, you will meet your Rabb with a greater disgrace on the Day of Judgement.

In the second section, Allah warned the Muslims not to treat their Friday as the Jews had treated their Sabbath. This section was sent down relating to the incident of a trade caravan, which arrived in Madinah right at the time of Friday congregation prayer. During the service when the people heard the din and drum, they left the Prophet's mosque and rushed to the caravan although the Prophet was delivering the Sermon. Thereupon, it was enjoined that when the call for the Friday Prayer is made, all trade, business and other transactions must stop. Upon hearing the call, believers should suspend every kind of transaction and hasten to the remembrance of Allah. However , when the prayer is over, they can go back and resume their normal business.

62: AL-JUMU'AH

This Sûrah, revealed at Madinah, has 2 sections and 11 verses.

In the name of Allah, the Compassionate, the merciful

SECTION: 1

All that is in the heavens and the earth declares the glory of Allah, the King, the Holy, the Mighty, the Wise.[1]   It is He Who has raised among the unlettered people, a Rasool of their own, who recites to them His revelations, purifies them, and teaches them the Book and Wisdom *(As-Sunnah)*, though, prior to this, they were in gross error,[2] *he is also sent* for others among them who have not yet joined them *(become Muslims)*. He is the Mighty, the Wise.[3] That is the grace of Allah, which He bestows on whom He pleases. Allah is the Lord of mighty grace.[4]   62:[1-4]

Allah appointed Muhammad as a Rasool

The example of those who were charged with the Tawrât, but failed to carry out their obligations, is that of a donkey who is carrying books *and does not know what is in those books*. Bad is the example of those who deny the revelations of Allah. Allah does not guide the wrongdoers.[5]   *Say to the Jews:* "O you, followers of the Jewish faith! If you claim that you are the favorites of Allah to the exclusion of other people, then wish for death, if what you say is true."[6]   But, because of what their hands have sent before *them for the Hereafter*, they will never wish for death. Allah knows these wrongdoers *very well.*[7] Tell them: "The death from which you are running away, will surely overtake you: then you will be sent back to Him Who knows the unseen and the seen; and He will tell you all that you have been doing."[8]   62:[5-8]

Allah rebutted the claim of Jews to be the favorites of God to the exclusion of others

SECTION: 2

O believers! When the call for Salah *(prayer)* is made on Friday *(the day of congregational prayer)*, hasten to the remembrance of Allah and cease your business. That is better for you if you but knew it.[9]   When you finish the Salah, then disperse through the land and seek the bounty of Allah *(go back to your normal business)*. Remember Allah frequently, so that you may prosper.[10] *Those who are still weak in Imân (faith),* when they see some bargain or some sport, they rush to it and leave you standing. *O Prophet* declare to them that what Allah has *in store for them* is far better than any sport and bargain, and Allah is the best provider.[11]   62:[9-11]

Commandment relating to the obligation of Friday Prayers

63: AL-MUNÂFIQÛN

Period of Revelation

This Sûrah was revealed either during the Prophet's return from his campaign against Bani Al-Mustaliq, or immediately after his arrival back at Madinah in Sh'abân CE 6.

Major Issues, Divine Laws and Guidance:

* Hypocrisy is such a sin against Islam and Muslims that even the Rasool's prayer cannot obtain forgiveness for them from Allah.
* Let not your riches or children divert you from the remembrance of Allah, lest you become a real loser.
* Spend in the Way of Allah before death approaches any one of you.

Before mentioning the particular incident about which this Sûrah was revealed, it is necessary to have a look at the history of the hypocrites of Madinah. The incident that occurred on this occasion was not a coincident, but had a whole series of events behind it.

Before the Prophet's migration to Madinah the tribes of the Aus and the Khazraj, fed up with their mutual rivalries and civil wars, had almost agreed on the leadership of one man and were making preparations to crown him their king. This was Abdullah bin Ubayy bin Salul, the chief of the Khazraj. Muhammad bin Ishâq has stated that among the people of Khazraj, his authority was never contested and never had the Aus and the Khazraj rallied behind one man before this.

When the Prophet arrived in Madinah, Islam had so deeply penetrated every house of the Ansâr that Abdullah bin Ubayy became helpless and did not see any other way to save his leadership than to become a Muslim. So, he entered Islam along with many of his followers from among the chiefs and leaders of both the tribes, although their hearts were burning with rage from within. Ibn Ubayy in particular was filled with grief, for the Prophet (peace be upon him) had deprived him of his kingship. For several years, his hypocritical faith and grief of being deprived of his kingdom manifested itself in different ways. On the one hand, when on Fridays the Prophet (peace be upon him) took his seat to deliver the Sermon, Abdullah bin Ubayy would stand up and say "O people, the Rasool of Allah is present among you, by whom Allah has honored you; therefore, you should support him, listen to what he says and obey him." (Ibn Hisham, vol. III, p. 111). On the other hand, his hypocrisy was being exposed day by day. The true Muslims were realizing that he and his followers bore great malice against Islam, the Prophet and the Muslims.

Following is a summary of the hypocrites' behavior:

1. Once, when the Prophet was passing along the way, Abdullah bin Ubayy spoke to him in harsh words. When the Prophet complained after it to Sayyidunâ Sa'd bin Ubadah, he said: "O Rasool of Allah, don't be hard on him, for when Allah sent you to us, we were about to crown him, and, by Allah, he thinks that you have robbed him of his kingdom."
    (Ibn Hisham vol: II, pp. 237-238)

2. After the Battle of Badr when the Prophet (peace be upon him) invaded the Jewish tribe of Bani Qainuqa for breaking their agreement and unprovoked revolt, this man stood up in support of them, and holding the Prophet by his armor, said: "These 700 fighters have been helping and protecting me against every enemy; would you cut them down in one morning? By Allah, I will not leave you until you pardon my clients." The Prophet (peace be upon him) did pardon and spare their lives.
    (Ibn Hisham, vol. III, pp. 51-52)

3. On the occasion of the Battle of Uhud, this man committed open treachery and withdrew from the battlefield with 300 of his companions. One should note that at this critical moment when he so acted, the Quraish had marched against Madinah with 3,000 troops and the Prophet had marched out with only 1,000 men to resist them. Of these 1,000, this hypocrite broke away with 300 men and the Prophet was left with only 700 men to meet 3,000 troops of the enemy on the battlefield. After this incident, the common Muslims of Madinah came to realize that he was certainly a hypocrite and so were his companions. That is why, when on the very first Friday, after the Battle of Uhud, this man stood up as usual to make a speech before the Prophet's Sermon, the people pulled at his garment, saying "Sit down you are not worthy to say any thing." That was the first occasion in Madinah when this man was publicly disgraced. Thereupon, he was so filled with rage that he left the mosque jumping over the people. At the door of the Mosque some of the Ansâr said to him, "What are you doing? Go back and ask the Prophet (upon whom be Allah's peace) to pray for your forgiveness." He retorted, "I do not want him to pray for my forgiveness."
    (Ibn Hisham, vol. III, p. 111)

4.   *In A. H. 4, the Battle of Bani an-Nadir took place. On this occasion, he and his companions supported the enemies of Islam even more openly. On the one side, the Prophet (peace be upon him) and his devoted companions were preparing for war against their enemy, the Jews, and on the other side, these hypocrites were secretly sending messages to the Jews: "Stand firm, we are with you: if you are attacked, we will help you, and if you are driven out, we too will go out with you." The secret of this intrigue was exposed by Allah Himself, as has been explained in Sûrah Al-Hashr verses 11-17. In spite of being so exposed, the reason why the Prophet (peace be upon him) was still treating him kindly, was that he had a large band of the hypocrites behind him. Many of the chiefs of both the Aus and the Khazraj were his supporters. At least a third of the population of Madinah consisted of his companions, as became manifest on the occasion of the Battle of Uhud. Under such conditions, it was not prudent to wage a war against these internal enemies. On this account, in spite of being fully aware of their hypocrisy, the Prophet continued to deal with them based on their claim to be Muslims.*

5.   *In A.H. 6, when Abdullah bin Ubayy, and like minded hypocrites, got an opportunity to accompany the Prophet (peace be upon him) in his campaign against the Bani Al- Mustaliq, they engineered two great mischiefs which could shatter the Muslim unity to pieces. However, by virtue of the wonderful training in discipline that the Muslims had received through the pure teaching of the Qur'an and the companionship of the Prophet (peace be upon him), both mischiefs were stopped in time, and the hypocrites themselves were disgraced instead. One of these, was the mischief that is mentioned in Sûrah An-Nûr, and the other in this Sûrah. These incidents are related by Bukhâri, Muslim, Ahmed, Nasâi, Tirmidhi, Baihaqi, Tabari, Ibn Marduyah, Abdur Razzaq, lbn Jarir Tabari, Ibn Sa'd and Muhammad bin Ishâq through many reliable channels.*

63: AL-MUNÂFIQÛN

This Sûrah, revealed at Madinah, has 2 sections and 11 verses.

In the name of Allah, the Compassionate, the Merciful

SECTION: 1

When the hypocrites come to you, they say: "We bear witness that you are indeed the Rasool of Allah." Allah knows that you are indeed His Rasool, and Allah bears witness that the hypocrites are liars.[1]   They use their oaths as a shield, and thus debar others from the Way of Allah. Evil is indeed what they do.[2] This is because they believed and then renounced their faith. Their hearts are sealed, therefore, they are devoid of understanding.[3] When you see them, their good stature pleases you; and when they speak, you listen to what they say. Yet, they are as *worthless as hollow* pieces of propped up timber. Every shout they hear, they think it to be against them. They are your enemies, so guard yourselves against them. May Allah destroy them! How perverse they are![4]   When it is said to them: "Come, the Rasool of Allah will pray for your forgiveness," they shake their heads and you see them turning away with arrogance.[5]   It is the same, whether you pray for their forgiveness or not, Allah is not going to forgive them. Surely, Allah does not guide the transgressors.[6]   They are the same people who say: "Do not give anything to those who follow the Rasool of Allah until they have deserted him." To Allah belongs the treasures of the heavens and the earth; but the hypocrites cannot understand.[7]   They say: "When we return to Madinah, the honorable will soon drive out the meaner." But the honor belongs to Allah, to His Rasool and to the believers; but the hypocrites do not know.[8]   63:[1-8]

SECTION: 2

O believers! Let neither your riches nor your children divert you from the remembrance of Allah. Those who will do so, it is they who shall be the real losers.[9]   Spend, *in charity and in the Cause of Allah*, out of the sustenance which We have bestowed on you before death comes to anyone of you, and then he says: "O my Rabb! If only you would give me respite for a little while then I would give charity, and be among the righteous."[10]   But Allah grants respite to no soul when its term comes to an end. Allah is well aware of all your actions.[11]   63:[9-11]

Hypocrites are such enemies of Islam and Muslims that even the Rasool's prayer cannot obtain forgiveness for them from Allah

Let not your riches or children divert you from the remembrance of Allah, lest you become a real loser

64: AT-TAGHÂBUN

Period of Revelation

This Sûrah was revealed during the early stage of the Prophet's residence at Madinah.

Major Issues, Divine Laws and Guidance:

* To Allah belongs the kingdom of the heavens and the earth, and He knows all that you conceal and or reveal.
* Surely, there will be life after death, the Day of Judgement will take place to reward for good and bad deeds. That will be the Day of gain or loss, victory or defeat, winning or losing.
* No affliction can ever befall anyone except by the leave of Allah.
* Among your wives and children, there are some who are your enemies, be aware of them.

The theme of this Sûrah is an invitation to the Faith, obedience (to Allah) and the teaching of good morals. The sequence followed is that the first four verses are addressed to all men; verses 5-10 to those men who do not believe in the invitation of the Qur'an; and verses 11- 18 to those who accept and believe in this invitation. In the verses addressed to all men, they have been made aware of the following four truths:

1. That the universe in which you live is not Godless, but its Creator, Master and Ruler is an All-Powerful Allah, and everything in it testifies to His being, Who is perfect and absolutely faultless.

2. That the universe is not without purpose and wisdom. Its Creator has created it to manifest the truth. No one should be under the delusion that it is just a show, which began without a purpose and will come to an end with out a purpose.

3. That the excellent form that Allah has created you with, and the choice that He has given you to choose between belief and unbelief, is not a useless and meaningless activity so that it may be of no consequence whether you choose belief or unbelief. In fact, Allah is watching as to how you exercise your choice.

4. *That you have not been created irresponsible and unanswerable. You are to return ultimately to your Creator, and will meet the Being who is aware of everything in the universe, from Whom nothing is hidden, and to Whom even the innermost thoughts of peoples' minds are known.*

After stating these truths about the Universe and the Human being, the address turns to the disbelievers and their attention is drawn to the two causes of prior nations' destruction:

A. *They refused to believe in the Rasools, whom Allah sent for their guidance. As a result Allah left them to themselves, they invented their own philoso- phies of life and went on groping their way from one error to another.*

B. *They rejected the doctrine of the Hereafter, and thought this worldly life to be an end in itself. They believed that there was no life hereafter, where they will render an account of their deeds before Allah. This corrupted their attitude towards life, their morals and character became so polluted that eventually the scourge of Allah came and eliminated them from the scene.*

After stating these historical facts, the disbelievers are admonished to wake up, believe in Allah, His Rasool and the Light of Guidance that Allah has sent in the form of the Qur'an, if they want to avoid the fate met by the former people. They are warned that the Day shall eventually come when all the former and the latter generations will be gathered in one place and the misdeeds committed by each will be exposed before all mankind. Then addressing the believers, a few important instructions are given:

i. *Whatever affliction befalls a person in the world, it befalls with Allah's leave. Whoever in this state of affliction remains steadfast to the Faith, Allah blesses his heart with guidance.*

ii. *The believer is not only required to affirm the Faith with the tongue, but after the affirmation, he should practically obey Allah and His Rasool. If he turns away from obedience he would himself be responsible for his loss.*

iii. *The believer should place his trust in Allah alone and not in any other power of this world.*

iv.   *Worldly goods and children are a trial, for it is their love that generally distracts man from the path of Allah and His obedience. Therefore, the believers should beware of this fact about their children and spouses lest they directly or indirectly become robbers on their Way to Allah. They should spend their wealth for the sake of Allah so that their self remains safe against the temptations of Satan.*

v.   *Every person is responsible only to the extent of his/her power and ability. Allah does not demand that man should exert himself beyond his power and ability. However, the believer should try his best to live in fear of Allah as much as possible, and should see that he does not transgress the limits set by Allah in his speech, conduct and dealings.*

64: AT-TAGHÂBUN

This Sûrah, revealed at Madinah, has 2 sections and 18 verses.

In the name of Allah, the Compassionate, the Merciful

SECTION: 1

All that is in the heavens and the earth glorifies Allah. To Him belongs the kingdom and to Him is due all praise; and He has power over all things.[1]   It is He Who has created you; yet, some of you are unbelievers and some are believers. Allah is observant of all your actions.[2]   He created the heavens and the earth to manifest the truth. He shaped you and shaped you well, and to Him you shall all return.[3]   He knows all that is in the heavens and the earth. He knows what you conceal and what you reveal, and Allah knows what is in your hearts.[4]   Have you not heard of those who disbelieved before you? So they tasted the evil result of their deeds, and *in the Hereafter* there shall be a painful punishment for them.[5] That is because, when their Rasools came to them with clear revelations, they said: "Are human beings going to guide us?" So they disbelieved and paid no heed. Allah has no need *of such people*. Allah is free of all needs, worthy of all praise.[6]   The unbelievers claim that they shall not be raised to life again. Tell them: "Indeed, by my Rabb, you shall surely be raised to life again! Then you shall be told of all that you have done; and that is easy for Allah."[7]   Therefore, believe in Allah and His Rasool, and in the Light which We have revealed. Allah is well aware of all your actions.[8]   The Day when He will gather you all will be the Day of Assembly, which shall be the Day of At-Taghâbun *(mutual loss and gain among the people)*. As for those who believe in Allah and do good deeds, He will remove from them their sins and admit them to gardens beneath which rivers flow, to live therein forever, and that will be the supreme achievement.[9]   *As for* those who disbelieved and deny Our revelations, they will become the inmates of hell, wherein they shall live forever, and that is an evil abode.[10]

64:[1-10]

SECTION: 2

No affliction can ever befall except by the leave of Allah. He that believes in Allah, his heart is guided to the Right Way. Allah has the knowledge of every thing.[11]   Obey Allah and obey His Rasool; but if you pay no heed, *then you should know that* Our

---

To Allah belongs the kingdom of heavens and earth, and He knows all that you conceal and reveal

Surely there will be life after death, Day of Judgment and reward for good and bad deeds

No affliction can ever befall except by the leave of Allah

Among your wives and children there are some who are your enemies, be aware of them

Rasool's responsibility is only to convey the message plainly.[12] Allah! There is none worthy of worship but He, therefore, in Allah *Alone* let the believers put their trust.[13]   O believers! Surely, among your wives and your children there are some who are your enemies: so beware of them. But if you pardon, overlook and forgive *their faults*, then Allah is Forgiving, Merciful.[14]   Your wealth and your children are but a trial. It is Allah with Whom is the greatest reward.[15]   Therefore, fear Allah as much as you can, listen *to His message* attentively, be obedient, and be charitable: this is for your own good. Those who are saved from the covetousness of their own souls, it is they who are truly successful.[16]   If you lend to Allah a goodly loan, He will pay you back manifold, and will forgive you *your sins*. Allah is Appreciative and Forbearing.[17]   He has the knowledge of the unseen and the seen, He is the All-Mighty, the All-Wise.[18]   64:[11-18]

65: AT-TALÂQ

Period of Revelation

It is difficult to determine precisely when this Sûrah was revealed. However, it appears that it was revealed when the people started making errors in understanding the commandments in Sûrah Al-Baqarah, and began to commit mistakes, Allah sent down these instructions.

Major Issues, Divine Laws and Guidance:

* Laws of divorce (for details see below).
* Iddat (waiting period before the divorce takes effect) is commanded to be three menstruation periods, three months if menstruation is not applicable, and in case of pregnancy, it is the delivery of child.
* Rebellion against Allah's commandment may bring stern reckoning or exemplary punishment, so fear Allah and adhere to His laws.

In order to understand the commandments of this Sûrah, it is useful to refresh one's memory about the regulations which were given concerning divorce and the waiting period (Iddat).

"Divorce may be pronounced twice; then the wife may either be kept back in fairness or allowed to separate in fairness."   (Al Baqarah 229)

"And the divorced women (after the pronouncement of the divorce) must wait for three monthly courses... and their husbands are fully entitled to take them back (as their wives) during this waiting period, if they desire reconciliation."   (Al Baqarah 228)

"Then, if the husband divorces his wife (for the third time), she shall not remain lawful for him after this divorce, unless she marries another man..."   (Al-Baqarah : 230)

"When you marry the believing women, and then divorce them before you have touched them, they do not have to observe a waiting period, the completion of which you might demand of them."   (Al-Ahzâb : 49)

"And if those of you who die, leave wives behind, the women should abstain (from marriage) for four months and ten days." (Al-Baqarah 234)

The rules prescribed in these verses are as follows:

1. *A man can pronounce at the most three divorces on his wife.*

2. *In case, the husband has pronounced one or two divorces, he is entitled to take the woman back as his wife within the waiting period, and if after the expiration of the waiting period the two desire to remarry, they can re marry and there is no condition of legalization (tahlil). But if the husband has pronounced three divorces, he forfeits his right to keep her as his wife within the waiting period, and they cannot remarry unless the woman marries another man and he subsequently divorces her of his own free will.*

3. *The waiting period of the woman, who menstruates and marriage with whom has been consummated, is that she should pass three monthly courses. The waiting period in case of one or two divorces is that the woman is still the legal wife of the husband and he can take her back as his wife within the waiting period. But if the husband has pronounced three divorces, this waiting period cannot be taken advantage of for the purpose of reconciliation, but is only meant to restrain the woman from remarrying another person before it comes to an end.*

4. *There is no waiting period for the woman, who is divorced before the marriage is consummated. She can remarry, if she likes, immediately after the divorce.*

5. *The waiting period of the woman whose husband dies is four months and ten days before she is allowed to remarry.*

One should understand that Sûrah At-Talâq was not sent down to annul or amend any of these rules, but was sent down for two purposes:

A. *The man who has been given the right to pronounce divorce should be taught such judicious methods of using this right so that it may not needlessly lead to separation. However, if separation does take place, it should only be when all possibilities of mutual reconciliation have been exhausted. In Divine Law, provision for divorce has been made only as an unavoidable necessity. Allah does not approve of the dissolution of a marriage. The Prophet (peace be upon him) has said:*

"Allah has not made lawful anything more hateful in His sight than divorce."   *(Abu Daûd)* And:

"Of all the things permitted by the Law, the most hateful in the sight of Allah is the divorce."   *(Abu Daûd)*

B.   *The object was to complement this section of the family law of Islam by supplying answers to the questions that remained after the revelation of the commandments in Sûrah Al-Baqarah. Answers are given to the following questions:*

   i.   *What would be the waiting period of women, marriage with whom has been consummated and who no longer menstruate or those who have not yet menstruated, in case they are divorced?*

   ii.   *What would be the waiting period of the woman who is divorced, if she is pregnant or a woman whose husband dies?*

   iii.   *What arrangements would be made for the maintenance and lodging of the different categories of divorced women, and for the fosterage of the child whose parents have separated on account of a divorce?*

65: AT-TALÂQ

This Sûrah, revealed at Madinah, has 2 sections and 12 verses.

In the name of Allah, the Compassionate, the Merciful

SECTION: 1

Laws of divorce and Iddat (waiting period) before the divorce takes effect

O Prophet! If you *and the believers* divorce your wives, divorce them at their prescribed periods, and count their prescribed periods *accurately*. Fear Allah, your Rabb. Do not expel them from their homes *during their waiting period*, nor they themselves should leave, unless they have committed an open lewdness. These are limits set by Allah; he that transgresses the limits of Allah will wrong his own soul. You never know, Allah may, thereafter, bring about some new situation *of reconciliation*.[1] Then, when their waiting period ends, either keep them honorably or part with them in an honorable way. Call to witness two honest persons among you, and *O witnesses*, bear witness equitably for the sake of Allah. This advice is being given to all who believe in Allah and the Last Day. He that fears Allah may be provided a way out *by Him,*[2] and given sustenance from the sources he could never expect: for Allah is all sufficient for the person who puts his trust in Him. Surely, Allah brings about what He pleases, and Allah has set a measure for all things.[3]

Iddat (waiting period) is three menstruation periods or three months and delivery in case of pregnancy

If you have any doubt concerning those *of your wives* who have ceased menstruating, then *you should know that* their waiting period will be three months, and the same will apply to those who have no menstruation *due to young age or a disease.* As for those who are pregnant, their waiting period will end with delivery. Allah will ease the hardship of those who fear Him.[4] This is the command of Allah which He has sent down to you. He that fears Allah, will have his sins removed and his reward enlarged.[5] Let those women, *during their waiting period ('Iddat),* live where you yourselves live according to your means. You shall not harass them so as to make life intolerable for them. If they are pregnant, maintain them until their delivery: and if, after that, they suckle your offspring, compensate them and settle the matter *of compensation* with mutual consultation and in all fairness. But, if you cannot bear with each other then let another woman suckle the baby for you.[6] Let the rich man give according to his means, and the poor man give according to *what Allah has given* him. Allah does not charge a man with more than He has given him; soon Allah may bring ease after hardship.[7]

65:[1-7]

SECTION: 2

How many townships have rebelled against the commandments of their Rabb and His Rasools! Stern was Our reckoning with them and exemplary was Our punishment.[8]   So they tasted the fruit of their misdeeds, and the fruit of their misdeeds was perdition.[9]   Allah has prepared for them a severe punishment *in the Hereafter*. Therefore, fear Allah! O men of understanding who have believed. Allah has indeed sent down to you an admonition,[10] a Rasool reciting to you the revelations of Allah containing clear guidance, so that he may lead the believers who do good deeds from darkness to light. He that believes in Allah and does good deeds, shall be admitted to gardens beneath which rivers flow, to live therein forever; and Allah has indeed granted for him an excellent provision.[11]   It is Allah Who has created seven heavens and of the earth a similar number. His commandment descends between them, *this is being explained to you,* so that you may know that Allah has power over every thing, and that Allah encompasses every thing in His knowledge.[12]   65:[8-12]

Rebellion against Allah's commandment may bring stern reckoning or exemplary punishment, so fear Allah and adhere to His laws.

66: AT-TAHREEM

Period of Revelation

This Sûrah was revealed in A.H. 7, after the conquest of Khaiber.

Major Issues, Divine Laws and Guidance:

* *Do not make something unlawful which Allah has made lawful.*
* *Wives of the Prophet (peace be upon him) are admonished on their behavior with him.*
* *Believers are commanded to turn to Allah in sincere repentance if they want to be forgiven.*
* *Example of the wives of Nûh (Noah) and Lût (Lot) who will go to hell and the example of Fir'aun's (Pharaoh's) wife and Maryam who will go to paradise.*

This is a very important Sûrah in which guidance is provided relating to questions of grave significance in reference to some incidents concerning the wives of the Prophet (peace be upon him), rules relating to lawful and unlawful and that kinship to the Prophet is not the criteria for salvation:

1. *The powers to prescribe the bounds of the lawful and the unlawful, the permissible and the forbidden, are entirely and absolutely in the hands of Allah and nothing of this sort has been delegated even to the Prophet of Allah, much less any other person.*

2. *The position of a Prophet is very delicate. A minor incident experienced by an ordinary man in his life may not be of any consequence, but it assumes the status of law when experienced by a Prophet. That is why, the lives of the Prophets have been kept under close supervision by Allah, so that none of their acts, not even a most trivial one, may deviate from Divine Will.*

3. *The Prophet (peace be upon him) was checked on a minor thing, which was not only corrected but also recorded. It gives us complete satisfaction that whatever actions, commands and instructions we now find in the documented life of the Prophet concerning which there is nothing on record in the nature of criticism or correction from Allah, we can trust that they are wholly based on truth, are in complete conformity with Divine Will and that guidance can be drawn from them with full confidence and peace of mind.*

4. It has been stated in this Sûrah that the Prophet, whose reverence and respect Allah Himself has enjoined as a necessary part of the faith of His servants, once during his sacred life, he made a thing declared lawful by Allah unlawful for himself only to please his wives. Allah severely reproved the error and admonished the wives of the Prophet, whom Allah Himself has declared as mothers of the faithful; worthy of the highest esteem and honor. Further, this criticism of the Prophet and the administration of the warning to his wives was made not secretly but included in the Book, which the entire Ummah has to read and recite forever. Obviously, the intention of making mention of this instance in the Book of Allah was not, nor could it have been, that Allah wanted to degrade His Rasool and the mothers of the faithful in the eyes of the believers. It is also obvious that no Muslim has lost respect for them after reading this Sûrah of the Qur'an. There cannot be any other reason of mentioning this instance in the Qur'an other than that Allah wants to acquaint the believers with the correct manner of reverence for their personalities. A Prophet is a Prophet, not God, and he may commit error. Respect for the Prophet has not been enjoined because he is infallible, but because he is a perfect representative of Divine Will, and Allah has not permitted any of his errors to pass unnoticed. This gives us the satisfaction that the noble pattern of life left by the Prophet wholly and fully represents the Will of Allah.

5. It is made explicitly clear that Allah's religion is absolutely fair and just. It has for every person just the recompense of which he becomes worthy of, on the basis of his faith and works. No relationship or connection, even with the most righteous person or the most evil person, can be beneficial or harmful for him in any way. In reference to this, three kinds of women have been cited as examples before the Prophet's wives in particular.

   A. One example is of the wives of the Prophets Nûh (Noah) and Lût (Lot), who, if they had believed and cooperated with their illustrious husbands, would have occupied the same rank and position in the Muslim community which is enjoyed by the wives of the Prophet Muhammad (peace be upon him). Since they were disbelievers, their being the wives of the Prophets is not going to save them from hell.

   B. The second example is of the wife of Pharaoh, who in spite of being the wife of a staunch enemy of Allah believed and chose a path of action separate from that followed by the Pharaoh's people. Her being the wife of a staunch disbeliever did not cause her *any harm, and Allah made her worthy of Paradise.*

C.   *The third example is of Sayyidah Maryam (Mary) (peace be upon her), who attained to her high rank because she submitted to the severe test Allah decided to put her to. Apart from Maryam, no other chaste and righteous woman in history has been put to such a difficult test. In spite of being unmarried, she was miraculously made pregnant by Allah's command and she was informed of the service that her Rabb willed to take from her. When Sayyidah Maryam accepted this decision, and agreed to bear, like a true believer, everything that she inevitably had to bear in order to fulfil Allah's Will, then Allah exalted her to the noble rank of "Sayyidah-tun-Nisâ' Fil-Jannah (Leader of the women in Paradise)."*

(Musnad Ahmed)

We also learn from this Sûrah that the Prophet (peace be upon him) did not receive from Allah only that knowledge which is included and recorded in the Qur'an, but was additionally given information about other things also by revelation, which was not recorded in the Qur'an. Clear proof of this is found in verse 3 of this Sûrah. In which we are told that the Prophet (peace be upon him) confided a secret to one of his wives, and she told it to another. Allah informed the Prophet of this secret. Then, when the Prophet warned his particular wife on this mistake of disclosure, she said: "Who has informed you of this mistake of mine?" He replied: "I have been informed of it by Him Who knows everything and is All-Aware." Is there any verse in which Allah has said: "O Prophet, the secret that you had confided to one of your wives has been disclosed by her to another person?" There is no such verse in the Qur'an. Thus it is an express proof of the fact that some times revelation that descended on the Prophet was not included in the Qur'an, and refutes the claim of the deniers of Hadith, who allege that nothing was revealed to the Prophet (peace be upon him) apart from the Qur'an.

66: AT-TAHREEM

This Sûrah, revealed at Madinah, has 2 sections and 12 verses.

In the name of Allah, the Compassionate, the Merciful

SECTION: 1

O Prophet! Why do you make something unlawful, which Allah has made lawful to you in seeking to please your wives? Allah is Forgiving, Merciful.[1]   Allah has already given you absolution from your oaths. Allah is your Master and He is the Knowledgeable, the Wise.[2]   When the Prophet confided a secret to one of his wives, she disclosed this secret to another and Allah informed him about it, *the Prophet* made known *to the said wife* a part of it and avoided mentioning the rest. So when he told her about this *disclosure*, she asked: "Who told you this?" He replied: "I was informed by Him Who is All-Knowing, All-Aware."[3] If you both *(Hafsah and 'Aisha)* turn in repentance to Allah - for your hearts have sinned - *you shall be pardoned;* and if you back up each other against him *(the Prophet)*, then *you should know that* his protectors are Allah, Gabriel and all righteous people; furthermore, the angels too are his supporters.[4]   It may well be that, if he divorces you all, his Rabb will give him in your place better wives than yourselves, submissive, faithful, obedient, penitent, worshippers and keepers of fasting, be they previously married or virgins.[5]   O believers! Save yourselves and your families from Hellfire, whose fuel is people and stones, in the charge of severe and mighty angels who never disobey Allah's command and who promptly do what they are commanded to do.[6]   *Then it will be said:* "O unbelievers! Make no excuses for yourselves this Day. You are being rewarded according to your deeds."[7]   66:[1-7]

SECTION: 2

O believers! Turn to Allah in sincere repentance. It may well be that your Rabb will remove from you your sins and admit you to gardens beneath which rivers flow. On that Day, Allah will not humiliate the Prophet and those who believe with him. Their light will shine in front of them and on their right, and they will say: "Our Rabb! Perfect our light for us and grant us forgiveness, for You have power over all things."[8]   O Prophet! Make Jihad

Do not make something unlawful which Allah has made lawful

Wives of the Prophet are admonished on their behavior with him

O believers! Turn to Allah in sincere repentance if you want to be forgiven

Example of the wives of Nûh and Lût who will go to hell and example of Fir'aun's wife and Maryam who will go to paradise

(struggle including war) against the unbelievers and the hypocrites and deal sternly with them. Hell shall be their home, and that is an evil abode![9]   Allah has set an example to the unbelievers in the wife of Nûh *(Noah)* and the wife of Lût *(Lot)*. They were married to two of Our righteous servants, but they betrayed them *(in their religion)*. In no way could *their husbands* protect them from Allah. *Both of* them were told: "Enter the fire, along with those who enter."[10]   And for the believers Allah has set an example in the wife of Fir'aun *(Pharaoh)*, who said: "My Rabb! Build for me a house as a special favor from You in paradise, deliver me from Fir'aun and his misdeeds, and save me from the wicked nation."[11] *Another example is in the life of* Maryam, the daughter of 'Imrân, who guarded her chastity, and into whose womb, We breathed of Our *created* spirit. She believed in the words of her Rabb and His scriptures, and was one of the obedient.[12]   66:[8-12]

JUZ (PART): 29

67: AL-MULK

Period of Revelation

It is not known from any authentic tradition when this Sûrah was revealed, but the subject matter and the style indicate that it is one of the earliest Sûrahs revealed during the life of the Prophet's residence at Makkah.

Major Issues, Divine Laws and Guidance:

* The Kingdom of the universe belongs to Allah.
* The lower heaven is decorated with lamps (stars).
* The dwellers of hell will wish: "Had we only listened to the call of Islam, we would have not been among the inmates of hell."
* No one can help you against Allah, nor can any one save you from the punishment of Allah.

In this Sûrah the basic teachings of Islam are briefly mentioned. In a most effective way, people are made to realize that the universe in which they live is a well organized and fortified Kingdom in which no fault, weakness or flaw can be detected no matter how hard they may try. This Kingdom has been created from nothing and is brought into existence by Allah Almighty Himself. All of the powers of controlling, administering and ruling it are also entirely in the hands of Allah. This system is not created without any purpose and the people have been sent here for a test. In this test they can succeed only by their righteous deeds and conduct. Then the dreadful consequences of disbelief, which will appear in the Hereafter, are mentioned. The people are told that Allah, by sending His Prophets, has fore-warned them of these consequences.

Emphasis is made on the fact that the Creator is aware of each open and hidden secrets of men, even the innermost ideas of their hearts. The right basis of morality, is that man should avoid evil and fear the accountability by his Creator. Those who adopt such conduct will deserve forgiveness and a rich reward in the Hereafter. Reference is made to those common truths of daily occurrence to which man does not pay much attention. He is told that the earth on which he moves about with full satisfaction and peace of mind, and from which he obtains his sustenance, is subdued for him by Allah. This earth might at any time start shaking suddenly so as to cause his destruction, or a typhoon might occur, which may annihilate him completely. Look at the birds that fly in the air: it is Allah Who is sustaining them in the air. Then man is reminded: "Look at your own means and resources. If Allah wills to inflict you with a scourge, none can save you from it; and if Allah wills to close the doors of sustenance on you, none can open them for you. These things are there to make you aware of the truth, but you see them like animals, which are unable to draw conclusions from observations, and you do not use your sight, hearing and minds which Allah has bestowed on you as a human being. You have to ultimately appear before your Rabb. It is not for the Prophet to tell you the exact time and date of that event. His only duty is to warn you before-hand of its inevitable occurrence."

Finally a response is given to what the disbelievers of Makkah said against the Prophet (peace be upon him) and his Companions. They cursed the Prophet and prayed for his and his follower's destruction. To this, it has been said: "Whether those who call you to the right way are destroyed, or shown mercy by Allah, how will their fate change your destiny? You should look after yourselves and consider who would save you if you were overtaken by the scourge of Allah? You regard those who believe in Allah and put their trust in Him as the misguided. A time will come when it will become evident as to who was really misguided?"

In conclusion, the people are asked this question and left to ponder over it: "If the water which has come out from the earth at some place in the desert or hill-country of Arabia and upon which depends your whole life's activity, should sink and vanish underground, who, besides Allah, can restore this life giving water to you?"

JUZ (PART): 29

67: AL-MULK

This Sûrah, revealed at Makkah, has 2 sections and 30 verses.

In the name of Allah, the Compassionate, the Merciful

SECTION: 1

Blessed be He in Whose hands is the Kingdom *of the universe* and has power over all things.[1]   The One Who created death and life, so that He may put you to test, to find out which of you is best in deeds: He is the All-Mighty, the All-Forgiving.[2] The One Who created the seven heavens, one above another, you will not see any fault in the creation of the Compassionate. Look once again, do you see any flaw?[3]   Then look still another time, yet, again your sight will come back humbled while it is fatigued.[4] We have decorated the heaven of this world with lamps *(stars)* and We made them as missiles for pelting the shaitâns and prepared for them the torment of the blazing fire.[5]   *As for* those who disbelieve their Rabb, there will be the punishment of hell, which is an evil abode.[6]   When they are plunged into its fire, they will hear its roaring and boiling,[7]   as though bursting with rage. Every time a group is plunged therein, its guards will ask: "Did not a Warner come to you?"[8]   They will answer: "Yes indeed, a Warner did come to us, but we rejected him and said, Allah has revealed nothing - you are merely in gross error."[9]   They will *further* say: "Had we only listened or used our intelligence, we would have not been among the inmates of the blazing fire."[10]   Thus shall they confess their sin; so away *from the mercy of Allah* will be the dwellers of hell.[11]   As for those who fear their Rabb, *although* they have not seen *Him*, shall have forgiveness and a great reward.[12]   Whether you speak in secret or aloud, surely, He is aware of all that is in the hearts.[13]   Would He, Who has created them, not know? He is Most Courteous and Well-Aware of all things[14]

67:[1-14]

SECTION: 2

It is He Who has made the earth subservient to you, to walk through its tracts and eat of His provided sustenance. To Him is the return at resurrection.[15]   Do you feel secure that He Who is in the heaven will not cause the earth to cave in beneath you and start

Kingdom of the universe belongs to Allah

The lower heaven is decorated with the lamps (stars)

Conversation between the dwellers of hell and its guards

No one can help you against Allah

shaking suddenly?[16]   Or do you feel secure that He Who is in the heaven will not send against you a stone-charged tornado; then you shall know how *terrible* My warning was![17]   Those who have gone before them likewise disbelieved, then see how terrible was the way I rejected them?[18]   Do they not observe the birds above them spreading their wings and folding them? None uphold them except the Compassionate *(Allah);* surely, it is He Who watches over all things.[19]   Who is the one that has the force to help you besides the Compassionate? In fact, the unbelievers are suffering from delusion.[20]   Or who is there that can provide you if He withholds His provision? Yet, they persist in rebellion and aversion *from the truth*.[21]   *Just think,* who is rightly guided: he who walks with his face bent down, or he who walks properly on a straight path?[22]   Say: "It is He Who has brought you into being, gave you the faculties of hearing, seeing and understanding: yet, you are seldom thankful."[23]   Say: "It is He Who has multiplied you in the earth, and before Him you shall all be assembled."[24] They ask: "When will this promise be fulfilled, if what you say is true?"[25]   Tell them: "Allah Alone has the knowledge of that; my mission is only to warn you plainly."[26]   But, when they shall see it close at hand, the humiliation and gloom shall become apparent on the faces of the disbelievers, and it will be said to them: "This is what you were calling for."[27]   *Further* say: "Have you ever considered that even if Allah destroys me as well as those with me or bestows His mercy on us; who will save the disbelievers from a painful punishment?"[28]   Say: "He is the Compassionate; in Him we have believed, and in Him we have put our trust. Soon you will find out, which one of us is in the manifest error."[29]   Say: "Have you ever considered that if all the water you have, sink down in the ground, who then can bring you the clear-flowing water?"[30]

6:[15-30]

No one can provide you sustenance besides Allah

No one can save you from the punishment of Allah

68: AL-QALAM

Period of Revelation

This is one of the earliest Sûrahs revealed in Makkah at a time when opposition to the Prophet (peace be upon him) had grown very harsh and tyrannical.

Major Issues, Divine Laws and Guidance:

* Allah declared Muhammad (peace be upon him) to be of the highest moral character.
* Commandment of not yielding to any disbelieving oath-monger, slanderer and wicked person.
* Example of the arrogant stingy owners of a garden who did not want to pay charity and as a result, their garden was destroyed.
* Allah is not going to treat the Muslims as He will treat the criminals.
* Those who do not believe in Allah's revelations are led step by step towards destruction.
* There are three important themes of this Sûrah:
   1. Response to the opponents' objections.
   2. Warning and admonition to the disbelievers.
   3. Exhortation of patience to the Prophet (peace be upon him) .

The Prophet is addressed, as if to say: "The disbelievers call you a madman whereas the Book that you are presenting and the sublime conduct that you practise are by themselves sufficient to refute their false accusations. Soon they will see as to who was crazy and who was sane."

The disbelievers are admonished that well-being in the Hereafter inevitably belongs to those who are Allah-conscious. It is utterly against reason that in the Hereafter, the obedient servants should meet the same fate as the criminals. Those who are being called upon to bow before Allah in this world and they refuse to do so, would be unable to prostrate themselves on the Day of Resurrection, even if they wanted to do so, and thus would stand disgraced and condemned. They have no reasonable ground for opposing the Rasool, they can neither make the claim that they know with certainty that he is not a true Rasool, nor that what he says is false.

In conclusion, the Prophet (peace be upon him) has been exhorted: "Bear with patience the hardships that you may have to face in the way of preaching the Faith until Allah's judgement arrives, and avoid the impatience which caused suffering and affliction to the Prophet Yûnus (Jonah), peace be upon him."

68: AL-QALAM

This Sûrah, revealed at Makkah, has 2 sections and 52 verses.

In the name of Allah, the Compassionate, the Merciful

SECTION: 1

Allah has declared Muhammad to be of the highest moral character

Nûn. By the pen and what they write.[1] You *(O Muhammad)* are not, by the grace of your Rabb, a madman,[2] and indeed, for you will be a never- ending reward.[3] You *(O Muhammad)* are of the highest noble character.[4] Soon you will see - as they will see[5] - which of you is afflicted with madness.[6] Surely, it is your Rabb Who knows best those who have strayed from His Way, as He knows best those who are rightly guided.[7] So do not yield to the unbelievers.[8] They desire you to compromise a little, so they too would compromise.[9] Neither yield to any mean oath-monger,[10] defaming slanderer,[11] opponent of good, transgressor, sinful,[12] wicked oppressor, and above all, illegitimate pretender,[13] though he be possessing wealth and children.[14] When Our revelations are recited to him , he says: "*They are nothing but* the tales of the ancients."[15] Soon We shall brand him on the snout.[16]

Do not yield to any disbelieving oath-monger, slanderer or wicked person

68:[1-16]

What happened to the arrogant stingy owners of a garden who did not want to pay charity?

Surely, We have tried them as We tried the owners of the garden when they swore that they would pluck its fruit the next morning,[17] without adding any reservation (*such as Allah willing).*[18] So a calamity *(fire)* from your Rabb came down upon it while they slept,[19] and by the morning it was like a dark desolate spot *(as if it had been already harvested).*[20] At daybreak they called out to one another,[21] saying: "Go out early to your crop, if you want to pick its fruit."[22] So they went, whispering to one another:[23] "Let no needy person enter in the garden today."[24] Thus they went out, fixed in their *stingy* resolve *(not to give any fruit to the poor people),* as if they had the full control *over harvesting the fruit.*[25] But when they saw the garden, they cried: "Surely, we must have lost our way![26] Nay, we have been deprived *of its fruit.*"[27] The most upright among them said: "Did I not tell you *to glorify Allah?* Why did you not glorify *Him by saying: "If Allah wills"?*"[28] *Then* they said: "Glory be to our Rabb! Surely, we were unjust,"[29] and they started blaming one another.[30] *Finally* they said: "Woe to us! Surely, we had become rebellious.[31] It may be that our Rabb will give us in exchange a better *garden* than this: surely, to our Rabb do we make our humble petition."[32]   Such is the punishment *in this life*; but the punishment in the Hereafter is even greater, if they but knew it.[33]

68:[17-33]

SECTION: 2

Surely, the righteous will be rewarded with gardens of delight by their Rabb.[34]   *What do the disbelievers think?* Shall We treat the Muslims as We treat the criminals?[35]   What is the matter with you? What kind of Judgment do you make?[36]   Or do you have a Book from which you read,[37]   that you shall be given whatever you choose?[38]   Or do you have a sworn covenant - a covenant binding on Us till the Day of Resurrection - that you shall have whatever you demand?[39]   Ask if any of them will vouch for that.[40]   Or do they have other gods *who could help them against Allah*? If so, let them produce their other gods, if they are truthful.[41] The Day the shin will be uncovered *(confront the hardship of the Day of Judgement)*, and they are called upon to prostrate themselves, they shall not be able to do so.[42]   They shall stand with eyes downcast, utterly humbled; because during their safe and sound *earthly* life they were called upon to prostrate themselves *but they refused to do so.*[43]   68:[34-43]

O Prophet, leave to Me those who reject this revelation. We shall lead them step by step to their ruin, in ways that they cannot perceive.[44]   I shall *even* put up with them for a while; for My plan is strong indeed.[45]   Or have you, *O Prophet,* demanded a compensation from them, that they are overburdened with debt?[46] Or do they have the knowledge of the unseen that they are writing it down?[47]   So wait with patience for the Judgment of your Rabb and be not like the companion of the fish *(reference is to the Prophet Jonah who was swallowed by a whale)*, who cried when he was in distress.[48]   Had his Rabb not bestowed on him His grace, he would certainly have been *left in the stomach of whale, but we forgave him, so he was* cast off on the naked shore, while he was reprimanded.[49]   But his Rabb chose him and included him among the righteous.[50]   The unbelievers would almost trip you up with their eyes when they hear Our revelations *(the Qur'an)*, and say: "He *(Muhammad)* is surely crazy."[51]   But this *(the Qur'an)* is nothing else than a Reminder to all the people of the world.[52]

68:[44-52]

Allah is not going to treat the Muslims as He will treat the guilty. Why don't the disbelievers understand this?

Those who do not believe in Allah's revelations are led step by step towards destruction

69: AL-HÂQQAH

Period of Revelation

This Sûrah was revealed at Makkah at the time when opposition to the Prophet (peace be upon him) had started but had not yet become tyrannical.

Major Issues, Divine Laws and Guidance:

* Description of the Day of Resurrection and the Day of Judgement.
* Righteous people and their reward.
* Sinful people and their punishment.
* Al-Qur'an is the word of Allah and not of the Prophet, and that it is a reminder for those who fear Allah.

The first section is about the Hereafter and the second about the Qur'an being a revelation from Allah and the Prophet being a true Rasool of Allah. The first section opens with the assertion that the coming of the Resurrection and the occurrence of the Hereafter is a truth, which is destined to take place inevitably. The real object why Allah has destined a second life for mankind after the present worldly life is described, depicting a scene from the Day of Judgement when all men shall appear in the court of their Rabb, where no secret of theirs shall remain hidden and each man's record will be placed in his hand. Those who spent their lives in this world with the realization that one day they would have to render an account of their deeds before their Rabb, had worked righteously and provided for their well being in the Hereafter, will rejoice when they see that they have been acquitted and blessed with the eternal bliss of paradise. On the contrary, those who neither recognized the rights of Allah, nor discharged the rights of men, will have no one to save them from the punishment of Allah, and they will be cast into hell.

In the second section the disbelievers of Makkah are addressed and told: "You think this Qur'an is the word of a poet or soothsayer, whereas it is a Revelation sent down by Allah, which is being presented by His noble Rasool. The Rasool by himself has no power to add or delete a word in it. If he forges something of his own composition into it, We will cut off his jugular vein."

69: AL-HÂQQAH

This Sûrah, revealed at Makkah, has 2 sections and 52 verses.

In the name of Allah, the Compassionate, the Merciful

SECTION: 1

The Inevitable Reality![1]   What is the Inevitable Reality?[2]   And what will make you understand what the Inevitable Reality *(the Day of Resurrection)* is?[3]   The Thamûd and the 'Ad people denied the striking calamity *(the Resurrection)*.[4]   As for Thamûd, they were destroyed by a terrible storm of thunder and lightening.[5]   As for 'Ad they were destroyed by a furious windstorm[6] - which He let loose on them for seven nights and eight *successive* days. *Had you been there,* you would have seen them lying over thrown as though they were hollow trunks of palm-trees.[7]   Now, do you see any of them alive?[8]   Fir'aun *(Pharaoh)* and those before him, and the inhabitants of the overthrown cities also committed similar sins[9]   and disobeyed the Rasools of their Rabb, so He gripped them with a tight grip.[10]   *Just consider the great flood of Nûh,* when the water rose high, We carried you *(O mankind)* in the floating Ark,[11]   that We may make that event a warning for you so that all attentive ears may retain its memory.[12]   *As for the doomsday, it shall come,* when the Trumpet will be blown with a single blast[13]   and the earth with all its mountains will be lifted up and crushed into pieces with a single stroke[14] - On that day the Great Event will come to pass,[15]   heaven shall split asunder, and shall become flimsy on the day.[16]   The angels will stand all around and eight of them will be carrying the Throne of your Rabb above them.[17]   That shall be the day when you will be brought *before your Rabb*, and none of your secrets shall remain hidden.[18]   69:[1-18]

Description of the Day of Resurrection and the Day of Judgment

Then he, who will be given his Book *of Deeds* in his right hand, will say: "Here it is, read my Book *of deeds*!"[19]   I knew that I would certainly face my account."[20]   So he will have a life of pleasure,[21] in a lofty garden,[22]   with clusters of fruit within his reach.[23]   *We shall say to him:* "Eat and drink to your heart's content; this is a reward for what you did in the days gone by."[24]   While he, who will be given his Book *of Deeds* in his left hand, will say: "Woe to me, would that I had not been given my Book *of Deeds*[25]   nor known what my account was![26]   Would that my

Righteous people and their reward

Sinful people and their punishment

death had ended all![27] My wealth had availed me nothing,[28] and my authority has gone away from me."[29] *We shall say:* "Seize him and put a chain *around his neck*,[30] then cast him in the blazing fire,[31] then fasten him with a chain seventy cubits long.[32] For he did not believe in Allah, the Most High,[33] nor did he care or urge to feed the poor.[34] Today he neither has a true friend here,[35] nor any food except the pus from the washing of wounds,[36] which none but the wrongdoers shall eat."[37]

69:[19-37]

SECTION: 2

The Qur'an is the word of Allah and not of the Prophet, and is a reminder for those who fear Allah (God)

Nay! I swear by all that you can see,[38] and all that you cannot see,[39] that this *Qur'an* is the word of *Allah recited by* a noble Rasool.[40] It is not the word of a poet - little is it that you believe,[41] - nor is it the word of a soothsayer - little admonition is that you take.[42] This is a revelation from the Rabb of the worlds.[43] Had he *(Muhammad)* invented false statements concerning Us,[44] We would certainly have seized him by his right hand[45] then cut off his main artery *(aorta)*,[46] and none of you could prevent it![47] Surely, this *Qur'an* is a reminder to the Godfearing.[48] We know that there are some among you who deny it,[49] and for such disbelievers, it will be indeed a cause of regret *on the Day of Resurrection*.[50] Yet, surely, it is the absolute truth.[51] So glorify the name of your Rabb, the Most High.[52]

69:[38-52]

70: AL-MA'ÂRIJ

Period of Revelation

This Sûrah was revealed during the early period of the Prophet's residence at Makkah when opposition had started but had not yet become severe.

Major Issues, Divine Laws and Guidance:

* The Day of Judgement will be equal to fifty thousand years.
* Disbelievers will wish to save themselves from the punishment, at the expense of their children, wives, brothers and relatives, but it will not happen.
* Paradise is not for the disbelievers.
* Disbelievers will have downcast eyes and countenances distorted with shame.

In this Sûrah, Allah admonished and gave warning to those disbelievers who were making fun of the Resurrection, the Hereafter, the hell and the heaven, and challenged the Prophet (peace be upon him) to resurrection take place, if what he said was true.

The whole Sûrah is meant to answer this question saying: "Resurrection, which they desire to be hastened out of jest and fun, is terrible, and when it will comes, it will cause great distress to the culprits. At that time they will even be prepared to give away their wives, then children and their nearest kinfolks in ransom to escape the punishment, but they will not be able to escape from it. On that Day, the destinies of mankind will be decided strictly on the basis of their belief and their conduct. Those who turn away from the Truth in this world, amass wealth and withhold it from the needy, will be doomed to hell; and those who fear the punishment of Allah, believe in the Hereafter, establish Salah (offer five times daily prayers), fulfill the rights of the needy out of their wealth, avoid immoral and wicked deeds, practise honesty in all their dealings, fulfill their pledges and bear true witness, will have a place of honor in paradise"

In conclusion, the disbelievers of Makkah are warned: "If you do not believe, Allah will replace you by other people who will be better than you," and the Prophet (peace be upon him) is consoled, so as to say: "Do not take to heart their mockery and jesting; leave them to indulge in their idle talk and foolish conduct, if they choose to face the disgrace and humiliation on the Day of the Resurrection."

70: AL-MA'ÂRIJ

This Sûrah, revealed at Makkah, has 2 sections and 44 verses.

In the name of Allah, the Compassionate, the Merciful

SECTION: 1

The Day of Judgment will be equal to fifty thousand years

Someone *from among the unbelievers* asked about the punishment which is bound to befall[1]   the disbelievers, which none can avert,[2]   coming from Allah, the Owner of the Ways of Ascent.[3]   The angels and the Rûh (Gabriel) ascend to Him in a Day the measure of which is fifty thousand years.[4]   Therefore, endure with graceful patience.[5]   They see it *(Day of Judgment)* to be far-off:[6]   but We see it quite near.[7]   On that Day, the sky shall become like molten brass[8]   and the mountains like flakes of wool;[9]   even a close friend will not ask about his friend,[10]   though they will see each other. To save himself from the punishment of that Day, the culprit *(disbeliever)* will wish to give his children,[11]   his wife, his brother,[12]   his relatives - who gave him shelter - [13]   and all that is in the earth, in ransom to save himself.[14]   By no means! It will be the fire of hell,[15]   eager to pluck out the scalp-skin;[16]   it will be calling all those who rejected the Truth and turned their backs *during their worldly life*,[17]   who collected *wealth* and withheld it *without giving out the due right*.[18]   Indeed, man has been created impatient,[19]   when evil befalls him, he becomes despondent;[20]   but when blessed with good fortune, he becomes stingy;[21]   with the exception of those who offer the Salah *(prayer)*,[22]   remain steadfast in their Salah,[23]   set aside a known right in their wealth[24]   for the beggars and the deprived *(who do not begg)*,[25]   accept the truth of the Day of Judgment,[26]   dread the punishment of their Rabb[27] - for none is secure from the punishment of their Rabb - [28]   and guard their private parts,[29]   except from their wives and those whom their right hands possess, for in their case they are not blameworthy.[30]   As for those who seek to go beyond this, they are transgressors.[31]   Those who keep their trusts and honor their promises,[32]   who stand firm in their testimonies[33]   and who strictly guard their Salah.[34]   It is they who shall live with honor in paradise.[35]   70:[1-35]

Disbelievers will wish to save themselves from the punishment at the expense of their children, wives, brothers and relatives, but it will not happen

SECTION: 2

Paradise is not for the disbelievers

What is the matter with the disbelievers that they are rushing towards you,[36]   from the right and from the left, in groups?[37] Are they each seeking to enter the garden of bliss?[38] By no means! Surely, We have created them out of that what they *(unbelievers)* know.[39] But nay! I swear by the Rabb of the easts and the wests, that We have the power[40] to *destroy them and replace them with others better than them, and nothing can hinder Us from doing so.*[41] Therefore, leave them to plunge in vain talk and amuse themselves until they face that Day of theirs which they are being promised.[42] The Day when they shall rush forward from their graves, as if they were racing towards a goal,[43] with downcast eyes, distorted with shame. Such will be the Day, which they are being promised.[44] 70:[36-44]

Disbelievers will have downcast eyes and countenances distorted with shame

71: NÛH

Period of Revelation

This Sûrah was revealed at Makkah during the period when opposition to the Prophet had grown to be very strong and active.

Major Issues, Divine Laws and Guidance:

* The Prophet Nûh's preaching and submission to Allah after exhausting all his efforts.
* The Prophet Nûh prayed not to leave any unbeliever on the surface of the earth - Allah granted his prayer.

In this Sûrah, the story of the Prophet Nûh (Noah) is told to warn the disbelievers of Makkah: "O people of Makkah, you are adopting towards Muham-mad (peace be upon him) the same attitude as the people of the Prophet Nûh had adopted towards him; if you do not change this attitude, you too might meet with the same end."

This Sûrah starts with a brief explanation of how the Prophet Nûh began his mission and what he preached. Then, after suffering hardships and troubles in fulfilling his mission for 950 years, the submission that he made to his Rabb is given in vv. 5-20. In it, he states how he had been trying to bring his people to the right path and how his people had stubbornly opposed him. After this, the Prophet Nûh prays to Allah, saying: "These people have rejected my invitation: they are blindly following their chiefs, who have devised a tremendous plot of deceit and cunning. Time has come when these people should be deprived of every grace." This was not an expression of impatience by the Prophet Nûh, but when after hav-ing preached his message under extremely trying circumstances for 950 years, he became utterly disappointed with his people, he formed the opinion that no chance was left of their coming to the Right Way. His opinion fully conformed to Allah's own decision.

In the concluding verse, the Prophet Nûh's supplication that he made to Allah when the torment descended, has been recorded. He seeks forgiveness for himself and all the believers, and submits to Allah: "Do not leave any of the disbe-lievers alive on the earth for they have become utterly devoid of every good; they will not beget any but disbelieving and wicked descendents."

71: NÛH

This Sûrah, revealed at Makkah, has 2 sections and 28 verses.

In the name of Allah, the Compassionate, the Merciful

SECTION: 1

We sent Nûh *(Noah)* to his people, *saying:* "Give warning to your people before there comes to them a painful punishment."[1] He said: "O my People! I am sent towards you as a plain Warner.[2] Worship Allah, fear Him and obey me.[3]   *If you will do so,* He will forgive you your sins and give you respite for an appointed term. The fact is that when the term given by Allah arrives, it cannot be deferred. If you could understand!"[4]   *After exhausting all his efforts Nûh* said: "O my Rabb! I have called my people night and day,[5]   but my plea has only added to their aversion.[6]   Each time I called on them to seek Your pardon, they thrust their fingers in their ears and drew their cloaks over their heads, persisting *in sin* and puffing themselves up with insolent pride.[7]   I have called them aloud,[8]   appealed to them openly in public and secretly in private,[9]   saying: "Seek forgiveness of your Rabb, He is ever ready to forgive you.[10]   He will send abundant rain for you from heaven,[11]   help you with wealth and sons, and provide you with gardens and flowing rivers.[12]   What is the matter with you that you do not regard the greatness of Allah[13]   when He has created you in gradual stages?[14]   Can you not see how Allah created the seven heavens one above the other,[15]   placing in them the moon as a light and the sun as a glorious lamp?[16]   Allah has caused you to grow as a growth from the earth.[17]   He will return you to the same earth and then raise you back *to life* again *on the Day of Resurrection?*[18]   Allah has made the earth for you as a wide expanse[19]   so that you may walk in its spacious paths."[20]

71:[1-20]

SECTION: 2

Finally, Nûh *(Noah)* submitted: "O my Rabb! *My people* have disobeyed me, and followed those *chiefs* whose wealth and children have added to them nothing but loss.[21]   They have devised an outrageous plot,[22]   and said *to each other*: 'Do not leave your gods; especially Wadd, Suwâ', Yaghûth, Ya'ûq and Nasr *(the names of their idols)*.'[23]   They have already misled many, *so O my Rabb,* do not increase the wrongdoers in anything but deviation."[24]   Because of their wrong doings they were

The Prophet Nûh's preaching and submission to Allah after exhausting all his efforts

The Prophet Nûh's prayer not to leave any unbeliever on the surface of the earth drowned *in the great flood* and made to enter the fire. They found no one besides Allah to help them.[25]   As Nûh had prayed: "O my Rabb! Do not leave a single unbeliever on *the surface of* the earth.[26]   For if You spare any of them, they will mislead your servants and beget none but wicked disbelievers.[27]   O my Rabb! Forgive me, my parents and any who enter my house as a believer, and all believing men and believing women. As to the wrongdoers, grant them increase in nothing but destruction."[28]

71:[21-28]

72: AL-JINN

Period of Revelation

This Sûrah was revealed during the early stages of the Prophet's residence at Makkah.

Major Issues, Divine Laws and Guidance:

* A beautiful speech of the jinn who embraced Islam after hearing the Qur'an.
* Jinns also have different religions and sects, there are some who are Muslims and some who are deviators from the truth.
* The reality of Jinn (for details see the following pages).
* Mosques are built for the worship of Allah, so invoke no one else besides Him.
* Rasools do not have the power to harm or benefit anyone, their mission is just to convey Allah's message.
* Only Allah knows the unseen, He reveals what He wants to whom He chooses from the Rasools.

Verses #8-10 indicate that, before the appointment of Muhammad (peace be upon him) as a Rasool, the jinns had the opportunity to eavesdrop in the heavens in order to hear news from the unseen. But after the appointment of Muhammad (peace be upon him) they suddenly found that angels had been set as guards and meteorites were being shot at them from every side, so much so that they could find no place of safety from where they could hear the secret news. Then they started searching for the unusual things that occurred on the earth, or were going to occur, because of which security measures were tightened up. Probably since then, many groups of the jinns must have been moving around in search of any unusual occurrence and one of them, after having heard the Qur'an from the Prophet (peace be upon him), must have formed the opinion that it was the thing for the sake of which all the gates of the heavens had been shut against the jinns.

This Sûrah reflects the impact of the Qur'an on the company of the jinns when they heard it and what they said to their fellow jinns when they returned to them. Allah, in this connection, has not cited their whole conversation but only those particular things which were worthy of mention. That is why the style is not that of a continuous speech but sentences have been cited so as to indicate that they said this and that. If one studies these sentences spoken by the jinns carefully, one can easily understand the real object of the narration of this event, of their affirming the faith and mentioning this conversation of theirs with their people in the Qur'an.

The people are admonished: "If you refrain from polytheism and firmly follow the way of righteousness, you will be blessed; otherwise, if you turn away from the admonition sent down by Allah, you will meet with a severe punishment." The disbelievers of Makkah are reproached: "When the Messenger of Allah calls you towards Allah, you surround and mob him from every side, whereas the only duty of the Messenger is to convey the messages of Allah. He does not claim to have any power to bring any gain or cause any harm to the people." The disbelievers are further warned: "Today you are trying to overpower and suppress the Rasool seeing that he is helpless and friendless, but a time will come when you will find out who is in fact helpless and friendless. Whether that time is far off, or near at hand, the Messenger has no knowledge thereof, but it will surely take place."

In conclusion, the people are told: "The Knower of the unseen is Allah Alone. The Rasool receives only that knowledge which Allah is pleased to give him. This knowledge pertains to matters connected with the performance of the duties of Prophethood and it is delivered to him in absolute security.

REALITY OF JINN

Many people have the misunderstanding that the jinns are not real, but an ancient superstition and myth. Their opinion is not based on the realities and truths about the universe and they have no direct knowledge that the jinns do not exist nor can they claim to possess any such knowledge. They have assumed, without reason and proof, that nothing exists in the universe except what they can see, whereas the sphere of human perception in accordance with the vastness of this great universe is not even comparable to a drop of water in the oceans. The person who thinks that what he does not see, does not exist, and what exists must necessarily be perceived, in fact, provides a proof of the narrowness of his own mind. With this mode of thought, not to speak of the jinn, man cannot even accept and acknowledge any reality which he cannot directly experience and observe, thus he does not admit the existence of God (Allah), not to say of admitting any other unseen reality.

Those Muslims who have been influenced by such opinions have given strange interpretations of the clear statements of the Qur'an about the jinn Iblees, called Shaitân (Satan). They say that the word jinn does not refer to any hidden creature, which may have its own independent existence, but it sometimes implies man's own animal forces, which have been called Satanic, and it sometimes implies savage and wild mountain tribes, and to the people who used to listen to the Qur'an secretly. But the statements of the Qur'an, in this regard, are so clear and explicit that these interpretations bear no relevance. The Qur'an frequently mentions the jinns and the men in a manner as to indicate that they are two separate creatures. For example:

Sûrah Al-A'râf: 12, Al Hijr : 26-27 and Ar-Rahmân : 14-19, expressly state that man was created out of clay and jinn out of fire.

Sûrah Al-Hijr: 27, states that the jinn had been created before man. The same thing is testified by the story of Adam and Iblees, which has been cited at seven different places in the Qur'an, and at every place it confirms that Iblees was already there at the time of creation of man.

Sûrah Al-K'ahf: 50, states that Iblees was a jinn. Sûrah Al-A'râf: 27, states in clear words that the jinn see human beings, but human beings do not see them.

Sûrah Al-Hijr: 16-18, Sûrah As-Sâffât: 6-10 and Sûrah Al-Mulk: 5, state that the jinn can ascend to the heavens but they cannot exceed a certain limit; if they try to ascend beyond that limit and try to hear what is going on in the heavens, they will not be allowed to do so. If they try to eavesdrop they will be driven away by meteorites. By this, the belief of the polytheistic Arabs that the jinn possess knowledge of the unseen, or have access to Divine secrets, has been refuted.

Sûrah Sabâ: 14, affirms the same facts.

Sûrahs Al-Baqarah: 30-34 and Al-K'ahf: 50, state that Allah has entrusted man with the vicegerency of the earth and that mankind is superior to the jinn. Although the jinn also have been given certain extraordinary powers and abilities, an example of which is found in Sûrah An-Naml: 39, the animals likewise have been given some powers greater than man, but these provide no argument that the animals are superior to man.

The Qur'an also explains that the jinns, like men, are a creation and are given the power and authority to choose between right and wrong, obedience and disobedience, belief and disbelief. This fact has been confirmed by the Qur'an in the story of Adam, where Iblees (Satan) refused to obey Allah's order to bow down to Adam. A similar event where jinn affirmed Faith, is stated in Sûrahs Al-Ahqâf and Al-Jinn. At various places in the Qur'an, it has also been stated that Iblees, at the very creation of Adam, had resolved to misguide mankind, and since then, the Satanic jinns have been persistently trying to mislead men, but they do not have the power to overwhelm them or forcibly make them do something. However, they tempt men with evil suggestions, beguile them and make evil fair seeming to them. (Examples of this phenomenon are given in Sûrah An-Nisâ': 117-120, Al-A'râf: 11-17, Ibrâheem: 22, Al-Hijr: 30-42, An-Nahl 98-100, Bani Israel 61-65.) The Qur'an also states that in the pre-Islamic ignorance and the polytheistic Arabs regarded the jinns as associates of God, worshipped them and thought they had descended from God. For reference see Sûrahs Al-An'am: 100, Sabâ : 40-41, As-Sâffât: 158.

From these details, it becomes clear that the jinns have their own existence, are an invisible creature and of an entirely different nature. Because of their mysterious qualities, ignorant people have formed various notions and concepts about them and their powers, and have even worshipped them.

72: AL-JINN

This Sûrah, revealed at Makkah, has 2 sections and 28 verses.

In the name of Allah, the Compassionate, the Merciful

SECTION: 1

O Prophet say: "It has been revealed to me that a band of Jinns listened *to the Qur'an, then returned to their folk* and said: 'We have heard a wonderful Qur'an, [1] which guides to the Right Way. We have believed in it and *henceforth* we shall worship none besides Our Rabb.[2] Surely, our Rabb's Majesty is exalted: He has neither taken a wife nor a son.[3] Our foolish liar (Iblees) has been uttering atrocious lies about Allah,[4] and we had presumed that no man or jinn could tell a lie concerning Allah.[5] Indeed, some individuals among mankind used to seek protection with some individuals among the Jinns, so they caused them to become more arrogant,[6] *as a result,* they presumed as you presumed that Allah would not send anyone *as a Rasool*.[7] We searched the heaven, and found it filled with stern guards and shooting stars.[8] *Before this,* we used to find a seat in heaven for eavesdropping, but now eavesdroppers find shooting stars lying in ambush for them.[9] We did not know whether an evil was intended for the dwellers of the earth or whether their Rabb intended to guide them.[10] There are some among us who are righteous and some to the contrary; we have sects following different ways.[11] We know that we can neither frustrate Allah in the earth nor frustrate Him by flight.[12] As for us, when we listened to the guidance, we believed in it; so he that believes in his Rabb shall have neither the fear of loss nor of injustice.[13] Surely, there are some among us who are Muslims and some who are deviators from the truth. Those who have adopted Islam have found the Right Way *to salvation*,[14] and those who have deviated *from the truth* will become the fuel for hell."[15]
72:[1-15]

O Prophet, say: "If they steadfastly follow the Right Way, We will certainly vouchsafe them abundant water,[16] and thereby put them to test. He that gives no heed to the Reminder of his Rabb *(the Qur'an)*, shall be made to undergo severe punishment.[17] Mosques are built for Allah's worship; therefore, invoke not anyone along with Allah.[18] And that when Allah's servant *Muhammad* stood up to invoke Him, they made around him a dense crowd."[19]
72:[16-19]

A beautiful speech of the jinns who embraced Islam after hearing The Qur'an

Jinns also have different religions and sects, there are some Muslims and some deviators from the truth

Mosques are built for the worship of Allah, so invoke no one else besides Him

SECTION: 2

Rasools do not have the power to harm or benefit anyone, their mission is just to convey Allah's message

O Prophet, say: "I pray only to my Rabb and associate none as a partner with Him."[20]   Say: "I have no power to cause you harm or bring you to the Right Way."[21]   Say: "If I were *to disobey Him,* no one can protect me from Allah, nor can I find any refuge besides Him.[22]   *My mission is* only to deliver what I receive from Allah and make His messages known. *As for those* who disobey Allah and His Rasool, they shall be put in the fire of hell to live therein forever."[23]   When they shall see *the punishment* that they are being threatened with, then they shall find out whose helpers are weak and whose *supporters* are fewer in number.[24] Say: "I do not know whether *the punishment* that you are threatened with is near or whether my Rabb has set for it a distant term.[25]   He *Alone* knows the unseen. He does not reveal His secrets to anyone[26]   except to the Rasool whom He may choose *for that purpose*, and then He appoints guards, who march before him and behind him,[27]   *so* that He may know that they *(the Rasools)* have indeed delivered the messages of their Rabb. He comprehends whatever is with them and keeps a count of each and everything."[28]   72:[20-28]

Only Allah knows the unseen, He reveals it to whom He chooses from the Rasools

73: AL-MUZZAMMIL

Period of Revelation

The two sections of this Sûrah were revealed in two separate periods.

The first section (vv. 1-19) is unanimously a Makki Revelation. This is supported both by its subject matter and by the traditions. This section was revealed at a time when the Prophet (peace be upon him) had openly started preaching Islam and the opposition to him at Makkah had grown active and strong.

About the second section, (v. 20) although many commentators have expressed the opinion that this too was revealed at Makkah, some other commentators regard it as a Madani Revelation. This same opinion is confirmed by the subject matter of this section. It mentions fighting in the way of Allah and, obviously, there was no fighting at Makkah. It also contains the command to pay the obligatory Zakah, and it is confirmed that paying Zakah at a specific rate and with an exemption limit (Nisâb) was enjoined at Madinah.

Major Issues, Divine Laws and Guidance:

* Allah ordered the Prophet not to stand in prayer the whole night.
* Those who oppose the Prophet will be treated with heavy fetters and blazing fire.
* The Qur'an is a reminder for those who want to find the Right Way.
* Read from the Qur'an as much as you easily can.
* Whatever you spend in the way of Allah, you will find it in the Hereafter.

In the first seven verses, the Prophet (peace be upon him) has been commanded: "Prepare yourself to shoulder the responsibilities of the great Mission that has been entrusted to you; its practical form is that you should rise during the hours of night and stand up in Prayer for half the night, or for a little more or less of it. Devote yourself exclusively to Allah Who is the Owner of the whole universe and entrust all your affairs to Him with full satisfaction of the heart. Bear with patience whatever your opponents may utter against you. Do not be intimate with them. Leave their affair to Allah: He Himself will deal with them." The people of Makkah are warned: "We have sent a Messenger to you, as We had sent a Messenger to the Pharaoh. Just consider what fate Pharaoh met when he did not accept the invitation of the Messenger of Allah. Even if you are not punished by a torment in this world, how will you save yourselves from the punishment on the Day of Judgment?"

The second section, according to a tradition from Sayyidunâ Sa'eed bin Jubair, was revealed ten years later, and in it, the initial command given in connection with the Tahajjud (late night prayer), in the beginning of the first section, was curtailed. The new Command enjoined, "Offer as much of the Tahajjud Prayer as you easily can, but what the Muslims should particularly mind and attend to, are the five times obligatory prayers a day; they should establish it regularly and punctually; they should pay their Zakah dues accurately; and they should spend their wealth with sincere intentions for the sake of Allah.

In conclusion, the Muslims are exhorted: "Whatever good works you do in this world will not go waste, they are like the provisions which a traveller sends in advance to his permanent place of residence. Whatever good you send forth from this world, you will find it with Allah. The provisions thus sent forth will not only be much better than what you will have to leave behind in this world, but Allah will also give you an extra and richer reward from His Own bounty."

73: AL-MUZZAMMIL

This Sûrah, revealed at Makkah, has 2 sections and 20 verses.

In the name of Allah, the Compassionate, the Merciful

SECTION: 1

O Muzzammil *(folded in garments - one of the nick names of the Prophet Muhammad)*![1]   Stand in prayers at night, but not the whole night,[2]   half of it or a little less,[3]   or a little more; and recite the Qur'an with measured tone.[4]   Soon We are going to send you a weighty message.[5]   Surely, the getting up at night for prayer is most effective for controlling the self and most suitable for understanding the Word of Allah *(the Qur'an)* as well;[6]   because, during the day you are hard pressed with manifold engagements.[7] Remember the name of your Rabb and devote yourself to Him exclusively.[8]   He is the Rabb of the east and the west: there is none worthy of worship but He; therefore, take Him Alone as your Protector.[9]   Bear patiently with what they say and leave their company in a polite manner.[10]   Let me deal with rejecters who are enjoying the comforts of this life, so put up with them for a while.[11] We have in store for them heavy fetters and a blazing fire,[12] choking food and a painful punishment.[13]   On the day when the earth with all its mountains will be in a violent commotion, and the mountains will crumble into heaps of shifting sand.[14]   *O mankind,* We have sent towards you a Rasool, to bear witness *for you or against you*, as We had sent a Rasool towards Fir'aun *(Pharaoh)*.[15] Fir'aun disobeyed Our Rasool; so We seized him with a firm grip.[16]   If you persist in unbelief, how will you save yourselves on that Day which shall turn the children grey-haired *(old)*;[17]   the heaven shall split asunder *because of the dreadfulness of that Day*; and His promise shall be fulfilled?[18]   Surely, this is but a reminder, so let him who wills, take the Right way to His Rabb.[19]

3:[1-19]

SECTION: 2

Surely, your Rabb knows that you stand *in prayers* nearly two thirds of the night, and sometimes one half or one third of it, as do others among your companions. Allah has the measures of the night and the day. He knows that you will not be able to keep it up *(to pray the whole night)*, so He has turned to you *in mercy;* therefore, read from the Qur'an as much as you easily can. He

Allah ordered the Prophet not to stand in prayer the whole night

Those who oppose the Prophet will be treated with heavy fetters and blazing fire

The Qur'an is a reminder for those who seek to find the Right Way

Read from the Qur'an as much as you easily can

Whatever you spend in the way of Allah, you will find it in the Hereafter

knows that there may be some sick people among you, and some others who travel through the land to seek Allah's bounty; and yet, some others fighting for the cause of Allah. Therefore, read as much *of the Qur'an* as you easily can. Establish the Salah *(five time daily prayers)* and pay the Zakah *(obligatory charity)*, and give to Allah, a goodly loan. Whatever good you will send before you for yourselves, you will find it with Allah much better and greater in reward. Seek Allah's forgiveness, surely, Allah is Oft-Forgiving, Most Merciful.[20]   73:[20]

74: AL-MUDDATHTHIR

Period of Revelation

The first seven verses of this Sûrah were revealed during the early period at Makkah. The rest of the Sûrah (vv. 8-56) was revealed on the occasion of the first Hajj, after the Prophet started preaching Islam openly.

Major Issues, Divine Laws and Guidance:

*   Instructions to the Prophet for cleanliness and patience.
*   The Day of Judgement will be very difficult, especially for those who deny Allah's revelations and oppose His cause.
*   Actions which lead to the hellfire are: Not offering Salah, not feeding the poor, wasting time in vain talk and denying the Day of Judgement.

The earliest revelation to the Prophet (peace be upon him) was the first five verses of Sûrah Al-'Alaq, in which it was said: "Read! In the name of your Rabb, Who created, created man from a leechlike mass. Read; and your Rabb is Most Gracious, Who taught by the pen, taught man what he knew not."

This was his first experience of revelations, therefore, in this Message it was not told what great mission he was being entrusted with and what duties he had to perform in the future. He was only acquainted with it and then left alone for a while in order to absorb the great strain this experience had caused him and allowing him to become mentally prepared for receiving the revelations and performing the Prophetic mission in the future. After this intermission, when the revelation was resumed, the first seven verses of Sûrah Al-Muddaththir were revealed. In these verses, he was commanded to arise and warn the people about the consequences of the way of life that they were following and to proclaim the greatness of Allah in a place where others were being magnified without any justification. He was given this instruction: "The demand of the unique mission that you are to perform is, that your life should be pure in every respect and you should carry out the duty of reforming your people sincerely." Then, in the last sentence, he is exhorted to endure with patience, for the sake of his Rabb, all the hardships and troubles that he might have to face while performing his mission.

In the implementation of this Divine Command, when the Prophet began to preach Islam and recite the Qur'anic Sûrahs revealed, the people of Makkah felt alarmed, and it created a great storm of opposition and hostility. A few months passed in this state until the Hajj season approached. The people of Makkah feared *that if Muhammad (peace be upon him) started visiting the caravans of the pilgrims coming from all over Arabia at their resting places reciting the spell binding and unique verses of the Qur'an to their assemblies, his message would eventually reach every part of Arabia and influence countless people. Therefore, the Quraish chiefs held a conference and decided that they would start a propaganda campaign against the Prophet (peace be upon him) among the pilgrims as soon as they arrive. After they had agreed on this, Waleed bin Al-Mugheerah said to the assembled people: "If you say contradictory things about Muhammad, we all would lose our trust among the people. Therefore, let us agree upon one opinion, which we should all say without dispute. They all requested Waleed to come up with some statement and he said: "Let me think it over for awhile." Then, after prolonged thought and consideration, he said: "The nearest thing to the truth is that you tell the Arabs that he is a sorcerer, who has brought a message by which he separates a man from his father, and from his brother, and from his wife and children, and from his family." They all agreed on what Waleed had proposed. Then, in accordance to the scheme, the men of Quraish spread out among the pilgrims of Hajj and warned everyone that they should avoid the sorcery of Muhammad through which he stirs up division among the families." But the plan, which the Quraish chiefs carried out, yielded results contrary to what they had expected and actually favored the Prophet and his name became known throughout Arabia.*

(Ibn Hisham, pp. 288-289)

In conclusion, this Sûrah clearly states: "Allah does not stand in need of anybody's faith. The Qur'an is an admonition that has been presented before the people openly; now whoever wants, may accept it. Allah has the right that the people should fear Him and He Alone has the power to forgive the one who adopts piety and Allah consciousness, even though one may have committed many acts of disobedience in the past."

74: AL-MUDDATHTHIR

This Sûrah, revealed at Makkah, has 2 sections and 56 verses.

In the name of Allah, the Compassionate, the Merciful

SECTION: 1

O Muddaththir *(the one enveloped - one of the nicknames of the Prophet Muhammad, peace be upon him)*![1] Stand up and warn.[2] Proclaim the greatness of your Rabb,[3] purify your clothes,[4] keep yourself away from abomination *(idolatry)*,[5] do not favor others to expect a gain,[6] and be patient for the sake of your Rabb.[7]

74:[1-7]

When the Trumpet will be sounded,[8] that Day will be a very difficult Day,[9] not easy for the disbelievers.[10] Leave Me and the one *(Waleed bin Mugheerah, a staunch opponent of the Prophet)* whom I created, alone.[11] I gave him abundant wealth,[12] many children to be by his side,[13] and made his life smooth and comfortable.[14] Yet, he hopes that I give him more.[15] By no means! Because he has stubbornly denied Our revelations.[16] Soon I shall make him suffer mounting calamities,[17] surely, he pondered and devised a plot.[18] May he perish, how he plotted![19] Again, may he perish, how he plotted![20] He looked around,[21] frowned and scowled,[22] then he turned his back in *scornful pride*[23] and said: "This is nothing but a magic from that of old,[24] this is nothing but the word of a human being."[25] Soon, I shall cast him into Saqar.[26] What will make you understand, what Saqar is?[27] It *is burning fire which* leaves nothing and spares none.[28] It shrivels human flesh.[29] It is guarded by nineteen guards.[30] We have appointed none but angels as wardens of the fire; and We have made their number a trial for the unbelievers, so that the People of the Book may be convinced and the faith of the true believers may be increased, and that no doubts will be left for the People of the Book and the believers, and that those in whose hearts there is a disease and the disbelievers may say: "What could Allah mean by this parable?" Thus, Allah leaves to stray whom He wills and guides whom He pleases. No one knows the forces of your Rabb except He, and this *(hell)* had been mentioned as a reminder so that the people may take heed.[31]

74:[8-31]

Instructions to the Prophet for cleanliness and patience

The Day of Judgment will be very difficult, especially for those who deny Allah's revelations and oppose His cause

SECTION: 2

Actions which lead to hellfire are: Not offering Salah, not feeding the poor, wasting time in vain talk and denying the Day of Judgment

Nay! By the moon,[32] by the departing night[33] and by the coming of dawn,[34] surely, this *Hellfire* is one of mighty scourge,[35] a warning to mankind;[36] to any of you who chooses to go forward or to lag behind.[37] Every soul is held in pledge for its deeds,[38] except the people of the right hand,[39] who shall be in paradise, asking[40] the culprits:[41] "What brought you into hell?"[42] They will answer: "We did not use to offer the Salah *(prayers)*,[43] nor did we use to feed the poor;[44] but we used to join those who wasted their time in vain talk,[45] and we used to deny the Day of Judgment,[46] until death overtook us."[47] *On that Day,* no intercession of any intercessors shall profit them.[48] Then what is the matter with them that they turn away from this admonition?[49] Like frightened donkeys[50] fleeing from a lion.[51] Nay, each of them wants a scripture of his own to be unrolled before him.[52] By no means! The fact is that they do not fear the Hereafter.[53] Nay! Surely, this *Qur'an* is an admonition.[54] Let him who wills, take heed.[55] But none takes heed except by the will of Allah. He *Alone* is worthy to be feared and He *Alone* is worthy of forgiving *those who fear Him*.[56]   74:[32-56]

75: AL-QIYÂMAH

Period of Revelation

There is no tradition to indicate this Sûrah's period of revelation. However the subject matter of this Sûrah indicates that it was revealed during the Makkan period.

Major Issues, Divine Laws and Guidance:

* The Day of Judgement is certain, there is no escape from it.
* Allah Himself took the responsibility of preserving the Qur'an.
* The last moments of disbeliever's death.
* Take Allah's warning about the Day of Judgement seriously.

This Sûrah addresses the deniers of the Hereafter and replies are given to each of their doubts and objections. Strong arguments are given to prove the possibility, occurrence and necessity of the Resurrection and the Hereafter, and it has been pointed out clearly that the actual reason of people's denying the Hereafter is not that they regard it as impossible rationally, but because their selfish motives do not allow them to affirm it.

After verse 15, the discourse is suddenly interrupted and the Prophet (peace be upon him) is told: "Do not move your tongue hastily to memorize this Revelation. It is Our responsibility to have it memorized and read. Therefore, when it is being recited, listen to its recital carefully. Again, it is Our responsibility to explain its meaning." Then, from verse 20, the same theme which was interrupted at verse 15, is resumed. This passage, according to both the context and the traditions, has been interjected here for a reason. That is, when the Angel Gabriel was reciting this Sûrah to the Prophet, the Prophet, lest he should forget its words later, was repeating them at the same moment. This, in fact, happened at the time when the receipt of Revelation was a new experience for him and he was not yet fully used to receiving it calmly. There are two other instances like this in the Qur'an. First, in Sûrah Tâ-Hâ, the Prophet (peace be upon him) was told: "And see that you do not hasten to recite the Qur'an before its revelation is completed to you." (v. 114). Second, in Sûrah Al-A'lâ, it has been said: "We shall enable you to recite, then you shall never forget." (v. 6). When the Prophet became fully used to receiving the Revelation, there remained no need to give him such instruction. That is why, except for these three instances, there are no other instructions like this in the Qur'an.

75: AL-QIYÂMAH

This Sûrah, revealed at Makkah, has 2 sections and 40 verses.

In the name of Allah, the Compassionate, the Merciful

SECTION: 1

Be aware of the Day of Resurrection and Judgment, from which there is no escape

I swear by the Day of Resurrection,[1] and I swear by the self reproaching soul![2] Does man think that We shall not be able to put his bones together?[3] Indeed, We are able to put together, in perfect order, the very tips of his fingers.[4] But man wishes to keep on doing evil in the future as well.[5] He questions: "When will this Day of Resurrection be?"[6] Well, it will come when the sight is dazed,[7] the moon eclipsed,[8] and the sun and the moon joined together[9] - on that Day, man will ask: "Is there any way to escape?"[10] Nay! There will be no refuge.[11] On that Day, the final return will be towards your Rabb.[12] On that Day, man shall be told *about all his deeds*, from the first to the last.[13] Indeed, man shall bear witness against himself,[14] even though he shall plead with excuses.[15]   75:[1-15]

There is no escape from it

O Prophet, do not move your tongue to hasten in *memorizing* this *revelation*,[16] It is Our responsibility to collect it *in your memory*, and make you recite it.[17] Therefore, when We are reciting it *through by Gabriel*, listen to its recital carefully.[18] Again, it is for Us to explain its meaning.[19] - Nay, *the fact is that* you *people* love this fleeting life[20] and are heedless of the Hereafter.[21] On that Day, some faces shall be bright,[22] looking towards their Rabb.[23] And on that Day, some faces shall be gloomy,[24] thinking that some backbreaking calamity is about to be inflicted on them.[25] Nay, when a man's soul is about to leave and reaches to the collar-bone,[26] and *those around him* cry: "Is there any enchanter *to help*?"[27] Then man will conclude that it was the time of departure *from this world*.[28] while one leg will twist around the other leg *(agony will heap on agony)*;[29] that will be the Day of driving towards your Rabb.[30]   75:[16-30]

Allah Himself took the responsibility of The Qur'an

The last moments of disbelievers' death

SECTION: 2

The disbelievers do not believe because they never

But *in this life,* he neither believed, nor offered Salah *(prayed)*;[31] but on the contrary he denied the truth and turned away.[32] Then he went to his family elated with pride.[33] Woe to you, *O man!* Woe to you.[34] Again woe to you, *O man!* Woe to you.[35]   Does man think that he will be left *to wander around* without any purpose?[36]   Was he not once a drop of emitted semen?[37]   Then he became a leechlike mass, then Allah created him and fashioned him in due proportion,[38]   and made him either of the two sexes, male and female.[39]   Has He not then the power to bring the dead to life?[40]   75:[31-40]

took Al-Islam seriously

76: AL-INSÂN / AD-DAHR

Period of Revelation

This Sûrah was revealed at the early stage of Prophet's Makki life which began just after the revelation of the first seven verses of Sûrah Al-Muddaththir.

Major Issues, Divine Laws and Guidance:

* The universe was there before mankind existed, then Allah created man, provided him with guidance and let him use his free will: either to believe or to disbelieve.
* An exemplary life in paradise for those who choose to believe.
* Allah gradually sent this Qur'an according to the issues faced by mankind
* This Qur'an is an admonition for those who want to adopt the way to their Rabb (Allah).

In this Sûrah, man is reminded that there was a time when he was nothing; then, a humble beginning of him was made with a mixed drop of sperm and ovum of which even his mother was not aware; even she did not know that he had been conceived nor anyone else seeing the microscopic cell could say that it was a man, who in the future would become the best of creation on the earth. After this, man has been warned: "Beginning your creation in this way, We have developed and shaped you into what you are today in order to test you in this world. That is why, unlike other creatures, you were made intelligent and sensible, and shown both the way of gratitude and the way of ingratitude. So that you may prove in this test; whether you are a grateful servant or an unbelieving, ungrateful wretch!" Then, just in one sentence, it has been stated decisively what the fate will be in the Here-after for those who emerged as unbelievers from this test.

In the first section, the blessings with which those who do full justice by serving in the world, are mentioned. Not only have their best rewards been mentioned, but they have also been told briefly what are those actions on the basis of which they would become worthy of those rewards. After introducing the funda-mental beliefs of Islam, those moral qualities and virtuous acts which are praise-worthy according to Islam, have been mentioned, and also those evil deeds which Islam strives to cleanse from human life. These two things are not mentioned with a view to show what good or evil result is entailed by them in the transitory life of this world, but they have been mentioned to point out what enduring results they will produce in the eternal and everlasting life of the Hereafter, irrespective of whether an evil quality may prove useful or a good quality may prove harmful during their life in this world.

In the second section, addressing the Prophet (peace be upon him), three things are stated:

1. In fact We are intentionally revealing this Qur'an piecemeal to you. This is intended to inform the disbelievers, not you, that the Qur'an is not being fabricated by Muhammad (peace be upon you), but it is We, Who are revealing it, and it is Our Own wisdom that We are revealing it piece by piece and not all at one time.

2. No matter how long it may take for the decree of your Rabb to be enforced, and no matter what afflictions may befall you in the mean time, in any case, you should continue to perform your mission of Risâlat (conveying the Message) patiently, and not yield to the pressure tactics of any of these wicked and unbelieving people.

3. Remember Allah day and night, perform the Prayer and spend your nights in the worship of Allah, for it is these things which sustain and strengthen those who call to Allah in the face of iniquity and disbelief.

In conclusion, it is said: "the Qur'an is an admonition; whoever wills may accept it and take the path to his Rabb. But man's own will and desire is not everything in this world. No one's will and desire can be fulfilled unless Allah (also) so wills. And Allah's willing is not haphazard; whatever He wills, He wills it on the basis of His knowledge and wisdom. He admits into His mercy whomever He regards as worthy of His mercy on the basis of His knowledge and wisdom, and He has prepared a painful torment for those who are unjust and wicked."

76: AL-INSÂN / AD-DAHR

This Sûrah, revealed at Makkah, has 2 sections and 31 verses.

In the name of Allah, the Compassionate, the Merciful

SECTION: 1

The universe was there before mankind existed, then Allah created man, provided him with guidance and gave him free will; either to believe or to disbelieve

Has there not passed over man, a period of time when he was nothing--not even mentioned?[1] Indeed, We have created man from the mixed sperm drop *containing both sexes*, so that We may test him. *Therefore,* We gave him the faculties of hearing and sight.[2] Then We guided him to the *Right* Way: *Now, it is his choice* either to be grateful or to be a disbeliever.[3] For the disbelievers, We have prepared chains, fetters and a blazing fire.[4] The righteous shall be *in paradise* drinking from a cup *of wine* mixed with Kâfoor *(camphor-water),*[5] from a gushing spring at which the servants of Allah will refresh themselves, and shall be able to take out its channels *at their will.*[6] They are those who keep their vows and dread the Day of widespread terror,[7] who feed the poor, the orphan and the captive for the love *of Allah,*[8] *saying*: "We feed you for the sake of Allah Alone; we seek from you neither reward nor thanks,[9] for we dread our Rabb's torment of a very distressful Day."[10] So Allah will deliver them from the evil of that Day, and bestow on them brightness and joy,[11] and reward them, for their steadfastness with paradise and *garments of* silk.[12]   76:[1-12]

An exemplary life in paradise for those who choose to believe

There they shall be reclining upon high couches; they shall feel neither scorching heat nor bitter cold.[13] *The trees of* paradise will spread their shade upon them, and their fruits will hang in clusters within their easy reach.[14] They shall be served with silver dishes, goblets of crystal,[15] and goblets made of crystal-clear silver, filled *according to their wishes* in due measure.[16] They will also be given to drink a cup *of wine* mixed with Zanjabeel *(ginger-flavored water),*[17] from a fountain, called Salsabeel *(for its fluent palatability).*[18] They shall be attended by boys graced with eternal youth: when you see them, they would seem like scattered pearls.[19] And which ever direction you will look, you will see blessings and the splendor of a great Kingdom.[20] They *(the residents of paradise)* shall be arrayed in the garments of fine green silk and rich brocade, adorned with bracelets of silver, and their Rabb will give them pure wine to drink.[21] *O believers,* that's how you will be rewarded, and your endeavors appreciated.[22]   76:[13-22]

SECTION: 2

Surely, it is We Who have sent down this Qur'an to you through gradual revelations,[23]   therefore, await with patience the command of your Rabb and do not yield to any sinner or disbeliever from among *the unbelievers*.[24]   Glorify the name of your Rabb, morning and evening;[25]   prostrate before Him at night and glorify Him during the long hours of night.[26]   These unbelievers love the transitory life *of this world* and neglect the heavy Day *that is coming ahead*.[27]   It is We Who created them and made their joints strong; but if We please, We can replace them with others like them with a complete replacement.[28]   This is indeed an admonition, so let him who will, adopt the Way to his Rabb,[29]   but you cannot will, except by the will of Allah. Surely, Allah is All-Knowledgeable, All-Wise.[30]   He admits to His mercy whom He wills; as for the wrongdoers, He has prepared a painful punishment.[31]

76:[23-31]

Allah sent this Qur'an gradually according to the issues faced by mankind

This is an admonition for those who want to adopt the way to their Rabb (God)

77: AL-MURSALÂT

Period of Revelation

This Sûrah was revealed in the early period during the Prophet's residence at Makkah. If this Sûrah is read together with the two Sûrahs preceding it, namely Al-Qiyâmah and Ad-Dahr, and the two Sûrahs following it, namely An-Nabâ and An-Nazi'ât, it becomes clear that all these Sûrahs are the revelations of the same period, and they deal with one and the same theme, which has been impressed on the people of Makkah in different ways.

Major Issues, Divine Laws and Guidance:

* Allah swears in the name of life giving winds, rain and angels that the Day of Judgement will be established.
* On that Day, the disbelievers will be asked to walk towards hell which they used to deny, and the righteous will be given all that they desire.
* A warning to the disbelievers, and a question as to what statement after this Qur'an (the last revelation) will they believe?

The theme of this Sûrah is to affirm the Resurrection and Hereafter and to warn the people of the consequences which will ultimately follow either the denial or the affirmation of these truths.

In the first seven verses, the system of winds is presented as an evidence of the truth that the Resurrection which is being foretold by the Qur'an and the Prophet Muhammad (peace be upon him) must come to pass. The power of All-Mighty Allah Who has established this wonderful system on the earth, is not helpless in bringing about the Resurrection. The express wisdom which underlies this system bears evidence that the life Hereafter and Day of Judgment must take place, for no act of an All-Wise Creator is vain and purposeless, and if there was no life Hereafter, it would mean that this life is useless and purposeless.

In vv. 16-28 arguments are given for the occurrence and necessity of the Resurrection and the life Hereafter. Man's own history, his own birth, and the structure of the earth on which he lives, bear the testimony that the coming of the Resurrection and the establishment of the Hereafter are possible as well as the demand of Allah Almighty's wisdom. History tells us that the nations which denied the Hereafter, ultimately became corrupted and met with destruction. This means that the Hereafter is a truth which, if denied and contradicted by a nation through its conduct and attitude, will cause it to meet the same fate as that of a blind man who rushes headlong towards an approaching train. It also means that in the Kingdom of the universe, not only physical laws are at work, but also moral laws, under which the process of retribution is operating. But, since in the present life of the world, retribution is not taking place in its complete form, the moral law of the universe necessarily demands that there should come a time when it should take its full course, and all those good works and evil deeds, which could not be rewarded here, or which escaped their due punishment, should be fully rewarded and punished. For this purpose, it is inevitable that there should be a second life after death. If man only considers how he takes his birth in this world, his intellect, provided it is sound intellect, cannot deny that Allah, Who began his creation from an insignificant sperm drop and developed him into a perfect human being, is able to create the same human being once again.

In conclusion, the deniers of the Hereafter and those who turn away from Allah's worship, are warned: "Enjoy your short-lived worldly pleasure as you may, but your end will ultimately be disastrous." The discourse ends with the assertion that the one who fails to obtain guidance from the Qur'an, can have no other source of Guidance.

77: AL-MURSALÂT

This Sûrah, revealed at Makkah, has 2 sections and 50 verses.

In the name of Allah, the Compassionate, the Merciful

SECTION: 1

By the emissary *winds*, *which are* sent forth one after another.[1] By the raging hurricanes.[2] By *the winds* that lift up and scatter *the clouds* to their distant places,[3] then separate them one from another.[4] By those who bring down the reminder,[5] either to remove the excuse or to convey the warning.[6] Surely, that which you are being promised, shall be fulfilled.[7] *It is going to be fulfilled* when the stars will lose their light,[8] heaven will cleft asunder,[9] the mountains will crumble into dust,[10] and when the Rasools will be brought together at the appointed time.[11] For what Day has all this been deferred?[12] For the Day of Judgment![13] And how would you know, what the Day of Judgment is?[14] Woe on that Day to the disbelievers![15] Did We not destroy the former generations *for their evil deeds?*[16] And *We shall do the same* to later generations who will follow them.[17] Thus do We deal with the guilty.[18] Woe on that Day to the disbelievers![19] Have We not created you from an unworthy fluid,[20] which We placed in a secure resting-place *(womb)*,[21] for an appointed term?[22] We have determined its term - and We are the best to determine.[23] Woe on that Day to the disbelievers![24] Have We not made the earth a home for both[25] the living and the dead,[26] set on it lofty mountains, and given you sweet water to drink?[27] Woe on that Day to the disbelievers![28]   77:[1-28]

On the Day of Judgment it will be said to the disbelievers: "Walk towards *hell* which you used to deny![29] Walk towards the shadow *of smoke* ascending in three columns,[30] giving neither coolness nor shelter from the flames,[31] throwing up sparks as huge as castles,[32] as if they were yellowish *black* camels."[33] Woe on that Day to the disbelievers![34] On that Day, they shall not be able to speak,[35] nor be given permission to offer their excuses.[36] Woe on that Day to the disbelievers![37] Such will be the Day of Judgment. We shall assemble you and your former generations.[38] Now if you have a plot, use it against Me.[39] Woe on that Day to the disbelievers![40]   77:[29-40]

Sidebar notes:

Allah swears in the name of life-giving winds, rain and angels that the Day of Judgment will be established

Woe on that Day to the disbelievers!

On that Day; the disbelievers will be asked to walk towards hell which they used to deny

SECTION: 2

Surely, the righteous shall dwell amidst cool shades and springs[41] and shall have whatever fruits they desire.[42] *We shall say to them:* "Eat and drink to your heart's content, this is the reward for your good deeds."[43] Thus, shall We reward the righteous.[44] Woe on that Day to the disbelievers![45]

77:[41-45]

The righteous will be given all that they desire

Eat and enjoy yourselves for a little while. Surely, you are criminals.[46] Woe on that Day to the disbelievers![47] When they are asked to bow down *before Allah*, they do not bow down.[48] Woe on that Day to the disbelievers![49] In what statement after this *Qur'an*, will they believe?[50]

77:[46-50]

A warning to the disbelievers

JUZ (PART): 30

78. AN-NABÂ'

Period of Revelation

This Sûrah was revealed during the early period of the Prophet's residence at Makkah.

Major Issues, Divine Laws and Guidance:

* Creation of the heavens , earth, mountains and vegetation clearly points out towards the Day of Judgement.
* Resurrection and man's accountability in the court of Allah.
* The righteous will be well pleased, while the disbelievers will be put in hell, where they will be treated with scalding water and decaying filth.

The theme of this Sûrah is to affirm the resurrection and hereafter, and to warn the people of the consequences of disbelieving it. When the Prophet (peace be upon him) first started to preach Islam at Makkah, his message consisted of three elements:

1. Do not associate any one with Allah in His Godhead;

2. Allah has appointed him as His Rasool (Messenger);

3. This world will come to an end one day and then another world will be established. All the former and the latter generations will be resurrected with the same bodies in which they lived and worked in this world. They will be called to account for their beliefs and deeds, and those who emerge as believing and righteous in this accountability will go to paradise and those who are proved to be disbelieving and wicked will live in hell for ever.

Of these, the first elements was highly unpleasant for the people of Makkah, they were not disbelievers in the existence of Allah. They believed in His Being, the Supreme Sustainer, Creator and Providence and also admitted that all those beings whom they regarded as their deities, were themselves Allah's creatures. Therefore, in this regard the only thing they disputed was whether the deities had any share in the attributes and powers of Divinity and in the Divine Being itself or not.

As for the second element, the people of Makkah were not prepared to accept it. However, they could not deny that during the 40-year of life, that the Prophet (peace be upon him) had lived amongst them before his claim to be a Prophet, they had never found him lying or deceitful or one who would adopt unlawful methods for selfish ends.

As for the third element, resurrection, they mocked it the most and expressed unusual wonder at it. They regarded it as remote from reason and impossible. They talked about it as incredible, even inconceivable, in their assemblies. Therefore, reference is made to the common talk and the doubts that were being expressed in the streets of Makkah and in every assembly of the people on hearing the news about Resurrection. Then, the deniers have been asked: "Don't you see this earth which We have spread as a carpet for you? Don't you see the high mountains which We have so firmly placed in the earth? Don't you consider your own selves, how We have created you as pairs of men and women? Don't you consider your sleep by which We make you seek a few hours rest after a few hours of labor and toil so as to keep you fit for work in this world? Don't you see the alternation of the night and the day which We are so regularly perpetuating precisely according to your needs and requirements? Don't you see the strongly fortified system of the heavens above you? Don't you see the sun by means of which you are receiving your light and heat? Don't you see the rain which fall from the clouds and help produce vegetables and gardens? Do these things tell you that the power of the Almighty Allah Who has created them, will be unable to bring about Resurrection and establish the Day of Judgment? Then, from the supreme wisdom which is clearly working in this world around you, do you only understand that even though each of these functions is for a purpose, life is yet meaningless? Nothing could be more absurd and meaningless than to say that, man, after being granted vast powers of appropriation in this world, would not be held accountable for his actions. He should neither be rewarded for satisfactory work, nor punished for unsatisfactory performance.

In conclusion, the Divine Court in the Hereafter has been depicted, making it clear that there will be no question about somebody's getting his followers and associates forgiven. None will speak without leave, and leave for intercession will be given only for those who had acknowledged the Truth in this world; rebels of Allah and rejectors of the Truth will deserve no intercession at all.

JUZ (PART): 30

78: AN-NABA'

This Sûrah, revealed at Makkah, has 2 sections and 40 verses.

In the name of Allah, the Compassionate, the Merciful

SECTION: 1

The creation of heavens, earth, mountains and vegetation clearly points towards the Day of Judgment

About what are they asking?[1]   About the mighty news [2] - about which they are in disagreement.[3]   Very soon they shall come to know;[4]   We repeat, very soon they shall come to know.[5]   Is it not true that We have spread the earth like a bed,[6]   and the mountains as pegs,[7]   created you in pairs,[8]   provided you rest in sleep,[9]   made the night a mantle,[10]   made the day to work for earning your livelihood,[11]   built above you seven firmaments,[12]   placed therein a shining lamp,[13]   sent down abundant water from the clouds,[14]   bringing forth grain, vegetation[15]   and gardens of thick growth?[16]   The Day of Judgement is already fixed.[17]   On that Day, the Trumpet shall be sounded and you shall come forth in multitude.[18]   The sky shall be opened, and it will become gateways.[19]   The mountains shall vanish, as if they were a mirage.[20]   For sure, hell is place of ambush,[21]   a home for the transgressors.[22]   There, they shall live for ages,[23]   and there, they shall taste neither refreshment nor drink,[24]   except scalding water and decaying filth:[25]   a fitting recompense *for their deeds*.[26]   For they never expected to be accountable,[27]   and wittingly rejected Our revelations.[28]   But We had recorded everything in a Book.[29] *It will be said:* "Taste *the fruits of your deeds!* You shall have nothing but increase in punishment."[30]   78:[1-30]

Resurrection and man's accountability in the court of Allah

SECTION: 2

The righteous will be well pleased and disbelievers will wish that they could remain merely dust

On that Day, the righteous will certainly achieve *their Heart's desires:*[31] beautiful gardens, vineyards;[32] and maidens of the same age,[33] and a full cup;[34] they shall hear there no vanity nor any falsehood:[35] - a recompense and a generous gift from your Rabb,[36] the Rabb of the heavens, the earth and all that lies between them, the Compassionate, before Whom no one shall be able to speak.[37] On that Day, the Spirit *(Gabriel)* and the angels shall stand in their ranks; none shall speak except the one to whom the Compassionate *(Allah)* shall grant permission to speak, and he will speak straight to the point.[38]   That Day is a sure reality. Let him who desires, seek a way back to his Rabb.[39]   Indeed, We have forewarned you of an *imminent* punishment which lies close-at-hand, on the Day when man shall see what his hands have sent forth and the unbeliever will cry: "Woe to me! Would that I were *merely* dust."[40]   78:[31-40]

79: AN-NAZI'ÂT

Period of Revelation

This Sûrah was revealed after Sûrah An-Nabâ. It was revealed during the early period of the Prophet's residence at Makkah.

Major Issues, Divine Laws and Guidance

* Death, the Day of Resurrection and life after death.
* The story of the Prophet Musa (peace be upon him) when he called Fir'aun (Pharaoh) towards his Rabb, he denied Allah and was subsequently punished.
* The creation of man is not harder than the creation of the heavens, earth and its contents.
* Punishment and reward on the Day of Judgement.

The theme of this Sûrah is resurrection, life after death and a warning about the consequences of rejecting the Prophet of Allah. The Sûrah opens with oaths by the angels who take the soul at death, who hasten to carry out Allah's Commands and those who conduct the affairs of the universe according to the Divine Will, in order to assure that the Resurrection will certainly come to pass and the life after death will certainly take place.

Then, briefly relating the story of Prophet Musa (Moses) and Fir'aun (Pharaoh), the fate that Fir'aun met in consequence of denying the Rasool and rejecting the guidance brought by him. The people of Makkah are warned that if they do not learn a lesson from this story and change their ways and attitude accordingly, they may also meet the same fate.

Arguments are then given in support of the Hereafter and the life after death. Attention is drawn to the earth and provisions that have been arranged in it for the sustenance of various creatures. It is further clarified that everything testifies to the fact that it has been created with great wisdom by Allah in fulfillment of some special purpose. After pointing out this, the question has been left to the intellect of man to ponder and to form an opinion of whether calling man to account for his sins after delegating authority and responsibility, would be in keeping with the demands of a wise system, or should man's life end without accountability after committing all sorts of misdeeds in the world? Should he perish and mix in the dust forever and never be called to account for the responsibility and the authority entrusted to him?

79: AN-NAZI‘ÂT

This Sûrah revealed at Makkah, has 2 sections and 46 verses.

In the name of Allah, the Compassionate, the Merciful

SECTION: 1

By those *angels* who violently pull out *the souls of the wrongdoers*.[1]   By those who gently draw out *the souls of the righteous*.[2]   By those who glide about swiftly *through space*,[3] and race each other in a race *to carry out the commands of Allah*,[4] and those who regulate the affairs of the world *by Allah's command*![5]   The Day on which the quake shall cause a violent commotion,[6]   which will be followed by another *violent commotion*.[7]   On that Day, some hearts shall be pounding with terror[8] and their sights shall be downcast.[9]   The *unbelievers* say: "Shall we really be restored to our former state *(life)*,[10]   when we shall have become decayed bones?"[11]   They *further* say: "It would then be a fruitless restoration!"[12]   *They should know that* it shall be only a single shout,[13]   and they will be *back to life* in open plain.[14]
79:[1-14]

Death, Day of Resurrection and Life after death

Have you heard the story of Musa *(Moses)*?[15]   When his Rabb called him in the sacred valley of Tuwâ,[16]   and said: "Go to Fir‘aun *(Pharaoh)* for he has indeed transgressed all bounds,[17] and tell him, `Have you the desire to purify yourself?[18]   *If so*, I shall guide you towards your Rabb, so that you may fear Him.'"[19]   Then *Musa* showed *Fir‘aun* the mighty sign,[20]   but he denied and disobeyed.[21]   Then he quickly turned back,[22]   assembled his people and made a proclamation;[23]   "I am your lord, the most high."[24]   Consequently, Allah seized him for punishment, both in the Hereafter and in this life.[25]   Surely, in this, there is a lesson for those who fear *Allah*.[26]
79:[15-26]

The story of Musa when he called Fir'aun to his Rabb, he denied Allah and was seized for punishment

SECTION: 2

O mankind, is your creation harder than the heaven that He built?[27]   He raised its canopy and fashioned it to perfection,[28]   He gave darkness to the night and brightness to the day.[29]   After that, He spread out the earth,[30]   then from it, He brought forth its water and its pasture,[31]   set its mountains,[32]   and made them a provision for you and your cattle.[33]
79:[27-33]

The creation of man is no harder than the creation of heavens, earth and its contents

Punishment and reward on the Day of Judgment

When the great disaster will strike,[34] the Day when man will call to mind all that he had striven for.[35] When hell shall be placed in full view of all;[36] then he who had rebelled[37] and preferred the life of this world[38] shall have his abode in hell.[39] But he who had feared standing before his Rabb and curbed his evil desires[40] shall have his home in paradise.[41] They ask you about the Hour: "When will it come?"[42] But it is not for you to know or tell its timing.[43] Only your Rabb knows when it will come.[44] You are but a Warner to him who fears it.[45] On that Day, when they shall see it, they shall feel as if they had stayed *in this world* only one evening or one morning.[46]   79:[34-46]

80: 'ABASA

Period of Revelation

The commentators and traditionalists are unanimous in pointing out that the revelation of this Sûrah was during the early stages of the Prophet's residence at Makkah.

Major Issues, Divine Laws and Guidance

* The commandment that the seekers of guidance should be given preference in conveying Allah's message
* Man is reminded to recognize his Creator.
* On the Day of Judgement, man will be so concerned about himself that he will not even care about his own mother, father, brother or children.

Upon reading the opening words of this Sûrah, one feels, that in this Sûrah Allah has expressed His displeasure against the Prophet (peace be upon him) for his treating the blind man with indifference and attending to the big chiefs exclusively. But in reading the whole Sûrah objectively, one finds that the displeasure, in fact, is expressed against the disbelieving Quraish, who, because of their arrogant attitude and indifference, were rejecting the message of truth with contempt.

The error in the method that the Prophet (peace be upon him) adopted at the start of his mission is pointed out. His treating of the blind man with neglect and disregard, and consequently devoting all his attention to the Quraish chiefs, was not because he regarded the rich as noble and a poor blind man as contemptible. Naturally, when a caller to the Truth embarks on the mission of conveying his message to people, he wants the most influential people of the society to accept the message so that his task may become easier. Almost the same attitude the Prophet (upon whom be peace) had adopted in the beginning, an attitude of sincerity and a desire to promote his mission, and not out of respect for the rich people and hatred for the poor. But Allah made him realize the correct method of extending invitation of Islam from his mission's point of view: every man, who was a seeker of the truth, was important, even if he was weak or poor, and every man, who was heedless to the truth, was unimportant, even if he occupied a high position in society.

80: 'ABASA

This Sûrah revealed at Makkah, has 1 section and 42 verses.

In the name of Allah, the Compassionate, the Merciful

The seekers of guidance should be given preference in conveying Allah's message

He *(the Prophet)* frowned and turned away[1] when there came to him the blind man *(Ibn Umme Maktûm, who came to the Prophet and interrupted his conversation with the chiefs of Makkah).*[2] How could you *(O Muhammad)* tell? He might have sought to purify himself[3] or become reminded and might have benefited from Our reminder.[4] As for him who thinks himself without need,[5] to whom you are giving all your attention.[6] You will not be held responsible, if he would not purify himself.[7] Yet, to him who came to you with zeal *on his own*[8] and with fear *of Allah in his heart,*[9] you gave no heed.[10] Nay! *It should not be so.* Surely, this is but an admonition;[11] let him who wants, pay attention to it.[12] It is written in scrolls, which are honored,[13] exalted, purified,[14] *and which remain* in the hands of scribes,[15] who are noble and virtuous.[16]   80:[1-16]

Recognize your Creator and fulfill your obligations

Woe to *disbelieving* man! How ungrateful he is![17] Out of what *Allah* has created him?[18] Out of a semen-drop! *Allah* created him and then fashioned him in due proportion,[19] then makes the way easy for him,[20] then causes him to die and stows him in a grave.[21] Then He will surely bring him back to life when He pleases.[22] By no means has he fulfilled the duty that *Allah* had assigned him.[23] Let man reflect on the food he eats.[24] We pour down rainwater in abundance[25] and cleave the soil asunder.[26] We bring forth grain,[27] grapes and vegetables;[28] olives and dates,[29] lush gardens,[30] fruits and herbage,[31] as a means of sustenance for you and your cattle.[32]   80:[17-32]

On the Day of Judgment, no one shall care about his own mother, father, brother or children

Finally when there will come the deafening blast,[33] on that Day each man shall flee from his own brother,[34] his mother and his father,[35] his wife and his children.[36] For each one of them, on that Day, shall have enough concern *of his own* to make him indifferent to the others.[37] Some faces on that Day shall be shining,[38] smiling and joyful.[39] And some faces on that Day shall be dusty[40] and veiled with darkness.[41] These shall be *the faces of* the disbelieving wicked.[42]   80:[33-42]

81: AT-TAKWEER

Period of Revelation

This Sûrah is one of the early Sûrahs revealed at Makkah.

Major Issues, Divine Laws and Guidance

* A scene from the scenes of the Doomsday.
* The Qur'an is conveyed to the Prophet through angel Gabriel.
* This message of the Qur'an is for all the people of the world.

This Sûrah has two themes:
1. The Hereafter and
2. The Institution of Risâlat (Prophethood).

The first six verses mention the first stage of the Doomsday, when the sun will lose its light, the stars will scatter, the mountains will be uprooted and dispersed, the people will become heedless of their dearest possessions, the beasts of the jungle will be stupefied and gather together, and the seas will boil up. The next seven verses mention the second stage when the souls will be reunited with their bodies, the records will be laid open, the people will be called to account for their deeds, the heavens will be unveiled, and the Hell and the Heaven will be brought into full view. After depicting the Hereafter this way, man has been left to ponder over his own deeds, saying: "Then each man shall himself know what he has brought with him."

The people of Makkah are addressed: "Whatever Muhammad (peace be upon him) is presenting before you, is not the bragging of a madman, nor an evil suggestion inspired by Satan, but the word of a noble, exalted and trustworthy messenger (Gabriel) sent by Allah, whom Muhammad (peace be upon him) has seen with his own eyes in the bright horizon of the clear sky in broad day light."

81: AT-TAKWEER

This Sûrah, revealed at Makkah, has 1 section and 29 verses.

In the name of Allah, the Compassionate, the Merciful

A dreadful scene of the Doomsday

When the sun ceases to shine;[1]   when the stars lose their luster;[2]   when the mountains are blown away;[3]   when the ten-month pregnant she-camels are left unattended;[4]   when the wild beasts are brought together;[5]   when the oceans are set ablaze;[6] when the souls are reunited *with the bodies*;[7]   when the infant girl buried alive *(here reference is made to the Pre-Islamic Arab barbarism of burying new born girls alive)* is questioned[8]   for what sin she was killed;[9]   when the record is laid open;[10]   when the heaven is stripped away;[11]   when hell is kindled;[12]   and when paradise is brought near,[13]   then each soul shall know what it has brought.[14]   81:[1-14]

The Qur'an is conveyed to the Prophet through angel Gabriel

This message is for all the people of the world

But no! I do swear by the retreating *stars*;[15]   that run their course and hide;[16]   by the night as it dissipates;[17]   by the morning when it breathes again:[18]   surely, this is the Word *(the Qur'an brought by)* a most honorable Messenger *(Gabriel)*,[19]   possessor of mighty power, having very high rank with the Owner of the Throne *(Allah)*,[20]   who is obeyed *in heaven*, and is trustworthy.[21] *O people of Makkah!* Your companion has not gone mad;[22]   he *(Muhammad)* indeed saw him *(Gabriel)* in the clear horizon[23]   and he *(Muhammad)* is not to withhold the knowledge of the unseen *(i.e. whatever was revealed by Allah)*.[24]   This *(Qur'an)* is not the word of an accursed Shaitân.[25]   Where then is your imagination taking you?[26]   This is but a Reminder to *all* the people of the world,[27]   to each one you who wills to follow the Right Way.[28] And you cannot will without the will of Allah, the Rabb of the worlds.[29]   81:[15-29]

82: AL-INFITÂR

Period of Revelation

This Sûrah and the Sûrah At-Takweer closely resemble each other in their subject matter and were sent down in the same period, which is the early stage of the Prophet's residence at Makkah.

Major Issues, Divine Laws and Guidance

* A description as to what will happen on the Day of Judgement.
* Guardian angels are assigned to each individual. They are recording each and every action.
* Allah Himself will be the Judge on the Day of Judgement.

The theme of this Sûrah is the Hereafter. After describing the Day of Resurrection, it is pointed out that every person will see whatever he has done in this world. Then man is asked to ponder upon the question as to what has deluded him into thinking that Allah (God), Who brought him into being and by Whose favor and bounty, he possesses the finest body, limbs and features among all creatures, is only bountiful and not just? His being bountiful and generous does not mean that man should become fearless of His justice. Man is warned that he should not have any misunderstanding about his accountability on the Day of Judgment because his complete record is being prepared. Two angels have been assigned to each person. They are the trustworthy writers. They are writing down whatever he is doing.

In conclusion, it is stated that the Day of Resurrection will surely take place and on that Day the righteous shall enjoy every kind of bliss in paradise and the wicked shall be punished in hell. On that Day, no one shall avail anyone anything. All powers of reward and punishment shall be with Allah.

82: AL-INFITÂR

This Sûrah, revealed at Makkah, has 1 section and 19 verses.

In the name of Allah, the Compassionate, the Merciful

Description of what will happen on the Day of Judgment

When the heaven is cleft asunder;[1] when the stars fall and scatter;[2] when the oceans are blown out;[3] and when the graves are laid open,[4] then each soul shall know what it has sent forth and what it has left behind.[5] O man! What has lured you away from your gracious Rabb,[6] Who created you, fashioned you, proportioned you,[7] and molded you in whatever form He pleased?[8] Nay! In fact you deny the Day of Judgment![9] *You should know that* guardian *angels* have indeed been appointed over

Guardian angels are recording all actions

you,[10] who are noble writers,[11] they know all that you do.[12] *On that Day,* the righteous will surely be in bliss;[13] while the wicked will indeed be in hell,[14] in which they will be burnt on the Day of Judgment,[15] and from which they will not be able to escape.[16] What could make you understand what the Day of Judgment is?[17] Again, what could make you understand what the

Allah Himself will be the Judge

Day of Judgment is?[18] It is the Day when no one will have the power to do anything for another, and when the entire command will be with Allah.[19]

82:[1-19]

83: AL-MUTAFFÎFEEN

Period of Revelation

This Sûrah was revealed in the early stage of the Prophet's residence at Makkah, when Sûrah after Sûrah was being revealed to impress the doctrine of the Hereafter upon the people's minds. This Sûrah was revealed when the disbelievers started ridiculing the Muslims and disgracing them publicly in the streets and in their assemblies, but persecution and manhandling of the Muslims had not yet started.

Major Issues, Divine Laws and Guidance

* On the Day of Judgment defrauders will be called to account and punished while the righteous will be rewarded with soft couches, the choicest wine and special spring water.
* Today disbelievers laugh at the believers, a Day will come when they themselves will be laughed at.

The theme of this Sûrah is the Hereafter. In the first six verses, the people are taken to task for the evil practice that was prevalent in their commercial dealings. When they were to receive their due from others, they demanded that it be given in full, but when they had to measure or weigh for others, they would give less than what was due. Taking this one evil as an example out of countless evils prevalent in their society, it is pointed out that it is an inevitable result of the heedlessness of the Hereafter. Unless the people realize that one Day they will have to appear before Allah and account for each single act that they are performing in this world, it is not possible that they would adopt piety and righteousness in their daily affairs. Even if a person might practise honesty in some of his less important dealings in view of "honesty is the best policy", he would never practise honesty on occasions when dishonesty would seem to be "the best policy". Man can develop a true and enduring honest nature only when he fears Allah and sincerely believes in the Hereafter, for then he would regard honesty not merely as "a policy" but as "a duty" and obligation, and his being consistent in it would not be dependent on its being useful or useless in this world.

In conclusion, the believers are consoled and the disbelievers warned, that the people who are disgracing and humiliating the believers today, will, on the Day of Judgement, meet the most evil end in consequence of their conduct, and the believers will feel comforted when they will see their fate.

83: AL-MUTAFFÎFEEN

This Sûrah, revealed at Makkah, has 1 section and 36 verses.

In the name of Allah, the Compassionate, the Merciful

Defrauders will be called to account and punished while the righteous will be rewarded with soft couches, choicest wines and special spring water

Woe to those who defraud,[1] who when, they take by measure from men, take the full measure,[2] but when they give by measure or by weight to others, they give less than due.[3] Do they not think that they will be raised to life again[4] on a Mighty Day,[5] a Day when all mankind will stand before the Rabb of the worlds?[6] Indeed not! The record of the wicked is in Sijjeen *(register for the wicked ones)*,[7] what could make you understand what Sijjeen is?[8] It is a written book *of hell.*[9] Woe on that Day to the disbelievers,[10] who deny the Day of Judgment![11] None denies it except every sinful transgressor.[12] *Who*, when Our revelations are recited to him, says: "These are the tales of the ancients."[13] Nay! In fact, their misdeeds have cast a veil over their hearts.[14] Nay! Surely, on that Day, they shall be debarred from the vision of their Rabb.[15] Then they shall certainly burn in hell,[16] and be told: "This is what you used to deny."[17] Nay! Surely, the record of the righteous is in 'Illiyyeen *(register of exalted ones)*,[18] and what could make you understand what the 'Illiyyeen is?[19] It is a written book *of paradise.*[20] Attested by those who are nearest *to Allah (angels).*[21] Surely, the righteous will be in bliss,[22] reclining on soft couches, looking *all around*,[23] and you will recognize in their faces the brightness of bliss.[24] Their thirst will be quenched with pure sealed wine,[25] the seal which will be of musk. Those who wish to excel *above others*, let them excel in this.[26] That *wine* shall have a mixture of Tasneem,[27] a spring, at which those nearest to Allah will drink.[28] 83:[1-28]

Today the disbelievers laugh at the believers , a Day will come when they will be laughed at

During their life on earth, those who were criminals used to mock at the believers,[29] and wink at one another as they passed them by.[30] When they returned to their own people, they returned jesting.[31] And when they saw *the believers*, they used to say: "These are the people who have surely gone astray,"[32] although they had not been sent as guardians over them.[33] On that Day, the believers shall be laughing at the unbelievers,[34] as they recline on couches, looking around them.[35] "Have not the unbelievers been fully rewarded for what they used to do?"[36] 83:[29-36]

84: AL-INSHIQÂQ

Period of Revelation

This is also one of the early Sûrahs revealed at Makkah. The persecution of the Muslims had not yet started; however, the message of the Qur'an was being openly opposed, the people were refusing to acknowledge that resurrection would ever take place and that they would have to appear before Allah to render an account of their deeds.

Major Issues, Divine Laws and Guidance

* On Doomsday, heaven will split asunder and earth will be spread out.
* The books of deeds will be distributed, the righteous will be happy while disbelievers will be wishing for death.
* The people are asked to believe, while they have time, during their life on earth.

The theme of this Sûrah is the Resurrection and Hereafter. In the first five verses the state of resurrection is described and the argument of its being true and certain is also given: that, one Day, the heavens will split asunder, the earth will be spread out plain and smooth, and it will throw out whatever lies inside it. It will be so because it will be the command of Allah, the Rabb of the heavens and the earth.

On that Day, all human beings will be divided into two groups:

1. Those whose records will be given in their right hands, will be forgiven without any severe reckoning.

2. Those whose records will be given to them from behind their back, they will wish for death but they will not die; instead they will be cast into hell. They will meet with this fate because during their life on earth, they remained heedless about appearing before Allah to render an account of their deeds.

In conclusion, the disbelievers who oppose the teachings of the Qur'an instead of bowing down to Allah when they hear it, are forewarned of a grievous punishment, while the good news of limitless rewards has been given to the believers and the righteous.

84: AL-INSHIQÂQ

This Sûrah, revealed at Makkah, has 1 section and 25 verses.

In the name of Allah, the Compassionate, the Merciful

On Doomsday, heaven will split asunder and earth will be spread out

When heaven is split asunder,[1] obeying its Rabb's command as it ought to;[2] when the earth spreads out[3] and casts out all that is within it and becomes empty,[4] obeying its Rabb's command as it ought to,[5] then O mankind! Surely, you are returning towards your Rabb *with your good or bad deeds,* a sure returning, and you are about to meet Him.[6] Then he who is given his Book *of deeds* in his right hand,[7] shall have a quick and easy reckoning[8] and shall return to his people rejoicing.[9] But he who is given his book *of deeds* from behind his back,[10] shall soon be calling for death,[11] and shall be made to enter a blazing fire;[12] for he used to live happily with his family[13] and thought that he would never return *to Allah for accountability*.[14] O yes! Indeed, his Rabb has ever been watching *over his misdeeds*.[15] I swear by the glow of sunset;[16] by the night and all that it gathers together;[17] by the moon, when it grows full,[18] that you shall gradually pass from one stage to another.[19]   84:[1-19]

Books of Deeds will be distributed; the righteous will be happy while disbelievers will be calling for death

People are asked to believe while there is still time

What is the matter with the people that they do not believe,[20] and when the Qur'an is recited to them, they do not prostrate?[21] Nay, but the unbelievers will deny *it*;[22] and Allah knows what they are hiding *in their hearts*.[23] Therefore, proclaim to them, a painful punishment,[24] except those who embrace the true faith and do good deeds; for them there will be a never-ending reward.[25]   84:[20-25]

85: AL-BURÛJ

Period of Revelation

This Sûrah was revealed in Makkah during the period when persecution of the Muslims was at its peak and the disbelievers of Makkah were trying their utmost by tyranny and coercion to turn the new converts away from Islam.

Major Issues, Divine Laws and Guidance:

* Those who torture the believers will be given the punishment of conflagration on the Day of Judgement
* He Who created you for the first time, will bring you back to life again for accountability.

This Sûrah warns the disbelievers of the evil consequences of persecution and tyranny, and consoles the believers that if they remain firm and steadfast against tyranny and coercion, they will be rewarded for it, and Allah Himself will avenge their persecutors. In this connection, the story of the makers of the ditch (Ashâb al-Ukhdud), who had burnt the believers to death by casting them into pits full of fire is related. By means of this story, the believers and the disbelievers have been taught a few lessons:

(1) Just as the makers of the ditch became worthy of Allah's curse and punishment, the chiefs of Makkah are also becoming worthy of it.
(2) Just as the believers at that time, willingly accepted to sacrifice their lives by being burnt to death in the pits of fire instead of turning away from their faith, so also should the believers endure persecution and not to give up faith.
(3) Allah, to Whom belongs the Kingdom of the heavens and the earth, is Praiseworthy and is watching what the two groups are striving for.

It is made clear that the disbelievers will not only be punished in Hell for their disbelief but, in addition to that, they will also suffer punishment of fire as a fit recompense for their tyranny and cruelty. The believers who are firm in their belief and do good deeds will be rewarded with paradise, which indeed, will be the supreme success. The disbelievers are warned that Allah's grip is very severe. If they are proud of the strength of their hosts, they should know that the hosts of Pharaoh and Thamûd were even stronger and more numerous. Therefore, they should learn a lesson from the fate, these people of the past met. No one can escape Allah's jurisdiction and the Qur'an that they are belying is unchangeable: it is inscribed in the Preserved Tablet, which cannot be destroyed.

85: AL-BURÛJ

This Sûrah, revealed at Makkah, has 1 section and 22 verses.

In the name of Allah, the Compassionate, the Merciful

Those who torture the believers will be given the punishment of conflagration on the Day of Judgment

By the heaven with its constellations![1]   By the promised Day *of Judgment*![2]   By the witnesses and that which is being witnessed![3]   Doomed be the makers of the ditch,[4]   who lit the fuel-fed fire[5]   and sat around it,[6]   to watch what they were doing to the believers.[7]   They tortured them for no other reason than that they believed in Allah, the All-Mighty, the Praise Worthy,[8]   the One to Whom belongs the Kingdom of the heavens and earth, and Allah is Witness to all things.[9]   Those who persecute the believing men and believing women and do not repent, shall receive the punishment of hell, wherein they shall have the punishment of conflagration.[10]   As for those who believe and do good deeds, they shall have gardens beneath which rivers flow; which will be the greatest success.[11]   Surely, the seizure of your Rabb is very severe.[12]   Surely, He, it is Who originates *the creation of everything*, and *He, it is Who* will repeat it *on the Day of Resurrection*.[13]   He is the Forgiving, the Loving,[14]   the Owner of the Throne, the Glorious,[15]   the executor of His own will.[16]   Have you not heard the story of the warriors[17]   of Fir'aun *(Pharaoh)* and of Thamûd?[18]   Yet, the unbelievers persist in denying *the truth*,[19]   although Allah has encircled them from all around.[20]   Surely, this is a Glorious Qur'an,[21]   inscribed on Al-Lauh Al-Mahfûz *(Imperishable Tablet)*.[22]

He Who created you for the first time will bring you back to life again for accountability

85:[1-22]

86: AT-TÂRIQ

Period of Revelation

This is one of the early Sûrahs revealed at Makkah. It was sent down at a stage when the disbelievers of Makkah were employing all sorts of devices and plans to defeat and frustrate the message of Islam.

Major Issues, Divine Laws and Guidance

* Allah has appointed a guardian angel over each soul .
* The Qur'an is the decisive Word of Allah.

This Sûrah discuses two themes:

(1) Man has to appear before Allah after death;

(2) The Qur'an is a decisive Word, which no plan or device of the disbelievers can defeat or frustrate.

The stars of the heavens are cited as an evidence that there is nothing in the universe that may continue to exist and survive without a guardian over it. Then man is asked to consider his own self as to how he has been brought into existence from a mere sperm drop and shaped into a living human being. Then it is said that Allah, Who brought him into existence, certainly has the power to create him once again to scrutinize all of the secrets of man which remained hidden in this world. At that time, man will neither be able to escape the consequences of his deeds by his own power, nor will anyone else come to his rescue.

In conclusion, it is pointed out that just as the falling of rain from the sky, the sprouting of plants and crops from the earth are not child's play, but a serious task, similarly the truths expressed in the Qur'an are no jest, but a firm and unchangeable reality. The disbelievers think that their plans and devices will defeat the invitation of the Qur'an, but they do not know that Allah too is devising a plan which will void all their plans. Then, a word of consolation is provided to the Prophet (peace be upon him) and a warning is given to the disbelievers that very soon they will themselves find out whether they have been able to defeat the Qur'an by their schemes or whether the Qur'an has dominated them in the very place where they are exerting their efforts to defeat it.

86: AT-TÂRIQ

This Sûrah, revealed at Makkah, has 1 section and 17 verses.

In the name of Allah, the Compassionate, the Merciful

By the heaven and by the nightly visitant,[1]   and what could make you understand what the nightly visitant is?[2]   It is the star of piercing brightness.[3]   *(Just as Allah Almighty is taking care of each star in the galaxies, similarly)* over each soul there is a guardian *angel*.[4]   Let man consider from what he is created![5] He is created from an emitted fluid[6]   that is produced from between the loins and the ribs.[7]   Surely, He *(the Creator)*, has the power to bring him back to life,[8] on the Day when the hidden secrets will be brought to scrutiny;[9]   then he will have neither power of his own nor any helper *to save him from the punishment of Allah*.[10] By the sky *(having rain clouds)* which sends down rain[11] and by the earth which is ever bursting *with new growth*;[12]   surely, this *Qur'an* is a decisive word,[13]   and it is no joke.[14]   These *unbelievers* are plotting a scheme:[15]   and I, too, am plotting a scheme.[16]   Therefore, leave the unbelievers alone. Leave them alone for a while.[17]   86:[1-17]

Over each soul there is an appointed guardian angel

The Qur'an is a decisive word of Allah

87: AL-A'LÂ

Period of Revelation

This Sûrah is one of the earliest Sûrahs revealed at Makkah, and the words: "We shall enable you to recite, then you shall never forget" of verse 6 also indicates that it was revealed in the period when the Prophet (peace be upon him) was not yet fully accustomed to receiving Revelation, and at the time of receiving the Revelations, he feared he might forget the words.

Major Issues, Divine Laws and Guidance

* Tawheed: Allah, the One and Only, has created all things and perfected them, always glorify Him.
* Allah has taken the responsibility of Prophet's memorization of the Qur'an by assuring him that he will not forget any portion of it.
* Those who heed Allah's reminders will be successful in the Hereafter.

In the first verse, the doctrine of Tawheed (God is One and Only) is compressed into a single sentence, saying that Allah's name should be glorified and exalted, and He should not be remembered by any name which might reflect a deficiency, fault, weakness, or likeness with created beings.

Then, the Prophet (peace be upon him) is told: "You are not responsible to bring everyone on to the right path; your only duty is to convey the message. The simplest way of conveying the message is to admonish him who is inclined to listen to the admonition and accept it. The one who is not inclined to it, should not be pursued. The one who fears the evil consequences of deviation and falsehood, will listen to the truth and accept it, and the wretched one who avoids listening to and accepting it, will himself see his evil end."

In conclusion, it is said that success is only for those who adopt purity of belief, morals and deeds, remember the name of their Rabb and perform the Prayer. On the contrary, most people are lost in seeking the ease, benefits and pleasures of this worldly life, instead of endeavoring for their well being in the hereafter. This world is transitory and the Hereafter everlasting, and the blessings of the Hereafter are far better than the blessings of this world. This truth has not been expressed only in the Qur'an, but also in the books of the Prophet Ibrâheem (Abraham) and Musa (Moses) peace be upon him.

87: AL-'A'LÂ

This Sûrah, revealed at Makkah, has 1 section and 19 verses.

In the name of Allah, the Compassionate, the Merciful

Glorify the name of your Rabb, the Most High,[1] Who has created all things and perfected them.[2] Who has set their destinies and guided them.[3] Who brings forth green pasture,[4] then reduces it to black rubbish.[5] Soon, We shall make you recite *Our revelations,* so you shall forget none of them[6] except what Allah wills. Surely, He knows what is open and what is hidden.[7] We shall make it easy for you to follow the easy way.[8] Therefore, admonish them if admonition be beneficial.[9] He who fears *Allah* will heed the reminder,[10] and he who is unfortunate will avoid it.[11] The one *who will avoid*, shall burn in the gigantic fire,[12] where he shall neither die nor live.[13] The one who *will take admonition and* purify himself shall be successful,[14] who remembers the name of his Rabb and prays.[15] But *O men!* You prefer the life of this world;[16] while the Hereafter is better and everlasting.[17] Surely, the same was *said* in the earlier scriptures;[18] the scriptures given to Ibrâheem *(Abraham)* and Musa *(Moses)*.[19]

87:[1-19]

Glorify Allah; Allah has taken the responsibility of the Prophet's memory about The Qur'an

It is a reminder and those who heed its reminders will be successful in the hereafter

88: AL GHÂSHIYAH

Period of Revelation

This is one of the early Sûrahs revealed at Makkah during the period when the Prophet (peace be upon him) had started preaching his message publicly, and the people of Makkah were hearing it and ignoring it carelessly and thoughtlessly.

Major Issues, Divine Laws and Guidance

* The condition of the disbelievers and the believers on the Day of Judgement.
* The wonders of nature, admonition and accountability.

To understand the subject matter of this Sûrah, one should keep in view the fact that in the initial stage, the preaching of the Prophet (peace be upon him) mostly centered around two points which he wanted to instill in the peoples' minds:

1.   Tawheed (God is One and Only), and
2.   The Life after Death.

Guidance is provided through questions, inviting people to think, such as: do these people not observe the common things which they experience in their daily lives? Do they not consider how the camels, on whom their daily life's activity in the Arabian desert depends, came into being? How they were endowed precisely with the same characteristics required to live the desert life? When they go on their journeys, they see the sky, the mountains, and the earth. Do they not ponder over these three phenomena and consider as to how the sky was stretched above them, how the mountains were erected and how the earth was spread beneath them? Has all this come about without the skill and craftsmanship of an All-Powerful, All Wise Designer? If they acknowledge that a Creator has created all this with great wisdom and power, and that no one else is an associate with Him in their creation, then why do they refuse to accept Him Alone as their Sustainer?

In conclusion, the people are reminded that if they acknowledge that Allah (God) had the power to create all this, then on what ground do they hesitate to acknowledge that Allah also has the power to bring about resurrection, to recreate man, to take the accountability, and to make hell for punishment and heaven for reward?

88: AL-GHÂSHIYAH

This Sûrah, revealed at Makkah, has 1 section and 26 verses.

In the name of Allah, the Compassionate, the Merciful

Condition of the disbelievers and the believers on the Day of Judgment

Has the news of the over shadowing event *of resurrection* reached you?[1]   On that Day some faces shall be downcast,[2] in hard labor, worn out,[3]   scorching in the blazing fire,[4] given to drink from a boiling fountain.[5]   They shall have no food except bitter thorny fruit,[6] which will neither provide nourishment nor satisfy hunger.[7] While some faces on that Day shall be radiant,[8] well pleased with their endeavors,[9] in a lofty garden.[10]   Therein, they shall hear no loose talk.[11] Therein, they shall have running springs.[12] Therein, they shall be reclining on raised soft couches,[13] with goblets placed before them;[14]   cushions arranged in order[15] and fine carpets richly spread.[16]   88:[1-16]

Wonders of nature, admonition and accountability

Do they not look at the camels, how they are created?[17] The sky, how it is raised high?[18]   The mountains, how they are firmly set?[19]   And the earth, how it is spread out?[20]   So keep on giving admonition, for you are an admonisher[21]   not a taskmaster over them.[22]   As for those who turn their backs and disbelieve,[23] Allah will punish them with the mighty punishment.[24]   Surely, to Us is their return,[25]   then surely, it is for Us to take their account.[26]   88:[17-26]

89: AL-FAJR

Period of Revelation

This Sûrah was revealed during the period when persecution of the new converts to Islam had begun at Makkah.

Major Issues, Divine Laws and Guidance

* The admonition for social welfare through the examples of prior nations.
* What should be avoided to do real social welfare?
* The Day of Judgement will be too late to heed the admonition.

The theme of this Sûrah is to affirm the rewards and punishments in the Hereafter through swearing oaths by the dawn, the ten nights, the even and the odd, and the departing night. The disbelievers are told that these things are a symbol of the regularity that exists in the night and day, and after swearing oaths by these things a question is asked: "Even after witnessing this wise system established by Allah, do you still need any other evidence to show that it is not beyond the power of that Allah, Who has brought about this system, to establish the Hereafter?" Reasoning is given from man's own history. The evil end of 'Ad, Thamûd and Pharaoh are cited as examples showing that when they transgressed and spread corruption in the land, Allah laid upon them the scourge of His chastisement. This is a proof of the fact that the system of this universe is not being run by deaf and blind forces, but by a Wise Ruler, the demand of Whose wisdom and justice is continuously visible in man's own history.

After this, an appraisal of human society is made criticizing the materialistic attitude of people; they overlook the morality of good and evil; they regard only the achievement of worldly wealth, rank and position or the absence of it, as the criterion of honor or disgrace; and have forgotten that neither riches are a reward nor poverty a punishment. Allah is testing man in both conditions to see what attitude he adopts when blessed with wealth and how he behaves when afflicted by poverty. This discourse is concluded with the assertion that accountability shall certainly be held and it will be held on the Day when the Divine Court will convene. At that time, the deniers of the Day of Judgement will regret, but their regrets will not save them from Allah's punishment. As for the people who have accepted the truth, which the Qur'an and the Prophet has presented to the world, Allah will be pleased with them and they will be well pleased with the rewards that will be bestowed on them by Allah. They will be called upon to join the righteous and enter paradise.

89: AL-FAJR

This Sûrah, revealed at Makkah, has 1 section and 30 verses.

In the name of Allah, the Compassionate, the Merciful

Admonition for social welfare through the examples of prior nations

By the morning,[1] and the ten nights *(first ten days of Dhul-Hijja)*,[2] the even and the odd,[3] and the night when it departs![4] Is there not in these oaths, *enough evidence* for those who use their common sense?[5] Have you not seen how your Rabb dealt with 'Ad?[6] *The residents* of Iram, the city of lofty pillars,[7] the like of which had never been built in the whole land.[8] And with the people of Thamûd who hewed out *their dwellings* in the rocks of the valley?[9] And with Fir'aun *(Pharaoh)* the owner of stakes?[10] They all transgressed beyond bounds in the land,[11] and committed great mischief therein.[12] Therefore, your Rabb let loose on them His scourge of torment.[13] Surely, your Rabb is ever watchful.[14]   89:[1-14]

What should be avoided to do real social welfare?

As for man, when his Rabb tries him through giving him honor and blessings, he says: "My Rabb is bountiful to me."[15] But when He tries him through restricting his provisions, he says: "My Rabb has humiliated me."[16] Nay! But you did not show kindness to the orphan,[17] nor did you encourage each other in feeding the poor.[18] Greedily you lay your hands on the inheritance *of the weak*,[19] and you love wealth with all your hearts.[20]

89:[15-20]

Day of Judgment will be too late to heed the admonition

Nay! *You should know*, when the earth is pounded to powder,[21] your Rabb will come, with angels standing in ranks,[22] and hell shall be brought in sight. On that Day man will remember his deeds, but how is that remembrance going to profit him?[23] He will say: "Alas! Would that I had sent forth *some good deeds* for this life of mine."[24] None can punish as *Allah* will punish on that Day,[25] and none can bind as He will bind.[26]

Allah's address to the believers

To the righteous soul it will be said: "O fully satisfied soul![27] Return to your Rabb, well pleased with Him and well-pleasing to Him.[28] Join My servants,[29] and enter My paradise."[30]   89:[21-30]

90: AL-BALAD

Period of Revelation

This Sûrah was revealed in the period when the disbelievers of Makkah started to oppose the Prophet (peace be upon him) through tyranny and excesses against him.

Major Issues, Divine Laws and Guidance

* An admonition to the disbelievers.
* Allah has given you two eyes, one tongue and two lips to control your tongue.
* The qualities of a righteous person: Freeing a slave, feeding the hungry, being patient, advising others about piety and compassion.

This Sûrah compressed a vast subject into a few brief sentences. It is a miracle of the Qur'an that a complete ideology of life which could hardly be explained in a thick volume has been abridged most effectively in few brief sentences of this short Sûrah. Its theme is to explain the true position of man in the world and of the world in relation to man and tell that Allah has shown man, both, the Highway of good and the Highway of evil. Allah has also provided for him the means to judge, see and follow them. Now it rests upon man's own effort and judgement whether he chooses the path of virtue and reaches felicity or adopts the path of evil and meets with doom.

After this, man's misunderstanding that he is all in all in this world and that there is no superior power to watch what he does and to call him to account, has been refuted. The Highway which leads to moral depravity is easy and pleasing to the self and the Highway which leads to moral heights is steep like an uphill road for which man has to exercise self-restraint.

Finally the people are advised to give up spending for ostentation, display and pride, and should spend their wealth to help the orphans and the needy. They should believe in Allah, join the company of believers and participate in the construction of human society. As a result, they would become worthy of Allah's mercy, while those who will follow the wrong way would become the fuel of hell from which there is no escape.

90: AL-BALAD

This Sûrah, revealed at Makkah, has 1 section and 20 verses.

In the name of Allah, the Compassionate, the Merciful

Admonition to the disbelievers of Makkah

I swear by this City *(Makkah - where to harm anyone is prohibited,*[1] *but to assassinate) you (O Muhammad)* have been made lawful in this city,[2] and I swear by your father *(Adam)* and the children he begot *(mankind)*,[3] certainly, We have created man to be in stress.[4] Does he think that none has power over him?[5] He may boast: "I have squandered wealth in abundance!"[6] Does he think that no one observes him?[7] Have We not given him two eyes *to observe*?[8] One tongue *to talk* and two lips *to control it*?[9]

Allah has given you one tongue and two lips *to control it*

Then, We have shown him the two High Ways *(good, leading towards paradise and evil, leading towards hell)*?[10] Yet, he has not attempted to tackle the 'Aqabah *(steep path)*![11] And what could make you understand what the 'Aqabah is?[12] It is the freeing of a neck *(slave)* from bondage;[13] or the giving of food in a day of famine[14] to an orphan relative,[15] or to a needy in distress;[16] besides this, he should be of those who believe, enjoin fortitude, encourage kindness and compassion.[17] Such are the people of the right hand *(going towards paradise)*.[18] But those who disbelieve Our revelations, they are the people of the left hand *(going towards hell)*,[19] having fire all around them.[20]

Qualities of a righteous person

90:[1-20]

91: ASH-SHAMS

Period of Revelation

This Sûrah was revealed, in the early stage at Makkah, when opposition to the Prophet (peace be upon him) had grown very strong and intense.

Major Issue, Divine Law and Guidance

* Success depends on keeping the soul pure and failure depends on corrupting it, people of Thamûd were leveled to the ground for that very reason.

This Sûrah teaches that:

(1) Just as the sun and the moon, the day and the night, the earth and the sky are different from each other and contradictory in their effects and results, so are good and evil different from each other and contradictory in their effects and results; they are neither alike in their outward appearance nor can they be alike in their results.

(2) Allah, after giving the human his body, sense and mind has not left him uninformed in the world. He has instilled into his subconscious, by means of a natural inspiration, the distinction between good and evil, right and wrong.

(3) The future of man depends on recognizing these differences, developing the good and suppressing the evil tendencies of the self. If he develops good inclinations and frees himself of evil inclinations, he will attain eternal success, and if, on the contrary, he suppresses good and promotes evil, he will meet with disappointments and failures.

This Sûrah relates the story of the people of Thamûd to show that a Rasool is raised in the world; because the inspirational knowledge of good and evil that Allah has placed in human nature is, by itself, not enough for the guidance of man; rather on account of his failure to understand it, man has invented a wrong criteria, and theories of good and evil, and has gone astray. The example of Thamûd relates that Prophet Sâleh (peace be upon him) was sent to that nation, but the people overwhelmed by their evil became so rebellious that they rejected him. When he presented before them the miracle of the she camel, which was demanded by them, the one who was the most wretched of them, hamstrung her in accordance with the will and desire of the people. Consequently, the entire nation was overtaken by the wrath of Allah.

91: ASH-SHAMS

This Sûrah, revealed at Makkah, has 1 section and 15 verses.

In the name of Allah, the Compassionate, the Merciful

Success depends on keeping the soul pure and failure depends on corrupting it

By the sun and its brightness;[1] by the moon, as it follows it *(the sun)*;[2] by the day, as it shows its splendor;[3] by the night as it draws a veil over it;[4] by the heaven and Him Who built it;[5] by the earth and He Who spread it;[6] by the soul and He Who perfected it[7] and inspired it with knowledge of what is wrong for it and what is right for it:[8] indeed successful will be the one who purifies it,[9] and indeed unsuccessful the one who corrupts it![10]

91:[1-10]

The corrupted people of Thamûd were leveled to the ground

The people of Thamûd denied the truth because of their arrogant transgression[11] when the most wicked man among them was deputed *to kill the she-camel*.[12] The Rasool of Allah warned them, saying: "This is Allah's She-camel *do not harm her*! Let her drink *on her turn*."[13] They disbelieved him and hamstrung her. Therefore, for that crime, their Rabb let loose His scourge upon them and leveled them to the ground.[14] For He *(Allah)* has no fear of its consequences.[15]

91:[11-15]

92: AL-LAIL

Period of Revelation

This Sûrah so closely resembles Sûrah Ash-Shams that each Sûrah seems to be an explanation of the other. It is one and the same thing which has been explained in Sûrah Ash-Shams in one way and in this Sûrah in another. This indicates that both these Sûrahs were revealed in about the same period, which is early stage of the Prophet's residence at Makkah.

Major Issues, Divine Laws and Guidance

* For good people, Allah will facilitate the easy way and for the wicked, the hard way.
* What benefit will one get from his wealth if he himself is doomed?

This Sûrah identifies two different ways of life and explains the contrast between their ultimate ends and results. The first way is of the one who spends his wealth, adopts God-consciousness and piety, and acknowledges the good as good. The second way is of the one who is a miser, does not care for Allah's pleasure or displeasure, and repudiates what is good and right. It is stated that these two modes of action, which are clearly opposite to each other, cannot be equal and alike in respect of their results. Just as they are different in their nature, so are they different in their results. After this the following three realities are stated briefly:

1. Allah has not left man uninformed in the examination hall of the world, but has taken on Himself the responsibility to tell him which one is the straight and Right Way out of the different ways of life. There is no need to point out that by sending His Rasools and His Books, He has fulfilled His responsibility.

2. The Master of both, this world and the Hereafter, is Allah Alone. If you seek this world, it is He Who will give it, and if you seek the Hereafter, again it is He Who will give it. Now, it is for you to decide what you should seek from Him, one or both.

3. The wretched one who rejects good, presented through the Rasool and the Book, and turns away from it, will have a blazing fire ready for him. As for the God-fearing person who spends his wealth in a good cause, without any selfish motive and only for the sake of his Rabb's pleasure, his Rabb will be pleased with him and will bless him with so much that he will be well pleased with his Rabb.

92: AL-LAIL

This Sûrah, revealed at Makkah, has 1 section and 21 verses.

In the name of Allah, the Compassionate, the Merciful

For good people Allah will facilitate the easy way and for the wicked the hard way

What benefit will he get from wealth, if he himself is doomed?

By the night, as it covers *with darkness*;[1] and by the day, as it spreads its brightness;[2] and by Him Who created the male and the female;[3] surely, your efforts are directed towards various ends.[4] So for him who gives *in charity,* fears *Allah*[5] and testifies to goodness,[6] We shall facilitate for him the Path to good.[7] As for him who is stingy and considers himself independent *of Allah*[8] and rejects the goodness,[9] We shall facilitate for him the Path to evil.[10] What benefit will he get from his wealth, if he himself is doomed.[11] Surely, it is for Us to give guidance,[12] and surely, to Us belong the end and the beginning.[13] Therefore, I warn you of the blazing fire,[14] in which none shall burn except the most wretched,[15] who denies the truth and gives no heed.[16] But the pious believer will be kept away from it,[17] the one who spends in charity for self-purification,[18] not seeking any favor from anyone for which a reward is expected in return,[19] except seeking the good pleasure of his Rabb, the Most High.[20] *Such a person* shall soon be well-pleased *with Allah*.[21]   92:[1-21]

93: AD-DHUHÂ

Period of Revelation

This Sûrah was revealed during the early period at Makkah, when the revelation was suspended for a time in the initial stage of Prophethood due to the fact that Muhammad (peace be upon him) was not yet accustomed to bearing the intensity of revelation.

Major Issue, Divine Law and Guidance

* Good news to the Prophet Muhammad (peace be upon him) that the later period will be better for him than the earlier.

The theme of this Sûrah is to console the Prophet (peace be upon him) and its object is to remove his anxiety and distress, which was caused by the suspension of revelation. The Prophet is reassured: "Your Rabb has not forsaken you, nor is he displeased with you." Then, he is given the good news that the hardships that he was experiencing in the initial stage of his mission will not last long and the later period of life for him will be better than the former. Before long, Allah will bless him so abundantly that he will be well pleased. This is one of the express prophecies of the Qur'an, which proved literally true later on. When this statement was made, there seemed not to be the remotest chance that the helpless and powerless man who had come out to wage a war against ignorance and paganism would ever achieve such wonderful success.

The Prophet (peace be upon him) is then told: "What made you think that your Rabb has forsaken you, and that He is displeased with you? Whereas the fact is that He has been good to you with kindness after kindness ever since the day of your birth. You were born an orphan, He made the best arrangement for your upbringing and care: you were unaware of the Right Way, He showed you the Right Way; you were indigent, He made you rich. All this shows that you have been favored by Him from the very beginning and His grace and bounty has been constantly focussed on you." These are similar words which Allah said to console Prophet Musa (Moses) when he was sent to Pharaoh as described in Sûrah Tâ-Hâ vv. 37-42: "We have been looking after you with kindness ever since your birth; therefore, you should be satisfied that you will not be left alone in this dreadful mission. Our bounty will constantly be with you."

93: AD-DUHÂ

This Sûrah, revealed at Makkah, has 1 section and 11 verses.

In the name of Allah, the Compassionate, the Merciful

Good news to Muhammad (pbuh) that the later period will be better for him than the earlier

By the morning day light,[1] and by the night when it grows dark and still,[2] your Rabb has neither forsaken you, *O Muhammad*, nor is He displeased with you.[3] Certainly, the later life shall be better for you than the earlier.[4] Soon your Rabb shall grant you something with which you will be well-pleased.[5] Did He not find you an orphan and gave you shelter?[6] Did He not find you lost *(unaware of the faith, the Qur'an, and the Prophethood)* and gave you guidance?[7] Did He not find you poor and made you self-sufficient?[8] Therefore, do not treat the orphan with harshness[9] and do not chide away the beggar,[10] and speak gratefully about the bounty of your Rabb.[11]   93:[1-11]

94: AL-INSHIRÂH

Period of Revelation

This Sûrah was revealed during the same period as Sûrah Ad-Dhuhâ, the early stage of the Prophet's residence at Makkah.

Major Issue, Divine Law and Guidance

* Allah expanded the breast of the Prophet, relieved his burden and exalted his fame.

This Sûrah is also to console and encourage the Prophet (peace be upon him). He never had to encounter the conditions which he suddenly had to face after embarking on his mission of inviting people to Islam. This was by itself a great revolution in his life. When he started preaching the message of Islam, the same society which had esteemed him with unique honor, turned hostile to him. The same relatives and friends, the same clansmen and neighbors, who used to treat him with the highest respect, began to shower him with abuse and insult. No one at Makkah was prepared to listen to him. He was being ridiculed and mocked in the streets and on the roads. At every step, he had to face new difficulties. Although, he gradually became accustomed to the hardships, even as they became more severe, yet the initial stage was very discouraging for him. That is why, Sûrah Ad-Dhuhâ was revealed earlier to console him, and then this Sûrah.

This Sûrah states that Allah has bestowed three major favors on the Prophet: the first is the blessing of Sharh Sadr (opening up of the breast), the second by removing from him the heavy burden that was weighing down his back before the call, and the third by exalting his renown, the like of which has never been granted to anyone before him.

Finally, the Prophet is instructed: "You can develop the power to bear and resist the hardships of the initial stage only by one means, and it is: `When you are free from your daily tasks, you should devote yourself to the labor and toil of worship, and turn all your attention exclusively to your Rabb."

94: AL-INSHIRÂH

This Sûrah, revealed at Makkah, has 1 section and 8 verses.

In the name of Allah, the Compassionate, the Merciful

Allah expanded the chest of the Prophet, relieved his burden and exalted his fame

O Prophet! Have We not expanded your breast for you[1] and relieved you from the burden[2]   which weighed down your back,[3]   and exalted your fame?[4]   Surely, with every difficulty there is relief.[5]   Surely, with every difficulty there is relief.[6] Therefore, when you are free *from your daily task*, devote your time to the labor *of worship*[7]   and turn all your attention towards your Rabb.[8]   94:[1-8]

95: AT-TEEN

Period of Revelation

There are two different views relating to this Sûrah: first that it is a Makki Sûrah, and second that it is Madani Sûrah. The majority of scholars regard it as a Makki revelation, a manifest symbol of which is the use of the words 'Hâdhal-Baladil-Ameen' (this city of peace) for Makkah.

Major Issue, Divine Law and Guidance

*   Man is the best creature of all, except the disbelievers.

The theme of this Sûrah is concerning the rewards and punishments in the Hereafter. For this purpose, first swearing an oath by the two food items, which are the nourishment to the body and the two sacred places (Mount of Tûr and Makkah, where Allah revealed His message to the Prophet Musa (Moses) and the Prophet Muhammad, peace be upon them), which are nourishment to the Soul and the source for its Guidance. Then it is stated that Allah has created man in the most excellent of molds, therefore, he is expected to keep balance in the nourishment of the body and the soul, following the guidance received from his Creator, and not to associate anyone else with Him. This signifies that man has been blessed with such excellent capabilities that he can attain the highest position which has not been attained by any other creature. Then, two kinds of men are pointed out:

First kind are those who in spite of having been created in the finest of molds, become inclined to evil and their moral degeneration causes them to be reduced to the lowest of the low. **Second kind** are those, who by adopting the way of faith and righteousness, remain secure from degeneration and are consistent with the noble position, which is the necessary demand of their having been created in the best of molds. The existence among mankind of both these kinds is a factual thing, which no one can deny. It has been observed and experienced in society everywhere at all times.

In conclusion, this reality of the two kinds of men, is used as an argument to prove that when among the people, there exist two separate and quite distinct kinds, how can one deny the judgement, and the reward and punishment for deeds. If the morally degraded people are not punished and the morally pure people are not rewarded (both end in the dust alike), it would mean that there is no justice in the Kingdom of Allah, whereas human nature and common sense demands that a judge should do justice. How then can one conceive that Allah, Who is the most just of all judges, would not do justice?

95: AT-TEEN

This Sûrah, revealed at Makkah, has 1 section and 8 verses.

In the name of Allah, the Compassionate, the Merciful

Man is the best creatures of all, except the disbelievers

By the fig and by the olive,[1] by the mount of Sinai[2] and by this city of peace *(Makkah)*.[3] We have indeed created man in the best stature,[4] then We return him to the lowest of the low[5] - except those who believe and do good deeds - for they shall have a never ending reward.[6] So, what causes you - *O disbelievers* - to deny the Day of Judgment?[7] Is not Allah the most just of all Judges?[8] 95:[1-8]

96: AL-'ALAQ

Period of Revelation

This Sûrah, revealed at Makkah, has two parts: the first part consists of the very first revelation sent down to the Prophet. The second part, when the Prophet began to perform the prescribed Prayer in the precincts of the Ka'bah and Abu Jahl, a Quraish chief, tried to prevent him from this with threats.

Major Issues, Divine Laws and Guidance

* The very first revelation 'Iqra bismi Rabbi kal-ladhi khalaq --- Mâlam Y'alam' (Read in the name of your Rabb Who created ---what he did not know)."
* Read in the name of Allah, Who created man and taught him by the pen.
* Those who forbid others from the worship of Allah will be dragged to hell by their forelock.

When the Prophet (peace be upon him) experienced this extraordinary event of receiving the first revelation, he returned home to his wife Sayyidah Khadijah, trembling with fear, and said to her: "Cover me, cover me," and he was covered. When terror left him, he said: "O Khadijah, what has happened to me?" Then he narrated to her what happened, and said: "I fear for my life." She took him to her tribe's learned man, Waraqah bin Naufal, who had become a Christian in pre-Islamic days, had transcribed the Gospel in Arabic and Hebrew, and had become blind through old age. Waraqah said: "This is the same Namûs (the Angel assigned to bring revelations) which Allah had sent down to Moses (peace be upon him). Would that I were a young man during your Prophethood! Would that I were alive when your tribe would expel you!" The Holy Prophet said: "Will they expel me?" Waraqah said: "Yes, never has it so happened that a person brought what you have brought and was not treated as an enemy. If I live till then I will help you with all the power at my command." But not very long after this, Waraqah died.

(For details see the Prophet's life at Makkah at page #24)

This narrative is enough to clarify that when Waraqa bin Naufal, who was a Christian, heard the Prophet's experience, he did not regard it as an evil suggestion. This means that even according to him, Muhammad (peace be upon him) was such a sublime person that there was nothing surprising in his being elevated to the rank of Prophethood.

The second part of this Sûrah vv. 6-19 was revealed when the Prophet began to perform his prayer in the Islamic way. The other people were watching it with curiosity, but Abu Jahl in his arrogance and pride threatened the Prophet and forbade him to worship that way in the Ka'bah.

96: AL-'ALAQ

This Sûrah, revealed at Makkah, has 1 section and 19 verses.

In the name of Allah, the Compassionate, the Merciful

Read in the name of Allah, Who created man and taught him by the pen

Those who forbid from the worship of Allah will be dragged to hell by their forelock

Read! In the name of your Rabb Who created[1] - created man from a leechlike mass.[2]   Read! Your Rabb is the Most Gracious,[3]   Who taught by the Pen,[4]   taught man what he knew not.[5]   Nay! Indeed, man transgresses all bounds,[6]   whenever he considers himself to be self-sufficient;[7]   although, surely, towards your Rabb is his return.[8]   Have you seen the one *(Abu Jahl)* who forbids[9]   a servant *(Muhammad)* from offering Salah *(prayer)*?[10]   Have you considered if he was on the right guidance,[11]   or was enjoining true piety, *why he would forbid someone from prayer*?[12]   Have you considered if he *(Abu Jahl)* denies the truth and turns away, *what will happen?*[13]   Does he not know that Allah is observing *all things*?[14]   Nay! *Let him know that* if he does not stop, We will drag him by the forelock,[15]   a lying, sinful forelock.[16]   So let him call his supporters for help.[17]   We too shall call the guards of hell *to deal with him.*[18]   Nay! Do not obey him! Prostrate yourself and bring yourself closer *to your Rabb.*[19]   96:[1-19]

97: AL-QADR

Period of Revelation

This Sûrah is one of the early Sûrahs revealed at Makkah.

Major Issue, Divine Law and Guidance

* The night of Qadr, in which the Qur'an was revealed, is better than one thousand months.

The theme of this Sûrah is to acquaint man with the value, worth and importance of the Qur'an. Being placed just after Sûrah Al-'Alaq in the arrangement of the Qur'an by itself explains that in the Holy Book, the revelation of which began with the first five verses of Sûrah Al-'Alaq, was sent down in a destiny-making night, which is also called the Night of Power. It is a glorious Book and its revelation for mankind is full of blessings.

The Night of Qadr (destiny) has two meanings, and both are implied here. First, it is the night during which destinies are decided. Second the revelation of this Book in this night is not merely the revelation of a book, but an event which will change the destiny of the entire world. In other words, this is a night of unique honor, dignity and glory; so much so that it is better than one thousand months. Thus, the disbelievers of Makkah have been warned: "You, on account of your ignorance, regard this Book, which Muhammad (peace be upon him) has presented, as a calamity for yourselves and complain that a disaster has befallen you, whereas the night in which it was decreed to be sent down was such a blessed night that it is worth more than one thousand months. In other words, a task was accomplished in it for the well-being of mankind which had not been accomplished   before during one thousand months of human history.

Finally, it is stated that during this night, the angels along with angel Gabriel, descend with all decrees by the leave of their Rabb. There is be peace from evening till morning; that is, there is no interference of evil in it, for all decrees of Allah are intended to promote good.

97: AL-QADR

This Sûrah, revealed at Makkah, has 1 section and 5 verseS.

In the name of Allah, the Compassionate, the Merciful

The night of Qadr is better than one thousand months

Surely, We have revealed this *(Qur'an)* in the night of Qadr.[1] And what could make you understand what the night of Qadr is![2] The night of Qadr is better than one thousand months.[3] The angels and the Spirit *(Gabriel)* come down, by the leave of their Rabb, with all Decrees.[4] *That night is the night of* Peace, till the break of dawn.[5] 　　　　　　　　　　　　　　　　97:[1-5]

98: AL-BAIYYINAH

Period of Revelation

Ibn 'Abbâs and Qatadah are reported to have expressed two views, first that it is Makki Sûrah, second that it is Madani Sûrah. As for its contents, there is nothing in it to indicate whether it was revealed at Makkah or at Madinah.

Major Issues, Divine Laws and Guidance

* The People of the Book (Jews and Christians) did not divide into sects until after receiving guidance.
* The People of the Book were also commanded to establish Salah (Prayer) and pay Zakah (Obligatory Charity) as it is commanded in the Qur'an.

In this Sûrah, the need of sending a Rasool is explained, then errors of the followers of earlier Books are pointed out. The cause of their straying into different creeds was not that Allah had not provided any guidance to them, but that they strayed after a clear statement of the True religion had come to them. From this, it automatically follows that they themselves were responsible for their error and deviation. If after the coming of the clear statement through Prophet Muhammad (peace be upon him) they continued to stray, their responsibility would further increase.

The Prophets who came from Allah and the Books sent down by Him, did not enjoin anything but that the way of sincere and true service to Allah be adopted; apart from all other ways, no one else's worship, service or obedience be mixed with His; the Salah (prayer) be established and the Zakah (obligatory charity) be paid. This has always been a part of the true religion and the followers of the earlier scriptures, straying from this true religion, have added extraneous things to it, which are false, and Allah's Rasool has come to invite them back to the same original faith.

In conclusion, it is pointed out that the followers of the earlier Books and the idol worshippers who would refuse to acknowledge this Message are the worst of all creatures. Their punishment will be an everlasting hell; and the people who would believe and act righteously, are the best of all creatures. Their reward will be an eternal paradise, wherein they will live forever. Allah will be well pleased with them and they will be well pleased with Allah.

98: AL-BAIYYINAH

This Sûrah, revealed at Madinah, has 1 section and 8 verses.

In the name of Allah, the Compassionate, the Merciful

The People of the Book did not divide into sects until after receiving guidance

Those who are unbelievers from among the people of the Book and from the Mushrikeen were not going to desist *from their unbelief* until the clear proof came to them,[1]   *that is,* a Rasool of Allah reciting to them holy scriptures from purified pages,[2] containing infallible books.[3]   Those who were given the Book before this *(Qur'an)* did not divide into sects until after there came to them a clear proof.[4]   Yet, they were commanded nothing but to worship Allah, with their sincere devotion to Him, being True in their faith; to establish Salah *(prayers)*; and to pay Zakah *(obligatory charity)*; and that is the infallible true Religion.[5]   Surely, those who disbelieve from among the people of the Book and the Mushrikeen shall be in the fire of hell, to dwell therein forever. They are the worst of all creatures.[6]   Surely, those who believe and do good deeds, are the best of all creatures.[7]   Their reward with their Rabb shall be the gardens of eternity, beneath which rivers flow, to dwell therein forever. Allah shall be well pleased with them and they shall be well pleased with Him. That is for him who fears his Rabb.[8]

They were also commanded to establish Salah and pay Zakah

98:[1-8]

99: AZ-ZALZALAH

Period of Revelation

Whether this Sûrah was revealed at Makkah or Madinah is disputed. Ibn Mas'ud, Ata, Jâbir, and Mujâhid say that it is a Makki Sûrah, a statement of Ibn 'Abbâs also supports this view, however, most other scholars consider it to be a Madani Sûrah.

Major Issue, Divine Law and Guidance

* On the Day of Judgement, the earth will report whatever happened on her and human beings shall be shown their Books of Deeds.

The theme of this Sûrah is the life after death and the presentation of man's full record of deeds done by him during his life on earth. The first three verses explain briefly how life after death will take place and how confounding it will be for man. In the next two verses, it is said that the earth, on which man has lived and performed all kinds of deeds thoughtlessly, and about which he never could fancy that this lifeless thing would at some time in the future bear witness to his deeds, will speak out on that Day by Allah's command and will state in respect of each person what act he had committed at a particular time and place. Then, it is said that men on that Day, rising from their graves, will come out in their varied groups from all corners of the earth and will be shown their book of deeds for accountability.

Presentation of their deeds will be so complete and detailed that not an atom's weight of good or evil will be left unnoticed or hidden. The words used in the verses are: "whoever has done an atom's weight of good, shall see it there and whoever has done an atom's weight of evil, shall see it there." The words " see it there" are worth pondering upon. We can understand it better today as compared to prior generations. Today in video technology, we can see split second movement or action to know exactly what happened in a game or event. Allah's technology is infinite times more sophisticated than human technology to see even an atom's weight, which normally cannot be seen without a powerful microscope. May be the angels assigned to each individual are audio and video recording all actions to be produced as a book of deeds, so that every one, whether learned or illiterate shall be able to see exactly what he or she did during his or her life in this world.

99: AZ-ZALZALAH

This Sûrah, revealed at Madinah, has 1 section and 8 verses.

In the name of Allah, the Compassionate, the Merciful

The earth will report whatever happened on her and men shall be shown their Books of Deeds

When the earth is shaken to its utmost convulsion,[1] and the earth brings out all its inner burdens,[2] man shall say: "What is happening to it?"[3] On that Day, it shall report whatever had happened *on it*,[4] for your Rabb shall have commanded it *to do so*.[5] On that Day, men shall proceed in sorted out groups to be shown their Deeds.[6] Then, whoever has done an atom's weight of good shall see it there,[7] and whoever has done an atom's weight of evil shall see it there.[8]

99:[1-8]

100: AL-'ÂDIYÂT

Period of Revelation

Whether this Sûrah is a Makki or a Madani is disputed. But the subject matter of the Sûrah and its style clearly indicate that it is not only Makki, but was revealed in the early stage of the Prophet's residence at Makkah.

Major Issue, Divine Law and Guidance

* An example of horses that they are more grateful to their owners than men are to their Rabb (Allah).

The object of this Sûrah is to make the people realize, how evil a man becomes when he denies the Hereafter, or becomes heedless of it, and also to warn them that in the Hereafter, not only their visible and apparent deeds, but the secrets hidden in their hearts will also be subjected to scrutiny. For this purpose, the general chaos and confusion prevailing in Arabia: bloodshed, looting and plundering; tribes subjecting other tribes to raids, no one could have a peaceful sleep at night out of fear that some enemy tribe might raid his settlement early in the morning, is pointed out. Every Arab was conscious about this state of affairs and realized that it was wrong. Although the plundered bemoaned his miserable, helpless state and the plunderer rejoiced, but when the plunderer himself was plundered, he too realized how abject was the condition of the society in which he was involved. Referring to this state of affairs, it is said: all this is happening because the people are not aware about their life after death and their accountability before Allah.

Then an example of stallions (horses used in war) is given to reflect on human attitude towards Allah. Stallions to whom man provides only food and water, are so grateful to him that they jump into the valley of death on his command, while man whom Allah has given life, faculties, food and other provisions is ungrateful to Allah and he himself is a witness to this fact. This example shows that an ungrateful person is worse than an animal. Such a person is so blinded by the love of worldly wealth that he tries to obtain it by every means, however impure and filthy it may be. He would never have behaved so, had he known the time when the dead would be raised from their graves for accountability. On that Day, the intentions and motives with which they had done all sorts of deeds in the world would be exposed and brought out before everyone to see by their Lord and Sustainer   (Allah).

100: AL-'ADIYÂT

This Sûrah, revealed at Makkah, has 1 section and 11 verses.

In the name of Allah, the Compassionate, the Merciful

An example of horses who are more grateful to their owners than men are to their Rabb

By the snorting steeds *(horses that are used in wars),*[1] dashing off sparks by the strike *of their hoofs,*[2]   making raids in the morning,[3]   and leaving a trail of dust[4]   as they dash into the middle of the *enemy* troops![5]   Surely, man is ungrateful to his Rabb;[6]   and surely, he himself bears witness to it,[7]   and surely, he is ardently devoted in his love of this worldly wealth.[8]   Is he not aware that when those who lie in the graves will be raised *to life,*[9] and that which is in their hearts will be made known,[10]   surely, their Rabb on that Day, shall be Well-Acquainted with them.[11]

100:[1-11]

101: AL-QÂRI'AH

Period of Revelation

This Sûrah was revealed at Makkah and is one of the early Sûrahs.

Major Issue, Divine Law and Guidance

*   A scene from the scenes of the Day of Judgement.*

The theme of this Sûrah is the Resurrection and the Hereafter. The people are warned: "The Great Disaster! What is the Great Disaster? And do you know what the Great Disaster is?" Thus preparing the listeners for the news of the dreadful calamity, then the incident of resurrection is depicted, that on that Day, people will be running around in confusion and bewilderment, just like scattered moths around a light, and the mountains will be uprooted and flung about like carded wool. Then Allah's Court will be established and the people will be called upon to account for their deeds. The people whose scale of good deeds will be heavier than their evil deeds, will be blessed with bliss and happiness, and the people whose good deeds will be lighter than their evil deeds, will be cast into the burning fire of hell.

101: AL-QÂRI‘AH

This Sûrah, revealed at Makkah, has 1 section and 11 verses.

In the name of Allah, the Compassionate, the Merciful

A scene
explaining the Day
of Judgment

The Striking Calamity![1]   What is the Striking Calamity?[2] And what could make you understand what the Striking Calamity *(the Day of Resurrection)* is?[3]   It is that Day when men shall be like scattered moths[4]   and the mountains like colorful carded wool.[5] *On that Day*, he whose scale of good deeds is heavy,[6]   shall live a pleasant luxurious life.[7]   But he whose scale of good deeds is light,[8]   his abode shall be Hâwiyah;[9] and what could make you understand what it *(Hâwiyah)* is?[10]   It is a blazing fire.[11]

101:[1-11]

102: AT-TAKÂTHUR

Period of Revelation

This Sûrah, according to all commentators, is Makki. Its contents and style indicate that it is one of the early Sûrahs revealed at Makkah.

Major Issue, Divine Law and Guidance

* *The cause of man's destruction is mutual rivalry for worldly gains, and real success is in working for the life Hereafter.*

In this Sûrah the people are warned about the evil consequences of selfish worldly gains when they spend their lives in acquiring more and more of worldly wealth, material benefits and pleasures, position and power. Rivalry with one another, bragging and boasting about their acquisitions is not going to end until they get to their graves. This pursuit has occupied the people so much that they are left with no time or opportunity for pursuing the spiritual and higher things in life. After warning the people of its evil, they are told: "These blessings which you are amassing and enjoying thoughtlessly, are not mere blessings but are also a means of your trial. For each one of these blessings and comforts, you will surely be called to account on the Day of Judgement. You will be asked as to how you used your faculties, your eyes, your hands, your time, your wealth, your health, your youth and opportunities provided to you for doing good and refraining from evil."

Mankind is told: "As soon as you close your eyes (die), you will find out the reality of this world and what you are going to face in the life hereafter. I wish that you believe in the knowledge that has been provided to you in this Qur'an, because if you do not, you will find out the reality when you will see the Hell with your own eyes but at that time it will be too late to believe. It will be the time of your accountability and Judgement for awarding you Paradise or dumping you into Hell."

102: AT-TAKÂTHUR

This Sûrah, revealed at Makkah, has 1 section and 8 verses.

In the name of Allah, the Compassionate, the Merciful

The cause of man's destruction is mutual rivalry for worldly gains.

O mankind, you have been distracted by the *rivalry of piling up* worldly gains *against one another*.[1] *You will never be satisfied* until you get to the grave.[2] Nay! You shall soon come to know.[3] Again, Nay! You shall soon come to know.[4] Nay! Would that you knew through the real knowledge *provided to you in this Qur'an and care about your life in the Hereafter*.[5] Because *on the Day of Judgment* when you see the Blazing Fire *(hell)*,[6] and see it with the certainty of your own eyes[7] - *you shall believe it, but that belief is going to do you no good because* - on that Day, you shall be questioned about the blessings *(faculties and resources that you were given in the worldly life - as to how you used them?)*[8]

Real success is in working for the life hereafter

102:[1-8]

103: AL-'ASR

Period of Revelation

Although scholars such as Mujâhid, Qatadah and Muqatil regard it as a Madani Sûrah, a great majority of the commentators are of the opinion that it is a Makki Sûrah. Its subject matter also testifies that it must have been revealed during the early stage at Makkah, when the message of Islam was being presented in a brief but highly impressive way so that the listeners who heard these verses once could not forget them even if they wanted to, because these verses will be committed to memory right away.

Major Issue, Divine Law and Guidance

* The formula for the way to salvation is to become a believer, do good deeds, be truthful and patient, and advise the same to others.

This Sûrah is a matchless example of comprehensiveness and brevity. A whole world of meaning has been compressed into its few brief words, which are too vast in content to be fully expressed even in a book. The way towards true success for mankind is clearly stated, as is the way towards ruin and destruction. Imam Shaf'e has said, "if the people comprehend this Sûrah well, it alone would suffice them as guidance." How important this Sûrah was in the sight of the companions can be judged from the tradition cited from Sayyidunâ Abdullah bin Hisn Ad-Darimi Abu Madinah, according to which, whenever any two of them met, they would not part company until they had recited Sûrah Al-'Asr to each other.

(This narration is taken from Tabarani)

103: AL-'ASR

This Sûrah, revealed at Makkah, has 1 section and 3 verses.

In the name of Allah, the Compassionate, the Merciful

Formula for the way to salvation

By the time *through the ages*![1] Surely, mankind is in loss,[2] except those who believe and do good deeds; those who exhort one another to the truth and exhort one another to patience.[3]

103:[1-3]

104: AL-HUMAZAH

Period of Revelation

This Sûrah was revealed at Makkah and is one of the early Sûrahs.

Major Issue, Divine Law and Guidance

*   *The slanderer, defamer and stingy shall be thrown into the blazing fire.*

This Sûrah condemns the evils which are prevalent among the materialistic hoarders of wealth. After stating this kind of ugly character, the ultimate end of such a people in the Hereafter is told. Both of these things (i. e., the character and one's fate in the Hereafter) are depicted in a way which makes the listener reach the conclusion that such a man deserves to meet such an end. And since in the world, people of such character may not suffer and appear to be thriving instead, the occurrence of the Hereafter becomes absolutely inevitable.

If this Sûrah is read in the sequence from the Sûrahs beginning with Az-Zalzalah, one can fully understand the fundamental beliefs of Islam. In Sûrah Az-Zalzalah, it was said that in the Hereafter, man's full record will be placed before him and not an atom's weight of good or evil done by him in the world will have been left unrecorded. In Sûrah Al-'Âdiyât, attention was drawn to the plunder, loot, bloodshed and vandalism, prevailing in Arabia before Islam; then making the people realize, that the way the powers given by Allah were being abused, was indeed an expression of sheer ingratitude to Him which deserves punishment. In Sûrah Al-Qâri'ah, after depicting the Resurrection, the people were warned that in the Hereafter, a man's good or evil end will be dependent on whether the scale of his good deeds was heavier, or the scale of his evil deeds was heavier. In Sûrah At- Takâthur the people were taken to task for their materialistic mentality because of which, they remained occupied in seeking increase in worldly benefits, pleasures, comforts and position. They were warned that they would have to render an   account to their Rabb and Sustainer as to how they obtained it and how they used it. In Sûrah Al-'Asr, it was declared that each member, each group and each community of mankind, even the entire world, was in manifest loss, if its members were devoid of faith, righteous deeds and the practice of exhorting others to truth and patience. Immediately after this comes Sûrah Al-Humazah, in which, after presenting a specimen of leadership of the pre-Islamic age of ignorance, the people are asked the question: "What should such character deserve, if not loss and perdition?"

104: AL-HUMAZAH

This Sûrah, revealed at Makkah, has 1 section and 9 verses.

In the name of Allah, the Compassionate, the Merciful

The slanderer, defamer and stingy shall be thrown into the blazing fire

Woe to every slanderer and backbiter,[1] who amasses wealth and keeps on counting it.[2] He thinks that his wealth *will make him last* forever![3] By no means! He shall be thrown into Hutamah.[4] What could make you understand what Hutamah is?[5] It is the fire of Allah, kindled to blaze,[6] which shall rise right to the hearts,[7] closing in upon them from every side[8] in out-stretched columns.[9]

104:[1-9]

105: AL-FEEL

Period of Revelation

This Sûrah was revealed in the very early stage at Makkah.

Major Issue, Divine Laws and Guidance

*   An example of Allah's saving His house (Al-Ka'bah) by destroying
    an army of 60,000 with elephants, through a flock of birds.

In this Sûrah, Allah's punishment which was inflicted on the people of the
elephant is referred to and described very briefly because it was an event of recent
occurrence, and everyone in Makkah and Arabia was fully aware of it. That's why
the Arabs believed that the Ka'bah was protected in this invasion, not by any god
or goddess, but by Allah Almighty Himself. Then Allah Alone was invoked by the
Quraish chiefs for help, and for quite a few years, the people of Quraish, having
been impressed by this event, had worshipped none but Allah. Therefore, there was
no need to mention the details in Sûrah Al-Feel, but only a reference to it was
enough.

History of attack on Ka'bah and how Allah saved it

According to Arab historians, the Abyssinian army that invaded Yemen
had two commanders, Aryat and Abraha. Aryat was killed in an encounter, and
Abraha took control of the country; then somehow he persuaded Negus (the Abyssinian king) to appoint him his viceroy over Yemen. Abraha was the slave of a
Greek merchant of the Abyssinian seaport of Adolis, who, by clever diplomacy,
had come to wield great influence in the Abyssinian army occupying Yemen. After
the death of the king, his successor was reconciled to accept him as his vicegerent
of Yemen. Through passage of time, Abraha became an independent ruler of Yemen. He acknowledged the sovereignty of the Negus only in name and portrayed
himself as his deputy.

After stabilizing his rule in Yemen, Abraha turned his attention to the objective which from the very beginning of this campaign had been, before the Byzantine empire and its allies, the Abyssinian Christians. This was to spread Christianity in Arabia and to capture the trade that was carried out through the Arabs
between the eastern lands and the Byzantine dominions. The need for this increased

because the Byzantine struggle for power against the Sasanian empire of Iran had blocked all the routes of the Byzantine trade with the East.

To achieve this objective, Abraha built in Sana, the capital of Yemen, a magnificent cathedral called by the Arabian historians, Al-Qalis. After completing the building, he wrote to king Negus, saying: "I shall not rest until I have diverted the Arabs pilgrimage to it. So, in 570 or 571 A. D., he took 60,000 troops and 13 elephants (according to another tradition, 9 elephants) and set off for Makkah. According to Muhammad bin Ishâq, when he was within three miles of Makkah at a place called 'Al- Mughammas,' Abraha sent his vanguard, who brought him the plunder of the people of Tihamah and Quraish, which included two hundred camels of Abdul Muttalib, the grandfather of the Prophet Muhammad (peace be upon him). Then, he sent his envoy to Makkah with the message that he had not come to fight the people of Makkah, but only to destroy the House (i. e. the Ka'bah). If they offered no resistance, there would be no cause for bloodshed. Abraha also instructed his envoy that if the people of Makkah wanted to negotiate, he should bring their leader to him. The leader of Makkah at that time was Abdul Muttalib. The envoy went to him and delivered Abraha's message. Abdul Muttalib replied: "We have no power to fight Abraha. This is Allah's House. If He wills, He will save His House." The envoy asked him to come with him to Abraha. He agreed and accompanied him to Abraha. Abdul Muttalib was such a dignified and handsome person, that when Abraha saw him, he was much impressed; he got off his throne and sat beside him on the carpet. Then, he asked him what he wanted. Abdul Muttalib replied that he only wanted the king to return his camels which he had taken. Abraha said: "I was much impressed when I saw you, but your reply has brought you down in my eyes; you only demand your camels, but you say nothing about this House which is your sanctuary and the sanctuary of your forefathers." He replied: "I am the owner of camels, therefore, I am requesting you to return them. As for the House, it has its own Owner; He will defend it." When Abraha said that He would not be able to defend it against him, Abdul Muttalib said that it rested between Him (Allah) and him (Abraha). With this, Abdul Muttalib left Abraha who had returned his camels to him.

One thing which becomes evident from this narration, is, that the tribes living in and around Makkah did not have the power to fight such a big force and save the Ka'bah. Therefore, obviously, the Quraish did not try to put up any resistance. - The Quraish on the occasion of the Battle of the Trench (Ahzâb) had hardly been able to muster ten to twelve thousand men in spite of the alliance with the pagan and Jewish tribes; they could not have resisted an army of 60,000 strong. - Muhammad bin Ishâq says that after returning from the camp of Abraha, Abdul

Muttalib ordered the Quraish to withdraw from the city and go to the mountains along with their families for fear of a general massacre. Then, he went to the Ka'bah along with some chiefs of the Quraish and holding the iron ring of the door, prayed to Allah Almighty. Ibn Hishâm, in his book 'Life of the Prophet,' has cited the prayer of Abdul Muttalib:

"O Allah, a man protects his house, so protect Your House; Let not their cross and their craft tomorrow overcome Your craft. If You want to leave them and our Qiblah to themselves, You may do as You please. My Lord, I do not cherish any hope from anyone against them except You. O my Lord, protect Your House from them. The enemy of this House is Your enemy. Stop them from destroying Your settlement."

After making this supplication Abdul Muttalib and his companions also went off to the mountains. The next morning Abraha prepared to enter Makkah, but his special elephant, Mahmud, which was in the forefront, knelt down. It was beaten with iron bars, goaded, but it would not get up. When they made it face south, north, or east, it would immediately start off, but as soon as they directed it towards Makkah, it knelt down. In the meantime swarms of birds appeared carrying stones in their beaks and claws and showered these on the troops. Whoever was hit would start disintegrating. Ibn 'Abbâs says that whoever was struck by a pebble, would start scratching his body resulting in breaking of the skin and falling off of the flesh. In another tradition, Ibn 'Abbâs says that the flesh and blood flowed like water and bones in the body became visible. The same thing happened with Abraha too. Nufail bin Habeeb, whom they had brought as guide from the country of Khatham, was searched out and asked to guide them back to Yemen, but he refused and said: "Now where can one flee when Allah pursues? The split nose (Abraha) is the conquered; not the conqueror."

According to Sayyidah Umme Hani and Sayyidunâ Zubair bin Al-Awwam, the Prophet (peace be upon him) said: "The Quraish did not worship anyone but Allah, the One and Only, for ten years. The Arabs describe the year in which this event took place as 'Am Al-Feel (the year of the elephants). It was the same year when the Prophet of Allah, Muhammad (peace be upon him) was born.

105: AL-FEEL

This Sûrah, revealed at Makkah, has 1 section and 5 verses.

In the name of Allah, the Compassionate, the Merciful

Allah has the power to defeat an army with elephants through the flock of birds

Have you not considered how your Rabb dealt with the owners of the Elephant *(reference is made to the elephant army which came from Yemen under the command of Abraha intending to destroy the Ka'bah at Makkah in the year of the Prophet Muhammad's birth)?*[1] Did He not make their treacherous plan a flop?[2] And sent against them flocks of birds,[3] which pelted them with stones of baked clay,[4] thus rendered them like the chewed-up chaff.[5]   105:[1-5]

106: QURAISH

Period of Revelation

This Sûrah was revealed during the very early stage at Makkah.

Major Issue, Divine Law and Guidance

*   An Admonition to believe in Allah, Who is the provider of your sustenance.

To understand this Sûrah, it is necessary to know the historical background of the tribe of Quraish. It was scattered throughout Hijâz until the time of Qusayy bin Kilâb, the ancestor of the Prophet (peace be upon him). First of all, Qusayy gathered his tribe in Makkah and the tribe was able to gain authority over the Ka'bah. On that basis, Qusayy was called Mujammi (uniter, assembler) by his people. This man, by his sagacity and wisdom, founded a city state of Makkah and made excellent arrangements for the welfare of the pilgrims coming from all over Arabia, as a result, the Quraish were able to gain great influence among the Arabian tribes. After Qusayy's death, the state of Makkah was divided between his sons, Abdi Manâf and Abd ad-Dar. Of the two, Abdi Manâf gained greater fame, and was held in high esteem throughout Arabia.

Abdi Manâf had four sons; Hashim, Abdi Shams, Al-Muttalib, and Naufal. Of these, Hashim, father of Abdul Muttalib and grandfather of the Prophet, got the idea to take part in the trade passing between the eastern countries, Syria and Egypt, through Arabia. He also purchased the necessities of life for the Arabs so that the tribes living by the trade route could buy these items from them and the merchants living in the interior of the country were attracted to the market of Makkah. This was the time when the Sasanian kingdom of Iran had gained control over the international trade that was carried out between the northern lands, the eastern countries and the Byzantine empire through the Persian Gulf. This boosted the trade activity on the trade route leading from southern Arabia to Syria and Egypt, along the Red Sea coast. The Quraish took advantage of the fact that the tribes on this route held them in high esteem because of their status of being Keepers of the Ka'bah. They stood indebted to them for the great generosity with which the Quraish treated them during the Hajj season. That is why the Quraish felt no fear that their caravans would be robbed or harmed any where along the way. The tribes along the way did not even charge them the heavy transit taxes that they demanded from the other caravans. Hashim, taking advantage of this, prepared the trade scheme and made his three brothers partners in it. Thus, Hashim obtained trade privileges from the Ghassanide king of Syria, Abdi Shams from the

Negus, Al-Muttalib from the Yemenite nobles and Naufal from the governments of Iraq and Irân, and their trade began to flourish. That is how the four brothers became famous as traders and were called Ashâb Al-Eelâf (generators of love and affection), on account of their friendly relations with the tribes and states in the surrounding areas.

Because of their business relations with Syria, Egypt, Iraq, Iran, Yemen and Abyssinia, the Quraish became the most affluent tribe in Arabia and Makkah, and Makkah became the most important commercial center of the Arabian peninsula. Another great advantage that accrued from these international relations, was, that the caravans brought tile script from Iraq, which was used for writing down the Qur'an. No other Arabian tribe could boast of so many literate people as Quraish. For these very reasons, the Prophet (peace be upon him) said: "The Quraish are the leaders of men." (Musnad Ahmed: Marwiyat Amr bin al-As).

The Quraish were thus prospering and flourishing when the event of Abraha's invasion of Makkah took place. Had Abraha succeeded in capturing Makkah and destroying the Ka'bah, the glory and renown of not only the Quraish, but of the Ka'bah itself, would have suffered a great setback. The belief of pre-Islamic Arabia that the House indeed was Allah's House, would have been shattered, and the high esteem in which the Quraish were held, for being keepers of the House, throughout the country would have been tarnished. Then, after the Abyssinian advance to Makkah, the Byzantium also would have taken the initiative to gain control over the trade route between Syria and Makkah. The Quraish would have been reduced to a plight worse than that in which they were involved before Qusayy bin Kilâb. But when Allah showed the manifestation of His power and swarms of birds destroyed 60,000 Abyssinian troops brought by Abraha by pelting them with stones, they continued falling and dying by the wayside from Makkah to Yemen. The faith of the Arabs that the Ka'bah indeed was Allah's House, increased manifold, and the glory and renown of Quraish was also enhanced considerably throughout the country. Now the Arabs were convinced that they were under Allah's special favor. They, therefore, visited every part of Arabia fearlessly and passed through every land with their trade caravans unharmed. No one would dare touch them with an evil intention. Not to speak of touching them, even if they had a non-Quraishite under their protection, he too was allowed to pass unharmed. That is why in this Sûrah, the Quraish are simply asked to consider; "When you yourselves acknowledge this House (i. e., the Ka'bah) to be Allah's House, and not of the idols, and when you fully know that it is Allah Alone Who has granted you peace by virtue of this House, made your trade and commerce flourish, and favored you with prosperity, you should then worship none but Him Alone!"

106: QURAISH

This Sûrah, revealed at Makkah, has 1 section and 4 verses.

In the name of Allah, the Compassionate, the Merciful

For the covenant of security *enjoyed* by the Quraish *(as the caretakers of the House of Allah)*,[1] *they enjoy* safety during their trade journeys of winter and summer.[2] So, they should worship the Rabb of this House,[3] Who provided them with food against hunger and made them secure against fear.[4]   106:[1-4]

Believe in Allah Who is the provider of your sustenance

107: AL-MÂ'ÛN

Period of Revelation

There is a difference of opinion relating to this Sûrah's place of revelation. Ibn Marduyah has cited Ibn 'Abbâs (may Allah bless them both) as saying that this Sûrah is Makki, and the same also is the view of Ata and Jâbir. But Abu Hayyan in Al-Bahr Al-Muhit, has cited Ibn 'Abbâs, Qatadah and Dahhak as saying that this Sûrah was revealed at Madinah. There is also a piece of evidence in the Sûrah itself, which points to its being a Madani revelation. It states a threat of destruction to those who offer the Salah (prayers) but are unmindful of their Salah since they want only to be seen offering the prayers. These kind of hypocrites were only at Madinah. Allah knows best. Since most the ulema have written this Sûrah as Makki Sûrah, therefore, we tabulate as such.

Major Issues, Divine Laws and Guidance

*   Disbelief in the Hereafter is the main cause of moral decay.
*   God consciousness, social welfare and caring about other people's necessities of life are the main purposes of Salah (prayers).

The theme of this Sûrah is to point out what kind of morals a man develops when he refuses to believe in the Hereafter. In vv 2-3 the condition of the disbelievers, who openly deny the Hereafter, is described. In the last four verses, the state of those hypocrites who apparently are Muslims but do not believe in the Hereafter, the Day of Judgement, reward and the punishment, has been described. The objective of depicting the attitude and conduct of two kinds of people is to stress the point that man cannot develop a strong, stable and pure character in himself unless he believes in the Hereafter

Those people who offer Salah (prayers), but do not practice good behavior with other believers and neighbors, and do not provide a helping hand when they are needed to do so, have not understood the very reason for which congregational Salah (prayers) are made obligatory. Therefore, it is pointed out that their prayers are nothing but a show and are not acceptable to Allah and such people may very well end up in the hellfire.

107: AL-MÂ'ÛN

This Sûrah, revealed at Makkah, has 1 section and 7 verses.

In the name of Allah, the Compassionate, the Merciful

Have you seen the one who denies the Day of Judgment?[1] He it is who drives away the orphan *with harshness*[2] and does not encourage the feeding of the poor.[3] So woe to those who offer Salah *(prayers)*,[4] but are neglectful of their Salah *(who neither observe the Salah as it ought to be observed, nor observe it on its prescribed timings)*;[5] those who make show *of piety*[6] but refuse to offer help *to the needy*.[7] 107:[1-7]

Disbelief in the Hereafter is the main cause of moral decay and lack of caring about others

108: AL-KAUTHAR

Period of Revelation

This Sûrah was revealed at Makkah during the early stages, when the Prophet was enduring extremely difficult conditions.

Major Issue, Divine Laws and Guidance

* Allah has made the name of Prophet Muhammad (peace be upon him), everlasting

The disbelieving Quraish used to say: "Muhammad (peace be upon him) is cut off from his community and reduced to a powerless and helpless individual. Muhammad bin Ishâq says: "Whenever the Prophet (peace be upon him) was mentioned before 'As bin Wa'il, the chief of Makkah, he used to say: Leave him alone for he is only a childless man (abtar) with no male offspring. When he dies, there will be no one to remember him." (Reported by Ibn Jareer). Ibn Sa'ad and lbn 'Asâkir have related that Sayyidunâ Abdullah bin 'Abbâs said; "The eldest son of the Prophet (peace be upon him) was Qâsim; next to him was Zainab, next to her Abdullah and next to him three daughters; Umme Kulthûm, Ruqayyah, and Fâtimah. Of them, first Qâsim died and then Abdullah. Thereupon 'As bin Wa'il said: "His line has come to an end; now he is abtar (i. e. cut off from the root)." Abu Jahl also had said similar words on the death of the Prophet's son, Abdullah.

Such were the disturbing conditions under which Sûrah Al-Kauthar was sent down. The Quraish were angry with him because he worshipped and served only Allah and repudiated their idolatry publicly. For this very reason, he was deprived of the rank, esteem and honor that he enjoyed among his people before Prophethood and was now cut off from his community. The handful of his Companions were helpless poor people who were also being persecuted and tyrannized. The Prophet (peace be upon him) was grieved by the death of his two sons, one after the other, whereas the near relatives and the people of his clan were rejoicing and uttering such words which were disheartening and disturbing for the Prophet (peace be upon him), who had treated even his enemies most kindly. At this occasion, Allah in just one sentence of this brief Sûrah, gave him the good news - better news than which has never been given to any one in this world. It will be his opponents who will be cut off from their roots and not him.

108: AL-KAUTHAR

This Sûrah, revealed at Makkah, has 1 section and 3 verses.

In the name of Allah, the Compassionate, the Merciful

O Muhammad, surely, We have granted you the Kauthar *(countless blessings - it is also the name of a special fountain which will be granted to Prophet Muhammad on the Day of Judgment)*.[1] Therefore, offer Salah *(prayer)* to your Rabb and sacrifice.[2] Surely, your enemy is the one who will be cut off from the root.[3]

108:[1-3]

Allah has made Muhammad's name everlasting

109: AL-KÂFIRÛN

Period of Revelation

There is a difference of opinion whether this Sûrah is Makki or Madani. However, according to the majority of commentators, it is a Makki Sûrah. Its subject matter also points to its being a Makki revelation.

Major Issue, Divine Law and Guidance

* Allah's commandment not to compromise in the matters of religion.

This Sûrah was not revealed to preach religious tolerance as some people of today seem to think, but was revealed in order to exonerate the Muslims from the disbelievers' religion, their rites of worship, and their gods; to express their total disgust and unconcern with them; to tell them that Islam and Kufr (unbelief) had nothing in common and that there was no possibility of their ever being combined and mixed into one entity. Although it was initially addressed to the disbelieving Quraish in response to their proposals of compromise, it is not confined to them only. Having made it a part of the Qur'an, Allah gave the Muslims the eternal teaching stating that they should exonerate themselves by word and deed from the creed of Kufr (disbelief), wherever and in whatever form it may be, and that they should declare without any reservation that they cannot make any compromise with the disbelievers in matters of Faith.

Sayyidunâ Khabbâb says: "The Prophet (peace be upon him) said to me; 'when you lie down in bed to sleep, recite Qul Yâ-Ayyuhal Kâfirûn, this was the Prophet's own practice when he lay down to sleep.'" - (Reported by Bazzar, Tabarani, Ibn Marduyah). According to Ibn 'Abbâs, the Prophet (peace be upon him) said to the people: "Should I tell you the word which will protect you from polytheism? It is that you should recite Qul Yâ-Ayyuhal Kâfirûn when you go to bed." (Reported by Abu Ya'la, Tabarani). Sayyidunâ Anas says that the Prophet said to Sayyidunâ Mu'adh bin Jabal: "Recite Qul Yâ-Ayyuhal-Kâfirûn at the time you go to bed, for this is immunity from polytheism." (Reported by Baihaqi in Ash-Shu'aib).

The Issue of Belief and Disbelief

There was a time in Makkah when although a storm of opposition had arisen in the pagan society of Quraish against the message of Islam preached by the Prophet (peace be upon him), the Quraish chiefs had not yet lost hope that they would reach some sort of a compromise with him. Therefore, from time to time they would visit him with different proposals of compromise so that he may accept any compromise and the dispute between them may end. In this connection, different narration have been related in the Hadith.

According to Sayyidunâ Abdullah bin 'Abbâs, the Quraish proposed to the Prophet: "We shall give you so much wealth that you will become the richest man at Makkah. Further, we shall give you whichever woman you like in marriage and we are prepared to follow and obey you as our leader on the condition that you will not speak ill of our gods. If you do not agree to this, we present another proposal which is to your and our advantage." When the Prophet asked what it was, they said that if he would worship their gods, Lât and Uzza, for a year, they would worship his God (Allah) for the same span of time. The Prophet said: "Wait awhile let me see what my Rabb commands in this regard." Thereupon this revelation came down. According to another tradition from Ibn 'Abbâs, the Quraish said to the Prophet, peace be upon him: "O Muhammad, if you kiss our gods (idols), we shall worship your God." Thereupon, this Sûrah was sent down. Yet in another narration Sa'id bin Mina (the freed slave of Abul Bakhtari) has related that Waleed bin Mughirah, 'As bin Wa'il, Aswad bin Al-Muttalib and Umayyah bin Khalaf met the Prophet (peace be upon him) and said to him: "O Muhammad, let us agree that we would worship your God and you would worship our gods, and we would make you a partner in all our works. If what you have brought is better than what we possess, we would be partners in it with You, and have our share in it, and if what we possess is better than what you have brought, you would be partner in it with us and have your share of it." At this Allah revealed: Qul Yâ-Ayyuhal-Kâfirûn (Ibn Jareer, Ibn Abi Hâtim, Ibn Hishâm also have related this incident in the Seerah (biography) of the Prophet Muhammad (peace be upon him).

Because of these repeated dialogues, there was a need that the Quraish be given a definite and decisive reply so that their hope of Muhammad (peace be upon him) coming to terms with them on the principle of "give and take" would be frustrated for ever.

109: AL-KÂFIRÛN

This Sûrah, revealed at Makkah, has 1 section and 6 verses.

In the name of Allah, the Compassionate, the Merciful

The commandment not to compromise in the matters of religion

Say: O unbelievers![1]   I do not worship that which you worship,[2]   nor do you worship that which I worship.[3]   I shall never worship that which you worship,[4]   nor will you ever worship that which I worship.[5]   You have your religion, and I have mine.[6]   109:[1-6]

110: AN-NASR

Period of Revelation

Sayyidunâ Abdullah bin 'Abbâs says that this is the last Sûrah of the Qur'an which was revealed, i. e. no complete Sûrah was revealed to the Prophet after this. (Reported by Muslim Nasâi, Tabarani, Ibn Abi Shaibah, Ibn Marduyah). According to Sayyidunâ Abdullah bin Umar, this Sûrah was revealed on the occasion of the Farewell Pilgrimage at Mina, and after it, the Prophet rode his she camel and gave his farewell Sermon. Mother of the Believers, Sayyidah Umme Habeebah, says that when this Sûrah was revealed, the Prophet said that he would leave the world that year. Upon hearing this, the Prophet's daughter Sayyidah Fâtimah wept. Thereupon, he said: "From among my family, you will be the first to join me." Hearing this she laughed. (Reported by Ibn Abi Hâtim and Ibn Marduyah).

Major Issues, Divine Laws and Guidance

*   Victory is not an occasion of exultation, but to glorify Allah , it comes with the help of Allah.
*   Indication is given that the mission of the Prophet has been fulfilled.

In this Sûrah, Allah has informed His Rasool (peace be upon him) that when Islam attained complete victory in Arabia and the people started entering Allah's religion (Islam) in great numbers, it would mean that the mission for which he was appointed in this world, had been fulfilled. He was then enjoined to busy himself in praising and glorifying Allah by Whose bounty he had been able to accomplish such a great task, and should implore Him to forgive whatever failings and shortcomings he might have shown in the performance of His service.

Here, one can easily see the great difference that there is between a Prophet and a common worldly leader. If a worldly leader, in his own lifetime, is able to bring about a revolution, which has been the aim and objective of his struggle, this would be an occasion for exultation for him. But here, we witness quite another phenomenon. The Rasool of Allah, in a brief space of 23 years, revolutionized an entire nation regarding its beliefs, thoughts, customs, morals, civilization, ways of living, economy, politics and fighting ability, and raised it from ignorance and barbarism, enabled it to conquer the world and become the leader of nations. Yet, when he had accomplished this unique task, he was not enjoined to celebrate it but to glorify and praise Allah, and to pray for His forgiveness. He busied himself humbly in the implementation of that command.

110: AN-NASR

This Sûrah, revealed at Madinah, has 1 section and 3 verses.

In the name of Allah, the Compassionate, the Merciful

Victory comes with
the help of Allah

When there comes the help of Allah and the victory,[1] you see people embracing Allah's religion *(Islam)* in multitudes.[2] So, glorify your Rabb with His praises, and ask for His forgiveness: surely, He is ever ready to accept the repentance *and forgive*.[3]

110:[1-3]

111: AL-LAHAB

Period of Revelation

This Sûrah was revealed at Makkah during the period when Abu Lahab had transgressed all limits in his hostility to the Prophet (peace be upon him), and his attitude was becoming a serious obstruction in the progress of Islam.

Major Issue, Divine Law and Guidance

* Allah has cursed Abu Lahab and his wife who were the opponents of the Prophet Muhammad (peace be upon him)

Background of Allah's Curse by Name

This is the only place in the Qur'an where a person from among the enemies of Islam has been condemned by name, even though in Makkah, as well as in Madinah after the migration, there were many people who were in no way less harmful to Islam and the Prophet Muhammad (peace be upon him) than Abu Lahab. The question is, what was the special trait of the character of this person, which became the basis of this condemnation by name? To understand this, it is necessary that one understands the Arabian society of that time and the role that Abu Lahab played in it.

In ancient days there prevailed chaos, confusion, bloodshed and plunder throughout Arabia. The condition of Arabia for centuries was that a person could have no guarantee of the protection of life, honor and property except with the help and support of his clansmen and blood relations. Therefore, silah rehmi (good treatment of the kindred) was esteemed most highly among the moral values of the Arabian society and the breaking off of connections with kindred was regarded as a great sin. Under the influence of this Arabian tradition, the Prophet (peace be upon him) began to preach the message of Islam. The other clans of Quraish and their chiefs resisted and opposed him tooth and nail, but the Bani Hashim and the Bani Al-Muttalib (children of Al-Muttalib, brother of Hashim) not only did not oppose him but continued to support him openly, even though most of them had not yet believed in his Prophethood. The other clans of Quraish regarded this support by the Prophet's blood relations as perfectly in accordance with the moral traditions of Arabia. That is why they never taunted the Bani Hashim and the Bani   Al-

Muttalib, even though they seemingly had betrayed their ancestral faith by supporting a person who was preaching a new faith. They knew and believed that they could in no case hand over an individual of their clan to his enemies, and their support and aid of a clansman was perfectly natural in the sight of the Quraish and the people of Arabia.

This moral principle, which the Arabs in the pre-Islamic days of ignorance, regarded as worthy of respect and inviolable was broken only by one man in his enmity of Islam, and that was Abu Lahab, son of Abdul Muttalib, a real uncle of the Prophet, peace be upon him. In Arabia, an uncle represented the father especially when the nephew was fatherless. The uncle was expected to look after the nephew as one of his own children. But this man in his hostility to Islam and love of Kufr trampled over all of the Arab traditions with his actions.

Before the proclamation of Prophethood, two of the Prophet's daughters were married to two of Abu Lahab's sons, Utbah and Utaibah. When the Prophet began to invite people to Islam, Abu Lahab said to both his sons: "I would forbid myself seeing and meeting you until you divorce the daughters of Muhammad (peace be upon him)." Both of them subsequently divorced their wives.

Whenever the Prophet went to preach the message of Islam, Abu Lahab followed him and forbade the people to listen to him. Târiq bin Abdullah Al-Muharibi says: "I saw in the fair of Dhul-Majâz, the Prophet (peace be upon him) exhorting the people saying: `O people, say Lâ Ilâh ill-Allah, you will attain success.' Behind him there was a man who was casting stones at him until his heels bled and he was telling the people: 'Do not listen to him, he is a liar.' I asked the people who he was. They said he was his uncle, Abu Lahab." (Reported by Tirmidhi).

In the 7th year of Prophethood, when all of the clans of Quraish socially and economically boycotted the Bani Hashim and the Bani Al- Muttalib, both of these clans, who remained steadfast in the Prophet's support, were besieged in Shi'b Abi Tâlib. Abu Lahab was the only person who sided with the disbelieving Quraish against his own clan. This boycott continued for three years, so much so that the Bani Hashim and the Bani Al- Muttalib began to starve. This, however, did not move Abu Lahab. When a trade caravan came to Makkah and a besieged person from Shi'b Abi Tâlib approached it to buy some food, Abu Lahab shouted out to the merchants to demand a forbidding price, telling them that he would make up for any loss that they incurred. Thus, they would demand exorbitant rates and the poor customer would return empty handed to his starving children. Then Abu Lahab would purchase the same articles from them at the market rates.

(Reported by Ibn S'ad and Ibn Hishâm)

On account of these misdeeds Abu Lahab was condemned in this Sûrah by name. It was against the established traditions of Arabia that an uncle would oppose his nephew without a reason or pelt stones at and bring false accusations against him publicly. Therefore, people were influenced by what Abu Lahab said and were in doubt about the Prophet (peace be upon him). But when this Sûrah was revealed, Abu Lahab filled with rage started uttering nonsense, the people realized that what he said in opposition to the Prophet was not at all reliable and was out of hostility to his nephew.

When the Prophet's uncle was condemned by name, the people's expectations that the Rasool (peace be upon him) could treat some relative leniently in the matter of religion, was frustrated forever. When the Prophet's own uncle was taken to task publicly, the people understood that there was no room for preference or partiality in their faith. A non-relative could become a near and dear one if he believed, and a near relation may become non-relative if he disbelieved. Thus, there is no place for preferring the ties of blood in Islam if the relative is an unbeliever.

111: AL-MASAD / AL-LAHAB

This Sûrah, revealed at Makkah, has 1 section and 5 verses.

In the name of Allah, the Compassionate, the Merciful

Curse of Allah on Abu Lahab and his wife, the opponents of the Prophet

Perish be the hands of Abu Lahab! And perish be he![1] His wealth and whatever he earned *(children)* shell not avail him anything.[2] Soon he shall be burnt in a flaming fire *(a pun on the meaning of Abu Lahab, "father of flames")*,[3] and his wife, the carrier of firewood *(to put thorns in the Prophet's path and slander him - the word firewood was used by Arabs to allude to slander and backbiting)*,[4] shall have a rope of palm-leaf fibre around her neck.[5] 111:[1-5]

112: AL-IKHLÂS

Period of Revelation

This Sûrah was revealed during the early period at Makkah when detailed verses of the Qur'an dealing with the essence and attributes of Allah Almighty had not yet been revealed. The people, hearing the Prophet's invitation to Allah, wanted to know what his God, Whose worship and service he was calling them to, was like.

Major Issue, Divine Law and Guidance

*   The unique attributes of Allah

It is important to know what the religious concepts of the world were about God (Allah), at the time the Prophet began to preach the message of Tawheed (God is One and Only)! The idolatrous polytheists were worshipping gods made of wood, stone, gold, silver and other substances. These gods had forms, shapes and bodies and the gods and goddesses were descended from each other. No goddess was without a husband and no god without a wife. They stood in need of food and drink and their devotees arranged these for them. A large number of the polytheists believed that God assumed human form and there were some people who descended from Him. Although the Christians claimed to believe in One God, they also believed that their God had at least one son, Isa (Jesus). That the Son and the Holy Ghost also had the honor of being associated with Godhead. The Jews also claimed to believe in One God, but their God too was not without physical, material or other human qualities and characteristics. He went for a stroll, appeared in human form, wrestled with a servant of His, and was father of a son, Ezra. In addition to these religious communities, the Zoroastrians (fire worshippers) and the Sabians (star worshippers), also existed. Under such conditions when the people were invited to believe in Allah, the One and Only, Who has no associate, it was inevitable that questions arose in their minds as to what kind of God He was, Who was the One and Only and Whose invitation to believe in Him was being given at the expense of all other gods and deities. It is a miracle of the Qur'an, that in a few brief words it answered all questions and presented such a clear concept of the Being of Allah that all polytheistic concepts were destroyed, leaving no room for the ascription of human qualities to His Being.

That is why the Prophet (peace be upon him) held this Sûrah in such great esteem. This made the Muslims realize its importance in different ways and exhorted them to recite it frequently and disseminate it among the people. It states *the foremost and fundamental doctrine of Islam (Tawheed) in four brief sentences, impresses on human memory and can be read and recited easily. There are a great number of Hadith which show that the Prophet, on different occasions and in different ways, told the people that this Sûrah is equivalent to one third of the Qur'an. Several Ahâdith (narrations from the Prophet, peace be upon him) on this subject have been related in Bukhâri, Muslim, Abu Daûd, Nasâi, Tirmidhi, Ibn Mâjah, Musnad Ahmed, Tabarani and other books. Commentators have also given many explanations of the Prophet's saying. In the opinion of Abul A'lâ Maudûdi, a well known mufassir, it simply means that the religion presented by the Qur'an is based on three doctrines: Tawheed (God is One and Only), Risâlat (Prophets were assigned for the guidance of people) and the Âkhirah (accountability of people in the Hereafter). This Sûrah teaches Tawheed, pure and undefiled. Therefore, the Prophet (peace be upon him) regarded it, equal to one-third of the Qur'an.*

112: AL-IKHLÂS

This Sûrah, revealed at Makkah, has 1 section and 4 verses.

In the name of Allah, the Compassionate, the Merciful

Say: "He is Allah the One and Only;[1] Allah is the Self-Sufficient *(independent of all, while all are dependent on Him)*;[2] He begets not, nor is He begotten *(he has no child, nor is He a child of any one)*;[3] And there is none comparable to Him."[4]   112:[1-4]

Tawheed - the unique attribute of Allah

113: AL-FALAQ & 114: AN-NÂS

Period of Revelation

There is a difference of opinion relating to the place and period of these Sûrahs' revelation. According to Sayyidunâ Hasan Basri, 'Ikrimah, 'Ata' and Jâbir bin Zaid these Sûrahs are Makkan. Ibn S'ad, Imam Baihaqi, 'Abd bin Humaid and others are of the opinion that these Sûrahs were revealed in A.H. 7, when the Jews had worked magic on the Prophet (upon whom be peace) in Madinah and he had fallen ill under its effect. The subject matter of these Sûrahs is explicit that they were sent down at Makkah when, for the first time, opposition to the Prophet had grown very intense. Later, when at Madinah storms of opposition were raised by the hypocrites, Jews and polytheists, the Prophet was instructed to recite these Sûrahs, as has been mentioned in the above cited tradition from Sayyidunâ Hasan Basri. After this, when magic was worked on the Prophet (peace be upon him) and his illness grew intense, Gabriel came and instructed him by Allah's command to recite these Sûrahs. Therefore, the view held by the commentators who describe both these Sûrahs as Makkan is more reliable.

Major Issues, Divine Laws and Guidance

*   Seek refuge with Allah from all evils.
*   Seek refuge with Allah from the slinking whisperers.

As soon as the Prophet (peace be upon him) began to preach the message of Islam, it seemed as though he had provoked all classes of the people around him. As his message spread, the opposition of the disbelieving Quraish also became more and more intense. As long as they had any hope that they would be able to prevent him from preaching his message by throwing some temptation in his way, or concluding some bargain with him, their hostility did not become very active. But when the Prophet (peace be upon him) completely disappointed them by the fact that he would not accept any kind of compromise with them in the matter of Faith, and in Sûrah Al-Kâfirûn they were plainly told: "I do not worship those whom you worship, nor, are you worshippers of Him Whom I worship; for you is your religion and for me mine," the hostility reached its extreme limits. More particularly, the families whose members (men, women, boys or girls) had accepted Islam, were burning with rage against the Prophet (peace be upon him). They were cursing him, holding secret consultations to kill him quietly in the darkness of the night so that the Bani Hashim could not discover the murderer and take revenge; magic and charms were being worked on him so as to cause his death, make him fall ill, or become mad; shaitâns from among the men and jinns spread *everywhere to whisper one or another evil into the hearts of the people against him and the Qur'an he had brought, to incite suspicion so that he might run away. There were many people who were burning with jealousy, for they could not tolerate that a man from a different family or clan should flourish and become prominent. For example, the reason why Abu Jahl was crossing every limit in his hostility to the Prophet (peace be upon him) was explained by him: "We and the Bani Abdi Manâf (to which the Prophet belonged) were rivals of each other: they fed the poor, we too fed the poor; they provided conveyances to the people, we too did the same; they gave donations, we too gave donations, so much so that when they and we have become equal in honor and nobility, they now proclaim that they have a Prophet who is inspired from heaven; how can we compete with them in this field? By God, we will never acknowledge him, nor affirm faith in him."*

(Ibn Hishâm, vol. I, pp. 337-338)

Under these conditions, the Prophet (peace be upon him) was commanded to tell the people: "I seek refuge with the Rabb (Lord) of the dawn, from the evil of everything that He has created, and from the evil of the darkness of night and from the evil of magicians, men and women, and from the evil of the jealousy," and to tell them: "I seek refuge with the Rabb of mankind, the King of mankind, and the God of mankind, from the evil of the whisperer, who returns over and over again, who whispers (evil) into the hearts of men, whether he be from among the jinns or men." This is similar to what the Prophet Musa (peace be upon him) had been told to say when Pharaoh had expressed his desire to kill him before his full court: "I have taken refuge with my Rabb and your Rabb against every arrogant person who does not believe in the Day of Reckoning." (Sûrah Al-Mu'min / Ghâfir: verse 27), and, "I have taken refuge with my Rabb and your Rabb against you injuring me." (Sûrah Ad-Dukhân: verse 20).

On both situations, these illustrious Prophets of Allah (peace be upon them) were confronted with well-equipped, resourceful and powerful enemies. They stood firm on the message of Truth against their strong opponents, even though they had no material power on the strength of which they could fight them, and utterly disregarded the threats, dangerous plans and hostile devices of the enemy, saying: "We have taken refuge with the Rabb of the universe against you." Obviously, such firmness and steadfastness can be shown only by the person who has the conviction that the power of His Rabb is the supreme power, that all powers of the world are insignificant against Him, and that no one can harm the one who has taken His refuge. Only such a person can say: "I will not give up preaching the Word of Truth. I care the least for what you may say or do, for I have taken refuge with my Rabb and your Rabb and Rabb of the whole universe."

113: AL-FALAQ

This Sûrah, revealed at Makkah, has 1 section and 5 verses.

In the name of Allah, the Compassionate, the Merciful

Seek refuge with Allah from all evils

Say: "I seek refuge with the Rabb of the dawn[1] from the evil of all that He has created,[2] and from the evil of darkness when it overspreads,[3] from the evil of those who blow in knots,[4] and from the evil of the envier when he envies."[5]   113:[1-5]

114: AN-NÂS

This Sûrah, revealed at Makkah, has 1 section and 6 verses.

In the name of Allah, the Compassionate, the Merciful

Seek refuge with Allah from the retreating whisperers

Say: "I seek refuge in the Rabb of mankind,[1] the King of mankind,[2] the real God of mankind,[3] from the evil of the retreating whisperer *(Shaitân or his worker)*[4] who whispers into the hearts of mankind,[5] *whether he be* from among the jinns or from among mankind."[6]   114:[1-6]

PRAYER
AT
THE COMPLETION OF AL-QUR'AN

O Allah! In my grave change my fear into love! O Allah! Have mercy on me in the name of this Great Qur'an; and make it for me a Guide and Light and a source of Your Guidance and Mercy; O Allah! Make me remember what of it I have forgotten; make me know of it that which I have become ignorant of; and make me recite it in the hours of the night and the day; and make it an argument in my favor, O Sustainer of all the worlds!

Â'meen!

REFERENCES

The following dictionaries, seerah of the Prophet Muhammad (peace be upon him), history of Islam, translations and tafãseer were used during the research and translation process to understand the Divine Message in the light of historical background of Arabian society and the issues which the Prophet Muhammad (pbuh) and his companions were facing at the time of Divine Revelations. Please note that in some cases one verse of this Holy Book took us three to four weeks of proper research to finalize the translation of its meanings. We noted in our research that most of the time the translation of Shabbir Ahmed Usmani and Abul A'la Maududi were very useful in arriving at the final wordings. May Allah bless all the following Ulema whose work helped us to complete this Translation and Qur'anic Subject Index for conveying the Message of Allah Subhanahu Wa Ta'ala.

* Vocabulary of the Holy Qur'an by Abdullah Abbas Nadwi.
* Lughatul Qur'an - Arabic and Urdu by Abdul Karim Parekh.
* Elias Modern Dictionary - Arabic English by Elias & Edward E. Elias.
* Mutâlab-e-Qur'an by Ya'qoob Sarosh.
* Lughat-ul Munjid - Arabic and Urdu by A Group of Ten Ulema.
* Mufridat-ul-Qur'an by Imam Raghib Asfahâni.
* Ahkâmul Qur'an by Chaudhry Nazar Muhammad
* Maudu'at-e-Qur'an and Human Life by Khawaja Abdul Waheed
* Index Of Qur'anic Topics by Ashfaque Ullah Syed

* Translation and Commentary of The Holy Qur'an by Abdullah Yûsuf Ali.
* The Meaning of the Glorious Koran by Mohammed Marmaduke Pickthall.
* Tafheem-ul-Qur'an by Syed Abul A'la Maududi.
* Tafseer Ibn Katheer by Allama Ibn-e-Katheer Dimashqi.
* Al-Qur'an Al-Karim by Shabbir Ahmed Usmani.
* English Translation of The Qur'an by M. H. Shakir.
* The Koran translation with notes by N. J. Dawood.
* Translation and Commentary of the Holy Qur'an by Abdul Majid Daryabadi.
* The Message of The Qur'an by Muhammad Asad.
* Interpretation of the meaning of The Noble Qur'an by
        Muhammad Taqi-ud Din Al-Hilali & Muhammad Mohsin Khan.
* The Qur'an translation and commentary by T. B. Irving.
* Dars-e-Qur'an by Dars-i-Qur'an Board of Idara-e-Islaho Tabligh.
* Asan Tarjumah of Qur'an Majeed by Hafiz Nazar Ahmed.
* Tadrees Lughatul Qur'an by Abu Masood Hasan Alwi.
* A Strudy of Al-Qur'an-ul-Karim by La'l Muhammad Chawla.
* Bayãn-al-Qur'an by Ashraf Ali Thhanwi.
* Dars-e-Qur'an by Al-Hãjj Muhammad Ahmed.

* Seerat-un-Nabi by Allama Shibli Nu'mani and Sayed Sulaiman Nadwi.
* History of Islam by Professor Masudul Hasan.

INTERNATIONAL ISLAMIC UNIVERSITY

ISLAMABAD-PAKISTAN

P.O.Box. 1243   Telegram:ALJAMIA   Telex.54068 IIU. PK,   Telephone:

No. IIU (VP-Acad)/96-386
Dated: January 02, 1996

Mr. Muhammad Farooq-I-Azam Malik,
Vice President,
Islamic Society of Greater Houston,
3110 Eastside Drive,
Houston, Texas 77098

My dear brother in Islam,

      Assalam-o-Alaikum wa Rehmatullah wa Barakatuhu

      I hope this letter will find you in the best of health and the Islamic spirit worthy of you. It is in connection with the English translation of the Holy Qur'an undertaken by you, an effort which is undoubtedly encouraging and useful. Your translation of the Qur'an is undoubtedly a step forward in the direction of making the Holy Book understandable to English readers. Your style is lucid and clear. The introduction of suras given by you will also help the reader in understanding the historical contexts in which it was revealed. I pray Almighty Allah to give you strength, time and resources to complete this project and to circulate it on a wide scale.

      With best regards and wishes,

Sincerely yours,

(Dr. Mahmood Ahmad Ghazi)
Vice President (Academics)

بسم الله الرحمن الرحيم

AL - AZHAR AL - SHARIF
ISLAMIC RESEARCH ACADEMY
GENERAL DEPARTMENT
For Research, Writting & Translation

الأزهــر الشريف
مجمع البحوث الاسلامية
الادارة العامـــــة
للبحــوث والتـأليف والترجمـة

السيد الاستاذ / محمد فاروق عزام مالــــــــــك

نائب رئيس المركز الاسلامي / هيوستن / امريكــــــــا

السلام عليكم ورحمة الله وبركاتـــــه ٠٠٠٠ وبحـــــد :

فبناء على ماجاء بكتابكم المؤرخ في ٢١/٢/ ١٩٩٤ والموجه لفضيلة الامام الاكبر شيخ الازهر

بشأن مراجعة وفحص الكتب الاتيـــــــــة :ـ

١ ــ القرآن هداية للنــــــــــــــــــــاس ٠

٢ ــ الوصية الاسلاميـــــــــــــــــــة ٠

٣ ــ الزكاة وهو من تأليفكم باللغة الانجليزيـــــة ٠

نفيد بالاتــــــــــــــــــــى :ـ

أولا : بفحص كتاب القرآن هداية للناس يتبين أنه يحتوى على معلومات علمية ودينية مفيــــــــدة
ولا مانـــــع من نشره وتداوله على أن يراعى الالتزام بكتابة المصطلحات العربيــــــــة
الاسلامية بالحروف اللاتينيـة في الطبعات القادمـــــة ٠

ثانيا : أما كتاب الوصية الاسلامية فقد تبين أن الوصية ضرورية في بلدكم وعليـــــــــــه
فلا مانع من نشره وتداوله بشرط التأكد على ان يكون للذكر في هذه الوصيـــــــــــة
مثل حظ الانثيين تنفيذا لقوله تعالى: " يوصيكم الله في أولاد ٣م للذكر مثل حظ ثــــــ
الانثيين "س٤ أية رقم ١١ ٠

ثالثا : وبالنسبة لكتاب الزكاة فقد تبين أنه يحتوى على معلومات علمية مفيدة ولا مانـــــــــع
من نشره وتداوله بشرط التأكيد على ان نصاب الذهب هو ٨٥ خمسة وثمانون جرامـــــا
والتى تعادل ل ٣ ثلاث اوقيات من الذهـــــــــب ٠
النصف
ونصاب للفضة هو ٥٩٥ خمسمائة وخمسة وتسعون جراما وهى تعادل ل إحدى وعشريـــــن
أوقية من الفضة الخالصة ويسجل ذلك ى الكتاب عند إعادة الطبـــــــــع ٠

رجاء الاحاطة

وفقكم الله لخدمة الاسلام والمسلمين ٠
والســــلام عليكم و رحمــة اللـــه و بركاتـــه ٠٠٠٠
مـبديسـر عـــام
البحوث و التأليف و الترجمة

٥/٩/١٤١٥هـ
١١/١/١٩٩٤م

" فتـح اللـــه يـــس جـد "

١٨٧
٢٢ ١١ ٩٢

TESTIMONIALS

Peace and blessing of Allah be upon the Prophet who provided us an opportunity to be rightly guided. We bear witness that there is no god except Allah and we bear witness that Muhammad, peace be upon him, is His Rasool. The best of the statements is the Book of Allah and the best of the guidance is the guidance provided by the Prophet Muhammad, peace be upon him. We can not find appropriate words to thank Allah, *Subhanahu Wa Ta'ala*, for giving us toufeeq to publish this fourth edition of Translation of the Meanings of Al-Qur'an, the guidance for Mankind. Of the hundreds of letters that we received during the last 3½ years, a few testimonials are being tabulated for your information as follows:

"…Demand for the copies of the translation of the Qur'an is in millions and millions are ready to read and benefit from Al-Qur'an. There are libraries and schools who are looking to get the copies of the Qur'an. Al-Qur'an is an excellent translation in local American language…"
  Dr. Sayyid M. Syeed, Secretary General, The Islamic Society of North America

"...Alhumdulillah, what a beautiful translation. …your summaries and notes are exactly what we were looking for. …"   *Fatima Bhyat, South Africa*

"… your translation is the best Da'wah tool available to us in the United States. …"
  Dr. Aslam Abdullah, Editor-in-Chief, The Minaret

"… it is with great pleasure and honor to certify that I have proofread the revised edition of Al-Qur'an for more than once and Insha Allah to the best of my knowledge there is no error in this final manuscript...you have indeed accomplished a wonderful job..."   *G. A. Khan, Reviewer of Abdullah Yusuf Ali's Translation*

"… It has several key features, which make it my number one choice for new Muslims. The format is exquisite… His (translator's) goal is to help the reader understand the meaning, appreciate the beauty of the Qur'an, and catch the grandeur of the original Arabic. In my opinion he certainly succeeded; it would be very hard to improve on this translation, especially as Da'wah for non-Muslims (in addition to new Muslims)   *Betty (Batul) Bowman, The Sun is Rising in the West, page 255*

"…I commend your efforts to build a bridge between the Muslim and non-Muslim community. As translated Al-Qur'an has already become very popular reading among my staff, I would like to request three additional copies..."
  Rodeny Ellis, Senator – Chairman, Jurisprudence Committee

"...Allah Subhanahu Wa Ta'ala opened my heart to another wonderful translation of the Qur'an in English... I have in my personal collection some five thousand books on Islam and related subjects including over fifty different translation of the Qur'an in English alone. .. It is worth mentioning that I am more than delighted with your innovative method of presenting the Qur'an to English-reading public. ...I honestly believe that such an important, accurate and useful translation of the Qur'an will bring the new generation, English-reading public, one step closer to a better understanding and appreciation of the Holy Qur'an. ..."

Mohammed Jaffar, Blangah Court, Singapore

"...I have reviewed your translation with great interest and attention. Language is lucid and clear, format is exquisite and style is excellent. I found the usage of the words, sentences and phrases to be the closest to the meanings the Qur'an. ..."

Mufti Basharat Ahmed, Gujrat, Pakistan

"...I recently obtained a copy of your "new' translation of Al-Qur'an. In a word its Wonderful! It will truly make a great impression on other American Muslims like myself...."

Alfonso Cowels, N. Charleston, South Connecticut

"...It is so powerful that he (other person) won't put it down long enough for me to study it. ..."

Devery A. Russell, Lagrange, Kentucky

"...When the students ask me, which translation of the Qur'an do you recommend for us to use? I tell them Farooq Malik's...."

Dr. Muzammil H. Siddiqi, President, The Islamic Society of North America

"... It is excellent. We normally do not have enough funds that we need for our projects. When we have enough funds, I would like to sponsor and promote this translation..."

Imam W. D. Muhammad, Chicago, Illinois

"...We find this translation rather unique compared to others in the market. The translator has done a very marvelous and splendid job in translating few ayahs and incorporating the notes together. ...The introduction given before the start of each Surah is in detail and very informative...We would like to introduce this translation to our brothers and sisters in Malaysia and also to promote it overseas..."

A. S. Noordeen, holybook@tm.net.my, Kuala Lumpur, Malaysia

"... I was thrilled to see this translation on ISL's Alim (6) software CD along with margin notes and English audio readings by J.D.Hall in American accent..."

Dr. Abdul Ghafoor, Rawalpindi, Pakistan

Recording and Preservation of the Qur'an

The very first word revealed to the Prophet Muhammad, peace be upon him (pbuh), was "lqra" which means read or recite (Sûrah 96, Ayah 1).Thus, it is not surprising that as soon as a verse was revealed, he would memorize it so that he could recite it to others, and Ayât 4 and 5 emphasized the use of pen, "Who taught by the pen, taught man what he knew not." Therefore, the revealed verses were not only memorized but also put in writing.

Among the companions of the Prophet (pbuh) some of the most literate were Abu-Bakr, Ali-bin-Abi-Talib, Othman-bin-Affan, Zaid-bin-Thabit, and Umar-bin-Khattab. They were all very pious and righteous people, full of integrity and honesty. In addition to acting as his scribes, some of them also memorized the Qur'an directly from the Prophet (pbuh). As soon as a portion of the Qur'an was revealed, the Prophet (pbuh) would call his scribe, from among his companions, to record it in writing. The Prophet (pbuh) would than ask the scribe to read the portion to ensure that what was written down was verbatim word of Allah. Once satisfied with the written text, the Prophet (pbuh) would instruct the scribe about the name of the Sûrah and the location where the just revealed portion (verse or verses) were to be inserted, to ensure that the textual order of the Qur'an was in accordance with the Divine plan.

His scribes used leather, parchments, leaves and tablets to write down the verses. These manuscripts were kept in the house of the Prophet (pbuh). It was quite common for many companions to also make their own personal copies. Thus the Qur'anic verses were not only memorized by the Prophet (pbuh) and many of his companions, but also existed in written form during the lifetime of the Prophet (pbuh), unlike any other scriptures in the history. It is reported that every year during the month of Ramadan, Angel Gabriel would come to the Prophet (pbuh) and hear him recite the Qur'an (whatever was revealed to date). And in the last year, before the Prophet (pbuh)'s death, Angel Gabriel came to hear him recite the whole Qur'an two times, thus, ensuring that the words of Allah have not been forgotten or changed. The Prophet (pbuh), while leading the prayers, used to recite some portions of the Qur'an each time, which became an excellent means of ensuring that his followers would not forget what they had memorized.

The Prophet (pbuh), in his last sermon, is reported to have said: "I am leaving behind me two things, the Book of Allah (the Qur'an) and my examples (the Sunnah) and if you follow these you will never go astray." If the Qur'an was not in written form during the lifetime of the Prophet (pbuh), he would never have said: "I am leaving behind the Book of Allah (Al-Qur'an)." Hence, unlike any other scripture, the Qur'anic verses were recorded and written down during the lifetime of the Prophet Muhammad, peace be upon him.

The First Official Copy of the Qur'an

Since Muhammad (peace be upon him) was the "Living Qur'an" and many Muslims during his lifetime who had memorized the Qur'an were "Living Copies" of the Qur'an, there was no need or urgency to put the manuscripts together to form the first official copy.

However, after the death of the Prophet (pbuh), more than seventy memorizers of the Qur'an, called Huffaz, were martyred in the battle of Al-Yamamah. This caused a great deal of concern to Umar-bin-Khattab (one of the close companions of the Prophet (pbuh)), who was deeply concerned at this sudden loss of the "Oral Copies" of the Qur'an. He approached Abu-Bakr, the first caliph, to start the process of gathering the manuscripts of the Qur'an under one official volume for reference. Abu-Bakr commissioned one of the main scribe and memorizer of the Qur'an, Zaid-bin-Thabit with the task.

Zaid-bin-Thabit had memorized the Qur'an, he was one of the main scribes and had heard the Prophet (pbuh) recite the Qur'an to Angel Gabriel during Ramadan. He was also a man of piety, integrity and honesty, as such; he had all the credentials needed to undertake such a supreme task.

Zaid, along with other trustworthy and competent colleagues, collected the manuscripts from many people and started to compile them in accordance with the Prophet (pbuh)'s original instructions. Even though he was an authority in the Qur'an, he took many steps to check, cross-check with other memorizers and with manuscripts from many other companions to guarantee that the final compiled version was authentic and that no alteration or modifications were made.

Just to illustrate how authentic his compilation of the Qur'an was, here is one example: every Sûrah in the Qur'an begins with "Bismillah" (In the name of Allah). However, Sûrah nine is the only exception - it does not begin with "Bismillah". It is the natural tendency of all human beings to follow the most normal and common practice. Zaid and other companions of the Prophet (pbuh) would have been tempted to add "Bismillah" to make it consistent with all the other 113 Sûrah in the Qur'an, but they refrained from such alteration or addition. Chronologically speaking the revelation of Sûrah eight and Sûrah nine are separated by an interval of seven years. Although the Prophet (pbuh) had instructed that Sûrah nine should follow Sûrah eight, it was not clear whether the Ayât (verses) were to form a separate Sûrah or to form a part of Sûrah eight. As such, Zaid treated it as a separate Sûrah (Sûrah 9), but the "Bismillah" was not prefixed to it, as there was no warrant for supposing that the Prophet (pbuh) used the "Bismillah" before it in his recitation of the Qur'an. This methodology proves how honest and truthful Zaid was in his compilation. Thus, the first official copy was prepared under the supervision of Zaid, and was put in the custody of Abu-Bakr, the first Caliph. Before his death, he passed this copy to Umar-bin-Khattab, the second Caliph, who in turn passed it to Hafsah, one of the widows of the Prophet (pbuh).

Copies of the Qur'an from the Original

During the time of Othman-bin-Affan, the third Caliph, Islam spread fast and many companions moved out of Arabia. Amongst the many countries and provinces that accepted Islam were Syria and Iraq, but their language was not Arabic. One of Prophet (pbuh)'s companions, Hudaifah-ibne-Yaman, during his visit to Syria and Iraq observed that people were reciting the Qur'an in different modes and styles. This disturbed him very much and upon his return he requested Othman to order for making several copies the Qur'an and distribute to distinct locations to help Muslims read or recite the Qur'an in a single consistent manner.

Othman appointed twelve members, headed by Zaid to write the Qur'an in the mode of the Quraish, the mode used by the Prophet (pbuh) in his recitation. Zaid along with the other colleagues reproduced a number of copies based on the original volume produced during the time of Abu-Bakr. The handwriting was to agree with the Arabic dialect of the Quraish. These copies maintained the order of the Sûrahs and the Ayât (verses) within the Sûrahs as was laid down by the Prophet (pbuh) himself. Of the completed official copies Othman ordered three to be sent to Syria, Iraq and Makkah respectively and one to be kept in Medina. The original manuscript was returned to Hafsah. Othman then ordered that all the other Qur'anic materials whether written in fragmentary manuscripts or whole copies be burnt. This was a precautionary measure taken by him to prevent any future conflict in the mode of reciting the Qur'an and from any possible fabrication or corruption. The preservation of the Qur'an has also been assured by Allah in the following verse:

"We have without doubt sent down the Message and We will assuredly preserve It."

(Sûrah 15, Ayah 9)

RIGHTS OF THE QUR'AN

"It is the month of Ramadhân in which the Qur'an was revealed, a guidance for mankind with clear teachings showing the Right Way and a criterion of truth and falsehood."- (2:185). Ramadhân is the month of the Qur'an, as the Prophet (peace be upon him) has said, and that the Qur'an has four rights: *Qir'at* (to read it), *Tilawat* (to understand and act upon its guidance), *Tadabbur* (to comprehend its teachings) and *Balaghat* (to preach and convey its Message).

Al-Hamdulillah, this publication, Al-Qur'an - the Guidance for mankind, is meant to fulfill all these four rights of the Qur'an. - It's Arabic text is to read (Qir'at), translation of its meanings in contemporary easy American Language is to understand and act upon its guidance (*Tilawat)*, information about Major Issues, Divine Laws and Guidance prior to the translation of each Sûrah is to comprehend its teachings (*Tadabbur*), and its distribution to Public Libraries, Muslims and non-Muslims at large is to convey its Message (*Balaghat).*

The Qur'an's right of *"Balaghat"* - was made a mandatory Assignment for the Muslim Ummah

The Prophet Muhammad, peace be upon him, has clearly stated this assignment of the Muslim Ummah in the following words:

"Ballaghû Annee Walo Âyah - Convey from me even if you have the knowledge of one Âyah."

"O Muslims: The best among you are those who learn and teach the Qur'an."
At *Hajja-tul-Wid'a* he said:

"O you, who are here, convey this message to those who are not here."

To comply with this commandment / assignment we started this project and we are inviting every one to join us in this mighty effort personally or through sponsoring its free distribution. Since all personal working for this project are volunteers, therefore, 100% of the contributions are used for printing Al-Qur'an and making it available to Muslims and non-Muslims. *Zaka-tul-Mall* can also be used for this purpose. If you would like to sponsor its printing and distribution, make your checks payable to 'Al-Qur'an Trust Fund' and send to the Institute of Islamic Knowledge, P. O. Box 8307, Houston, Texas 77288-8307.

Allah (SWT) has said in the Qur'an:

O believers! Be the helpers of Allah, just as Isa (Jesus) the son of Maryam said to his disciples: "Who will be my helper in the cause of Allah?" And the disciples responded: "We will be your helpers in the cause of Allah."   (Sûrah 61, Ayah 14)

AL-QUR'AN'S SUBJECT INDEX

Peace and blessing of Allah be upon the Prophet Muhammad, peace be upon him, who provided us an opportunity to be rightly guided and follow Allah's commandments as they should be followed. I bear witness that there is no god except Allah and I bear witness that Muhammad (peace be upon him) is His Rasool. The best of the statements is the Book of Allah (Al-Qur'an) and the best of the guidance is the guidance provided by the Prophet Muhammad, peace be upon him.

Please note that given the depth and sublimity of the Qur'an, it is not possible to list all the themes, subjects and topics. Al-Qur'an has provided a complete Guidance for every aspect of human life, may it be personal, family, social, economic, cultural, national or international. It has provided every thing we, as human beings, need to know about our lives here on Earth and the life Hereafter. I have been trying to compile the Subject Index for over four years and now for the last six months on full time basis. Every time I read the Qur'an I noted that I have missed many topics and updated the list accordingly. I am sure as many times as I shall read the Qur'an again I shall have the same experience. Since I do not know how long I can live, therefore, it is necessary to publish what I have compiled so far and hope to keep on updating in the future editions.

I have tried to make it very easy for the reader through providing a list of the topics in two pages. You may select a topic and go directly to that page for reference. The scheme followed in the Subject Index is first to tabulate the topics relating to 'Human Life,' then the fact that Allah has given the 'Freedom Of Choice' to believe or to disbelieve. Then the fact that the only 'Way Of Life' acceptable to Allah is Al-Islam, therefore, Al-Islam is listed next, followed by the Responsibilities Of The Believers, The Articles Of Faith, The Pillars Of Islam, specific topics relating to Faith And Belief, General Topics relating human life and interaction, Rewards And Punishment for good and bad deeds, Allah's Creations in general, Natural Phenomenon / Scientific Facts and Stories Of The Past Generations not listed under Rasools And Their Nations.

Please note that it is a Subject Index and not a Word Index as is in the Translation of Abdullah Yusuf Ali, may Allah bless his soul. The listing is not in alphabetical order in the categories of Human Life, for logical reasons, and in The Articles Of Faith and The Pillars Of Islam because these were fixed by the Prophet, peace be upon him, himself. In other categories the listing is in alphabetical order for easy reference and is not in the order of preference or importance; such as, even though Muhammad, peace be upon him, was the last Rasool of Allah but in alphabetical order he is listed earlier and Nûh, peace be upon him, who was the first Rasool of Allah is listed after him. Another important thing to know is that the Subject Index is based on the theme of the Âyât, therefore, the specific word or title may not appear in the referenced Âyah or Sûrah; such as, word 'Muhammad' (peace be upon him) is mentioned in only four Âyât of the Holy Qur'an but you will find the reference about him in hundreds of Âyât in various Sûrahs.

Finally, please note that I have not listed the page numbers of this Translation in the detailed Index listing so that the readers may use any Translation they like, because the Sûrah numbers and Âyah numbers in every Translation are the same. In this Translation, however, the Sûrah number and Âyah numbers are listed after each paragraph and on each page for easy reference. Furthermore, if anyone would like to copy or print this Index for Da'wah, he / she is hereby allowed to do so.

AL-QUR'AN'S SUBJECT INDEX

AL-QUR'AN'S SUBJECT INDEX

1. Relating To The Human Life:

A. Personal Aspect:

i. Creation:

Creation Of Man	2:30; 4:1; 6:2; 6:98; 7:11; 7:189; 15:26; 15:28-29; 15:33; 16:4; 18:37; 19:67; 22:5; 23:12-14; 25:54; 30:20; 30:54; 32:7-9; 35:11; 36:36; 36:77-78; 37:11; 38:71-72; 39:6; 40:57; 40:64; 40:67; 45:4; 49:13; 50:16; 53:45-46; 55:3-4; 55:14; 56:57-59; 67:23; 71:14; 74:11; 75:36-39; 76:1-2; 76:28; 77:20-23; 78:8; 79:27; 80:18-19; 82:7-8; 86:5-7; 90:4-9; 96:2
Human Helplessness	3:185; 4:78; 7:188; 10:49; 50:19; 53:24-25; 55:26-27; 62:8; 63:11
Human Honor	2:30-31; 2:34; 5:44; 7:11; 7:19; 7:26; 7:31; 17&0; 33:72
Human Nature	32:49-51; 42:27; 43:15; 70:19-2175:5; 75:20-21; 96:6-7; 100:6-8
Human's Responsibility	2:286; 6:94; 30:44-45; 32:46; 34:25; 35:18; 39:41; 42:30; 45:15; 53:33-41; 74:38
Life On Earth	3:185; 4:77; 6:32; 6:70; 9:38; 23:112-114; 29:64; 31:33; 40:39; 47:36; 57:20
Purpose Of His Creation	2:21; 4:1; 21:16-17; 40:115; 51:49; 51:56; 67:1-2; 76:1-2
Self-Preservation / Self-Defense	2:195; 2:286; 5:105; 6:12; 6:153; 16:126; 18:6; 35:8; 39:13; 39:15; 39:53-54; 42:39; 42:41; 59:18; 64:16; 66:6

ii. Attributes:

Determination	3:159; 3:186; 20:115; 46:35;
Efforts	2:148; 3:132; 17:19; 20:15; 21:94; 23:60-61; 53:39-40; 62:9; 88:8-9
Hope And Expectation	12:87; 15:55-56; 17:83; 30:36; 32:49; 39:53
Intention	5:89; 33:5
Patience	2:152; 2:177; 2:249-250; 3:186; 3:200; 16:126; 22:34-35; 28:54; 29:59; 30:60; 31:17; 39:10; 47:35; 50:39; 74:7; 76:24; 90:17; 103:1-3
Steadfastness	2:250; 3:8; 4:66; 8:11; 8:45; 11:112; 12:111; 16:94; 47:7
Superstitions	2:189; 7:131; 16:47

iii. Purpose Of Life:

Allah Has Shown Two Highways	86:3; 90:10
Fulfill The Trust Undertaken By Man	83:72
Freedom Of Choice – Belief Or Disbelief	2:256; 6:107; 10:99; 18:29
Jinn And Human Being Are Created To Worship Allah	51:56
Life On Earth IsAn Examination	67:2

iv. Elements Of Good Life:

Action Followed By Statement	2:44; 61:2-3
Ihsân (Going An Extra Mile In Doing Good)	5:13; 74:6-7
Being Fair And Just	4:135; 5:8; 5:42; 6:152; 7:29; 16:90; 42:15; 49:9; 57:25
Being Good To Others	2:58; 2:195; 3:148; 4:36; 5:13; 9:120; 11:115; 16:90; 28:77
Being Thankful To Allah	2:152; 5:6; 14:28-31; 16:78; 27:40; 27:73; 28:73; 31:12; 34:13; 93:9-11; 100:6-8
Controlling The Anger	3:133-134; 3:159; 42:36-37
Dedication	2:139; 7:29; 39:2-3; 39:11; 40:65; 98:5
Doing Good In Response To Bad	4:148-149; 25:96-98; 28:53-54; 41:34-35;
Fair Dealing With Enemy	5:2; 5:8; 32:34
Fear Of Allah	67:12; 70:27-28; 79:17-19; 21:48-49; 26:183-184; 31:33;

Investigate Before Jumping To Conclusion	4:94; 49:6
Invite People To Faith With Wisdom	16;125; 29:46
Keep Your Faith And Trust In Allah All The Times	3:160; 5:11; 22:11; 41:51; 33:21; 60:6
Let Allah Deal With Those Who Reject Faith	74:11
Make Room For Others	58:11
Miserliness (Do Not Be A Miser Or Stingy)	4:37; 47:38
Mockery And Sarcasm (Do Not Mock Or Be Sarcastic)	49:11
Never Use Profanity In Allah's Name	7:180
Parable Of Those Who Did Not Rely On Allah	68:17-33
Peace And Reconciliation	8:61; 9:6; 9:9; 49:10
Say *Bismillah* (In The Name Of Allah) Before Starting Any Thing	27:29-31
Say *Insha-Allah* (Allah Willing) For Any Future Activity	18:23-24
Scandal (Do Not Be A Part Of Any Scandal)	24:19; 58:9-10
Self-Defense	42:39-43
Sincerity And Devotion To Allah	7:29; 31:32; 37:40-41; 37:73-74; 37:159-160; 38:83; 39:2-3; 39:11; 39:14; 40:65; 49:15; 49:17; 57:19; 59:7-8; 98:5
Slander And Backbiting	49:12; 104:1-9
Supporter Or Rejecter Of Good Cause	4:85
Taking Precautions	4:71
Tolerance And Respect For Others	4:94; 6:108; 49:13
Trustworthiness (Do Not Violate Trust)	4:58
Truthfulness (Ascertain Truth Before Passing A Judgment)	49:6
Turning Foes Into Friends	41:34

ix. Necessities Of Life:

Acquisition Of Knowledge	2:30-33; 2:67; 2:247; 2:269; 9:122; 12:76; 20:114; 29:43; 35:28; 39:9; 58:11
Dress	7:31-32
Food	5:3; 5:96; 6:118-119; 6:142; 7:31; 22:30; 24:61; 34:15; 67:15

B. Family Aspects:

Abortion	6:137; 6:140; 6:151; 17:31; 60:12
Adopted Child	33:4-5
Cutting Of Matrimonial Relationship (Eela)	2:226-227; 5:89
Difference Between Man And Woman	2:222; 2:228; 2:282; 4:11; 4:34
Divorce	2:228-232; 2:236-237; 2:241; 4:20-21; 33:49; 65:1-2; 65:4-7
Unacceptable Way Of Divorce (Zihaar)	33:4; 58:2-4
Dovery (Mehr)	2:229; 2:237; 4:4; 4:19-21; 4:24-25; 33:49; 60:10-11
Iddat - Waiting Period Before Marriage	2:228; 2:234-235; 2:240; 33:49; 65:1-4; 65:6-7
Marriage	2:221; 4:22-25; 24:32-33; 33:37
Marriage Disputes And Reconciliation	4:19; 4:34-35; 4:128; 4:130
Married Life	2:187; 2:222-223; 2:233; 20:132; 57:20; 64:14-15; 65:6; 66:6
Menstruation	2:222
Purpose Of Creating Man And Woman	2:187; 2:223; 16:72; 30:21
Relationship - Father, Mother And Children	2:215; 14:41; 17:23-24; 19:12-14; 29:8; 31:14-15; 37:102; 46:15; 63:9; 71:28
Relationship With Wives	2:187; 2:223; 2:226; 2:228; 2:231-234; 2:237; 2:240-241; 4:19-21; 4:25; 4:34-35; 4:128-130; 30:21; 33:49; 64:14-15; 65:2-3; 65:6-7; 66:3
Relatives	2:83; 2:177; 4:8; 16:90; 17:26; 24:22; 30:38; 42:23
Respect Of Women	2:231; 3:42; 3:45-46; 24:4; 24:23; 66:11-12
Responsibilities Of The Head Of the Household	66:6-7
Restriction On Opposite Sexes:	
Inside The Household	24:27; 24:30-31; 24:58-60; 33:32-33; 33:53
Outside The Household	33:33; 33:59
Restriction On Number Of Wives	4:3; 4:129
Rights Of Man And Woman	2:228; 3:195; 4:32; 4:124; 5:38; 9:68; 9:71-72; 16:97;

F. Political Aspect:

i. National:

3. Religion Of Islam (Deen)

Accept Islam Wholeheartedly	2:208
Allah Has Chosen Islam As A Favor To Mankind	5:3; 24:55; 49:17
An Introduction To Islam	2:112; 3:9-20; 3:95; 3:102; 4:125; 6:14; 6:71; 6:125; 10:105; 11:14; 16:81; 21:108; 22:34; 27:31; 27:42; 27:44; 27:81; 27:91; 29:46; 39:12; 39:22; 39:54; 40:66; 41:33; 43:68-69
Believers Are To Protect One Another	8:73
Difference Between Islam and Belief	49:14-15
Do Not Be Fanatical In Religion	4:171; 5:77
Do Not Create Division In The Religion	3:103; 3:105; 6:159; 21:92-93; 30:31-32; 42:13
Fellowship Of Believers	5:55; 9:6
Islam Is A Single Brotherhood	21:92; 23:52; 49:10
Islam Is Not A New Religion	16:123; 42:13
Islam Is The Final Disposition	3:85; 3:102; 5:3; 48:28
Islam Is The Religion Of All The Prophets (pbut)	2:130-133; 2:135; 3:65-66; 3:68; 3:95; 4:125; 6:161; 22:78; 42:13
Islam Is The Religion Of Truth	9:29; 9:33; 48:28; 61:9
Islam Is The Right Religion	30:30; 30:43; 45:18; 98:5
No Compulsion In Religion	2:256; 10:99; 22:78; 50:45; 64:11-12
No Difficulty Imposed In Islam	22:78
Rejecting The Call To Islam Is The Worst Thing	61:7
Religion Is Not A Play Or Amusement	6:70; 7:51;
Study Islam And Teach Others	9:122; 103:1-3
Those Who Disregard Religion	6:21; 8:22; 29:61-64
Unbelievers Will Wish They Had Accepted Islam	15:2

4. Responsibilities Of the Believers

Avoid The Company Of Bad People	4:140; 4:144; 6:68; 28:55; 76:24
Believe And Do What You Preach	2:44; 9:107-109; 61:2-3; 62:5
Confrontation In The Case Of Prophet Isa (Jesus)	3:61
Conveying The Message Of Allah	3:104; 3:110; 4:63; 4:88; 5:79; 6:51-52; 6:69-70; 7:164-165; 7:181; 7:199-201; 9:71; 9:102-104; 9:122; 10:108-109; 11:116; 12:103-104; 16:2; 16:44; 16:125; 16:127; 38:67-68; 38:86-88; 18:27; 20:40-44; 21:108-111; 22:94-96; 22:41; 22:67; 25:51-52; 25:56-57; 26:214-216; 27:91-92; 28:87-88; 29:46-47; 30:52-53; 31:17-19; 41:33; 42:15; 43:63-65; 50:45; 51:52-53; 52:29; 61:14; 74:1-7; 80:1-12; 87:8-13; 88:21-24; 90:8-17; 103:2-3;
Cooperation In Doing Good Deeds	4:105-109; 5:2; 5:119; 68:7-15
Excelling In Good Deeds	2:148; 5:48; 25:55; 57:21; 83:25-26
Follow The Rules Of Propagation And Discussion	16:125; 29:46
Good Intention And Making Efforts Accordingly	9:107-109; 17:19
Not To Create Divisions In The Religion	3:105-106; 6:159; 6:164; 10:19; 10:99; 11:118-119; 21:92-94; 25:52-53; 30:31-32; 42:14; 42:16; 98:4
Not To Sell The Âyât Of Allah	2:41; 2:79; 2:174; 3:77; 3:187; 3:199; 5:44; 16:95
Not Yielding To The Pressure For Wrongdoing	2:120; 24:21; 45:18; 68:7-15; 76:23-24; 96:9-10; 96:19
Opposing The Wrongdoers	4:105-109; 5:2; 68:7-15; 68:10-16
Self Evaluation	2:44; 3:105
Service Of Humanity Irrespective Of Religion	76:8-10
Struggle In The Path Of Allah (Make Jihâd)	2:218; 3:83; 3:142; 4:125; 5:35; 5:54; 8:74; 9:11-12; 9:20; 9:24; 9:33; 9:41; 9:73; 10:104-105; 16:38-39; 22:78; 25:52; 29:5-6; 29:69; 30:30-32; 42:13; 49:15; 53:39-41; 61-11
Taking A Stand For The Truth	3:200; 5:119; 9:119; 11:112; 12:108; 18:29-30; 33:23-24; 33:35; 33:70-71; 39:33-35

5. Relating To The Articles Of Faith:

i. Belief In Allah:

Belief In Allah — 2:62; 2:177; 2:256; 3:179; 3:193; 4:38-39; 4:59; 4:136; 4:152; 4:162; 4:171; 4:175; 5:62; 7:158; 9:18-19; 9:44-45; 24:2; 24:62; 36:25; 40:84; 48:13; 49:15; 57:7-8; 57:19; 58:4; 58:22; 60:4; 60:11; 61:11; 64:8; 64:11; 65:2; 67:29; 72:13; 85:8

All — Beings Declare His Glory 17:44; 21:20; 21:79; 24:41; 57:1; 59:1; 59:24; 61:1; 62:1; 64:1

All Bounties Are In His Hand — 3:73

All Good Is From Him — 4:79; 16:30; 16:53

All Honor Is With Him — 4:139; 10:65; 63:8

All Things Are From Him — 4:78; 15:21

As Portrayed By The Qur'an — 2:255; 6:103; 24:35; 31:27, 33:15; 39:62; 40:3; 57:23; 59:25; 112:2; 113:3; 112:4

Does Not Abrogate His Revelation — 2:106; 39:23

Does Not Get Tired Of Creating Anything — 46:33

Forgives Whom He Pleases — 2:284; 3:129; 6:16; 8:4

Gives Life And Death — 2:28; 2:243; 2:258-260; 3:27; 7:158; 9:116; 10:31; 10:56; 15:23; 16:38; 16:70; 22:5-6; 22:66; 23:80-81; 30:40; 32:7-9; 36:12; 36:68; 36:77-79; 40:68; 42:9; 44:8; 45:26; 6:33; 50:43; 53:44; 57:2; 67:2; 75:40; 80:18-22

Has Knowledge Of The Heavens And The Earth — 3:29; 5:97; 6:59; 11:123; 14:38; 16:77; 17:55; 18:26; 21:4; 22:70; 25:6; 27:65; 29:52; 34:2; 35:38; 49:16; 49:18; 57:4; 58:7; 64:4

Is All Wise — 2:32; 2:129; 2:209; 2:220; 2:228; 2:240; 3:62; 3:126; 4:17; 4:24; 4:26; 4:130; 4:165; 4:170; 5:38; 5:118; 6:18; 6:73; 6:83; 6:128; 8:10; 8:63; 8:71; 9:15; 9:28; 9:40; 9:98; 9:106; 11:1; 12:83; 12:100; 15:23; 16:60; 22:52; 24:10; 24:18; 24:58-59; 27:6; 27:9; 29:26; 29:42; 30:27; 31:9; 31:27; 34:1; 34:27; 35:2; 39:1; 31:27; 34:1; 34:27; 35:2; 39:1; 41:42; 42:3; 42:51; 43:84; 45:2; 45:37; 46:2; 48:4; 48:7; 48:19; 51:30; 57:1; 59:1; 59:24; 60:5; 60:10; 61:1; 62:1; 62:3; 64:18; 66:2; 76:30

Is Close To Everyone — 2:186; 50:16

Is Free Of All Wants — 4:131; 31:12; 47:38

Is Perfect In Knowledge And Wisdom — 2:29; 2:32; 3:27; 12:100; 15:25; 34:1; 43:84; 35:2; 45:37; 48:7; 64:18

Is The Knower Of All Affairs — 2:30; 2:33; 2:115; 2:158; 2:247; 2:255; 3:5; 4:26; 4:147-149; 5:109; 5:116; 6:3; 6:13; 6:18; 6:59; 6:73; 6:101; 6:103; 9:115; 10:61; 11:111; 13:8-10; 15:24; 15:86; 16:19; 16:23; 16:70; 16:91; 17:55; 18:26; 21:4; 21:110; 20:7; 20:110; 21:28; 22:70; 22:75-76; 23:92; 23:118; 24:21; 24:35; 24:51; 24:64; 26:220; 27:65; 27:74-75; 24:78; 28:69; 28:85; 29:11; 29:60; 31:16; 31:23; 31:28; 31:34; 32:6; 33:54; 34:2; 35:8; 35:38; 36:12; 39:7; 40:16; 40:19-20; 41:47; 42:11-12; 42:25; 43:80; 43:85; 49:18; 50:16; 53:30; 53:32; 57:3-4; 57:6; 58:7; 64:4; 64:18; 66:2; 67:13-14

Is Worthy Of All Praise And Glory — 1:2-3; 1:5; 4:131; 10:10; 11:73; 13:15; 17:42-44; 22:64; 24:35-36; 28:70; 31:26; 34:1; 35:1; 35:10; 35:15; 35:34; 40:64; 42:5; 42:28; 43:12; 43:13; 43:82; 45:36-37; 55:26-27; 55:78; 59:1; 59:23-24; 62:1; 64:1

Knower Of The Hidden And Open — 2:33; 6:59; 6:73; 9:94; 9:105; 10:20; 11:123; 13:9; 16:77; 18:26; 18:27; 18:65; 23:92; 27:65; 32:6; 34:3; 35:38; 39:46; 49:18; 59:22; 62:8; 64:18; 72:26

Knows All Things — 2:224; 2:227; 2:256; 2:265; 3:34; 3:73; 4:12; 4:17; 4:24; 4:26; 4:32; 4:39 4:70; 4:147-148; 4:170; 4:176; 5:76; 5:97; 6:13; 6:83; 6:96; 6:101; 6:115; 6:128; 8:17; 8:42, 8:53; 8:61; 8:71; 8:75; 9:15; 9:28; 9:98; 9:103; 9:106;

	9:115; 10:36; 10:65; 12:76; 12:83; 12:100; 15:25; 1586 214 22:52 22:59; 24:18; 24:21; 24:28; 24:35; 24:41; 24:58-60; 24:64; 26:220; 27:6; 27:78; 29:5; 29:60; 29:62; 30:54; 31:23; 31:34; 33:40; 33:34; 33:51; 34:26; 35:8; 35:38; 35:44; 36:79; 36:81; 40:2; 41:12; 41:36; 42:12; 42:50; 43:9; 43:84; 44:6; 48:4; 48:26; 49:1; 49:16; 51:30; 57:3; 58:7; 60:10; 62:7; 64:11; 66:2-3; 67:13; 76:30
Signs Of Allah's Existence	2:117; 2:129; 2:164; 2:260; 6:63-65; 6:96-97; 7:57; 9:26; 9:40; 10:22; 10:24; 10:67; 13:3; 13:12-13; 13:17; 15:22; 16:12-17; 16:40; 16:67-79; 17:12; 17:66-67; 17:99; 20:53; 20:54-55; 22:61; 22:65; 23:15-22; 24:43-44; 25:45-50; 25:53; 25:61-62; 27:61-64; 27:86; 27:88; 28:73; 29:19-20; 29:63; 30:25; 30:27; 30:46; 30:48; 31:10; 31:29-31; 34:9; 35:9; 35:11-13; 35:16-17; 35:27; 36:79-80; 36:82-83; 40:61; 41:10-12; 41:39; 42:28-29; 42:32-34; 42:50; 43:9-12; 50:6-8; 51:47-49; 53:43-54; 54:49-50; 55:19-25; 56:57-76; 56:83-87; 57:6; 57:9; 57:17; 64:3; 64:11; 65:12; 67:5; 67:15-24; 70:40-41; 78:6-16; 79:27-33; 87:1-5; 88:17-20; 88:20; 90:8-10; 96:3-5; 105:1-5
The One (There Is No God But Allah)	2:133; 2:163; 2:255,8:2; 3:6; 8:18; 3:62; 4:87; 5:78; 6:102; 6:106; 7:59; 7:65; 7:85; 7:158; 9:31; 9:129; 11:14; 11:50; 11:61; 11:84; 16:2; 17:42; 20:8; 20:14; 20:98; 21:22; 21:25; 21:87; 23:23; 23:32; 23:116- 117; 27:26; 27:60-64; 28:70; 28:88; 35:3; 38:65; 39:6; 40:3; 40:62; 40:65; 44:8; 47:19; 52:43; 59:22-23; 64:13
The Provider Of All Things	2:29; 5:22; 5:58; 5:114; 7:32; 16:81; 17:20; 17:30; 23:72; 29:60; 29:62; 30:23; 31:20; 34:39; 40:13; 42:27; 25:13; 51:58; 62:11; 67:15; 106:3-4
The Supreme Creator	2:117; 2:164; 3:47; 3:59; 6:1-2; 6:73; 7:54; 10:6; 13:2; 13:16; 15:16; 15:85; 16:3; 16:40; 17:99; 19:35; 21:16; 21:30-32; 24:42; 25:59; 27:60; 29:44; 30:22; 31:10; 31:25; 32:4; 35:1; 36:81; 36:82; 39:5; 40:68; 41:9; 42:11; 41:29; 43:9; 44:38-39; 45:22; 46:33; 50:38; 57:4; 67:3

ii. Belief In Angels:

Belief In The Angels	2:177; 2:285; 4:136
Angels	2:161; 2:210; 2:248; 3:18; 3:39; 3:45; 3:42; 3:80; 3:87; 4:166; 6:8-9; 6:11; 6:111; 6:158; 11:12; 13:23; 15:7-8; 16:32-33; 17:40; 17:92; 17:95; 19:17; 21:103; 22:75; 23:24; 25:7; 25:21-22; 37:1-3; 41:14; 43:60; 53:26-27; 66:4; 79:1-5
Angel Jibrâ'el (Gabriel)	2:97-98; 66:4
Angel Malik, The Angel In Charge Of Hell	43:77
Angel Mika'el (Michael)	2:98
Angels And Adam	2:30; 2:34; 7:11; 15:28-30; 17:61; 18:50; 38:71-73
Angels And Allah Send Blessings To The Believers	33:43
Angels And Allah's Salutation To Muhammad (pbuh)	33:56
Angels And The Day of Judgment	34:40-41; 39:75; 50:21; 69:17; 78:38; 89:22
Angels Appointed As Guardians To Each Person	6:61; 13:11; 50:17-18; 82:10
Angels Given Female Names By The Pagans	53:27-28
Angels Help The Believers Against The Unbelievers	3:124-125; 8:9; 8:12; 9:26
Angels Implore Forgiveness For All Beings	40:7-9; 42:5
Angels In Charge Of Hell Fire	39:71; 43:77; 66:6-7; 67:8; 74:30-31; 96:18
Angels Record Our Deeds	50:17-18; 82:11-12
Angels Serve And Worship Allah	2:30; 4:172; 13:13; 16:49-50; 21:19-20; 37:164-166; 39:75; 40:7; 42:5
Angels Take The Soul Of The Dying	4:97; 6:61; 6:93; 7:37; 8:50; 16:28; 16:32; 32:11; 47:27;

	79:1-2
Ascent Of Angels	70:4
Creation Of The Angels	35:1; 37:150; 43:19
Descent Of Angels	16:2; 19:64-65; 25:25; 41:30-32; 97:4

iii. Belief In Holy Books:

The Holy Books	2:285; 4:136; 6:92

The Tawrah (Torah)	5:4; 5:48; 5:65; 3:97; 5:44; 5:46; 5:66; 5:110; 6:91; 6:146; 7:144-145; 7:157; 9:111; 11:17; 46:12; 48:29; 61:6; 62:5
Confirmed By Jesus	61:6
Confirmed By The Injeel *(Gospel)*	5:46
Confirmed By The Qur'an	46:12
Mention Of Muhammad In	7:157
Revelation Of	7:144-145

The Zaboor (Psalms)	4:163; 17:55; 21:105

The Injeel (Gospel)	3:4; 3:48; 3:65; 5:46-47; 5:66; 5:110; 7:157; 9:111; 48:29; 57:27
Mention Of Muhammad In The Gospel	7:157

The Qur'an:

The Qur'an Is The Words Of Allah	4:82; 9:111; 10:15-16; 11:1; 12:1-3; 15:1; 13:31; 14:1; 15:1; 15:91; 17:41; 17:89; 18:54; 21:106; 25:30; 26:2; 27:1; 28:2; 30:58; 36:69-70; 39:27; 43:44; 47:20; 47:24; 50:45; 55:2; 69:43-51; 86:13-14
Belief In The Qur'an	2:177; 5:69; 17:107; 42:15; 72:2; 77:50
Allah Commands That His Message Be Proclaimed	96:1-5
Allah Will Preserve The Qur'an From Corruption	2:106; 5:48; 15:9; 41:42
Challenge To Produce The Like Of The Qur'an	2:23; 10:38; 11:13-14; 17:88; 26:210-211; 52:34
Confirms Earlier Scriptures	2:97; 3:3; 5:48; 6:92; 10:37; 46:10; 46:12
Deaf Dumb And Blind Are Those Who Do Not Understand	2:171; 7:179; 8:22;
Do Not Have Doubts On Allah's Revelation	3:60
Follow The Best Meaning In The Qur'an	39:18; 39:54-55
Is A Book Of Guidance	2:2; 2:159; 11:17; 12:111; 16:64; 16:89; 16:102; 17:9; 27:2; 27:76-77; 31:3; 34:6; 41:44; 42:52; 45:20; 72:2
Is A Book Of Wisdom	10:1; 31:2; 36:2; 43:4
Is A Guide And A Mercy For The Doers Of Good	31:2-4
Is A Message For The Living	36:69-70
Is A Source Of Healing And Mercy	6:157; 7:204; 10:57; 17:82; 20:2; 27:77; 28:86; 29:51; 38:29; 41:44; 45:20
Is For All Mankind	6:92; 14:1; 14:52; 17:89; 18:54; 21:10; 38:86; 38:87-88; 39:41; 42:7; 68:52
Is Full Of Admonition And Full Of Blessings	38:1; 38:29
Is Heard By Jinn	46:29-32; 72:1-2
Is Imperishable	85:21-22
Is Made Easy	44:58; 54:17; 54:21; 54:32; 54:40
Is Message For The Heart	50:37
Is Message To All The Worlds	38:87; 68:52; 81:26-28
Language Of The Qur'an	12:2; 13:37; 16:103; 20:113; 26:195; 39:28; 41:3; 41:44; 42:7; 43:3; 46:12
Listen With Silence When It Is Read	7:204; 41:26; 46:29
Men Of Understanding Will Grasp The Message	2:269; 3:7; 14:52; 38:29; 39:18; 40:54
Qur'an Guides Those Who Want To Be Guided	47:17; 50:37
Qur'an To Be Read, Recited And Understood	2:121; 7:205; 16:98; 17:45; 17:106-107; 18:27; 20:114; 23:68;28:52-53; 29:45; 32:15; 33:34; 35:29; 38:29; 39:18; 46:29; 59:21; 73:1-4; 73:20; 75:16

Read The Qur'an Regularly	35:29; 73:20
Recitation Of The Qur'an	10:61; 16:98; 17:45-46; 17:106; 18:27; 27:92; 29:45; 35:29; 56:80; 73:4; 73:20; 75:18; 84:21; 96:1; 96:3
Revelation Of The Qur'an	2:176; 2:185; 2:213; 2:231; 3:3; 3:7; 4:105; 4:113; 5:48; 5:101; 6:19; 6:114; 6:155-157; 7:2-3; 14:1; 15:87; 16:64; 17:82; 17:105-106; 18:1;20:2-4; 20:114; 21:10; 24:1; 25:6; 25:82; 26:192-199; 29:51; 32:2; 36:5; 38:29; 39:1-2; 39:23; 40:2; 41:2-4; 42:17; 44:3-6; 45:2; 46:2; 69:43; 75:16-19; 87:6-7
Seek Allah's Protection Before Reading The Qur'an	16:98; 85:22
Teach The Qur'an To Others	7:2; 51:55
The Mother Of The Book	5:7; 15:39; 43:4
The Qur'an As Defined By Allah	10:37; 11:1; 13:31; 36:2; 36:5; 38:67; 43:4; 56:77; 80:13-16; 85:21-22
The Qur'an Confirms Previous Revelation	5:48; 6:92; 10:37; 46:10; 46:12
The Qur'an Is Easy To Understand And Remember	44:58; 54:17; 54:22; 54:32; 54:40
The Qur'an Is Pure And Holy	98:2-3
The Qur'an Is The Book Of Guidance	2:2; 2:121; 2:159; 2:185; 3:138; 4:174; 5:15; 6:90; 6:155; 7:3; 7:52; 10:57; 11:1-2; 11:17; 12:1-2; 12:111; 14:1; 14:52; 15:1; 16:64; 16:89; 16:102; 17:9; 17:89; 18:2; 18:3; 18:54; 19:97; 21:10; 21:106; 22:54; 24:1; 24:34; 27:1-2; 27:76-77; 30:58; 31:3-4; 32:3; 34:6; 36:2; 36:5-6; 36:69-70; 38:1; 38:29; 38:86-88; 39:28; 39:41; 39:55; 40:54; 41:3-4; 41:44; 42:17; 42:52; 43:3-4; 43:44; 44:58; 45:11; 45:20; 46:12; 50:45; 51:23; 57:16; 59:21; 68:52; 69:51; 72:2; 75:17-18; 86:13-14
The Qur'an Is The Book Of Power	13:31; 39:23; 41:41-42; 59:21
The Qur'an Is The Book Of Wisdom	10:1; 31:2; 36:2; 43:4
The Qur'an Makes Things Clear	15:1; 25:33; 26:1-2; 27:1; 28:1-2; 36:69-70; 43:2; 44:2
The Qur'an Revealed In Stages	17:106; 20:114; 25:32; 76:23
The Qur'an Revealed To Muhammad (Pbuh)	2:97-98; 3:3; 3:7; 4:82; 4:105; 5:15-16; 5:48; 5:67; 6:19; 6:92; 7:2; 10:37; 12:3; 13:1; 13:36-37; 14:1; 15:87; 16:64; 16:89; 16:102; 16:123; 17:85; 17:105; 18:1; 20:2-4; 20:99; 20:113; 25:32-33; 26:192-196; 26:210-211; 27:6; 27:91-92; 28:44; 28:85; 29:47-49; 29:51; 32:2-3; 35:31-32; 36:5; 39:1-2; 40:2; 41:2; 41:41-42; 42:7; 42:17; 42:52; 43:43; 44:3-6; 45:2; 46:2; 46:9; 55:2; 56:80-81; 69:38-39-48; 72:1; 76:23; 87:6
The Qur'an To Be Cared And Respected	4:82; 7:204; 17:107; 32:15; 53:59-62; 56:78-79
The Qur'an To Be Recited Properly	73:1-4; 75:16
The Qur'an Without Discrepancies	4:82
There Is No Crookedness In The Qur'an	18:1-2; 39:28
Those Who Reject The Qur'an Will Be Punished	3:4; 7:182
Toward Understanding The Qur'an	2:164; 2:121; 2:219; 2:230; 2:242; 3:7; 7:26; 12:2; 16:90; 23:68; 38:29; 39:18; 41:3; 44:58

iv. Belief In Rasools (Prophets)

Rasools/ Prophets/ Messengers, Peace Be Upon Them

All Prophets Were Humans	6:50; 7:188; 18:110; 25:20
Do Not Make Distinctions Between Prophets	2:285; 4:152
Difference In Status Among Rasools / Prophets	2:253; 4:150-151; 17:55
Prophets Came To Every Group Of People	5:48; 10:47; 13:7; 13:38; 14:4; 16:36; 16:63; 16:84; 22:67; 35:24
Prophets Cannot Help The Un-Believers	11:42-46
Some Prophets Were Exalted Over The Others	2:253; 38:40

Rasools (Prophets) Mentioned In The Qur'an, Their Stories And Their Nations

Some Rasools Stories Are Related And Some Are Not	4:164; 40:78
Objective In Relating The Stories Of The Rasools	11:120; 12:111; 14:5

Adam, Peace Be Upon Him

Creation Of Adam	2:30-34; 7:11; 15:26; 15:28-30; 15:30; 15:33; 17:61; 18:50; 20:116; 38:71-73
Angels Prostrated To Him	2:34; 7:11; 15:30; 17:61; 18:50; 20:116; 38:72-73
Allah Taught The Names Of Things	2:31
Chosen By Allah	3:33
Covenant With Allah	20:115
His Disobedience To Allah (Seduced By Shaitân)	2:35-39; 7:19-25; 20:116-123
His Decent From Paradise	2:36; 7:22-25; 7:27; 20:120-123
His Repentance	2:37; 7:23
His Progeny	7:172-173; 19:58
Story Of The Two Sons Of Adam	5:27-31

Al Yasa' (Elisha), Peace Be Upon Him

	6:86; 38:48

Ayyûb (Job), Peace Be Upon Him

	4:163; 6:84; 21:83-84; 38:41-44

Daûd (David) And Sulaimân (Solomon), Peace Be Upon Them

Animals Talk To Each Other	27:18
Story Of Daûd And Sulaimân	27:15-44; 38:17-26; 38:30-40
Adjudicated	21:78; 38:21-26
Celebrated Allah's Praises	21:79; 27:15; 34:10; 38:18-19
Cursed The Children Of Israel	5:78
Killed Goliath	2:251
Given Power And Wisdom	2;251; 27:15; 38:20
Given Sulaimân (Solomon)	38:30
Given The Psalms	4:163; 17:55
Guided by Allah	6:84
His People Could Understand Bird's Speech	27:26
His People Were Able To Read And Write	27:28-30
Made Chain Mail	21:80; 34;10-11
Man Of Strength	38:17

Dhu Al-Kifl, Peace Be Upon Him

	21:85-86; 38:48

Hûd, Peace Be Upon Him

Story Of Prophet Hûd (Pbuh)	7:65-68; 11:50-60; 26:123-140; 41:16
People of Hûd (Pbuh) A'd	7:65-72; 7:74; 9:70; 11:50-60; 11:89; 14:9; 22;42; 25:38; 26:123-140; 29:38;32:15-16; 41:13-16; 46:21-26; 50:13; 51:41-42; 53:50; 54:18-21; 69:6-8; 89:6-8

Idrees (Idris)

	19:56-57; 21:85-86

Ibrâheem (Abraham) , Peace Be Upon Him (Pbuh):

Ibrâheem, Peace Be Upon Him	2:133; 2:136; 2:140; 2:260; 3:33; 3:84; 4:54; 6:74-84; 12:6; 12:38; 19:41; 21:51; 29:27; 33:7; 37:83
Allah's Order To Follow The Ways Of Ibrâheem	16:121-123
Promised Prophethood To Him And His Offspring	2:124; 19:49; 21:72-73; 29:27; 37:112-113; 57:26
Allah Saved Ibrâheem (Pbuh) From The Fire	21:68-71; 29:24; 37:98-99
Allah Showed His Signs To Ibrâheem (Pbuh)	2:260
And His Father	4:74, 6:74; 9:114; 19:42-47; 21:52; 26:70-82; 37:85-90; 43:27
Denounced Idol Worshipping	14:35; 19:48-49; 21:51-71; 26:70-82, 29:17-18; 29:24-25; 37:85-98; 43:26-28
Did Not Hesitate To Offer His Son As Sacrifice	37:100-111
Is Allah's Friend	4:125
Prayed For Forgiveness	14:40-41; 60:4-6
Prayer	2:126-129; 14:35-41; 26:8389; 37:100; 60-5
Religion Of Ibrâheem And Muhammad Is Islam	2:130-135; 3:6568; 3:95; 4:125; 6:161; 22:78; 42:13
Station Of Ibrâheem - The Ka'bah	2:125-127; 3:96-97; 14:35; 22:26

Was A Devoted Muslim	2:130-132; 16:122; 26:83; 29:27; 38:47
Was Given A Revelation (Book)	4:163-164; 57:26
Was Tested By Allah	2:124; 37:106
Worshipped Allah	2:135-136; 2:258; 3:67; 3:95; 6:74; 3:95; 6:74-82; 6:161; 14:35-36; 16:120; 16:123; 29:16; 43:27-28

Ilyâs (Elias)   6:85; 37:123-132

Isa (Jesus), Peace Be Upon Him

Allah Blessed Isa (Jesus) With Holy Spirit	2:87; 2:253; 5:110
Cursed The Children Of Israel	5:78
Did Not Die Nor Was He Crucified	4:157-158; 19:15; 19:33
Given The Revelation	2:136; 3:48; 3:84; 5:46; 19:30; 57:26-27
His Miracles	3:45-49; 5:110-115; 19:28-29
His Miraculous Birth	3:35-47; 3:59; 5:75; 5:110; 19:2-34
Is Not God	5:17; 5:72; 9:30-31
Mary, Mother Of Jesus (Pbuh)	3:42
Messenger To The Children Of Israel	3:49-51; 5:46; 5:72; 43:59; 61:6; 61:14
Proclaimed That There Is No God But Allah	3:51; 4:172; 5:116-117; 43:63-64
Prophesized The Coming Of Muhammad (Pbuh)	6:16
Similitude Of Jesus Is Like That Of Adam (Pbut)	3:59
Some Believed In Him Others Plotted Against Him	3:52-55; 43:57-58; 43:65; 57:27; 61:14
Some Israelites Disobeyed Him	2:87-88; 3:183-184; 5:78; 61:14
Spoke In Infancy	3:46; 5:110
Was A Prophet (Pbuh)	5:46; 5:75; 43:59; 43:63
Was Given Wisdom	43:63
Was Sent To Israelites As A Prophet (Pbuh)	3:54-53; 4:156-159; 5:46; 5:110; 43:57-59; 43:54-65

Ishâq (Isaac)   2:136; 2:140; 3:84; 4:163; 6:84; 11:71; 12:6; 12:38; 14:39; 19:49; 21:72-73; 29:27; 37:112-113; 38:45-47; 51:28

Isma'il (Ishmael)   2:136; 2:140; 3:84; 6:86; 14:39; 19:54-55; 31:85-86

And The Ka'bah	2:125-127
And The Sacrifice	37:100-107
Was Sent Revelation	4:163

Lût (Lot), Peace Be Upon Him

Story Of Lût (Lot), Peace Be Upon Him	7:80-84; 15:61-77; 21:74-75; 26:160-175; 27:54-58; 29:26-35

Lût's People

6:86; 7:80-84; 11:69-83; 11:89; 11:95; 14:9; 15:51-77; 17:59; 21:71; 21:74-75; 22:42; 25:38; 26:141-158; 26:160-175;   27:45-53; 27:54-58; 29:6; 29:28-35; 29:38; 37:133-134; 38:13; 40:31; 41:13; 41:17; 50:12; 51:43; 53;51; 54:23-31; 54:36; 69:4-5; 88:18; 89:9; 91:11-14

Musa (Moses) And Haroon (Aaron), Peace Be Upon Them

His Meeting With Allah	4:164; 7:142-145; 20:9-48; 20:83-85; 27:7-14; 28:29-35; 79:15-19
His Miracles	2:60; 7:106-108; 7:160; 20:69; 26:32-33
His Prayer	7:151; 7:156; 10:88-89; 20:25-36; 28:16-17
His Religion Was Same As That Of Other Prophets	42:13
Musa And The Learned Servant Of Allah	18:60-82
Musa And The Pharaoh	7:103-137; 7:137; 10:75-83; 11:96-97; 20:47-79; 23:45-48; 26:10-51; 28:36-42; 40:23-45; 43:46-56; 51:38-40; 61:5; 79:15-26
Pharaoh And His People Were Punished	73:16; 79:21-26
Pharaoh's Body Is Saved For Generations To See	10:92

	21:45; 22:49; 25:56; 27:92; 8:46; 29:50; 32:3; 33:45; 34:28; 34:46; 35:23-24; 36:6; 38:65-70; 46:9; 48:8; 51:50-51; 61:13; 67:86; 74:2; 79:45
Is A True Prophet And Messenger Of Allah	2:119; 5:19; 5:92; 7:182-184; 7:188; 11:57; 13:7; 15:89; 27:92; 29:50; 33:45; 34:46; 5:23-24; 38:65; 46:9; 48:8; 50:2; 51:52; 53:56; 79:45
Is Close To The Believers	33:6
Is Mercy For Mankind	9:61; 21:107; 28:46
Is Not A Poet	21:5; 36:69; 37:36-37; 52:30; 69:41
Is Not A Soothsayer	52:29; 69:42
Is Not Astray	53:2
Is Not Harsh	3:159
Is Not Mad Or Possessed	7:184; 23:70; 34:46; 37:36-37; 52:29; 68:2; 81:22
Is Not Responsible For Arranging The Affairs Of People	6:66; 6:104; 6:107; 10:108; 10:108; 16:82; 17:54; 26:216; 39:41; 42:6; 42:48; 88:21-22
Is Not The Father Of Any Of Your Men	33:40
Is On The Right Way And Right Religion	36:4; 43:43; 45:18; 48:2
Is One Of The Rasools (Messengers)	36:3
Is The Seal Of The Prophets	33:40
Is The Unlettered Prophet	7:157-158; 29:48; 62:2
Is The Rasool (Messenger) Of Allah	33:40; 48:28-29; 49:7; 63:1
Messenger To The People Of The Book	5:15; 5:19; 98:2
Most Kind And Merciful To The Believers	3:159; 9:128; 15:88
Nearest Of Kin To Ibrâheem (Abraham)	3:68
No Difficulty In Duty To Allah	33:38
No More Than A Rasool (Messenger)	3:144; 17:94
Obey Him	3:32; 4:59; 4:64; 4:69; 5:92; 8:1; 8:20-21; 8:46; 9:71; 24:51-54; 24:56; 33:33; 33:36; 33:71; 47:33; 48:16-17; 49:14; 58:13; 60:12; 64:12;
Prayed For His Own Salvation	17:80; 23:93-98
Proclaim The Praises Of his Rabb (Lord)	52:29
Prophet (Muhammad, Pbuh) And The Believers	2:104; 2:108; 3:31; 4:100; 8:24; 24:63; 33:53; 33:56; 49:1-5; 59:7
Sanctifies The People	62:2
Sent By Allah With Guidance And True Religion	61:9
Sent To Proclaim The Message Of Allah	2:151; 5:67; 5:92; 5:99; 6:105; 9:33; 11:2-3; 13:40; 15:94; 16:35-36; 16:44; 16:82; 6:125; 17:81; 22:67; 24:54-55; 25:56; 42:7; 42:48; 42:52; 42:35; 46:35; 64:12; 72:23; 73:15; 96:1
Speak To Him With Respect	2:104; 4:46; 24:62; 33:56-57; 49:1-5; 58:8
Take What He Assigns To You	59:7
The Jews' And Christians' Attitude Towards Him	2:120; 2:145; 5:79-82
Unbelievers Caused Him Grief And Pain	6:33; 36:76
Universal Messenger	34:28
Wars During The Life Of The Prophet Pbuh):	
Badr	3:13; 3:122-127; 3:172-175; 8:5-19; 8:41-44; 8:47-48; 8:67-71
Bani Qainuqa	59:15
Uhud	3:121-122; 3:128; 3:139-145; 3:151-158; 3:165-175
Banu Nadheer	59:2-6; 59:11-12
Ditch	33:9-27
Treaty Of Hudaibia	48:1-7; 48:18; 48:20; 48:22-23
Khaiber	33:27; 48:15-16; 48:19
Conquest Of Makkah	8:57; 9:1-2; 9:5; 9:12-15; 48:12; 48:25; 57:8; 48:24; 48:27; 110:1-3
Hunain	8:56; 9:25-27
Tabuk	9:38-39; 9:41-59; 9:81; 9:83; 9:86-87; 9:90-96; 9:117-118; 9:120-121
Was A Human Being	6:50; 7:188; 18:110; 25:7; 41:6
Was Falsely Accused By His Enemies	7:184; 21:5; 23:70; 36:69; 37:36-37; 52:29-30; 53:2; 68:2; 69:41-42; 81:22

vi. Belief In Life After Death:

All Beings Will Be Resurrected	2:259-260; 6:36; 7:57; 19:93; 22:5-7; 30:19; 30:25; 31:28; 35:9; 36:12; 36:51-53; 42:29; 43:11; 50:42; 53:47; 54:6-8; 67:15; 70:43; 71:18; 75:3-4; 80:22
Animals Will Be Resurrected	6:38
Every One Will Recognize Each Other	10:45
Man Will Be Resurrected As A New Creation	13:5; 14:19; 17:49; 17:98; 21:104; 32:10; 34:7; 35:16; 53:47; 56:6061
Resurrection From Grave	36:51-52
Resurrection Is Denied By Unbelievers	6:29; 11:7; 15:5; 16:58; 17:49-52; 17:98; 19:66; 25:35-58; 25:82-83; 25:40; 27:67-68; 32:10; 35:7-8; 36:78; 57:16-17; 37:53; 44:34-56; 45:24-26; 50:5; 56:47-48; 64:7; 72:7; 79:10-12
To Allah Is Our Return	2:28; 2:46; 2:156; 2:245; 2:285; 3:14; 3:28; 3:55; 4:87; 5:18; 5:105; 6:12; 6:22; 6:60; 6:94; 6:108; 8:24; 10:4; 10:23; 10:45-46; 10:70; 11:4; 13:36; 16:93; 16:52; 19:80; 19:93; 20:55; 21:35; 21:93; 22:5-7; 23:15-16; 23:60; 23:99-100; 24:64; 28:39; 28:70; 29:8; 29:17; 31:15; 31:23; 32:5; 24:26; 36:51-52; 36:79; 36:83; 39:7; 40:43; 40:77; 41:21; 41:39; 43:85; 45:15; 45:26; 46:6; 50:11; 54:6-7; 58:18; 60:4; 67:15; 75:1-6; 78:39; 84:14; 85:3-6; 86:8
Trumpet Of The Day Of Judgment	6:73; 18:99; 20:102; 23:101; 27:87; 36:51-52; 39:68; 50:20; 69:13; 74:8; 78:18; 79:7; 80:83
Waking Up From Sleep Is Like The Resurrection	6:60

6. Relating To The Pillars Of Islam:

1. Tawheed (The One And Only God – Allah):

Allah, The One And Only God	2:133; 2:163; 4:171; 5:73; 6:19: 9:31; 12:39; 13:16; 14:48; 14:52; 16:22; 16:51; 18:110; 21:108; 29:46; 37:4; 38:65; 39:4; 40:16; 41:6; 112:1
Allah, There Is No God But He,	2:183; 2:163; 2:255,8:2; 3:6; 8:18; 3:62; 4:87; 5:78; 6:102; 6:106; 7:59; 7:65; 7:85; 7:158; 9:31; 9:129; 11:14; 11:50; 11:61; 11:84; 16:2; 17:42; 20:8; 20:14; 20:98; 21:22; 21:25; 21:87; 23:23; 23:32; 23:116- 117; 27:26; 27:60-64; 28:70; 28:88; 35:3; 38:65; 39:6; 40:3; 40:62; 40:65; 44:8; 47:19; 52:43; 59:22-23; 64:13
Allah Begetteth Not, Nor Is He Begotten	112:3
Allah Has No Partner	6:163; 7:190-198; 9:31; 10:66; 17:111; 23:91; 25:2; 34:27; 35:40; 42:21; 68:41; 72:3
Allah Has No Son	2:116; 4:171; 6:101; 9:30; 10:68; 17:111; 18:4; 19:35; 19:88-92; 21:26; 23:91; 25:2; 37:152; 39:4; 43:81-82; 72:3
Allah Is Rabb (Lord) Of The Worlds	1:2; 2:131; 5:28; 6:45; 6:71; 6:162; 7:54; 7:61; 7:67; 7:104; 7:121; 10:10; 10:37; 26:16; 26:23; 26:47; 26:77; 26:98; 26:109; 26:127; 26:145; 26:164; 26:180; 26:192; 27:8; 27:44; 28:30; 32:2; 37:87; 37:182; 39:75; 40:64-66; 41:9; 43:46; 45:36; 56:80; 59:16; 69:43; 81:29; 83:6
Associate No Partners With Allah	3:64; 4:36; 4:48; 4:116; 5:72; 6:14; 6:81; 6:88; 6:106; 6:136-137;6:148; 6:151; 9:31; 10:28-29; 12:108; 13:16; 13:33; 13:36; 16:51.57; 16:73; 16:86; 17:22; 17:39-40; 17:56-57; 18:12; 18:110; 22:31; 23:59; 23:117; 24:55; 25:68; 28:87-88; 29:8; 30:31; 31:13; 35:13-14; 39:64-65;

	40:41-43; 40:66; 41:6; 43:15; 43:45; 46:4-6; 50:26:
	51:51; 60:12; 72:2; 72:18
To Allah Belongs The Dominions of The Heavens And The Earth	2:107; 2:116; 3:109; 3:189; 4:126; 4:131; 4:132; 4:170;
	4:171; 5:17; 5:18; 5:40; 5:120; 5:181; 6:12; 7:158; 9:116;
	10:55; 11:123; 13:15; 13:16; 14:2; 16:49; 16:52; 16:77;
	19:65; 20:6; 21:19; 22:64 24:42; 24:64; 25:2; 26:24;
	30:26; 31:26; 35:13; 36:83; 37:5; 38:6; 39:38; 39:44;
	42:4; 42:49; 43:85; 45:27; 48:14; 53:31; 57:2; 57:5; 64:1;
	64:4; 67:1; 78:37; 85:9
To Allah Belongs The Heritage Of The Heavens And The Earth	3:180; 15:23; 1940; 57:10
To Allah Is The Final Goal	2:285; 5:18; 5:105; 6:164; 22:48; 24:42; 35:18; 40:3;
	42:15; 50:43; 53:42; 60:4; 64:3
To Allah All Shall Be Brought Back	2:28; 2:46; 2:156; 2:281; 3:158; 5:48; 5:96; 6:12; 6:36;
	6:38; 6:60; 6:164; 8:24; 10:4; 10:23; 10:45; 10:56; 11:3;
	11:4; 15:25; 19:40; 21:35; 23:79; 23:115; 24:64; 28:70;
	28:88; 29:8; 29:57; 30:11; 31:15; 32:11; 36:22; 36:32;
	36:83; 39:44; 43:85; 45:15; 67:24; 96:8

2. Salah (Prayer):

Allah Discounts Salah Of Those Who Show Off And Neglect Neighborly Needs	107:4-7
Allah Listens To Prayer	2:186; 14:39; 40:60
As Taught By Allah	2:239; 7:29; 7:31; 73:8
Be Steadfast In Prayer	2:3; 2:43; 2:110; 2:177; 4:103; 5:55; 6:72; 7:55; 7:170;
	9:71; 9:112; 13:22; 14:31; 20:14; 21:73; 22:26; 22:78;
	24:37; 24:41; 24:56; 27:3; 29:45; 30:31; 33:33; 53:59-
	62; 58:13; 87:15
Do Not Approach Prayer In A State Of Intoxication	4:43
Face In The Direction Of The Ka'bah While Praying	2:142-144; 2:149-150
Friday Prayer	62:9-10
Guard Strictly The Mid-Day Prayer	2:238
In Travel And Warfare	2:239; 4:101-103
Is For Allah Alone	6:162; 13:14; 14:39; 14:40
Of Muhammad	26:218-219; 52:48-49; 73:2-4; 73:20; 108:2
Perform Ablution Before Prayer	4:43; 5:6
Perform In A Moderate Tone	17:110
Prayer Without Faith Is Useless	13:14; 40:50
Prayer (Du'a)	13:14; 14:39-40; 17:11; 32:16; 39:8; 39:49; 41:51; 46:15;
	52:28; 72:19-20
Punishment For Not Praying	68:43; 74:43; 75:31; 77:48; 107:4-6
Restrains From Shameful And Unjust Deeds	29:45
Reward	4:162; 7:170; 23:1-4; 23:9; 31:4; 33:35; 48:29
Salah (Prayer)	2:3; 2:43; 2:153; 2:177; 2:238-239; 4:43; 4:142- 143;
	4:162; 5:12; 5:55; 5:91; 6:72; 6:162; 7:29; 7:170; 8:3;
	9:18; 9:71; 9:112; 10:87; 13:22; 14:31; 14:37; 14:40;
	17:110; 19:31; 19:55; 19:59; 20:14; 20:132; 21:73;
	22:26; 22:35; 22:41; 22:77-78; 23:2; 23:9; 24:37; 24:56;
	27:3; 30:31; 31:4; 31:17; 33:33; 35:18; 35:29; 42:38;
	58:13; 62:9-10; 70:22-23; 70:34; 73:20; 87:15
Seek Allah's Help Through Patience And Prayer	2:153
Short Salah Allowed Under Certain Circumstances	4:101
Tahajjud (Pre-Dawn) Salah	17:79; 39:9; 50:40; 51:17-18; 52:48-49; 73:1-6; 73:20;
	76:26; 25:63-64
Take Precautions From Attack Even While Praying	4:102; 4:43
Times Of Salah	2:238; 11:114; 17:78-79; 20:130; 25:69; 30:17-18;
	33:41-42; 39:9; 40:55; 50:39-40; 50:39; 51:18; 52:48-49;
	73:2-4; 73:6; 73:20; 76:25-26
Unbelievers Take Salah As Mockery	5:58
Was Prescribed Before Muhammad (Pbuh)	2:83; 5:12; 7:128; 19:31; 19:55

3. Zakah (Obligatory Charity):

Zakah (Obligatory Charity)
2:43; 2:83; 2:110; 2:177; 2:270-274; 2:277; 4:77; 4:162; 5:12; 5:55; 7:156; 9:71; 19:31;19:55; 21:73; 22:41; 22:78; 23:4; 23:60; 24:37; 24:56; 27:3; 28:54; 30:39; 32:16; 33:33; 33:35; 35:29; 36:47; 41:7; 57:7; 57:10; 58:13; 63:10; 64:16; 70:24- 25; 93:10; 98:5

Sadaqah (Optional Charity):
Charity Is Considered A Beautiful Loan To Allah   2:245; 5:12; 57:11; 57:18; 64:17; 73:20

4. Siam (Fasting):

Fasting As Prescribed By Allah   2:183-185; 2:187; 33:35
Fasting As Penance   2:196; 4:92; 5:89; 5:95; 58:3-4
Conjugal Relationship During Ramadân   2:187

5. Hajj (Pilgrimage):

Hajj (Pilgrimage)   2:189; 2:196-203; 3:97; 5:1-2; 5:95-96; 9:3; 22:30
Abstain From Fighting (Unless Compelled) At The Ka'bah 2:191; 2:217
And Unbelievers   8:34-35; 9:7; 9;17; 9:28; 22:25; 48:25
Built By Ibrâheem And Isma'il   2:125-127; 3:96-97; 9:107-108; 14:37
Hunting Of Land Game Prohibited During Hajj   5:96
Ka'bah   2:144; 2:149-150; 2:158; 3:96-97; 5:2; 5:05-97; 9;19; 17:1; 22:29; 22:33; 48:27; 52:4; 106:3
Ka'bah, The Sacred House   22:26-32
Pagans Are Not Permitted To Enter The Ka'bah   9:28
Pilgrim Garb (Ihrâm)   5:1; 5:95-96
Pilgrimage (Hajj) And Umrah Ordained By Allah   2:196-200; 3:97; 22:26-30
Sacrifice Animal (During Hajj) And Use It For Food   22:36-37
Safa And Marwah Part Of Ka'bah   2:158
Short Hajj Allowed Under Specific Condition   2:203
Umrah   2:158; 2:196
Was Instituted By Abraham   2:125; 22:26-29

7. Relating To The Faith And Belief :

Allah's Signs:
2:73; 2:242; 2:251; 3:103; 3:108; 4:155; 5:75; 5:89; 6:33; 6:35; 6:37; 6:157-158; 7:26; 7:40; 7:175-177; 8:2; 10:71; 16:104-105; 17:1; 18:9; 18:17; 18:57; 18;105; 19:58; 19:73; 19:77; 20:22-23; 20:42; 20:126-128; 21:37; 22:52; 23:30; 23:58; 24:1; 25:73; 27:13-14; 27:93; 32:22; 32:24; 33:34; 34:4; 36;46; 39:52; 40:4; 40:13; 40:34:35; 40:63; 40:81; 41:15; 42:35; 43:69; 45:6-9; 45:31; 46:27; 57:9; 62:2; 65:41; 68:15; 74:16

Allah's Attributes:

All-Embracing (Cares For All)   2:115; 2:247; 2:261; 2:268; 3:73; 4:130; 5:54; 24:32; 53:32;
Answers The Prayers And Petitions   11:61; 37:75
Aware (Well-Acquainted)   2:234; 2:271; 3:153; 3:180; 4:35; 4:94; 4:128; 4:135; 5:8; 6:18; 6:73; 6:103; 9:16; 11:1; 11:111; 17:17; 17:30; 17:96; 22:63; 24:30; 24:53; 25:58; 25:59; 27:88; 31:16; 31:29; 31:34; 33:2; 33:34; 34:1; 35:14; 35:31; 42:27; 48:11; 49:13; 57:10; 58:3; 58:11; 58:13; 59:18; 63:11; 64:8; 66:3; 67:14; 100:11
Beneficent   52:28
Best Of Judges   6:57
Best Of Those Who Show Mercy   7:151; 12:64; 12:92; 21:83; 23:109; 23:118
Bestower Of Forms And Colors   59:24
Best To Decide   7:87; 10:109; 11:45; 12:80; 95:8
Blots Out Sins   4:43; 4:99; 4:149; 22:60; 58:2
Calls To Account   4:6; 4:86; 6:62; 17:14; 21:47; 33:39

Cherisher And Sustainer	1:2; 6:45; 6:162-163; 7:54; 7:58; 7:61; 7:67; 10:10; 10:32; 13:16, 18:42; 21:92; 23:52; 26:16; 26:23-28; 26:77; 29:59; 37:126; 37:182; 39:6; 4.4:8; 45:36; 81:29; 96:1; 98:8; 114:1
Creator	6:102; 13:16; 15:28; 15:86; 35:3; 36:81; 37:125; 38:71; 39:62; 40:62; 59:24
Disposer Of Affairs	4:171; 6:102; 17:65; 28:28; 33:3; 33:48; 39:62; 73:9
Eternal, Absolute	112:2
Evident	57:3
Evolver	59:24
Exalted In Power And Might	2:209; 2:220; 2:228; 2:240; 3:6; 3:18; 3:62; 3:126; 4:56; 4:158; 4:165; 5:38; 5:118; 6:96; 8:10; 8:63; 9:71; 9:40; 9:128; 9:129; 11:66; 14:14; 14:47; 16:60; 22:40; 22:74; 26:9; 26:104; 26:122; 26:140; 26:159; 26:175; 26:191; 26:217; 27:9; 27:78; 29:26; 29:42; 30:27; 31:9; 31:27; 32:6; 33:25; 34:6; 34:27; 35:2; 35:28; 36:5; 38:9; 38:66; 39:1; 39:5; 39:37; 40:2; 40:42; 41:12; 42:3; 42:19; 43:9; 44:42; 45:2; 45:37; 46:2; 48:7; 48:19; 54:42; 57:1; 57:25; 58:21; 59:1; 59:23-24; 60.5; 61:1; 62:1; 62:3; 64:18; 67:2; 85:8
First	57:3
Forbearing	2:225; 2:235; 2:263; 3:155; 4:12; 5:101; 17:44; 22:59; 33:51; 35:41; 64:17
Forgives Again And Again	20:82; 38:66; 39:5; 40:42; 71:10
Free From All Wants	4:131; 6:133; 10:68; 14:8; 22:64; 27:40; 29:6; 31:12; 31:26; 35:15; 39:7; 47:38; 57:24; 60:6; 64:6
Full Of Bounty	2:105; 2:243; 2:251; 3:74; 8:29; 10:58; 10:60; 27:73; 40:61; 57:21; 62:4
Full Of All Glory	11:73; 85:15
Full Of Kindness	2:143; 2:207; 3:30; 9:117; 9:128; 16:7; 16:47; 22:65; 24:20; 57:9; 59:10
Full Of Loving-Kindness	11:90; 85:14
Full Of Majesty, Bounty, And Honor	55:27; 55:78
Full Of Mercy	6:133; 6:147; 18:58
Hears All Things	2:224; 2:27; 2:256; 3:34; 4:58; 4:134; 4:148; 5:76; 6:13; 6:115; 8:17; 8:42; 8:53; 8:61; 9:103; 10:65; 14:39; 17:1; 21:4; 22:61; 22:75; 24:21; 24:60; 26:220; 29:5; 29:60; 31:28; 34:50; 40:20; 40:56; 41:36; 42:11; 44:6; 49:1; 58:1
Maker Of The Heavens And Earth	6:14; 12:101; 14:10; 35:1: 39:46: 42:11
Master Of The Day of Judgment	1:4
Master All The Kingship	3:26
Most Appreciative	35:30; 35:34; 42:23: 64:17
Most Bountiful	96:3
Most Gracious	1:1; 1:3; 2:163; 13:30; 17:110; 19:18; 19:26; 19:45; 19:58; 19:61; 19:69; 19:75: 19:78; 19:85; 19:87-88; 19:91-93: 19:96; 20:5: 20:108-109; 21:26: 21:36; 21:42; 21:112; 25:26; 25:59-60; 26:5; 27:30; 36:15: 36:23; 36:52: 41:2: 43:17: 43:20; 43:33; 43:36; 43:45; 43:81: 50:33; 55:1; 59:22; 67:3: 67:19-20; 67:29; 78:37-38
Most Great	4:34; 13:9; 17:43: 22:62; 31:30; 34:23: 40:12
Most High	2:255: 4:34; 13:9: 22:62; 31:30; 34:23: 40:12; 42:4; 42:51; 87:1
Most Merciful	1:1; 1:3; 2:160; 2:163; 2:192; 2:218; 2:226; 3:31; 3:89: 4:16: 4:23: 4:25: 4:29; 4:96; 4:100; 4:105; 4:110; 4:129; 4:152: 5:3 ; 5:4; 5:39: 5:74; 5:98; 6:145; 6:165; 7:153; 7:167; 9:91; 9:99; 9:102; 9:104; 9:117-118; 10:107: 11:90; 12:98: 15:49; 16:7; 16:18; 16:47; 16:110: 16:115; 16:119; 15:66; 22:65; 24:5: 24:20: 24:22; 24:33: 24:62; 25:6; 25:70: 26:9; 26:104; 26:122; 26:140: 26:159;

	26:175; 26:191; 26:217; 27:11; 27:30: 28:16: 32:6: 33:5; 33:24; 33:43; 33:50; 33:73; 34:2: 36:5; 36:58: 39:53; 41:2; 41:32; 42:5; 44:42: 46:8; 48:14; 49:5; 49:12: 52:28; 57:9; 57:28; 58:12; 59:10; 59:22: 60:7; 60:12: 66:1: 73:20
Most Merciful Of Those Who Show Mercy	7:151; 12:64; 12:92; 21:83
Most Near	2:186; 11:61; 34:50
Oft-Forgiving	2:170; 2:182; 2:192; 2:218; 2:225-226; 2:235; 3:31; 3:89; 3:129; 3:155; 4:23; 4:25; 4:96; 4:100; 4:105; 4:110; 4:129: 4:152; 5:3; 5:34; 5:39; 5:74; 5:98; 5:101: 6:145; 6:165; 7:153: 7:167; 9:91; 9:99; 9:102; 9:104; 10:107; 12:98; 15:49: 16:18; 16:110; 16:115; 16:119; 17:25; 17:44; 18:58: 22:60; 23:5; 24:22: 24:33; 24:62; 25:6; 25:70; 27:11: 28:16: 33:5; 33:24; 33:50; 33:73; 34:2; 35:28: 35:30; 35:34; 39:53; 41:32; 42:5; 42:23; 46:8: 48:14; 49:5; 49:14; 57:28; 58:2: 60:7; 60:12; 64:14; 66:1; 67:2; 73:20
Oft-Returning	2:37; 2:54; 2:160; 4:16: 4:64: 9:104; 9:118: 24:10; 49:12; 103:3
One God	2:133; 2:163; 4:171; 5:73; 6:19: 9:31; 12:39; 13:16; 14:48; 14:52; 16:22; 16:51; 18:110; 21:108; 29:46; 37:4; 38:65; 39:4; 40:16; 41:6; 112:1
Originator Of The Heavens And Earth	2:117; 6:101
Prevails Over All Things	18:45; 43:42; 54:42
Protector	2:107; 2:120; 2:148; 2:257; 2:286; 3:68; 3:50; 3:51; 3:70; 4:45; 4:75; 6:14; 6:62; 7:155; 7:196; 8:40; 9:51; 9:116; 12:101; 22:78; 34:41; 42:9; 42:28; 45:19; 47:11; 66:2; 66:4
Provider Of Sustenance	5:22; 5:58; 5:114; 23:72; 34:39; 51:58; 62:11
Quick In Punishment	6:165; 7:167
Rabb Of Grace	2:105; 3:174; 8:30; 57:21; 57:29; 62:4
Rabb Of Honor	37:180
Rabb Of Power	51:58
Rabb Of Retribution	3:4; 14:47; 39:37
Rabb Of Dawn	113:1
Rabb Of The East And The West	26:28: 37:5; 55:17; 70:40; 73:9
Rabb Of The Heavens And Earth	18:14; 19:65; 21:56; 37:5; 38:66; 43:82: 44:7; 45:36; 51:23; 78:37
Rabb Of The Throne Of Glory Supreme	9:129; 17:42; 21:22; 23:86-87; 23:116; 27:26; 40:15; 43:82; 85:15
Rabb Of The Ways Of Ascent	70:3
Rabb Of The Worlds	1:2; 2:131; 5:28; 6:45; 6:71; 6:162; 7:54; 7:61; 7:67; 7:104; 7:121; 10:10; 10:37; 26:16; 26:23; 26:47; 26:77; 26:98; 26:109; 26:127; 26:145; 26:164; 26:180; 26:192; 27:8; 27:44; 28:30; 32:2; 37:87; 37:182; 39:75; 40:64-66; 41:9; 43:46; 45:36; 56:80; 59:16; 69:43; 81:29; 83:6
Sees All Things	4:58; 4:134; 8:72; 17:1; 17:18; 17:30; 17:96; 22:61; 22:75; 25:20; 31:28; 33:9; 34:11; 35:31; 35:45; 40:20; 40:44; 40:56; 41:40; 42:11; 42:27; 48:24; 49:18; 57:4; 58:1; 60:3; 64:2; 67:19; 84:15
Self-Subsisting Eternal	2:225; 3:2; 20:111
Source Of Peace	59:23
Steadfast	51:58
Strict In Punishment	2:165; 2:196; 2:211; 3:11; 5:2; 5:98; 8:25; 8:48; 8:52; 13:6; 40:3; 40:22; 59:4; 59:7
Strong	8:52; 11:66; 22:40; 22:74; 33:25; 40:3; 42:19; 57:25; 58:21
Swift In Taking Account	2:202; 3:19; 3:199; 5:4; 6:62; 13:41; 14:51; 24:39; 40:17
The Helper	3:150; 4:45; 8:40; 9:116; 22:78; 25:31; 40:51
The Hidden	57:3

The Holy One	59:23; 62:1
The Inheritor	15:23
The Irresistible	59:23
The King (Sovereign)	1:4; 3:26; 20:114; 23:116; 54:55; 59:23; 62:1; 114:2
The Knower Of The Hidden And Open	2:33; 6:59; 6:73; 9:94; 9:105;10:20; 11:123; 13:9; 16:77; 18:26; 18:27; 18:65; 23:92; 27:65; 32:6; 34:3; 35:38; 39:46, 49.1
The Knower Of The Finest Mysteries	6:103; 12:100; 22:63; 30:16; 33:34; 42:19; 67:14
The Knows All Things	2:224; 2:227; 2:256; 2:265; 3:34; 3:73; 4:12; 4:17; 4:24; 4:26; 4:32; 4:39 4:70; 4:147-148; 4:170; 4:176; 5:76; 5:97; 6:13; 6:83; 6:96; 6:101; 6:115; 6:128; 8:17; 8:42, 8.53; 8:61; 8:71; 8:75; 9:15; 9:28; 9:98; 9:103; 9:106; 9:115; 10:36; 10:65; 12:76; 12:83; 12:100; 15:25; 1586 214 22:52 22:59; 24:18; 24:21; 24:28; 24:35; 24:41; 24:58-60; 24:64; 26:220; 27:6; 27:78; 29:5; 29:60; 29:62; 30:54; 31:23; 31:34; 33:40; 33:34; 33:51; 34:26; 35:8; 35:38; 35:44; 36:79; 36:81; 40:2; 41:12; 41:36; 42:12; 42:50; 43:9; 43:84; 44:6; 48:4; 48:26; 49:1; 49:16; 51:30; 57:3; 58:7; 60:10; 62:7; 64:11; 66:2-3; 67:13; 76:30
The Last	57:3
The Light Of The Heavens And The Earth	24:35
The Living	2:255; 3:2; 20:111; 25:58; 40:65
The Most Honorable	23:116; 27:40; 27:44; 27:49; 82:6
The One To Decide	34:26
The Praiseworthy	4:131; 11:73; 14:1; 14:8; 22:24; 22:64; 31:12; 21:26; 34:6; 35:15; 41:42; 42:28; 57:24; 60:6; 64:6; 85:8
The Preserver	59:23
The Supreme	2:255; 42:4; 56:74; 59:23; 56:96; 69:52
The Truth (Al-Haqq)	18:44; 20:144; 22:6; 22:62; 23:116; 24:25; 31:30
The Watcher	5:117
The Wise	2:32; 2:129; 2:209; 2:220; 2:228; 2:240; 3:62; 3:126; 4:17; 4:24; 4:26; 4:130; 4:165; 4:170; 5:38; 5:118; 6:18; 6:73; 6:83; 6:128; 8:10; 8:63; 8:71; 9:15; 9:28; 9:40; 9:98; 9:106; 11:1; 12:83; 12:100; 15:23; 16:60; 22:52; 24:10; 24:18; 24:58-59; 27:6; 27:9; 29:26; 29:42; 30:27; 31:9; 31:27; 34:1; 34:27; 35:2; 39:1; 31:27; 34:1; 34:27; 35:2; 39:1; 41:42; 42:3; 42:51; 43:84; 45:2; 45:37; 46:2; 48:4; 48:7; 48:19; 51:30; 57:1; 59:1; 59:24; 60:5; 60:10; 61:1; 62:1; 62:3; 64:18; 66:2; 76:30
The Wisest Of All Judges	95:8
The Witness To All Things	4:33; 4:79; 4:166; 5:117; 6:19; 10:46; 13:43; 17:96; 29:52; 33:55; 34:47; 41:54; 46:8; 48:28; 58:6; 85:9
Âyatul Kursi (Glorification Of Allah)	2:255

Believers

Believers	2:3-5; 2:62; 2:136; 3:16-18; 8:2-4; 13:19-22; 13:28; 16:42; 22:54; 23;1-11; 23:57-61; 24:51-52; 24:62; 25:63-65; 25:67-74; 28:53-55; 29:59; 29:69; 31:4-5; 32:15-16; 34:6; 35:34; 37:164-166; 39:9; 40:7; 48:29; 49:7-8; 49:15; 50:33; 51:17-19; 70:19-30; 70:32-34; 76:7-10
Allah Always Rescues The Believers	10:103; 26:118-119; 27:53; 41:18; 51:35-36; 52:18; 52:27; 76:11
Allah Guides Those Who Are God Conscious And Wants To Be Guided	8:29; 19:76
Allah Has Purchased The Life And Wealth Of Believers	9:111
Allah Is Nearer To Man Than His Own Jugular Vain	50:16
Allah Is With Them	8:19; 47:35
Allah Is With You At All Times	50:16; 57:4; 58:7
Allah Loves The Righteous	2:195; 2:222; 3:134; 3:148; 3:159; 5:13; 9:4; 9:7; 19:96;

Fear Of Allah

Fear Of Allah	2:2; 3:102; 3:175; 3:200; 4:77; 4:131; 5:8; 5:11; 5:96; 5:100; 6:69; 6:72; 7:56; 7:63; 9:13; 9:18; 16:51; 22:1; 23:52; 23:57; 32:16; 33:37; 35:28; 39:10; 39:23; 49:12; 58:9; 59:18; 59:21; 60;11; 64:16; 65:1-2; 65:4-5; 65:10; 70:27-28; 71:3; 79:26; 79:40; 87:10; 92:5; 98:8
Fear, As Motive For Reclamation	2:74; 39:16
In Signs Of God	17:59
Unseen	35:18; 36:11; 50:33; 67:12

Grave

Standing At Grave And Seeking Allah's Forgiveness For The Buried	9:84
Punishment In Grave	4:97; 8:50; 16:28-29; 23:99-100; 40:45-46
Resurrection From Grave	36:51-52

Intercession (Shafa'a)

False Gods And Intercession	2:48; 2:123; 2:254; 6:94; 7:53; 10:18; 26:100-101; 30:13; 36:23; 39:43; 40:18
Allah Alone Has The Power To Intercede	2:254; 10:3; 39:43-44
Intercession By Allah's Permission Alone	2:254-255; 10:3; 19:87; 20:109; 21:28; 34:23; 39:43-44; 53:26

Lailatul Qadr (The Night Of Power)

The Night Of Power	97:1-5

Life

Life in General	6:142; 7:10; 8:24; 16:97; 21:30; 21:34; 22:5; 24:45; 25:54; 35:10; 26:68; 40:67-68; 42:29; 45:21; 46:15; 67:2; 71:17; 75:20; 76:27; 77:26; 84:6; 84:19
Belief In The Life Hereafter	2:4; 6:92; 6:113; 6:150; 7:45; 11:19; 16:23; 17:19; 27:3; 31:4; 34:21; 39:45; 41:8 Better Than Worldly Life, 2:86; 2:102; 2:201; 3:77; 3:152; 4:74; 6:32; 6:169; 9:38; 13:26; 14:27; 16:30; 17:21; 18:46; 20:131; 28:80; 29:64; 33:29; 40:39; 42:20; 43:35; 57:20; 87:17; 93:4
Life Of This World	2:86; 2:200-201; 2:212; 2:220; 3:14; 3:117; 4:74; 4:77; 4:94; 4:134; 6:32; 7:169; 9:37; 9:69; 10:7; 10:23-24; 10:64; 10:88; 11:15; 12:101; 13:34; 14:27; 16:30; 16:107; 16:122; 18:27; 18:46; 20:72; 22:11; 24:14; 24:19; 24:23; 28:60-61; 28:77; 28:79; 29:27; 29:64; 30:7; 33:28; 39:10: 40:43; 41:16; 41:31; 42:20; 43:32; 53:29; 59:3; 68:33; 79:38; 87:16; 102:1
Life Of This World Is A Little Enjoyment	3:197; 10:23; 10:70; 10:98; 13:26; 17:18; 20:131; 26:205; 40:39; 42:36; 43:35; 46:20; 77:46
Life Of This World Is But A Deception	2:204; 3:185; 6:70; 6:130; 7:51; 31:33; 35:5; 45:35; 47:36; 57:20
Man Is Tempted By The Allurements Of This World	6:130; 23:33; 23:64-67; 30:7; 31:33; 45:35
Similitude Of The Life Of This World	3:117; 10:24; 18:45; 57:20
The Reality Of This Life	4:77; 10:7-8; 18:7; 21:16-18; 21:35; 21:110; 39:49; 43:32-36; 75:20-21; 76:27; 89:15-16; 102:1-4
This Life Is Insignificant Compared To The Life In The Hereafter	9:38; 10:45; 13:26; 17:52;
There Is A Life Hereafter	2:94; 2:200-201; 2:220; 3:22; 3:85; 3:145; 3:148; 4:77; 4:134; 6:135; 9:69; 10:64; 12:57; 12:101; 13:34; 16:107; 16:122; 17:72; 20;127; 22:11; 22:15; 24:14; 24:19; 24:23; 27:66; 29:27; 38:46; 39:9; 39:26; 40:43; 41:16; 41:31; 59:3; 60:13; 68:33; 75:21
Those Who Desire Only This Life Will Be Doomed	2:85-86; 7:50-52; 10:7-8; 11:16; 16:106-108; 17:18-19; 41:40; 42:20; 62:11
Unbelievers May Only Enjoy The Life Of This World	46:20

Worldly Wealth Is Not An Indication Of Allah's Pleasure	9:55; 9:85; 9:109; 16:96-97; 21:34-35; 28:61; 43:32-35; 93:4

Record

All Things Are Being Recorded And Are Known To Allah	6:59; 10:61; 11:6; 22:70; 27:75; 34:3; 36:12; 50:4; 54:53; 57:22; 78:29 Of Deeds, 17:13-14; 17:71; 18:49; 36:12; 45:28-29; 50:17- 18; 50:23;54:52; 69:19-20; 69:25-26; 81:10; 83:7-9; 83:18-21; 84:7-10; 99:6-8

Sacrifice

Allah Only Accepts The Sacrifice Of The Righteous	5:27; 22:37
Animal Sacrifice	2:67-71; 5:2; 22:27-28; 37:100-111

Shaitân (Iblees / Satan)

Cannot Harm The Believers	58:10
Do Not Follow Or Obey Or WorshipHim	2:168; 2:208; 6:142; 19:44-45; 22:3-4; 24:21; 36:60
Enemy Of Man	12:5; 12;100; 17:53; 18:50; 20:117; 25:29; 35:5; 36:60; 43:62
Fails In His Promise	14:22
Fears Allah	8:48; 59:16
Has No Authority Over Allah's Servants	15:42; 16:99-100; 17:65; 34:21
Makes Sins Fair-Seeming	6:43; 8:48; 15:39; 16:63; 27:24; 29:38
Misleads And Deceives	4:117-121; 15:39; 17:62-68; 20:120; 34:20; 36:62; 57:14; 59:16
Party of Shaitân Will Perish	58:19
Shaitân	2:268; 2:275; 3:155; 3:175; 4:38; 4:60; 4:83; 6:68; 12:42; 22:52-53; 31:21; 47:25
Shaitân (Iblees) Is A Jinn	18:50; 26:95
Shaitân Disobeyed Allah	2:34; 7:11—18; 15:31-38; 17:61-65; 18:50; 20:116; 38:71-85
Shaitân's Handiwork	5:90-91; 28:15
Shaitân Leads Man To Disobedience And Sin	2:35-36; 4:60; 4:117-120; 6:43;7:16-22; 15:39-43; 16:63; 17:61-64; 19:44; 20:120; 24:21; 28:15
Seek Refuge With Allah From	7:200-201; 16:98; 41:56
Tempted Adam And Eve	7:20-22
Whisperer Of Evil	114:4

The Day of Judgment

A Day Of Distress	25:26; 74:9-10
A Day Of Mutual Loss And Gain	64:9
A Day Well-Known	56:50
All Mankind Will Stand Before The Rabb Of The Worlds	83:4-6
Appointed Time Of The Hour	7:187; 10:48-51; 11:104; 16:61; 16:77; 18:21; 18:36; 20:15; 21:38-40; 27:71-72; 31:34; 32:28-30; 33:63; 34:3; 34:29-30; 36:48-50; 40:59; 41:47; 42:17-18; 43:61; 43:66;43:85; 45:32; 47:18; 51:12-14; 54:1; 56:1; 67:25-26; 70:67; 72:25; 78:17; 79:42-46
Awe, Dread, Horror, And Terror	21:97; 22:1-2; 27:87; 34:23; 34:51; 69:4; 73:17; 75:7; 79:6-9; 101:4
Belief In The Day Of Judgment	2:177; 3:114; 4:38-39; 4:59; 4:136; 4:141; 4:162; 5:69; 9:18-19; 9:44-45; 24:2; 40:27; 42:18; 58:22; 65:2; 70:26
Day Of Account (Or Reckoning)	14:41; 38:16; 38:26; 38:53; 40:27
Day Of Assembly	42:7; 64:9
Day Of Eternal Life	50:34
Day Of Gathering	50:44
Day Of Judgment	1:4; 2:281; 3:9; 3;25; 3:73; 3:106; 3:161; 3:185; 3:194; 4:87; 4:109; 5:14; 6:12; 6:16-17; 6:22-23; 7:53; 7:59; 7:167; 10:45; 10:93; 11:3; 11:84; 11:103-108; 14:31; 14:41-42; 14:48-51; 16:25;16:27-34; 16:92; 16:124; 17:13-14; 17:36; 17:97; 18:98-101; 18:105;19:37-40; 20:100-109; 22:7; 22:56; 22:61; 23:16; 23:100; 25:17-30; 26:82; 26:87-102; 30:12-16; 30:43-44; 30:55-57;

	39:15; 39:31; 39:4748:39:67-75; 40:15-20; 42:45-47; 43:65-77; 45:26-35; 55:39-41; 56:1-56; 58:6-7; 58:18; 60:3; 60:6; 66:7-8; 67:27; 68:42:43; 69:13-37; 70:1-4; 75:7-15; 77:29-49; 78:17-40; 79:34-46; 80:33-42; 81:1-14; 4:1-15; 85:2; 86:9-10; 89:21-30; 99:1-8; 100:9-11; 102:8
Day Of Noise And Clamor	101:1-11
Day Of Requital	56:56
Day Of Resurrection	50:42; 75:1; 75:6
Day Of Sorting Out	37:19-74; 44:40-42; 55:7; 77:13-15; 77:38; 78:17; 81:7; 99:6
Every Thing Shall Belong To Allah	1:4; 25:26; 82:19
Friends Will Be Foes On The Day of Judgment	43:67
Great News	78:1-5
Is Coming Closer And Closer	21:1; 40:18; 53:57-58; 54:1; 70:7
It Will Happen Suddenly	16:77; 36:51-52
No One Can Avert The Day of Judgment	18:21; 40:59; 42:47; 43:61; 52:1-8; 78:40; 77:7; 78:17
No Excuses Shall Be Accepted	66:7; 75:13-15
No One Can Avail Another	31:33; 34:37; 44:41; 70:10-15; 80:34-37; 82:19
No One Shall Be Able To Speak	11:105; 77:35-36; 78:37-38
No One Shall Bear The Burden Of Another	6:164; 17:15; 35:18; 39:7; 53:38
No One Shall Help On The Day Of Judgment	2:48; 2:123; 3:10; 14:31; 21:39; 29:25; 26:88-89; 26:100-101; 31:33; 34:41-42; 35:14; 35:18; 39:47; 40:18; 44:41; 60:3; 80:33-37; 82:17-19
No Ransom Will Profit Anyone	3:91; 5:36; 6:70; 10:54; 13:18; 39:47; 57:15
No Where To Hide	42:47
Only Allah Knows When It Will Happen	7:187; 20:15; 31:34; 33:63; 43:85; 46:23; 67:25-26
People Will Say That They Were On Earth For Only An Hour	30:55
Prophets And Leaders Will Be Called As Witnesses	10:47; 16:84; 16:89; 17:71; 39:69
Record Of Our Deeds Will Become Manifest	3:30; 4:42; 10:23; 17:13-14; 17:71; 18:49; 20:15; 22:69; 24:23-25; 24:64; 39:69; 41:20-24; 45:28-29; 69:18-19; 78:29; 83:7-9; 99:6-8
Shall Be A Single Mighty Blast	36:49; 36:53; 38:15; 50:42; 69:13; 79:13-14
Souls Will Not Be Unjustly Dealt With	16:11; 17:71; 18:49; 19:60; 21:47; 36:54; 39:69-70; 40:17; 43:76; 45:22; 50:29
The Caller Will Call Out From A Place Quite Near	50:41; 54:6
The Deafening Noise	80:33
The Great Overwhelming Event	79:34-46; 88:1-16
The Scenes Of The Judgment Day	7:46; 7:47-53; 7:187; 11:105; 14:42; 14:48; 16:77; 18:47; 18:99; 20:102-111; 21:104; 22:2; 25:25-29; 27:87-88; 30:43; 30:45; 30:57; 36:49-54; 37:19 38:15; 39:55; 39:67-69; 39:75; 40:16; 43:67; 44:9-11; 44:40-42; 45:27; 47:181 50:20-21; 50:30; 50:41-44; 52:1-12; 54:1; 54:7-8; 55:37; 55:39; 56:1-10; 68:42-43; 69:13-17; 70:8-15; 70:14-15; 73:14; 73:16-19; 74:8-10; 75:7-15; 75:20-30; 77:7-13; 78:17-20; 78:38;79:7-8; 79:46;80:34-41; 81:1-18; 82:1-5; 84:1-6;89:21-23; 99:1-8; 100:9-11; 101:1-5; 102:8
The Sure Reality	69:1-3; 78:39
The Sworn	39:68; 52:45
There Shall Be No Favor Or Injustice	3:25; 3:161; 3:185; 10:47; 14:51; 16:84; 16:111; 17:71; 21:47; 32:25; 34:26; 36:54; 39:69; 39:70; 40:17; 50:29; 51:5-6
Tongues, Hands, Feet, Hearing, Sight, Skins, All Shell Bear Witness	24:24; 36:65; 41:20-22
Unbelievers / Wrong-Dowers Will Dispute With One Another	14:21; 25:26-29; 34:31; 36:65; 37:26-34; 50:27-29
Unbelievers/Wrongdoers Will Be Questioned	6:22; 16:25; 16:27; 18:52; 27:83-85; 28:61-66; 28:74; 37:19-31; 37:31; 45:31; 46:34

Unbelievers/Wrongdoers Will Be Rejected By Allah	2:174; 18:105; 23:101; 25:22; 28:41-42; 36:59; 40:52; 42:8; 45:34; 52:45-46; 69:35
Veil Is Removed From Your Sight	50:22
Will Surely Come To Pass	51:5-6; 52:7-8; 56:1; 69:15; 74:47; 77:7

Trials And Tests

Ibrâheem (Pbuh) Was Tested By Allah	2:124; 37:106
This World Is A Place Of Trial	4:77; 18:7; 21:16-18; 21:35; 39:49; 47:36; 75:20-21; 76:27; 89:15-16; 102:1-4
Trials And Tests	2:49; 2:124; 2:155; 2:214; 2:249; 3:142; 3:152-154; 3:186; 5:48; 5:94; 6:53; 6:165; 7:141; 7:155; 7:163; 7:168; 8:17; 8:28; 8:41; 9:49; 9:126; 11:7; 11:9-10; 14:6; 16:92; 16:110; 17:60; 18:7; 20:85; 20:90; 21:35; 21:111; 21:135; 22:11; 22:52; 22:53; 23:30; 24:63; 25:20; 27:47; 29:2-3; 33:11; 34:21; 37:106; 39:49; 44:17; 47:4; 47:31; 49:5; 57:25; 60:5; 60:10; 64:15; 67:2; 68:17; 72:17; 74:31; 76:1-2; 89:15-16
Trial In Ranks And Status	4:32; 6:165; 16:71; 16:75; 43:32
Trial In Suffering And Pain	2:214; 2:177; 6:42-43; 7:94-95

8. General Topics:

Adultery, Fornication And Lewdness

Adultery/ Fornication	7:33; 16:90; 1732; 24:2-3;25:68-69
False Charge Of Adultery Condemned By Allah	24:11-26
Lewdness	4:15-16; 4:19; 65:1
Premarital Sex And Prostitution Are Condemned	24:33
Repentance Shall Save The Fornicators/Adulterers	4:16; 25:68-70
The Condition Of Marriage For Adulterers	24:3; 24:26
The Condition Prescribed For Alleged Adultery	24:4-10

Arrogance

Arrogance - A Detestable And Punishable Action	2:206; 4:172-173; 7:36; 7:40-41; 7:133; 7:146; 16:29; 28:39-40; 31:7; 39:72; 40:35; 40:60; 40:76; 45:8-9; 46:20
The Arrogant Is Disliked By Allah	4:36; 7:48; 7:133; 10:75; 16:22-23; 17:37; 25:21; 27:14; 31:18; 44:19; 57:23

Bribery

Bribery Condemned	2:188

Business Or Trade

Deal Justly In Business Or Trade	38:23-24
Earn Your Living By Seeking Allah's Bounties	30:23; 30:46; 62:9-10
Trade Is Encouraged	2:283; 4:29; 9:24; 62:9-10

Charity

Allah Punishes Those Who Do Not Give Charity	9:34
Allah Will Multiply What You Spend In Charity	2:265; 2:276; 2:280; 30:39; 34:39; 35:29; 57:11; 57:18; 64:17
Charity Done In Secret Is Better	2:271
Charity Given Is Like A Loan To Allah	2:245; 5:12; 57:11; 57:18; 64:17; 73:20
Charity Is For The Needy	2:273
Charity Prescribed Even Before Islam	2:83; 5:12; 19:31; 19:55
Distribution of Charity	2:177
Exemption From Charity	9:91
Do Not Give Out Every Thing In Charity	17:29
Give Regular Charity	2:3; 2:43; 2:100; 2:177; 2:195; 2:254; 2:267; 2:277; 5:55; 9:71; 13:22; 14:31; 21:73; 22:41; 22:78; 24:37; 24:55; 24:56; 27:3; 30:38; 31:4; 33:33; 47:38; 57:7; 57:10; 58:12-13; 63:10; 64:16

Fostering

Call Fostered Children By Their Father's Name   33:4-5; 33:37

Fraud

Fraud Is Highly Condemned   26:181; 83:1-3

Gardens Of Paradise

Gardens Of Paradise

3:15; 3:133; 3:136; 3:195; 3:198; 4:57; 4:122; 5:85;
5:119; 7:19; 7:42-43; 7:49; 9:21-22; 13:35; 15:45-48;
18:31; 18:107-108; 20:76; 22:14; 22:23; 25:10; 25:15-
16; 25:24; 29:58; 30:15; 31:8-9; 35:33-35; 26:26; 36:55-
58; 38:49-54; 39:72-73; 40:40; 43:70-73; 44:51-57;
51:15; 52:17-28; 54:54; 56:11-40; 76:5- 22; 77:41-44;
78:31-36; 79:41; 89:30

A Garden On High   69:22-24; 88:10-16
A Home That Will Last   35:35
A Position Of Security   44:51; 44:55
A Realm Magnificent   76:20
All Sorrow Removed   35:34
Assembly Of Truth   54:5 5
Brought Nigh   50:31-35; 81:13
Carpets In Paradise   55:54; 55:76; 88:16
Companions Of Paradise   36:55; 59:20
Drink In Paradise   37:45-47; 38:51; 46:15; 52:23; 56:18-19; 76:5-6; 76:15-
18; 76:21; 77:43; 78:34; 83:25-28; 88:14
Female Companions In Paradise (*Hûr*).   57:48-49; 38:52; 44:54; 52:20; 55:56- 58; 55:70-76;
56:22-23; 56:35-38; 78:33
Food In Paradise   2:25; 19:62; 35:57; 37:41-42; 38:51; 43:73; 44:55;
47:15; 52:22; 55:52-54; 55:68; 56:20-21; 56:32-33;
69:23-24; 76; 14; 77:42-43; 80:24-32
Four Gardens   55:46-47
Garden Of Abode   53:15
Garden Of *Firdaus*   18:107-108; 23:11
Gardens Of Bliss, Felicity, And Delights   5:65; 10:9; 22:56; 26:85; 31:8; 37:43-49; 5:12; 56:89;
68:34; 76:20
Gardens Of Everlasting Bliss (*'Adn*),   9:72; 13:23; 16:31; 18:31; 19:61; 20:76; 35:33; 38:50;
40:8; 61:12; 98:8
Greetings In Paradise   10:10; 13:24; 14:23; 15:46; 16:32; 19:62; 21:103; 25:75;
33:44; 36:58; 39:73; 56:26; 56:91; 57:12
Home Of Peace   6:127; 10:25
In The Presence Of Allah   10:25; 50:35; 66:11; 68:34; 73:20
Lofty Mansions   39:20; 61:12; 66:11
No Toil Nor Weariness   35:35
Parable Of Paradise   47:15
Reclining On Throne Of Dignity   18:31; 36:56; 52:20; 56:15-16; 56:34; 76:13; 83:23;
83:35; 88:13
Rest And Satisfaction   56:89
The Eternal Garden   25:15
Width Of The Heaven And Earth   57:21
Youths Of Paradise   52:24; 56:17; 76:19

Gender Equity

Equality Of Sexes In The Sight Of Allah   9:71-72; 16:58-59; 16:97; 24:30-31; 33:35; 33:58; 33:73;
40:40; 47:19; 48:5-6; 57:12; 57:18
Men And Women Are Entitled To Their Own Earnings   4:32
Men And Women Are Protectors Of One Another   9:71
Originally Created From One Soul   4:1

Good Deeds

Allah Will Ignore Some Bad Deeds Of The Doers Of Good   46:13-16; 47:2

Allah Is With Those Who Do Good Deeds	16:128; 7:56; 34:37
Allah Multiplies Good Deeds	4:40; 6:160; 27:89; 28:84; 35:7; 39:10; 39:34-35; 42:23
Best In The Sight Of Allah Are The Doers Of Good	19:76; 20:75; 49:13; 4:128; 18:46; 35:32
Compete Others Only In Good Deeds	2:148; 2:197; 5:48; 23:57-61
Faith Without Good Deeds Is Of No Avail	18:103-105; 18:108
Foremost In Good Deeds Is The Highest Grace	35:32-35
Good Word Versus Evil Word	14:24-26
Most Honorable Are Those Who Do Good Deeds	35:32; 49:13
Multiple Reward For Good Deeds	34:37
People Of The Book And Good Deeds	3:113-115
Piety And Righteousness	2:177; 2:132; 2:135; 3:95; 4:125; 16:123
Worship Without Good Deeds Is Useless	107:1-7

Greed

Do Not Be Greedy	2:188; 3;14; 4;2; 4:10; 17:26; 30:39; 70:18-19; 74:11-15; 89:19-20; 100:8; 102:1-8; 104:1-9

Hell

Hell	in General 2:206; 3:12; 3:103; 3:131; 3:151; 3:191-192; 3:197; 4:56; 4:121; 7:18; 7:38; 39:35; 9:81; 14:16; 14:28-30; 15:43-44; 16:29; 17:97; 18:29; 21:98-100; 22:19-22; 23:103-108; 25:65-66; 29:54-55; 32:20; 36:63-64; 38:55-64; 39:16; 39:60; 40:71-76; 43:74-77; 44:43-50; 45:10; 50:24-26; 42:13-16; 54:48; 55:43-44; 56:41-56; 56:94; 57:15;58:8; 59:3; 69:30-37; 70:15-18; 72:23; 73:12-13; 74:26-31; 74:42-48; 76:4; 77:29-33; 82:14-16; 83:16-17; 88:4-7; 90:20; 102:6-7
A Place Of Ambush	78:21-30
Blazing In Fury	25:11-12; 67:7-8; 77:31-33; 81:12; 92:14-16; 101:11; 111:3 Breaks To Pieces, 104:4-9
Filled With Jinn And Men	7:18; 7:179; 11:119; 32:13; 38:85
Fuel Is Men And Stones	2:24; 66:6
Inhabitant May be Viewed By Former Companion In Paradise	37:51-59
Insatiable	50:30
Neither Dying Nor Living Therein	14:17; 20:74; 35:36; 43:77; 74:28; 84:11; 87:13
Penalty Of Eternity	10:52; 32:14; 41:28
Placed In Full View	79:36-39; 89:23
Will Break To Pieces	104:4-9

Hoarding

Hoarding Is Condemned	10:57-58

Homosexuality

Homosexuality Is A Call For Utter Destruction	26:165-174; 27:55; 29:28-30

Hûr (**Companions In Paradise**)	57:48-49; 38:52; 44:54; 52:20; 55:56- 58; 55:70-76; 56:22-23; 56:35-38; 78:33

Hypocrites

Hypocrites Deceive None But Themselves	2:9; 4:63; 9:78; 9:101; 9:107; 29:11
If They Would Have Obeyed Allah !	4:66-88
Punishment For The Hypocrites	2:10; 2:15; 4:138; 2:140; 4:145; 9:68-69; 9:73; 9:81-82; 9:101; 33:24; 33:60-61; 33:73; 48:6; 57:13-17; 63:2-3; 66:9
Repentance May Save Them	9:74
Who Are The Hypocrites?	2:8; 2:11; 2:14; 2:16-20;3: 165-168; 3:119; 4:61-62; 4:141-143; 8:49; 9:56; 9:64-67; 9:74-77; 9:81-83; 9:93-96; 9:107; 24:47-50; 29:10-13; 33:12; 58:8; 59:11-17; 63:1-8

Inheritance

Custodian Of Will Must Discharge It Honestly	2:181-182; 4:9
Debt To Be Paid Before Distributing Inheritance	4:12

Moderation
Moderation (Spend According To Your Means)   65:7
Wastage And Extravagance Condemned   4:6; 6:141; 7:31; 17:26-27; 25:67; 26:151

Modesty
Modesty In Looks And Clothing   24:30-31; 24:58-60; 33:32-33; 33:35; 33:53; 33:55; 33:59

Modesty In Walk   31:19

Monasticism
An Invention Of Christians   5:82; 57:26-27

Mosques
To Be Maintained By Believers   9:17-18

Muslims
2:128; 2:132; 2:136; 3:52; 3:64; 3:80; 3:84; 3:102; 4:131; 5:111; 6:109; 6:163; 7:126; 8:26; 10:72; 10:84; 10:90; 11:14; 12:101; 16:89; 16:102; 22:78; 28:53; 33:35; 41:33; 43:69; 46:15; 66:5; 68:35; 72:14

Mutual Consultation
Decide The Affairs With Mutual Consultation   3:159; 42:38

Night And Day Alterations
2:164; 3:27; 3:190; 7:54; 10:6; 10:67; 13:3; N. 190; 16:12; 17:12; 22:61; 23:80; 24:44; 25:47; 25:62; 27:86; 28:71-73; 31:29; 35:13; 36:37; 36:40; 39:5; 40:61; 41:37; 45:5; 56:6; 73:20; 74:33-34; 78:10-11; 79:29; 81:17-18; 84:16-17; 89:1-5; 91:4-5; 92:1-2; 93:1-2; 97:5

Oaths
Oaths To Be Fulfilled   16:91-92; 16:94; 23:8; 48:10; 70:32
Penalty For Breaking Oaths   5:89

Obedience To Allah And The Prophet
Follow The Example Of The Prophet Muhammad (Pbuh)   33:21
Non-Believers Of Muhammad (Pbuh) Will Perish   9:80; 108:3
Nothing To Be Dearer Than Allah And Muhammad (Pbuh)   9:24
Obey Allah And The Prophet Muhammad (Pbuh)   3:31-32; 3:101; 3:132; 3:179; 4:59; 4:69; 4:136; 4:170; 5:56; 5:92; 7:157; 8:1; 8:20-24; 8:27; 8:64; 24:54; 33:36; 33:57; 33:70-71; 47:33; 48:8-10; 49:1; 49:14; 57:21; 57:28; 61:10-11; 64:11-12; 72:22-23; 73:15-17

Oppression
Defend Yourself Against Oppression   8:39; 42:39-42
Oppression Condemned   2:191; 2:217; 42:39; 42:42

Orphan, Wayfarer And The Indigent
Orphans And Their Property   4:2; 4:6; 6:8-10; 6:152; 17:26; 17:34; 30:33:38
Orphans, Wayfarer And The Indigent   4:3; 59:7
They Are To Be Helped   2:177; 2:215; 4:2; 8:41
Treat Them With Kindness   2:83; 2:220; 4:3; 4:5; 4:8; 4:36; 4:127; 17:34; 30:38; 93:6-9

Parent And Children
Be Good To Your Parents   2:83; 2:215; 4:36; 6:151; 17:23-24; 19:14; 19:32; 29:8; 31:14-15; 46:15; 71:28

Breast Feeding A Child May Be Up To Two Years   2:233
Children   7:189-190; 8:28; 13:38; 16:72; 17:64; 24:31; 25:58-59; 42:49-50; 46:15; 60:3; 63:9; 64:14-15; 71:12; 90:3

Do Not Kill Your Children   6:137; 6:140; 6:151; 17:31; 60:12
Obligations To Parents   2:83; 2:215; 4:36; 6:151; 17:23-24; 17:28; 29:8; 31:14-15; 46:15-16

Parents   90:3
Save Yourself And Your Family From Hell   66:6
Their Shares Of Inheritance   2:180; 4:7; 4:11; 4:33

Wealth , Children And Closeness To Allah	31:15; 34:37; 63:9; 64:15
Wicked Children	18:80-81; 46:17-18
Your Spouses And Children May Be Your Enemies	64:14

Patience And Perseverance

Allah Is With Those Who Have Patience	7:137; 8:46; 8:65; 11:115; 13:22-24; 16:96; 16:110; 21:85-86; 22:35; 23:111; 25:75; 28:54; 28:80; 29:58-59; 29:59; 30:60; 39:10; 41:35; 76:12-13
Patience And Persevere	2:45; 2:153; 2:155-156; 2:177; 2:249; 3:17; 3:186; 3:200; 6:34; 7:87; 7:126; 128; 7:137; 8:46; 10:109; 11:11; 11:49; 11:115; 12:83; 14:5; 14:12; 16:42; 16:110; 16:126-128; 19:65; 20:130; 21:85; 22:11; 25:20; 30:17; 30:60; 31:17; 31:31; 32:24; 37:102; 38:17; 38:44; 40:55; 40:77; 41:35; 42:33; 42:42-43; 46:35; 47:31; 49:5; 50:39; 52:16; 52:48; 54:27; 68:48; 70:5; 73:10; 74:7; 76:24; 90:17; 103:2-3
Relief After Every Difficulty - So Have Patience	94:5-6; 65:7; 94:5
Reward For Patience	16:96; 22:34-35; 23:111; 25:75; 28:54; 29:58- 59; 33:35; 39:10; 76:12
Seek Allah's Help Through Patience And Prayer	2:153

People Of The Book

Allah Chose The Children Of Israel Above All Nations	44:32
Allah Did Special Favors To Israelites	2:49-50; 2:56-60; 5:20-26; 7:138; 10:87-93; 14:6—8; 20:77-82; 26:52-68; 44:30-32
Allah Reminds Them Of His Past Favors To Them	2:40; 2:47-48; 2:56-59;2:93;2:122-123; 10:93; 20:80-81; 44:30-33
Allah Reminds Them Of Their Covenants And Behavior	2:63-64; 2:83; 2:100; 3:187; 4:154-155; 5:12-13; 5:70; 20:80-81
Allah Warns The Jews And The Christians	2:48; 2:84-86; 2:92-95; 2:120; 2;135; 2:1390144; 3:64-69; 3:98-99; 3:110; 4:46; 5:47; 5:59; 5:63; 5:65-66;5:77; 16:24; 32:23-27; 57:29
Among Them Are Those Who Believe	2:62; 3:113-115; 3:199; 4:162; 5:66; 5:83; 28:53; 29:47; 57:27-29
Among Them Are Unbelievers	59:2; 59:11; 98:1; 98:6
Differed Among Themselves	2:213; 3:19; 3:66; N. 2159; 27:76; 32:25; 41:45; 42:14; 43:65; 45:17; 59:14; 98:4
Do Not Exceed The Bounds	5:77
Do Not Take Them For Friends And Protectors	5:51; 5:57
Isa (Jesus, Pbuh) Was Sent As A Prophet	3:45-53; 4:156-159; 5:46; 5:110; 43:57-59; 43:64-65
Jews Believe Only A Part Of The Book	2:85; 2:145
Many Disbelieved In Allah And His Messengers (Pbut)	2:87-88; 5:17; 5:64; 5:72-73; 9:30-33; 10:68-70; 18:4
Many Of The Children Of Israel Are Greedy	2:96
Many People Of The Book Reject The Qur'an	2:89-91; 2:101; 2:146-147; 5:61-62; 5:68; 5:104; 6:20; 6:156-157; 6:20; 6:91; 13:36; 26:197-201; 46:9-10
People Of The Book	2:148; 3:20; 3:98; 3:110-115; 3:187; 4:51; 4:123; 4:131; 4:153; 4:171; 4:159; 5:65-66; 5:68; 6:20; 74:31
Required To Believe In The Qur'an And Muhammad (Pbuh)	2:41-44; 2:89-90; 2:151-152; 3:20; 3:64; 5:15; 5:19; 5:61; 7:105; 27:76-77; 98:5-6
Some Believed In Jesus Others Plotted Against Him	2:87-88; 3:52-55; 3:183-184; 5:78; 43:57-58; 43:65; 57:27; 61:14
Some Children Of Israel Disobeyed Moses (Pbuh)	4:153; 4:160-161; 6:15
Some Children Of Israel Violated Allah's Commands	2:51-52; 2:54-55; 2:61; 2:63-66; 2:92-93; 7:138-141; 7:141; 7:148-156; 7:161-169; 10:93; 20:83-98; 34:153
Some Of The People Of The Book Believe And Are Righteous	3:75-76; 3:113-115; 3:110; 3:199; 4:46; 4:162; 5:66; 29:47; 46:10
Their Attitude Towards Muhammad (Pbuh) And Islam	2:120; 2:145; 5:79-82
Their Priests	9:31; 9:34
Their Relationship To Muslims	3:64-80; 3:99-101; 4:44; 5:5; 5:15-16; 5:19; 5:57-59; 5:82; 9:29; 29:46

| Their Treachery | 33:26-27; 59:2-4 |

Preordainment (Fate And Destiny)

Allah Does Not Wrong Any Soul	3:117; 4:79; 4:111; 6:70; 9:70; 10:44; 11:101; 16:33; 24:50; 30:9; 35:32; 39:41
Misfortune Is Due To Your Own Deeds	4:79; 42:30; 42:48
You Can Change Your Own Condition	13:10-11
Your Action Is A Reflection Of Your Destiny	4:79; 42:30; 42:48

Previous Revelations

| Believe In The Qur'an And Previous Revelations | 2:62; 5:69; 7:157; 7:170 |

Property And Wealth

| Property And Wealth | 2:188; 3:14; 4:29; 4:33; 8:28; 8:72; 9:24; 9:85; 9:88; 9:111; 11:87; 17:64; 18:34; 18:39; 18:46; 19:77; 23:55; 28:76-79; 34:34-35; 34:37; 44:27; 51:19; 58:17; 59:7; 61:11; 63:9; 64:15; 68:14; 69:28; 71:12; 71:21; 74:12; 89:20; 90:6; 92:11; 92:18; 100:8; 104:2-3; 111:2 |

Prosperity And Success

| Success Or Failure Is Based On The Purification Of Soul | 62:2; 91:7-10 |
| Who Will Prosper As Defined By Allah | 2:2-5; 2:189; 3:130; 5:35; 5:90; 5:100; 7:8; 7:69; 7:157; 8:45; 9:88; 22:77; 31:2-5; 62:10; 87:10-14 |

Purification

By Allah	24:21; 33:33
Of The Soul	3:42; 5:41; 9:103; 9:108; 20:76; 35:18; 79:18; 80:3; 80:7; 87:14; 91:9; 92:18
Purification In General	2:222; 3:43; 5:6; 8:11; 74:4
Purify Your Souls	62:2; 91:7-10

Remembrance Of Allah

Effect On Hearts	8:2; 13:28; 22:35; 39:23; 39:45
In The Reading And Listening Of Al-Qur'an	17:46
Is The Greatest Act Of Worship	29:45
It Was Commanded To Isa (Jesus), Pbuh	5:110
It Was Commanded To The Children Of Israel	2:40.; 2:47; 2:122; 5:20; 14:6
Lack Of Remembrance	4:142; 18:28; 18:101; 21:36; 21:42; 39:22; 43:36; 53;29; 59:19; 63:9; 72:17;
Remembrance Of Allah *(Dhikr),*	2:114; 2:152; 2:198; 2:200; 2:205; 2:239; 5:41; 5:155; 3:191; 4:105; 6:138; 7:205; 8:45; 18:24; 20:14; 20:54; 20:42; 21:60; 22:28; 22:54-56; 22:40; 24:36-57; 25:62; 26:227; 29:65; 53:21; 55:55; 33:41; 58:12; 57:16; 62:9-10; 73:8; 76:25; 87:15
Remembrance Of Allah's Is Commanded	2:251; 3:103; 5:7; 5:11; 7:69; 7:74; 53:9; 35:3; 43:15
Shaitân's Hindrance From The Remembrance Of Allah	5:91; 12:42; 58:19

Repentance

Repentance In General	2:54; 2:160; 3:89-90; 4:17-18; 5:34; 5:74; 6:54; 7:155; 9:3; 9:112; 9:118; 9:126; 11:3; 11:52; 11:61; 11:90; 13:27; 16:119; 17:25; 19:60; 24:5; 25:70-71; 28:67; 30:31; 30:33; 39:8; 9:17; 39:54; 40:7; 46:15; 0:32-33; 60:4; 66:4-5; 66:8; 68:32; 85:10
Accepted By Allah	40:3; 42:25
Of Adam And Eve	2:37; 7:23
Of Moses	7:43

Righteous And Righteousness

| Loved By Allah | 9:4; 9:7; 19:96 |
| Righteous | 3:15-17; 4:69; 6:69; 6:85; 7:35; 7:128; 7:169-170; 13:23; 13:35; 16:30; 16:97; 16:122; 21:72; 21:75; 21:105; 25:74; 26:83; 27:19; 28:27; 29:9; 29:27; 37:112; 43:35; 43:67; 44:51-57; 45:19; 49:7; 50:31-35; 51:15-19; 52:17-28; 54:34; 66:4; 68:34; 68:50; 76:5-22; 77:41-44; |

Allah Sets A Seal On The Hearts Of Unbelievers	6:25; 6:125; 6:127; 24:39-40
Are Astray	1:7; 4:136-137; 6:110; 14:3; 14:18; 17:48; 17:72; 23:106; 25:9; 25:34; 25:44; 27:4; 42:18; 42:44; 43:40; 48:23; 46:32; 105:2
Are Cursed	2:89; 2:161; 4:52
Are Cut Off	108:3
Are Deaf, Dumb, And Blind	2:18; 2:171; 6:89; 17:72; 17:97; 20:124-126; 21:45; 22:46; 27:66; 27:80-81; 28:66; 30:52- 53; 31:7; 41:40; 47:23
Are Despair Of Mercy	12:87; 15:56; 41:49
Are Despair Of The Hereafter	60:15
Are Granted Respite	22:44; 68:45
Characteristics Of UnbelieversAnd Hypocrites	2:14; 2:17; 2:76; 6:23-24; 6:28; 6:93; 9:56-58; 10:42-43; 30:33
Covered With Shame	3:112; 8:192; 16:27; 59:5; 68:43; 70:44
Deny The Day of Judgment,	18:36; 34:8; 41:50; 42:18; 45:82; 52:11; 64:7; 82:9; 83:10-18; 84:18-15; 107:1
Do Not Obey Them	3:149; 33:48; 96:19
Do Not Take Them For Friends Or Helpers	3:28; 4:189; 4:144; 5:57; 9:23; 60:1-2; 60:9; 60:15
Doubt Allah's Message (Revelation)	6:7-8; 6:25; 16:101; 25:4-8; 30:58; 54:31; 37:12-17; 37:35-56; 37:170; 38:5-8; 40:70; 43:31; 45:11; 48:25; 50:2; 52:30-44; 67:9; 68:15; 74:24-25; 84:20-22
Fuel For The Fire	3:10-12; 3:151; 5:10; 5:86; 21:98; 22:19; 40:6; 57:19; 64:40; 67:10-11; 72:15
No Ransom Will Be Accepted	3:91; 5:36; 13:18
Parable For Those Who Reject Faith	2:74; 7:176; 15:80-84; 24:41
Play With Vanities	43:83; 52:12
Plotting And Planning	8:30; 13:42; 14:46; 52:42; 71:22; 74:18-20; 86:15-17; 105:2
Protectors Of One Another	8:73; 45:19
Repentance, Faith And Good Deeds May Save Them	3:89; 8:38; 28:67; 32:21; 35:7; 39:54; 85:10
Satan (Evil Ones) Are Friends Of The Unbelievers	7:27
Slander And Calumnies	68:11; 104:1
Some Unbelievers Will Never Believe	2:6-7; 2:10; 2:13; 2:17-18; 2:171; 6:7; 6:39; 6:111; 7:193; 7:198; 10:96-97; 13:31
Summoned To Bow, But Will Not Be Able To Do So	68:42-43; 77:48
Take Their Own Desires As Their God	45:23
Their Deeds Are Fruitless	47:1; 47:8-9
Their Deeds Are Like A Mirage	24:39
Their Faces Will Be Turned Upside Down	33:66
Their Hearts Are Diseased	2:10; 5:52; 8:49; 9:125; 22:53; 24:50; 33:12; 33:60; 47:20; 47:29; 74:31
Their Hearts Are Sealed	2:7; 7:101; 10:74; 16:108; 30:59; 40:35; 45:23; 47:24; 63:3; 83:14
Their Mutual Recriminations On The Day of Judgment	34:31-33; 37:24-32; 38:59-64; 40:47; 41:29
Their Wrong Deeds Seem Pleasing To Them	6:122; 8:48; 9:37; 27:4; 35:8
There Is A Covering Over Their Hearing And Sight	2:7; 17:45-46; 18:57; 36:9; 41:5; 45:23
There Will Be Yokes On Their Necks	34:33; 36:8; 40:71
They Are In Delusion	67:20:21
They Are The Worst Of All Creatures'	98:6
They Are Warned By Allah	9:125-126; 11:121-122; 14:44-45; 15:2-3; 19:80-84; 20134-135; 21:11-15; 21:43; 25:41-42; 35:44; 36:41-45; 37:171-177; 39:46-52; 46:27; 52:39-47; 53:28—29
They Deny Resurrection	6:29; 11:7; 15:5; 16:58; 17:49-52; 17:98; 19:66; 25:35-58; 25:82-83; 25:40; 27:67-68; 32:10; 35:7-8; 36:78; 57:16-17; 37:53; 44:34-56; 45:24-26; 50:5; 56:47-48; 64:7; 72:7; 79:10-12
They Do Not Believe In The Day Of Judgment	6:31; 16:60; 17:10; 17:49-51; 18:48; 22:47; 23:35-37; 23:81-83; 25:11; 25:21; 25:40; 30:8; 30:33-35; 32:12; 32:28; 34:3; 34:7; 34:29-30; 36:7; 36:78; 37:16; 34:7; 37:17-18; 42:18; 44:34-37; 45:26; 45:32; 46:17-18; 50:3;

	54:1-6; 56:47-48; 67:7; 70:6; 79:10-11; 83:10-12
They Forbid Their Votaries To Pray	96:9-10
They Have Lost Their Own Souls	6:12; 6:20; 11:21; 39:15; 42:45
They Laugh At The Believers	83:29-36
They Persecute The Believers	85:4-8; 85:10
They Protect One Another	8:73
They Reject Allah And Commit Shirk (Assign Partners)	6:1; 7:194; 8:23; 10:34-35; 10:60; 11:101; 11:109; 16:1; 16:20-21; 17:42-43; 21:18; 21:21-26; 22:71; 23:91; 25:77; 26:77; 26:4-6; 29:41-42; 29:65; 34:22; 34:40-42; 35:40; 37:12-15; 37:35; 38:5-7; 39:3; 39:36; 39:67; 40:71-76; 41:47-48; 58:20
They Reject Allah's Signs	6:39; 6:49; 8:31; 10:17; 13:30; 16:105; 17:98; 18:56-57; 18:105-106; 19:73-74; 19:77-79; 22:72; 23:66-67; 23:105; 26:7-8; 28:47-48; 29:23; 29:47; 29:49; 29:61; 30:10; 30:16; 30:58; 31:7; 31:32; 32:22; 32:26-27; 34:5; 34:38; 34:43; 36:71-74; 37:13; 37:170; 39:63; 40:4-5; 40:21-22; 40:69; 40:81; 42:35; 45:9-10; 45:26; 83:13-14
They Reject The Prophet Muhammad (Pbuh)	6:10; 7:184; 9:61; 10:41; 11:27; 13:27; 13:43; 16:113; 17:90 96; 30:9; 30:58; 34:8; 35:25-26; 35:42; 36:30; 36:48; 37:36; 38:8; 38:14; 43:23-25; 44:12-16; 47:13; 47:16; 50:2-5; 51:52-53; 52:30-31; 58:5-6
They Reject The Qur'an	2:89-90; 2:99; 5:104; 6:7; 6:25; 7:185; 8:32; 9:127; 10:15-16; 10:94; 11:12-14; 13:31; 16:24; 16:101; 16:103; 17:41; 17:46; 21:5; 21:45; 21:50; 22:42-44; 23:66-68; 25:3; 23:70; 25:4-6; 25:32; 26:199-201; 29:48-52; 30:58; 34:31; 34:34; 37:170; 38:1-2; 41:44; 41:52-53; 43:30-31; 45:11; 46:7-8; 47:24; 52:33-34; 69:49-50; 56:82; 68:44-46; 84:20-23
They Rely On Shaitân (Satan)	8:48; 14:22; 31:21; 34:20-21
They Spend Extensively To Hinder The Believers	8:36
They Will Be Humiliated	58:5-6; 58:20
They Will Be Led To Hell In Crowds	29:71-72; 41:19
They Will Wish That They Were Muslims	15:2
They Will Wish They Had Believed In Allah	15:2
Those Who Reject The Call To Islam	61:7
Turn Away From Them	51:54; 54:6
Unbelievers	8:156; 5:176-178; 5:196;4 :42; 4:76; 4:84; 4:151; 6:1; 8:30-40; 8:55; 9:78; 16:107; 22:72; 29:68; 32:2; 40:4; 61:8; 66:9-10; 74:43-53; 7531-35; 78:40; 80:42; 88:28-24; 109:1-6
Unbelievers Caused The Prophet (Pbuh) Grief And Pain	6:33; 36:76
Who Are The Unbelievers?	2:16; 2:204-206; 3:22; 3:120; 3:101; 5:58; 6:25-26; 6:29; 6:100; 8:22; 8:73; 9:37; 9:59; 9:62; 9:125-126; 10:18; 10:36; 10:42-43; 13:7; 13:14; 14:3; 14:18; 15:6-7; 15:11-13; 16:22-24; 16:35; 16:56-57; 16:58-59; 16:101; 16:103; 17:40-41; 17:47-48; 17:73; 17:76; 19:81; 19:88-89; 20:133; 21:2-6; 21:41; 22:12-13; 23:71; 23:73-75; 23:117; 24:39-40; 24:47-48; 25:7-10; 25:43-44; 25:55-56; 25:60; 27:4-5; 29:12-13; 29:66-67; 30:29; 37:149-160; 38:4; 40:10-11; 41:5; 41:26; 43:15; 43:20-22; 43:79-80; 45:7-8; 45:21; 45:25; 46:3; 47:14; 47:18; 47:25-26; 47:29-30; 52:35-47; 53:27-29; 78:1-5; 83:29-33; 85:17-20; 86:15-17; 92:8-11
Will Be Forbidden Paradise	7:50; 70:38-39
Will Never Triumph	8:59; 23:117
Will Not Be Forgiven	47:34

Usury

Interest Or Usury Prohibited	2:275-279; 3:130; 4:161; 30:39

Vain Or Idle Talk

Refrain From Such Acts	9:69; 23:1-3; 28:55; 74:41-45

Wastage And Extravagance

Wastage And Extravagance Condemned   4:6; 6:141; 7:31; 17:26-27; 25:67; 25:151

Weigh And Measure

Give Due Measure   6:152; 7:85; 11:84-85; 17:35; 55:7-9

Widows

Maintenance For Widow   2:240
Waiting Period Before Their Remarriage   2:234-235

Will and Testament

Amending Someone's Will Is Forbidden   2:181-182
Prepare Will Before Death   2:180; 2:240
Preparation Of Will   2:180; 2:240; 5:106-108

Wars

Rules Of Warfare   8:15-16; 8:45-47; 8:57-58; 8:60-61; 8:65; 8:70- 72; 9:5-6; 49:9; 59:5

Fighting (And Striving) In The Cause Of Allah   2:190-193; 2:216-218; 2:244; 2:246; 3:142; 3:146; 4:71-77; 4:84; 4:95-96; 4:104; 5:54; 8:72; 9:12-14; 9:19-20; 9:24-26; 9:29; 9:36; 9:38-39; 9:41- 47; 9:73; 9:81;9:86-88; 9:111; 9:120-123; 16:110; 22:39-40; 22:78; 47:4; 47:20; 48:15-17; 57:10; 59:6; 61:4; 73:20

Striving,   17:19; 21:24; 29:5-6; 29:69; 47:31; 53:39-41; 76:22; 88:9; 92:4

Worship None But Allah

Adore Not The Sun And The Moon   41:37
Associate No Partners With Allah   3:64; 4:36; 4:48; 4:116; 5:72; 6:14; 6:81; 6:88; 6:106; 6:136-137; 6:148; 6:151; 6:163; 7:33; 7:190-191; 9:31; 10:18; 10:28-29; 10:66; 12:38; 12:108; 13:16; 13:33; 13:36; 16:1; 61:3; 16:51-57; 16:73; 16:86; 17:22; 17:111; 17:39-40; 17:56-57; 18:110; 22:26; 22:31; 23:59; 23:92; 24:55; 25:2; 25:68; 27:59; 27:63; 28:68; 28:87-88; 28:8; 30:31; 30:40; 31:15; 35:13; 35:14;35:40; 39:64; 39:65; 39:67; 40:41-43; 40:66; 40:6; 43:15; 43:45; 46:4-6; 50:26; 51:51; 52:43; 69:12; 72:2

Do Not Worship Shaitân (Satan)   19:44; 36:59-61
Every Thing Worships Allah   2:116; 13:15; 16:49-50; 22:18; 38:18; 42:5; 57:1; 59:1
Those Deities Who Some Worship Can Do Nothing   22:73; 22:62
Worship None But Allah And Seek His Help   2:21; 2:163-165; 4:36; 4:172; 7:56; 7:158; 8:24; 9:112; 10:2; 10:104; 10:106; 11:2-3; 11:123; 13:30; 13:36; 16:36; 16:72-74; 16:123; 17:22; 19:65; 22:18; 22:31; 22:73-74; 22:77; 23:32; 26:213; 28:88; 29:56; 30:17-18; 30:31; 30:42; 33:41-43; 35:3; 36:60; 37:4; 40:55-56; 40:60; 41:37; 42:13; 47:19; 51:51; 60:4-7; 64:13; 66:8

9. Reward And Punishment

According To Best Of Action   16:97; 29:7
According To The Best Of Your Deeds   16:96-97; 23:102; 24:38; 29:7; 39:35; 45:30; 46:16

Allah Has Always Warned Before Destroying A Nation   17:15-16
Boiling Fluid, As A Form Of Punishment   6:70; 10:4; 14:15-20; 37:67; 38:57-58; 40:70-72; 44:43-46; 47:15; 44:43-49; 55:43-44; 56:41-42; 56:52-56; 56:92-93; 78:24-25; 88:1-5

Both Males And Females Shall Be Rewarded   3:195; 4:124; 9:72; 16:97; 33:35; 40:40; 48:5
Family Members May Reunite In Paradise   13:22-24; 36:55-56; 43:70

For Struggling In Allah's Cause (Perform Jihâd)	2:218; 3:170-174; 3:195; 4:74; 4:95-96; 4:100; 8:74; 9:20-22; 9:88-89; 9:111-112; 9:120-121; 16:41; 16:110 25:58; 47:4-7; 48:16; 48:18-20; 61:12-13
For Those Who Are Patient	11:11; 13:22-24; 16:41-42; 25:75-76; 39:10
For Those Who Believe And Do Good Deeds	2:25; 2:62; 2:82; 2:112; 2:277; 3:57; 4:57; 4:122; 4:124-125; 4:173; 5:9; 5:58; 7:42; 7:56; 9:100; 9:120; 10:4; 10:9; 10:103; 11:11; 11:23; 13:29; 14:23; 12:56; 16:30-32; 16:97; 17:25; 18:2-3; 18:30-31; 18:107-108; 19:60-63; 19:96; 20:75-76; 20:112; 21:94; 21:101-103; 22:14; 22:23; 22:50; 22:56; 23:102; 24:55; 27:89; 29:7; 29:9; 29:58; 30:15; 30:45; 35:10; 39:10; 39:34-35; 40:40; 40:58; 41:8; 42:22-23; 42:26; 45:30; 47:2; 47:12; 47:35; 52:19; 53:31; 64:9; 65:11; 77:41-44; 84:24-25; 85:11; 95:4-8; 101:6-7; 103:1-3
For Those Who Believe And Mend Their Ways	6:48
For Those Who Do Right And Refrain From Wrong	3:172; 3:179; 9:112; 10:26
For Those Who Fulfill Trust And Perform Salah	2:277; 23:8-11
For Those Who Give Charity	2:262; 2:270; 2:274; 3:17; 4:162; 9:71-72; 13:29-30; 23:1-4; 30:39; 31:4; 33:35; 35:29-30; 35:33; 42:38; 57:7; 57:10-11; 57:18; 58:12; 92:5-7
For Those Who Guard Against Evil	10:63-64; 13:22-24; 19:63; 19:72
For Those Who Obey Allah And The Prophet	3:179; 4:13; 4:69-70; 4:152
For Those Who Seek Forgiveness In The Early Hours	3:15-17
Foremost In Faith Will Be Foremost In The Paradise	56:10
Friends Of Allah Have No Fear	10:62
Hell Fire, As A Form Of Punishment	2:23-24; 2:39; 2:81; 2:126; 2:257; 3:10; 3:131; 3:151; 3:181-182; 3:197; 4:14; 4:56; 4:115; 4:121; 4:168-169; 5:10; 5:36-37; 5:86; 6:27; 8:14; 8:50; 9:17; 9:34-35; 9:63; 9:68; 9:113; 10:27; 11:98-99; 11:106; 13:5; 13:35; 14:49-51; 16:28-29; 16:62; 17:97; 18:29; 18:53; 21:39-40; 21:98-100; 22:8-10; 22:51; 23:104; 24:57; 25:11-14; 26:91-95; 27:90; 29:25; 31:21; 32:20; 33:64-68; 34:40-42; 35:36-37; 36:63-64; 37:21-23; 37:68; 38:27; 38:55-56; 38:59; 38:64; 39:8; 39:16; 40:6; 40:46-50; 41:19; 41:27-28; 44:47; 45:34-35; 46:20; 46:34-35; 47:12-13; 50:29; 51:11-14; 52:13-16; 54:46-48; 55:35; 56:42-43; 56:92-95; 57:15; 15:19; 58:8; 59:3; 69:30-31; 70:10-16; 73:12-13; 76:4; 79:34-39; 82:14-16; 83:15-16; 84:10-12; 85:10; 87:10-13; 92:14-17; 101:8-11
Multiple Reward For Good Deeds	34:37
Punishments At Law	5:35; 5:38; 17:33; 24:2; 24:4; 24:8
Punishment For Disbelief And Misdeeds	2:90; 2:114; 3:4; 3:11-12; 3:21; 3:56; 3:178; 4:18; 4:97; 4:115; 4:151; 6:30; 7:41; 7:182-183; 8:13; 8:35; 8:36; 8:37; 9:55; 9:61; 9:73; 10:7-8; 10:13; 10:52; 11:9; 11:102; 13:18; 13:32; 13:34; 14:2; 14:29-30; 14:49; 16:25-29; 16:39; 16:45-47; 16:63; 16:84-88; 16:106; 16:109; 18:59; 18:100-102; 19:68-72; 19:86; 20:74; 20:100-101; 20:124; 20:127; 21:29; 21:41; 22:25; 22:55-57; 23:103; 25:34; 25:68-69; 29:53-55; 31:6; 31:24; 32:13-14; 32:29; 33:8; 33:60-61; 33:73; 34:33; 34:51-54; 36:7-10; 36:31-32; 39:47; 39:71-72; 40:21; 40:82-85; 41:29; 41:48; 42:16; 42:21; 42:26; 42:44; 42:22; 42:45-46; 43:36-39; 43:74-78; 46:27-28; 47:27-28; 58:16-20; 67:6; 76:31
Punishment Of The Wrongdoers On The Day Of Judgment	2:85; 3:106; 3:180; 4:42; 7:50; 18:100; 20:124; 21:9; 22:45-48; 25:23; 25:26-27; 25:68-70; 29:13; 29:55; 30:12; 30:43-44; 32:14; 36:59-68; 36:74-75; 37:38-39; 37:62-64; 37:66; 39:24-26; 39:47; 39:60; 39:71-72; 43:65; 45:33; 46:35; 50:22-26; 51:59-60; 54:6; 55:41; 55:43-44; 56:42-56; 57:13-14; 58:14-15; 64:10; 66:7; 69:25-37; 70:42-44; 77:15-19; 77:23-40; 77:45-50;

10. Allah's Creations:

Ungrateful	2:243; 7:10; 7:17; 10:60; 14:7; 14:34; 16:54; 16:83; 17:67-69; 17:84; 22:65; 23:78; 25:50; 27:73; 30:33-34; 30:51; 32:9; 34:17; 40:61; 42:48; 67:23; 74:15; 76:3; 100:6-7
Unity	2:213; 6:98; 10:19; 11:118; 16:93; 39:6; 42:8; 49;13
Women	2:222-223; 3:14; 3:195; 4:15; 4:19-25; 4:32; 4:34; 4:124; 4:127; 9:71; n. 2103; 24:26; 24:31; 24:60; 33:32; 33:35; 33:73; 40:40; 47:19; 48:5; 48:25; 65:1-2; 65:6; 66:5; 71:28

Planets

Created To Serve Man	2:189; 6:96-97; 10:5; 14:33; 16;12; 16:16; 25:61; 71:16
Orbiting - Move Under The Divine Law And Order	7:54; 13:2; 14;33; 16:12; 21:33; 29:61; 31:29; 35:13; 36:38-40; 55:5

Plants, Vegetation And Fruits

Crops	6:99; 6:136; 6:138; 6:141; 7:57-58; 10:24; 26:148; 27:60; 32:27; 39:21; 44:26; 50:9; 56:63-67; 57:20; 78:15-16
Dates And Date-Palms	6:99; 6:141; 13:4; 16:11; 16:67; 17:91; 18:32; 19:23-25; 20:71; 23:19; 26:148; 41:47; 50:10; 55:11; 55:68; 80:27-32
Fruits	6:9; 6:141; 14:3-4; 14:32; 14:37; 16:11; 16:67; 23:19-20; 26:147-148; 34:16; 36:34-35; 50:10-11; 80:31
Gardens	6:141; 13:4; 23:19; 26:57; 25:134; 26:147; 34:15-16; 44:25; 50:9; 71:12; 78:16; 80:30
Grain	6:99; 12:43; 12:46-47; 13:4; 16:10-11; 26:147-148; 36:33; 50:9; 55:12; 78:15; 80:27
Grapes And Grapevines	2:266; 6:99; 13:4; 16:11; 16:67; 17:91; 18:32; 23:19; 36:34; 78:32; 80:28
Plants	6:95; 6:99; 13:4; 16:11; 20:53; 22:5; 31:10; 37:146; 39:21; 50:7; 50:9-10; 55:6; 55:12; 79:30-31; 80:28

Stars

Stars	6:76; 7:54; 12:4; 16:12; 22:18; 37:88; 53:49; 77:8; 81:2; 82:2; 86:1-3
Are For Guidance For Direction And To Find The Way	6:97; 16:16
Retreat	52:49
Setting	6:76; 53:1; 56:75-76
Sun And Moon As Indicators Of Time	2:189; 6:96; 10:5
Sun -The Primary Source Of Light	25:61; 71:16
Used As A Flaming Fire To Repel Evil Ones	37:6-10; 67:5; 72:8-9

11. Natural Phenomenon And Scientific Facts

Ageing And Biology

All Living Things Are Made From Water	21:30; 24:45; 25:54
Process Of Ageing	16:70; 22:5; 30:54; 36:68

Astronomy

Celestial Organization	7:54; 10:5; 21:33; 31:29; 36:37; 36:40; 39:5; 43:38; 55:17; 70:40
Evolution And Expansion Of Heavens	13:2; 31:29; 35:13; 39:5; 36:38; 51:47
Nature Of Heavenly Bodies	6:76; 21:32; 24:35; 25:61; 37:6-7; 41:12; 67:5; 71:15-16; 78:12-13; 82:1-2; 86:1-3
Sky, Sun, Moon And Stars	6:96-97; 10:5; 13:2; 14:33; 16:12; 16:16; 31:10; 22:65; 36:39; 45:13; 50:6; 55:5; 55:7;

Hurricanes And Tornados
Allah Sends Tornado   17:68; 29:39-40; 54:34; 67:17
The Hurricane Sent Down As Scourge   33:9; 51:41-42; 54:19-20; 69:6-7

Life And Death
Allah Gives Life And Death   2:28; 2:243; 2:258-260; 3:27; 7:158; 9:116; 10:31; 10:56; 15:23; 16:;38; 16:70; 22:5-6; 22:66; 23:80-81; 30:40; 32:7-9; 36:12;36:12; 36:68; 36:77-79; 40:68; 42:9; 44:8; 45:26; 46:33; 50:43-44; 53:44; 57:2; 67:2; 75:;40; 80:18-22

Angels Take The Soul At Death   4:97; 6:61; 6:93; 7:37; 8:50; 16:28; 16:32; 32:11; 47:27; 79:1-2

Every Soul Will Taste Death   21:35; 29:57; 39:30
Know One Knows Ones Place Of Death   31:34
State Of Affair At Death   8:50; 16:28-29; 23:99-100
Time And Place Of Death Is Fixed   3:145; 4:78; 62:8; 63:11

Metals, Nature And Natural Resources
Brass   34:12-13
Coral   55:21-22
Gold And Silver   3:14; 9:34
Gold As Precious Metal   3:14; 9:34; 18:31; 22:23; 35:33-34; 43:53; 43:71
Iron   18:96; 34:10; 57:25
Mountains   13:3; 15:19; 16:15; 16:81; 21:31; 26:149; 31:10; 33:72; 50:7; 78:6-7; 79:32; 88:10-19

Pearl   35:33; 52:22; 52:24; 76:19
Trees   27:60; 36:80; 55:6; 56:72

Mountains
General   13:3;13:31; 15:19; 15:82; 16:81; 17:36; 21:31; 21:79; 22:18; 26:149; .31:10; 33:72; 38:18; 50:7; 7:27; 79:32; 88:19

As Pegs   78:6-7
As Stabilizers Of Earth   16:15

Oceans, Seas And Rivers
Oceans And Seas   6:97; 10:22; 14:32; 16:14; 17:66-67; 17:69-70; 24:40; 25:53; 31:31; 35:12; 36:41-44; 45:12; 55:19-20; 55:22; 55:24

Barrier Between Fresh And Salt Water   25:53; 35:12; 55:19-20; 55:22
Deep Sea Condition   24:40
Rivers   13:3; 16:15

Pregnancy And Women's Courses
Male Or Female Child Based On Allah's Plan   42:49
Pregnancy, A Natural Phenomenon   7:189; 13:8; 31:34; 32:6-8; 39:6; 41:47; 53:32
Sex Education   2:187; 2:197; 2:222-223; 65:4;
Women's Courses   2:222

Water And Wind
Water   13:4; 13:17; 15:22; 21:30; 24:45; 25:48; 25:50; 25:53-54; 35:12; 38:42; 54:12; 54:28; 55:19-20; 56:68-70; 67:29-30; 77:27; 80:24-25

Water Cycle And The Seas   7:57; 13:17; 15:22; 23:18-19; 25:48-49; 30:48; 35:9; 36:34; 39:21; 45:5; 50:9-11; 56:68-70; 67:30

Wind   2:164; 7:57; 10:22; 15:22; 21:81; 25:48; 27:63; 30:46; 30:48; 30:51; 34:12; 35:9; 38:36; 41:16; 42:33; 45:5; 46:24; 46:25; 51:1-5; 51:41-42; 54:18-20; 69:6-7; 77:2-6

12. Past Generations

A. Past Generations

2:134; 2:141; 6:6; 10:13; 10:94; 10:102; 11:100-101; 11:116; 13:30; 16:63; 17:17; 19:74; 20:51-52; 20:128; 21:6; 21:11-15; 22:42; 24:34; 28:58; 28:78; 29:18; 30:9; 32:26;36:31; 38:3; 39:50; 40:5; 43:6-8; 46:18; 46:27-28; 47:13; 50:12-15; 50:36; 51:59; 53:50-54; 54:51; 57:16; 645-6; 65:8-10; 77:16-19

B. Why Prior Nations Were Destroyed?

5:29; 5:60; 6:42-45; 6:109-110; 6:123; 6:147; 7:4-5; 7:34; 7:94; 7:96-100; 9:38-39; 10:11-14; 11:100-107; 11:117; 12:105-107; 13:11; 13:31-32; 19:74-75; 14:13-17; 14:28-30; 14:42-46; 15:4-5; 16:26-29; 16:33-34; 16:45-47; 16:61; 16:112-113; 17:15-16; 18:57-59; 19:98; 20:128; 21:6; 21:11-15; 21:41; 22:45-46; 22:48; 23:63-67; 6:208-209; 28:58-59; 29: 38-40; 30:9-10; 30:47; 34:34-38; 36:31-32; 40:21-22; 47:13; 47:38; 50:12-14; 58:5-6; 65:8-10; 67:18; 68:17-33; 89:6-20

C. Prior Nations (Also See #4: Articles Of Faith under Rasools And Their Nations):

i.	Children Of Israel	2:61; 3:112; 5:12-13; 5:20-26; 7:161-162; 7:165-166
ii.	Companions Of The Cave	18:8-20
iii.	Companions Of The City	36:13-30
iv.	Fir'aun (Pharaoh)	7:130-133; 7:134-137; 8:50-54; 11:96-99; 26:65-68; 28:1-6; 28:36-42; 40:45-46; 79:15-26
v.	Karoon (Korah)	28:76-82
vi.	Lûqman	31:12-19
vii	Residents Of Al-Hijr	15:80-84
viii.	Sheba (Saba)	34:15-19
ix.	Zul-Qarnain And Ya'juj Wa Ma'juj	18:83-100

Lucky and fortunate are those
whom Allah has blessed to serve His Message
"Al-Qur'an"

*Please note, we are under obligation to convey Allah's Message to the rest
of mankind. If we neglect this duty, our fellow human beings
will hold us responsible on the Day of Judgment for not
conveying Allah's Message to them.*

After reading this translation, if you feel that the translator was able to
increase your understanding of the Message of the Qur'an, please make it
available to your friends, colleagues and as many local Public, University,
College and School libraries as possible. You may obtain copies
directly from our printers at 713-526-6364 or fax
your request at 713-526-9090 or send an
e-mail at: cc12@swbell.net

*To reach mankind at large we have made this Translation and Al-Qur'an's
Subject Index available at www.al-quraan.org. To listen to its reading by a
reputable American and to see its comparison with other three most
popular English Translations (i.e. by Abdullah Yusuf Ali,
Muhammad Asad and Mamaduke Pickthal) please
refer to "Alim" software's new release
at www.alim.org*

**Any individual or organization who would like to help in its improve-
ment, printing and distribution, they are most welcome. They are
requested to please contact the Institute through
telephone, fax, mail or e-mail address listed
on the second page of
this publication.**